THE GREEN GUIDE

Northern France
and the Paris Region

Bacôves in the Audomarois, near St-Omer, Y. Tierny/ MICHELIN

General Manager　　　　　Cynthia Clayton Ochterbeck

THEGREENGUIDE **NORTHERN FRANCE AND THE PARIS REGION**

Editor	Rachel Mills
Principal Writer	Françoise Klingen, Heather Stimmler-Hall
Production Manager	Natasha G. George
Cartography	Stéphane Anton, Andrew Thompson
Photo Editor	Yoshimi Kanazawa
Interior & Cover Design	Chris Bell
Layout	Therese Schneider
Cover Design	Chris Bell, Christelle Le Déan
Cover Layout	Michelin Apa Publications Ltd.

Contact Us

The Green Guide
Michelin Maps and Guides
One Parkway South
Greenville, SC 29615
USA
www.michelintravel.com

Michelin Maps and Guides
Hannay House
39 Clarendon Road
Watford, Herts WD17 1JA
UK
✆01923 205240
www.ViaMichelin.com
travelpubsales@uk.michelin.com

Special Sales

For information regarding bulk sales,
customized editions and premium sales,
please contact our Customer Service
Departments:
USA　　1-800-432-6277
UK　　　01923 205240
Canada 1-800-361-8236

Note to the reader Addresses, phone numbers, opening hours and prices
published in this guide are accurate at the time of press. We welcome
corrections and suggestions that may assist us in preparing the next edition.
While every effort is made to ensure that all information printed in this guide
is correct and up-to-date, Michelin Apa Publications Ltd. accepts no liability
for any direct, indirect or consequential losses howsoever caused so far as
such can be excluded by law.

HOW TO USE THIS GUIDE

PLANNING YOUR TRIP

The blue-tabbed PLANNING YOUR TRIP section at the front of the guide gives you **ideas for your trip** and **practical information** to help you organize it. You'll find tours, practical information, a host of outdoor activities, a calendar of events, information on shopping, sightseeing, kids' activities and more.

INTRODUCTION

The orange-tabbed INTRODUCTION section explores **The Region Today** including government, food and drink and folklore. The **History** section spans from the Celts and Romans through the Middle Ages, Revolution and World Wars. **Art and Culture** includes architecture, ceramics and painting, while the final section delves into **Nature**.

DISCOVERING

The green-tabbed DISCOVERING section features Principal Sights by region, featuring the most interesting local **Sights**, **Walking Tours**, nearby **Excursions**, and detailed **Driving Tours**. Admission prices shown are normally for a single adult.

ADDRESSES

We've selected the best hotels, restaurants, cafés, shops, nightlife and entertainment to fit all budgets. See the Legend on the cover flap for an explanation of the price categories. See the back of the guide for an index of hotels and restaurants.

Sidebars

Throughout the guide you will find blue, peach and green-colored text boxes with lively anecdotes, detailed history and background information.

A Bit of Advice

Green advice boxes found in this guide contain practical tips and handy information relevant to the sight in the Discovering section.

STAR RATINGS★★★

Michelin has given star ratings for more than 100 years. If you're pressed for time, we recommend you visit the ★★★, or ★★ sights first:

★★★	**Highly recommended**
★★	**Recommended**
★	**Interesting**

MAPS

- Driving Tours map, Places to Stay map and Sights map.
- Region maps.
- Maps for major cities and villages.
- Local tour maps.

All maps in this guide are oriented north, unless otherwise indicated by a directional arrow. The term "Local Map" refers to a map within the chapter or Tourism Region. A complete list of the maps found in the guide appears at the back of this book.

PLANNING YOUR TRIP

Michelin Driving Tours   **12**

When and Where to Go   **14**
When To Go..................... 14
Where To Go 14
Themed Tours.................. 15

What to See and Do   **18**
Outdoor Fun 18
Water Sports 21
Sightseeing 23
Spas........................... 27
Activities for Children........... 27
Shopping 28
Books.......................... 29
Films 30

Calendar of Events   **31**

Know Before You Go   **35**
Useful Websites 35
Tourist Offices.................. 35
International Visitors 37
Health 38
Accessibility.................... 38

Getting There   **39**
By Air.......................... 39
By Ship 39
By Train/Rail.................... 39
By Coach/Bus 40

Getting Around   **41**
By Public Transport.............. 41
By Car 41

Where to Stay and Eat   **45**
Where to Stay 45
Where to Eat 46

Useful Words and Phrases   **49**

Basic Information   **52**

INTRODUCTION TO NORTHERN FRANCE

The Region Today   **58**
21st Century 58
Population..................... 58
Local Government............... 59
Economy....................... 59
Food and Drink................. 62
Northern Folklore and Traditions . 64

History   **68**
Time line....................... 68

Art and Culture   **71**
Living like Kings 71
Religious and Civil Architecture .. 74
Monasteries in Île-de-France..... 86
Rural Housing in the North....... 88
Military Architecture............. 90
Faïence and Porcelain in
   Île-de-France................. 91
Landscape Painting.............. 94

Nature   **98**
Picardy 98
Nord-Pas-de-Calais............. 100
Artois......................... 100
Flanders 101
Île-de-France.................. 102
Forests........................ 103
Gardens in Île-de-France 106

DISCOVERING NORTHERN FRANCE

Paris and Surrounds   **110**
Paris.......................... 114
Château d'Écouen 148
Maisons-Laffitte................ 150
Marly-le-Roi................... 151
Meudon 155
Montmorency.................. 157
St-Cloud 159
St-Denis 162
St-Germain-en-Laye............ 166

CONTENTS

Sceaux 171
Sèvres 173
Château de Versailles 174
Parc du château de Versailles 191
Ville de Versailles 201

Île-de-France   **206**
Auvers-Sur-Oise 208
Barbizon 210
Musée de l'Air et de l'Espace
     du Bourget 212
Château de Breteuil 213
Chartres 214
Château de Dampierre 224
Disneyland Resort Paris 226
Château de Ferrières 233
Fontainebleau 235
Forêt de Fontainbleau 245
L'Isle-Adam 252
Abbaye de Jouarre 253
Jouy-en-Josas 255
Maintenon 257
Meaux 259
Milly-La-Forêt 261
Montfort-l'Amaury 263
Moret-Sur-Loing 265
Vallée de l'Ourcq 267
Poissy 270
Abbaye de Port-Royal-
     des-Champs 272
Provins 274
Rambouillet 278
Forêt de Rambouillet 280
La Roche-Guyon 283
Abbaye de Royaumont 285
Rueil-Malmaison 287
Château et Parc de Thoiry 289
Château de Vaux-le-Vicomte 291

Picardy   **294**
Abbeville 296
Albert 297
Amiens 299
Parc Astérix 312
Beauvais 313
Abbaye de Chaalis 318
Château de Chantilly 320
Chemin des Dames 328
Compiègne 329
Corbie 341
Coucy-Le-Château-Aufrique 342
Crécy-en-Ponthieu 344
Laon 345

Parc du Marquenterre 350
Morienval 352
Grottes-Refuges de Naours 353
Noyon 354
Péronne 356
Château de Pierrefonds 357
Château-Fort de Rambures 360
Senlis 361
Soissons 366
Baie de Somme 368
Forêt de St-Gobain 370
St-Leu-d'Esserent 371
St-Quentin 372
St-Riquier 374
St-Valery-sur-Somme 375
La Thiérache 376
Abbaye et Jardins de Valloires . . . 379
Villers-Cotterêts 381

Nord-Pas-de-Calais   **382**
Arras 384
Avesnes-sur-Helpe 392
Bailleul 397
Bavay 400
Bergues 401
Boulogne-sur-Mer 403
Calais 411
Cambrai 415
Cassel 419
La Côte d'Opale 421
Douai 424
Dunkerque 428
Guînes 432
Coupole d'Helfaut-Wizernes 433
Lille 434
Montreuil-sur-Mer 448
Colline de Notre Dame-
     de-Lorette 450
Château d'Olhain 450
Le Quesnoy 451
St-Amand-les-Eaux 452
St-Omer 454
Le Touquet-Paris-Plage 458
Valenciennes 462
Villeneuve-d'Ascq 463

Index 464
Maps and Plans 475
Map Index 476

Welcome to Northern France and the Paris Region

Extending from the trendy banks of the Seine River to the windy flatlands by the North Sea, Northern France and the Paris Region is a land of many contrasts. A wealth of preserved architectural treasures and easily reached peaceful landscapes largely makes up the charms of this lovely part of France.

Relaxing at a café in Saint-Germain-des-Prés

S. Sauvignier/MICHELIN

PARIS AND SURROUNDS
(p110–205)

Bristling along the banks of the Seine River and its many bridges, Paris grew from one ordinary Gallo-Roman burg with its (still standing) arenas to one of the few major political, cultural and artistic centres of attraction on earth. Drawing crowds of students from all over the world since the Middle Ages, it is also known for its relaxed day and night life, and taking in the city pulse while enjoying a café crème with a fresh croissant at one of its lively cafés is a pleasure one doesn't get easily tired of. Other must-dos include getting lost in the trendy Marais narrow streets crowned by scandalous Beaubourg Modern Art Centre; exploring the Louvre palace, one of the most impressive art museums in the world, and its impressionist neighbour, the Musée d'Orsay; tracing the history of the city, from outstanding Middle Age Notre-Dame Cathedral to Saint-Denis Basilica, burial site of the French kings. On to the sumptuous palace of Versailles, with its gardens and music fountains; climbing the Eiffel Tower and strolling along breathtaking Champs-Elysées Avenue. Spare time to visit Paris' hidden gems: neighbouring villages that were swallowed whole with their unique atmosphere, like Montmartre or Auteuil.

ÎLE-DE-FRANCE (p206–293)

Surrounding Paris, the Ile-de-France will appeal to those who seek to escape from crowded metropolises and yearn for peaceful landscapes and family outdoor activities. The region has a couple of beautiful forests: to the southeast, Fontainebleau, renowned for its tormented landscapes of gorges and rocky outcrops, draws hikers and climbers; to the southwest, Rambouillet, once a large royal hunting domain extending around a still standing castle, supports large herds of deer. The peaceful Vallée de Chevreuse harbours some of the finest castles of the region, as well as the remains of Port-Royal Abbey. In the eastern part of the region, the vast agricultural plains of the Beauce,

Landscape of the Vexin française

D. Pazery/ MICHELIN

Porte d'Ardor., Laon

known as the granary of France, are home to two of the most famous French cheeses: Brie and Coulommiers, and the most famous family attraction: Disneyland Resort. On a totally different note, some of the spirit of the impressionists still lingers in the picturesque guinguettes off the banks of Marne River and in the small town of Auvers-sur-Oise, in the northwest.

PICARDY (p294–381)

Cradle of Northern France gothic art, lying to the north of the Parisian Basin, Picardy includes several historical towns: the regional capital of Amiens, with its World Heritage cathedral and quaint water gardens; Carolingian Laon, nestled behind ramparts flanked by watchtowers; Chantilly, where a magnificent castle set in a park designed by Le Nôtre dominates a 15C forest; Merovigian Soissons, where the famous vase story took place... Home to some of the bloodiest battlefields of World War I, Picardy also keeps a faithful watch over the memories of the fallen. Rural flatlands make up most of its landscape, yet the region harbours one of Europe's largest remaining forests: Compiègne, maintained as a hunting ground and cherished by the kings of France. Enjoying a stable, yet fresh and windy climate, the coasts of Picardy exhibit one of France's best hidden natural wonders: the nature

preserve of Baie de Somme, a major stop for migrating water-birds and a shelter for harbour seals.

NORD-PAS-DE-CALAIS
(p382–465)

Lying along the Belgian border, with its capital city, Lille, only one hour away from Paris by train and its main cities easily accessible from London or Dover, Nord-Pas-de-Calais is a major European crossroad, with a strong and lively language and culture of its own. Fairs, like Lille's yearly braderie, draw merry crowds from all Flanders and beyond, around the local belfry. Colourful carnivals are a long standing tradition and hundreds of them happen year round: the one in Dunkerque, an old Flemish city of fishermen and privateers on the North Sea coast, lasts for two months! As a strategic stronghold on the coast of the English Channel, Nord-Pas-de-Calais has seen many a war until the 18C, and a host of beautiful fortified cities such as Boulogne, Calais and Bergues, stand witness of those times. More recent conflicts have also left their imprint on the region, especially on the coast, but lovely preserved sections, like the Côte d'Opale and its cliffy capes (Gris-Nez and Blanc-Nez), still remain. Dutch influence in the region left a wealth of navigable canals, an original way to discover the inner countryside.

Place d'Armes, Douai

9

Côte d'Opale, Pas-de-Calais
Y. Tierny/MICHELIN

Michelin Driving Tours

1 ROYAL PALACES OF ÎLE-DE-FRANCE

420km/261mi starting from St-Germain-en-Laye

This large circuit, centred on Paris, embraces the most impressive royal residences in France. Just on the outskirts of Paris, the Château of St-Germain-en-Laye is especially interesting for the prehistoric art collection. Écouen is home to the national museum of the Renaissance. Vaux-le-Vicomte displays wonderful symmetry and landscape design, while visitors are moved by the sad fate of the man who built it. Fontainebleau, on the edge of the large forest of the same name, evokes the imperial grandeur of Napoleon and echoes of his downfall, and Versailles, of course, is legendary for its splendour and its role in history.

2 FROM VERSAILLES TO CHARTRES THROUGH RAMBOUILLET FOREST

168km/104mi starting from Versailles

The forest of Rambouillet was once the favoured hunting ground of kings and, later, presidents of France.

Many parts are open to the public and the establishment of the Haute Vallée de la Chevreuse Regional Nature Park has preserved typical local villages and churches. Breteuil and Dampierre are in beautiful natural settings, ideal places to spend some time outdoors. On the way to Chartres, the forests give way to a vast plain, across which the cathedral spires, seen for some distance, pinpoint the city. It is not difficult to imagine how pilgrims must have felt as they neared this awesome building. After admiring the renowned stained-glass windows and the inlaid labyrinth, or maybe enjoying a tour with the cathedral guide, it is worth exploring the Old Town along the banks of the River Eure, with its beautiful half-timbered houses and narrow streets.

3 CASTLES AND CATHEDRALS

510km/317mi starting from Amiens

This tour meanders through the countryside of Picardy into Oise, a landscape that is easy on the eye, with huge expanses (and some very small ones, too, at the edge of villages) of barley and wheat, dotted with wildflowers. After Beauvais, you enter the distinctive landscape of the Bray, where groves and meadows alternate. The village of Gerberoy is one of 'The Most Beautiful Villages of France', a place of lovely half-timbered houses. And as you contemplate the many marvellous Gothic churches, don't forget to stop and enjoy the regional cuisine of Picardy, which includes many vegetable-based dishes such as hearty soups, and the tasty *ficelle Picarde*, a form of stuffed pancake.

4 THE VALLEYS OF PICARDY

350km/217.4mi starting from Amiens

This is a good tour to make when all the family is along for the ride, as there is something for everyone. Follow the meandering route of the River Somme from Amiens, and perhaps stop to visit the Samara Prehistoric Park or Naours, where an amazing network of underground passageways is big enough to shelter 3,000 people. When you reach the coast, the Parc Ornithologique du Marquenterre offers 3 000ha/7 413 acres of pine forests, sand and mud flats that are an irresistible invitation for thousands of migratory birds. Nearby, if you're not too squeamish, is the Escargotière du Marquenterre, where edible snails are bred and sold. Leave time for water play, or time for a snooze on the warm sand at Berck-sur-Mer or Le Touquet-Paris-Plage. The delightful gardens at Valloires are likely to be less crowded than the beach, and offer a lovely and restful interlude.

5 THE ARTOIS REGION

300km/186.4mi starting from Arras
This mining region has always shown a strong festive spirit and if you happen to visit at carnival time, you may even see jolly giants roaming the streets of Douai, and be carried away by the festivities. You may stop at any time to enjoy a moment in a traditional brasserie or listen to the chiming of a carillon, one of the many village bell towers found throughout northern France. In the Fine Arts Museum in Valenciennes, you can admire works by Bosch and Rubens. On your way to Lille and French Flanders, you may wish to take advantage of the natural benefits of the spring water at Saint-Amand. Then on to Béthune and its Grand Place, and south to the medieval castle of Olhain in the heart of the mining area.

6 THE OPAL COAST

250km/155mi starting from Boulogne.
Catch the fresh sea breezes as you drive along the cliff-top roads or stop to clamber in the dunes and play on the beaches of the Côte d'Opale. Join the sunbathers or sand-yachters along the vast sandy beaches of Paris-Plage at Le Touquet. Or see the live sharks and rays year-round at Nausicaä. Many travellers enjoy a tour of the busy harbours at Boulogne and Calais; there are also traditional craftsmen at work in the region: a stop-over in Desvres, for example, is a chance to see unique ceramics being made. Inland from Boulogne the countryside is a patchwork of fields, trees and hedgerows; the Audomarois wetlands are a protected area where you may visit the Regional Nature Park's exhibition areas or enjoy nature discovery walks. If you are feeling hot and tired, why not take a boat ride on the *watergangs*, canals running between the fields, and home to many species of waterfowl. Seafood lovers will find everything they crave here, and the fresh local produce is a lovely com-plement to other regional specialities.

7 BELFRIES IN FLANDERS

250km/155mi starting from Lille
Leave the friendly city of Lille behind and head out to the hills and dales of Flanders. This little region has a style of its own, as you will soon see by observing the architecture of the fortified villages, churches and mills, and inside the charming little eateries and watering holes known locally as *estaminets*. Local brewers contribute to the fun when traditional festivities are held. This corner of France is a favourite with those who love good beer. It's also an area rich in military history, from Vauban's forts and Hitler's missile launchpads to Villeneuve-d'Ascq's memorial and Dunkirk's daring evacuation. Let the world-famous belfries of French Flanders, 23 of them listed UNESCO World Heritage sites, lead the way throughout this unique landscape.

8 THE AVESNOIS COUNTRYSIDE

350km/217.4mi starting from St-Quentin
Heading east from St-Quentin, the road follows the Oise Valley, dotted with fortified churches. This is where Maroilles, a strong-tasting cheese, is produced. The drive then takes you through the region known locally as l'Avesnois, named after the main town, Avesnes-sur-Helpe, and close to the Belgian border. In fact, there are two rivers named Helpe, the Majeure and the Mineure, which flow through the Regional Nature Park. Since the Middle Ages, the landscape has been marked by small villages set around the mills and forges that sprung up beside powerful abbeys. There are plenty of opportunities to stop along this part of the itinerary and enjoy the amenities of the park. On your way south from Bavay and its Gallo-Roman remains, stop in Cateau-Cambrésis to admire works by Matisse. Between Cambrai and St-Quentin, the Riqueval tunnel runs through the plateau separating the Somme and Escaut rivers.

When and Where to Go

WHEN TO GO
SEASONS

Inland, the winters are chilly and darkness comes early in the northern latitudes. As spring turns to summer, the days become long and warm, and by June the sun lingers until after 10pm. Spring and autumn provide a chance to explore the valleys of the Aa, Canche, Authie and Somme, and the different regional nature parks.

Spring in Île-de-France offers a glorious contrast between the vivid yellow of rapeseed fields against the green background of the copses and forests, while autumn in the oak and beech woods of Compiègne, Rambouillet, Sénart or St-Germain is accompanied by the warm colours of changing leaves.

CLIMATE

While the beaches of the Opal Coast are spectacular, stretching out for 1km/0.6mi at low tide, the relatively cool weather and the chilly waters of the Channel are generally more appealing for shell-seekers, horse riders, landsailers and kite-flyers than for swimmers. In the winter months, the coast is often buffeted by strong winds. Statistically, June is the sunniest month on the coast, August the warmest. The highest period of rainfall is in November, and the lowest in April (for a total of 170 days per year). Peak summer temperatures usually hover around 25°C/77°F.

WEATHER FORECAST

National forecast: ℘32 50
Local forecast: ℘0 892 68 02 XX, where XX is the number of the *département* (e.g. for the Nord – ℘*0 892 68 02* **59**).
This information is also available on www.meteofrance.com.

WHERE TO GO
CITY BREAKS
Paris

If you have a long weekend in Paris, begin with a Seine River Cruise followed by one of the hop-on, hop-off coach tours to get an overview of the major sights. You'll want to explore the charming, history-packed streets of the Marais, St-Germain-des-Près and Montmartre on foot, where you'll find plenty of boutiques, cafés, and sights worth a closer look. Reserve a table in advance at one really great restaurant, and possibly an opera, dance or cabaret show. Pick one or two museums that fit your interests, or if the weather is right join the locals in one of the beautiful city parks.

Lille

Discover the unique charm of French Flanders with a long weekend in Lille. Start with a walk through the historic Old Town to get acquainted with the distinct Flemish architectural style of the 17C and 18C buildings. Shop for luxury goods, antiques, and second-hand books in the Vieille Bourse before peeking into the history museum in the ancient Hospice Comtesse. Art lovers should reserve the better part of a day to the world-class Palais des Beaux Arts, while fans of military fortifications can visit the Citadelle with advance reservations. In the evening enjoy the regional cuisine

What to Pack

As little as possible! Cleaning and laundry services are available everywhere. Most personal items can be replaced at reasonable cost. Try to pack everything into one suitcase and a small bag. Porter help is in limited or non-existent in rural France, and new purchases simply add to the original weight. If you think it may be necessary, take an extra bag for packing new purchases, shopping at the open-air market, carrying a picnic, etc. Be sure luggage is clearly labelled and old travel tags removed. Do not pack medication in checked luggage; keep it with you.

Aerial view of Bergues

and locally brewed beers, or a show at the Folies de Paris.

ONE WEEK

Using Paris as a base, explore the Île-de-France on day trips starting with Fontainebleau-Vaux-le-Vicomte and Barbizon. A morning in Chartres can be complemented by visits to Breteuil or Dampierre and the Abbaye de Port Royal des Champs. Spend a full day at Versailles, Disneyland or, to appeal to all ages, the medieval town of Provins. For a more relaxed day, visit the riverside village of Auvers-sur-Oise and L'Isle-Adam, followed by a tour of Napoléon's Malmaison. A day enjoying the artworks at the Château of Chantilly and an equestrian show at the living horse museum can be finished with a stroll through the romantic medieval streets of Senlis. If the weather is agreeable you can spend the final day hiking in the beautiful forests in Compiègne.

TWO WEEKS

A second week will give you time to visit the cathedral at Amiens, followed by an afternoon in the gardens of the Abbaye de Valloires. Spend a day exploring the Opal Coast, with an afternoon at the beach or the Nausicaä aquarium. Visits to St-Omer and Bergues can be combined with

stops at Second World War military sites like La Coupole d'Helfaut-Wizernes. A day in Lilles will show French Flanders at its best, while Arras shows off the best of the Artoise region. Enjoy the natural sights on your last day with a drive through the Avesnois Regional Nature Park and its charming villages.

THEMED TOURS
HISTORY TOURS

These are itineraries based, for the most part, on architectural heritage presented in its historical context. There are several historical routes in the area covered in this guide:

- ◆ **Route du Camp du Drap d'Or:** the 'Cloth of Gold' route from Calais to Arras. Information from the Association Route du Camp du Drap d'or, 20 rue Clemenceau, 62340 Guînes, &03 21 35 24 90.
- ◆ **Route des Archers:** evoking the battle of Agincourt, when the French knights were defeated by the English archers during the Hundred Years' War. Contact the Agincourt tourist office, &03 21 47 27 53.
- ◆ **Route des Valois:** the Valois dynasty in the heart of the forests of Retz and Compiègne. Contact M. de Montesquiou, abbaye

de Longpont, 02600 Longpont, 𝒞03 23 96 01 53.

- **Route du Lys de France et de la Rose de Picardie:** 'Lily of France and Rose of Picardy' route from St-Denis to Boulogne-sur-Mer, via Écouen, Royaumont, l'Isle-Adam, Gerberoy, Poix-en-Picardie, St-Riquier, Rue and Montreuil. Apply to the Château de Troissereux, 60112 Troissereux, 𝒞03 44 79 00 00.
- **Route du Roy Soleil:** châteaux occupied by the Sun King Louis XIV.

These and other special itineraries are the subjects of brochures that can be found in most local tourist offices.

CULTURAL HERITAGE

- **Route des Villes Fortifiées:** This itinerary was set up by an association for the promotion of the **walled towns** of the Nord-Pas-de-Calais region. It includes 13 of the area's main citadels: Arras, Avesnes-sur-Helpe, Bergues, Boulogne-sur-Mer, Calais, Cambrai, Condé-sur-l'Escaut, Gravelines, Lille, Maubeuge, Montreuil-sur-Mer, Le Quesnoy and St-Omer. The itinerary is 500km/311mi in length, but is subdivided into shorter sections that provide many possibilities for excursions and tours. Each of the towns has a *Route des Villes Fortifiées* signpost at its entrance, accompanied by a logo. A map and brochure telling the history of each town are available from the local tourist offices and from the **Comité Régional de Tourisme du Nord-Pas-de-Calais** (&see *Tourist Offices in France, p33*).
- **Route des Abbayes en Yvelines:** this tourist itinerary passes via the Cistercian abbey of Les Vaux-de-Cernay and the abbey of Port-Royal-des-Champs, associated with the history of Jansenism.
- **Chemins des Retables:** several tours enable visitors to discover the rich interior of churches in

the Flanders region. Contact the Association des Retables de Flandre, BP 6535, 59386 Dunkerque Cedex, 𝒞03 28 68 69 78.

- **Route des Maisons d'Écrivains:** this opens the door to residences of famous authors in the Île-de-France, including Chateaubriand, Zola and Dumas. Information centre: 13 avenue d'Eylau, 75116 Paris, 𝒞01 47 27 45 51.
- **Route des Jardins et Châteaux:** around Paris: parks and châteaux in Île-de-France, including Breteuil, Sceaux, Courances, Fontainebleau, and St-Cloud.
- **Route des Impressionnistes en Val d'Oise:** Impressionist painters in the Val d'Oise region, Auvers-sur-Oise, Pontoise, L'Isle-Adam, Vétheuil, La Roche-Guyon, Argenteuil … in the footsteps of Manet, Daubigny, Pissarro, Renoir and Van Gogh. Information: 𝒞01 30 29 51 00.
- **Balades au Pays des Impressionnistes:** nine municipalities situated along the River Seine form what is known as Impressionist country, including Carrières-sur-Seine, Bougival, Louveciennes, Marly-le Roi, le Port-Marly, Le Pecq-sur-Seine and Noisy-le-Roi. A leaflet is available from the tourist offices in these towns.

TRADITIONS

Windmills – Once a common sight in the region, surviving examples of windmills have been taken under the wing of a local association, which has begun to restore and develop them. The **Centre Régional de Moulinologie**, Musée des Moulins *(59650 Villeneuve-d'Ascq, 𝒞03 20 05 49 34)*, can provide brochures, maps and books on the subject. Most of the windmills cited in this guide are open to visitors. On the plains of the Beauce and Brie, a few sails still catch the wind from time to time, and you can buy freshly ground flour there. Listed below are a few operating windmills where visitors are welcome, at least for a look around the outside of the mill.

In the Beauce *(located off the A 10 "Allainville" exit or, from Orléans, the "Allaines-Chartres" exit):*

+ **Ouarville:** Open Sundays from Easter to 1 November 2.30–6pm. ✆02 37 22 13 87.
+ **Levesville-la-Chenard:** Sunday afternoons, June to August, or by appointment. ✆02 37 22 13 10.
+ **Sannois:** on Mont Trouillet *(near Enghien-les-Bains)*, open Sundays 1.30–6.30pm. Contact the Sannois town hall *(mairie)*. ✆01 39 98 20 00.

The following windmills are described in the *Discovering* section of this guide:

+ Moulins de CASSEL, Steenmeulen (at Terdeghem), Drievemeulen, Noordmeulen near Steenvoorde, Moulin Deschodt at Wormhout *(see CASSEL).*
+ Oudankmeulen at Boeschepe *(see BAILLEUL).*
+ Musée des Moulins *(see VILLENEUVE D'ASCQ).*

The association's annual windmill festival is held around the region in June.

Carillons – Chiming bells are part of everyday life in many towns in northern France and particularly in Flanders. A carillon consists of several bells hung in a bell-tower or belfry. The bells ring out different refrains to indicate the hour, the quarter and the half hour. The word comes from a medieval term 'quadrillon''', a peal of four bells ringing in harmony. In the Middle Ages, clocks were mechanical; they included small bells that the bell-ringer struck using a mallet or hammer. After a gradual increase in the number of bells, the mallet was replaced by a keyboard. The automatic system with cylinders, used in some places, is progressively being replaced by an electrical system that is easier to maintain.

The main carillons in the Nord-Pas-de-Calais area are as follows:

+ **Tourcoing** – Eglise St-Christophe: 61 bells
+ **Douai** – Town hall: 62 bells
+ **Bergues** – Belfry: 50 bells
+ **Avesnes-sur-Helpe** – Collégiale St-Nicolas: 48 bells
+ **Capelle-la-Grande** – Belfry: 49 bells
+ **Dunkerque** – Tour St-Eloi: 48 bells
+ **Le Quesnoy** – Town hall: 48 bells
+ **St-Amand-les-Eaux** – Tower on the abbey church: 48 bells
+ **Seclin** – Collégiale St-Piat: 42 bells
+ **Orchies** – Church: 48 bells

Carillon concerts are held regularly in certain towns *(for information, contact the local tourist office).*

LOCAL CRAFTS AND INDUSTRY

Below are a few suggestions for visits; it is usually necessary to make an appointment.

+ **Usine élévatoire de Tribardou** – Route de Charmentray, 77450 Tribardou, ✆01 60 09 95 00. *Guided tours year round, on request.* This factory, situated a few miles from Meaux, uses an impressive waterwheel to pump water from the River Marne and supply the Ourcq canal; an interesting insight into 19C technical methods.
+ **Météo-France** – Centre départemental des Yvelines, 3 rue Teisserenc-de-Bort, 78190 Trappes, ✆01 30 66 47 80. This regional weather station is open to the public on Thursdays.
+ **Verrerie d'art de Soisy-sur-École** – Le Moulin de Noues, BP 2, 91840 Soisy-sur-École, ✆01 64 98 00 03. Visit of the glassworks, exhibition centre and salesroom.
+ **Coca Cola Entreprise** – 1–3 rue J.J.-Rousseau, ZAC Les Radars, 91350 Grigny, ✆01 69 02 20 00; Monday to Friday 10am–5pm.

What to See and Do

OUTDOOR FUN
WALKING

There is an extensive network of well-marked footpaths in France which make rambling (la randonnée pédestre) a breeze. Several **Grande Randonnée (GR)** trails, recognisable by the red and white horizontal marks on trees, rocks and in town on walls, signposts etc, go through the region. Along with the GR, there are also the **Petite Randonnée (PR)** paths, which are usually blazed with blue (2hr walk), yellow (2hr15min–3hr45min) or green (4–6hr) marks. Of course, with appropriate maps, you can combine walks to suit your desires.

To use these trails, obtain the topo-guide for the area published by the **Fédération Française de la Randonnée Pédestre**. Their information centre is at 14 rue Riquet, 75019 Paris, ☎01 44 89 93 93, www.ffrp.asso.fr. Some English-language editions are available. Another source of maps and guides for excursions on foot is the **Institut National Géographique (IGN)**, which has a boutique in Paris at 107 rue de la Boétie (off the Champs-Elysées); to order from abroad, visit the website (www.ign.fr) for addresses

of wholesalers in your country. Among their publications, France 1M903 is a map showing all of the GR and PR in France (4.90€); the Série Bleue and Top 25 maps, at a scale of 1:25 000 (1cm = 250m), show all paths, whether waymarked or not, as well as refuges, camp sites, beaches, etc.

The **Conseil général du Nord** publishes, jointly with the **Association Départementale de la Randonnée**, itineraries covering various distances, with maps and information. Contact the **Comité Départemental de Tourisme du Nord** (for address, ♿see Tourist Offices in France, p33).

An association publishes a guide (Guide des Sentiers de Promenade dans le Massif Forestier de Fontainebleau) on the famous forest south-east of Paris – a popular spot for ramblers, climbers, mushroom hunters and cyclists on day trips – and provides guided tours that are open to all. For a programme, visit the bilingual website **Association des Amis de la Forêt de Fontainebleau** (26 rue de la Cloche, BP 14, 77301 Fontainebleau Cedex, ☎01 64 23 46 45, www.aaff.fr). To join up with fellow ramblers, try the **Randonneurs d'Île-de-France club** (92 rue du Moulin-Vert, 75014 Paris, ☎01 45 42 24 72, www.rifrando.asso.fr), which organises walks in the region (small membership fee).

Brisk walk along the Côte d'Opale

Y. Tierny/ MICHELIN

CYCLING

The network of country roads is ideal for cycling. Lists of cycle hire shops are available from local tourist offices. Bikes are carried free of charge on many regional trains and on the Paris-Amiens-Boulogne line. Cycle tours are easy to organise as there are cycle hire firms near or in train stations close to the main forests.

The **Fédération française de Cyclotourisme** (8 rue Jean-Marie-Jégo, 75013 Paris, ℰ01 44 16 88 88, www.ffct. org) supplies itineraries covering most of France, outlining mileage, the level of difficulty of routes and sights to see. Mountain biking *(VTT)*, or off-road cycling, has become very popular in France. There are many tracks laid out in the region, suitable for both new and experienced riders.

The **Office National des Forêts** edits publications for mountain bike enthusiasts – *Guides VTT Evasion* (numbers 1 to 8). They include itineraries covering between 15km/9mi and 30km/18.6mi. www.onf.fr.

The **Fédération Française de Cyclisme** (5 rue de Rome, 93561 Rosny-sous-Bois Cedex, ℰ01 49 35 69 24) also publishes a guide with over 43 452km/27 000mi of marked mountain biking tracks, available on their website: www.ffc.fr.

GOLF

Golfers can enjoy their favourite sport and take part in competitions in the region. Courses abound in the Nord-Pas-de-Calais region, in pleasantly rustic settings taking players up hill and over dale, on the edge of forests, or overlooking the sea. Contact the relevant Comité Régional de Tourisme *(for address, ⌂see Tourist Offices in France, p33)*. to obtain the brochure entitled *Golfs Nord-Pas-de-Calais*. Picardy has golf courses in Fort-Mahon, Quend-Plage, Grand-Laviers, Nampont-Saint-Martin, Salouel *(3km/2mi from Amiens)* and Querrieu *(7km/4.3mi from Amiens)*.

Horse riding on the Opal Coast

Y. Tierny/ MICHELIN

Ligue de Golf de Picardie, Rond-point du Grand Cerf, Lys-Chantilly, 60260 Lamorlaye, ℰ03 44 21 26 28. **Fédération Française de Golf**, 68 rue Anatole-France, 92309 Levallois-Perret Cedex, ℰ01 41 49 77 00, www.ffgolf.org.

HORSE RIDING

The Nord-Pas-de-Calais and Île-de-France regions have hundreds of miles of bridle paths running through forests or along the coast.

The **Comité National de Tourisme équestre**, 9 boulevard Mac-Donald, 75019 Paris, ℰ01 53 26 15 50, www. cnte.fr, publishes an annual review called *Cheval Nature, l'officiel du tourisme équestre en France*. It lists all the possibilities for riding by *région* and *département*.

Addresses of riding stables and information on bridle paths are available from:

- **Association Régionale de Tourisme équestre Nord-Pas-de-Calais,** Le Paddock, 62223 St-Laurent-de-Blangy, ℰ03 21 55 40 81.
- **Association Régionale de Tourisme équestre Picardie**, 8 rue Fournier-Sarlovèze, B.P. 20636, 60203 Compiègne Cedex, ℰ03 44 40 19 54.

🐎 **Association Régionale de Tourisme équestre d'Île-de-France (ARTEIF),** 1 rue Barbès, 95260 Beaumont-sur-Oise, ℰ01 34 70 05 34.
The brochure *Chevauchée en Île-de-France* lists the main centres in the region and their activities.

HORSE FARM

It is possible to visit the Haras national de Bréviaires, a few miles north of Rambouillet. G*uided tours (1hr30min) on first Saturdays of the month at 3pm. Closed August. 8€. ℰ01 34 57 85 38. www.haras-nationaux.fr.*

LANDSAILING

Landsailing, or sand yachting, uses a strange combination of a three-wheeled go-kart and a sail-boat. Powered solely by the wind, they may exceed 100kph/62mph on the vast stretches of fine, hard sand along the coasts of northern France. In addition to landsailers, there are also speedsail boards which resemble windsurfing boards on wheels.
For information, contact the **Fédération Française de Char à voile**, 19 rue des Sables, 62600 Berck-sur-Mer, ℰ03 21 89 99 10; www.ffcv.org.

KITE FLYING

This is another popular activity in northern France, particularly on the beaches. To obtain a good kite and

Landsailing

Having fun on the beach

learn how to fly it, it is advisable to join a club or an association *(addresses are available from local tourist offices).* For general information, contact the **Fédération française de vol libre** (hang-gliding, paragliding and kite-flying), 4 rue de Suisse, 06000 Nice, ℰ04 97 03 82 82; www.ffvl.fr.

ROCK CLIMBING

The Île-de-France area offers climbers numerous possibilities for all levels at a number of natural sites; the most renowned and best equipped for bouldering are to be found in and around **Fontainebleau Forest**.
The highest rocks are at Larchant and the Dame Jouanne. The Massif des Trois-Pignons offers remarkable scenery and many different levels of difficulty. Bouldering may look easy, but requires good technique and adherence to safety procedures, and is best practised with club or professional climbers.
Fédération Française de la Montagne et de l'Escalade, 8 quai de la Marne, 75019 Paris, ℰ01 40 18 75 50, www.ffme.fr.
Club alpin Île-de-France, 24 rue Laumière, 75019 Paris, ℰ01 53 72 88 00.
Centre européen d'escalade, 3 rue des Alouettes, Senia 219, 94320 Thiais, ℰ01 46 86 38 44.
Mur Mur, 55 rue Cartier-Bresson, 93500 Pantin, ℰ01 48 46 11 00, www.murmur.fr, or boulevard Garibaldi, 92130 Issy-les-Moulineaux, ℰ01 58 88 00 22. Good indoor installations.

Horse Racing

The Paris region has the largest number of race tracks anywhere in France, hosting all types of horse races. **France Galop** specialises in improving breeds of horses in France and manages the flat racing tracks in the Paris area: 46 place Abel-Gance, 92655 Boulogne Cedex, ℘01 49 10 20 30; www.france-galop.com.

Track	Trotting	Flat course	Steeplechase	Main races
Chantilly (June)	–	●	–	Prix du Jockey-Club
(June)				Prix de Diane-Hermès
Enghien (April)	●	–	●	Prix de l'Atlantique
				Prix d'Europe (July) Grand Steeple-Chase (October)
Longchamp (June)	–	●	–	Grand Prix de Paris
				Arc de Triomphe (October)
Maisons-Laffitte	–	●	Cross-country	Prix Robert Papin (July)
St-Cloud (July)	–	●	–	Grand Prix de St-Cloud Critérium de St-Cloud (October)

The region also includes the Parisian race tracks of Auteuil (steeplechases) and Vincennes (trotting races).

Rock climbing in Fontainebleau Forest

Ph. Gajic/MICHELIN

GO-KARTING

There are several tracks in the Paris region, including:
RKB Racing Kart Buffo, RN 19, BP3, 77390 Les Étards (35km/22mi from Paris), ℘01 64 07 61 66; . Kart rental available from age 7 upwards.
Aérodrome de Pontoise-Cormeilles, 95650 Boissy-l'Aillerie, ℘01 30 73 28 00; www.rkc.fr; three tracks including one for kids.

SKIING

In the north, Noeux-les-Mines has been converted into a ski resort without snow! Even so, the artificial runs are quite enjoyable.
Loisinord, rue Léon-Blum, 62290 Noeux-les-Mines, ℘03 21 26 84 84; two runs: a main one and one for learning; skiing instructor from the French skiing school available.

WATER SPORTS
SWIMMING

Bathing conditions are indicated by flags on beaches which are monitored by lifeguards (no flags means no lifeguards): green indicates it is safe to bathe and lifeguards are on duty; yellow warns that conditions are not that good, but lifeguards are still in attendance; red means bathing is forbidden as conditions are too dangerous. Quality control tests take place regularly from June onwards. Well-equipped beaches offer facilities such as swimming pools, water-skiing, diving, jet-skiing, landsailing, kite-flying, rowing, etc. Information is available from local tourist offices.

SAILING AND WINDSURFING

The Paris region boasts around 15 lakes and half a dozen locations on the River Seine and River Marne where sailing is available. There are a number of sports and recreation parks *(bases de loisirs)*, where windsurfing and dinghy or catamaran sailing are possible, occasionally combined with other activities such as tennis, swimming, horse riding, golf or water-skiing. Among others, these centres include **St-Quentin-en-Yvelines** *(D 912, 78190 Trappes, ℘01 30 62 20 12)*; **Moisson-Mousseaux** *(78840 Moisson, t01 34 79 33 34)*; **Jablines/Annet** *(77450 Jablines, ℘01 60 26 04 31)* and **Cergy-Neuville** *(rue des Étangs, 95001 Cergy-Neuville, ℘01 30 30 21 55)*.

There are sailing schools all along the coast of northern France from Bray-Dunes to Auly-Onival. Some of the inland lakes are also ideal for these sports, for example the Val-Joly recreation area in the Avesnois region

Fishermen along the lake

G. Crépel/MICHELIN

(⊙ see map under L'AVESNOIS), the Etangs de la Sensée and Escaut, and the Lac de Monampteuil near Soissons. For information, contact the:

- **Fédération Française de Voile**, 55 avenue Kléber, 75784 Paris Cedex 16. ℘01 45 53 68 00. www.ffvoile.org
- **France station Voile – Nautisme et Tourisme**, 17 rue Boissière. 75116 Paris. ℘01 44 05 96 55; www.france-nautisme.com.

CANOEING AND KAYAKING

Canoes, propelled by a single-bladed paddle, are ideal for family day trips from a base or down a river. **Kayaks**, propelled by a double-bladed paddle, are more suitable for exploring lakes and the lower part of rivers. **Sea-kayaks** are narrower and longer and beginners are advised to start out in the company of an experienced guide.

FRESHWATER FISHING

The area around Paris offers many lakes and rivers for anglers of all levels, moreover northern France is crossed by many rivers, waterways and lakes; a paradise for anglers, especially along the Somme, Course, Lys, Aisne, Oise, Aa rivers and in the Seven-valleys region (Canche, Authie, Ternoise, etc.). The map-brochure with commentary entitled *Pêche en France* can be obtained from the **Conseil Supérieur de la Pêche** *(134 avenue de Malakoff, 75016 Paris, ℘01 45 02 20 20)* or from the *Fédération de Pêche* (angling union) in each *département*. Obligatory fishing permits *(cartes de pêche)* are often for sale on site in cafés or sports shops located near popular spots. Between June and September, it is possible, in certain places, to obtain a special holiday fishing permit *(permis de pêche 'vacances')*, valid for a fortnight. Day permits are available for fishing in some of the region's lakes.

SEA FISHING

Day or half-day fishing trips are organised along the coast of northern France. The equipment is supplied by the

Chemin de Fer de la Baie de Somme

Th. Demont/ MICHELIN

organisers. Information can be obtained from:
Fédération Française des Pêcheurs en Mer, Résidence Alliance, centre Jorlis, 64600 Anglet. ℘05 59 31 00 73. www.ffpm-national.com.

SIGHTSEEING
TOURIST TRAINS

Le p'tit train de la Haute-Somme – South of Albert, 3km/2mi from Bray-sur-Somme, there is a narrow-gauge railway running from Froissy to Dompierre via the Cappy Tunnel *(300m/328yd)*. The round trip covers a distance of 14km/8.7mi and takes about 1hr30min. A visit to the railway museum rounds off the trip.

Le Chemin de Fer de la Baie de Somme – A train of old carriages with platforms runs through fields and salt marshes from Noyelles to Le Crotoy, St-Valéry-sur-Mer and Cayeux-sur-Mer.

Chemin de Fer Touristique du Vermandois – From St-Quentin to Origny-Ste-Benoîte *(44km/27mi round trip)* via Ribemont. A steam train or an old-fashioned rail motor car crosses and then runs alongside the Canal de la Sambre in Oise.

For information and bookings, contact **Laure Peillon** *(CFTV, BP 152, 02104 St-Quentin Cedex,* ℘03 23 07 88 38).

Chemin de Fer Touristique de la vallée de l'Aa – The journey runs for 15km/9mi from Arques to Lumbres along the old branch of the St-Omer to Boulogne-sur-Mer line. It enables a visit to the Fontinettes barge lift and stops at the Coupole d'Helfaut-Wizernes Second World War rocket-launching pad. Information can be found by calling ℘03 21 12 19 19, or visit http://www.cftva.c.la.

Tramway Touristique de la vallée de la Deûle – Trips by tram along a metre-gauge track over 3km/2mi between Marquette and Wambrechies in the suburbs of Lille. For information, contact AMITRAM, 1521 rue de Bourbourg, 59670 Bavinchove, ℘03 28 42 44 58. www.amitram.asso.fr.

COACH TOURS

Paris Vision – Day trips to many Île-de-France destinations: Thoiry, Provins, Fontainebleau, Vaux-le-Vicomte, Chantilly in minivans for up to 12 passengers, and coach tours to Versailles, Disneyland, Parc Asterix, Chartres and Giverny. 214 rue de Rivoli, 75001 Paris. ℘01 42 60 86 00. www.parisvision.com.

Viatours – Coach trips (1–3 days) to Northern France and Belgian battlefields (Somme, Ypres Salient, Vimy Ridge) Lille, Giverny and Versailles. ℘+1 (702) 648-5873 (USA). www.viator.com.

Cityrama – Full-day excursions to Barbizon, Auvers-sur-Oise, Chartres, Provins, Thoiry, Fontainebleau, Vaux-le-Vicomte, Chantilly and Disneyland. 149 Rue Saint Honoré, 75001 PARIS 01 44 55 61 00. www.pariscity rama.com.

BIRD'S-EYE VIEWS
Tourist Flights
A 35min plane flight is one of the highlights of a weekend break (2 days and nights) in the Oise *département*: contact Loisirs Accueil at the **Comité Départe-mentale du tourisme de l'Oise** (03 44 45 82 12). Other tourist flights are organised by the following: **Aéroclub de St-Omer** (*Plateau des Bruyères, BP 7, 62967 Longuenesse, 03 21 38 25 42, http://acsto.free.fr*) – flights over the Helfaut-Wizernes rocket-launching-pad area and the Marais audomarois.
ULM flights are available from Dreux or Viabon daily from April to October, depending on weather conditions; contact **Loisirs Accueil Eure-et-Loir** (*10 rue du Dr-Maunoury, BP 67, 28002 Chartres Cedex, 02 37 84 01 00. www. tourisme28.com*); also from Abbeville: contact **Ludair** (*Abbeville airport, 80132 Buigny-St-Maclou, 03 22 24 36 59, www.ludair.com*) – flights over the Baie de Somme.

Hot-air ballooning
Take off from Moret-sur-Loing with professional bilingual pilots on a tour of the landscapes which inspired the Impressionists or of the hunting grounds of the French kings: from April to October, mornings and evenings, depending on the weather:

France Montgolfières (*24 rue de Paris, 77240 Champs-sur-Marne, 01 47 00 66 44, www.franceballoons. com*). This company is certified by the civil aviation authority. Flights also available in other areas of France. Also available from La Roche-Guyon with **Airshow** (*6 rue du Faubourg-Poissonnière, 01 53 24 95 47, www. airshow.fr*); and from Hazebrouck with **Club Montgolfière Passion** (*253 rue d'Aire, 59190 Hazebrouck, 03 28 41 65 59*).

Tethered Balloon Rides
Tethered rides are organised outside the Parc préhistorique de Samara, near Amiens: **Samara**, 80310 La Chaussée-Tirancourt, 03 22 51 82 83.

CRUISING THE WATERWAYS
The rivers and canals once plied by well-laden barges constitute over 1 609km/1 000mi of navigable waterways providing holidaymakers with an opportunity to enjoy a cruise or hire their own boat; both excellent ways of visiting the region.
The **Comité Régional de Tourisme d'Île-de-France** has joined with the Paris Port Authority and Voies Navigables de France to publish a brochure on boating opportunities in Île-de-France, *Prenez le large en Île-de-France*. They can also provide the *Tourisme fluvial – Guide pratique*, which gives addresses of rental agencies and marina facilities. Likewise, the **Comité Regional de Tourisme du Nord-Pas-de-Calais** (*for address, see Tourist Offices in*

Tourist Passes

The **Paris Museum Pass** allows free direct entry to the permanent collections of 60 museums and monuments **in and around Paris**. Valid for 2 days (*32€*), 4 consecutive days (*48€*) or 6 consecutive days (*64€*), it can be purchased in participating museums and monuments, at major metro stations, the tourist information bureau at the Carrousel du Louvre, and at the National Tourist Bureau in the Champs Elysées. Information: 01 44 61 96 60.
Visit www.parismuseumpass.com for participating museums and hyperlinks.
Many other towns in Île-de-France, Nord and Pas-de-Calais have their own Passport offers for sightseeing, dining, or even accommodation. Be sure to ask at the local tourist offices.

France, p33) publishes a brochure on the area's inland waterway network.

Cruises and boat rentals:

Marne Loisirs –
Chemin des 2 rivières –
77 260 La Ferté sous Jouarre,
✆03 85 53 76 70,
www.marne-loisirs.fr.
Live-aboard boat rentals (no permit required) for 2–12 people.

Nogent-sur-Marne Marina –
Quai du Port, 94130 Nogent-sur-Marne, ✆01 48 71 41 65.
Pedal boats and small motor boats for hire.

Arques Plaisance –
Base nautique, rue d'Alsace,
62510 Arques, ✆03 21 98 35 97.
River launches for hire for a day, a weekend or a week; river permit or pilot on board.

Locaboat Plaisance –
Small barges for hire on the River Somme (departure from Cappy); reservations: Port au Bois,
BP 150, 89303 Joigny Cedex,
✆03 86 91 72 72,
www.locaboat.com.

Somme Plaisance –
27 rue Georges-Clemenceau,
80110 Moreuil, ✆03 22 09 75 50.
Boat rental (4–10 people),
departure from Corbie.

Maps of waterways are available from:
Éditions Grafocarte-Navicarte,
125 rue Jean-Jacques-Rousseau,
BP 40, 92132 Issy-les-Moulineaux
Cedex, ✆01 41 09 19 00.

Éditions du Plaisancier, 43 porte
du Grand-Lyon, 01700 Neyron,
✆04 72 01 58 68.

Boat trips

In the Audomarois region
(*see ST-OMER*).

Around the market garden district of Amiens (*see AMIENS: Hortillonnages*).

Paris Canal –
Bassin de La Villette, 9–21 quai de la Loire, 75019 Paris, ✆01 42 40 96 97, www.pariscanal.com. On

On the Loing canal
S. Sauvignier/MICHELIN

the canals of Paris and along the meanders of the Marne (Paris-Chennevières-Paris).

Un canal, deux canaux –
BP 69, 77440 Lizy-sur-Ourcq,
✆01 60 01 13 65.

Tourisme Accueil Val-d'Oise –
Château de la Motte, rue François-de-Ganay, 95270 Luzarches,
✆01 30 29 51 00. Boat trips, lunch or dinner cruises from La Roche-Guyon, Auvers and Pontoise.

NATURE PARKS AND RESERVES

Regional nature parks have brought a breath of fresh air to the landscapes of the Île-de-France region and northern France. They are promoted as protected areas, not only in regard to the natural environment but also for traditional lifestyles, crafts and trades. Information can be obtained from the *Maison du Parc* associated with each one.

South of Paris, the Château de Dampierre, the Château de Breteuil and the Abbaye de Port-Royal-des-Champs (*see description in the Discovering section*) are within the **Parc naturel régional de la Haute Vallée de Chevreuse**, created in 1985 *(Maison du Parc, Château de la Madeleine, BP 73, 78460 Chevreuse, ✆01 30 52 09 09, www.parc-naturel-chevreuse.org)*. Woods and farmlands alternate on the plateau along with

Ferries crossing the Channel
F. Bocquet/MICHELIN

Excursions to the UK

Many visitors to Northern France take advantage of the close proximity to the UK by taking a quick trip over the Channel to Kent or even London (passport required):

From Calais – 75min by ferry to Dover *(see Getting There: By Ship).*

The **Eurotunnel** is situated at Coquelles *(3km/2mi from the coast).* For those travelling by car, the **Shuttle** links Calais with Folkestone in Kent, 24hr 7 days a week. The journey lasts 35min, 28 of which are spent in the tunnel. 09 90 35 35 35, www.eurotunnel.com.

From Paris or Lille – For those travelling by train, **Eurostar** takes around 2.5hr for the journey from Paris-Gare du Nord to London St Pancras, or around 1.5hr from Lille-Europe (www.eurostar.com).

To obtain tourist information in Paris, contact the **Office du tourisme de la Grande Bretagne**, BP 154-08, 75363 Paris Cedex 08, 01 58 36 50 50, www.visitbritain.com/fr.

---

lush valleys. The park offers over 200km/125mi of blazed hiking trails. The **Parc naturel régional du Vexin français**, created in 1995 just north of Paris *(Maison du Parc, Château de Théméricourt, 01 34 48 66 30 www.pnr-vexin-francais.fr),* offers 500km/310mi of marked footpaths as well as cycling tracks and bridle paths.

In the **northern area** covered in this guide, discover dunes, forests, bays and wetlands by following itineraries on foot, horseback or bike in the region's nature parks which include the **Parc naturel régional de l'Avesnois** *(Maison du Parc, Grange Dîmière, 4 cour de l'Abbaye, 59550 Maroilles, 03 27 77 90 20, www.parc-naturel-avesnois.fr);* the **Parc naturel regional des Caps et Marais d'Opale** *(Maison du Parc, le Grand Vannage, 62510 Arques, 03 21 87 90 90, www.parc-opale.fr);* the **Parc naturel regional Scarpe-Escaut** *(Maison du Parc, Le Luron, 357 rue Notre-Dame-d'Amour, 59230 St-Amand-les-Eaux, 03 27 19 19 70, www.pnr-scarpe-escaut.fr).*

CONSERVATION AREAS

To protect coastal areas, the **Conservatoire du Littoral** *(Corderie Royale, rue Jean-Baptiste Audebert, 17300 Rochefort, 05 46 84 72 50)* was set up in 1975 to safeguard and maintain ecological balance.
There are now 339 protected sites, including the dunes at Garennes-de-Lornel in Pas-de-Calais, the first to be covered by preservation measures. Various other organisations and centres are aimed at safeguarding ecological systems:

- **Centre Permanent d'Initiatives pour l'Environnement Vallée de Somme**, 32 route d'Amiens, 80480 Dury, 03 22 33 24 27, www.cpie80.com *(guided walks, guided tours of the Samara marshland).*
- **Conservatoire des Sites Naturels de Picardie**, 1 place Ginkgo, Village Oasis, 80044 Amiens Cedex 1, 03 22 89 63 96, www.conservatoirepicardie.org.
- **Conservatoire des Sites Naturels du Nord-Pas-de-Calais**, 4 allée Saint-Éloi, ZA La Becquerelle,

59118 Wambrechies,
*&*03 28 04 53 45.

🔯 **Centre Ornithologique Île-de-France** (CORIF), *&*01 48 51 92 00; birdwatching in the Paris region.

🔯 **Ferme pédagogique de Versailles**, In the Hameau de la Reine, *&*01 40 67 10 04, www.ferme-pedagogique.com.

WILDLIFE RESERVES

These areas are protected by virtue of the rare or remarkable flora and fauna found there, exceptional geological characteristics, or their role as a way station for migratory species. Some reserves are vast while others are quite modest. Waymarked footpaths allow visitors to observe the natural habitat.

🔯 **le Marais d'Isle**, Aisne (*see St-Quentin)*; Maison de la Nature, *&*03 23 05 06 50; a footpath enables visitors to walk round the marsh, a sanctuary for migratory birds.

🔯 **la Baie de Somme** (the largest reserve in the region). Information at the Parc Ornithologique du Marquenterre, *&*08 36 68 80 21.

SPAS
SPECIALISED CENTRES

Enghien-les-Bains has the only spa centre in Île-de-France. It specialises in throat ailments, skin conditions and rheumatism, but there are also programmes purely for relaxation.
Les Thermes, 87 rue du Général-de-Gaulle, 95880, *&*01 39 34 12 00.
In the northern part of the region, **St-Amand-les-Eaux** specialises in respiratory complaints and rheumatism.
Les Thermes, 1303 route Fontaine-Bouillon, *&*03 27 48 25 00.
Chaîne thermale du Soleil/Maison du Thermalisme, 32 avenue de l'Opéra, 75002 Paris, *&*01 44 71 37 00; www.chainethermale.fr.

SEA-WATER THERAPY

Le Touquet is a well-known seaside resort with a sea-water therapy *(thalassothérapie)* centre offering

a wide range of treatments (health, fitness, post-natal, dietetics, personalised programmes, etc.).
Institut Thalassa, sea front, *&*03 21 09 86 00; **Centre Thalgo**, Park Plaza hotel, 4 boulevard de la Canche, *&*03 21 06 88 84.
Fédération Mer et Santé, 8 rue d'Isly, 75008 Paris, *&*01 44 70 07 57, www.mer-et-sante.asso.fr.

ACTIVITIES FOR CHILDREN

The region abounds in parks, and various attractive sites and features as well as leisure activities which will appeal to children; in the Sights section, the reader's attention is drawn to these features by the symbol 🏃. Below is a selection from this guide.

NORTHERN FRANCE

Olhain, Parc départemental de Nature et de Loisirs (*see Château d'OLHAIN)*.
Prés du Hem, 7 avenue Marc-Sangnier, 59280 Armentières, 15km/9mi north-west of Lille, *&*03 20 44 04 60 (*see LILLE)*.
Val Joly, Parc départemental, 59132 Eppe-Sauvage, *&*03 27 61 83 76 (*see AVESNES-SUR-HELPE)*.
Loisinord, 62290 Nœux-les-Mines, *&*03 21 26 89 89. Water sports and downhill skiing on an artificial slope.

ÎLE-DE-FRANCE

Parc Astérix, 60128 Plailly, *&*08 92 68 30 10; www.parcasterix.fr (*see Parc ASTÉRIX)*.
Disneyland Resort Paris, 77777 Marne-la-Vallée, *&*01 60 30 60 30. Advance booking, schedules and prices at www.disneylandparis.com (*see DISNEYLAND RESORT PARIS)*.
Mer de Sable, 60950 Ermenonville, *&*03 44 54 18 48 (*see Abbaye de CHAALIS)*.
Thoiry, 78770 Thoiry, *&*01 34 87 52 25 (*see THOIRY)*.

Puppets

The north is an area traditionally known for its puppets (marionnettes) and a few theatres continue to give shows, to the great delight of children and adults alike:

Théâtre Le Grand Bleu,
36 avenue Max-Dormoy, Lille,
℘03 20 09 88 44.
Théâtre Louis Richard,
26 rue du Château, Roubaix,
℘03 20 73 10 10.
Théâtre du Broutteux,
11 bis place Ch.-Roussel, Tourcoing,
℘03 20 27 55 24.
Musée des Marionnettes du monde,
Buire-le-Sec, ℘03 21 81 80 34.
Théâtre "Chès Cabotans d'Amiens",
rue E.-David, Amiens,
℘03 22 22 30 90.

SHOPPING
OPENING HOURS

Most of the larger shops are open Mondays to Saturdays from 9am to 6.30 or 7.30pm. Smaller shops may close during the lunch hour. Food shops (grocers, wine merchants and bakeries) are generally open from 8am to 6.30 or 7.30pm; some open on Sunday mornings. Many food shops close between noon and 2pm and on Mondays. Hypermarkets usually stay open non-stop until 9pm or later.

Booze Cruise

The English associate Northern France with a dash across the channel to stock up on wine and beer bargains. The streets of Calais around the port are lined with discount shops, but these are a good place to start:

Calais Vins *(Zone Curie, rue Gutenbert, ℘03 21 46 40 40, www.calais-vins.com)*

Franglais *(CD 215 Frethun, ℘03 21 85 29 39, www.franglais-wine.com)*

Majestic Wine & Beer World *(rue de Judee, ZA Marcel Doret, ℘03 21 97 63 00, www.majesticinfrance.co.uk)*

Check your limits with customs regulations; you will need to prove that any amount you are carrying is for personal use only.

Plant products or fresh food, including fruit, cheeses and nuts cannot be brought into the USA except for tinned products or preserves.

VALUE ADDED TAX (VAT)

There is a **Value Added Tax** (VAT) in France of 19.6% on almost every purchase. VAT **refunds** are available to visitors from outside the EU only if purchases exceed 175€ on one day in one store; the VAT cannot be refunded for items shipped. The system works in large stores which cater to tourists, in luxury stores and other shops advertising Duty Free. Show your passport, and the store will complete a form which is to be stamped by a customs agent at the airport or at whatever point you are leaving the EU. You may have to show the agent the items purchased, so don't pack them in checked luggage. www.douane. gouv.fr.

LOCAL SPECIALITIES
Food and Drink

The famous **Brie** cheese comes from Meaux, east of Paris, but also from Coulommiers and Melun further south. Meaux also produces a gourmet **mustard** made according to a traditional recipe. Northern France's cheeses include the mild **Mont-des-Cats** and the stronger-flavoured **Maroilles**, first produced by monks in the 10C, and often used in regional dishes. **Beer** is Northern France's traditional drink and there are many varieties to be enjoyed along the "route des Brasseurs" (the brewers' trail).

Liqueurs

Liqueurs from Île-de-France include the **Noyau de Poissy**, made from brandy flavoured with apricot stones, and the famous **Grand Marnier** produced in Neauphle-le-Château, west of Versailles.

Handicrafts

There is a wide choice of beautiful objects to take home: **porcelain** manufactured in Sèvres (a Paris suburb) and in Arras; **earthenware** from Desvres; **pottery** from Sars-Poteries; **glassware** and **crystal** from Arques; **lace** from Calais; **puppets** from Amiens.

BOOKS
THE MONARCHY

Memoirs Duc De Saint-Simon: 1710–1715 (Lost Treasures) by Lucy Norton, Editor (Prion Books, 2000). The Duc de Saint-Simon was at the very centre of Louis XIV's court at Versailles, and later played an important role in the regency of the Duc d'Orléans. He stood out amid the intrigue and scheming as a truly pious and honest man.

Marie Antoinette: The Journey by Antonia Fraser (Anchor Books, 2002). Also a film starring Kirsten Dunst. The Queen was much-maligned by rumour in her own time, and many stories of her alleged outrages have persevered, but this book shows how difficult her position was and provides a thoughtful consideration of a woman whose story never fails to fascinate.

Versailles: A Novel by Kathryn Davis (Houghton Mifflin Co, 2002). The viewpoint of this historical novel belongs to Queen Marie Antoinette, who arrived in France at age 14 to marry Louis, a distracted young man destined to become the 16th French monarch of that name, and who was to take his wife to the guillotine with him.

The Many Lives & Secret Sorrows of Josephine B. by Sandra Gulland (Scribner, 1999). The first historic novel in a trilogy about the life of Napoléon Is first wife, Joséphine de Beauharnais, and her experience of the French Revolution, her imprisonment, her marriage to Napiléon and the rise of the First Empire.

THE WORLD WARS

Suite Française by Irène Némirovsky (Vintage Books, 2007). Set in the year France fell to Germany, the book depicts a group of Parisians as they flee the Nazi invasion, then follows the inhabitants of a small rural community under occupation. The author Irène Némirovsky died in Auschwitz before the book was published.

A Storm in Flanders: The Ypres Salient, 1914-1918: Tragedy and Triumph on the Western Front by Winston Groom (Grove Press, 2003). The author describes "the most notorious and dreaded place in all of the First World War, probably of any war in history": the Ypres salient. Groom draws on the journals of men and women who were there to depict the terrifying new tactics and technologies employed at Ypres, the ineffable horror of trench warfare and also the heroism and humanity that somehow survived.

Battle of the Somme by Gerald Gliddon (Sutton Publishing, 2000). Gerald Gliddon is an author and bookseller specialising in the history of the First World War. His book is well researched and covers all of the battles of the Somme, 1916. There are useful descriptions of the many Commonwealth War Graves in the region, and a full list of all military units.

Good-Bye to All That: An Autobiography by Robert Graves (Anchor, 1958). This book serves as a memoir for the whole generation of Englishmen who suffered in the First World War. The rough scenes of atrocities, suicides, murders and heroic rescues follow one another and build up to an emotional charge that defines Graves' experience. The book shows how the battlefield left the survivors numb and "shell-shocked" long after they had returned home.

GENERAL INTEREST

Calais, An English Town in France by Susan Rose (Boydell Press, 2008). The story of Calais during the English governance, from its capture in 1347 until its surrender to the French in 1558. Rose argues that Calais played an important role both diplomatically and economically for the English, even if its militarily strategic significance can be rightfully questioned.

More More France Please by Helena Frith Powell (Gibson Square, 2007). What do you do when a semi-feral dog bites off the nose of a guest at your first French dinner? Where do you go if you don't want to see any compatriots? What do you do when your well dries up? In this book, the author writes about the real life sotires of herself and fellow Brits in France, revealing some surprising details about what goes on behind the façades in France.

Universe of Stone: A Biography of Chartres Cathedral by Philippe Ball (Harper, 2008). A story of the creation of one of the greatest gothic cathedrals in the world, how 12C masons "turned geometry into stone". Includes the secrets of how they achieved the famous blue stained glass, and how architects discovered how to virtually overcome gravity at a time when religious fervor was at its height in France.

FILMS

Dangerous Liaisons, 1988. Starring Glenn Close, John Malkovitch, Michelle Pfeiffer. Based on the pre-Revolutionary novel by Choderlos de Laclos of bored aristocrats living in mansions around the Île-de-France, playing high-stakes games of passion and betrayal. Amazing costumes and settings in Chateau de Maisons-Lafitte, the Opéra Garnier and Abbaye du Moncel.

Germinal, 1993. Starring Gérard Départdieu. After the book by Émile Zola (Viking Press; Reprint 1954). Misery at its most miserable. This film is based on the novel, a realistic depiction of the living conditions of the miners of northern France in the 1860s. The hero is a newcomer who tries to force improvements by organising resistance to the mine owners. The consequences are terrible as the authorities supress their actions.

Vatel 2000. Starring Gérard Depardieu, Uma Thurman. This lush period piece tells the story of a doomed Head Steward in love with a Lady in Waiting. The tale of Vatel, *maître d'hôtel* to the Grand Condé at the château of Chantilly is both true and tragic. The over-the-top festivities, Baroque showgirls and the decadence of the aristocracy leave little to the imagination.

Bienvenue Chez les Ch'tis (Welcome to the Sticks), 2008. Starring Dany Boon and Kad Merad. One of the most popular films in recent French history tells the story of a hapless French postal worker from the South of France who gets transferred to the Northern France town of Bergues, where he's surrounded by rednecks who speak in the incomprehensible dialect called Ch'ti. He eventually warms to the locals; and vice versa!

Calendar of Events

FESTIVALS AND FAIRS
FEBRUARY–MARCH

Chambly *Bois-Hourdy* folk festival dating back to the 13C. ✆0139 37 44 00. www.ville-chambly.fr.

Maubeuge – Jazz Manège: international festival of jazz. ✆03 27 65 65 40. www.lemanege.com.

END OF MARCH

Amiens International jazz festival. ✆03 22 97 79 79. www.amiensjazzfestival.com.

MARCH–APRIL

Seine-Saint-Denis Banlieues Bleues jazz festival. ✆01 49 22 10 10. www.banlieuesbleues.fr.

SATURDAY APRIL–DECEMBER

Chartres *Les samedis musicaux de Chartres* (classical music, jazz, folk music). ✆02 37 27 18 52. http://lessamedismusicaux.free.fr.

APRIL

Abbeville et baie de Somme Bird Film Festival (screenings, exhibits, nature walks, lectures). ✆03 22 24 02 02. www.festival-oiseau-nature.com.

Valenciennes Action and Adventure film festival. ✆03 27 29 55 40. www.festival-valenciennes.com.

PALM SUNDAY WEEKEND (FRIDAY TO MONDAY)

Coulommiers Cheese and wine fair. ✆01 64 03 88 09. www.foire-fromages-et-vins.com.

LAST SUNDAY IN APRIL

Fortified towns in the Nord-Pas-de-Calais Regional fortified towns festival. ✆03 28 82 05 43. www.nordmag.fr.

MAY

Boulogne-sur-Mer Music & Ramparts. ✆03 21 10 88 10.

Marly-le-Roi Fête du parc. ✆01 30 61 61 35.

2ND SUNDAY IN MAY

Rambouillet Lily-of-the-Valley festival. ✆01 34 83 21 21. www.rambouillet.fr.

WHITSUN WEEKEND

St-Quentin *Fêtes du Bouffon*. www.les-fetes-du-bouffon.com.

END OF MAY

Lille *Montgolfiades* balloon festival. ✆03 20 05 40 62. http://montgolfiades.ec-lille.fr.

Laon Euromédiévales (banquet, displays, medieval markets). ✆03 23 22 30 34. www.laon-ville.net.

Tourcoing Medieval market, European Knights Tournament. ✆03 20 28 13 20.

MAY–JUNE

Auvers-sur-Oise International Music Festival. ✆01 30 36 77 77. www.festival-auvers.com.

1ST WEEKEND IN JUNE

Bièvres Photo fair. ✆01 43 22 11 72. www.foirephoto-bievre.com.

MID JUNE (ODD-NUMBERED YEARS)

Aérodrome du Bourget International Air and Space Show. ✆01 53 23 33 33). www.paris-air-show.com.

Medieval festival, Provins

S. Sauvignier/MICHELIN

Red fruit market, Noyon

©jpgilson.fr/Office Du Tourisme du Pays Noyonnais

SATURDAY OR SUNDAY JUNE–SEPTEMBER

Royaumont Concerts at the abbey.
    ✆01 34 68 05 50.
    www.royaumont.com.

JULY

Côte d'Opale Music Festival.
    ✆03 21 30 40 33.
St-Riquier Classical music festival.
    ✆03 22 28 82 82
Desvres Fête de la faïence
    (earthenware festival).

1ST SUNDAY IN JULY

Noyon Red fruit market.
www.noyon-tourisme.com.

3RD WEEKEND IN JUNE

Lille *Fêtes de Lille*:
    various events around the city.
Provins Medieval festival.
    ✆01 64 67 02 60.

3RD SUNDAY IN JUNE

Gerberoy *Fête des roses*.
Windmills around the region
    National Windmill Day.
    ✆03 20 05 49 34.
    http://asso.nordnet.fr/aramnord.

23 JUNE

Long *Feux de la Saint-Jean*
    mid-summer festival.
    ✆03 21 31 80 21.

JUNE–JULY

Saint-Denis Festival of classical music.
    ✆01 48 13 06 07.
    www.festival-saint-denis.com.

LATE JUNE–MID AUGUST

St-Germain-en-Laye *Fête des Loges*
    fun fair. ✆01 30 87 21 70.

AROUND 14 JULY

Bray-Dunes World Folklore Festival.
    ✆03 28 26 61 09.

JULY–AUGUST

Hardelot Classical Music Festival.
    ✆03 21 83 51 02.

4TH SUNDAY IN JULY

Buire-le-Sec Crafts and Trades Fair.

TUESDAY, THURSDAY AND SATURDAY AT 9.15PM IN LATE JULY AND AUGUST

Chartres *Soirées Estivales*
    (summer nights festival).
    ✆02 37 18 26 26.

JULY–SEPTEMBER

Sceaux *Festival de l'Orangerie*.
    ✆01 46 60 07 79.
    www.festival-orangerie.fr.

ONE WEEK IN MID AUGUST

Wimereux Wimereux during
    the Belle Époque.

Les Nieulles

The name of these little biscuits (pronounced *nee-uls*) comes from the Spanish *niola*, which means 'crumb'. In 1510, a banquet was held in the reception rooms of the Hôtel de Ville, presided by the Count of Luxembourg, Lord of Armentières. When the guests had finished feasting, the Count stepped out on the balcony. A crowd of children gathered below, holding their hands out for alms. The Count flung the crumbs from the cake at them, as if they were hungry birds.

FIRST FORTNIGHT IN AUGUST
Le Touquet International music festival.
📞03 21 06 72 00.

AUTUMN
Versailles Baroque music concert series.
📞01 39 20 78 10.

SEPTEMBER–OCTOBER

Throughout Île-de-France Festival:
concerts. 📞01 58 71 01 01.
In Picardie *Festival des cathédrales*.
📞03 22 22 44 94.

1ST SUNDAY IN SEPTEMBER
Arleux Garlic Fair.
Melun Antiques Fair and Brie
cheese market.

1ST WEEKEND IN SEPTEMBER
Lille *Grande braderie*: largest
regional flea market.

2ND SUNDAY IN SEPTEMBER
Armentières *Fête des Nieulles*.

**LAST WEEKEND IN SEPTEMBER
(ODD-NUMBERED YEARS)**
Senlis *Rendez-vous de Septembre*:
car-free city, music festival in the
streets on odd-numbered years,
last weekend in the month.
📞03 44 53 06 40.

**LATE SEPTEMBER–
EARLY OCTOBER**
Chatou *Foire nationale
à la brocante et aux jambons*
(ham and antiques fair).
📞01 47 70 88 78.
www.sncao-syndicat.com/
sncao/chatou/foire/acc.htm.

1ST WEEKEND IN OCTOBER
Steenvoorde Hops festival.

1ST SUNDAY IN OCTOBER
Suresnes *Fête des Vendanges*:
Grape harvest festival.
📞01 41 18 18 76.

Fête des Nieulles, Armentières

Office de Tourisme d'Armentières

OCTOBER–NOVEMBER

Barbizon Painting awards.
📞01 60 66 40 24.

3RD SUNDAY IN OCTOBER
Sains-du-Nord Cider festival.

MID-OCTOBER–MID-NOVEMBER
Tourcoing Jazz Festival.
📞03 20 28 96 99.

NOVEMBER–DECEMBER

St-Jean-de-Beauregard Fairs:
Past and Present Vegetables.
📞01 60 12 00 01.

2ND WEEKEND IN DECEMBER
Licques Turkey festival.

24 DECEMBER
Boulogne-sur-Mer *Fête des Guénel*s
(a *guénel* resembles a jack-o'-
lantern, carved out of a beetroot!).

PAGEANTS, SON ET LUMIÈRE,
FOUNTAINS
APRIL–OCTOBER

Provins Falconry show.
📞01 64 20 26 26.
www.provins.net.

**2ND AND LAST SATURDAY
OF THE MONTH**
Vaux-le-Vicomte Fountains in the
garden. 📞01 64 14 41 90. 3–6pm.

SUNDAY
Versailles Fountains and music in the
palace garden. 📞01 39 24 88 88.
11am–noon, 3.30–5pm.

33

Soirées aux chandelles, Château Vaux-le-Vicomte

Château Vaux-le-Vicomte

MAY–SEPTEMBER
3RD SUNDAY OF THE MONTH
Parc de Marly-le-Roi Grand fountain.
🕿 01 30 61 61 35.

MAY-MID OCTOBER

**SATURDAY BETWEEN 8PM
AND MIDNIGHT**
Vaux-le-Vicomte Candlelight tour
of château and gardens.
🕿 01 64 14 41 90.
www.vaux-le-vicomte.com.

SUNDAY IN JUNE–JULY
St-Cloud Fountains. 🕿 01 41 12 02 90.

MID-JUNE–AUGUST
Provins Jousting tournament in
the moat. 🕿 01 64 60 26 26.

MID-JUNE–MID-JULY, LATE AUGUST AND FIRST THREE WEEKS IN SEPTEMBER
FRIDAY AND SATURDAY
Meaux *Son et Lumière*.
🕿 01 64 33 02 26.

3RD WEEKEND IN JUNE
Chantilly *Nuits de Feu*. International
fireworks competition, on
even-numbered years.
🕿 03 44 45 18 18.

CERTAIN SATURDAYS JULY–SEPTEMBER
Versailles *Grandes Fêtes de Nuit
au bassin de Neptune*, fireworks,
fountains and music in the
palace garden.
🕿 01 30 83 78 88.

SEPTEMBER
Moret-sur-Loing *Son et Lumière*.
🕿 01 60 70 41 66.

SPORTING EVENTS
FEBRUARY
Le Touquet *Enduro des sables*.
Motorbike endurance race.
Liévin International athletics meeting
(mid-month).

END MARCH–END NOVEMBER
Fontainebleau *La Solle* racetrack
open. 🕿 01 60 74 99 99. Sunday
11am–noon, 3.30–5pm.

Son et Lumière at Meaux

©Yves Belin/Office de Tourisme de Meaux

Know Before You Go

USEFUL WEBSITES

www.ambafrance-uk.org
The French Embassy's website offers basic information (geography, demographics, history), a news digest and business-related information. It offers special pages for children, and pages devoted to culture, language study and travel.

www.visiteurope.com
The European Travel Commission provides useful information on travelling to and around 27 European countries, and includes links to some commercial booking services.

www.franceguide.com
The French Government Tourist Office site is packed with practical information and tips for those travel-ling to France. The homepage has a number of links to more specific guidance, for American or Canadian travellers for example, or to the FGTO's London pages.

www.FranceKeys.com
A useful portal that takes you straight to the individual regions, tourist boards, leading hotels and sights.

www.franceway.com
An online magazine, which focuses on culture and heritage. For each region, there are also suggestions for activities and practical information on where to stay and how to get there.

www.northernfrance-tourism.com
The regional tourism office website for Pas de Calais and Nord *départements* in English. Lodging, dining, sightseeing and events, with an excellent photo album showing the diversity of the northern France landscape.

www.pas-de-calais.com
The regional tourist office site, with a complete English version. On it, you will find maps, useful addresses, scheduled events, and information for booking *gîtes*, other furnished accommodation, and bed and break-fast establishments. There is a space for emailing your specific questions for reply.

www.picardietourisme.com/ www.picardy.org
Two sites dedicated to promoting Picardy, and provide masses of information not only on basics like accommodation and where to eat, but on history, culture and recreation.

TOURIST OFFICES
FRENCH TOURIST OFFICES ABROAD

For information, brochures, maps and assistance in planning a trip to France, travellers should apply to the official French tourist office in their own country:

Australia – New Zealand
- **Sydney** – BNP Building, 12 Castlereagh Street, Sydney, New South Wales 2000. ℘(02) 9 231 52 44. Fax (02) 9 221 86 82.

Canada
- **Toronto** – 30 St Patrick's Street, Suite 700, Toronto, ONT M5T 3A3. ℘(416) 979 7587.
- **Montreal** – 1981 McGill College Avenue, Suite 490, Montreal PQ H3A 2W9. ℘(514) 288-4264. Fax (514) 845 48 68.

Eire
- **Dublin** – 10 Suffolk St, Dublin 2. ℘(1) 679 0813, Fax (1) 679 0814.

United Kingdom
- **London** – 178 Piccadilly, London W1J 9AL. ℘(09068) 244 123. Fax (020) 793 6594.

United States
- **East Coast: New York** – 444 Madison Avenue, NY 10022. ℘212-838-7800. Fax (212) 838 7855.
- **Midwest: Chicago** – 676 North Michigan Avenue, Suite 3360,

Chicago, IL 60611. &(312) 751 7800. Fax (312) 337 6339.
- **West Coast: Los Angeles** – 9454 Wilshire Boulevard, Suite 715, Beverly Hills, CA 90212. &(310) 271 6665. Fax (310) 276 2835.

TOURIST OFFICES IN FRANCE
Visitors may also contact local tourist offices for more precise information, and to receive brochures and maps. The addresses, telephone numbers, and websites of local tourist offices are listed after the symbol 🛈 in the Orient Panels of the Principal Sights in the *Discovering* section of this guide. Below are addresses for the regional tourist offices of the *départements* and *régions* covered in this guide.

Regional Tourist Offices
- **Île-de-France** – Comité Régional du Tourisme, 11 r. du Faubourg-Poissonnière – 75009 Paris. &01 73 00 77 00. www.new-paris-ile-de-france.co.uk.
- **Nord-Pas-de-Calais** – Comité Régional du Tourisme, 6 place Mendès-France, 59028 Lille.

&03 20 14 57 57. www.tourisme-nordpasdecalais.fr.
- **Picardie** – Comité Régional du Tourisme, 3 rue Vincent Auriol, 80011 Amiens 1. &03 22 22 33 63. www.picardietourisme.com.

Departmental Tourist Offices
PICARDY
- **Aisne** – 24-28 avenue Charles-de-Gaulle, 02007 Laon. &03 23 27 76 76. www.evasion-aisne.com.
- **Oise** – 19 rue Pierre-Jacoby, BP 80822, 60008 Beauvais. &03 44 45 82 12. www.oisetourisme.com.
- **Somme** – 21 rue Ernest-Cauvin, 80000 Amiens. &03 22 71 22 71. www.somme-tourisme.com.

NORD-PAS-DE-CALAIS
- **Nord** – 6 rue Gauthier-de-Châtillon, BP 1232, 59013 Lille. &03 20 57 59 59. www.cdt-nord.fr.
- **Pas-de-Calais** – route La Trésorerie, BP 79, 62126 Wimille. &03 21 10 34 60. www.pas-de-calais.com.

ÎLE DE FRANCE
- **Essonne** – 19 rue Mazières, 91000 Evry. &01 64 97 35 13. www.tourisme-essonne.com.

EMBASSIES AND CONSULATES IN FRANCE		
Australia	Embassy	4 rue Jean-Rey, 75015 Paris &01 40 59 33 00. www.france.embassy.gov.au
Canada	Embassy	35 avenue Montaigne, 75008 Paris &01 44 43 29 00. www.international.gc.ca
Ireland	Embassy	4 rue Rude, 75016 Paris &01 44 17 67 00. www.embassyofireland.fr
New Zealand	Embassy	7 rue Léonard-de-Vinci, 75016 Paris &01 45 00 24 11. www.nzembassy.com/france
South Africa	Embassy	59 quai d'Orsay, 75007 Paris &01 53 59 23 23. www.afriquesud.net
UK	Embassy	35 rue du Faubourg St-Honoré, 75008 Paris &01 44 51 31 00. http://.ukinfrance.fco.gov.uk/en
	Consulate	16 bis rue d'Anjou, 75008 Paris &01 44 51 31 00
	Consulate	353 boulevard du Président Wilson, 33073 Bordeaux &05 57 22 21 10
USA	Embassy	2 avenue Gabriel, 75008 Paris &01 43 12 22 22. http://france.usembassy.gov
	Consulate	2 rue St-Florentin, 75001 Paris. &01 43 12 22 22

- **Eure-et-Loir** – 10 rue du Docteur Maunoury, BP 67, 28002 Chartres. ℘02 37 84 01 00. www.tourisme28.com.
- **Hauts-de-Seine** – 8 place de la Défense, Courbevoie, 92974 Paris-la-Défense. ℘01 46 93 92 92. www.tourisme-hautsdeseine.com.
- **Seine-et-Marne** – 11 rue Royale, 77300 Fontainebleau. ℘01 60 39 60 39. www.tourisme77.net.
- **Seine-St-Denis** – 140 avenue Jean-Lolive, 93695 Pantin. ℘01 49 15 98 98. www.tourisme93.com.
- **Val de Marne** – 38 quai Victor-Hugo, 94500 Champigny-sur-Marne. ℘01 55 09 16 20. www.tourisme-valdemarne.com.
- **Val-d'Oise** – Château de la Motte, 95270 Luzarches. ℘01 30 29 51 00. www.val-doise-tourisme.com.
- **Yvelines** – 2 place André-Mignot, 78012 Versailles. ℘01 39 07 71 22. www.tourisme.yvelines.fr.

Tourist Information Centres
The **Espace du tourisme d'Île-de-France** *(Carrousel du Louvre, 99 rue de Rivoli, 75001 Paris, ℘08 26 16 66 66)* is a handy tourist information bureau.
The **Espace du tourisme d'Île-de-France et Seine-et-Marne** *(place des Passagers du Vent, 77700 Chessy-Marne-la-Vallée, ℘01 60 43 33 33)* is a tourist information kiosk close to the RER station at Disneyland/Disney Village.
The **Espace accueil tourisme CDT Seine-St-Denis** *(Stade de France, porte H, 93216 St-Denis-La-Plaine, ℘01 49 46 08 11)* is an information centre located in the stadium.

INTERNATIONAL VISITORS
ENTRY REQUIREMENTS
Passport – Nationals of countries within the European Union entering France need only a national identity card; in the case of the UK, until such time as there may be national identity cards, this means your passport. Nationals of other countries must be in possession of a valid national **passport**. In case of loss or theft,

☙ Plan Your Itinerary ☙

Local tourist offices *(Syndicats d'Initiative)* provide information on craft courses and itineraries with special themes – wine tours, history tours, artistic tours. Nineteen towns and areas, labelled **Villes et Pays d'Art et d'Histoire** by the Ministry of Culture, are mentioned in this guide (Amiens, Arras, Beauvais, Boulogne-sur-Mer, Cambrai, Compiègne, Douai, Laon, Lille, Meaux, Noyon, Pontoise, Provins, St-Denis, St Germain-en-Laye, St-Omer, St Quentin, Senlis and Soissons). They are particularly active in promoting their architectural and cultural heritage and offer guided tours by qualified guides as well as activities for children. More information is available from www.vpah.culture.fr *(French only)*.

report to your embassy or consulate and the local police.
Visa – No **entry visa** is required for Canadian, US or Australian citizens travelling as tourists and staying less than 90 days, except for students planning to study in France. If you think you may need a visa, apply to your local French Consulate.
US citizens should consult the government website http://travel.state.gov, which provides useful information on visa requirements, customs regulations, medical care etc for international travellers. General passport information is available by phone toll-free from the Federal Information Center (item 5 on the automated menu), ℘800-688-9889.

CUSTOMS REGULATIONS
Apply to the Customs Office (UK) for a leaflet on customs regulations and the full range of duty-free allowances; available from HM Customs and Excise, Thomas Paine House, Angel Square, Torrens Street, London EC1V 1TA, ℘08450 109 000. The US Customs Service offers a publication *Know Before You Go* for US citizens online

DUTY-FREE ALLOWANCES	
Spirits (whisky, gin, vodka, etc.)	10l/2.6gal
Fortified wines (vermouth, port, etc.)	20l/5.2gal
Wine (not more than 60l sparkling)	90l/23.7gal
Beer	110l/29gal
Cigarettes	800
Cigarillos	400
Cigars	200
Smoking Tobacco	1kg/2.2lb

at http://www.cbp.gov. There are no customs formalities for holidaymakers bringing their caravans into France for a stay of less than six months. No customs document is necessary for pleasure boats and outboard motors for a stay of less than six months, but the registration certificate should be kept on board. Americans can take home, tax-free, up to US$ 400 worth of goods (limited quantities of alcohol and tobacco products); Canadians up to CND$ 300; Australians up to AUS$ 400 and New Zealanders up to NZ$ 700. Residents from a member state of the European Union are not restricted with regard to purchasing duty-paid goods for private use or personal consumption.

HEALTH

First aid, medical advice and chemists' night service rotas are available from chemists (pharmacie) identified by a green cross sign. All prescription drugs should be clearly labelled; it is recommended that you carry a copy of the prescription. It is advisable to take out comprehensive travel insurance which also covers medical expenses as medical treatment in French hospitals or clinics is not free. **Nationals of non-EU countries** should check with their insurance companies about policy limitations. Reimbursement can then be negotiated with the insurance company according to the policy held.

British and Irish citizens should apply to the Department of Health and Social Security **before travelling** for a EuropeanHealth Insurance Card, which entitles the holder to urgent treatment for accident or unexpected illness in EU countries – see www.nhs.uk. A refund of part of the costs of treatment can be obtained on application in person or by post to the local Social Security Offices (Caisse Primaire d'Assurance Maladie).
Americans concerned about travel and health can contact the International Association for Medical Assistance to Travelers, which can also provide details of English-speaking doctors in different parts of France: ℘(716) 754-4883.
✚ **The American Hospital of Paris** has English-speaking staff, at 63 boulevard Victor-Hugo, 92200 Neuilly-sur-Seine, ℘01 46 41 25 25.
✚ **The British Hospital** is just outside Paris in Levallois-Perret, 3 rue Barbès, ℘01 46 39 22 22.

ACCESSIBILITY

The sights described in this guide that are easily accessible to people of reduced mobility are indicated by the ♿ symbol.
On TGV and Corail trains operated by the national railway (SNCF), there are special wheelchair slots in 1st class carriages available to holders of 2nd class tickets. On Eurostar and Thalys, special rates are available for accompanying adults. All airports are equipped to receive physically disabled passengers. Information for slow walkers, mature travellers and others with special needs is online at www.access-able.com.
For information on museum access for the disabled contact Les Musées de France, Service Accueil des Publics Spécifiques, 6 rue des Pyramides, 75041 Paris Cedex 1, ℘01 40 15 80 72.
The Michelin Guide France and the **Michelin Camping France** indicate hotels and campsites with facilities suitable for travellers with physical disabilities.

Getting There

BY AIR

Various international and other independent airlines operate services to Paris (Charles-de-Gaulle/Roissy located 25km/15.5mi north of Paris, Orly located 16km/10mi south, and Beauvais-Tillé). There are also direct flights from London to Lille-Lesquin Airport, located 15min from the centre of Lille in northern France. Contact airlines and travel agents for information on **package-tour** flights with rail or coach link-ups or **fly-drive** schemes.

PRACTICAL ADVICE

Practical advice for travelling by plane, specifically as regards carrying liquids, gels, creams, aerosols, medicines and food for babies is provided on www.franceguide.com. Some countries impose restrictions on liquids bought in duty-free shops when transferring to a connecting flight. Aéroports de Paris recommends that passengers contact individual airline companies for further information. www.aeroportsdeparis.fr.

BY SHIP
FROM THE UK OR IRELAND

There are numerous **cross-Channel services** (passenger and car ferries, hovercraft) from the United Kingdom and Ireland, and also the rail Shuttle through the Channel Tunnel (**Le Shuttle-Eurotunnel**, ☎0990 353 535, www.eurotunnel.com). For details apply to travel agencies or see box overleaf. between London St Pancras and Paris in 3hr *(bookings and information ☎0345 303 030 in the UK; ☎1-888-EUROSTAR in the US; www.eurostar.co.uk)*. In Paris it links to the high-speed rail network **(TGV)** which covers most of the country and which has recently been extended to the south of France *(for details call ☎0836 676 869)*.

P&O Ferries	In the UK: ☎08716 645 645.
	In France: ☎0825 120 156
	www.poferries.com
Norfolkline	In the UK: ☎0844 847 5042
	Outside the UK: ☎+44 208 127 8303
	www.norfolkline-ferries.co.uk
Brittany Ferries	In the UK: ☎0871 244 0744
	In France: ☎08 25 82 88 28
	In Ireland: ☎021 427 7801
	www.brittany-ferries.com
Irish Ferries	In the UK: ☎08717 300 400
	In Ireland: ☎0818 300 400
	In France: ☎01 70 72 03 26
	In the US: ☎(772) 563 2856
	www.irishferries.com
Seafrance	In the UK: ☎0871 423 7119
	In France: ☎0825 082 505
	www.seafrance.com

BY TRAIN/RAIL

All rail services throughout France can be arranged through **Rail Europe** in the UK. ☎08708 304 862. www.raileurope.co.uk.
Eurostar runs from **London** (St-Pancras) to **Paris** (Gare du Nord) in under 3hr (up to 20 times daily), or **Lille** (Europe) in 2hr (up to 10 times daily). There is a once-daily service (every day of the year) running directly from the UK to **Marne La Vallée Disneyland**, taking 3hr. In Paris it links to the high-speed rail network **(TGV)** (☎0836 676 869). The main towns served by the TGV network are Lyon, Avignon, Valence, Montpellier, Aix-en-Provence, and Marseille.
Bookings and information:
☎08705 186 186 *(booking fee)* in the UK, www.eurostar.com. Rail Europe can also book Eurostar travel on ☎08708 303 862 or visit www.raileurope.co.uk.

Eurostar in Lille-Europe station
©Eurostar

☺Tickets must be validated (composter) by using the orange automatic date-stamping machines at the platform entrance (☺failure to do so may result in a fine).

Eurailpass, **Flexipass** and **Saverpass** are three of the travel passes which may be purchased by residents of countries outside the European Union. In the US, contact your travel agent or Rail Europe *(2100 Central Avenue, Boulder, CO, 80301; ℘1-800-4-EURAIL)* or **Europrail International** *(℘1 888 667 9731; www.europrail.net)*. If you are

a European resident, you can buy an individual country pass, if you are not a resident of the country you are buying it for. In the UK, contact Europrail *(179 Piccadilly London W1V OBA; ℘0990 848 848)*. Information on schedules can be obtained on websites for these agencies and the **SNCF**, respectively: www.raileurope.com, www.voyages-sncf.com. At the SNCF site, you can book ahead, pay with a credit card, and receive your ticket in the mail at home free of charge (seven days minimum before leaving in the case of foreign countries, four days for France).

The French railway company, SNCF, operates a telephone information, reservation and prepayment service in English from 7am to 10pm (French time). In France call ℘08 36 35 35 39 (when calling from outside France, drop the initial 0).

BY COACH/BUS

Eurolines (UK), 4 Cardiff Road, Luton, Bedfordshire, LU1 1PP. ℘08705 143219, Fax 01582 400694.

Eurolines (Paris), 22 rue Malmaison, 93177 Bagnolet. ℘01 49 72 57 80, Fax 01 49 72 57 99.

www.eurolines.com is the international website with information about travelling all over Europe by coach (bus).

Gare du Nord, Paris
©Eurostar/Lydia Shalet

RER trains

D. Pazery/ MICHELIN

Getting Around

BY PUBLIC TRANSPORT

Metro lines are identified by a number. Some of them extend into the suburbs: St-Denis or Asnières on line 13, Créteil on line 8.

For **RER** lines A, B, C, D, E, which extend into the outer suburbs, cost depends on the distance travelled. Six Parisian railway stations (Austerlitz, Est, Lyon, Montparnasse, Nord, St-Lazare) provide suburban train links to the towns of the Île-de-France region. Stations are open from 6am to 9pm. The cost of travelling on the *transilien SNCF* (Île-de-France regional network) varies according to length of journey, ℰ01 53 90 20 20 (6am–10pm). There is a very frequent service to Lille by **TGV** (1hr) from the Gare du Nord. Arras is under an hour away from the capital, again by TGV. Travel to Amiens takes 1–2hr, depending on the number of stops made, while Beauvais takes a little over 1hr. Information: ℰ08 36 35 35 35, www.sncf.fr.

BY CAR

The area covered in this guide is easily reached by main motorways and national routes. **Michelin map 726** indicates the main itineraries as well as alternate routes for avoiding heavy traffic during busy holiday periods, and gives estimated travel times. **Michelin map 723** is a detailed atlas of French motorways, indicating tolls, rest areas and services

along the route; it includes a table for calculating distances and times. The latest Michelin route-planning service is available on **www.Via Michelin.com**. Travellers can calculate a precise route using such options as shortest route, route avoiding toll roads or a Michelin-recommended route and gain access to tourist information (hotels, restaurants, attractions). The service is available on a pay-per-route basis or by subscription.

The roads are very busy during the holiday period (particularly weekends in July and August) and, to avoid traffic congestion, it is advisable to follow

😊 Travel Passes 😊

The **Paris Visite** pass allows unlimited travel on the entire RATP network in the Paris and Île-de-France area and includes the metro, RER, bus, tram and suburban trains, depending on the geographical zone (1–3 for the inner zone and 1–5, 6, 7 or 8 for the outer suburbs of Île-de-France). Valid for 1, 2, 3 or 5 consecutive days, it can be purchased in main metro and all RER stations, or abroad. Information: ℰ08 36 68 77 14, www.ratp.fr. Other passes are also available on the RATP network, including the *carte navigo découverte* for travel from daily in zones 1–8, or the **Mobilis** card, issued with a voucher, and valid for one day.

RENTAL CARS – RESERVATIONS IN FRANCE		
Avis France:	☎0820 05 05 05 (UK)	www.avis.fr
Europcar:	☎0825 35 83 58 (UK)	www.europcar.com
Budget France:	☎0825 00 35 64 (UK)	www.budget.com
Hertz France:	☎0825 861 861 (UK)	www.hertz.com
SIXT:	☎0820 00 74 98 (UK)	www.e-sixt.com
CITER:	☎0825 16 12 20 (UK)	www.citer.fr
Thrifty:	☎01494 751 500 (UK)	www.thrifty.com
Nova Car Hire:	☎0800 018 6682 (UK)	www.novacarhire.com

the recommended secondary routes (signposted as *Bison Futé – itinéraires bis*). The motorway network includes rest areas *(aires de repos)* and petrol stations *(stations-service)*, usually with restaurant and shopping complexes attached, about every 40km/25mi, so that long-distance drivers have no excuse not to stop for a rest every now and then.

DOCUMENTS
Drivng licence
Travellers from other European Union countries and North America can drive in France with a valid national or home-state driving licence. Always carry your passport and UK driving licence with you when motoring abroad. Remember, you may be asked to produce these at any time in addition to your motor insurance and vehicle registration documents. An **international driving licence** is useful because the information on it appears in nine languages (keep in mind that traffic officers are empowered to fine motorists). An international licence is available in the UK from the AA or the RAC, or in the US from the National Automobile Club, 1151 East Hillsdale Blvd., Foster City, CA 94404, ☎650-294-7000 or, www.nationalautoclub.com; or contact your local branch of the American Automobile Association. For the vehicle, it is necessary to have the registration papers (logbook) and a nationality plate of the approved size.

INSURANCE
Many motoring organisations offer accident insurance and breakdown service schemes for members. Check with your current insurance company regarding cover while abroad. If you plan to hire a car using your credit card, check with the company, which may provide liability insurance automatically (and thus save you having to pay the cost for optimum coverage).

ROAD REGULATIONS
The minimum driving age is 18. Traffic drives on the right. All passengers must wear **seat belts**. Children under the age of 10 must ride in the back seat. Headlights must be switched on in poor visibility and at night; use sidelights only when the vehicle is stationary. Do not drive using only sidelights. In the case of a **breakdown**, a red warning triangle or hazard warning lights are obligatory, as is a high-visibility vest.
In the absence of stop signs at intersections, cars must **yield to the right**. Traffic on main roads outside built-up areas (priority indicated by a yellow diamond sign) and on roundabouts has right of way. There are many **roundabouts**, especially on the edge of towns; you must slow down when you approach one and yield to the cars in the circle. Vehicles must stop when the lights turn red at road junctions and may filter to the right only when indicated by an amber arrow.

The regulations on **drinking and driving** (limited to 0.50g/l) and **speeding** are strictly enforced – usually by an on-the-spot fine and/or confiscation of the vehicle.

Speed Limits
Although liable to modification, these are as follows:

- toll motorways (*autoroutes*) 130kph/80mph (110kph/68mph when raining);
- dual carriageways and motorways without tolls 110kph/68mph (100kph/62mph when raining);
- other roads 90kph/56mph (80kph/50mph when raining) and in towns 50kph/31mph;
- outside lane on motorways during daylight, on level ground and with good visibility – minimum speed limit of 80kph/50mph.

Parking Regulations
In town there are zones where parking is either restricted or subject to a fee; tickets should be obtained from the ticket machines (*horodateurs* – you need a *carte stationnement* from any Tabac to pay) and displayed inside the windscreen on the driver's side; failure to display may result in a fine, or your vehicle being towed away and impounded. Other parking areas in town may require you to take a ticket when passing through a barrier. To exit, you must pay the parking fee (usually there is a machine located by the exit – *sortie*) and insert the paid-up card in another machine which will lift the exit gate.

Tolls
In France, most motorway sections are subject to a toll (*péage*). You can pay in cash or with a credit card (Visa, MasterCard).

CAR RENTAL
There are car rental agencies at airports, railway stations and in all large towns throughout France. European cars have manual transmission; automatic cars are available in larger cities only if

an advance reservation is made. Drivers must be over 21; between ages 21–25, drivers are required to pay an extra daily fee; some companies allow drivers under 23 only if the reservation has been made through a travel agent. It is relatively expensive to hire a car in France; it is worth checking, when you buy your air ticket, to check whether it is possible to take advantage of **fly-drive offers**. There are many online services that will look for the best prices on car rental around the globe. **Nova** can be contacted at www.rentacar-worldwide.com or ✆0800 018 6682 (free phone UK) or ✆44 28 4272 8189 (calling from outside the UK). All of the firms listed opposite have Internet sites for reservations and information.

MOTORHOME RENTAL
Worldwide Motorhome Rentals offers fully equipped campervans for rent. You can view them on the company's website.
✆888-519-8969 *US toll-free*
✆530-389-8316 *outside the US*
Fax 530-389-8316.
www.mhrww.com
Overseas Motorhome Tours Inc. organises escorted tours and individual rental of recreational vehicles:
✆800-322-2127 *US*
✆1-310-543-2590 *outside the US*

PETROL/GASOLINE
French service stations dispense:
- *sans plomb 98* (super unleaded 98)
- *sans plomb 95* (super unleaded 95)
- *diesel/gazole including high grade diesel* (diesel)
- *GPL* (LPG).

For US citizens: gasoline is more expensive in France than in the USA. Prices are listed on signboards on the motorways; it is usually cheaper to fill up after leaving the motorway; check hypermarkets on the outskirts of town. You can pay at the pump using credit/debit cards.

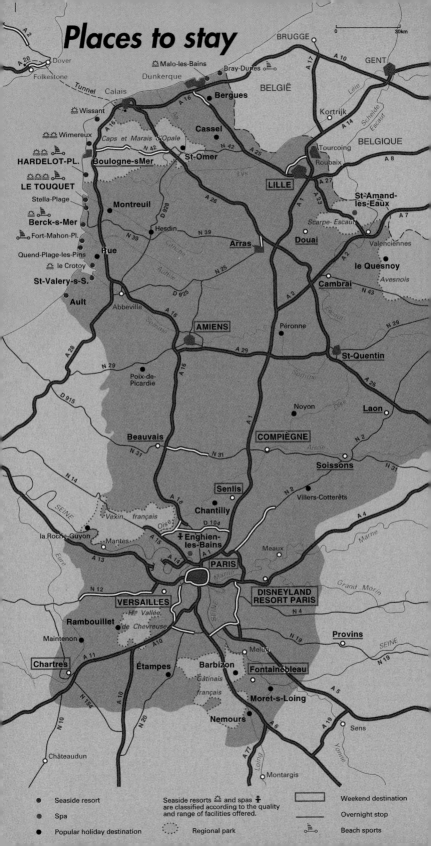

Places to stay

Where to Stay and Eat

Hotel and Restaurant listings fall within the description of each region. &*For coin ranges, see the Legend on the cover flap.*

WHERE TO STAY

The map opposite illustrates a selection of holiday destinations that are especially recommended for their accommodation and leisure facilities, and their pleasant setting. It shows **overnight stops**, fairly large towns that should be visited and that have good accom-modation facilities, as well as traditional destinations for a **short break**, which combine accommodation, charm and a peaceful setting. As far as Paris and Lille are concerned, the influence they exert in the region and the wealth of monuments, museums and other sights to which they are home make them the ideal setting for a **weekend break**.

FINDING A HOTEL

Turn to the **Addresses** within individual sight listings for descriptions and prices of typical places to stay **(Stay)** with local flair. The key on the front cover flap of the guide explains the symbols and abbreviations used in these sections. We have reported the prices and conditions as we observed them, but of course changes in management and other factors may mean that you will find some discrepancies. Please feel free to keep us informed of any major differences you encounter.

Use the **Map of places to stay** *(opposite)* to identify recommended places for overnight stops. For an even greater selection, use the **Michelin Guide France**, with its famously reliable star-rating system and hundreds of establishments all over France. Book ahead to ensure that you get the accommodation you want, not only in tourist season but year round, as many towns fill up during trade fairs, arts festivals, etc. Some places require an advance deposit or a reconfirmation. Reconfirming is especially important if you plan to arrive after 6pm.

For further assistance, **Loisirs Accueil** is a booking service that has offices in some French *départements* – for further information, contact local tourist offices or the **Fédération nationale des services de réservation Loisirs-Accueil**, 280 boulevard St-Germain, 75007 Paris, &01 44 11 10 44, www.resinfrance.com.

A guide to good-value, family-run hotels, **Logis et Auberges de France**, is available from the French Tourist Office, as are lists of other kinds of accommodation such as hotel-châteaux, bed-and-breakfasts, etc.

Relais et châteaux provides information on booking in luxury hotels with character: 15 rue Galvani, 75017 Paris, &01 45 72 90 00; likewise **Chateaux and Hotels de France**, &01 72 72 92 02, www.chateauxhotels.com.

Economy Chain Hotels

If you need a place to stop en route, these can be useful, as they are inexpensive (around 45€ for a double room) and generally located near the main road. While breakfast is available, there may not be a restaurant; rooms are small, with a television and bathroom. Central reservation numbers:

- **Akena** &01 69 84 85 17 www.hotels-akena.com
- **B&B** &01 72 36 51 06 www.hotel-bb.com
- **Etap Hotel** &0892 688 900 www.etaphotel.com
- **Hotel Formula 1** &0892 685 685 www.hotelformule1.com
- **Accor Hotels** &0825 88 00 00 www.accorhotels.com/fr
- **Villages Hôtel** &03 80 60 92 70 www.villages-hotel.com

The chain hotels listed below are slightly more expensive (from 58€) and offer a few more amenities and services. Central reservation numbers:

- **Campanile** &01 64 62 59 70 www.campanile.com
- **Etap** &0892 688 900

www.etaphotel.com
✉ **Ibis** ✆0892 686 686
www.ibishotel.com

COTTAGES, BED & BREAKFASTS

The **Maison des Gîtes de France** is an information service on self-catering accommodation in the Northern France region (and the rest of France). *Gîtes* usually take the form of a cottage or apartment decorated in the local style where visitors can make themselves at home, or bed-and-breakfast accommodation *(chambres d'hôtes)* which consists of a room and breakfast at a reasonable price.
Contact the **Gîtes de France office** in Paris *(59 rue St-Lazare, 75439 Paris Cedex 09, ✆01 49 70 75 75)*, or their representative in the UK, **Brittany Ferries**. The website **www.gites-de-france.fr**, has a good English version. From the site, you can order catalogues for different regions illustrated with photographs of the properties, as well as specialised catalogues (bed and breakfasts, farm stays etc). You can also contact the local tourist offices which may have lists of available properties and local bed and breakfast establishments.
The **Fédération nationale Clévacances** *(54 boulevard de l'Embouchure, BP 2166, 31022 Toulouse Cedex 09, ✆05 61 13 55 66, www. clevacances.com)* offers a wide choice of accommodation (rooms, flats, chalets and villas) throughout France.
The **Fédération des Stations vertes de vacances et Villages de neige** *(6 rue Ranfer-de-Bretenières, BP 71698, 21016 Dijon Cedex, ✆03 80 54 10 50, www.stationsvertes.com)* is an association, which promotes almost 600 rural localities throughout France, selected for their natural appeal as well as for the quality of their environment, their accommodation and the leisure activities available.

Farm Holidays

Three guides, *Guide des Fermes Auberges, Bienvenue à la Ferme* and *Vacances et week-ends à la Ferme*, list the addresses of farms providing guest facilities which have been vetted for quality and for meeting official standards. For more information, apply to local tourist offices.

HOSTELS, CAMPING

To obtain an **International Youth Hostel Federation card** (there is no age requirement, and there is a senior card available too), you should contact the IYHF in your own country for inform-ation and membership applications (US ✆1 301 495 1240; UK ✆01629 592 700; Australia ✆61 2 9283 7195). There is a booking service online *(www.hihostels.com)*, which you may use to reserve rooms as far as six months in advance.
There are two main youth hostel *(auberges de jeunesse)* associations in France, the **Ligue Française pour les Auberges de Jeunesse** *(67 r. Verg-niaud, 75013 Paris; ✆01 44 16 78 78; www.auberges-de-jeunesse.com)* and the **Fédération Unie des Auberges de Jeunesse** *(27 r. Pajol, 75018 Paris; ✆01 44 89 87 27; www.fuaj.org)*.
The Féderation's informative website provides an online booking service. There are numerous officially graded **campsites** with varying standards of facilities.

The **Michelin Camping France** guide lists a selection of camp sites. Much of France is popular with campers in the summer months, so it is wise to book in advance.

WHERE TO EAT

A selection of places to eat **(Eat)** in the different locations covered in this guide can be found in the **Addresses** appearing in the *Discovering* section of this guide. The Legend at the back of this guide explains the symbols and abbreviations used in these sections. Use the **Michelin Guide France**, with its famously reliable star-rating system and hundreds of establishments all over France, for an even greater choice. If you would like to experience a meal in a highly rated restaurant from the red-cover **Michelin Guide**, be sure to book ahead! In the countryside, restaurants usually serve lunch between noon and 2pm and dinner between 7.30 and 10pm. It is not always easy to find something in between those two meal times, as the non-stop restaurant is still a rarity in rural France. However, a hungry traveller can usually get a sandwich in a café, and ordinary hot dishes may be available in a *brasserie*.

For information on local specialities, see the section on food and drink in the *Introduction*.

In French restaurants and cafés, a service charge is included. Tipping is not necessary, but French people often leave the small change from their bill on their table or about 5% for the waiter in a nice restaurant.

Chez Gégène

©Emilio Suetone/hemis.fr/World Pictures/Photoshot

"GUINGUETTES" IN ÎLE-DE-FRANCE

After the golden age of Impressionism in the late 19C, dance halls located along canals and rivers in the country-side around Paris, known as *guingettes*, gradually disappeared from Île-de-France. These dance halls, serving drinks and meals, with music provided by a band, were reintroduced as part of regional policy and as a result of the enthusiasm of the Culture Guingette association. They are now springing up again on the banks of the Marne and Seine, bringing back to life the picturesque atmosphere of the turn of the century. You may prefer to be a casual spectator, enjoying simple fare at a riverside table. But if you have your dancing shoes on, dress with flair as the regulars do (men may need a tie to enter the ballroom). Brush up on your passo doble, tango and cha-cha-cha, and they'll be sure to take you for a native.

Association Culture Guinguette
🛈 ✆*01 45 16 37 51.*
www.culture-guinguette.com.
This association for the promotion of these traditional gathering places

can inform tourists of special events. Dance styles ranging from athletic rock to energetic polka by way of the classic waltz are practised in the member clubs:

- ◆ **Domaine Ste-Catherine**
  22-24 allée Centrale, Pont de Créteil, Île de Brise-Pain, 94000 Créteil. ✆01 42 07 19 18.
- ◆ **L'Île du Martin-Pêcheur**
  41 quai Victor-Hugo, 94500 Champigny-sur-Marne.
  ✆01 49 83 03 02.
- ◆ **Le Moulin Vert**
  103 chemin du Contre-Halage, 94500 Champigny-sur-Marne.
  ✆01 47 06 00 91.
- ◆ **Quai 38**
  8 quai du Viaduc, 94500 Champigny-sur-Marne.
  ✆01 47 06 24 69.
- ◆ **La Goulue**
  17 quai Gabriel-Péri, 94340 Joinville-le-Pont, ✆01 48 83 21 77.
- ◆ **Le Petit Robinson**
  164 quai de Polangis, 94340 Joinville-le-Pont.
  ✆01 48 89 04 39.
- ◆ **Chez Gégène**
  162 quai de Polangis, 94340 Joinville-le-Pont.
  ✆01 48 83 29 43.
  www.chez-gegene.fr.
- ◆ **La Grenouillère**
  68 avenue du 11-Novembre,

St-Maur-des-Fossés, 94210 La
Varenne-St-Hilaire. ℘01 48 89 23 32.

- **Le Canotier**
  2 rue du Bac, 77410, Précy-
  sur-Marne. ℘01 60 01 62 12.
- **L'Auberge Charmante**
  20 quai de la Rive-Charmante,
  93160 Noisy-le-Grand.
  ℘01 45 92 94 31.

FERMES-AUBERGES

These farm inns may or may not
offer accommodation. They serve
farm produce and local speciality
dishes. They are open at weekends
but advanced booking is required.
Contact the **Association des
Fermiers Aubergistes de France**,
Ferm'Auberge, Les Perriaux, 89350
Champignelles. ℘03 85 45 13 22.

BRASSERIES IN NORTHERN FRANCE

The best place to discover the friend-
liness of people in the north of France
is in one of the many **brasseries** (the
name derives from the French for
'brewery'; hot and cold dishes are
usually available all day) often located
on the main square. This is also the best
place to taste inexpensive traditional
dishes like *moules et frites*, or a brown-
sugar tart, washed down with a glass
of beer. The ambience is often lively
well into the night.

ESTAMINETS

Food and drink are also served in cafés
known locally as *estaminets* (originally,
a café where smoking was permitted).
The warm, unpretentious atmosphere
is typical of the region, as is the good
beer served there.

- ℘/ **De Vierpot**
  125 Complexe Joseph-Decanter,
  59299 Boeschepe (⌖see BAILLEUL).
- ℘/ **Het Blauwershof**
  9 rue d'Eecke, 59270
  Godewaersvelde (⌖see CASSEL).
- ℘/ **'T Kasteelhof**
  8 rue St-Nicolas, 59670 Cassel
  (⌖see CASSEL).
- ℘/ **La Taverne Flamande**
  34 Grand'Place (⌖see CASSEL).

GASTRONOMY IN NORTHERN FRANCE

The Coast

Boulogne is France's leading fresh
fish port. In addition to the gourmet
restaurants serving fish soup, turbot
with cream sauce, *sole meunière*,
or a fish platter known as *la gainée*
consisting of three different types
of fish with a shrimp sauce, there are
also fishmongers' stalls selling cod,
herring and fresh eels.

Picardy

Soup has pride of place in this region
and one of the best-known is the
soupe des hortillons, made with fresh
vegetables. Water fowl is used in
many different ways, for example
duck or snipe pâté. The *ficelle picarde*
is a ham pancake rolled up and filled
with mushrooms then smothered in
bécha-mel sauce and baked in the
oven until the top is crisp and golden.
Leek quiche also forms part of a simple
but delicious meal.

Gourmet guide

The Picardy region boasts places that
appeal to the gourmet tourist interested
in discovering local specialities. Among
the spots that have been awarded the
Site remarquable du goût (for "remarkable
taste sensations") distinction are Houille,
Loos and Wanbrechies, on the outskirts
of Lille, known for *genièvre* (a juniper-
flavoured eau-de-vie similar to gin);
the port of Boulogne famous for its
fish; the market gardens of the Marais
Audomarois in St-Omer; and the
Hortillonnages marshland in Amiens,
for fruit and vegetables (traditional
floating market on the 3rd Sunday in
June, canal festival in September).
You can obtain detailed information
on local gastronomy by contacting:

- **Comité de Promotion Nord-
  Pas-de-Calais** 5 avenue Roger-
  Salengro, BP 39, 62051, St-Laurent-
  Blangy Cedex, ℘03 21 60 57 86;
  www.saveurs-npdc.com
- **Comité de Promotion Picardie**
  19 bis rue A.-Dumas,
  80026 Amiens Cedex 3.

Useful Words and Phrases

ARCHITECTURAL TERMS
See Introduction: Architecture.

Sights

	Translation
Abbaye	Abbey
Beffroi	Belfry
Chapelle	Chapel
Château	Castle
Cimetière	Cemetery
Cloître	Cloisters
Colombage	Half-timbering
Cour	Courtyard
Couvent	Convent
Écluse	Lock (Canal)
Église	Church
Fontaine	Fountain
Gothique	Gothic
Halle	Covered market
Jardin	Garden
Mairie	Town Hall
Maison	House
Marché	Market
Monastère	Monastery
Moulin	Windmill
Musée	Museum
Pan de Bois (En)	Timber-framed
Parc	Park
Place	Square
Pont	Bridge
Port	Port/harbour
Porte	Gateway
Quai	Quay
Remparts	Ramparts
Romain	Roman
Roman	Romanesque
Rue	Street
Statue	Statue
Tour	Tower

Natural Sites

	Translation
Abîme	Chasm
Aven	Swallow-hole
Barrage	Dam
Belvédère	Viewpoint
Cascade	Waterfall
Col	Pass
Corniche	Ledge
Côte	Coast, Hillside
Forêt	Forest
Grotte	Cave
Lac	Lake
Plage	Beach
Rivière	River
Ruisseau	Stream
Signal	Beacon
Source	Spring
Vallée	Valley

On the Road

	Translation
Car Park	Parking
Diesel	Diesel/gazole
Driving licence	Permis de conduire
East	Est
Garage (For Repairs)	Garage
Left	Gauche
Lpg	Gpl
Motorway/Highway	Autoroute
North	Nord
Parking meter	Horodateur
Petrol/gas	Essence
Petrol/gas station	Station d'essence
Right	Droite
South	Sud
Toll	Feu tricolore
Tire	Pneu
Unleaded	Sans plomb
West	Ouest
Wheel Clamp	Sabot
Pedestrian Crossing	Passage clouté

"Couteau" and "Fourchette"

©Andrew Johnson/iStockphoto.com

Time

	Translation
Today	Aujourd'hui
Tomorrow	Demain
Yesterday	Hier
Winter	Hiver
Spring	Printemps
Summer	Été
Autumn/fall	Automne
Week	Semaine
Monday	Lundi
Tuesday	Mardi
Wednesday	Mercredi
Thursday	Jeudi
Friday	Vendredi
Saturday	Samedi
Sunday	Dimanche

Numbers

	Translation
0	zéro
1	un
2	deux
3	trois
4	quatre
5	cinq
6	six
7	sept
8	huit
9	neuf
10	dix
11	onze
12	douze
13	treize
14	quatorze
15	quinze
16	seize
17	dix-sept
18	dix-huit
19	dix-neuf
20	vingt
30	trente
40	quarante
50	cinquante
60	soixante
70	soixante-dix
80	quatre-vingt
90	quatre-vingt-dix
100	cent
1000	mille

Shopping

	Translation
Antiseptic	Antiseptique
Bank	Banque
Bakery	Boulangerie
Big	Grand
Bookshop	Librairie
Butcher's	Boucherie
Chemist's/drugstore	Pharmacie
Closed	Fermé
Cough mixture	Sirop pour la toux
Cough sweets	Cachets pour la gorge
Entrance	Entrée
Exit	Sortie
Fishmonger's	Poissonnerie
Grocer's	Épicerie
Newsagent	Maison de la Presse, Marchan de Journaux
Open	Ouvert
Painkiller	Analgésique
Plaster (Adhesive)	Pansement Adhésif
Post office	Poste
Pound (Weight)	Livre
Push	Pousser
Pull	Tirer
Shop	Magasin
Small	Petit
Stamps	Timbres

Food And Drink

	Translation
Beef	Bœuf
Beer	Bière
Butter	Beurre
Bread	Pain
Breakfast	Petit-déjeuner
Cheese	Fromage
Chicken	Poulet
Dessert	Dessert
Dinner	Dîner
Duck	Canard
Fish	Poisson
Fork	Fourchette
Fruit	Fruits
Glass	Verre
Grape	Raisin
Green salad	Salade verte
Ham	Jambon
Ice cream	Glace

Jug of water	Carafe d'eau
Jug of wine	Pichet de vin
Knife	Couteau
Lamb	Agneau
Lunch	Déjeuner
Meat	Viande
Mineral water	Eau minérale
Mixed salad	Salade composée
Orange juice	Jus d'orange
Plate	Assiette
Pork	Porc
Red wine	Vin rouge
Salt	Sel
Sparkling water	Eau gazeuse
Spoon	Cuillère
Still water	Eau plate
Sugar	Sucre
Tap water	Eau du robinet
Turkey	Dinde
Vegetables	Légumes
Water	De l'eau
White Wine	Vin blanc
Yoghurt	Yaourt

Personal Documents and Travel

	Translation
Airport	Aéroport
Credit Card	Carte de crédit
Customs	Douane
Passport	Passeport
Platform	Voie, Quai
Railway Station	Gare
Shuttle	Navette
Suitcase	Valise
Train/plane ticket	Billet de train/ d'avion
Wallet	Portefeuille

Clothing

	Translation
Coat	Manteau
Jumper	Pull
Raincoat	Imperméable
Shirt	Chemise
Shoes	Chaussures
Socks	Chaussettes
Stockings	Bas
Suit	Costume/tailleur
Tights	Collant
Trousers	Pantalon

USEFUL PHRASES

	Translation
Goodbye	Au Revoir
Hello/ Good Morning	Bonjour
How	Comment
Excuse Me	Excusez-moi
Thank You	Merci
Yes/no	Oui/non
I Am Sorry	Pardon
Why	Pourquoi
When	Quand
Please	S'il vous plaît

Do you speak English?
Parlez-vous anglais?

I don't understand
Je ne comprends pas

Talk slowly
Parlez lentement

Where's...?
Où est...?

When does the ... leave?
À quelle heure part...?

When does the ... arrive?
À quelle heure arrive...?

When does the museum open?
À quelle heure ouvre le musée?

When is the show?
À quelle heure est la représentation?

When is breakfast served?
À quelle heure sert-on le petit-déjeuner?

What does it cost?
Ça coûte combien?

Where can I buy a newspaper in English?
Où puis-je acheter un journal en anglais?

Where is the nearest petrol/ gas station?
Où se trouve la station essence la plus proche?

Where can I change travellers' cheques?
Où puis-je échanger des traveller's cheques?

Where are the toilets?
Où sont les toilettes?

Do you accept credit cards?
Acceptez-vous les cartes de crédit?

I need a receipt
Je voudrais un reçu

Basic Information

BUSINESS HOURS

National museums and art galleries are closed on Tuesdays; municipal museums are generally closed on Mondays. Shops hours are usually Monday to Saturday 10am to 6pm. In smaller towns, shops may also close for lunch and off-season. Churches, especially in secluded areas or small villages, are often only opened for services or on request.

DISCOUNTS

Significant discounts are available for senior citizens, students, young people under the age of 25, teachers, and groups for public transportation, museums and monuments and for some leisure activities such as the cinema (at certain times of day). Bring student or senior cards with you, and bring along some extra passport-size photos for discount travel cards. The **International Student Travel Confederation** (www.isic.org), global administrator of the International Student and Teacher Identity Cards, is an association of student travel organisations around the world. ISTC members collectively negotiate benefits with airlines, governments, and providers of other goods and services for the student and teacher community, both in their own country and around the world. The non-profit association sells international ID cards for students, under-25-year-olds and teachers (who may get discounts on museum entrances, for example). The ISTC is also active in a network of international education and work exchange programmes. The corporate headquarters address is Herengracht 479, 1017 BS Amsterdam, The Netherlands ℘31 20 421 28 00; Fax 31 20 421 28 10.

ELECTRICITY

The electric current is 220 Volts/50Hz. Circular two-pin plugs are the rule. Adapters and converters (for hairdryers, for example) are best bought before you leave home. If you have a rechargeable device, read the instructions carefully. Sometimes these items only require a plug adapter, in other cases you must use a voltage converter.

EMERGENCIES
Police (Gendarme) 17
Fire (Pompiers) 18
Ambulance (SAMU) 15

INTERNET ACCESS

Internet access is often easiest to find in hotels in larger towns, where WiFi is becoming standard (often free) and dial-up access is virtually nonexistent. Most towns have many wireless hotspots in cafés, bars and libraries, as well as a few internet cafés for those travelling without a computer. You can look online at **www.easyinternetcafe.com** to find your nearest internet café.

MAIL/POST

Main post offices open Monday to Friday 8am to 7pm, Saturday 8am to noon. Smaller branch post offices generally close at lunchtime between noon and 2pm and at 4pm.

Postage via airmail:
- ✉ UK: letter (20g) 0.70€
- ✉ North America: letter (20g) 0.85€
- ✉ Australia, NZ: letter (20g) 0.85€

Stamps are also available from newsagents and *bureaux de tabac*. Stamp collectors should ask for *timbres de collection* in any post office.

MONEY
CURRENCY

There are no restrictions on the amount of currency visitors can take into France. Visitors carrying a lot of cash are advised to complete a currency declaration form on arrival, because there are restrictions on currency export.

BANKS
Banks are open from 9am to noon and 2pm to 4pm and branches are closed either on Monday or Saturday. Banks close early on the day before a bank holiday. A passport is necessary as identification when cashing traveller's cheques in banks. Commission charges vary and hotels usually charge more than banks for cashing cheques. One of the most economical ways to use your money in France is by using **ATM/cash machines** to get cash directly from your bank account or to use your credit cards to get cash advances. Before you leave home, check with the bank that issued your card about emergency replacement procedures, and ask them to note that your credit card is likely to be used abroad for a while.

Be sure to remember your 4-digit PIN, you will need it to use cash dispensers and to pay with your card in most shops, restaurants, etc. ATM code pads are numeric; use a telephone pad to translate a letter code into numbers. Visa is the most widely accepted credit card, followed by MasterCard; other cards (Diners Club, Plus, Cirrus) are also accepted in most cash machines. Most places post signs indicating the cards they accept; if you don't see such a sign, and want to pay with a card, ask before ordering or making a selection.

Cards are widely accepted in shops, hypermarkets, hotels and restaurants, at tollbooths and in petrol stations. If your card is lost or stolen in France, call one of the following 24-hour hotlines (**Ⓒ**see box):

American Express ✆01 47 77 70 00	
Visa ✆08 36 69 08 80	
MasterCard/Eurocard ✆01 45 67 84 84	
Diners Club ✆01 49 06 17 50t	

You must report any loss or theft of credit cards or traveller's cheques to the local police who will issue you with a certificate (useful proof to show the issuing company).

PUBLIC HOLIDAYS
There are 11 public holidays in France. In addition, there are other religious and national festivals days, and local saints' days, etc. On all these days, museums and monuments may vary their hours of admission.

In addition to the usual school holidays at Christmas and in the spring and summer, there are long mid-term breaks (ten days to two weeks) in February and early November.

1 January	New Year's Day (*Jour de l'An*)
	Easter Day and Easter Monday (*Pâques*)
1 May	May Day (*Fête du Travail*)
8 May	VE Day (*Fête de la Libération*)
Thurs 40 days after Easter	Ascension Day (*Ascension*)
7th Sun–Mon after Easter	Whit Sunday and Monday (*Pentecôte*)
14 July	France's National Day (*Fête de la Bastille*)
15 August	Assumption (*Assomption*)
1 November	All Saint's Day (*Toussaint*)
11 November	Armistice Day (*Fête de la Victoire*)
25 December	Christmas Day (*Noël*)

SMOKING
Smoking is banned inside all public spaces, including hotel rooms, bars, and clubs, since January 2008. It is still permitted on outdoor café terraces and in specially-built fumoirs.

TELEPHONES
PUBLIC TELEPHONES
Most public phones in France use pre-paid phone cards (*télécartes*), rather than coins. Some telephone booths

TO USE YOUR PERSONAL CALLING CARD	
AT&T	☎0-800 99 00 11
Sprint	☎0-800 99 00 87
MCI	☎0-800 99 00 19
Canada Direct	☎0-800 99 00 16

accept credit cards (Visa, MasterCard/
Eurocard). *Télécartes* (50 or 120 units)
can be bought in post offices, branches
of France Télécom, *bureaux de tabac*
(cafés that sell cigarettes) and newsagents
and can be used to make calls in France
and abroad. Calls can be received at
phone boxes where the blue bell sign is
shown; the phone will not ring, so keep
your eye on the small digital screen.

INTERNATIONAL CALLS

French telephone numbers have 10
digits. Paris and Paris region numbers
begin with 01; 02 in northwest France;
03 in northeast France; 04 in southeast France and Corsica; 05 in southwest France.

To call France from abroad, dial the
country code (33) + 9-digit number
(omit the initial 0). When calling abroad
from France dial 00, then dial the country
code followed by the area code and
number of your correspondent.
International information:
US/Canada: 00 33 12 11
International operator:
00 33 12 + country code
Local directory assistance: 12

INTERNATIONAL DIALLING CODES			
(00 + code)			
Australia	☎61	New Zealand	☎64
Canada	☎1	United Kingdom	☎44
Ireland	☎353	United States	☎1

MOBILE/CELL PHONES

In France these have numbers that
begin with 06. Two-watt (lighter,
shorter reach) and eight-watt models
are on the market, using the Orange,

Bouygtel or SFR networks. *Mobicartes*
are prepaid phone cards that fit into
mobile units. Mobile phone rentals
(delivery or airport pickup provided):
World Cellular Rentals:
www.worldcr.com

TIME

WHEN IT IS NOON IN FRANCE, IT IS	
3am	in Los Angeles
6am	in New York
11am	in Dublin
11am	in London
7pm	in Perth
9pm	in Sydney
11pm	in Auckland

In France "am" and "pm" are not used but
the 24-hour clock is widely applied.

TIPPING

Since a service charge is automatically
included in the price of meals and
accommodation in France, any
additional tipping is up to the visitor,
generally small change, and generally
not more than 5%. Hairdressers are
usually tipped 10–15%.

As a rule, prices for hotels and
restaurants as well as for other goods
and services are significantly less
expensive in the French regions
than in Paris.

Restaurants usually charge for meals
in two ways: a *forfait* or *menu*, that is
a fixed price menu with two to three
courses, sometimes a small pitcher of
wine, all for a set price, or *à la carte*,
the more expensive way, with each
course ordered separately.

Cafés have very different prices,
depending on where they are located.
The price of a drink or a coffee is
cheaper if you stand at the counter
(comptoir) than if you sit down *(salle)*
and sometimes it is even more
expensive if you sit outdoors *(terrace)*.
In some big cities, prices go up after
10pm in the evening.

CONVERSION TABLES

Weights and Measures

1 kilogram (kg) 6.35 kilograms 0.45 kilograms	**2.2 pounds (lb)** 14 pounds 16 ounces (oz)	**2.2 pounds** 1 stone (st) 16 ounces	*To convert kilograms to pounds, multiply by 2.2*
1 metric ton (tn)	**1.1 tons**	**1.1 tons**	
1 litre (l) 3.79 litres 4.55 litres	**2.11 pints (pt)** 1 gallon (gal) 1.20 gallon	**1.76 pints** 0.83 gallon 1 gallon	*To convert litres to gallons, multiply by 0.26 (US) or 0.22 (UK)*
1 hectare (ha) **1 sq. kilometre (km²)**	**2.47 acres** 0.38 sq. miles (sq.mi.)	**2.47 acres** 0.38 sq. miles	*To convert hectares to acres, multiply by 2.4*
1 centimetre (cm)	**0.39 inches (in)**	**0.39 inches**	*To convert metres to feet, multiply by 3.28; for kilometres to miles, multiply by 0.6*
1 metre (m)	3.28 feet (ft) or 39.37 inches or 1.09 yards (yd)		
1 kilometre (km)	**0.62 miles (mi)**	**0.62 miles**	

Clothing

Women					Men			
	35	4	2½			40	7½	7
	36	5	3½			41	8½	8
	37	6	4½			42	9½	9
Shoes	38	7	5½		**Shoes**	43	10½	10
	39	8	6½			44	11½	11
	40	9	7½			45	12½	12
	41	10	8½			46	13½	13
	36	6	8			46	36	36
	38	8	10			48	38	38
Dresses	40	10	12		**Suits**	50	40	40
& suits	42	12	14			52	42	42
	44	14	16			54	44	44
	46	16	18			56	46	48
	36	06	30			37	14½	14½
	38	08	32			38	15	15
Blouses &	40	10	34		**Shirts**	39	15½	15½
sweaters	42	12	36			40	15¾	15¾
	44	14	38			41	16	16
	46	16	40			42	16½	16½

Sizes often vary depending on the designer. These equivalents are given for guidance only.

Speed

KPH	10	30	50	70	80	90	100	110	120	130
MPH	6	19	31	43	50	56	62	68	75	81

Temperature

Celsius (°C)	0°	5°	10°	15°	20°	25°	30°	40°	60°	80°	100°
Fahrenheit (°F)	32°	41°	50°	59°	68°	77°	86°	104°	140°	176°	212°

To convert Celsius into Fahrenheit, multiply °C by 9, divide by 5, and add 32.
To convert Fahrenheit into Celsius, subtract 32 from °F, multiply by 5, and divide by 9.
NB: Conversion factors on this page are approximate.

INTRODUCTION TO NORTHERN FRANCE AND THE PARIS REGION

Grand-Place Lille
S. Sauvignier/ MICHELIN

ARTOIS

The Region Today

21ST CENTURY

Northern France and the Paris Region make up for an interesting array of similarities and differences.

Culturally speaking, Picardy has much more in common with Nord-Pas-de-Calais than with its southern neighbour, Île-de-France. Its traditional language, 'Picard', so closely resembles its northern counterpart, 'Chtimi', than they are nearly undistinguishable. But its geography closely links it with the Parisian Basin, its agricultural flatlands and forests. Many Parisians seek to escape the Capital for peaceful weekend hideways in nearby Oise, while many Picards may be attracted by the Paris employment *eldorado*.

On the other hand, the culture of Nord-Pas-de-Calais has some unique features of its own, like the still wide use of flemish. Its rich privateer past has given birth to some of the wildest festive Carnival celebrations, not to mention a tradition of hospitality that is proverbially unequalled in France, and the famous football rivalry between Lens 'Blood-red and Golden' and Lille's 'Mastiffs'.

But be reassured: a narrow link of nearly impassable muddy cobblestone exists between the three regions: the Paris-Roubaix, one of France's oldest and most popular cycling races which run almost each year since 1896.

POPULATION
NORD-PAS-DE-CALAIS

Nord-Pas-de-Calais is one of France's most populated regions. With a birth rate significantly higher than the rest of the country, its demography is one of the youngest and most dynamic. Its dense population is mostly urban: 9 out of 10 inhabitants live in one of the numerous city centres. Among those, Lille emerges as a metropolis, attracting workers from no less than fifteen medium-sized neighbouring towns.

Belgians came there before 1910, but it is the huge 1920s immigration wave of Italians and Poles, who did the hard work in coal mines, that comes to mind when speaking about migratory currents in the area. With the decline of the mining industry, the migrating trend has slackened, but the region still attracts many North-African migrants.

PICARDY

A vivid contrast with its northern neighbour, Picardy has one of the weakest demographic growth rate of the country, despite one of the highest birth rate in Europe. Stuck between two greatly attractive industrial basins, the region steadily loses its inhabitants. Only the southern *département* of Oise

Paris-Roubaix – bicycle race on cobblestones

Jean-luc Barbat/MICHELIN

The Villages of Paris: An Urban Exception

Take advantage of a nice, sunny day to step away from the hustle and bustle of the city and its tourist landmarks, and discover a more intimate side of the Capital. Paris harbours a wealth of small-sized neighbourhoods, sometimes just a couple of buildings tucked away in some forgotten alley. These are remnants of long-absorbed villages which miraculously escaped Haussmann's urban renovation of Paris. As a sampler, walk half a mile from busy Porte de Bagnolet, and you'll come across the village of **Charonne**, complete with its church and cemetery. Stroll along the calm streets and villas of the **Mouzaïa** district, a former craftsmen township near the Parc des Buttes-Chaumont. Visit secluded and libertarian **Butte aux Cailles**, Montmartre's southern sister hidden on a hill of the 13th arrondissement. Around the popular Rue du Commerce, look for the former hamlet of **Grenelle**, a mere hunting ground until the 19C. Finally, enjoy the lively ambience of the **village d'Auteuil**, largely unchanged since the 19C.

sees an increase in its population, many former inhabitants of neighbouring Île-de-France or Paris settling there to escape rising real estate prices while retaining the ability to work in their original region.

PARIS AND ÎLE DE FRANCE

Although Île-de-France covers only 2.2% of the surface area of France, over 18% of the French population resides in the region. This huge concentration of around 12 million inhabitants has gradually focused around the natural junctions of the Seine, Marne and Oise river basins. These large, slow rivers separate vast plateaus bearing rich countryside including the Brie and Beauce areas, and the large forests of Fontainebleau, Halatte, Rambouillet, Marly and St-Germain.

These natural areas have somehow managed to escape the urban sprawl which, today, tends to concentrate around the new towns of Cerg, Pontoise, Créteil, Évry, St-Quentin-en-Yvelines, Marne-la-Vallée and Melun-Sénart.

LOCAL GOVERNMENT

Metropolitan France is divided into 22 **administrative regions** (including Nord-Pas-de-Calais, Picardy and Île-de-France) which are further divided into **départements**. The regions are ruled by regional parliaments with extended budgetary powers. Those were created in the 1980s, in an effort by the state to counterbalance the otherwise overwhelming power of the capital city.

Oddly enough, Paris is a département city, with **20 local mayors** and a Parliament, the Conseil de Paris, whose counsellors appoint the **mayor of Paris**. Still, the Police Commissioner, a highly ranked civil servant, prevails over the mayor in public order matters. This situation originates in the aftermath of 19C Commune de Paris, when Paris revolted once more against the state and elected its own parliament. Horrified by the ensuing bloodsheds, Third Republic conservative legislators decided to make short of the freedom of action of the Conseil de Paris. They also decided that the Paris budget be approved by the state, effectively making the city a penniless beggar. Laws in the early 1980s have fortunately changed that.

ECONOMY
NORD-PAS-DE-CALAIS

A long-standing major trading area, with havens lying on one of the main maritime trade routes to Northern Europe, Nord-Pas-de-Calais acquired wealth from textiles and trade since medieval times and thus enjoyed a great deal of autonomy throughout history. Although industrial employment is now decreasing overall, the area's small and medium-size enterprises modernise in order to tackle the export market and

Coal Mines

Mining in the coal fields of Nord-Pas-de-Calais started in the 18C. The deposit lay at the western end of a large coal depression, which extended into Belgium and Germany. The pits employed up to 220 000 people in 1947, but the production started to decline from then on. In 1959, when productivity still reached 29 million tonnes, a plan of progressive shutdown was implemented which led to the closure of the last pit on 21 December 1990.

A wide variety of industries has developed around the ruined mines: production of oval coal briquettes, foundry and special coke; manufacture of facing bricks; sale of mine gas; production of electricity in power stations, which run largely on fuel products, gathered from the slag heaps; use of shale, also from slag heaps, for road foundations and as ballast for railway lines. About 70 slag heaps could be exploited in that way.

take full advantage of the proximity of vast European markets and the ease of access afforded by the Nord-Europe high-speed train, the Channel Tunnel and the dense network of roads. This ideal localisation has attracted a great deal of foreign investments, with the likes of Coca-Cola, MacCain or Rank Xerox settling in.

Going back to the Middle Ages, the textile and clothing industries now find it hard to cope with massive low cost imports from low-wage countries, such as China. Despite these difficulties, the Nord-Pas-de-Calais area still supplies the entire national production of linen (Lys Valley) and high-quality products like famous Calais and Caudry lace.

The glassware and crystal industries still number a few regional jewels, the best-known of all being the internationally renowned Arques works.

Coal extraction in Nord-Pas-de-Calais started in the 18C. With the increasing needs of 19C Industrial Revolution, the coal mining industry became an essential element of the region's economy. The conical black **slag heaps** (terrils), of which 300 now remain, became a distinctive feature of the landscape, along with brick-houses miners townships. Competition from emerging cheap labour countries and a drop in productivity in the post WW II era led to the decline of the northern mines. Seen by many as a regional drama, the last pit closed down in 1990.

Closely connected regional iron and steel industry also suffered from competitive imports of raw materials with higher mineral content. The local government is actively looking for alternative solutions to make up for the job losses and to transform the mining landscapes (Ⓒ see box). Successes include the steelworks in Dunkerque or the ultra-modern Pechiney aluminium plant in Gravelines.

French rail equipment is produced mainly in the Valenciennes and Douai areas. The now threatened automotive industry has plants in Douai (Renault), Maubeuge (MCA), Douvrain (Française de Mécanique) and Hourdain (Peugeot-Fiat). Services, such as logistics, distribution or tourism account for more than half of total jobs. Mail order is also an important sector of employment, with half of the ten largest French companies, including La Redoute and Trois Suisses, operating from the area.

Food-processing industry is now the region's leading industrial sector. Regional produce supplies flour mills and biscuit factories in the Lille area. The sugar beetroot industry has shaped a new specific industrial landscape on the plains near Cambrai and Thumeries. Canning factories produce 30% of the total national production of tinned vegetables and ready prepared meals and 50% of canned fish, the latter specifically around Boulogne, France's leading fishing port.

PICARDY

Agriculture is still the best known aspect of the economy of Picardy. A mainly rural area, with over two-thirds of its rich soil dedicated to open plains, Picardy holds, as one may expect, the French first rank for sugar beet and plays a prominent role in the production of other staples, such as like potatoes, peas and grain.

Food processing plays an important role in many areas: canning factories, based in the Santerre area at Estrée, Rosières and Péronne, are essential local job providers and so are Saint-Louis sugar refineries in Roye and Eppeville.

But Picardy has a powerful and long-standing, if less obvious, industrial tradition in many other domains: over 300 small and medium-sized plants employing about 20 000 people operate in the **plastic** transformation, **rubber** and **composite materials** industries. **Metallurgy** accounts for one half of the region's industrial workforce and more than 1 700 enterprises. Five internationally recognised and government-aided industrial groupings exist in the region: **light metallurgy** in Vimeu; **glass transformation** in the Bresle Valley; **machine-tooling** in Albert; **industrial boilers** in Ham and **car components** in Thiérache.

One of the region's most remarkable features is the strength of its **craft industry**, an ancient yet very lively tradition, especially in the domain of tapestry, stained-glass windows, etc.

Finally, new sectors like **logistics** or **call-centres** have recently appeared in Picardy. Located in one of the best connected areas of Europe, they will certainly have an important impact on local job forces in the years to come.

PARIS AND ÎLE-DE-FRANCE

France's economic heavyweight champion, Île-de-France's Gross Regional Product, accounts for one third of the country's GNP, exceeding those of Sweden or Belgium. The region concentrates more than five million jobs (over 15% of the national labour force), of which four million are in the private sector. Its **educational system** welcomes 60 0000 students at university level each year. Nearly 75 000 new companies are registered yearly; to assist them in their development, government-sponsored agencies called *pépinières d'entreprises* have been created in the region.

Covering more than 50% of the regional territory, highly mechanised agriculture only accounts for 0.5% of the local workforce, which says something about the size of the average farmland. The western plains of **Brie** and the seemingly endless plateau of **Beauce**, south-west of Paris, are nicknamed the granary of France, and for good reason: their silt soils are among France's best for the massive production of wheat and colza, a non-drying oil. Other regional produce includes beetroots and other fresh vegetables, decorative plants and flowers, especially Brie's roses. Animal production of meat or dairy is negligible, with Seine-et-Marne famous Brie cheeses making a notorious exception.

The food-processing industry is understandably strong in the region, with more than 500 companies present.

France's foremost industrial area, with more than 650 000 jobs in various branches, Île-de-France is paradoxically one of the country's least industrialised regions, with a scant 14% of the workforce and 6% of the companies engaged in industrial activity. Nor is that a temporary phenomenon: the sector has been steadily losing plants in the region since the 1980s.

The automotive industry is the leading actor, French carmakers Renault and PSA, along with their vast network of suppliers, generating one regional industrial job out of four.

The aerospace and defence industry also plays a prominent role, with companies like EADS, Dassault Aviation, Arianespace or Safran plants and research centres recruiting amongst the students of 17 regional universities and numerous high-level specialised engineering schools.

Energy specialised companies, like Total or EDF, the French national electricity producer, are also major employers.

Business and services make up for the overwhelming majority (more than 80%) of Francilian jobs and companies. Education and social welfare employs 1.5 million regional civil servants. Private enterprise includes electricity, phone or water-supplying companies as well as a host of consulting companies, the latter a fast-growing actor in the region's economy, accounting for nearly 500 000 jobs. Banking and other financial activities account for little more than one half of that job tally (270 000 jobs), telling much about the region's lack of specialisation.

One of the most visited cities in the world, Paris' largest economic sector is tourism. The capital attracts 31% of Île-de-France's jobs in the private sector, with average wages slightly higher than in the rest of the region but well above the country's average. Geographic inequalities are also reflected within the city: wages offered in the 8th *arrondissement* are 82% higher than in the more popular 20th *arrondissement*.

FOOD AND DRINK
THE CUISINE OF PICARDY

Soups are the great local specialities, in particular those made from tripe, pumpkin *(potiron)* or frogs *(grenouilles)*, as well as the famous vegetable soup *soupe des hortillons* and the stuffed pancakes in a creamy mushroom sauce

Mont-des-Cats cheese

S. Sauvignier/MICHELIN

(ficelle Picarde). The people of Picardy and Artois love their vegetables: beans from Soissons, Laon artichokes, St Valery carrots, peas from the Vermandois and leeks, which are used in a delicious pie, the tarte aux poireaux.

Starters include duck pâté in a pastry case *(pâté de canard en croûte)* – prepared in Amiens since the 17C – snipe pâté *(pâté de bécassines)* from Abbeville and Montreuil, eel pâté *(pâté d'anguilles)* from Péronne.

Duck, snipe and plover, eel, carp and pike from the River Somme are often on the menu. Seafood (shrimps known as *sauterelles*, cockles called *hemons*) is common, as well as sole, turbot, fresh herring and cod, often cooked with cream.

FLEMISH CUISINE

Flemish cooking, washed down with beer and often followed by a glass of gin or a *bistouille* (coffee with a dash of alcohol), contains several typical dishes:

- ✕ rabbit with prunes or raisins and pigeon with cherries;
- ✕ home-made potted meat made from veal, pork fat, rabbit and sometimes chicken *(potjevleesch)*;
- ✕ mixed stew of veal, mutton, pork offals, pork fat and vegetables *(hochepot)*;
- ✕ braised beef in a beer sauce flavoured with onions and spices *(carbonade)*;
- ✕ eel sautéed in butter and stewed in a wine sauce with herbs *(anguille au vert)*;
- ✕ small, smoked herrings, a speciality of Dunkirk *(craquelots)*.

Among the other specialities of the north of France are chitterling sausages *(andouillettes)* from Arras and Cambrai, trout from the River Canche and River Course, and cauliflowers from St-Omer.

CHEESES OF THE NORTH

Local cheeses, except for the one from **Mont des Cats**, are strong. Most come from the Thiérache and Avesnois region rich in pastureland. The best is

Maroilles, created in the 10C by monks from Maroilles Abbey: it has a soft centre with a crust soaked in beer, similar to cheese from Munster. The other cheeses in the region are derived from it: **Vieux Lille**, also called Maroilles Gris (grey Maroilles); **Dauphin** (Maroilles with herbs and spices); **Cœur d'Avesnes** or Rollot; and the delicious **Boulette d'Avesnes** (Maroilles with spices, rolled in paprika). **Flamiche au Maroilles**, a creamy, highly flavoured quiche, is one of the most famous dishes from the northern region of France.

Moule-frites

S. Sauvignier/MICHELIN

BRIE

The Brie region in Île-de-France is famous for its soft cow's milk cheeses with surface mould. There are two types, Brie and double- or triple-cream cheeses (**Lucullus**, **Grand Vatel**, **Gratte-Paille**, etc.) often made from the fat left over from the production of Brie, a legendary cheese that has enjoyed a reputation for excellence since the 13C. Brie was as popular with the commoners of Paris as with royalty, and it was the outright winner of a competition organised during the Congress of Vienna in 1815 bringing together all the best cheeses from throughout Europe. There are certain characteristics common to all Brie cheeses: they are made from partially skimmed raw cow's milk; the rind is white with reddish marks; the cheese is soft in texture and pale yellow in colour; the fat content is approximately 45%; and the maturing period does not exceed seven weeks. Setting these features aside, several varieties of Brie have developed and they differ depending on the area of production. The best-known are Brie de Meaux and Brie de Melun.

CAKES

The local pancakes *(crêpes)*, waffles and sweet breads (*tartines* and *brioches*) can make entire meals in themselves; the brioches with bulging middles are called

The Brewing Process

Beer is obtained by the mashing and fermentation of a mixture of water and malt, flavoured with hops. Barley grains are soaked in water (malting) until they germinate. The malted barley, dried and roasted in a kiln, becomes **malt**. This is powdered and then mixed with pure water and hops and cooked, according to each manufacturer's secret procedure. This operation, called brewing, transforms the starch in the malt into sugar and makes it possible to obtain the **wort**. With the addition of a raising agent, the wort begins to ferment.

Beer brewing was formerly undertaken simply by a brewer, with his boy handling a sort of pointed shovel *(fourquet)*, but is now a large and sophisticated industry.

Much French beer and lager (paler, 'aged' beer containing more bubbles and often less alcohol) is produced in the Pas-de-Calais region, which is rich in water, barley and hops. The hops grown in Flanders have a particularly strong flavour. The largest breweries are in the areas around Lille-Roubaix and Armentières, and the Scarpe and Escaut (Scheldt) river valleys. Today, there are only 17 left, although many small breweries are now operating locally. Different beers have their own characteristics: the slightly bitter lager *(bière blonde)* of the north; the relatively sweet and fruity dark beer *(bière brune)* or the richly flavoured, amber-red beer *(bière rousse)*.

coquilles.Tarts, such as the delicious tartes au sucre sprinkled with brown sugar, are often served for dessert. Sweets are accompanied by the light, chicory coffee which people from the region drink at any time of the day.

BEER

Gambrinus, the king of beer, is greatly revered in the north of France, as is St Arnould, the patron saint of brewers. Beer *(la bière)* was already known in Antiquity. In Gaul it was called *cervoise*. During the Middle Ages brewing beer was a privilege of the monasteries. It spread enormously in Flanders under John the Fearless, Duke of Burgundy and Count of Flanders, who developed the use of hops.

GIN

Gin is still produced in Houlle, Wambrechies and Loos. Another drink produced in Loos is an apéritif called *chuchemourette*, consisting of *crème de cassis* and gin.

WINE

A rather demanding plant in terms of sun exposure and soil quality, grape never made it to the plains of Picardy or Nord-Pas-de-Calais. Quite unexpectedly however, in the early 19C, the vineyards of Île-de-France were the country's largest. West of Paris, beyond the skyscrapers of La Défense, is a suburb called Argenteuil, which produced a wine known as **Piccolo**.

Massively consumed by Parisians in the guinguettes off the banks of the Seine River in the 19C, the beverage gave its name to the French word for 'boozing': *picoler*. By the end of the Second World War, the vineyards of Île-de-France had almost completely disappeared, fallen victim to merciless phylloxera, and unable to compete with the increasingly popular wine production from southern France. Only a few patches remain today, the largest being the **Clos Montmartre**, grown on the slopes of Paris Butte Montmartre, on a little plot beneath the famous Sacré-Coeur Basilica. The small annual production (roughly 850 half-bottles) is sold at the Grape Harvest Festival held in October.

NORTHERN FOLKLORE AND TRADITIONS

For dates of festivals and other events, see the Calendar of Events in the Practical information section.

The people of Picardy and the north of France belong to the 'Picardy nation' that used to spread from Beauvais to Lille and from Calais to Laon, extending as far as Tournai and Mons. The common language of this 'nation' formed a bond between its inhabitants, who are known for being hard workers with a taste for good food and lively merrymaking. Even now, the slightest excuse is found to celebrate or get together in an estaminet (the Walloon word for a café) for a beer or two. Natives of Flanders, Artois, Lille and Picardy all have this same fondness for gatherings which is reflected in their many group activities: carnivals, celebrations, patron saint's days, village fairs and associations (each village has its own band).

THE DUCASSE OR KERMESSE

The words *ducasse* (from *dédicace*, meaning a Catholic holiday) and *kermesse* ('church fair' in Flemish) now both designate a town or village patron saint's day. This holiday has preserved aspects of its religious origins (Mass and procession) but today also includes stalls, competitions, traditional games, jumble sales, etc.

CARNIVALS

Carnival time is an occasion to dress up in costume and watch parades of floats and giant figures. It traditionally takes place on Shrove Tuesday *(Mardi Gras)* – as in Dunkirk, where it lasts for three days – but in reality, carnival parades take place throughout the year in the North of France.

FAMOUS GIANTS

Giants originate from various myths, legends and stories, and include:
♦   **legendary founders**, such as Lydéric and Phinaert in Lille

Yan den Houtkapper *Steenvoorde*

Martin and Martine *Cambrai*

Gayant and his wife *Douai*

The Sailor's wife *Grand-Fort Philippe*

Mother Reuze *Cassel*

R. Corbel/ MICHELIN

Carnival in Dunkirk

©Pierre Cheuva/Photononstop/Tips Images

- **famous warriors** like the Reuzes from Dunkirk and Cassel, said to originate from Scandinavia
- **historic figures**, such as Jeanne Maillotte in Lille, the inn-keeper who fought off the 'Howlers'; the beautiful Roze in Ardres, who saved the town from dragonnades; the Elector of Bergues, portraying Lamartine; Roland in Hazebrouck, one of Baudouin of Flanders' Crusaders, who distinguished himself at the taking of Constantinople
- **famous couples**, like Martin and Martine, the two 'Jack o' the Clocks' of Cambrai; Colas and Jacqueline, the gardeners of Arras; Arlequin and Colombine in Bruay; Manon and Des Grieux in Hesdin
- **popular figures**, like Gédéon, the bell ringer of Bourbourg, who saved the belfry chimes from being stolen; the pedlar Tisje Tasje of Hazebrouck, symbol of the Flemish spirit, with his wife Toria and his daughter Babe Tisje; Pierrot Bimberlot in Le Quesnoy; and Ko Pierre, a drum major, in Aniche
- **legendary heroes**: Gargantua in Bailleul; Gambrinus, the king of beer, in Armentières; Yan den Houtkapper, the woodcutter who made a pair of wooden boots for Charlemagne, in Steenvoorde;

Gayant of Douai, said to have delivered the town from brigands
- **representatives of trades**, like the vegetable gardener Baptistin in St-Omer; the miner Cafougnette in Denain; and the fisherman Batisse in Boulogne
- or simply a **child**, like the famous Binbin in Valenciennes.

Giants are often accompanied by their families – as they do marry and are given large families – and are surrounded by skirted horses, devils, bodyguards and wheels of fortune. Sometimes they have their own hymn, such as the Reuzelieds in Dunkirk and Cassel.

Materials – Traditionally the giants' bodies are made from a willow frame on which a painted papier-mâché head is placed. Once dressed in their costumes, the giants are then carried by one or more people, who make them dance in the procession. The tallest is Gayant in Douai, who is 8.4m/28ft tall.

As giants are often now made of heavier materials (steel tubing, cane, plastic), they are frequently pulled along in carts or on wheels, rather than being carried.

TOWN CHIMES

Chimes in town belfries, which regularly sound out their melodic tunes, lend a rhythm to life in northern French towns. Since the Middle Ages, when four bells were tapped by hand with a hammer, there have been many additions: a mechanism, a manual keyboard, pedals, all of which have made it possible to increase the number of bells (62 in Douai) and to increase the variety of their sounds.

Carillon concerts are held in Douai, St-Amand-les-Eaux and Maubeuge (east of Valenciennes).

TRADITIONAL GAMES AND SPORTS

Traditional entertainments remain popular: marionettes, ball games, real tennis, ninepins, darts, lacrosse (an ancestor of golf), archery (which is also a traditional sport of the Valois area), cock-fighting, pigeon-breeding, etc. A popular bar game is the *billard Nicolas*, where players squeeze a bulb to blow a marble across a round playing area.

Archery – In the Middle Ages archers were already the pride of the counts of Flanders, who would have the archers accompany them on all their expeditions. As soon as individual towns were founded, the archers formed associations or guilds. They appeared at all public ceremonies, dressed in brightly coloured costumes, brandishing the great standard of their association. Today archery is practised in several ways. A method particular to the North is vertical or 'perch' shooting, which consists of firing arrows upwards to hit dummy birds attached to gratings suspended from a pole. At the top of this pole, about 30m/98ft off the ground, is the hardest target of all, the **poppinjay** *(papegaï)*. Archers must hit this bird with a long, ball-tipped arrow and the winner is proclaimed 'King of the Perch'. In winter the sport is practiced indoors: arrows are shot horizontally at a slightly tilted grating. Still grouped in brotherhoods, the archers gather every year to honour their patron, St Sebastian.

Crossbow – The art of the crossbow, which also dates from the Middle Ages, has its own circle of enthusiasts organised in brotherhoods. Their gatherings, colourful events featuring

Chimes of the belfry in Douai

S. Sauvignier/MICHELIN

these curious weapons from another time, are often given evocative names such as the King's Crossbow Shoot.

Javelin – This feathered arrow measuring 50–60cm/20–24in is thrown into a tightly tied bundle of straw which serves as a target. It is the same principle as for the game of darts, which is played in many cafés.

The Game of 'Billons' – A *billon* is a tapering wooden club about 1m/3ft long, weighing about 2–3kg/4–7lb. Two teams throw their *billons* in turn towards a post 9m/29.5ft away. The aim is to land the narrower end of the club nearest to the post and this may be achieved by dislodging the *billons* of the opposing team.

Bouchon – Teams face each other in cafés, and knock down the cork and wood 'targets' with their metal paddles. The best players participate in competitions at local festivals.

Pigeon-Breeding – Pigeon fanciers *(coulonneux)* raise their birds to fly back to the nest as quickly as possible. For pigeon-racing competitions, which are very popular, the birds are carried in special baskets to a distance of up to 500km/310mi and must then return to their dovecote at record speed. A pigeon can fly over 100km/62mph on average.

Singing Finch Competitions – Finches have also become part of the folklore in the north of France, where they participate in trilling contests. Some can trill as many as 800 times an hour.

History

TIME LINE
CELTS AND ROMANS

Circa 300 BC The north of Gaul occupied by a Celto-Germanic tribe, the Belgae.

153 BC First Roman soldiers enter Gaul.

57 BC Belgian Gaul conquered by Caesar. Bavay, Boulogne and Amiens become important Roman centres.

AD 1C–3C Roman peace. Northern France becomes part of the province of Second Belgium (capital at Reims).

406 German tribes invade Gaul.

MEROVINGIANS AND CAROLINGIANS

486 Territory from the Somme to the Loire rivers occupied by Clovis following the defeat of the Roman army at Soissons: his kingdom was called Francia in Latin.

534–36 Franks conquer Burgundy and acquire Provence.

6C and 7C Creation of bishoprics and founding of many abbeys.

751 Pepin crowned first Carolingian king of the Franks.

800 Charlemagne crowned Holy Roman Emperor.

9C and 10C Norman and Hungarian invasions. Withdrawal of the abbeys into the towns.

911 The Duchy of Normandy created after the Treaty of St Clair-sur-Epte, ending the Normans' ambitions in Île-de-France.

987 Hugh Capet, duke and suzerain of the land extending from the Somme to the Loire rivers, crowned the first King of France, in Senlis.

THE MIDDLE AGES

11C and 12C Period of prosperity. Development of the clothmaking industry in Flanders, Artois and Picardy. Towns obtain charters and build belfries.

1066 William, duke of Normandy, conquers England.

1095 Pope Urban II preaches the first crusade at Clermont.

1154 Henry II becomes king of England and establishes the Angevin Empire of Britain and western and southern France.

1214 Battle of Bouvines: victory for Philippe Auguste over the Count of Flanders and his allies King John of England, the Holy Roman Emperor Otto IV and the counts of Boulogne and Hainault.

Gallo-Roman ruins in Champlieu near Morienval

S. Sauvignier/MICHELIN

1272 Ponthieu under the authority of the kings of England.

1314 Flanders annexed by Philip the Fair.

1337 Beginning of the Hundred Years' War (1337–1453). The death of Philip the Fair and his three sons ('the accursed kings') results in a problem of succession: Philip the Fair's nephew, Philip de Valois, preferred by the French barons over his grandson, Edward III, King of England. The following century marked by battles between the French and the English who lay claim to the French Crown, as well as between the Armagnacs, supporters of the family of Orléans, and the Burgundians, supporters of the dukes of Burgundy.

1346 Battle of Crécy: victory for Edward III of England.

1347 Calais surrendered to the English with the famous episode of the Burghers of Calais.

1348 The Black Death

1369 Marriage of Philip the Bold, Duke of Burgundy, with Marguerite, daughter of the Count of Flanders: Flanders under Burgundian authority.

1415 Battle of Agincourt: victory for Henry V of England.

1420 The Treaty of Troyes signed by Isabeau of Bavaria, wife of the mad king Charles VI, depriving the Dauphin of his rights of succession and designating her son-in-law, Henry V of England, heir to the French throne.

1422 — Death of Charles VI. France divided between the English, the Burgundians and the Armagnacs. Charles VII, the legitimate heir, resident in Bourges.

1430 Joan of Arc taken prisoner at Compiègne, and burned at the stake in 1431, in Rouen.

1435 Reconciliation of France and Burgundy in the Treaty of Arras.

1441 English supremacy over Île-de-France ends with the liberation of Pontoise.

1477 Invasion of Picardy, Artois, Boulonnais and Hainault by Louis XI following the death of Charles the Bold; only Picardy subsequently held. Marriage of Marie of Burgundy, daughter of Charles the Bold, to Maximilian of Austria: Flanders brought under Hapsburg control.

FROM THE BOURBONS TO THE REVOLUTION

16C Through the House of Hapsburg, Flanders included in the empire of Charles V of Spain.

1520 Meeting between Henry VIII of England and François I at the Field of the Cloth of Gold, Guînes.

1529 Peace of Dames signed at Cambrai: claims to Artois and Flanders renounced by François I.

1557 St-Quentin taken by the Spanish.

1558 Calais taken from the English by the Duke of Guise.

1562 Beginning of the Wars of Religion (1562–98).

1585 Philip II of Spain allied with the Catholic League (Treaty of Joinville).

1593 Henry of Navarre converts to Catholicism after capturing most of Île-de-France; crowned King Henri IV of France.

1598 Edict of Nantes grants religious tolerance to the Huguenots.

1659 Following the Treaty of the Pyrenees, marriage agreed between Louis XIV and Maria-Theresa of Spain; Artois brought under French sovereignty.

1661 The construction of a huge palace at Versailles commissioned by Louis XIV.

1663 Marriage of Louis XIV with Maria-Theresa, who according to local custom was to inherit all of the Brabant region from her mother. When the inheritance passes to another heir, Louis XIV declares the war of 'Devolution' on the Spanish Low Countries.

1668 Walloon Flanders given to Louis XIV by the Treaty of Aix-la-Chapelle.

1678 Louis XIV allowed to annex the other northern towns by the Treaty of Nimegen.

1713 The borders of northern France established definitively (Treaty of Utrecht).

1789 The French Revolution. Declaration of the Rights of Man, Storming of the Bastille and formation of the National Assembly.

FROM THE FIRST TO THE SECOND EMPIRE

1802 Treaty of Amiens: peace with Britain.

1803 Napoleon's army mustered at the Boulogne Camp for a possible invasion of England.

1804 Napoleon crowns himself Emperor of France.

1814 France invaded. Unconditional abdication by Napoleon at Fontainebleau. Louis XVIII, returned from exile in England, is enthroned in 1815.

1840 Attempted uprising against King Louis-Philippe organised by Louis-Napoleon in Boulogne.

1848 Louis-Napoleon elected President of the Republic; crowned Emperor (Napoleon III) in 1852.

1870–71 Franco-Prussian War. End of the Second Empire signalled by the defeat at Sedan: the Third Republic proclaimed. Paris besieged by Prussians: Alsace and part of Lorraine given up under the Treaty of Frankfurt.

20TH CENTURY

1914 Outbreak of the First World War. France attacked by German armies through neutral Belgium; four years of bloody trench warfare follow.

1915–18 Battles throughout northern France and Flanders: in Artois (Neuville-St-Vaast, Vimy), in Picardy (Somme Valley, Chemin des Dames in the Aisne Valley, St Quentin) and in Île-de-France (Ourcq Valley, Battle of the Marne).

1918 11 November: armistice signed in Compiègne Forest.

British army patrols the town of Cambrai on the 9 October 1918

©Imagestate/Tips Images

1919	End of the war with the Treaty of Versailles.
1939	Outbreak of the Second World War. In June 1940 France overrun by the German army; occupation of much of the country. The 'French State', established at Vichy, collaborates closely with the Germans. The north of France cut off from the rest of the country by a boundary. France's honour saved by General de Gaulle's Free French forces and by the courage of the men and women of the Resistance. By 1942 all France occupied; the French fleet scuttled at Toulon. Allied landing in Normandy in June 1944, and in the south of France in August: Paris liberated. The 'Dunkirk pocket' retaken by the Allies. The German surrender signed at Reims on 7 May 1945.
1976	Creation of the 'Île-de-France' administrative region.
1987	Start of building works for the Channel Tunnel linking France and England.
1994	6 May: official opening of the Channel Tunnel.

1996	Inauguration of Evry Cathedral.
1998	Inauguration of the Stade de France in St-Denis for the World Cup, won by the French team.

21ST CENTURY

2004	Lille is designated a European Capital of Culture, a distinction that gives cities a chance to showcase its cultural life and development.
2007	Nicolas Sarkozy is elected President of France: the 6th President of French Fifth Republic, the 23rd President of the French Republic and Co-Prince of Andorra. One of his first 'social' acts was to admit singer Barbra Streisand the Office of Légion d'Honneur. Paris is one of ten venues in France to host the 2007 Rugby World Cup.
2009	The **global financial crisis** reaches Picardy and Nord-Pas-de-Calais regions, causing job losses in services for the first time in years.

Art and Culture

LIVING LIKE KINGS

After the 15C, medieval castles were converted from fortresses into residential châteaux. Windows were enlarged, doors and openings were richly adorned. Towers, once strategic elements of the defensive structure, became decorative features, along with crenellated battlements and moats. By the second half of the 16C, such characteristics had become superfluous. Façades were embellished with statues and rows of superimposed columns. Roofs were high and presented a single slope.

The Château d'Écouen is a fine example of the French Renaissance style, as is the Richelieu Pavillon of the Louvre (1546–1654), in Paris. The style, which succeeded Gothic as the style dominant in Europe after the mid-16C, first developed in Italy. The name describes the 'rebirth' of interest in Roman and Greek art and learning. By the early 17C, the Classical style of architecture had emerged, as expressed in the magnificence of royal palaces.

FRANÇOIS I
(R. 1515–47)

The early phase of the French Renaissance culminated in the François I style (*& see FONTAINEBLEAU*). The decorative aspects mingle Gothic embellishments with elements inspired by Italian art, and

INTERIOR DECORATION

Fontainebleau – Galerie François I, fresco by Primaticcio

Renaissance: First Fontainebleau School – Ornate decoration in a free interpretation of the Italian masters. The frescoes framed by stuccowork are above the wainscoting. Coffered ceilings and rafters.

Grosbois – Dining Room

Louis XIII style – The decorative features are more restrained. Above the wainscoting are huge tapestries or frescoes. The ceiling rafters are visible but in most instances the coffering has disappeared.

Versailles – Salon de Vénus

Louis XIV style – The decoration is luxurious in the materials used but understated in design. Marble panels decorate the walls. The ceiling is divided into painted compartments separated by gilded stuccowork.

Champs – Mme de Pompadour's bedchamber

Louis XV style – Right angles have been banished. Curves, scrolls and arabesques soften straight lines. Light-coloured wainscoting has replaced the marble panels. Mouldings with plant and floral motifs, volutes, cartouches and shells.

Versailles – Louis XVI's gaming room

Louis XVI style – The decoration is still elegant and light in colour, but straight lines have come back into fashion. The severity of the rectangular panels is relieved by reeds and ribbons or garlands.

Compiègne – Napoleon's bedchamber

Empire style – Antique green or crimson-red hangings have replaced the wainscoting. Straight lines and semicircular arches predominate. Heavy mouldings and motifs stand out against the dark woodwork.

the design features round arches and symmetrical composition. Many of the elegant buildings erected by the monarch bear his distinctive emblem: a crowned salamander.

HENRI IV (R. 1589–1610) – LOUIS XIII (R. 1610–43)

Louis XIII was strongly influenced by the Henri IV style (Place des Vosges, Paris), which marked the beginnings of the Classical period of French architecture. The principal characteristics of this style, which prevailed during the first half of the 17C, are the exact symmetry of the main building and the use of brick panels set into white stonework. Carved ornamentation is limited and sober. Most often, the design is a central block flanked by two end pavilions (&see Château de COURANCES). Louis XIII built the first palace in Versailles in this style, in brick, stone and slate.

LOUIS XIV (R. 1643–1715)

Under the skilful hand of François Mansart, civil architecture gave up its straightforward character and acquired a less domestic, nobler appearance. The early period shows columns and pilasters that stand the height of a single floor of the château. Triangular and arched pediments top doorways and windows. Numerous chimneys sprout from the high roofs (& see Château de MAISONS-LAFITTE).

Châteaux built during the second period are characterised by a high ground floor, a very high first floor and a relatively low second floor. A balustrade conceals the roof. The horizontal lines of the building are broken by rows of sturdy columns and tall windows. Ornamental sculpture is limited to the rooftop and the summit of the front pavilions, and inspired by classical models. Versailles represents the culmination of the high Classical period.

LOUIS XV (R. 1715–74)

After 1700, the Louis XIV style and its harsh angles were mellowed by soft, rounded contours. Under Louis XV, oval spaces and curved surfaces were favoured. Windows and pediments display intricate ornamentation, while the rest of the façade remains austere, without columns; the roof is formed by two sloping planes (&see the stables at CHANTILLY). Over time, Classical yielded more and more to Rococo (also known as Baroque classicism in France), which is distinguished by profuse, often semi-abstract ornamentation, and lightness of colour and weight.

LOUIS XVI (R. 1774–92)

The influence of the elegant Louis XV style is still apparent in works of this period, but over-abundant curves are replaced by right angles. Columns make a conspicuous comeback, placed on unadorned façades. This phase is known as 'Classicist', for many of the decorative motifs are inspired by Antiquity, a trend that introduced the so-called Pompeian and the Empire styles that followed (&see VERSAILLES: Petit Trianon). The French Revolution brought an abrupt end to building in this style.

RELIGIOUS AND CIVIL ARCHITECTURE

Île-de-France and the regions north of Paris offer a rich variety of architectural styles: Gallo-Roman at Bavay; Romanesque at Morienval, Rhuis and Chartres; Gothic architecture throughout Île-de-France, where it was born, and the later Flamboyant Gothic mainly in Picardy; Renaissance influence at Amiens and Cassel; Classical architecture in and around Paris; and Baroque in Flanders. Many of the earliest buildings of note were constructed for religious purposes, and the development of architectural styles is best understood through them. A church consisted basically of a chancel reserved for members of the clergy, where the high altar and the reliquaries were located, and of a nave for the congregation. This simple layout characterised the early churches, built on a basilical plan. During the Romanesque period the plan of the church developed into the shape of a cross. The vestibule (narthex) at the entrance received those who had not been baptised, and the nave was enlarged with aisles. In places of pilgrimage, an ambulatory and side aisles were added to the chancel to facilitate processions. Architects followed this layout as it was convenient for celebrating Mass and easy to build.

ROMANESQUE (11C–12C)

Architects in Romanesque times knew how to build huge, lofty churches, but as the heavy stone vaulting often caused the walls to settle or cave in, they made the windows as small as possible and added aisles surmounted by galleries to support the sombre nave.

One of the main types of roofing in Romanesque churches is groined vaulting, in which two identical barrels meet at right angles. The barrel, in line with the nave, is supported by the transverse arch, while the one set at a right angle is supported by the main arch or by a recess in the wall. Rhuis and Morienval churches and the Royal Doorway of Chartres Cathedral are splendid examples of Romanesque art worth seeing.

GOTHIC (12C–15C)

The transition from Romanesque to Gothic architecture – which originated in Île-de-France – was a slow, natural process that developed in response to the demand for wider, higher and lighter churches. Gothic art, typified by quadripartite vaulting and the use of pointed arches, evolved from sombre 12C Romanesque sanctuaries into light 13C churches and the extravagantly ornate buildings of the 15C. It is rare to find a church with entirely unified features reflecting a given period in history. Building a church was a costly and lengthy operation subject to changes in public taste and building methods as the work progressed. Towards the late 13C, famous personalities and guilds were granted the privilege of having a chapel built in their honour in one of the side aisles. In exchange they were expected to make a generous contribution towards the building or its maintenance.

Architects – The names of the architects of great religious edifices are known to us only from the Gothic period onwards, through texts or through inscriptions carved around the 'labyrinths' outlined on cathedral floors. That is how Robert de Luzarches was revealed as responsible for the plans of Amiens Cathedral.

The most outstanding master builder in the north of France, however, was undoubtedly **Villard de Honnecourt**, born near Cambrai. The towers of Laon Cathedral, Vaucelles Abbey *(south of Cambrai)*, and the chancels at St-Quentin and Cambrai *(no longer extant)* have all been attributed to him.

West fronts – Most main façades were set facing west. Nave and aisles had their own doorway flanked by buttresses that were bare in the 12C and 13C, ornate in the 15C. The tympanum featured ornamentation, and in the 14C its gable was elaborately carved. In the 13C, rose windows were fairly small; in the 14C they were enlarged across the west front to provide light for the nave. As windows grew larger, façades became more delicate. A gallery was built at the base of the towers to break the rigid vertical perspective created by the buttresses and bell towers; in the 15C this was reduced to a balustrade and the gables further embellished.

Ideally, west fronts were to be richly decorated with stone carvings, but in many cases they were the last part to be completed. Architects were often obliged to forego ornamentation, and even towers, owing to insufficient funds. In other cases, even the transepts were given remarkable façades (see CHARTRES).

Spires – After lightening the façades of Gothic churches, architects turned to the spires. By the Flamboyant period the open-work masonry was markedly ornate. In the 19C many bell towers in the region were given a spire by followers of Viollet-le-Duc.

Flying buttresses – In Early Gothic churches the pillars in the nave were supported by masonry concealed in the galleries. During the 12C these walls were reduced to arches (see p80) supported by sturdy piers. Soon afterwards the galleries themselves were

ARCHITECTURAL DRAWINGS

Religious architecture

MANTES-LA-JOLIE – Ground plan of Notre-Dame (12C-14C)

Basilical plan without transept: the sacristy was added in the 13C, the radiating chapels and the Chapelle de Navarre in the 14C.

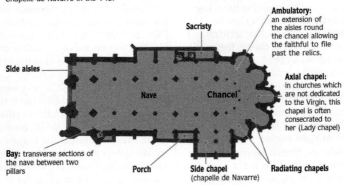

Ambulatory: an extension of the aisles round the chancel allowing the faithful to file past the relics.

Sacristy

Side aisles

Axial chapel: in churches which are not dedicated to the Virgin, this chapel is often consecrated to her (Lady chapel)

Nave　　**Chancel**

Bay: transverse sections of the nave between two pillars

Porch

Side chapel (chapelle de Navarre)

Radiating chapels

CHARTRES – Notre-Dame Cathedral

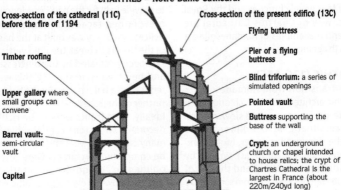

Cross-section of the cathedral (11C) before the fire of 1194

Cross-section of the present edifice (13C)

Flying buttress

Pier of a flying buttress

Timber roofing

Blind triforium: a series of simulated openings

Pointed vault

Upper gallery where small groups can convene

Buttress supporting the base of the wall

Barrel vault: semi-circular vault

Crypt: an underground church or chapel intended to house relics; the crypt of Chartres Cathedral is the largest in France (about 220m/240yd long)

Capital

RAMPILLON – Main doorway of the church (13C)

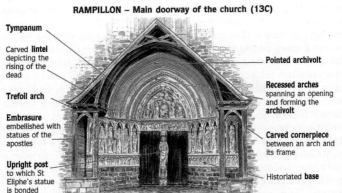

Tympanum

Carved **lintel** depicting the rising of the dead

Pointed archivolt

Trefoil arch

Recessed arches spanning an opening and forming the **archivolt**

Embrasure embellished with statues of the apostles

Carved cornerpiece between an arch and its frame

Upright post to which St Eliphe's statue is bonded

Historiated base

R. Corbel/MICHELIN

AMIENS – West front of the cathedral (13C)

The vast cathedral is the edifice which best reflects the blossoming of Rayonnant Gothic architecture.

Kings' gallery decorating the west front of many cathedrals: it includes 22 statues representing Christ's royal lineage

Finial: a flower-shaped ornament finishing off a pinnacle

Gargoyle: a rainwater spout

Great rose-window

Openwork **gallery** consisting of **trefoil arches** surmounted by quatrefoil openings

Tympanum made of four **historiated** bands

Gable: a steeply pitched ornamental pediment surmounting doorways and windows, here decorated with **crockets.**

Recessed arches spanning an opening and forming the **archivolt**

Jambs: uprights supporting the archivolt

Band: a carved ornamental strip

Upright post to which a statue is generally bonded (here the "Beau Dieu")

Door leaf

Embrasure embellished with statues carved in the **round**

Canopy: a richly decorated baldaquin surmounting a statue

R. Corbel/MICHELIN

77

BEAUVAIS – East end of the cathedral (13C)

In spite of the missing spire (which collapsed in 1573) and nave (never built owing to lack of funds), the cathedral has a magnificent chancel representing the apogee of Gothic building techniques with vaulting soaring to a height of 48m/157ft.

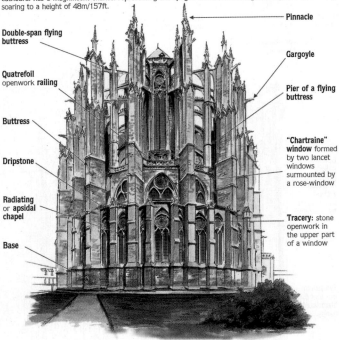

Pinnacle

Double-span flying buttress

Gargoyle

Quatrefoil openwork railing

Pier of a flying buttress

Buttress

"Chartraine" window formed by two lancet windows surmounted by a rose-window

Dripstone

Radiating or apsidal chapel

Tracery: stone openwork in the upper part of a window

Base

SENLIS – Notre-Dame Cathedral (12C-13C)

Cell or quarter: a segment of vaulting defined by intersecting ribs

Intersecting ribs

Lunette: part of the ribbed vaulting which does not extend to the keystone

Pendant keystone

Transverse arch: a reinforcing arch under a vault

Tierceron: an intermediate rib

Tracery: delicate stone openwork in the upper part of a window

Clerestory window

Equilateral arch: a pointed arch whose radii are equal to its span

Gallery

Openwork railing

Composite pillar formed by several bonded columns

Pointed main arcade

R. Corbel/MICHELIN

AIRE-SUR-LA-LYS – Organ of the collegiate church (1653)

This richly carved organ comes from the former Cistercian abbey of Clairmarais near Aire-sur-la-Lys.

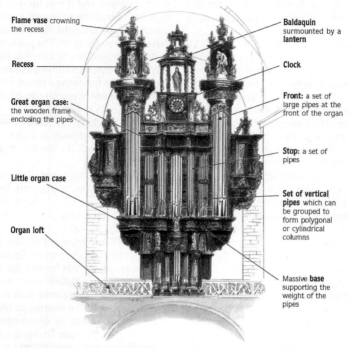

Flame vase crowning the recess

Recess

Great organ case: the wooden frame enclosing the pipes

Little organ case

Organ loft

Baldaquin surmounted by a **lantern**

Clock

Front: a set of large pipes at the front of the organ

Stop: a set of pipes

Set of vertical pipes which can be grouped to form polygonal or cylindrical columns

Massive **base** supporting the weight of the pipes

QUAËDYPRE – High altar and altarpiece of the church (late 17C)

In the 17C and 18C, altarpieces were architectural compositions towering above the altar and intended to channel the congregation's religious fervour.

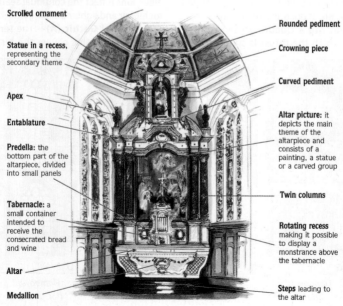

Scrolled ornament

Statue in a recess, representing the secondary theme

Apex

Entablature

Predella: the bottom part of the altarpiece, divided into small panels

Tabernacle: a small container intended to receive the consecrated bread and wine

Altar

Medallion

Rounded pediment

Crowning piece

Curved pediment

Altar picture: it depicts the main theme of the altarpiece and consists of a painting, a statue or a carved group

Twin columns

Rotating recess making it possible to display a monstrance above the tabernacle

Steps leading to the altar

R. Corbel/MICHELIN

replaced with a row of flying buttresses outside. A number of high openings could therefore be incorporated into the church interior, producing a far more luminous nave.

From then on, tall churches can be schematically described as stone frames consisting of columns supporting diagonal arches and resting on two or three levels of flying buttresses. The buttresses were in turn supported by a series of tall pillars bearing pinnacles.

Diagonal arches – Towards the end of the 11C, groined vaulting was extremely common; but, as it was difficult to build and liable to crack, a group of architects from England, Milan and Île-de-France decided to reinforce the groins.

They found that by building the diagonal arches first and by consolidating them with a small amount of rubble, vaulting that was both sturdy and light was achieved.

By supporting this vaulting on a series of arches, so that the weight of the masonry would have to be borne at the springing, the architects could dispense with the walls in between the arches and replace them with stained-glass windows; this in turn greatly enhanced the luminosity of the interiors.

This significant development heralded the age of quadripartite vaulting.

Vaulting – Quadripartite vaulting, in which the thrust is supported by four main arches, is easy to install in a square-shaped bay. In the 12C bays were enlarged and it was no longer possible to build them square, as the pillars propping up the walls would have been too far apart. The problem was initially resolved by covering the bays two by two, thus forming a square again. An extra transverse arch was then added and made to rest on slim pillars alternating with stout piers.

This type of vaulting – upheld by three diagonal arches – is known as sexpartite vaulting because of the number of its divisions.

When more sophisticated diagonal arches were made to support the vaulting above rectangular bays, the intermediary resting points were eventually discarded.

After the 15C, Flamboyant architects put in additional, decorative ribbing of complex design that formed purely decorative arches (called liernes and tiercerons) and subsequently stars and intricate networks. The main supporting arches were flanked by ornamental arches of no practical use. The keystones – usually pendant – grew thinner and longer.

Elevations (*see illustrations*) – Gothic elevations reflect the continual search for higher and lighter buildings.

Transitional Gothic (A) – The term Transitional Gothic covers the birth

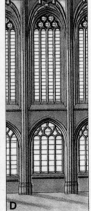

MICHELIN

| Transitional (12C) | Early Gothic (early 13C) | High Gothic (late 13C-early 14C) | Flamboyant (15C and 16C) |

and early stages of Gothic architecture, from about 1125 to 1190. The first use of diagonal vaulting in France appeared over the ambulatory in the Romanesque abbey church at Morienval.

Though some Romanesque details – such as semicircular arches – can still be observed in early Gothic buildings, there were several significant changes. The new interiors presented four-storey elevations consisting of high clerestory windows at the top lighting the nave directly, a triforium (a narrow, arcaded passageway below the clerestory), a gallery – instrumental in supporting the walls as high up as possible – and arcading at ground level. There were often openings behind the gallery but never behind the triforium.

The pillars of the main arches initially consisted of a thick column; this was later replaced by twinned columns supporting the arches and the colonnettes above. Laon Cathedral is a good example of Early Gothic architecture. Semicircular transept endings like the famous south arm at Soissons Cathedral were also a feature.

Early Gothic (B) – This great period (c. 1180–1250), when Gothic architecture was in its ascendancy, produced some of France's finest masterpieces, among them Chartres Cathedral (see illustration).

Characteristics include: arches and windows pointed and shaped like a lancet; clerestory windows surmounted by a round opening; the gallery replaced by external flying buttresses. The numerous colonnettes originating from the vaulting rested on the shaft that bore the weight of all the main arches. This pier was generally a large round column flanked by four colonnettes.

High Gothic (C) – This was the golden age of the great cathedrals in France, lasting from about 1250 and the reign of St Louis to around 1375 when the Hundred Years' War blocked the progress made by medieval architects.

At this time High Gothic, known as 'Rayonnant' in French, reached its peak: the three-storey elevation (large arcades, triforium – the wall at the back now pierced with stained glass – and

tall clerestory windows) lightened the nave and formed one huge single stained-glass window in the chancels of churches with no ambulatory; the wall area was reduced to a minimum and the springers supporting the vaulting were doubled by another series of arches. In many cases the colonnettes started from the ground, at the point where they surround the pillar of the main arches. Two slight mouldings – level with the main arches and the springers – were the only features to break the vertiginous ascent. Beauvais Cathedral is the most outstanding example of High Gothic (see illustration).

Flamboyant Gothic (D) – This last stage in Gothic architecture, which could develop no further, succumbed to ornamental excess, aided by the fine, easily worked Picardy stone.

The style owes its name to the flame shapes in the tracery of the bays and rose windows, and to the exuberant carved and sculpted decoration which tended to obscure the structural lines of the buildings: doorways were crowned with open-work gables, balustrades were surmounted by pinnacles, vaulting featured complex designs with liernes and tiercerons converging on ornately worked keystones. The triforium disappeared, replaced by larger clerestory windows. Arches came to rest on columns or were continued by ribbing level with the pillars. The latter were no longer flanked by colonnettes. In some churches, the ribs formed a spiral around the column.

Flemish civil architecture – From the late 13C the particular nature of Flemish Gothic architecture manifested itself in the civic buildings, belfries and town halls erected by the cities that had obtained charters.

Belfries – A symbol of the town's power, the belfry was either an isolated building (Bergues, Béthune) or part of the town hall (Douai, Arras, Calais). It was built like a keep with watchtowers and machicolations. The rooms above the foundations – which housed the prison – had various functions, such as guard room. At the top, the bell room

Civil architecture

Château de COURANCES (16C-17C)

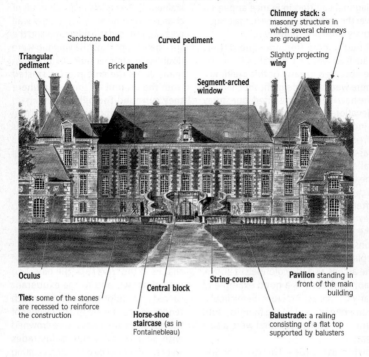

Chimney stack: a masonry structure in which several chimneys are grouped

Sandstone **bond**

Curved pediment

Slightly projecting **wing**

Triangular pediment

Brick **panels**

Segment-arched window

Segment-arched window

Oculus

Ties: some of the stones are recessed to reinforce the construction

Central block

Horse-shoe staircase (as in Fontainebleau)

String-course

Balustrade: a railing consisting of a flat top supported by balusters

Pavilion standing in front of the main building

Château de CHANTILLY stables – Dome (1721-1740)

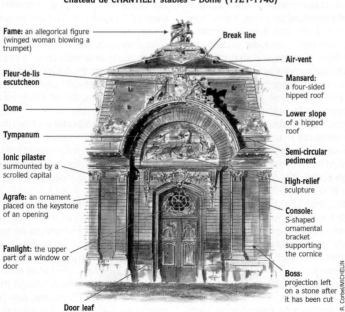

Fame: an allegorical figure (winged woman blowing a trumpet)

Break line

Air-vent

Fleur-de-lis escutcheon

Mansard: a four-sided hipped roof

Dome

Lower slope of a hipped roof

Tympanum

Semi-circular pediment

Ionic pilaster surmounted by a scrolled capital

High-relief sculpture

Agrafe: an ornament placed on the keystone of an opening

Console: S-shaped ornamental bracket supporting the cornice

Fanlight: the upper part of a window or door

Boss: projection left on a stone after it has been cut

Door leaf

R. Corbel/MICHELIN

RUE – Belfry (15C)

Symbolising the power of the city, the belfry was used as a watchtower as well as the aldermen's meeting place.

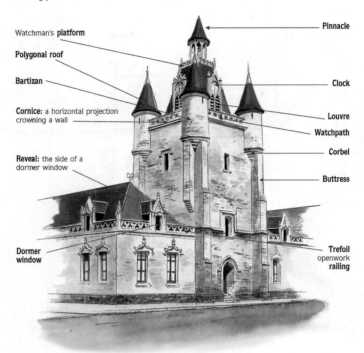

Watchman's **platform**

Polygonal roof

Bartizan

Cornice: a horizontal projection crowning a wall

Reveal: the side of a dormer window

Dormer window

Pinnacle

Clock

Louvre

Watchpath

Corbel

Buttress

Trefoil openwork **railing**

ARRAS – Façades overlooking the Grand'Place (15C-17C)

Left is the Hôtel des Trois Luppars (1467), the oldest house lining the square, right is a house dating from 1684.

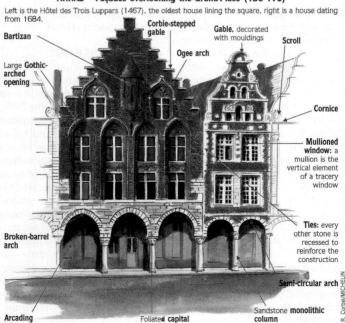

Bartizan

Corbie-stepped gable

Gable, decorated with mouldings

Scroll

Ogee arch

Large **Gothic-arched opening**

Cornice

Mullioned window: a mullion is the vertical element of a tracery window

Broken-barrel arch

Ties: every other stone is recessed to reinforce the construction

Arcading

Foliated capital

Semi-circular arch

Sandstone **monolithic column**

R. Corbel/MICHELIN

CHATOU – 19C pavilion

This type of pavilion, built of course-grained limestone, is characteristic of suburban domestic architecture.

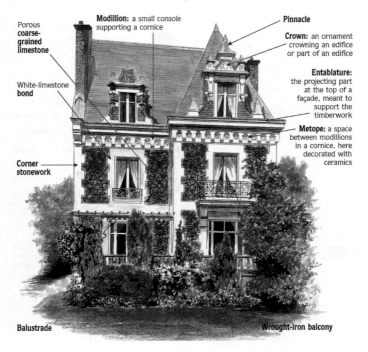

Modillion: a small console supporting a cornice

Porous **coarse-grained limestone**

Pinnacle

Crown: an ornament crowning an edifice or part of an edifice

Entablature: the projecting part at the top of a façade, meant to support the timberwork

White-limestone **bond**

Metope: a space between modillions in a cornice, here decorated with ceramics

Corner stonework

Balustrade

Wrought-iron balcony

enclosed the **chimes**. Originally, these consisted of only four bells. Today they often number at least 30 bells which play every quarter-hour, half-hour and hour. The bell room is surrounded by watchtowers from which the sentry looked out for enemies and fires. At the very top is a weather vane symbolising the city: thus the lion of Flanders stands at Arras, Bergues and Douai.

Town halls – Town halls are often imposing with striking, richly embellished façades: niches, statues, gables and pinnacles might adorn the exterior.

Inside, the large council chamber or function room had walls decorated with frescoes illustrating the history of the town.

The most beautiful town halls (Douai, Arras, St-Quentin, Hondschoote, Compiègne) were built in the 15C and 16C. Many suffered damage and modification over the centuries and some were completely rebuilt in their original style, as at Arras.

RENAISSANCE (16C)

Renaissance architecture, under the influence of Italian culture, favoured a return to classical themes: columns with capitals imitating the Ionic and Corinthian orders; façades decorated with niches, statues and roundels; pilasters flanking the windows. Quadripartite vaulting was replaced by coffered ceilings and barrel vaulting. Architects introduced basket-handled arches and semicircular or rectangular openings. Inverted brackets replaced flying buttresses. West fronts, and sometimes the north and south façades too, kept their heavy ornamentation. Spires were replaced by small domes and lantern towers.

Isolated examples of Renaissance art – not widely adopted in the north of France – are the Maison du Sagittaire

Versailles Classicism

During the reign of Louis XIV (1643–1715) the centralisation of authority and the all-powerful Royal Academy gave rise to an official art that reflected the taste and wishes of the sovereign. The Louis XIV style evolved in Versailles and spread throughout France, where it was imitated to a lesser degree by the aristocracy in the late 17C.

The style was characterised by references to Antiquity and a concern for order and grandeur, whether in architecture, painting or sculpture. French resistance to Baroque, which had but a superficial effect on French architecture, was symbolised by the rejection of Bernini's projects for the Louvre. One of the rare examples of the style is Le Vau's College of Four Nations (today's Institute of France), which consists of a former chapel with a cupola and semicircular flanking buildings.

In Versailles **Louis le Vau** and later **Jules Hardouin-Mansart** (1646–1708) favoured a majestic type of architecture: rectangular buildings set off by projecting central sections with twin pillars, flat roofs and sculptural decoration inspired by Antiquity. **Charles le Brun** (1619–90), the leading King's Painter, supervised all the interior decoration (paintings, tapestries, furniture and *objets d'art*), giving the palace remarkable homogeneity. There were dark fabrics and panelling, gilded stuccowork, painted coffered ceilings, and copies of Greco-Roman statues. The decoration became less abundant towards the end of the century.

In 1662, the founding of the **Gobelins**, the Royal Manufactory for Crown Furniture, stimulated the decorative arts. A team of painters, sculptors, goldsmiths, warp-weavers, marble-cutters and cabinet-makers worked under Charles le Brun, achieving a high degree of technical perfection. Carpets were made at the Savonnerie factory in Chaillot. The massive furniture of the period was often carved and sometimes gilded. Boulle marquetry, a combination of brass, tortoiseshell and gilded bronze, was one of the most sumptuous of the decorative arts produced at the time.

Versailles park, laid out by **Le Nôtre** (1613–1700), fulfilled all the requirements of French landscape gardening with its emphasis on rigour and clarity. Its geometrically tailored greenery, long axial perspectives, fountains, carefully designed spinneys and allegorical sculptures reflect the ideal of perfect order and control over nature.

Sculptures were placed throughout the gardens. Many of the works were by the two major sculptors of the time, **François Girardon** (1628–1715) and **Antoine Coysevox** (1640–1720) who drew upon mythology from Antiquity. The work of **Pierre Puget** (1620–94), another important sculptor, was far more tortured and Baroque – an unusual style for the late 17C.

in Amiens and the Hôtel de la Noble Cour in Cassel.

BAROQUE AND CLASSICAL (17C–18C)

Architecture – Through the 17C and 18C, architecture presented two different faces. One was Baroque, dominated by irregular contours, an abundance of exuberant shapes, generous carving and much ornamentation. The other was Classical, a model of stateliness and restraint, adhering strictly to the rules of Antiquity with rows of Greek columns (Doric, Ionic and Corinthian), pedimented doorways, imposing domes and scrolled architraves.

The Baroque style flourished in Flanders, Hainault and Artois which fell under Spanish influence, while the Classical style found favour in Picardy and Île-de-France.

Abbaye and gardens of Valloires

©CRT PICARDIE/Guy François

The Baroque Chapelle du Grand Séminaire in Cambrai is one of many religious buildings erected in the 17C following the influence of the Counter Reformation and its main engineers, the Jesuits. Civil buildings include the House of Gilles de la Boé in Lille and the Mont-de-Piété in Bergues. The Mint in Lille, with its bosses and richly carved ornamentation, exemplifies **Flemish Baroque**.

The Petit Trianon at Versailles is a famous example of Classical architecture.

In Arras, Baroque and Classical elements were combined for the town's splendid main squares framed by houses with arcades and volutes. Combined elements can also be seen at the abbeys in Valloires and Prémontré and at the Château de Long.

Sculpture – The finely grained and easily worked chalky stone found in Picardy was used for much decorative work. By the 13C the 'picture carvers' in Amiens and Arras were already displaying the specific Picardy traits discernible throughout later centuries: lively, finely detailed figures going about their everyday life. The calendar at Amiens is a good example of this engaging art. In the late 15C and early 16C the Picardy wood carvers *(huchiers)* became renowned through their work on the stalls in Amiens Cathedral; the door panels in St Wulfram's in Abbeville; and the finely worked frames of the 'Puy-Notre-Dame' paintings.

Baroque art favoured abundant decorative sculpture. Buildings were covered with a profusion of ornamental fruit, flowers, cornucopias, putti, niches, statues, vases, etc.

MONASTERIES IN ÎLE-DE-FRANCE

A considerable number of priory, convent and abbey ruins are to be found in Île-de-France, and numerous districts and street names recall the many religious communities that have not survived.

Abbeys in the history of Île-de-France – Abbeys would not exist if people didn't feel a strong calling to take up ecclesiastical duties. At the same time, there would be no abbeys if the clergy had not been given any land. After the 5C, when the victorious Franks divided up the Gallo-Roman territory, it would have been impossible for any religious community to survive without the help of donations. There were many aspiring monks in France up to the 18C, and the different communities were almost entirely dependent on the generosity of benefactors. As the suzerain of Île-de-France was none other than the supreme ruler of France, the king, this region was graced with an abundance of local monasteries.

In the early days of Christianity, during the late 4C, Île-de-France was covered with forests; but the land was also fertile and the area attracted monks who wanted to live in peace and escape the terrible famine ravaging the country. Soon afterwards the Merovingian monarchs, who had been strongly backed by the clergy, encouraged the creation of religious foundations, to which they made considerable contributions. The wealthy Carolingians continued to endow these abbeys, and the practice was kept up by the Capetians and their vassals for over 800 years (Chaalis and Royaumont).

French kings favoured monasteries because the monks used to reclaim uncultivated land and because the monasteries were constantly praying for their patrons. Religious faith was strong from the 10C to the 17C, and kings made donations to abbeys for a variety of reasons: to thank God for a victory, to seek expiation for an offence committed against the Church, to express their own personal belief or to offer a dowry to dowager queens or royal princesses about to take the veil.

Religious Orders – The term abbey does not apply to just any Christian community whose members lead a frugal, secluded life. In fact, it designates a group of men or women placed under the authority of an abbot or an abbess, who live according to a rule approved by the Pope. The monks' day is usually divided into chores related to community life, and spiritual and liturgical duties, which are the main purpose of the association.

All abbeys have an abbot or abbess, who generally enjoys the same rank as a bishop. He or she is elected by fellow companions and incarnates the spiritual and temporal leader of the abbey. After the 16C, the Pope gave the king of France the right to appoint abbots and abbesses. These prelates were called commendatory abbots and usually lived in the king's entourage.

Sometimes, to administer new domains or to fulfil the wish of a patron who wanted to receive monks on his land, the abbots would build a priory. This small community was supervised by a prior who was answerable to the abbey. The Cistercians set up many granges, farming colonies run by lay brothers.

Monastic Rules – The Benedictine Order – created by St Benedict in the 6C – was undoubtedly the order which flourished the most in France. Its members founded over 1 000 abbeys throughout the country. The Benedictine rule was subsequently reformed, leading to the creation of two additional orders.

The first originated in the late 10C from Cluny in Burgundy, but unfortunately all the Cluniac houses died out during the Revolution. The second – the Cistercian Order – was, and still is, extremely powerful. It was St Bernard of Cîteaux, also a native of Burgundy, who founded the order in the 11C. A firm believer in asceticism, he introduced a number of new rules: elaborate ceremonies

Church ruins, Abbaye de Chaalis

M.O.Bernard/ MICHELIN

and the decoration of churches were condemned; monks could no longer be paid tithes, nor receive or acquire land; strict rules were laid down on diet, rest was limited to seven hours and monks had to sleep in their clothes in a common dormitory.

They shared their time between liturgical worship (6–7 hours a day), manual labour, study and contemplation. In the 17C, Abbot de Rancé added further austerities to the Cistercian rule (silence, diet). This new rule was named after La Trappe, the monastery near Perseigne where it originated. It is presently enforced in abbeys of strict observance.

The other two main orders that founded abbeys in France were the Augustinian friars and the Premonstratensian canons, both dating from the 12C.

Other communities include the Carmelite Order, the Order of St Francis (Franciscans and Capuchins), the Order of Preachers and the Society of Jesus (Jesuits). They do not follow monastic rules, nor do they found abbeys. Their activities (missionary work, caring for the sick) bring them into contact with the lay world. They live in convents or houses under the authority of the prior, the Mother Superior, etc.

A collegiate church is occupied by a community of canons accountable to their bishop.

Monastic buildings – The cloisters are the centre of an abbey; the four galleries allow the nuns or the monks to take their walks under cover. One of the cloister walls adjoins the abbey church, while another gives onto the chapter house, where monks meet to discuss community problems under the chairmanship of the abbot. The third gallery opens onto the refectory and the fourth onto the calefactory, the only room with heating, where the monks study or do manual labour.

The dormitory is generally placed above the chapter house. It communicates with the church by means of a direct staircase, so that the monks could more readily attend early morning and nighttime Mass.

Lay brothers – These are believers who cannot or choose not to take holy orders and therefore have a different status. They spend most of their time in the fields and the workshops, and have their own dormitory and refectory. They may not enter the chapter house or the chancel of the church. Since the Vatican II Council (1962–65), lay brothers have become more and more involved in the life of the community.

Visitors are not allowed to enter the 'enclosure' and are lodged in the guest house. The poor are housed in the almshouse.

Monasteries also include an infirmary, a noviciate, sometimes a school, and the buildings needed to run the abbey: barns, cellars, winepress, stables and cowsheds.

RURAL HOUSING IN THE NORTH

The Coast, Inland Flanders and Artois – Whether in Picardy, Artois or Flanders, the same type of houses can be found along the coast: long and low to form a defence against the west winds, which often bring rain. They are capped by high-pitched roofs covered with Flemish S-shaped tiles called *pannes*. Their whitewashed walls are cheered by brightly coloured doors and shutters; the bases of the buildings are tarred against the damp.

Behind this apparent uniformity lie very different construction techniques.

In Picardy the walls consist of daubing on wood laths; in certain areas the surface is left plain, as in Ponthieu, but it is more usually whitewashed, giving a spruce look in summer to the flower-bedecked villages along the River Canche and River Authie.

In Flanders the usual building material is more generally brick, sandy coloured in maritime areas and ranging from red to purplish or brown farther inland. The great Lille and Artois regional farms, known as **censes**, are built around a courtyard with access through a carriage gateway often surmounted by a dovecote.

Windmill in Hondschoote

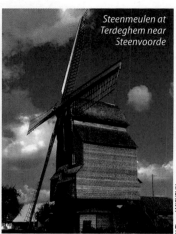

Steenmeulen at Terdeghem near Steenvoorde

Y. Tierny/ MICHELIN

Y. Tierny/ MICHELIN

Some large, partly stone-built farms in the Boulonnais hills are actually old seigniorial homes with a turret or fortifications, giving the impression of a manor house.

Hainaut, Avesnois, Thiérache and Soissonnais – In the Hainaut and Avesnois regions houses are massively built, usually consisting of one-storey brick buildings with facings and foundations in regional blue stone. Their slate roofs are reminiscent of the nearby Ardennes region.

Construction in the Thiérache region, the land of clay and wood, consists of daubing and brick with slate roofs. There are many old dovecotes in the region, either over carriage gates or free-standing in courtyards. Villages in close proximity to one another huddle around their fortified churches (&see La THIÉRACHE).

The houses in the Soissonnais region are similar to those of Île-de-France. Beautiful white freestone is used for walls and crow-stepped gables, contrasting with flat, red roof tiles which take on a patina with the years.

Windmills – In the early 19C there were nearly 3 000 windmills in northern France. Today no more than a few dozen still exist, registered, protected and restored by the Association Régionale des Amis des Moulins du Nord-Pas-de-Calais (ARAM).

Post mills – Built of wood, these mills are the most common in Flanders. The main body of the structure and the sails turn around a vertical post. On the exterior – the side opposite the sails – a beam known as the 'tail' is linked to a wheel which is turned to position the entire mill according to the wind direction. Some fourteen of this type remain in northern France, including those at Boeschepe, Cassel, Hondschoote, Steenvoorde, Villeneuve d'Ascq and St-Maxent.

On a **tower mill** (or smock mill when made of wood) only the roof, to which the sails are attached, turns. This type of mill is more massive and is usually built of brick or stone; the Steenmeulen at Terdeghem near Steenvoorde is the only one still in working order, but there are other fine specimens at Templeuve and Watten (Nord) as well as Achicourt, Beuvry, Guemps (Pas-de-Calais), and Louvencourt (Somme).

Water mills – Water mills can also be seen throughout the region, particularly in the Avesnois, Ternois, Thiérache and Valenciennes areas. The shape and size of the wheel, which is the essential part of the mill, depends on the rate of flow of the river and on the specific features of the site. Some of these mills are open to the public: Felleries, Sars-Poteries, Marly (Nord), Esquerdes, Maintenay, Wimille and Wissant (Pas-de-Calais).

Military architecture

LE QUESNOY – Fortifications (12C and 17C-19C)

These well-preserved fortifications, remodelled by Vauban from 1667 onwards, are set in green surroundings.

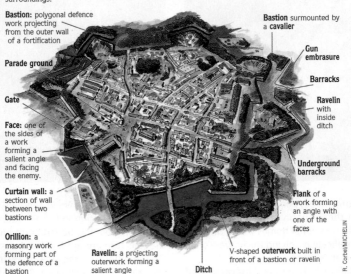

Bastion: polygonal defence work projecting from the outer wall of a fortification

Parade ground

Gate

Face: one of the sides of a work forming a salient angle and facing the enemy.

Curtain wall: a section of wall between two bastions

Orillion: a masonry work forming part of the defence of a bastion

Ravelin: a projecting outerwork forming a salient angle

Ditch

Bastion surmounted by a **cavalier**

Gun embrasure

Barracks

Ravelin with inside ditch

Underground barracks

Flank of a work forming an angle with one of the faces

V-shaped **outerwork** built in front of a bastion or ravelin

R. Corbel/MICHELIN

MILITARY ARCHITECTURE

Of the defensive systems in the north of France, relatively few date from the Middle Ages: the town walls of Boulogne and Laon, and the castles at Coucy, Rambures, Picquigny, Lucheux, Septmonts and Pierrefonds. In contrast, numerous 17C star fortifications along the northeastern border have been preserved, some in their entirety, as at Bergues and Le Quesnoy, others only partially: Avesnes, Maubeuge, Cambrai, Douai, St-Omer and Péronne.

Before Vauban – It was under the last of the Valois kings that the military engineers, who had studied Italian examples, adopted a system of curtain walls defended at the corners by bastions. Bastions in the shape of an ace of spades with projections were introduced to protect the men defending the curtain wall. This feature can be seen at Le Quesnoy. Bastions and curtain walls, usually with stone bonding, were crowned with platforms bearing cannon. Raised towers allowed the moats or ditches and surrounding area to be watched. In the 17C Henri IV employed an engineer, **Jean Errard**

(1554–1610) nicknamed the Father of French Fortification, who specialised in castrametation. In the north Errard fortified Ham and Montreuil and built the citadels at Calais, Laon, Doullens and Amiens which still stand today. In 1600 he published an authoritative *Treatise on Fortification* which served until Vauban's time.

The Age of Vauban – Inspired by his predecessors, **Sébastien le Prestre de Vauban** (1633–1707) established a system of his own characterised by bastions with half-moons surrounded by deep moats. Making the most of the natural obstacles and using local materials (brick in the north), he also tried to give an aesthetic quality to his works by adorning them with carved monumental stone gateways as at Bergues, Lille and Maubeuge.

On the coast and along the border of Flanders and Hainaut, Vauban established a long line of double defences, known as the **pré carré**. These two close lines of fortresses and citadels were designed to prevent the enemy's passage, and to ensure mutual backup in case of attack.

The first line consists of 15 sites from Dunkirk and Bergues to Maubeuge, Philippeville and Dinant. The second runs a little way behind and includes 13 towns extending from Gravelines and St-Omer to Avesnes, Marienbourg, Rocroi and Mézières. Some of these strongpoints were Vauban's own creations such as the citadel at Lille, which he himself called the 'Queen of Citadels'; others existed already and were remodelled.

For over a century this group of fortifications succeeded in defending the north of France, until the invasions of 1814 and 1815.

During the French campaign in 1940 Le Quesnoy, Lille, Bergues, Dunkirk, Gravelines and Calais all formed solid strongholds protecting the retreat of the Franco-British armies.

Atlantic Wall – The concrete bunkers of the Atlantic Wall that stretch along the coastline were erected by the **Todt Organisation**, which from 1940 used prisoners of war for the task. The Nord-Pas-de-Calais region was considered a war zone against England, and in 1944 about 10 000 constructions were counted on the French coast. In the deep forests of Eperlecques and Clairmarais enormous concrete installations were built for launching the V1 and V2 rockets on London. The Eperlecques Bunker (see ST-OMER), today designated a historic monument, is one of the most impressive examples of this type of monumental concrete architecture, along with the fort at Mimoyecques (see GUÎNES).

FAÏENCE AND PORCELAIN IN ÎLE-DE-FRANCE
FAÏENCE

This term is commonly applied to all ceramics made of porous clay and glazed with waterproof enamel. The enamel was initially transparent but, in the 9C, it became opaque thanks to the discovery in the Middle East of tin glaze. The Arabic influence throughout the Mediterranean Basin led to the development of faïence in Moorish Spain and Italy from the 15C onwards. The Spanish island of Majorca gave its name to 'Majolica ware', the term describing Italian Renaissance ceramics. The name 'faïence' may derive from Faenza, the Italian town renowned for its majolica.

Faïence developed in France in the 16C and 17C with leading pottery centres such as Nevers and Rouen. The latter influenced the early producers of faïence in Île-de-France such as Pierre Chicaneau who settled in St-Cloud in 1674. In the 18C, as porcelain became more popular, the number of potteries increased in the region and the first pieces of porcelain were produced. The famous ceramist Jacques Chapelle set up the works in **Sceaux** in 1748 and circumvented the Vincennes-Sèvres mono-poly on faïence by creating 'Japanese-style faïence'. The Rococo style, vivid colours, and original decorations, many of them in relief, brought success to Sceaux until the end of the 18C. This period was marked by the discovery in England of 'fine faïence' or white lead-glazed earthenware. Its reasonable cost and elegance, along with the exceptionally liberal conditions laid down in the Treaty of Vergennes (1786), ensured its popularity and it was massively imported into France. This know-how was gradually taken over in Île-de-France by the works in **Montereau**, **Creil** and **Choisy-le-Roi**. However, the end of the 19C confirmed the preference for porcelain, and faïence went into a decline.

PORCELAIN

Porcelain was discovered in China in the 12C. It is a thin, white ceramic ware that is slightly translucent. Body and glaze are fired together. In the 16C, the popularity of porcelain from the Far East led to numerous experiments in Europe to try and achieve a product that would rival it. The high level of imports by the French East India Company is indicative of European interest in this mysterious technique. Craftsmen did not know the exact nature of the paste used by the Chinese and they progressed by trial and error, using processes similar to the ones used for faïence. A very fine marl used on its own was vitrified by the introduction

12C-13C stained glass, Cathédrale de Chartres

S. Sauvignier/ MICHELIN

Stained Glass

Since the early Middle Ages, church windows have been adorned with coloured glass. Unfortunately, none of these very early works has survived.

During the Gothic period, master glassmakers played an important role in the completion and ornamentation of churches. Thanks to them, both the clergy and the congregation could appreciate the shimmering light that came streaming through the roundels. Stained glass is not purely decorative, however. To the Church it is an invaluable teaching aid, permanently communicating catechism, sacred history and the lives of the saints.

The art of making stained glass

Stained-glass windows consist of juxtaposed pieces of coloured glass held together by strips of lead. The window is divided into panels to ensure perfect solidity. When the various coloured pieces have been selected and cut to shape, the glassmaker completes the shading and details of the figures with touches of **grisaille**, a brownish pigment containing silica that is painted on and blends with the glass in the melt. The glass panels are then reassembled and fixed in place in the window. Patches of lichen may develop on stained-glass windows; it starts to attack the lead after 100 years and has been known to break through the glass after 300 to 400 years. However, it is man rather than erosion who is to blame for the disappearance of numerous early stained-glass windows: in the 18C many were dismantled and replaced by plain glass, which afforded a better view of the aisles.

The development of stained glass

Technical developments in glass-making were prompted by artistic trends but also by the search for greater economy and the wish to produce lighter tones.

of a sort of glass called frit. The resulting ceramic was 'soft-paste' porcelain that could be scratched by steel.

In the early 18C, the basic ingredient of porcelain, white china clay, was discovered in Saxony. The secrets of the production process were jealously kept in Meissen, near Dresden.

In France, it was not until 1769 that the output from a white china clay quarry near St-Yriex in the Limousin area enabled craftsmen to produce 'hard-paste' porcelain. Sèvres produced

porcelain exclusively from the beginning of the 19C onwards. This new product, in which body and glaze were fired together at a very high temperature (1 400°C/2 500°F), was very strong but more difficult to decorate.

Only five colours are suitable for high-temperature firing – blue, green, yellow, purplish brown and reddish orange.

The introduction of low-firing techniques revolutionised the production of faïence and porcelain. The enamel was fired in succession at low temperatures,

12C – Stained-glass windows were small, with fairly heavy borders. The ornamentation around the main figures was extremely limited.

13C – To ensure perfect cohesion between the panels and the leading, the iron armatures were fastened to the walls.

The clerestory windows presented tall, isolated figures. The lower windows, which could be observed more closely, had medallions depicting scenes from the lives of the saints. This genre is known as historiated stained glass. Panels included architectural features and embellishments. Borders were heavy and the scenes show a marked attempt at realism. Historiated roundels were set in a *grisaille* framework enhanced by brightly painted rose-windows. The daily lives of craftsmen were evoked in lively anecdotal scenes. The lower windows were generally divided into panels composing geometric motifs (stars, diamonds, clover-leaves).

14C – The loss of wealth led to a considerable increase in window space. For reasons of economy, more and more grisaille was produced, its starkness softened by delicate shading and graceful foliage motifs. Angels and rosy cherubs adorned the barer parts of the windows. Borders became smaller and lettering made an appearance. In the second half of the 14C glassmakers discovered that silver staining could be used to accentuate a variety of bright colours: yellow on a white background, light green on blue, amber on red, etc.

15C – The leading was no longer produced using a plane, but instead stretched on a wire-drawing bench: the lead strips were thinner, therefore more flexible and able to hold together larger and thinner panes of glass than previously. Glassmakers worked with a lighter type of glass, and the colours used in the decoration were less vivid. In some churches, two thirds of the window was taken up by grisaille. These panels featured Gothic canopies with high gables and openwork pinnacles. The craftsmanship was of a remarkable quality, and master glassmakers began to sign their own work, introducing original themes.

16C – Stained glass drew inspiration from the works of the great painters and contemporary engravings. Glassmakers had become masters at cutting glass from large sheets – using a diamond and no longer a red-hot iron – and they also excelled at painting with enamels. Stained-glass windows developed into large, transparent paintings in which minute attention was given to detail, perspective and design. In some buildings religious themes were replaced by classical scenes taken from Antiquity.

17C and 18C – The use of coloured glass decreased. Stained glass was painted and decorated with enamels.

enabling the use of a wide range of fresh, vivid colours.

The porcelain works in **St-Cloud** (1697–1766) were the first to master the techniques required to produce 'soft-paste' porcelain. It was famous for its 'white' ware and applied gilding that differed greatly from the technique used by Sèvres. Numerous porcelain works opened in quick succession in the 18C, with the backing of princes or the royal family. The works in **Chantilly** (1725–1800), for example, were set up by Cirquaire Cirou with the support of Louis-Henri de Bourbon, Prince de Condé. In **Mennecy**, it was the Duke de Villeroy who provided the necessary patronage in the face of ever-increasing privileges granted to some of the works. The one with the highest level of support was in **Vincennes**. Madame de Pompadour and Louis XV both took a keen interest in the company that set up works in **Sèvres** in 1756. The earliest designs were 'natural' flowers and the works gradually specialised in the production of dinner services, statuettes and even veritable pictures in porcelain. Because of the processes used, the decoration and enamel combined perfectly, giving an incomparable blending. In its early days, the Sèvres porcelain works enjoyed exclusive rights to the use of gold on all its products. Even now, unless there is some technical reason against it, all its products must include some gold. 'Biscuit-ware', another speciality of these works, is the term used to describe a production method in which the body of the paste is left unglazed so that the gracefulness of the statuettes is not altered.

LANDSCAPE PAINTING

Although many painters were employed in the internal decoration of châteaux and abbeys around Paris, it was not until the 19C that painters began to show an interest in the surrounding landscapes.

Until the 18C, French masters had used landscapes merely as a background to their work, either as a decorative element or to enhance the atmosphere through composition and colour. It was so poorly regarded that often a major artist painting a portrait or other subject would leave the background landscape to be painted by a studio assistant. The two most celebrated French landscape painters were the 17C classicists Nicolas Poussin and Claude Lorrain. Poussin gave his views the heroic qualities of his subject and Lorrain painted scenes of a lost, idyllic Antiquity.

CAMILLE COROT (1796–1875)

Corot was the pioneer of contemporary landscape painting in France. He lived in Barbizon from 1830 to 1835 and worked outdoors in Fontainebleau Forest and all over Île-de-France, studying the contrasts and soft hues of light in the undergrowth, along shaded paths and on the edge of the plain. He later took up painting lakes in a search for more delicate variations; the ponds at Ville-d'Avray *(south of St-Cloud)*, with their subtle reflections, were his favourites.

PAINTERS OF THE OISE

The group was founded in 1845 by two of Corot's followers, **Charles-François Daubigny** and **Jules Dupré**. Daubigny (1817–78) liked to paint the rippling waters of the River Oise and the greenery and blossoms of the orchards and groves. He led a peaceful life: his work paid well and received universal acclaim. He could often be found working on the Île de Vaux near Auvers, or in a small rowing boat he had converted into a studio. Jules Dupré (1811–89), a close friend of

Horsecart, Memory of Marcoussis near Montlhery (1855) by Jean-Baptiste-Camille Corot

©Imagestate/Tips Images

Théodore Rousseau, used darker colours and belonged to the Barbizon School. He seldom left his house in L'Isle-Adam.

In 1865 the lithographer and satirical cartoonist Honoré Daumier (1808–79) moved from the capital to Valmondois in Île-de-France, when he met with serious financial difficulties.

In 1866 **Camille Pissarro** (1830–1903) initially settled in Pontoise for two years. Uninterested in the nearby streams and rivers, he concentrated on meadows, grassy slopes, country villages and street scenes featuring peasant women, which he portrayed in a deliberately poetic manner. His gift for expressing light, his qualities as a teacher and his kindness made him the father figure of the Impressionist movement.

THE BARBIZON SCHOOL

Its representatives drew inspiration from the landscapes of Fontainebleau Forest and the nearby Bière plain. The founder of the movement was **Théodore Rousseau** (1812–67) who settled in a modest country cottage in 1847 and stayed there until his death. Diaz and Charles Jacque were among his close friends. They remained cheerful and humorous despite the lack of success of their paintings and their consequent penury. It was only towards the end of the Second Empire that their talent was acknowledged. Troyon (1810–65) specialised in rural scenes representing cattle. Barye, the highly respected animal sculptor, also took up landscape painting because of his love of nature. The charms and hardships of country life were portrayed particularly well in the work of **Jean-François Millet** (1814–75), who lived in Barbizon from 1849 until his death.

The artists of this school generally favoured the dark colours of tree bark and undergrowth, and their preferred subjects included dusk, soft lighting and stormy skies. These sombre tones were criticised by their detractors, who claimed they painted with 'prune juice'.

Around 1865 a new group of artists fell under the spell of these magical woodlands and Pierre-Auguste Renoir, Alfred Sisley and Claude Monet settled in Chailly. Though they did not associate themselves with the Barbizon community, they did accept advice from their elders. Diaz encouraged the young Renoir to work with lighter tones. Here. too. the seeds of Impressionism were being sown.

IMPRESSIONISM

The second-generation artists wanted their work to capture the essence of light itself and to reflect the vibrant quality of colour. The term 'Impressionist' was actually coined by a sarcastic journalist in 1874, but was adopted by the group as they felt it conveyed the double revolution they had brought about in the field of painting.

The Impressionist Revolution – The Impressionist movement revolutionised artistic conventions on two counts: it paid little attention to form and it invented a new technique. Until then, the representation of reality was fundamentally important, and no artist would have dared to neglect the lines and shapes of his subject, whether a portrait, still-life painting or landscape. Painters showed little concern for light and its effects, considered a minor component, and priority was given to subject matter. For the Impressionists, light and the analysis of its effects became the principal subject; all the rest – contours, scenes, people – was simply an excuse to paint light.

Religious and historical works, as well as family portraits and everyday scenes, were no longer interesting in themselves. The Impressionists' favourite subjects were those that played with light, such as water, snow, fabrics, flesh, flowers, leaves or fruit.

They wished to capture the infinite depths of the skies, the shimmering of light on water, a dress or a human face. When depicting the undergrowth, they wanted to show how the russet tones glitter in sunlight, how bright colours sparkle.

Such fleeting and indefinite concepts were no longer attainable using traditional techniques. As priority was

Boulevard Montmartre at Night (1897) by Camille Pissarro

©Imagestate/Tips Images

given to the vibration of light around the edges of objects, the process that applied paint along contours was banished. Traditionally, the layers of paint were applied slowly and acquired their definite colour after the oil had solidified. They were then coated with varnish to produce a transparent effect and to give depth to the colours. Naturally this technique was far too lengthy to capture the ephemeral quality of light. As a consequence, the Impressionists developed a technique more suited to their purpose that involved very little oil and dispensed with varnish. Their art consisted in applying quick, small dabs of colour. The exact shade was conveyed by the juxtaposition of touches of pure colour, the final effect being assessed by the eye of the viewer.

The Impressionists were harshly criticised, even insulted at times, and it was only after a 20-year struggle that their work was fully acknowledged. Île-de-France – with its rivers, lakes, gardens, orchards, showers of rain, mists, elegant ladies and regattas – provided them with countless sources of inspiration.

THE PAINTERS

The Impressionist School was founded in Honfleur where **Claude Monet** (1840–1926), a painter from Le Havre, was encouraged by the seascape specialist Eugène Boudin to paint landscapes. **Boudin** (1824–98), a friend of Corot's, was also a precursor of Impressionism: his paintings are full of air and light. Following his example, Monet and later the Dutch artist Jongkind worked on the luminosity of the landscapes around the Seine estuary. They were joined by Bazille and **Sisley**, whom they had befriended in Gleyre's studio, and began to paint around Fontainebleau Forest too, though they remained separate from the Barbizon School. Pissarro, Cézanne and Guillaumin, who met at the Swiss Academy, were called 'The Famous Three' *(Le Groupe des Trois)*.

The painters were strongly supported by **Édouard Manet** (1832–83), one of their elders who was upsetting artistic conventions and scandalising the public with his bold colours and compositions. It was Manet who encouraged the Impressionists to pursue their efforts at painting light. In 1863, following clashes between the artists and the official salons that refused to show these new works, a now-famous independent exhibition of the rejected works (Salon des Refusés) was set up on the orders of Napoleon III. It gave birth to, and led to the naming of, the Impressionist movement.

In 1871 small groups of amateur painters, pupils and friends, including **Paul Cézanne**, joined Pissarro at Pontoise and Docteur Gachet in Auvers. Another group based in Argenteuil and Louveciennes included **Renoir**, Monet, Sisley and Edgar Degas, who had originally studied under Ingres. Monet's innovative technique put him at the head of the movement and inspired both Manet and later Berthe Morisot.

In the 1880s, Renoir moved to Chatou just west of Paris, where he frequented the Maison Tomaise, a restaurant first opened in 1815 and now restored. After 1880 the group broke up, but its members remained faithful to painting with light colours. Sisley moved to Moret, drawn to the River Loing, while Monet settled in Giverny on the banks of the Epte (see The Green Guide NORMANDY). For practical reasons, Pissarro left the Oise Valley to live in Eragny, near Gisors. **Georges Seurat** (1859–91) remained in Paris but concentrated on the landscapes around the capital and along the Channel coast. His technique amounted to breaking down the subject matter into small dabs of colour, each consisting of a series of dots (points). Maximilien Luce (1858–1941) also experimented with this method – known as Pointillism or Divisionism – in the vicinity of Mantes. Cézanne later returned to Aix-en-Provence where, through the use of colour, tone and accentuated outlines, he developed stylised masses that laid the foundations for the Cubist movement.

Renoir travelled to Algeria and Venice, which inspired him to paint some of his finest works. Degas and Toulouse-Lautrec (1846–1901) lived in Paris. They were fascinated by circuses and theatres where swirling dancers and performers were bathed in complex illuminations created by artificial lighting.

THE DAWN OF THE 20C

The followers of the **Nabis** and **Fauve** movements, which preceded Cubism and the new art forms born in the wake of the First World War, also set up their easels – and sometimes even their studios – in the picturesque outskirts of Paris. On his return from a stay in Pont-Aven, where Paul Gauguin had shown him the magic of composing in flat, bold colours, Paul Sérusier converted his friends from the Académie Julian to the same style and formed the Nabis movement (a Hebrew word meaning prophet). **Maurice Denis** (1870–1943) became the leader of the group, which included Bonnard, Roussel, Vuillard, Maillol, Vallotton and others.

The early Fauves (meaning 'wild beasts') included extremely diverse artists – Matisse, Dufy, Braque, Derain, Vlaminck, Rouault, Marquet. Their paintings of bright, even violent colour created an uproar when they were first shown. The painters, never a coherent group, were influenced by the paintings of **Van Gogh**, who had died in 1890 leaving a collection of brilliant canvases composed of strong, vigorous brushstrokes of pure colour.

The coasts and countryside of the north of France and the region around Paris continue to attract many artists.

Nature

Artois, Picardy and Île-de-France (the region around Paris) all lie within a vast geological area known as the Paris Basin, which borders Flanders and the great plain of Northern Europe. The landscapes of the Basin comprise forests, lush alluvial valleys with slow-flowing rivers, and limestone plateaux providing rich arable land. The climate is mild in summer and temperate in winter, with damp springs and autumns.

PICARDY

This region, to the north of Île-de-France, comprises three separate *départements*: **Somme**, **Aisne** and **Oise**.

SOMME

Somme really is a land of contrasts, from the towering chalk cliffs of Mers-les-Bains and Ault to the leafy valleys of the Thiérache. It is a region with the best reserves of game-filled ancient forest in Northern Europe, its biggest tidal estuary, and the largest expanse of sand dunes. Wide skies, secretive marshlands, cosy villages nestling among rolling farmland and orchards, or the open country of the Haute Somme characterise the area.

AISNE

To the east, Aisne is identified by large farms, often complemented by a sugar refinery or a distillery. St-Quentin, the administrative and industrial centre of the *département*, is the principal town. The voluptuous landscape of Aisne is lush with cereals and the bocage of dairy cattle, rolling green hills and fields of gold that ripple away to the horizon. Among the folds, tiny communities, mostly of less than 100 souls, gather around a series of Middle Age fortified churches, built as a quick and temporary defence against the passage of plundering neighbours.

OISE

To the south, marking the transition to the Île-de-France, the Valois region of **Oise** has a mantle of forests and miles of wheat fields invariably bright in spring with poppies and other wildflowers. The Oise may be close to Paris, but it doesn't live in its shadow. In the **Vimeu** region, the chalk has decomposed into flinty clay, and the cold, damp ground has created a mixed landscape of farmland crisscrossed by hedges and trees, cider-apple orchards and small, scattered villages. Near Beauvais the chalky, silt-covered plateau suddenly reveals a verdant hollow: the **Pays de Bray**, a wooded area interspersed with meadows where stock-farming is the main activity.

Chalk cliffs of Ault

G. Targat/MICHELIN

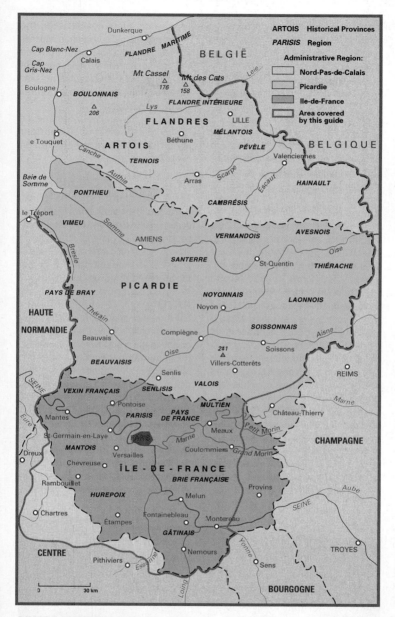

RIVERS AND VALLEYS

The verdant, wide-mouthed valleys are bisected by the Somme, Authie and Canche rivers.

These waters flow so slowly they have difficulty in making their way, losing themselves in ponds and marshes full of fish and waterfowl. The floors of the valleys are a mix of old peat bogs, rows of poplars, arable and stock-farming fields and in a few places, on the outskirts of towns like Amiens, floating vegetable gardens (hortillonnages) surrounded by canals.

Towns and cities have developed along the valleys: Montreuil on the Canche; Doullens on the Authie; Péronne, Amiens and Abbeville on the Somme.

The capital of Picardy is **Amiens**, a great industrial centre with factories producing tyres, electronics, video games, domestic appliances, car parts and chemical products. In Oise the main town is **Beauvais**, and in Aisne it's **Laon**.

MARITIME LANDSCAPE

To the south, near Ault, the Picardy plateau meets the sea, ending in a sharp cliff of white chalk banded with flint. The bay, not surprisingly, is a huge and dangerous place to be, though it does seem to be suffering from coastal erosion. In 1878, it comprised 86sq m/33sq mi; in 1993 that was down to 73sq km/28sq mi, and today is about 70sq km/27sq mi – one estimate puts it at 40sq km/15.4sq mi. The tide goes out as much as 14km/8.7mi, the second largest ebb in France, leaving behind tricky sandbanks, muddy channels and large expanses of sea grass; when it comes back in it does so rather more quickly than it went out.

North of the Somme Bay a maritime plain called the **Marquenterre** area has been created by debris torn from the Normandy coast and carried northward by the currents, gradually forming an offshore bar. Only the Somme, Authie and Canche rivers have carved a passage to the sea; there are therefore few large ports but several seaside resorts, the largest of them, Le Touquet, seated beside the dunes.

The coastal plain lies between the dunes and the old coastal bar, which is marked by a noticeable cliff. The drained and dried plain is now used for fields of wheat and oats, and for raising salt-pasture lambs on the grassy shores known as *mollières*.

In the past St-Valery-sur-Somme, Le Crotoy and Étaples were important ports; today they harbour only fishing boats and yachts.

NORD-PAS-DE-CALAIS

The northernmost region of France, Nord-Pas-de-Calais comprises two *départements*: **Nord** and **Pas-de-Calais**. Locally, but now generally throughout France, the region takes in the former provinces of Artois and Flanders, though the borders are not easy to define.

ARTOIS

The former province of Artois lies on an extension of the Picardy plateaux, a rise of land running northwest to southeast. It ends in an escarpment of about 100m/328ft (Vimy Ridge, Notre-Dame de Lorette Hill), which divides the Paris Basin from the Anglo-Belgian Basin. The great plain of Flanders begins at the foot of this escarpment.

The well-watered hills of Artois are however bare to the south-east, in the **Ternois** region where there are outcrops of chalk; to the north-west, the chalky top layer of soil has decomposed

Parc du Marquenterre

S. Sauvignier/MICHELIN

Landscape of the Boulonnais in spring

Y. Tierny/MICHELIN

into flinty clay resulting in lush, damp countryside, which includes Hesdin Forest and mixed agricultural and meadow land.

BOULONNAIS

The **Boulonnais** region forms an enclave in the chalk layer, revealing outcrops of harder, older rocks. The landscape here is very different from neighbouring areas. In the north, the Upper Boulonnais forms a chalky plateau which in places reaches over 200m/650ft in altitude. In the area where the land forms a hollow, the Lower Boulonnais, the wooded countryside is dotted with whitewashed farms. The clay has created meadows that are used for rearing the dappled-grey 'Boulonnais draughthorses' and for other stock-breeding. The soil also supports the Desvres and Boulogne forests, while the Hardelot Forest grows in sandier soil.

Boulogne, France's foremost fishing port, stands at the mouth of the River Liane. To the north, the edge of the calcareous plateau forms the cliffs of the Opal Coast (ⓘ *see La CÔTE D'OPALE*).

HAINAUT AND CAMBRÉSIS

Hainaut (capital: Valenciennes) and **Cambrésis** (capital: Cambrai) are extensions of the chalky plateaux of Artois and Picardy. They are also covered with a thick layer of silt that is ideal for growing sugar beets and wheat, with excellent per-acre harvests. The plateaux are divided by wide river valleys such as those of the Scarpe, Sambre, Selle and Escaut (Scheldt). Meadows of fodder crops and pasture give them the look of farming country. The forests of St-Amand and Mormal appear where there is flinty clay, the result of decomposition of the chalk.

THIÉRACHE AND AVESNOIS

These two relatively hilly regions form the tail of the Ardennes uplands, covered at the western end by marl and chalk mixed with marl. The **Thiérache** is a damp region, part forest and part pasture. When carefully drained the cold, non-porous ground provides pasture for cows. The dairies produce butter, cheese and condensed milk.

The **Avesnois** is crossed by the River Helpe Majeure and River Helpe Mineure, tributaries of the River Sambre. This region resembles the Thiérache, but is marked by summits rising to over 250m/820ft in places. It is also an area of pastureland famous for its dairy cows and cheeses, especially Maroilles.

FLANDERS

The Flemish plain, which continues into Belgium, is bounded to the south by the hills of Artois and to the east by the plateaux of Hainault and Cambrésis.

COASTAL FLANDERS

The wet and windy *Blooteland* (bare land protected by dunes separating the area from the sea) has been gradually reclaimed from the sea since the Middle Ages. The engineers, including the famous **Coebergher**, who came mostly from the Low Countries, drained the land gradually using great dams, canals and pumps, thus creating the marshes *(Moëres)*. Today it is a low-lying region where the grey clay yields crops of sugar-beets, cereals, flax and chicory, and the nearby pastures are grazed by sheep, pigs, horses and cattle. The flat countryside, scattered with great isolated farms built around square courtyards, is dominated by belfries, bell towers, windmills and, on the coast, the factory chimneys and harbour cranes of Dunkirk and Calais.

INLAND FLANDERS

Known as *Houtland* (wooded land) in contrast to the bare coastal area, the 'Flemish lowlands' consist of lush countryside divided by rows of poplars, willows or elms. The censes, white-walled Flemish farms with red roofs, stand out against this green background.

A series of summits extends into Belgium, comprising the **Monts des Flandres** range. In addition to providing beautiful meadows where cows, horses and pigs thrive, the rich soil is also used for growing various crops such as cereals, fruit and vegetables in gardens among the St-Omer canals, and plants for industrial processing (hops near Bailleul, flax in the Lys Valley, chicory, sugar beets).

However, two small areas between Lille and Douai are different: the bare plateaux of the **Mélantois** and the **Pévèle** regions. The coal fields (*see Economy*) stretching from Béthune to Valenciennes have given rise to a 'black country' marked by slag-heaps, brick mining towns and mine-shaft frames.

Between the Lys Valley and the River Escaut (Scheldt) lies the industrial conurbation of Lille-Roubaix-Tourcoing-Armentières. Once a major textile centre (*see LILLE*), it is currently undergoing extensive urban renewal.

ÎLE-DE-FRANCE
PAYS DE FRANCE

This arable plateau extending between St-Denis, Luzarches and the Dammartin-en-Goële ridge was in the heart of royal territory. The layer of marl covering the subsoil has made the area extremely fertile, and the huge fields are planted with wheat and beet.

PARISIS

Parisis lies between the River Oise and River Seine and the Pays de France. The area was once occupied by the Gauls, who gave it its name and christened the French capital. Parisis is an alluvial plain with few rivers that slopes toward the Seine. It is dominated by limestone hillocks covered in sand or grit.

Beyond the industrial suburbs of Paris, market gardens and orchards spread along the limestone slopes of the plain, while the sandy stretches are forested.

SENLISIS

Geographers and historians have often grouped this region with Valois, but in fact it was part of the Crown territory, the central core of Île-de-France. Senlisis, which is bordered by the Oise, the Dammartin-en-Goële ridge and the Valois itself, is one of the most picturesque regions near the capital. Arable land is found on the silty soils, while the sandy areas have favoured the development of forestry.

VALOIS

Valois is surrounded by Senlisis and the Oise, Automne and Ourcq rivers. It acquired strategic importance as early as Roman times and has remained one of the most important regions in French history. First a county, then a duchy, Valois was twice given to one of the king's brothers. On two occasions the descendants of this royal line, known as the Princes de Valois, acceded to the throne.

MULTIEN

Multien is an area of rolling landscapes and ploughed fields bounded by the River Marne, the Valois and the Goële ridge. It was the scene of fierce combat in September 1914.

FRENCH VEXIN

Three rivers border this limestone platform: the **Oise**, the **Epte** and the **Seine**. West of the River Epte is the Normandy Vexin. The loess covering is an extremely fertile topsoil which favours cereal cultivation, especially wheat, and vegetable crops. Cattle rearing is concentrated in the valleys planted with poplar trees. The Buttes de Rosne, a series of outliers stretching from Monneville to Vallangoujard, are wooded. They include the strip of land running north of the Seine.

MANTOIS

Mantois is an enormous plateau situated between the River Eure and River Oise. It consists of forests to the east and arable land to the west. The small towns dotting its many valleys are well worth a visit.

HUREPOIX

Bounded by Mantois, Beauce, Fontainebleau Forest and the Seine, the **Hurepoix** region has suffered from recent urbanisation. However, by avoiding major roads and referring to map no 106, you will enjoy exploring its varied landscapes.

GÂTINAIS

The **Gâtinais** is defined by the River Seine and the Hurepoix, Beauce and Champagne regions. The French Gâtinais, a clay plateau, lies east of the River Loing while the Orléanais Gâtinais (to the west) is an area of sand and sandstone. This second area is covered by Fontainebleau Forest, popular because of its splendid groves and sandstone boulders. The lush valley of the Loing, which attracted a number of well-known artists to the area (Corot, Millet), is dotted with charming small towns.

FRENCH BRIE

French Brie is located between the River Seine and River Grand Morin and has Champagne Brie as its northern border. Historically, the former belonged to the king of France, while the latter was the property of the Comte de Champagne. The area is watered by four meandering rivers – Seine, Marne, Petit Morin and Grand Morin – and has many large farms specialising in large-scale wheat, sugar-beet and vegetable cultivation. French Brie contains sites as varied as the Chateau de Vaux-le-Vicomte and Disneyland Paris.

FORESTS

Île-de-France has some magnificent forests, including Rambouillet, Compiègne and Fontainebleau, which feature among the finest in the country. The forests form a 'green ring' around Paris that is a delight for weekend hikers, bikers and horse riders, among others. Woods and forests have a timeless appeal: lush greenery in springtime, shaded groves in summer, the deep russet tones of autumn or the crisp frosts of winter. Forests also provide a multitude of fauna and flora to study, or flowers, fruit, nuts and mushrooms to harvest in season. Many also have charming picnic areas. Those who take time to understand the lifecycle of a forest also understand its infinite variety.

STATE AND PRIVATE FORESTS

Three types of forest exist in France: state, private and local. The most interesting for walkers are the state forests, as they have an extensive network of roads, paths and lanes, and their magnificent groves form a picturesque setting. The aim of the forest rangers is to preserve the natural habitat. The most beautiful French forests used to feature protected forest zones known as 'artistic reserves' in which unusually striking trees were left untouched by the axe, even when they died. This practice was given up in favour of 'biological reserves'. Forests on private estates are not open to the public, apart from the roads that run through them.

TREES

Like all living things, trees breathe, reproduce and need nourishment. Mineral nutrients are drawn from the earth by the roots and distributed to all parts of the tree via the sap running through the trunk and leaves.

Different trees require different kinds of soil. Chestnut trees, for instance, cannot survive on limestone sites, whereas oaks will flourish on a variety of soils.

Trees, like other plants, breathe through their leaves and reproduce through their flowers. Flowers will bear fruit if they are fertilised by pollen of their own species. Very few trees have hermaphrodite flowers – presenting both male and female characteristics – like roses, acacias, etc. Consequently the pollen is usually carried from the male flower to the female flower by insects, or sometimes by the wind. Trees may also reproduce by their shoots; thus, when a youngish tree trunk is razed to the ground, a number of stool shoots will emerge from the stump. Conifers do not produce offshoots.

The trees of Île-de-France fall into two categories: deciduous and coniferous.

Deciduous – These trees shed their leaves every autumn and grow them again in the spring. Beeches, oaks, hornbeams, birches and chestnut trees belong to this category.

Coniferous – In place of leaves, coniferous species have needles which they shed regularly throughout the year. The needles are renewed every four to five years. Their sap contains resin – they are also known as resinous trees – and the fruit is generally cone-shaped. Pines, cypresses, cedars and fir trees are all conifers, as is the larch, which loses its needles every year.

TREES OF THE ÎLE-DE-FRANCE FORESTS

Most species of deciduous trees can be found around Paris. The most common are listed below.

Oak – One of the most esteemed forest trees, the oak's hard but beautiful wood is used both for carpentry and ornamental woodwork. In former times oak bark was much sought after by local tanners. Some of the oaks tower 40m/132ft high with trunks over 1m/3ft in diameter. Trees can be felled up to the age of 250 years.

Beech – Although it resembles the oak in its habit, beech is slightly more elegant. The wood is mainly used for everyday furniture and railway sleepers but it is also popular as fuel. The trunk is cylindrical, the bark smooth and shiny; young shoots have a crooked, gnarled appearance. Beeches grow as tall as oaks but are not commercially viable beyond 120 years.

Hornbeam – A remarkably tough species, the hornbeam resembles the beech; it also lives to the same age, but is shorter and its bark features numerous grooves.

Chestnut – This tree can grow to great heights and can live for several hundred years, but is generally felled much younger as very old chestnut trees become hollow and prone to disease. Its wood was traditionally used by the cooperage industry for making staves, posts and stakes; nowadays it is used for the production of chipboard. Chestnut trees will grow only on siliceous soil.

Birch – Even when it reaches 25m/82ft in height the birch retains a graceful, slim trunk of white bark – which peels off in fine layers – and shimmering leaves. Damp, sandy soil is an excellent terrain for all varieties of birch. Although it is excellent firewood, it is mainly used in making wood pulp for the paper industry.

Scots Pine – This species, the most commonly found conifer in Île-de-France, is ideal for reafforestation, particularly in sandy terrain. Since the mid-19C it has been planted in plots of land where there is meagre or non-existent vegetation. Scots pines have short needles (4–6cm/1.5–2.5in) which grow in pairs, smallish cones (3–5cm/1–2in) and reddish-ochre bark.

Foresters often plant Scots pines alongside exotic or Mediterranean (maritime pine) resinous species. A great favourite is the Corsican pine, a tall, handsome tree with a perfectly

Scots pine and birch trees with boulders in Fontainebleau Forest

H. Le Gac/MICHELIN

straight trunk. It can grow to 50m/165ft, but old trees develop large grey patches on their bark.

THE SCIENCE OF FORESTRY

If a forest is not tended, it will invariably deteriorate. In order to develop fully and reach their proper size, trees must be given breathing space and be placed in an environment which meets their specific requirements. The first step in a reafforestation campaign is to plant fir trees, which have few needs and produce wood in a very short time. Their roots retain the earth, otherwise washed away by surface water, and the needles build up thick layers on the ground. Next, hornbeams, birches and beeches are planted to increase the fertility of the soil, and finally oaks. Many of the beech groves are left as this species is considered to be commercially profitable.

Rotations – The prime concern of foresters is always to have trees ready for felling. Consequently, when trees are felled foresters ensure they are immediately replaced with seedlings. For example, a forest may be divided into ten units, and every five years the unit with the oldest trees is cleared and then replanted. Thus, within 50 years the forest is entirely renewed while remaining commercially viable, a technique known as rotation.

Forest managers try to avoid exposing a large sector of the forest, as leafy plants such as hazel and mulberry trees can set in and choke the young shoots. Two, three or four groups within each sector are formed according to the trees' approximate age, and a programme of successive felling is planned. This ensures that only limited areas are deforested at any one time.

Whatever the rotation for a given forest, its appearance is bound to change depending on the thickness of the vegetation and the forestry techniques applied. There are three types of plantation in Île-de-France:

Groves – After the land has been sown, the weaker shoots are choked by the stronger ones in a process of natural selection. The trees, planted fairly close to one another, spread vertically.

After some time the land is cleared around the finer species to encourage them to develop, and eventually these are the only ones that remain. This grove, where the widely spaced trees are all the same age, is called a *futaie pleine*; the rotation is rather long, 50 or even 80 years for very tall trees. *Futaie jardinée* is another type of grove, in which the trees are planted and cut at different times, so that the sector features a variety of 'age groups'; older trees are always felled first.

A fully matured grove is a truly impressive sight, with its powerful trunks and its rich canopy of foliage producing subtle effects of light and shade.

Copses – The trees are younger. Rotation ranges from 5 to 30 years, depending on whether pit props, logs for heating or firewood is wanted. A copse is a sector of forest where a group of mature trees have been cut down. The shoots growing around the stump develop into a multitude of young, bushy, leafy trees.

Copses with Standards – If, when cutting a copse, the finest trees are left standing, these will dominate the new shoots. If they survive a series of fellings, they will grow to be extremely strong. The utilisation of copses with standards produces both fuel wood (from the copses) and timber for industrial purposes (from the older species).

FAUNA AND FLORA

Forests contain not only trees but also countless varieties of plants and animals. Hunts are still organised in certain forests.

Nature lovers will find forests fascinating as the rich, damp soil is remarkably fertile, sustaining moss, lichen, mushrooms, grasses, flowers, shrubs and ferns.

Flowers – April is the season of laburnum, hyacinths and daffodils. May brings hawthorn, lily-of-the-valley, columbine and the delightful catkins of the hazel tree. In June there is broom, heather, campanula, scabious and wild pinks. During the autumn, russet and gold leaves are as attractive as the forest flowers.

Fruit – Wild strawberries and succulent raspberries ripen during July and August, while blackberries can be harvested in August and September together with the new crop of hazelnuts. October is the time for sloes and sweet chestnuts.

Mushrooms – Some varieties of mushrooms – Russula virescens, chanterelle comestible and mousseron – are always edible. Other species are difficult to identify and may be dangerous. If in doubt, mushroom pickers should consult a professional mycologist or a local chemist *(pharmacien)*, who is trained to identify mushrooms.

GARDENS IN ÎLE-DE-FRANCE

Three successive trends defined the official canons of ornamental gardening in Île-de-France, the home of many royal residences.

16C

During the 16C gardens were not considered as an essential part of an estate, but merely in the same category as outbuildings. They were generally of geometric shape and resembled a chessboard, where each of the squares contained carefully trimmed spindle and box forming arabesques and other elaborate patterns. These motifs were called *broderies*. Gardens were enclosed within a sort of cloister made of stone or greenery, from which visitors could enjoy a good view of the garden. Paths featuring fragments of marble, pottery and brick cut through the grounds. Though water did not play any significant part in the general appearance of the gardens, there were basins and fountains encircled by balustrades or tall plants. They were there to be ob-served in their own right and for people to admire the ornamental statues and water displays.

Most of them have now disappeared, at least in Île-de-France. There is, however, an outstanding example in Villandry in the Loire Valley (ℭ *see The Green Guide, CHÂTEAUX OF THE LOIRE*).

17C–EARLY 18C: THE FORMAL GARDEN

Although **André le Nôtre** cannot be credited with 'inventing' the **formal French garden**, he was the one person who raised this art form to absolute perfection. Its purpose was twofold: to enhance the beauty of the château it surrounded and to provide a superb view from within. The garden's main features were fountains, trees, statues, terraces and a sweeping perspective.

The château was fronted by a 'Turkish carpet' of parterres, with flowers and evergreen shrubs forming arabesques and intricate patterns. These were flanked symmetrically by basins with fountains, usually adorned with statues. Fountains were also placed on the terrace bearing the château and the upper lawns, which was the starting-point of the central perspective along a canal or a 'green carpet of lawn' *(tapis vert)*, lined with elegant groves of pretty, tall trees.

The groups of trees planted along the perspective were designed to be perfectly symmetrical. They were crossed by a network of paths, with clearings at the intersections offering splendid vistas extending into the far distance. Hedges lined the paths, concealing the massive tree trunks and providing a backdrop for marble statues. As hedges were fragile and expensive to maintain, most were later removed or greatly reduced in height from their original 6–8m/20–26ft. Each grove of trees featured a 'curiosity': perhaps a fountain with elaborate waterworks, a colonnade or a group of sculpted figures.

The enormous variety of designs and styles used for the parterres and surrounding trees, bushes and hedges ensured that these formal gardens were never monotonous. They were conceived as an intellectual pursuit, giving pleasure through their stately proportions and perspectives, the skilful design and the sheer beauty of each detail.

LATE 18C–19C:
THE LANDSCAPE GARDEN

In the 18C, manipulating the landscape into rigid geometric patterns was no longer fashionable. The tendency instead was to imitate nature. The landscape garden – also called the Anglo-Chinese garden – consisted of lush, rolling grounds dotted with great trees and rocks, pleasantly refreshed by streams and tiny cascades. A rustic bridge might cross a river flowing into a pond or lake covered with water-lilies and surrounded by willow trees, and a mill or dairy might add the final touch to this Arcadian scene. The 18C fascination for philosophy, characteristic of the Age of Enlightenment, was also reflected in contemporary gardening, which saw the introduction of symbolic or exotic monuments or *fabriques* (a technical term originally referring to architectural works depicted in paintings).

Antique temples and medieval ruins were particular favourites, while tombs and mausoleums became popular just before the Revolution. Chinese and Turkish sculptures were also fashionable. An unfinished temple, for instance, would remind visitors of the limits of science, while an oriental pagoda standing beside a crumbling tower symbolised the fragility of human achievements.

Sentimentality, romance and melodrama were popular features of many art forms. Such trends also affected landscape gardens, giving rise to a number of new sights including the secret lovers' grotto, the bench of the tired mother, the grave of the rejected suitor, etc.

Most of these estates were ravaged during the Revolution, and few of their fragile monuments survived. Efforts are now being made to restore what was left. The most outstanding example of an 18C folly in the region is the Cassan Pagoda at L'Isle-Adam.

Particularly fine gardens may still be found at Versailles, Vaux-le-Vicomte, Chantilly, Courances, St-Cloud, Sceaux, Champs, Fontainebleau, Rambouillet and Ferrières.

Parterre de l'eau, Château de Versailles
S. Sauvignier/MICHELIN

Paris is France's most populated city, its national capital, and also the regional capital of Île-de-France. Lying on both banks of a loop of the Seine River, its location at a crossroads of trade routes in the heart of a rich agricultural region turned the ordinary Gallo-Roman village of Lutetia into one of the main cities of France during the 10C. Two hundred years later, its cultural influence was felt all over Europe. With the kings of France choosing it as their capital city, and the basilica of the neighbouring town of St-Denis as their necropolis, Paris' political weight grew to the point of making it a major focal point of the Christian world at the beginning of the 14C. As a centre of all powers in France, the only real challenge to Paris came from Versailles, where the royal court settled from the late 17C up to the French Revolution. World capital of arts and pleasures in the 19C and early 20C, Paris' unrivalled heritage and culture have given it the honour of becoming one of the world's most favourite tourist destinations.

Highlights

1. If you enjoyed the award-winning film *Amélie*, follow in her footsteps in **Montmartre** *(p134)*.

2. Visit one of the world's finest collections of Impressionist paintings at **Musée d'Orsay** *(p140)*.

3. Take a step back in history, walking among **St-Denis'** recumbent effigies of royal figures *(p163)*.

4. Visit the Queen's hamlet, Marie-Antoinette's private retreat from the pomp of **Versailles** *(p197)*.

A Parisian way of life

None of your days in Paris should begin without a *café-croissant*, weather-permitting, at a terrace, a Parisian institution since the 18C, when cafés attracted the likes of Voltaire and Rousseau. But the "City of Lights" has a lot more in store for you, and not just the *Grands Magasins!* Looking for a good film? You'll have to choose from a hundred venues, one of the most emblematic ones being Le Grand Rex. Home of the Comédie-Française (17C), Paris always has a great classic on stage, but it also harbours a multitude of small-sized avant-garde auditoriums. The musical scene ranges from classic concerts in Salle Pleyel or Salle Gaveau to jazz events at trendy New Morning Club. Two opera houses, 19C Opéra-Garnier and modern, more popular Opéra-Bastille, offer a rich and varied repertoire. What about night owls? Well, they may want to check the Champs-Elysées or the Bastille-République area as a starter, but just about anywhere they go in town, they will find loads of nightclubs, cabarets, variety shows, reviews, cafés-theatres or plain old bars!

Museums galore

Magnificently restored in the 1990s, the Louvre is one of the largest art museums in the world. Do not miss the new Egyptian and Assyrian sections, and pay a visit to French and Italian sculpture aisles! Right across the River, the Musée d'Orsay, a former glass and steel railway station, will reveal its outstanding collections of impressionist masterpieces. If Modern Art is more after your taste, make a stop at colourful Centre Georges-Pompidou; its temporary exhibits will always surprise you. Lesser known, Musée Guimet hosts a wealth of Asian Art pieces, whereas recently created Musée du Quai Branly is a vibrant tribute to indigenous arts from all around the globe. Outside of Paris, exploring World Heritage Palace of Versailles is a must! The National Museum of Archeology in St-Germain hosts unique sculptures from prehistoric France. Why not pay a visit to the workshops of the National Manufacture of Porcelain in Sèvres? You could also discover Rodin's house in Meudon, where the artist created some of his immortal pieces.

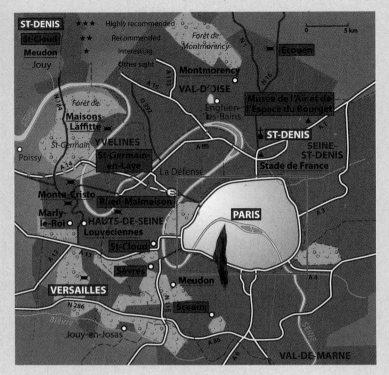

Urban landscape

Did you ever imagine you could have a picnic in the Gallo-Roman Arènes de Lutèce, right in the middle of the city? Or relax on a lounge chair in the heart of Paris, when each summer, several kilometres of a usually busy road by the Seine River are converted into Paris-Plage, a gold, sunny beach, complete with palm trees? Civil architecture in Paris and its surrounds ranges from the bizarre – witness 1970s colour pipes extravaganza of Centre Georges-Pompidou – to the utmost expressions of classicism, Versailles and the Louvre being perfect examples of this. Fashionable Marais abounds in quaint 17C mansions, but the city's dominant style is 19C Haussmanian cut stone buildings. Its very symbols, the Eiffel Tower and the Arc de Triomphe, both date back from this period. But do not think of Paris as a city living in its glorious past. The skyscrapers of La Défense, dominated by the Arche's intriguing cubic shape, and the newborn district of the Bibliothèque Nationale are here to remind us that Paris is a dynamic urban community that is constantly evolving.

Parks and Gardens

Paris' oldest public garden, the Jardin des Plantes, dates back to the early 17C, but most green spaces in Paris were actually created in the 19C, with outstanding examples such as the Buttes-Chaumont, and in the city's outskirts, the Bois de Vincennes and the Bois de Boulogne. The Parc André-Citroën is one of the rare 20C creations. But in order to discover perhaps one of the finest gardens of all times, you will have to leave for Versailles. Its magnificent 17C royal park is an amazing composition of gardens, musical fountains and canals, harbouring the recently restored domain of Queen Marie-Antoinette. On a smaller scale, quiet Parc de Sceaux with its rose gardens and Parc de St-Cloud, towering over the Seine River, are equally worth a visit. Do not miss the castle in St-Germain-en-Laye, the splendid terrace of its park commanding a sweeping view of the Capital.

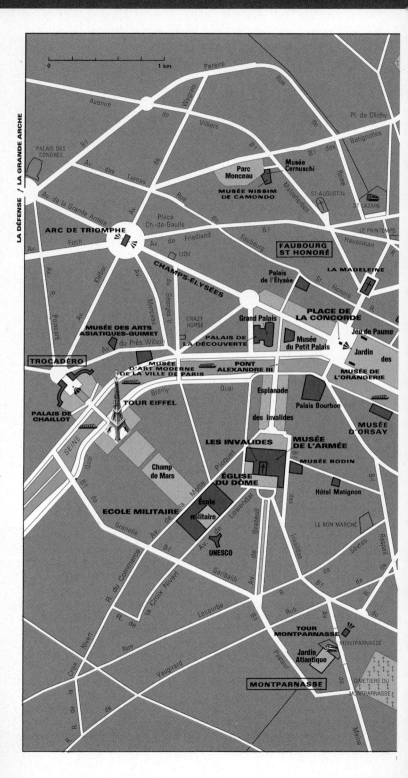

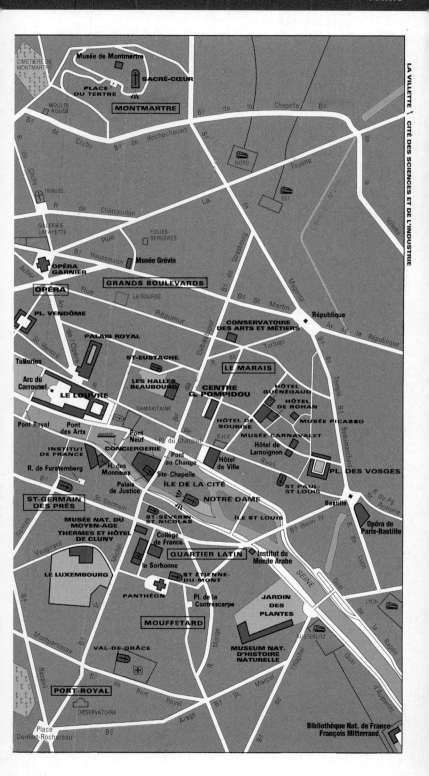

113

Paris★★★

The brilliance and greatness of Paris – its evocative spirit, the imposing dignity of its avenues and squares, its vast cultural wealth and unique flair and style – are known the world over. The dominance of Paris in France's intellectual, artistic, scientific and political life can be traced back to the 12C when the Capetian kings made it their capital.

A BIT OF HISTORY
Origins

At the time of the fall of the Roman Empire towards the end of the 5C, Paris was a modest township founded seven centuries previously by Gallic fishermen. Following its occupation by the **Romans**, the settlement had been extended south of the river to where the remains of the Cluny Baths and a 2C amphitheatre now stand: the **Quartier latin**. In the 3C, St Denis, Paris' first bishop, had met his martyrdom and the Barbarians had razed the place to the ground. This destruction, together with the threat posed by Attila's hordes (but supposedly averted by the intervention of St Geneviève, patron saint of the city), had caused the inhabitants to withdraw to the security of the Île de la Cité.

Clovis, King of **the Franks**, settled in Paris in 506. Two years later, he founded an abbey south of the Seine in honour of St Geneviève, just as 35 years previously a basilica had been erected over the tomb of St Denis. In 885, for the fifth time in 40 years, the Norsemen sailed up the river and attacked Paris; Odo, son of Robert the Strong, bravely led the local resistance, and was elected king of "France" in 888; from then on, the town became the royal seat, albeit with some interruptions.

The Capetian Dynasty (987–1328)

In 1136, Abbot Suger rebuilt the abbey church of St-Denis in the revolutionary Gothic style, an example soon followed by Maurice de Sully at Notre-Dame. Between 1180 and 1210, **Philippe**

▶ **Population:** 2 181 371
♿ **Michelin Local Map:** 312 D 2
🅱 **Info:** There are several branches of the tourist office in the city. The **main office** is at 25 rue des Pyramides. The other branches are located at place du 11 novembre 1918, **Gare de l'Est**; 20 bd Diderot, **Gare de Lyon**; 18 r. de Dunkerque, **Gare du Nord**; 72 bd Rochechouart, **Anvers**; 1 pl. de la Porte de Versailles, Paris Expo; Corner of ave des Champs-Elysées and ave Marigny, **Clémenceau**; 99 r. de Rivoli, **Carrousel du Louvre**; and 21 place du Tertre, **Montmartre**. ℘0892 68 30 00. http://en.parisinfo.com.
▶ **Location:** Paris is France's capital and its largest city. It lies in the middle of the Île-de-France region, which sits between the Centre, Bougogne, Champagne-Ardennes, Picardy and Haute Normandie regions. Paris is 85.6km/53mi SW of Compiègne and 69km/42.8mi NW of Fontainebleau.
▶ **Don't Miss:** Arc de Triomphe, Place de la Concorde, Eiffel Tower, Notre-Dame Cathedral, the Champs-Élysées, Quartier Latin, Montmartre, the Louvre and the Musée d'Orsay.
▶ **Kids:** La Villette encompasses the child-friendly Cité des Sciences et l'Industrie, the spherical cinema La Géode, Cité des Enfants, Jardin de Luxembourg, Palais de Découverte.

GETTING AROUND PARIS

Seine River flows east–west across the city. Places north of the river are on the *rive droite*, while those to the south are on the *rive gauche*. Paris is divided into 20 **arrondissements** (districts or neighbourhoods), each one with its own local government and characteristics. Each arrondissement is further divided into a number of neighbourhoods determined by history and the people who live there.

The métro is the easiest and most economical way of moving around the city. **Line 1**, which crosses Paris east–west, services many of the most famous attractions: the Louvre, the Champs-Élysées and the Arc de Triomphe. **Line 4** is useful for travelling across the city from north–south. The metro also services the immediate suburbs of Paris, but for those a bit farther out, use the **RER** suburban trains.

Auguste surrounded the growing city with a continuous ring of fortifications anchored on the Louvre fortress. In 1215 France's first university was founded on the Ste-Geneviève hill.

The House of Valois (1328–1589)

On 22 February 1358, Étienne Marcel, the merchants' provost, succeeded in rousing the townsfolk to break into the Law Courts (Palais de Justice); entering the Dauphin's apartments, he slew two of the future Charles V's counsellors before his very eyes. On becoming king, **Charles V** quit this place of ill memory. In 1370, he built himself a stronghold in the eastern part of the city, the Bastille, which became the centrepiece of a new ring of fortifications.

Paris was taken by the English in 1418. **Joan of Arc** was wounded in front of Porte St-Honoré trying to retake the city in 1429. Paris was won back for France eight years later by Charles VII.

In 1492, the discovery of America marked the first beginnings of a new outlook and the modern age. The Neapolitan artists brought back by **Charles VIII** from his campaigns in Italy were introducing new trends in taste and thought; the influence of the Renaissance became apparent in many new buildings. In the 1560s, the brothers Androuet Du Cerceau drew up the plans for the Flore Pavilion abutting the Louvre to the west, then set about the construction of the Pont Neuf (New Bridge), which today is the city's oldest surviving bridge.

On 24 August 1572, the bells rang out from the tower of St-Germain-l'Auxerrois to signal the start of the St Bartholomew's Day Massacre (of Protestants); Henry of Navarre, the future Henri IV, just married to Marguerite of Valois, barely escaped with his life. In 1589, Henri III was assassinated at St-Cloud in 1589 by the monk Jacques Clément. This violent act marked the end of the Valois line.

The Bourbons (1589–1789)

In 1594 Paris opened its gates to **Henri IV**, the new king who had renounced his Protestant faith and succeeded in pacifying the country. But on 14 May 1610 in the Rue de la Ferronnerie, this monarch too fell victim to an assassin.

Under **Louis XIII** (1610–43), Métezeau designed an imposing Classical west front for St-Gervais Church, the first of its kind in Paris; Salomon de Brosse built the Luxembourg Palace for Marie de' Medici; Jean Androuet Du Cerceau laid out the courtyards and gardens of the Hôtel de Béthune-Sully; as well as erecting a church for the Sorbonne with Classical columns on its courtyard side, Lemercier built the Palais-Royal for Richelieu. On the king's death in 1643, Anne of Austria became Regent, acting in concert with Mazarin and continuing the policies of Richelieu. Paris fell prey to the series of disturbances caused by unrest among the nobility and known as the Fronde; the young king came to the conclusion that it might be advantageous to separate Court from city.

The 23-year-old **Louis XIV** began his long and highly personal reign in 1661. Even more than the splendour of court life, it was the extraordinary advancement of the arts and literature at this time that gave Paris and France such prestige in Europe. Under the protection of a king keen to encourage artistic endeavour and promote creative confidence, writers, painters, sculptors and landscapers flourished as never before. In the space of 20 years, the great Le Nôtre redesigned the parterres of the Tuileries; Claude Perrault provided the Louvre with its fine colonnade and built the Observatory; Le Vau completed the greater part of both the Institut de France and the Louvre. France's "Century of Greatness" came to an end with Louis XIV's death in 1715.

The country now found itself, for the second time, under the rule of a five-year-old. The running of the country was therefore put into the hands of a regent, Philippe d'Orléans; the first action of the court was to pack its bags and quit the boredom of Versailles for the gaiety of the capital. A long period of peace accompanied the years of corruption; for 77 years France experienced no foreign incursions. Literary salons flourished, notably those of the Marquise de Lambert, Mme Du Deffand and Mme Geoffrin, all helping the spread of new ideas in what became known as the **Age of Enlightenment**. The Palais Bourbon (1722–28), which now houses the National Assembly, was erected at this time.

The personal rule exercised by **Louis XV** was discredited by his favourites, but Paris nevertheless witnessed a number of great personalities and important advances; such as Charles de la Condamine, a surveyor and naturalist responsible for the discovery of rubber (1751); Jussieu, incumbent of the Chair in Botany at the Botanical Gardens, responsible for a systematic classification of plants (1759) and for many advances in pharmacology; Diderot, author, together with d'Alambert, of the great *Encyclopaedia*, a splendid summary of the technology of the age; Chardin,

who had lodgings in the Louvre, devoted himself to working in pastel; Robert Pothier, who wrote the *Treatise of Obligations*; Ange-Jacques Gabriel, the last and most famous of a line of architects linked to Mansart and Robert de Cotte, who between them gave France a hundred years of architectural unity; it was he who designed the magnificent façades fronting the Place de la Concorde, the west front of St-Roch Church and the École Militaire (Military Academy). Finally there was Soufflot, creator of the dome which crowns the Panthéon.

Distinguished furniture-makers were at work too: Lardin with his cabinets and commodes with rosewood inlay, and Boudin with his virtuoso marquetry and secret compartments; they anticipate the masters who were to emerge in the following reign.

Revolution and Empire (1789–1814)

In 1788, King **Louis XVI (1774–92)** decided to convene the States-General. The delegates assembled at Versailles on 5 May 1789. As a result, on 17 June, the States-General transformed itself into a **National Assembly** which styled itself the Constituent Assembly on 9 July; the monarchy would eventually become a constitutional one.

On **14 July 1789**, in the space of less than an hour, the people of Paris took over the Bastille in the hope of finding arms there; the outline of the demolished fortress can still be traced in the paving on the west side of the Place de la Bastille (14 July became a day of national celebration in 1879). On 17 July, in the City Hall (Hôtel de Ville), Louis XVI kissed the recently adopted tricolour cockade. The feudal system was abolished on 4 August, and the Declaration of the Rights of Man adopted on 26 August; on 5 October, the Assembly moved into the riding-school of the Tuileries, and the royal family was brought from Versailles and installed in the Tuileries Palace.

On 12 July 1790 the Church became subject to the Civil Constitution for the

Clergy. Two days later, a great crowd gathered on the Champ-de-Mars to celebrate the anniversary of the fall of the Bastille; Talleyrand, Bishop of Autun as well as statesman and diplomat, celebrated mass on the altar of the nation and the king reaffirmed his oath of loyalty to the country.

After his attempt to join Bouillé's army at Metz had been foiled, Louis was brought back to Paris on 25 June 1791; on 30 September, he was forced to accept the constitution adopted by the Assembly which then dissolved itself.

The Legislative Assembly – The new deputies met the following day in the Tuileries Riding School. On 20 June 1792, encouraged by the moderate revolutionary faction known as the Girondins, rioters invaded the Tuileries and made Louis put on the red bonnet of liberty. On 11 July, the Assembly declared France to be in danger, and during the night of 9 August the mob (sans-culottes) instituted a "revolutionary commune" with the status of an organ of government; the next day the Tuileries were sacked and 600 of the Swiss Guards massacred. The Assembly responded by depriving the king of his few remaining responsibilities and confining him with his family in the tower of the Templar Prison (Tour du Temple).

Soon after, the "September Massacres" began; 1 200 prisoners, some "politicals", but most of them common offenders, were hauled from the city's jails and arbitrarily executed on the Buci crossroads in a frenzy of fear and panic precipitated by fear of invasion. This grisly event marked the beginning of the Terror. On 21 September, the day after the French defeat at the Battle of Valmy, the Legislative Assembly gave way to the Convention.

The Convention – At its very first meeting, the new assembly, now in the hands of the Girondins, formally abolished the monarchy and proclaimed the **Republic**. This day, 21 September 1792, became Day 1 of Year One in the new revolutionary calendar (which remained in force until 31 December 1805). At the end of May, beset by

difficulties at home and abroad and bereft of popular support, the Girondins fell, to be replaced by the "Mountain" (the extreme Jacobin faction, so-called because they occupied the upper tiers of seating in the Assembly).

In one of its first acts, the monarch was guillotined on 21 January 1793 in Place de la Concorde. On 17 September, the Law of Suspects was passed, legalising **the Terror**. The first to be executed by the revolutionary tribunals were the Girondins, in October 1793. On 8 June 1794, Robespierre the "Incorruptible" presided over the Festival of the Supreme Being. The event was orchestrated by the painter David, beginning in the Tuileries Gardens and proceeding to the Champ-de-Mars.

On 10 June (9 Prairial), the Great Terror began. Over a period of two months, the "national razor", as the guillotine was known, was to slice off 2 561 heads. Among those executed was Lavoisier, former Farmer-General and eminent chemist, responsible for the formulation of the theory of the conservation of mass on which much of modern chemistry rests, and André Chénier, the lyric poet who had condemned the excesses of the regime in his verse. The end of the Terror came with the fall and execution of Robespierre himself, on 27 July (9 Thermidor).

The Thermidorian Convention now attempted to put the sickening spectacle of the scaffold behind it with a policy calculated to promote stability. Among its most important achievements were measures designed to advance science and learning, including the founding of the École Polytechnique (School of Engineering); the creation of the Conservatoire des Arts et Métiers (National Technical Institution), and the setting up of the École Normale (the prestigious college). In 1795, the metric system was adopted and the Office of Longitudes founded. Just before the Assembly's dissolution on 25 October, public education was instituted and the Institut de France founded, embracing the nation's learned academies (including the Académie Française).

The Directory and the Consulate – The period of the Directory was marked, in 1798, by the very first Universal Exhibition, but was brought to an end with the *coup d'état* of 9 November (18 Brumaire) 1799, when the Council of Elders persuaded the legislature to move to St-Cloud as a precautionary measure against Jacobin plots. On the following day, **Napoleon Bonaparte** entered the chamber to address the delegates, but was booed; he was saved by the presence of mind of his brother Lucien, who used the guard to disperse the members. By the same evening, power was in the hands of three consuls; it was the end of the Revolution. In less than five years, the Consulate allowed Napoleon to centralise power, opening the way to the realisation of his Imperial ambitions.

The Empire – Proclaimed Emperor of the French by the Senate on 18 May 1804, Napoleon I was anointed on 2 December by Pope Pius VII at Notre-Dame, though it was he himself who actually put the crown on his head in a ceremony immortalised by David. His reign was marked by the promulgation in 1804 of the Civil Code, which he had helped draft himself when he was still First Consul, and which, as the *Code Napoleon*, has since formed the legal basis of many other countries. In order to make Paris into a truly imperial capital, Napoleon ordered the erection of a great column in the Place Vendôme; cast from the melted-down metal of guns taken at the Battle of Austerlitz (Slavkov), it commemorated the victories of his *Grande Armée*. Vignon was commissioned to design a temple which nearly became a railway station before ending up as the Madeleine Church; Chalgrin was put to work drawing up plans for a great triumphal arch (Arc de Triomphe); Brongniart built the Stock Exchange (Bourse); Percier and Fontaine, the promoters of the Empire style, constructed the north wing of the Louvre and the Carrousel Arch (Arc du Carrousel); Gros painted the battles and Géricault the cavalry of the *Grande Armée*.

On 31 March 1814, despite the strong resistance offered by Daumesnil at Vincennes, the Allies occupied Paris. On 11 April, the Emperor, "the sole obstacle to peace in Europe", put his signature to the document of abdication at Fontainebleau.

The Restoration (May 1814–February 1848)
The reign of Louis XVIII – **1814–24** The period of rule of Louis XVI's brother was interrupted by the Hundred Days of Napoleon's attempt to re-establish himself between his sojourn on Elba and his final exile to St Helena. During the years of Louis XVIII's reign, Laënnec invented the stethoscope, wrote his *Treatise on Mediate Auscultation* and founded the anatomo-clinical school together with Bayle and Dupuytren; Pinel studied mental illness at the Salpêtrière Hospital; Cuvier put biology on a sounder footing, formulated the principles of subordination of organs to their function and established a zoological classification; Bertholet studied the composition of acids, Sadi Carnot thermodynamics and temperature equilibrium, and Arago electromagnetism and the polarisation of light; Daguerre laid the foundations of his fame with his dioramas, and Lamartine conquered literary society with his *Méditations Poétiques* – its elegaic rhythms soothed Talleyrand's sleepless nights.

The reign of Charles X – **1824–30** Painting flourished with the brilliant sweep of Delacroix' great canvases and Corot's landscapes. At the same time, Laplace was establishing the fundamental laws of mathematical analysis and providing a firm basis for astronomical mechanics, and Berlioz was composing his *Fantastic Symphony*, the key work of the Romantic Movement in music.

On 21 February 1830, Victor Hugo's drama *Hernani* provoked a literary battle between "moderns" and "classicals" in which the latter were temporarily routed. In the summer, Charles' press ordinances provoked a crisis which led to his abdication; he was succeeded by

Louis Philippe, a member of the cadet branch of the Bourbons.

Reign of Louis-Philippe – 1830–48

During the 1830s, the mathematician Evariste Galois put forward the theory of sets; Victor Hugo wrote *Notre-Dame de Paris* and Alfred de Musset *Caprices*. Chopin, the darling of Parisian society, composed scherzos, waltzes and his celebrated Polonaises. In 1838, while on holiday in Paris, Stendhal wrote *The Charterhouse of Parma*, a masterpiece of psychological observation which can be read on a number of levels. The first news agency was founded by Charles Havas. In 1839, a railway line was opened between Paris and St-Germain. The 1840s saw the publication of the *Mysteries of Paris* by Eugène Sue, the *Count of Monte Cristo* and the *Three Musketeers* by Dumas and many of the works of Balzac's prodigious Human Comedy as well as the *Treatise on Parasitology* by Raspail; the abuses of the July monarchy were satirised in the drawings of Daumier.

At the age of 79, Chateaubriand brought his finely chiselled *Memories from beyond the Tomb* to a triumphant conclusion. On 23 February in 1848, the barricades went up on the Boulevard des Capucines and the monarchy fell; the next day, at the City Hall, amid scenes of wild enthusiasm, Lamartine saluted the tricolour "the flag which has spread the name of France, freedom and glory around the wide world".

Second Republic and Second Empire (1848–1870)

Second Republic

The abolition of the National Workshops in June 1848 led to rioting in the St-Antoine district, in which the archbishop of Paris was killed. In 1849, Léon Foucault proved the rotation and spherical nature of the earth by means of a pendulum (the experiment was repeated in 1855 from the dome of the Panthéon). On 2 December 1851 the short life of the Second Republic was ended by a *coup d'état*.

Second Empire – 1852–70

Two great exhibitions (in 1855 and 1867) proclaimed the prosperity France enjoyed under the rule of Bonaparte's nephew, Napoleon III. **Baron Haussmann**, Prefect of the *Département* of the Seine, was responsible for an ambitious programme of public works which transformed the capital, giving it many of the features which now seem quintessentially Parisian. Among them were the laying out of the Bois de Boulogne and the Bois de Vincennes, and the building of railway stations and the North Wing of the Louvre. But the Baron is remembered above all for the ruthless surgery he performed on the capital's ancient urban tissue, opening up new focal points (Place de l'Opéra) and linking them with great axial roadways (Grands Boulevards), splendid exercises in traffic engineering and crowd control.

In 1852, Alexandre Dumas wrote *The Lady of the Camellias* at the same time as Rudé was working on the memorial to Marshal Ney, which was to be placed on the spot where the great soldier had been executed in 1815; in Rodin's opinion, it was Paris' finest statue. In 1857 Baudelaire, the first poet of the teeming modern metropolis, published *Les Fleurs du Mal (The Flowers of Evil)*. In 1859, Gounod presented *Faust* at the Opéra Lyrique. In 1860, Étienne Lenoir registered his first patent for the internal combustion engine.

The year 1863 was marked by the scandals caused by Manet's *Déjeuner sur l'herbe* and *Olympia*; Baltard masked the masterly iron structure of the St-Augustin Church with the stone cladding still obligatory in a religious building. In 1896 Pierre de Coubertin created the International Olympic Committee.

Republican Continuity (1870 to the present day)

On 4 September 1870, the mob which had invaded the National Assembly was led by Gambetta to the City Hall where the Republic was proclaimed. The new government busied itself in preparing to defend Paris against the advancing Prussians; the St-Cloud château was set on fire and a fierce battle took place at Le Bourget.

Paris Commune – the Vendome Column was pulled down on 16th May 1871

The ensuing siege subjected the population of Paris to terrible hardships; food ran out and the winter was exceptionally severe. The city surrendered on 28 January 1871. The revolutionary **Commune** was ruthlessly suppressed by military force, not before the Communards had burnt down the City Hall, the Tuileries and the Audit Office (Cours des Comptes – on the site of what is now the Orsay Museum), pulled down the column in the Place Vendôme and shot their prisoners at the Hostages' Wall in the Rue Haxo. They made their last stand in the Père-Lachaise Cemetery, where those of their number who had survived the bitter fighting were summarily executed at the Federalists' Wall (Mur des Fédérés). But political institutions were re-established and the nation revived; the Republic was consolidated as France's political regime, notwithstanding Marshal Pétain's so-called French State (État Français), Nazi occupation and the provisional government following the end of World War II.

Third Republic – Carpeaux sculpted the Four Corners of the World for the Observatory Fountain, and Émile Littré completed the publication of his renowned *Dictionary of the French Language*. Bizet wrote *L'Arlésienne (the Woman of Arles)* for the Odéon theatre and followed it with *Carmen*, based on a short story by Mérimée.

In 1874, Degas painted *The Dancing Class* and Monet *Impression: Rising Sun*, which, when exhibited by his dealer Nadar, led to the coining of the initially derisive term Impressionism. Later, Renoir worked at the Moulin de la Galette, and Puvis de Chavannes decorated the walls of the Panthéon. The public applauded Delibes' innovatory *Coppélia* and *Lakmé*. Rodin created the *Thinker*, followed by figures of Balzac and Victor Hugo.

In 1879, Seulecq put forward the principle of sequential transmission on which television is based and Pasteur completed his vast body of work. Seurat's Grande Jatte heralded the establishment of the Pointillist school of painting. In the following year, 1887, Antoine founded the Free Theatre (Théâtre libre) based on spontaneous expression. The engineer Gustave Eiffel completed his great tower, centrepiece of the Universal Exhibition of 1889. In the century's final decade, Toulouse-Lautrec painted cabaret scenes and Pissarro Parisian townscapes, and Forain gained fame as a marvellous caricaturist. In the Catholic Institute, Édouard Branly discovered radio-conductors.

In 1891, René Panhard built the first petrol-engined motor car, which drove right across Paris. In 1898, the 21-year-old Louis Renault built his first car, then founded his Billancourt factory; in 1902 he patented a turbocharger. The factory turned out cars, lorries, planes and, in 1917, light tanks which contributed to the German defeat in 1918. Nationalised at the end of World War II, the firm continued to produce vehicles in large numbers.

In October 1898 Pierre and Marie Curie succeeded in isolating radium and established the atomic character of radioactivity; their laboratory was a shed which has since disappeared, but its outline is shown in the paving pattern in the courtyard of the school at No 10 Rue Vauquelin. At the same time, Henri Bergson was teaching philosophy at the Collège de France and Langevin was conducting his investigations into ionised gases (in 1915, he was to use ultrasonic waves in the detection of submarines); a combination of steel, stone and glass was employed by Girault in the construction of the exhibition halls (the Grand Palais and the Petit Palais) for the 1900 Exhibition; this occasion also saw the bridging of the Seine by the great flattened arch of the Pont Alexandre III.

In 1900, Gustave Charpentier put on a musical romance *Louise*; with its lyrical realism and popular appeal it was a great "hit" of the time. In 1902, Debussy's *Pelléas et Mélisande* was produced at the Salle Favart of the Comic Opera. In 1906, Santos-Dumont succeeded in taking off in a heavier-than-air machine, staying aloft for 21 seconds, and covering a distance of 220m/721.7ft.

Dalou's bronze group entitled *The Triumph of the Republic* graced the Place de la Nation, while at Montparnasse the re-erected Wine Pavilion from the 1900 Exhibition provided lodgings and studios for Soutine, Zadkine, Chagall, Modigliani and Léger; other innovative artists included the sculptor Maillol and the painter Utrillo, while Brancusi's work was evolving away from cubism towards abstraction *(The Sleeping Muse)*; the Perret brothers built the Théâtre des Champs-Élysées in reinforced concrete; its façade was adorned with eight relief panels by Bourdelle.

The theatre was opened in 1913 with a performance of Stravinsky's *Rite of Spring*; its music and choreography outraged an unprepared public.

In 1914 the construction of the Sacré-Cœur Church (begun in 1878 by the architect Abadie) on the Montmartre heights was completed. On the evening of 31 July, the eve of general mobilisation, Jean Jaurès was assassinated.

The World Wars

World War I (1914–18) put civilians as well as soldiers to the severest of tests; after three years of conflict, Clemenceau was made head of government, and, by restoring the country's confidence, earned the title of "Father of Victory".

In 1920, the interment of an unknown soldier at the Arc de Triomphe marked France's recognition of the sacrifices made by her ordinary soldiers, the unshaven "poilus" of the trenches.

In the course of the 1920s, Le Corbusier built the La Roche Villa, and Bourdelle sculpted *"France"* at the Palais de Tokyo; Georges Rouault, with his predilection for religious themes, completed his *Miserere*, and Landowsky carved the figure of St Geneviève for the Tournelle Bridge; in the course of a fortnight, Maurice Ravel composed *Boléro* for the dancer Ida Rubinstein; with its subtle instrumentation and rhythmic precision it popularised the name of this aristocratic composer; Poulbot created the archetypal Montmartre urchin; Cocteau wrote *Les Enfants Terribles*; the dynamism of the theatrical scene was marked by many fine actors and producers, notably the Cartel of Four (Cartel des Quatre) consisting of Charles Dullin (at the Sarah Bernhardt Theatre), Gaston Baty (at the Montparnasse), Louis Jouvet (at the Champs-Élysées then the Athénée) and Georges Pitoëff (at the Mathurins). At the end of the 19C, Émile Roux had studied the causes of and cure for diphtheria; he was now in charge of the Pasteur Institute, and brought to Paris the scientists Calmette and Guérin who had worked on vaccination against tuberculosis.

In 1934, André Citroën brought out the Traction Avant (Front-Wheel Drive) car; 15 years previously, his Type A had been Europe's first mass-produced car; 21 years later, he was to unveil the innovative DS 19.

In 1940, during **World War II**, Paris was bombed, then **occupied** by the German army. Between 16 and 17 July

1942, numerous French Jews, victims of the Nazi racial myth, were rounded up at the Vélodrome d'Hiver prior to their deportation eastwards for extermination; 4 500 members of the Resistance also met their deaths in the clearing on Mount Valérien where the National Memorial of Fighting France now stands. Finally, on 19 August 1944, Paris was **liberated**.

Fourth and Fifth Republics – In 1950, Alfred Kastler, working in the laboratories of the École Normale Supérieure, succeeded in verifying the principle of "optical pumping", which has subsequently become the basis of one of the methods of producing a laser beam. The *Symphony for a Single Man* by Maurice Béjart, presented at the Étoile Theatre on 3 August 1955, was danced to *musique concrète* composed by Pierre Henry and Pierre Schaeffer, and led to many innovations in ballet throughout Europe.

Since 1945 the influence of Le Corbusier (there are few examples of his genius in Paris: Villa La Roche, Cité Universitaire pavilions…), has given a new impetus to architecture: new forms (Maison de Radio-France), structures on piles (UNESCO), sweeping rooflines (CNIT building). The present trend is for glass buildings (GAN and Manhattan towers, Centre Georges-Pompidou, Institut du Monde Arabe).

The use of pre-stressed concrete led to technical advances (Palais des Congrès, Tour Montparnasse). But in the main architecture becomes an integral part of town planning: buildings are designed to fit into an overall plan: remodelling of an area (Maine-Montparnasse, les Halles, la Villette, Bercy) or new project (la Défense).

Grand new town-planning initiatives have also been implemented: the Opera house at la Bastille, the Ministry of Finance buildings at Bercy, the Grande Arche at la Défense and the Bibliothèque nationale de France François-Mitterrand at Tolbiac are distinctive modern landmarks.

THE CITY'S MONUMENTS
CIVIL ARCHITECTURE
Palais du Louvre★★★
 ♿ *See Musée du Louvre.*

Neither the Merovingians nor the Carolingians, nor even the Capet kings lived in the old Louvre, which then lay beyond the city limits; instead, they preferred the Law Courts (Palais de Justice), their *hôtels* in the Marais, the manor at Vincennes, their own châteaux or those of their liegemen in the Loire Valley.

Contributions of the Heads of State
Floor plan below shows the evolution of the Louvre Palace.

It was **François I** who had the old Louvre pulled down, and, in 1546, commissioned Pierre Lescot to build the palace which was to become the residence of the kings of France. Lescot's work 1 is regarded as the most prestigious part of the Louvre; it was he who brought the Italian Renaissance style, already flowering on the Loire, to the banks of the Seine; to the façade he built, sculptor Jean Goujon added the nymphs of the Fountain of the Innocents.

When Charles IX came to the throne at age ten, the Florentine **Catherine de' Medici** was made Regent. At first she lived in the Louvre on the floor since known as the Queens' Lodging (Logis des Reines), but ordered Philibert Delorme (succeeded by Jean Bullant) to build the Tuileries. The site of this new palace was some 500m/550yd away, just beyond the fortifications built by Charles V, and, to link it with the Louvre, Catherine requested a covered way following the line of the Seine, with a smaller gallery at right angles.

Charles IX completed the southwestern part of the Cour Carrée, the courtyard which is the most impressive part of the Old Louvre to remain, embellishing it with his monogram (K = Carolus).

Henri III was responsible for the southeastern part of the Cour Carrée (which bears the monogram H). **Henri IV**, from 1595, had the work on the Great Gallery (Grande Galerie) continued by Louis Métezeau. He also had the Flora Pavilion (Pavillon de Flore) built by Jacques II Androuet Du Cerceau, completed the Small Gallery (Petite Galerie) (its first floor was occupied by Marie de' Medici and Anne of Austria, hence the monogram AA), and erected the upper part of the Henri III wing in the Cour Carrée, marked by his monogram. **Louis XIII** continued with the construction of the Cour Carrée. At the same time as he was building the Sorbonne and the Palais-Royal, the architect Lemercier erected the Clock Pavilion (Pavillon de l'Horloge) together with the northwest corner of the courtyard, a Classical response to Lescot's work (the monogram LA = Louis and Anne). Anne of Austria lived in the Queens' Lodging; the bathroom designed for her by Lemercier now houses the Venus de Milo. In 1638, Charles V's rampart was razed and the moat filled in.

On the death of Louis XIII, Anne became Regent and moved to the Palais-Royal with the young **Louis XIV**. Nine years later, however, having been made aware of the palace's vulnerability by the uprising of the nobility (the Fronde), she took up residence in the Louvre again.The young king, who had married Maria-Theresa, moved into the Tuileries in 1664 for three years. The architect Le Vau, working on the Louvre, his personal style evident in the Small Gallery, started again after a fire in 1661, and in the Apollo Gallery; he continued the enclosure of the Cour Carrée by adding a storey onto the western part of the north wing (monogram LMT = Louis, Maria-Theresa) and by building the Marengo Pavilion (Pavillon Marengo) (with the monogram LB = Louis XIV de Bourbon).

But the palace still needed a monumental façade facing the city; **Colbert** had refused permission for a number of projects designed with this in mind. An appeal was made to the master-architect of the Italian Baroque, Bernini, already 67 years old. But his proposals were turned down too, since they would have either destroyed or clashed with Lescot's façade. In the end it fell to Claude Perrault, aided by Le Brun and Le Vau, to design an imposing colonnaded façade. In 1682, the king left Paris for Versailles. The Louvre now housed the Academy as well as a less desirable population. In 1715, the Court returned to Paris for a period of seven years; the young King Louis XV lived in the Tuileries and the Regent in the Palais-Royal. Coustou continued the work on the colonnade.

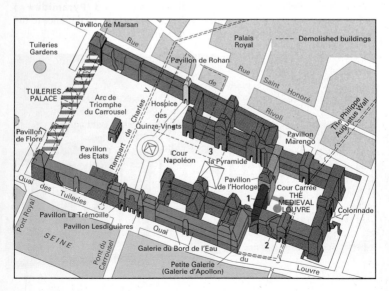

After the **Revolution**, the Convention used the Louvre theatre for its deliberations. The Committee of Public Safety (Comité du Salut public) convened in the state rooms of the Tuileries, which were subsequently appropriated for his own use by Napoleon.

Napoleon I took up residence in the Tuileries. Percier and Fontaine completed the Cour Carrée by adding a second floor to the north and south wings. They also provided a wing linking the Rohan and Marsan Pavilions and gave it a façade identical to Du Cerceau's Grande Galerie, as well as enlarging the Place du Carousel to enable Napoleon to review his legions and embellishing it with a triumphal arch commemorating the Emperor's victories, its design based on the Arch of Septimus Severus.

All of the "restored" monarchs lived in the Tuileries, as did **Napoleon III**, who decided to enclose the large courtyard on the north, confiding the task to Visconti, then to Lefuel, whose design was intended to conceal the disparity between the two wings; the architects razed the Hôtel de Rambouillet 3 which had housed the literary *Salon des Précieuses* under Louis XIII, replacing it with the present pavilions. They also restored the Pavillon de Rohan (the monogram LN = Louis Napoleon). Lefuel restored the Pavillon de Flore together with the wing extending it eastwards; his design is a not altogether successful copy of Métezeau's work; the gallery bears the monogram NE (= Napoleon, Eugénie).

During the night of 23 May 1871, the **Communards** burnt down the Tuileries and half of Napoleon I's North Wing (Aile Nord de Napoleon I), as well as the Pavillons Richelieu and Turgot and the East Wing (Aile Est) attached to the Pavillon de Flore.

In 1875, under **President MacMahon**, Lefuel continued the work of Visconti with some modifications; he restored and extended the North Wing (Aile Nord) as well as refurbishing the Pavillon de Marsan and providing it with the monogram RF (République Française); in addition, he rebuilt the Riverside Gallery (Galerie du Bord de l'Eau) and the Pavillons de La Trémoille and de Flore.

In 1883, under **President Jules Grévy**, the Palais des Tuileries was demolished; and the city was deprived of one of the key buildings in its history.

In 1984 **President Mitterrand** embarked on the "Grand Louvre and Pyramide" project. He commissioned the architect Ming Pei to expand the services and reception area of what had now become a world-famous art museum. Beneath the Cour Napoleon, a vast hall offering information and documentation services is lit up by the glass pyramid (**Pyramide★★**) which marks the main entrance to the museum.

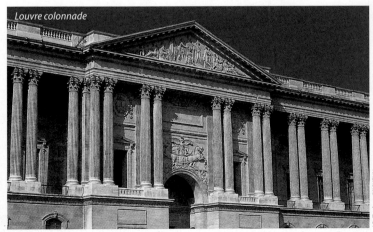
Louvre colonnade

J.P. Clapham/MICHELIN

Hôtel Nacional des Invalides★★★

129 r. de Grenelle. ♿🕐*Open daily Oct–Mar 10am–5pm (5.30pm Sun); Apr–Sept 10am–6pm (6.30pm Sun).* 🕐*Closed 1st Mon of the month in Oct–Jun, 1 Jan, 1 May, 1 Nov, 25 Dec.* ☞*8.50€ incl. audioguide; price includes Église du Dôme, Musée de l'Armée, l'Historial de Gaulle, Musée des Plans-Reliefs and Musée de l'Ordre de la Libération.* 👣*Guided tours available; call in advance:* ✆*01 44 42 38 77 or 0810 11 33 99.* ✆*01 44 42 33 75. www.invalides.org.*

The plans for the vast edifice were drawn up by Libéral Bruant between 1671–76; their implementation was placed under the direction of Louvois. The main façade, nearly 200m/650ft long, is majestic without being monotonous; it is dominated by an attic storey decorated with masks and dormer windows in the form of trophies. Napoleon used to parade his troops in the main courtyard (Cour d'honneur); here the South Pavilion (Pavillon du Midi) forms the façade of the Église St-Louis, the resting-place of some of France's great soldiers; the interior is hung with flags taken from the enemy. It was here, in 1837, that Berlioz' Requiem was performed for the first time.

Église du Dôme

MICHELIN

Église du Dôme★★★

🕐*Same as Hôtel Nacional.*

The church of Les Invalides, designed by the master of proportion, **Jules-Hardouin Mansart**, was begun in 1677. With its beautiful gilded dome, it is one of the great works of the Louis XIV style, bringing to a peak of perfection the Classicism already introduced in the churches of the Sorbonne and the Val-de-Grâce, an ecclesiastical equivalent of the secular architecture of Versailles.

1) Tomb of Joseph Bonaparte, elder brother of Napoleon, King of Spain.

2) Monument to Vauban by Etex. The Emperor himself commanded that the military architect's heart be brought to the Invalides.

3) Marshal Foch's tomb by Landowsky.

4) Ornate high altar surrounded by twisted columns and covered by a baldaquin by Visconti. Vaulting decoration by Coypel.

5) General Duroc's tomb.

6) General Bertrand's tomb.

7) At the back – the heart of La Tour d'Auvergne, first grenadier of the Republic; in the centre, the tomb of Marshal Lyautey.

8) Marshal Turenne's tomb by Tuby.

9) St Jerome's Chapel (carvings by Nicolas Coustou). The tomb at the foot of the wall is Jerome Bonaparte's, Napoleon's younger brother and King of Westphalia.

10) The Emperor's tomb.

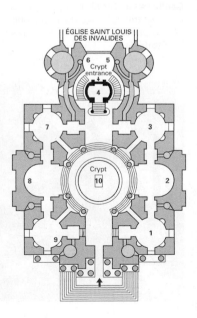

In 1735, Robert de Cotte completed the building by replacing the planned south colonnade and portico with the splendid vista offered by the Avenue de Breteuil. On the far side he laid out the Esplanade, and set up the guns captured at Vienna in 1805 by Napoleon to defend the gardens and fire ceremonial salvoes on great national occasions.

The church became a military necropolis after Napoleon had Marshal Turenne (d 1675) buried here. Note the memorial to Vauban, the great military architect, and the tomb of Marshal Foch. In Visconti's crypt of green granite from the Vosges stands the "cloak of glory", the unmarked **Tombeau de Napoleon** completed in 1861 to receive the Emperor's mortal remains. In 1940, the body of Napoleon's son, King of Rome and Duke of Reichstadt, was brought here too. Also housed in Hôtel nacional des Invalides is the **Musée de l'Armée** (*⊘same as Église du Dôme*).

Arc de Triomphe★★★

pl. Charles-de-Gaulle. ⊘Open daily Apr–Sept 10am–11pm; Oct–Mar 10am–10.30pm. ⊘Closed public holidays. ⊛9€. ℘01 55 37 73 77.
Together with the **Place Charles de Gaulle★★★** and its 12 radiating avenues, the great triumphal arch makes up one of Paris' principal focal points, known as the **Étoile** (Star).

The façades of the buildings around were designed in a harmonious style by Hittorff as part of Haussmann's plans for the metropolis.

The Arc de Triomphe was the scene on 14 July 1919 of the great victory parade and, on 11 November 1920, of the burial of the Unknown Soldier. Three years later the flame of remembrance was kindled for the first time. The arch is ornamented with sculpture, notably Rude's masterpiece of 1836 known as the *Marseillaise,* depicting volunteers departing to defend France from the invading Prussians (1792).

Place de la Concorde★★★

A perfect expression of the Louis XV style, it was designed by Ange-Jacques Gabriel in 1755 and completed over a period of 20 years. On 21 January 1793, near where the statue of Brest now stands, the guillotine was set up for the execution of Louis XVI and other victims of the Terror.

The square owes its monumental character to the colonnaded buildings defining it to the north, to its octagonal plan, and to the massive pedestals intended for allegorical statues of French cities. Two great urban **axes★★★** intersect here: one runs from the Église de la Madeleine to the Palais-Bourbon, the other from *Coysevox's Winged Horses (Chevaux ailés)*, which mark the entrance to the Tuileries, to the magnificent

View of the Place de la Concorde from the Tuileries

B. Kaufmann/MICHELIN

marble sculptures (copies) by Nicolas and Guillaume Coustou which flank the Champs-Élysées. The pink granite Luxor obelisk (Obélisque de Louksor), 3 300 years old, covered with hieroglyphics, was brought here from Egypt in 1836. The square's fountains adorned with statues are particularly fine.

♟♟ Tour Eiffel★★★

7 r. de Belloy. ◑Open daily. Lift: midJun–Aug 9am–12.45am; Sept–mid-Jun 9.30am–11.45pm. ◎8€; child 6.40 (elevator to 2nd floor), 13€, 9.90€ child (elevator to Top floor); Stairs 1st and 2nd floors only, 4.50€, 3.50€ child. ✆01 44 11 23 23. www.tour-eiffel.fr.

The Eiffel Tower is Paris' most famous symbol. The first proposal for a tower was made in 1884; construction was completed in 26 months and the tower opened in March 1889 for the Universal Exhibition (Exposition universelle) of that year.

The structure is evidence of Eiffel's imagination and daring; in spite of its weight of 7 000 tonnes and a height of 320.75m/1 051ft and the use of 2.5 million rivets, it is a masterpiece of lightness. It is difficult to believe that the tower actually weighs less than the volume of air surrounding it and that the pressure it exerts on the ground is that of a man sitting on a chair.

Palais de Justice and Conciergerie★★

*2 bd du Palais. **Palais** ◑open Mon–Sat 8.30am–6pm. ◑Closed public holidays. Visitors are normally allowed to attend a civil or criminal hearing. ✆01 44 32 52 52. **Conciergerie** ◑open daily Mar–Oct 9.30am–6pm; Nov–Feb 9am–5pm. ◑Closed 1 Jan, 1 May, 25 Dec. ◎7€. ✆01 53 40 60 80.*

Known as the Palace (Palais), this is the principal seat of civil and judicial authority. Before becoming the royal palace of the rulers of medieval France, it had been the residence of Roman governors, Merovingian kings and the children of Clovis, the mint of Dagobert and Duke Eudes' fortress.

The Capetian kings built a chapel and fortified the palace with a keep. Philippe le Bel (the Fair) entrusted Enguerrand de Marigny with the building of the Conciergerie as well as with the extension and embellishment of the palace; its Gothic halls of 1313 were widely admired. Later, Charles V built the Clock Tower (Tour de l'Horloge), the city's first public clock; he also installed Parliament here, the country's supreme court. Survivals from this period include the Great Hall (Salle des gens d'Armes) with its fine capitals, the Guard Room (Salle des Gardes) with its magnificent pillars, and the kitchens with their monumental corner fireplaces.

The great hall on the first floor was restored by Salomon de Brosse after the fire of 1618; it was refurbished again in 1840 and once more after the fire of 1871.

The First Civil Court is in the former Parliamentary Grand Chamber (Grand'chambre du parlement), the place where the kings dispensed justice, where the 16-year-old Louis XIV dictated his orders to Parliament, where that body in its turn demanded the convocation of the States-General in 1788, and where the Revolutionary Tribunal was set up under the public prosecutor, Fouquier-Tinville.

The entrance to the royal palace was once guarded by the twin towers gracing the north front of the great complex; this is the oldest part of the building, albeit now hiding behind a 19C neo-Gothic façade.

The **Conciergerie** served as antechamber to the guillotine during the Terror, housing up to 1 200 detainees at any one time. The Galerie des Prisonniers (Prisoners' Gallery), Marie-Antoinette's cachot (cell) and the Chapelle des Girondins (Girondins' Chapel) are particularly moving.

Palais-Royal★★

6 r. de Montpensie Palais Cardinal r.

In 1632, Richelieu ordered Lemercier to build the huge edifice which came to be known as the Palais Cardinal (Cardinal's Palace) when it was extended in 1639. It is remarkable for its impressive central façade, surmounted by allegorical statues and a curved pediment. On his deathbed, Richelieu bequeathed it to Louis XIII, whereupon its name was changed to the Palais-Royal. In 1783, Victor Louis laid out the charming formal gardens and the arcades which enclose them and which house a number of specialist shops and boutiques.

In 1986, Daniel Buren designed the arrangement of 260 columns, all of different height, which occupy the outer courtyard.

École Militaire★★

ave de Lowendal.

Though the original design could not be fully implemented because of lack of financial resources, the Military Academy by Jacques-Ange Gabriel is one of the outstanding examples of French 18C architecture. It was begun in 1752, financed in part by Mme de Pompadour, and completed in 1773. Under the Second Empire, cavalry and artillery buildings of nondescript design were added, together with the low-lying wings which frame the main building. True to its original function, it now houses the French Army's Staff College. The superb main courtyard **(cour d'honneur★)**, lined on either side by beautiful porticoes with paired columns, is approached via an exercise

Opéra Garnier

S. Sauvignier/MICHELIN

yard; the imposing central section and the projecting wings form a harmonious composition.

Panthéon★★

pl. du Panthéon. ○*Open daily Apr–Sept 10am–6.30pm; Oct–Mar 10am–6pm.* ○*Closed 1 Jan, 1 May, 25 Dec.* ⊕*8€.* ℘*01 44 32 18 00.* ○*Guided tours (1hr30min); reservations required.* ℘*01 44 54 19 30.*

In 1744, Louis XV had made a vow at Metz to replace the half-ruined church of St Geneviève's Abbey. Fourteen years later Soufflot began the construction of the new building on the highest point of the Left Bank. The scale of the building was such that its collapse was confidently predicted and the pretensions of its architect ridiculed. The present building has been much changed since Soufflot's day; its towers have gone, its pediments have been remodelled, its windows blocked up. In 1791, the Constituent Assembly closed the church to worshippers in order to convert it into the last resting place of the "great men of the epoch of French liberty". Successively a church, a necropolis, headquarters of the Commune, a lay temple, the Panthéon is representative of the time in which churches lost their dominant position in the urban landscape. Still crowned by Soufflot's dome, the great edifice is built in the shape of a Greek Cross. It has a fine portico with Corinthian columns and a pediment carved by David d'Angers in 1831. In the crypt are the tombs of the famous.

Opéra Garnier★★

1 pl. de l'Opéra. ○*Open daily 10am–5pm; last adm. 4.30pm.* ○*Guided tours Jul–Aug and school holidays Wed, Sat, Sun 11.30am and 2.30pm.* ⊕*8€; tour 12€.* ○*Closed 1 Jan, 1 May and for special events.* ℘*0892 89 90 90. www.operadeparis.fr.*

This is the National Academy of Music, and was until 1990 France's premier home of opera. It opened in 1875 and it is the work of Charles Garnier, who had dreamed of creating an authentic

Second Empire style. But the huge edifice, "more operatic than any opera" (Ian Nairn), magnificent though it was, lacked sufficient originality to inspire a new school of architecture. The interior, with its Great Staircase, foyer and auditorium, is of the utmost sumptuousness. Garnier used marble from all the quarries of France, and there is a ceiling by Chagall.

Palais de Chaillot★★
pl. du Trocadéro.
This remarkable example of inter-war architecture was built for the 1937 Exhibition. Its twin pavilions are linked by a portico and extended by wings which curve to frame the wide terrace with its statues in gilded bronze.
From here there is a wonderful **view**★★★ of Paris; in the foreground are the Trocadero Gardens with their spectacular fountains, and beyond the curving river the Eiffel Tower, the Champ-de-Mars, and the École Militaire.
The Palais houses the **Théâtre de Chaillot** *(✆01 53 65 30 00; www.theatre-chaillot.fr),* the **Musée de l'Homme**★★, *(∞7€; ✆01 44 05 72 72; www.mnhn.fr),* **Musée de la Marine**★★ *(∞9€; ✆01 53 65 69 69; www.musee-marine.fr),* **Musée des Monuments Français**★★ *(∞8€; ✆01 58 51 52 00; www.citechaillot.fr)* and **Musée du Cinéma Henri-Langlois**★ *(✆45 53 21 86; www.paris.org/Musees/Cinema).*

ECCLESIASTICAL ARCHITECTURE
Cathédrale Notre-Dame★★★
r. du cloître Notre-Dame.
🕐**Cathedral** *open Mon–Fri 8am–6.45pm, Sat–Sun 8am–7.15pm.* ∞*No charge.* •*Guided tours Wed & Thu 2pm, Sat 2.30pm.* **Towers** *open Apr–Sept 10am–6.30pm; Oct–Mar 10am–5.30pm; ∞6€. ✆01 53 10 07 00. www.notredamedeparis.fr.*
🖉 *Notre-Dame is the point from which distances to Paris are measured.*
People have worshipped here for 2 000 years and the present building has witnessed the great events of French history.

Where to Stay and Eat
For comprehensive suggestions of Where to Stay and Where to Eat in Paris, consult the red-cover *Michelin Guide Paris* and the *Michelin Green Guide Paris*.

Work on the cathedral was begun by Maurice de Sully in 1163. Notre-Dame is the last great galleried church building and one of the first with flying buttresses. In 1245 the bulk of the work was complete and St Louis held a ceremony for the knighting of his son and also placed the Crown of Thorns in the cathedral until the Sainte-Chapelle was ready to receive it. In 1250 the twin towers were finished.
In 1430, the cathedral was the setting for the coronation of the young Henry VI of England as King of France; in 1455, a ceremony was conducted to rehabilitate Joan of Arc; in 1558, Mary Stuart was crowned here on becoming Queen of France by her marriage to François II and, in 1572, the Huguenot Henri IV waited at the door as his bride, Marguerite de Valois, stood alone in the chancel; in 1594 the king converted to the Catholic faith.
The great building was not spared mutilations of various kinds; in 1699 the choir screen was demolished, and later some of the original stained glass was removed to let in more light, and the central portal demolished (18C) to allow processions to move more freely. During the Revolution statues were destroyed and the cathedral declared a Temple of Reason. It was in a much-dilapidated building that Napoleon Bonaparte crowned himself Emperor and the King of Rome was baptised. In 1831, public opinion was alerted by Hugo's novel Notre-Dame de Paris to the state of the building, and in 1841 Louis-Philippe charged Viollet-le-Duc with its restoration. In the space of 24 years, he completed his work in accordance with his own, idealised vision of the Gothic style; though open to criticism, it needs to be seen in the context of the

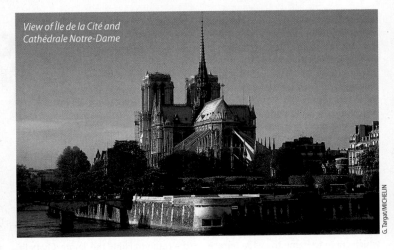

View of Île de la Cité and
Cathédrale Notre-Dame

G. Targat/MICHELIN

wholesale demolition of the medieval Île-de-la-Cité and its replacement with administrative buildings.

The magnificent Cloister Portal (Portail du Cloître–north transept) is 30 years older than the west front portals; with its richly carved gables and smiling figure of the Virgin – the only original large sculpture to have survived – it demonstrates clearly how far the art of sculpture had advanced over the period.

At the beginning of the 14C, the bold array of flying buttresses was sent soaring over ambulatory and galleries to hold in place the high vaults of the east end.

Above the Kings' Gallery is the great rose window, still with its medieval glass. An enterprise of considerable daring – it was the largest such window of its time – its design is so accomplished that it shows no sign of distortion after 700 years and has often been imitated. Inside, the rose window has particularly fine stained glass of a deep bluish-mauve.

Sainte-Chapelle★★★

4 bd du Palais. &⊙*Open Mar–Oct 9.30am–6pm; Nov–Feb 9.30am–5pm.* ⊙*Closed 1 Jan, 1 May, 1 and 25 Dec.* ⊛*8€.* ✆*01 53 40 60 80. www.monum.fr.*
Only 80 years separate this definitive masterpiece of the High Gothic from the Transitional Gothic of Notre-Dame, but the difference is striking; in the lightness and clarity of its structure, the Sainte-Chapelle pushes Gothic ideas to the limit. The chapel was built on the orders of St Louis to house the recently acquired relics of the Passion within the precincts of the royal palace; it was completed in the record time of 33 months.

The upper chapel resembles a shrine with walls made almost entirely of remarkable stained glass covering a total area of 618sq m/6 672sq ft; 1 134 different scenes are depicted, of which 720 are made of original glass. The windows rise to a height of 15m/49ft. By 1240, the stained glass at Chartres had been completed, and the king was thus able to call on the master-craftsmen who had worked on them to come to Paris; this explains the similarity between the glass of cathedral and of chapel, in terms of the scenes shown and the luminous colour which eclipses the simplicity of the design.

The theme is Christ's Passion, including its foretelling by the Prophets and by John the Baptist, together with the episodes which lead up to it. The original rose window is shown in a scene from the Très Riches Heures du Duc de Berry; the present rose window is a product of the Flamboyant Gothic, ordered by Charles VII, and showing the Apocalypse of St John. It is characteristic of its age in the design of its tracery and in the subtle variations of colour which had replaced the earlier method of juxtaposing a great number of small coloured panes. The glass of the Sainte-Chapelle has been much imitated, even in architecturally inappropriate situations.

Abbaye de St-Germain-des-Prés★★

pl. Saint-Germain des Prés.
This most venerable of the city's churches reveals more than visual delights to those who know something of the history of its ancient stones. With the exception of Clovis, the Merovingian kings were buried here. The church was subsequently destroyed by the Normans, but restored in the course of the 10C and 11C. Understandably, the tower rising above the west front has a fortress-like character. Around 1160, the nave was enlarged and the chancel rebuilt in the new Gothic style. "Improvements" followed in the 17C (triforium and chancel windows) and in 1822 a somewhat over-zealous restoration took place.

But the church's years of glory were between 1631 and 1789, when the austere Congregation of St Maur made it a centre of learning and spirituality: the monks studied ancient inscriptions (epigraphy) and writing (paleography); the Church Fathers (Patristics), archaeology, cartography... Their library was confiscated at the time of the French Revolution.

Église St-Séverin-St-Nicolas★★

3 r. Prêtres St Séverin.
www.saint-severin.com.
This much-loved Latin Quarter Church has features from a number of architectural styles. The lower part of the portal and the first three bays of the nave are High Gothic; while much of the rest of the building was remodelled in Flamboyant style (upper part of the tower, the remainder of the nave, the secondary aisle, the highly compartmentalised vaulting of the chancel and the famous spiral pillar in the ambulatory). In the 18C, the pillars in the chancel were clad in wood and marble.

Église St-Eustache★★

2 Impasse Saint-Eustache. Open Mon–Fri 9.30am–7pm, Sat 10am–7pm, Sun 9am–7pm. Audioguides available, suggested donation 3€. 01 42 36 31 05. http://saint-eustache.org.
This was once the richest church in Paris, centre of the parish which included the areas around the Palais-Royal and the Halles market; its layout was modelled on that of Notre-Dame when building began in 1532. But St-Eustache took over a hundred years to complete; tastes changed, and the Gothic skeleton of the great building is fleshed out with Renaissance finishes and detail.

The Flamboyant style is evident in the three-storeyed interior elevation, in the vaulting of the choir, crossing and nave, in the lofty side aisles and in the flying buttresses. The Renaissance is exemplified in the Corinthian columns and in the return to the use of semicircular arches, and Classicism in P. de Champaigne's choir windows and in Colbert's tomb, designed by Le Brun in collaboration with Coysevox and Tuby. In the Chapelle St-Joseph is the English sculptor Raymond Mason's colourful commemoration of the fruit and vegetable market's move out of Paris in 1969.

Église Notre-Dame-du-Val-de-Grâce★★

1 pl. Laveran. Open Mon–Sat 2–6pm, Sun 9am–noon, 2–6pm.
01 43 29 12 31.
After many childless years, Anne of Austria commissioned François Mansart to design a church in thanksgiving for the birth of Louis XIV in 1638. The work was completed by Lemercier and Le Muet. The church recalls the Renaissance architecture of Rome; the dome, rising above the two-tier west front with its double triangular pediment, is particularly ornate and obviously inspired by St Peter's. Inside, the spirit of the Baroque prevails; there is polychrome paving, highly sculptured vaulting over the nave, massive crossing pillars and a monumental baldaquin with six wreathed columns. The **cupola**★★

was decorated by Mignard with a fresco featuring 200 figures.

URBAN DESIGN

Since the sweeping away of much of medieval Paris in the 19C, three central districts have come to typify particular stages in the city's evolution.

Le Marais★★★

Renaissance, Louis XIII and Louis XIV. Charles V's move to the Hôtel St-Paul in the Marais district in the 14C signalled the incorporation of a suburban area into Paris. The area soon became fashionable, and Rue St-Antoine the city's finest street. It was here that that characteristic French town house, the hôtel, took on its definitive form with the collaboration of the finest architects and artists; it became the setting for that other distinctive feature of Parisian life, the literary or philosophical salon.

The **Hôtel Lamoignon**★ (24 r. Pavée) of 1584 is a typical example of a mansion in the Henri III style. For the first time in Paris, its architect, Jean-Baptiste Androuet Du Cerceau, used the Giant Order with its flattened pilasters, Corinthian capitals and sculpted string-course.

The Henri IV style makes its appearance in the **Place des Vosges**★★★ designed by Louis Métezeau and completed in 1612. The 36 houses retain their original symmetrical appearance with arcades, two storeys with alternate brick and stone facings and steeply pitched slate roofs pierced with dormer windows. The

Place des Vosges

A. Éli/MICHELIN

King's Pavilion (Pavillon du Roi) is sited at the southern end of the square, balanced by the Queen's Pavilion (Pavillon de la Reine) at the sunnier northern end.

Louis XIII's reign heralds the Classical style. In 1624, Jean Androuet Du Cerceau built the **Hôtel de Sully★** (62 r. Saint-Antoine) with a gateway framed between massive pavilions and a main courtyard **(cour d'honneur★★★)** with triangular and curved pediments complemented by the scrolled dormer windows; beyond is an exquisite inner courtyard.

The early Louis XIV style is seen in Mansart's **Hôtel Guénégaud★★** (60 r. des Archives) of 1648, where its plain harmonious lines, majestic staircase and small formal garden make it one of the finest houses of the Marais; in Le Pautre's **Hôtel de Beauvais★** (68 r. François Miron) with its curved balcony on brackets and its ingenious internal layout; in the **Hôtel Carnavalet★** (23 r. de Sévigné), a Renaissance house rebuilt by Mansart in 1655; and in Cottard's **Hôtel Amelot-de-Bisseuil★** (47 r. Vieille-du-Temple) of somewhat theatrical design with its cornice and curved pediment decorated with allegorical figures.

The later Louis XIV style features in two adjoining *hôtels* built by Delamair: the **Hôtel de Rohan★★** (87 r. Vieille-du-Temple) with its wonderful sculpture of the *Horses of Apollo (Chevaux frémissants d'Apollon à l'abreuvoir)* by Robert Le Lorrain; and the **Hôtel de Soubise★★** (60 r. des Francs-Bourgeois) with its horseshoe-shaped courtyard and double colonnade. They are characterised by their raised ground floors, massive windows, roof balustrades and by the sculpture of their projecting central sections.

La Voie Triomphale (From the Tuileries to the Arc de Triomphe)★★★

A great axis leading from the courtyard of the Louvre to St Germain had been planned by Colbert, but today's "Triumphal Way" was laid out under Louis XVI, Napoleon III and during the years of the Third Republic.

Arc de Triomphe du Carrousel★
pl. du Carrousel.

This delightful pastiche of a Roman arch is decorated with statues of Napoleonic military men in full uniform. An observer standing in the Place du Carrousel commands an extraordinary perspective which runs from the Louvre, through the arch, to the obelisk in the Place de la Concorde, then onward and upward to the Grande Arche at the Défense.

Jardin des Tuileries★
r. de Rivoli.

The gardens were first laid out in the 1560s by Catherine de' Medici in the Italian style. A century later, they were remodelled by Le Nôtre, who here created the archetypal French garden, a formal setting for the elegant pleasures of outdoor life. The Riverside Terrace (Terrasse du Bord de l'Eau) became the playground of royal princes and of the sons of the two Napoleons, then of all the children of Paris.

Champs-Élysées★★★

In 1667, Le Nôtre extended the axis from the Tuileries to a new focal point, the Rond-Point, which he laid out himself. The avenue was then a service road for the houses facing the Rue du Faubourg-St-Honoré, but very soon refreshment stalls were set up and crowds flocked to the area. In 1724, the Duc d'Antin planted rows of elms to extend the "Elysian Fields" up to the Étoile. In 1729, street lanterns lit the evening scene.

Forty-eight years on, and the avenue had descended the gentle slope beyond the Étoile to reach the Seine at the Pont de Neuilly. The buildings lining it included taverns and wine-shops, the later haunt of Robespierre and his friends. Finally, in 1836, the **Arc de Triomphe★★★** was completed by Louis-Philippe.

The Champs-Élysées became fashionable during the reign of Louis-Napoleon, when high society flocked to the restaurants (like Ledoyen's), to the theatres (like the Folies Marigny and the Bouffes d'Été where Offenbach's operettas were performed), or to receptions in the grand houses (like no 25, today occupied by the Travellers' Club, with its doors of bronze and its onyx staircase).

The avenue has undergone much change since 1914. Its character nowadays is determined by its luxury shops, expensive cafés, and motor showrooms; but it nevertheless remains the capital's rallying point at times of high national emotion (the Liberation, 30 May 1968, the funeral of De Gaulle in 1970, and annually on July 14).

La Défense★★

An outstanding architectural achievement, La Défense has nothing in common with the traditional business districts found in most city centres.

A 1 200m/3 937ft terraced podium, pleasantly punctuated with gardens, fountains and shaded spots, runs from the Seine up to La Grande Arche. It is lined with an impressive ensemble of huge towers (Tour Fiat: 178m/584ft) that compose a dazzling tableau of radiant light. It is also noted for many outdoor works by distinguished modern sculptors, which turn the district into an informal, open-air museum.

La Grande Arche★★

Open daily Sept–Mar 10am–7pm; Apr–Aug 10am–8pm. 10€. 01 49 07 27 27. www.grandearche.com.

The Danish architect Johan Otto von Spreckelsen designed this vast hollow cube which stands at the end of the esplanade and houses private firms as well as several ministries. The Cathédrale Notre-Dame with its spire could fit into the space between the walls of the arch. Each side of the cube is 110m/360ft long. Towering 100m/328ft above the esplanade, the 2.4 acres/1ha terrace-roof is partly taken up by temporary exhibition rooms. From the belvedere visitors will also be able to admire Paris and its suburbs. At the foot of the arch lies the Palais de la Défence (CNIT): it was the first to be built (1958) and has been "rejuvenated". Now it is an important business centre focusing on three main

La Défense seen from Arc de Triomphe, La Grande Arche in the middle

©naphtalina/iStockphoto.com

areas of activity: technology, world trade and corporate communication.

Bercy

The modernised Bercy district boasts a Palais Omnisports by architects Andrault, Parat and Gavan; the **Cinémathèque Française** *(51 r. de Bercy; www.cinema theque.fr)*, which hosts the largest archive of films in the world; the imposing buildings of the **Finance Ministry** designed by Chemetow and Huidobro – part of the structure rises above the Seine and the **Jardins de la Mémoire** with three planted areas.

Across the river, the **Bibliothèque nationale de France-François-Mitterrand★** *(Quai François-Mauriac; www.bnf.fr)* by Dominique Perrault – four tower blocks in the shape of open books – was the last of the "great projects" carried out under the former President.

La Villette★★

The **Parc★ de la Villette** is the largest architectural ensemble within the city. The 55ha/135 acre site houses an impressive urban complex featuring the **Cité des Sciences et de l'Industrie** (City of Science and Industry, ⚫ *see entry*) and its cinema La Géode, the Zenith concert hall, the Paris-Villette Theatre, La Grande Halle and the Cité de la Musique.

POLITICAL AND INTELLECTUAL SIGHTS

In addition to the city's famous monuments, churches and modern structures, other buildings and districts have come to be identified with the political and intellectual aspects of Paris.

Hôtel de Ville★
pl. de l'Hôtel de Ville.
It is from here that central Paris is governed. Municipal government was introduced in the 13C, under the direction of leading members of the powerful watermen's guild appointed by Louis IX.
The place has long been the epicentre of uprising and revolt. Throughout the French Revolution it was in the hands of the Commune, and in 1848 it was the seat of the Provisional Government. The Republic was proclaimed from here in 1870, and, on 24 March 1871, the Communards burnt it down. It was rebuilt from 1874.

Institut de France★★
quai Conti. ✆01 44 41 44 41.
www.institut-de-france.fr.
The Institute originated as the College of Four Nations founded by Mazarin for scholars from the provinces incorporated into France during his ministry (Piedmont, Alsace, Artois and Roussillon). Dating from 1662, its building was designed by Le Vau and stands on the far side of the river from the Louvre. The Institute is made up of five academies:
The Académie Française, founded 1635; Académie des Beaux-Arts, 1816; Académie des Inscriptions et Belles Lettres, 1663; Académie des Sciences, 1666; and Académie des Sciences morales et politiques, 1795.

Montmartre★★★
The "Martyrs' Hill" was a real village before becoming the haunt of artists and Bohemians in the late 19C, and it still has something of the picturesque quality of a village in its steep and narrow lanes and precipitous stairways. The "Butte",

On 19 December 1915, Édith Giovanna Gassion was born to abject poverty on the steps of no 72 r. de Belleville. She later sang in the streets, before becoming a radio, gramophone and music-hall success in 1935 under the name of **Édith Piaf**. Beloved for the instinctive but deeply moving tones of her voice, she came to embody the spirit of France (*La vie en rose, Les cloches*).

Another famous figure was Maurice Chevalier (1888–1972), film star, entertainer and cabaret singer *(chansonnier)*; he paired with Jeanne Mistinguett at the Folies Bergère (1911) and sang at the Casino de Paris between the wars. Before attaining fame on Broadway in blacktie and boater, he was known at home for songs that are rooted in Belleville: *Ma Pomme, Prosper and un gars du Ménilmontant*.

or mound, rises abruptly from the city's sea of roofs; at its centre is the **Place du Tertre**★★ with the former town hall at no. 3, still enjoying some semblance of local life, at least in the morning; by the afternoon, tourism has taken over, and the "art market" is in full swing.

Not far away from all this activity rises the exotic outline of the **Basilique du Sacré-Cœur**★★ *(r. du Chevalier-de-la-Barre;* ❧5€; ✆01 53 41 89 09; *www.sacre-coeur-montmartre.com)*, a place of perpetual pilgrimage. From here, particularly from the gallery of the dome, there is an incomparable **panorama**★★★ over the whole metropolitan area.

Palais de l'Élysée
55 r. du Faubourg Saint-Honoré.

The palace has been the Paris residence of the President of France since 1873. It was built in 1718 by Henri de La Tour d'Auvergne.

Palais Bourbon★
126 r. de l'Université.
The palace of 1722 has been the seat of the Lower House of France's parliament, the Assemblée Nationale, for more than 150 years.

Palais du Luxembourg★★
15 r. de Vaugirard.
This is the seat of the Senate, the French Upper House. The president of the Senate exercises the functions of Head of State if the Presidency falls vacant. It was constructed in the early 17C by the Regent, Marie de' Medici, who wished

Basilique du Sacré-Cœur atop Montmartre

S. Sauvignier/MICHELIN

to have a palace of her own which would remind her of the Pitti Palace in Florence.

Quartier Latin★★★

Lying on the left bank of the Seine, and on the slopes of the mount, **"Montagne" Ste-Geneviève**, and the surrounding area are concentrated many of the capital's most venerable institutions, notably the Sorbonne, the country's most illustrious university, founded 1253.

Around them is the ebb and flow of a perpetually youthful tide, the students and other young people who make up the population of the "Latin" Quarter (so-called because Latin was the language of instruction right up to the French Revolution).

The area abounds in publishing houses, bookshops, and terrace cafés, including the legendary Flore *(172 bd St Germain)*, Deux-Magots *(6 pl. St Germain des Prés)* and Procope *(13 r. Ancienne Comédie)*.

Quartier de St-Germain-des-Prés★★

Antique dealers, literary cafés, the night life of side streets all combine to create the reputation of this former centre of international Bohemian life.

MUSEUMS

The city has a total of 87 museums and over 100 art galleries. In addition, there are around 30 places where temporary exhibitions are held and a whole array of studios (particularly around the Rue St-Honoré, Avenue Matignon and the Rue de la Seine), as well as libraries and other institutions. Between them, they offer the visitor a continuously changing view of past and present artistic achievement and aspiration. The most famous include the Grand Palais, the Palais de Tokyo, the Pavillon des Arts, the Petit Palais, the Pompidou Centre and the Grande Halle de la Villette.

🏛️ MUSÉE DU LOUVRE★★★

🔆 *See Civil Architecture for the history of the Louvre Palace.* ⏰*Open Wed–Mon 9am–6pm (Wed and Fri 10pm), 24 and 31 Dec 9am–5pm.* ⏰*Closed 1 Jan, 1 May, 11 Nov, 25 Dec.* **Hall Napoleon** *open Wed–Mon 9am–10pm. Please check calender for unscheduled room closures.* *Permanent Collections with Musée Delacroix included 9€; Wed and Fri 6–9.45pm 6€; child and 14 Jul no charge; temporary exhibitions 9.50€; Combined tickets are 13€, Wed and Fri 6–9.45pm 11€; tickets can be bought in advance at Fnac (𝒫0892 68 46 94; 1.50€surcharge), and Ticketnet (𝒫0892 39 01 00; 1.10€ surcharge). www.louvre.fr.*

Palais du Luxembourg

J.P. Clapham/MICHELIN

The Louvre and the pyramid

S. Sauvignier/MICHELIN

THE LOUVRE: GENERAL INFORMATION

Info: General information ℘01 40 20 51 51 (recorded message); ℘01 40 20 53 17 to speak to someone at the desk (six languages); www.louvre.fr. Some galleries are closed on certain days (or for restoration); check the schedule of open rooms online or call in advance. Fourteen video screens in the hall provide information about daily events at the museum. There is also a general activity programme (six languages) available at the main information desk, which comes out every three months. **Audioguides** can be hired (six languages) on the mezzanine level in the various wings.

Location: The main entrance to the museum is at the Pyramid. There is also an entrance through the shopping mall of the Carrousel du Louvre (metro stop Palais-Royal-Musée-du-Louvre (lines 1 and 7)), on either side of the Arc du Carrousel, or at the Porte des Lions. You will find yourself in the well-lit **Napoleon Hall**, which leads you towards the three wings of the museum: Denon, Richelieu and Sully. There is a bookshop, restaurant and auditorium.

Parking: The closest underground car park (80 coaches, 620 cars) is **Parking Carrousel-Louvre**, located on avenue du Général Lemonnier.

Open daily 7am–11pm. Fees from 12.20€. After parking, enter the museum via the shopping mall of the Carrousel by the fortifications of Charles V.

Don't Miss: Of all the artworks inside the museum, probably the most famous are Leonardo's masterpiece, The *Mona Lisa* (here called La Joconde) and among the classical works, the *Victoire de Samothrace* and the *Vénus de Milo*. All three are in the Denon section.

Timing: The Louvre cannot be enjoyed in its entirety even in several visits, let alone one. From the list of artworks below, decide what you would like to see and head for your selections. The information desks offer a variety of aids and amenities to enhance your visit. Audio guides are available or choose one of the thematic trails (provided on leaflets) designed for all ages that allow you to discover both masterpieces and less well-known works while exploring a particular theme, such as the Da Vinci Code.

Kids: Children aged 4 and up can take part in one of the many workshops for young people or follow a Children's Route through the museum. Call or check the website for details.

Musée du Louvre★★★
Room by Room

Choose which section of the museum to visit:
Sully
- History of the Louvre: *Entresol.*
- Medieval Louvre: *Entresol.*
- Egyptian Antiquities: *Ground and 1st floors.*
- Greek Antiquities (Cariatides room, Hellenic period): *Ground floor.*
- Oriental Antiquities (Iran and art of the Levant): *Ground floor.*
- Greek Antiquities (Bronze room, Campana gallery): *1st floor.*
- 17–18C objets d'art: *1st floor.*
- 17–19C French painting, including Graphic arts: *2nd floor.*
- Beistegui collection (room A): *2nd floor.*

Denon
- Italian sculpture: *Entresol and Ground floor.*
- Scandinavian sculpture: *Entresol.*
- Roman and Coptic Egypt: *Entresol (rooms A, B and C).*
- Greek Antiquities: *Ground and 1st floors.*
- Etruscan and Roman Antiquities: *Ground floor.*
- Italian painting: *1st floor.*
- Spanish painting: *1st floor.*
- 19C French painting (large sizes): *1st floor.*
- Objets d'art (Apollon gallery): *1st floor.*

Richelieu
- Exhibitions-documents: *Entresol.*
- Islamic art: *Entresol (closed until 2010; will reopen in Denon).*
- French sculpture (Marly and Puget rooms): *Ground floor.*
- Oriental Antiquities (Mesopotamia): *Ground floor.*
- Objets d'art (including Napoleon III's apartments): *1st floor.*
- 14–17C French painting: *2nd floor.*
- Scandinavian schools: *2nd floor.*

Select what to see within the chosen section:
Oriental Antiquities
- Statues of *Gudea* and *Ur-Ningirsu* – Mesopotamia: c 2150 BC
- *Code of Hammurabi* – Babylon: c 1750 BC
- *Frieze of the Archers* from Darius' palace – Susa: 6C BC
- Low-reliefs from Nineveh and Khorsabad – Assyria: 7C BC
- Vase from Amathus – Cyprus: early 5C BC

Egyptian Antiquities
- Gebel-el-Arak knife – Egypt: c. 300–3200 BC
- *Sphinx* of the Crypt – Egypt: c. 2600 BC
- Jewellery of Rameses II – middle of second millennium
- *Seated Scribe* from Sakkara – Egypt: Fifth Dynasty
- Funerary chapel of Akhout-Hetep – Fifth Dynasty
- Fragments from the Coptic monastery of Bawit – 5C

Classical Antiquities

- *Kore* from the Temple of Hera at Samos – Greece: archaic period
- *La Dame d'Auxerre (Lady of Auxerre)* – Greece: c. 640–630BC
- *Apollo of Piombino* – Greece: 1C BC
- *Venus de Milo* – Greece: Hellenistic period
- Parthenon fragments (metopes) – Greece: Classical period
- *Etruscan terracotta* sarcophagus from Cerveteri, Italy: 6C BC
- *Victoire de Samothrace (Winged Victory)* – Greece: Hellenistic period

Sculpture

- Limewood *Madonna* from the Church of the Antonites, Isenheim – late 15C
- *Diana the Huntress* (fountain) from Château d'Anet – French Renaissance
- *The Three Graces* (funerary monument for Henri II) by Germain Pilon
- *The Four Evangelists* by Jean Goujon
- *Madonna and Child* (terracotta) by Donatello – Florence c. 1450
- Marble bust of *Voltaire* by Houdon: 1778
- *The Slaves* by Michelangelo – Florence: early 16C

Painting

- Malouel's circular *Pietà* – Dijon: c. 1400
- St Denis Altarpiece by Henri Bellechose – Dijon: c. 1415–1416
- Avignon *Pietà* by Enguerrand Quarton – c. 1455
- Portrait of *François I* by Jean Clouet – Loire Valley School
- *St Thomas* by Georges de La Tour – 17C *Gilles* by Watteau – c. 1718–1719
- Portrait of *Mme Récamier and Sacre de Napoleon I*
  (The Coronation of Napoleon) by David
- *La Baigneuse de Valpinçon (The Turkish Bath)* and *Grande Odalisque* by Ingres
- *Scène des massacres de Scio (Scenes of the Massacres of Chios)* by Delacroix – 1824
- *Le Radeau de la Méduse (Raft of the Medusa)* by Géricault – 1819
- *Maestà (Virgin with Angels and Saints)* by Cimabue – Florence: c. 1280
- *La Couronnement de la Vierge (Coronation of the Virgin)* by Fra Angelico –
  Florence: c. 1430
- *La Joconde (The Gioconda – Mona Lisa)* by Leonardo da Vinci –
- Florence: c. 1503–1506
- *Les Noces de Cana (The Wedding at Cana)* by Veronese – Venice: 1563
- *La Mort de la Vierge (Death of the Virgin)* by Caravaggio – Naples: early 17C
- *Le Jeune Mendiant (Young Beggar)* by Murillo – Seville: c. 1645–1650
- *La Vierge du chancelier Rolin (The Rolin Madonna)* by Jan van Eyck – Dijon: c. 1435
- *Charles I of England* by Van Dyck – England: 17C
- *Vie et règne de Marie de Médicis* – allegorical paintings of the *Life of Marie de'*
  Medici by Rubens
- *Les Pèlerins d'Emmaüs (Pilgrims at Emmaus)* by Rembrandt c. 1660

Objets d'art

- The Regent Diamond and Crown Jewels of France
- Ivory figure of the Virgin Mary from the Sainte-Chapelle, Paris: middle of the 13C
- The *Hunts of Maximilian* tapestries – Brussels: 1537
- The study of the Elector of Bavaria by Boulle – early 18C
- Clock in ebony case inlaid with tortoiseshell by Boulle – early 18C
- Monkey commode (gilded bronze) by Charles Cressent – 1740
- The *Loves of the Gods* tapestries – Gobelins: mid-18C
- Writing-desk, table and commode in the Oeben room – mid-18C
- Medici vase (Sèvres porcelain, bronzes by Thomire)

When the Grand Louvre was opened to the public in 1994, the different collections were divided into three large departments, **Sully**, **Denon** and **Richelieu**, which are located in the two wings and around the Cour Carrée.

OTHER MAJOR MUSEUMS
Musée d'Orsay★★★

62 r. de Lille. ♿🕐*Open Tue–Sun 9.30am–6pm, Thu 9.30am–9.45pm.* 🕐*Closed 1 Jan, 1 May, 25 Dec.* ✎*8€ for the permanent collection, 9.50€ for access to the permanent and temporary collections; no charge 1st Sun in the month.* ✆*01 40 49 48 14. www.musee-orsay.fr.*

The focus of the museum is the period 1848 to 1914. The upper floor is dedicated to the Impressionists, with one of the world's finest collections. There is a considerable collection of pre- and post-Impressionist works. Other sections include decorative arts and photography.

Highlights include:

La Source (The Spring) by Ingres – 1846
Un enterrement à Ornans (Burial at Ornans) by Courbet – c. 1849–50
Des Glaneuses (Gleaners) and *L'Angélus (Angelus)* by Jean-François Millet
Le Déjeuner sur l'herbe and *Olympia* by Manet – 1863
La Danse (The Dance), sculpture by Jean-Baptiste Carpeaux – 1868

Le golfe de Marseille vu de L'Estaque (Marseille Bay from L'Estaque) by Cézanne – c. 1878–1879
Les Danseuses bleues (Blue Dancers) and *Dans un café (The Absinthe Drinker)* by Degas
L'Église d'Auvers-sur-Oise (The church at Auvers-sur-Oise) and *Autoportrait (Self-Portrait)* by Van Gogh
Le Cirque (The Circus) by Seurat
Aréarea joyeusetés (Women of Tahiti) by Gauguin – 1892
Jane Avril dansant (Jane Avril Dancing) by Toulouse-Lautrec – 1892
Balzac by Rodin – 1898
The Mediterranean by Maillol – 1902
Pendant and chain by René Lalique
Héraclès Archer (Hercules the Archer) in bronze by Antoine Bourdelle – 1909
Les Baigneuses (Women Bathing) by Renoir – c. 1918–19

Musée National d'Art Moderne (Centre George Pompidou)★★★

pl. Georges-Pompidou. ♿🕐*Open daily 11am–9pm (last admission 1hr before closing).* **Atelier Brancusi** *Wed–Mon 2–6pm. Museum and exhibitions* ✎*12€; free 1st Sun in the month.* ✆*01 44 78 12 33. www.centrepompidou.fr.*

The Centre seeks to demonstrate that there is a close correlation between art and daily activities. For both the specialists and the general public, this multi-purpose cultural centre offers an astonishing variety of activities and modern communication techniques encouraging curiosity and participation. The Centre includes four departments: the **Bibliothèque Publique d'Information** (BPI), offering a wide variety of French and foreign books, slides, films, periodicals and reference catalogues; the **Musée National d'Art Moderne – Centre de Création Industrielle** (MNAM – CCI), the former presenting collections of paintings, sculptures and drawings from 1905 to the present time, and the latter demonstrating the relationship between individuals and spaces, objects and signs through

Musée d'Orsay,

©Musée d'Orsay/Sophie Boegly

Centre George Pompidou

S. Sauvignier/MICHELIN

architecture, urbanism, industrial design and visual communication; the **Institut de Recherche et Coordination Acoustique/Musique** (IRCAM), bringing together musicians, composers and scientists for the purpose of sound experimentation.

Highlights include:

La Rue pavoisée (Street Bedecked with Bunting) by Dufy – Fauvism: 1906

Le Guéridon (Table) by Braque – Cubism: 1911

Nus de dos (Nudes) by Matisse – beginnings of Abstraction: 1916

Arlequin (Harlequin) by Picasso – mature Cubism: 1923

La Vache spectrale (Spectral Cow) by Dali – beginnings of Hyper-realism: 1928

Le Phoque (Seal), sculpture by Brancusi – Surrealism in sculpture: c. 1943–46

Hôtel de Cluny (Musée du Moyen Âge)★★

Hôtel de Cluny, 6 Place Paul Painlevé. ○*Open Wed–Mon 9.15am–5.45pm; desk closes at 5.15pm.* ○*Closed 1 Jan, 1 May, 25 Dec.* ⊜*7.50€ (audioguide included); free 1st Sun in month (audioguide 1€).* ☏*01 53 73 78 16. www.musee-moyenage.fr.*

Highlights include:

Ivory casket – Constantinople: early 11C

Gilt altar-front made for Henri II – Basle cathedral: 11C

29 medallions from the stained glass of the Sainte-Chapelle – Paris: 13C

Limoges reliquaries in *champlevé* enamel – 13C

Golden rose given by Pope Clement V to the Prince-Bishop of Basle: early 14C

Eagle of St John (brass lectern) – Tournai cathedral: 1383

Life of St Stephen tapestry – Arras: mid-15C

Altarpiece from Limburg in painted and gilded wood – late 15C

Lady and the Unicorn tapestries – Brussels: late 15C

Mary Magdalene (probable likeness of Mary of Burgundy) – Flanders

Musée de l'Orangerie★★

Jardin des Tuileries. ♿○*Open Wed–Mon 9am–6pm.* ○*Closed 1 May, 25 Dec.* ⊜*7.50€; 2€ surcharge for temporary exhibitions; free 1st Sun in*

Paris Museum Pass

This pass is valid for 2, 4 or 6 consecutive days (⊜40€, 58€, 76€ respectively) and provides unlimited access to more than 70 museums in and around Paris. It is on sale at each of the museums and at city tourist offices. Passholders do not have to queue for admission. www.museums-in-paris.com/museum_pass.php.

month. 🔊Guided tours (1hr30min)
8€. ℘01 44 77 80 07. www.musee-
orangerie.fr.

Highlights include:
Portrait of Mme Cézanne by Cézanne
Baigneuse aux cheveux longs (Woman Bathing) and *Femme à la lettre (The Letter-Writer)* by Renoir
Nude on red background by Picasso – 1906
La Carriole du père Junier (Père Junier's Cart) by Douanier Rousseau – 1908
Maison de Berlioz (Berlioz' House) and *Église de Clignancourt* by Utrillo
Antonia by Modigliani
Nymphéas (Water-lilies) from Giverny by Claude Monet
Les Trois Soeurs (The Three Sisters) by Matisse
Le Petit Pâtissier (The Little Pastry-cook) and *Garçon d'étage (The Attendant)* by Soutine – 1922
Arlequin à la guitare (Harlequin with Guitar) and *Le Modèle blond (Blond Model)* by Derain

Musée de l'Armée (Hôtel des Invalides)★★★
🕯See *Église du Dôme*. ℘0810 11 33 99.
www.invalides.org.

Highlights include:
Seussenhofer's suit of armour for François I – 1539
Model of the city of Perpignan (one of a series ordered by Vauban in 1696)

Cité des Sciences et de l'Industrie

©CSI/Sophie Chivet

Napoleon's flag of farewell flown at Fontainebleau on 20 April 1814
The room where Napoleon died on St Helena (reconstruction)
The Armistice Bugle (which sounded the cease-fire at 9pm on 7 November 1918)

👥 Cité des Sciences et de l'Industrie★★★
30 ave Corentin-Cariou. 🕯🕐*Open Tue–Sat 10am–6pm, Sun 10am–7pm.* 🕐*Closed 1 May and 25 Dec.* 🎫*6€– 10.50€. ℘01 40 05 70 00. www.cite-sciences.fr.*
Built in response to the growing need of young and old alike to have a better understanding of the scientific and industrial world, this living museum encourages visitors to investigate, learn and have fun through a wide range of edifying and entertaining scenarios.

Highlights include:
L'Argonaute (a submarine formerly in use with the French Navy)
Le Nautile (full-size model of research submarine)
Voyager 2 space probe
Model of Ariane 5 rocket (scale 1:5)
Le Robot-mouche (a glimpse into the future development of bionics)

Cité des Enfants★
🕯 *See above for opening times.*
The ground floor of the Cité is desig-nated especially for young, encouraging scientific discovery through experimen-tation and play. It's cleverly divided into two sections: ages 2–7, and ages 5–12.

👥 La Géode★★★
In the park just outside the museum. The most comfortable viewing is from the top of the hall. 🕐*Open Tue–Sun 10.30am–8.30pm (hourly sessions).* 🎫*10.50€ (child 9€). ℘01 44 84 44 84. www.lageode.fr.*
The Cité's extraordinary reflective spherical cinema and its circular screen (diameter: 36m/118ft), which rests on a sheet of water, is a remarkable technical achievement, whose bold conception and perfect execution is the work of the engineer Chamayou.

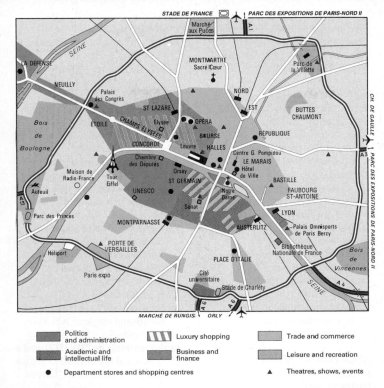

Politics and administration
Academic and intellectual life
● Department stores and shopping centres

|||| Luxury shopping
Business and finance

Trade and commerce
Leisure and recreation
▲ Theatres, shows, events

Musée du Quai Branly★★

37 quai Branly. ○*Open Tue, Wed, Sun 11am–7pm, Thu–Sat 11am–9pm.* ⊗*8.50€.* ✆*01 56 61 70 00.* *www.quaibranly.fr.*

Modern purpose built museum opened in 2006, located on the left bank of the Seine near the Eiffel Tower, exhibiting indigenous art from Africa, Asia, Oceania and the Americas.

♣♣ Palais de la Découverte★★

ave Franklin-D.-Roosevelt. ○*Open Tue–Sat 9.30am–6pm, Sun and public holidays 10am–7pm (last entrance 30min before closing).* ○*Closed 1 Jan, 1 May, 14 Jul, 15 Aug, 25 Dec.* ⊗*7€ (child 4.50€); Planetarium 3.50€.* ✆*01 56 43 20 20.*

This children's museum is a marvel of ingenuity and interest, with clever animators to bring the exhibits to life. **Highlights include:**
School of Rats
The Planetarium

Lunakhod (Soviet moon buggy) – 12 November 1970
Fragment of moon-rock – Apollo Mission XVII: 1972
The number Pi and the 703 prime numbers of the 16 000 000 decimals calculated

Musée du Quai Branly

©Bruno Bernier/Fotolia.com

Musée des Arts et Métiers★★

60 r. Réaumur. ○*Open Tue–Sun 10am–6pm (Thu 9.30pm).* ○*Closed 1 May, 25 Dec.* ∞*6.50€.* ℘*01 53 01 82 00. www.arts-et-metiers.net.*

Highlights include:

Microscope belonging to the Duke of Chaulnes – mid-18C
Cugnot's steam-carriage of 1771
Marie-Antoinette's automaton "Dulcimer-Player" – 1784
Jacquard loom
Thimonnier's sewing-machine – 1825
Foucault's pendulum (proving the rotation of the Earth)
L'Obéissante automobile by Amédée Bollée Snr – 1873
The Lumière brothers' cinemato-graphic apparatus – 1895
Transmitting station from the Eiffel Tower
Blériot's No 9 aeroplane (in which he made the first cross-Channel flight)

ADDITIONAL MUSEUMS

Musée Picasso *(5 r. Thorigny)*
Musée Rodin *(77 r. Varenne)*
Musée Carnavalet *(29 r. de Sévigné)*
Musée d'Art et Histoire du Judaïsme *(71 r. du Temple)*
Musée de la Magie *(11 r. Saint Paul)*
Musée Marmottan *(2 r. Louis Boilly)*
Musée d'Art Moderne de la Ville de Paris *(11 ave du Président Wilson)*

PARKS AND GARDENS

The city has as many as 450 parks, public gardens and green spaces, some perfect for a rest and some fresh air, or a place for children to play; other parks are prestigious and historic, and perhaps adorned with fine sculpture.

Highlights include:

Bois de Vincennes, 4 458 acre/995ha including the Parc Floral.
Bois de Boulogne, 2 090 acre/846ha with the Bagatelle, iris and rose gardens.
Jardin des Plantes, historic Botanic Gardens of Paris.
Jardin des Tuileries, with its ancient and modern stauray.
Jardin du Luxembourg, very agreeable Latin Quarter park with a circular pond alongside a palace, popular with students and with big play areas for children.
Parc Montsouris and Square des Batignolles, examples of "Jardins Anglais", with less formal layout.
Parc Paysager des Buttes-Chaumont, without doubt the most picturesque.
Jardin du Palais-Royal, a haven of silence and elegance in the very heart of Paris.
Jardin japonais de l'UNESCO, in the grounds of the UNESCO headquar-ters, it is also known as "Garden of Peace".
Jardin du Musée Rodin, ideal spot to prolong the museum visit and discover magnificent city view along its pathways.
Parc Monceau, where it is enjoyable to encounter statues of Musset, Maupassant, Chopin and others.
Parc André-Citroën, the most sophis-ticated.
Parc de La Villette, the largest in Paris.
Parc de Belleville, with views across the whole city.
Parc de Bercy, recalling the wine-dealing past of this modernised district.

ADDRESSES

🛏 STAY

🍴🛏 **Louvre Ste-Anne** – *32 r. Ste-Anne, 75001.* ⊙*Pyramides.* ✆*01 40 20 02 35. www.louvre-ste-anne.fr. 20 rooms.* In a street lined with Japanese restaurants, this hotel has small but well-equipped rooms decorated in pastel shades. Vaulted breakfast room.

🍴🛏 **Etats-Unis Opéra** – *16 r. d'Antin, 75002.* ⊙*Opéra.* ✆*01 42 65 05 05. www.hotel-paris-opera.com. 45 rooms.* Nestled by a quiet street, this hotel in a 1930s building offers modern, comfortable rooms. Breakfast is served in the inviting English-style bar.

🍴🛏 **Hôtel des Archives** – *87 r. des Archives, 75003.* ⊙*Temple.* ✆*01 44 78 08 00. www.hoteldesarchives.com. 19 rooms.* Charming hotel near the National Archives, with small yet prettily decorated, comfortable rooms. Some have original exposed beams.

🍴🛏 **Beaubourg** – *11 r. S. Le Franc, 75004.* ⊙*Rambuteau.* ✆*01 42 74 34 24. www.hotelbeaubourg.com. 28 rooms.* Nestled in a tiny street behind the Georges-Pompidou Centre. Some of the friendly rooms have exposed stone walls and wooden beams.

🍴🛏 **Familia** – *11 r. des Ecoles, 75005.* ⊙*Cardinal Lemoine, 75005.* ✆*01 43 54 55 27. www.familiahotel.com. 30 rooms.* Notre-Dame and the Collège des Bernardins provide the backdrop for rustic rooms adorned with sepia frescoes of the monuments of Paris.

🍴🛏 **Eiffel Park Hôtel** – *17 bis r. Amélie, 75007.* ⊙*La Tour Maubourg.* ✆*01 45 55 10 01. www.eiffelpark.com. 36 rooms.* From the Indian and Chinese artefacts to the ethnic fabrics, exoticism reigns through this elegant hotel. Rooftop summer terrace complete with bee hives.

🍴🛏 **Elysées Mermoz** – *30 r. J. Mermoz, 75008.* ⊙*Franklin D. Roosevelt.* ✆*01 42 25 75 30. www.hotel-elysees mermoz.com. 22 rooms.* This cosy hotel has rooms in sunny colours or shades of grey. Varnished wood panelling and blue stone in the bathrooms as well as a cane furnished lounge.

🍴🛏 **Nord et Est** – *49 r. Malte, 75011.* ⊙*Oberkampf.* ✆*01 47 00 71 70. www.paris-hotel-nordest.com. 45 rooms.* The warm family atmosphere and reasonable prices draw regulars to this hotel near Place de la République. Ask for one of the refurbished rooms.

🍴🛏 **Delambre** – *35 r. Delambre, 75014.* ⊙*Edgar Quinet.* ✆*01 43 20 66 31. 30 rooms.* French poet André Breton stayed in this hotel located in a quiet street close to Montparnasse railway station. The rooms are simple but bright, and many are spacious.

🍴🛏 **Aberotel** – *24 r. Blomet, 75015.* M°*Volontaires.* ✆*01 40 61 70 50. www.aberotel.com. 28 rooms.* A popular hotel with stylish rooms and an inner courtyard for summer breakfasts. It has a pleasant lounge adorned with paintings of playing cards.

🍴🛏 **Le Hameau de Passy** – *48 r. Passy, 75016.* ⊙*La Muette.* ✆*01 42 88 47 55. www.hameaudepassy.com. 32 rooms.* A private lane leads to this hamlet with a charming inner courtyard overrun with greenery. Quite nights ensured in the small, well-maintained rooms.

🍴 EAT

🍴🍴 **Pharamond** – *24 r. de la Grande-Truanderie, 75001.* ⊙*Châtelet-Les-Halles.* ✆*01 40 28 45 18. www.pharamond.fr.* An institution dating back to the heyday of Les Halles. The Pharamond still serves traditional dishes (tripes and offal a speciality). Authentic 1900s decor.

🍴🍴 **Vaudeville** – *29, r. Vivienne, 75002.* ⊙*Bourse.* ✆*01 40 20 04 62. www.vaudevilleparis.com.* This large Brasserie with its sparkling Art Deco details in pure Parisian style is especially lively after theatre performances. Classical menu.

🍴🍴 **Le Carré des Vosges** – *15 r. St-Gilles, 75003.* ⊙*Chemin Vert.* ✆*01 42 71 22 21. www.lecarredesvosges.fr.* Friendly bistro a stone's throw from the Rue des Francs-Bourgeois and its trendy boutiques. Well-prepared market cuisine with fish to the fore.

🍴🍴 **Bofinger** – *5 r. Bastille, 75004.* ⊙*Bastille.* ✆*01 42 72 87 82. www.bofinger paris.com.* The famous clients and remarkable decor have bestowed enduring renown on this brasserie created in 1864. The interior boasts a finely worked cupola and a room on the 1st floor decorated by Hansi.

⊜⊜**Atelier Maître Albert** – *1 r. Maître Albert, 75005.* ⋒*Maubert Mutualité.* ℘*01 56 81 30 01. www.ateliermaitrealbert.com.* A huge medieval fireplace and spits for roast meat take pride of place in this handsome interior. Guy Savoy is responsible for the mouth-watering menu.

⊜⊜**Florimond** – *19 av. La Motte-Picquet, 75007.* ⋒*Ecole Militaire.* ℘*01 45 55 40 38.* Pocket-sized restaurant named after Monet's gardener in Giverny. Bistro decor, popular with locals for its tasty traditional cooking.

⊜⊜⊟**La Maison de l'Aubrac** – *37 r. Marbeuf, 75008.* ⋒*Franklin D. Roosevelt.* ℘*01 43 59 05 14. www.maison-aubrac.fr.* Aveyron farmhouse-style decor, generous portions of rustic cuisine (with an emphasis on Aubrac beef) and an excellent wine list. Close to Champs-Elysées.

⊜⊜**Chardenoux** – *1, rue Jules Vallès, 75011.* ⋒*Charonne.* ℘*01 43 71 49 52.* Reopened under the chef Cyril Lignac on its 100th anniversary, this bistro is bringing back traditional cuisine. Decor of yesteryear: marble counter, zinc bar and painted ceiling.

⊜⊜⊟**La Coupole** – *102 boul. Montparnasse, 75014.* ⋒*Vavin.* ℘*01 43 20 14 20. www.flobrasseries.com.* The spirit of Montparnasse lives in this huge Art Déco brasserie opened in 1927. The 24 pillars were decorated by artists of the period, while the cupola sports a new contemporary fresco**.**

⊜⊜**Le Troquet** – *21 r. François Bonvin, 75015.* ⋒*Cambronne.* ℘*01 45 66 89 00.* An authentic Parisian bar: single set menu shown on the blackboard, retro-style dining room, and tasty market- based cuisine. For locals… and others.

⊜⊜**Bistro de la Muette** – *10 chaussée de la Muette, 75016.* ⋒*Mo La Muette.* ℘*01 45 03 14 84. www.bistrocie.fr.* The very attractive, all-inclusive formula of this elegant bistro explains part of its appeal in the neighbourhood. Warm, modern decor in brown colours. Veranda.

⌨ENTERTAINMENT

Consult publications such as *L'Officiel des Spectacles*, *Une Semaine à Paris* and *Pariscope*, and the daily press for details of time and place of exhibitions. The monthly booklet *Paris Selection*, edited by the Paris Tourist Office, lists exhibitions, shows and other events in the capital.

Paris may be said to be one huge "living stage", as it boasts a total of 100 **theatres** and other venues devoted to the performing arts, representing altogether a seating capacity of 56 000. Most of these are located near the Opéra and the Madeleine but from Montmartre to Montparnasse, from the Bastille to the **Latin Quarter★★★** and from Boulevard Haussmann to the Porte Maillot, state-funded theatres (**Opéra-Garnier★★**, Opéra-Bastille, Comédie Française, Odéon, Chaillot, La Colline) are to be found side by side with local and private theatres, singing cabarets and cafés-théâtres. Not to mention television studios and the large auditoriums where radio and TV programmes are regularly recorded in public.

Cinemas, more than 400 in number, are to be found in every part of the city, with particular concentrations in the same areas as the theatres and on the Champs-Élysées. There are also two open-air cinema festivals in the city in the summer: one at **Parc de la Villette★**; the other, **Cinéma au Clair de Lune**, is held in parks and squares across Paris.

Music-hall, **variety shows** and **reviews** can be enjoyed at such places as the Alcazar de Paris, the Crazy Horse, the Lido, the Paradis Latin, the Casino de Paris, the Folies Bergère and the Moulin Rouge. As well as the **Opéra-Garnier★★**, the Opéra-Bastille and the Comic Opera (Opéra-Comique), there are a number of concert halls with resident orchestras like the Orchestre de Paris at the Salle Pleyel, the Ensemble Orchestral de Paris at the Salle Gaveau, and the orchestras of the French Radio at the Maison de Radio-France. In addition there are many other halls in which full-scale performances are put on (Théâtre des Champs-Élysées, Châtelet, Salle Cortot,

Espace Wagram, Maison de la Chimie, Palais des Sports, Palais Omnisports de Bercy, Palais des Congrès, Théâtre de la Ville, Zénith…).

There are also nightclubs, cabarets, dens where *chansonniers* can be heard, *café-théâtres*, television shows open to the public, concerts and recitals in churches, circuses, and other entertainment.

🛒 SHOPPING

SHOPPING DISTRICTS

Most major stores are concentrated in a few districts, whose names alone are suggestive of Parisian opulence.

Champs-Elysées

All along this celebrated avenue and in the surrounding streets (**avenue Montaigne, avenue Marceau**), visitors can admire dazzling window-displays and covered shopping malls (**Galerie Elysée Rond-Point, Galerie Point-Show, Galerie Elysée 26, Galerie du Claridge, Arcades du Lido**) devoted to fashion, cosmetics and luxury cars.

Rue du Faubourg-St-Honoré

Here haute couture and ready-to-wear clothing are displayed alongside perfume, fine leather goods and furs.

Place Vendôme

Some of the most prestigious jewellery shops (**Cartier, Van Cleef & Arpels, Boucheron, Chaumet**) stand facing the Ritz Hotel and the Ministry of Justice.

Place de la Madeleine and r. Tronchet

An impressive showcase for shoes, ready-to-wear clothing, luggage, leather goods and fine tableware.

DEPARTMENT STORES

♿ *See map p 143*

For locals and visitors alike, the city's great department stores are the ideal way to find a vast choice of high-quality fashions and other goods under one roof. Most leading names are represented. Some have free fashion shows. Department stores are usually open from Monday–Saturday 9.30am–7pm.

Bazar de l'Hôtel de Ville (52 r. de Rivoli)
Galeries Lafayette (40 bd. Haussmann)
Printemps (64 bd Haussmann)
Le Bon Marché (r. de Sèvres)

ANTIQUE SHOPS AND DEALERS

Le Louvre des Antiquaires (1 pl. du Palais Royal), **Le Village Suisse** (r. du Général de Larminat), the **Richelieu-Drouot** auction room and the **rues Bonaparte** and **La Boétie** specialise in antique objects and furniture. Good bargains can also be found by browsing through the flea market at the **Porte de Montreuil and Porte de St-Ouen** (Sat–Mon).

FAIRS AND EXHIBITIONS

Paris hosts a great number of trade fairs and exhibitions all year round. The following events are among the most important.

Paris – Expo, *pl. de la Porte de Versailles. www.viparis.com.*
Over 200 exhibitions, conventions and events per year including the Paris Nautical Trade Show.

Parc International d'Expositions, *Paris-Nord Villepinte. www.viparis.com.* Trade Show for Crafts (SMAC) in March, the Maison & Objet home style expo, the International food industry exhibition (SIAL) and Japan Expo.

Parc des Expositions, *Le Bourget aerodrome. www.paris-air-show.com.* Paris Air Show (odd years, next 2011).

🏃 SPORT

Among the most popular sporting events held in and around Paris are the International Roland Garros Tennis Championships, the Paris Marathon, the legendary **Tour de France** with its triumphant arrival along the Champs-Elysées, and several prestigious horse races (Prix du Président de la République in Auteuil, Prix d'Amérique in Vincennes, Prix de l'Arc de Triomphe in Longchamp).

The **Parc des Princes stadium** (*24 r. Claude Farrère; www.leparcdesprinces.fr*) is host to the great football and rugby finals, attended by an enthusiastic crowd, and the **Palais Omnisport de Paris-Bercy** (*8 bd Bercy; www.bercy. fr*) organises the most unusual indoor competitions: indoor surfing, North American rodeos, ice figure-skating, tennis championships (Open de Paris), moto-cross races, martial arts, Six-day Paris Cycling Event, and also pop concerts by international stars.

Château d'
Écouen★★

Nestled in a 17ha/42 acre park overlooking the Île-de-France plain, the Château d'Écouen was originally built in the 16C for Constable Anne de Montmorency, supreme commander of the French Army. Confiscated during the Revolution, and salvaged by Napoleon I who founded here the first school for the daughters of members of the Légion d'Honneur, the castle now houses some of the most prestigious Renaissant Art collections in the country.

THE CASTLE

The Château d'Écouen reflects the transition of French art from the **Early Renaissance** period (Château of the Loire) to the **High Renaissance** (during Henri II's reign). The buildings feature pavilions at each corner, and are surmounted by elaborate dormer windows with carved pediments. The beautiful east range was destroyed in the 18C and replaced by a low entrance wing.

Porticoes with Classical-style columns decorate the buildings. The most outstanding one is to the left, on the south wing (Anne de Montmorency's residence), built by **Jean Bullant** to house Michelangelo's famous *Slaves* in the niches on the ground floor. The statues (*the originals are in the Louvre*) were a

Michelin Local Map:
305: F-6, map 101 fold 6
or 106 fold 19.
Parking: Cars must be parked at the entrance to the forest. Access is through the forest, on foot.

gift to Anne de Montmorency from King Henri II. From the North Terrace, you will get a sweeping **view** of the surrounding cereal-growing countryside.

Musée National de la Renaissance★★

  Open daily (except Tue) 9.30am – 12.45pm, 2–5.15pm (5.45pm in summer). Closed Jan 1, May 1 and Dec 25. 6.50€ (no charge 1st Sun in the month). ☎01 34 38 38 50. www.musee-renaissance.fr.

This outstanding museum presents a wide range of works dating from the 16C and early 17C, which introduce visitors to the various branches of the decorative arts: furniture, tapestries and embroideries, silver and gold work, ceramics, enamels , glasswork, stained glass, paintings, weapons etc. Most of the pieces, made in France, Italy or the Netherlands, were carefully selected to recreate the ambience in keeping with the life of wealthy nobility during the Renaissance.

The original interior decoration mainly consists of **grotesque paintings** on the friezes below the ceiling and the

Château d'Écouen

©JyFotolia.com

embrasures of the windows. But it is for its 12 **painted fireplaces**★ that Écouen is famed. Representative of the first Fontainebleau School, these chimney-pieces feature a central biblical scene painted on a medallion, surrounded by grotesques, garlands of fruit, motifs in leather, and hazy landscapes depicting antique ruins, fortresses and humble cottages.

Ground Floor – The monograms A and M (Anne de Montmorency and Madeleine of Savoy, his wife) were included in the decoration of the **chapel** (1544), covered with painted vaulting resting on diagonal arches. This heraldic motif reappears in different rooms of the castle. The Passion Altarpiece is adorned with enamelling and a copy of Leonardo da Vinci's *Last Supper*.

Several rooms are devoted to a particular trade or technique. Note a clock of German origin in the shape of a ship known as Charles V's clock, now incorporated into a 16C collector's cabinet and, in the reconstruction of a 16C goldsmith's workshop, a work bench set in an inlaid chest.

First Floor – In the south wing, visitors are shown round the constable's bedroom and Madeleine of Savoy's suite, with period furniture.

The west wing is almost entirely taken up by the **Tapestry of David and Bathsheba**★★★ (1510–20) which runs from the Abigail pavilion to the king's bedchamber, along the Psyche Gallery. The 75m/246ft hanging divided into 10 sections tells of the romance between King David and Bathsheba. The outstanding quality of the tapestry is equalled only by that of *The Hunts of Maximilian* in the Louvre, without doubt the two most precious examples of 16C Brussels tapestry work existing in France.

The hanging ends in the **King's Apartment**, situated in the northwest pavilion. The king's suite occupied the northern wing. Note the floor tiles made specially for the château in 1542 by Rouen potter Masséot Abaquesne, and two tapestries

which were part of the famous *Fructus Belli* made in Brussels to cartoons by Jules Romains.

Second Floor – In the northeast pavilion, many pieces of Iznik pottery (mid-16C to early 17C) illustrate the exotic tastes of 16C collectors. The first room in the north wing presents religious stained glass painted in *grisaille*; admire the Virgin and Child, dated 1544.

The second hall deals entirely with French ceramics. It features St-Porchaire ceramics, pieces by Bernard Palissy and Masséot Abaquesne, and a reconstruction of the second floor tiled floor designed for the château, showing the arms of the Constable, those of his wife, of Henri II and Catherine de' Medici.

The 15 **marriage chests** on show in the northwest pavilion form a remarkable ensemble. The west pavillion features beautiful enamel pieces by Léonard Limosin, while the southwest pavilion showcases silverware (cutlery, jewellery), mainly of German origin (note the extraordinary Daphné by the great Nuremberg goldsmith, Wenzel Jammitzer).

See also... – Rarely opened to the public *(ask for opening days)*, some rooms give an unusual insight into life in the Renaissance period. Among these, note the former **library** of Constable Anne *(above the chapel)* , with its original gilded wainscoting, and a suite of **private bathrooms** *(in the basement)* to which rain water from the central courtyard was ingeniously channelled.

ADDITIONAL SIGHT
Église St-Acceul

This is Ecouen's second architectural-masterpiece. The **chancel** by Jean Bullant is the most interesting part of the building. The complex rib patterns of the vaulting date it to the 16C. St-Acceul features several Renaissance **stained-glass windows**★. Those in the north aisle (1544) feature the Dormition and Assumption of the Virgin, the Annunciation and Visitation, the Nativity and the Adoration of the Magi.

Maisons-Laffitte★

Set on the westerly outskirts of Paris, in a loop on the River Seine, Maisons-Laffitte is a residential town lying on the edge of St-Germain Forest. Particularly famous for its castle, a manifesto of French neo-Classical architecture built by Mansart in the 17C, it is also known as the birthplace of horse racing in France.

▶ **Population:** 21 856
⚭ **Michelin Local Map:** 311: I-2, map 101 fold 13 or 106 fold 18.
🖩 **Info:** Office du tourisme de Maisons-Laffitte, 41 av. de Longueil, 78600. ℘01 39 62 63 64. www.tourisme-maisonslaffitte.fr.
▶ **Location:** From Paris, SNCF rail link from Gare St-Lazare or RER line A 3/A 5.

A BIT OF HISTORY

Maisons-Laffitte castle was built by **François Mansart** between 1642 and 1651 for **René de Longueil**, President of Paris Parliament, appointed Governor of the royal châteaux at Versailles and St-Germain. The castle was designed to receive royalty as it was one of the official places of residence assigned to French rulers. Louis XIV, who took up residence at St-Germain, paid frequent visits to Maisons, as did his successors. The Comte d'Artois, brother of Louis XVI, acquired the estate in 1777 and gave orders to build the world-famous racecourse.

In 1818, **Jacques Laffitte** (1767–1844) bought the estate. This powerful banker entertained the adversaries of the Restoration (the Marquis de Lafayette, Benjamin Constant etc.). He did much to secure Louis-Philippe d'Orléans' accession to the throne during the Revolution of July 1830 which overthrew Charles X. Made Prime Minister to the new king in 1830, Laffitte proved unable to calm the disturbances that had broken out in the capital. Mistrusted by both the Orleanists and the moderates, he was forced to resign in March 1831. Ruined, he dismantled the imposing stables and used the stone to build houses in the Grand Parc. The stables had been two long, beautiful buildings designed by Mansart and erected on the avenue du Château *(now avenue du Général-Leclerc)*. They provided a very impressive entrance to the Longueil's estate.

CHÂTEAU★

🕓*Open daily (except Tue) 10am–12.30pm, 2–5pm (summer 6pm).*
🕓*Closed Jan 1, May 1, Nov 1 and 11, Dec 25.* ⊜*7€ (no charge 1st Sun in the month Nov–Apr).* ℘*01 39 62 01 49. www.maisonslaffitte.net.*

Dating from the early part of Louis XIV's reign, the château has always been considered a model of French architecture. From the main driveway, formerly called the King's entrance, there is a splendid **view** of the high-pitched roofs.

The **façade** facing the Seine is fronted by a dry moat, a terrace and the main staircase. The stone exterior presents Classical ornamentation: Doric on the ground floor, Ionic on the first floor, and Corinthian on the attic storey level with the dormer windows. The alternating fluted columns and engaged pilasters form a pleasing, well-balanced composition.

The **interior** features harmonious volumes and refined decorations, with great highlights such as the Vestibule and Grand Staircase, and the Mirror Room.

ADDRESSES

⬗ EAT

⊜⊜⊜ **Tastevin** – *9 av. Eglé.* ℘*01 39 62 11 67. Closed Aug 3–26, Feb 2–Mar 8, Sun and Tue dinners, Wed.* Mansion on the edge of the park with attentive service. High quality produce and a fine wine list. Specialities of the house include venison and chocolate desserts.

Marly-le-Roi★

Although a number of major property developments have spread across the Grandes Terres plateau since 1950, stretching towards Le Pecq, the name of Louis XIV remains firmly attached to this town.
Marly was the Sun King's favourite residence. Unfortunately, its golden age lasted barely twenty years. After the First Empire, only the park remained, an impressive display of greenery bordering the old village, which has welcomed many writers and artists: Alexandre Dumas senior and junior, Alfred Sisley, Camille Pissarro, the sculptor Maillol and the tragedienne Mlle Rachel, to name but a few.

A BIT OF HISTORY

The early stages – Marly's construction was due to **Louis XIV**'s desire to retreat from the formal etiquette of Versailles. In 1678, at the peak of his glory, tired of the continual entertaining at Versailles, the king dreamed of a peaceful country residence, far from the madding crowd. His barony at Marly offered a deep, lush valley which seemed to suit the purpose and he entrusted **Jules Hardouin-Mansart** with the plans. Mansart came up with an ingenious idea: instead of designing one huge single pavilion, which he knew the king would refuse, he conceived a series of 13 separate units. The royal pavilion would stand on the upper terrace, while the other 12, smaller in size and all identical, would be arranged along a stretch of water.
To promote his idea, Mansart explained that the decoration of the king's pavilion could symbolise the sun – Louis XIV's emblem – and that the surrounding buildings could represent the 12 signs of the zodiac. To cut down on costs, it was agreed to replace the carved bas-reliefs by *trompe-l'œil* frescoes.
The King, delighted, gave orders to start building in 1679. It took nine years for the whole project to be completed. After working relentlessly all his life, Mansart died at the château in 1708.

▶ **Population:** 16 759
♿ **Michelin Local Map:** 311: I-2, map 101 fold 12 or 106 fold 17.
🚩 **Info:** Office du tourisme de Marly-le-Roi, 2 av. des Combattants, 78160. ☎01 30 61 61 35. www. marlyleroi-tourisme.fr.
◗ **Location:** From Paris, SNCF rail link from Gare St-Lazare.

Further embellishments – Right until the end of his reign, Louis XIV applied himself to the improvement of his Marly residence and kept a close watch on the various projects under way. He would even tell the gardeners how to trim the edges properly.
Behind the royal pavilion rose the steep, wooded slopes of the hillside. The Sun King gave orders to build the River, also called the **Grande Cascade**, the Wonder of Marly, which was served by the famous "Machine" (♿*see sidebar p154*): starting from the top of the hill, an impressive series of falls poured down a flight of 52 steps of pink marble set into the terraced slope. The whole ensemble – adorned with statues, porticoes and rockeries – was completed in 1699.
The same year, the King decided to clear the main perspective and raze the hillock that stood in the way, an enterprise that occupied 1 600 soldiers for a period of four years.

Life at Marly – Apart from his close relatives, Louis XIV brought very few guests to Marly; the facilities for accommodation were limited to **24 apartments**. It is estimated that 500 lords and 300 ladies altogether were invited to the château over a period of 30 years. The King himself drew up a list of the guests and he personally determined where they should stay; the nearer they were to the royal pavilion, the greater the honour. The "happy few" were not necessarily members of the aristocracy or high dignitaries, but lively, intelligent personali-

Famed "Marly horses"

Ph. Gajic/ MICHELIN

MARLY PARK★★

🕐 *Open daily year-round 8am–5.30pm, (summer 7.30pm, mid-may–mid-Sept 9.30pm).*

A large esplanade flanked by lime trees in the centre of the park marks the former site of the **royal pavilion**. A series of slabs defines the layout of the building; the large octagonal drawing room in the centre is surrounded by four corner rooms, separated by vestibules. The decoration in the King's rooms was red, the Dauphin's rooms were green (they were originally intended for the Queen but she never occupied them); the apartments for "Monsieur" (Louis XIV's brother) were blue and those of "Madame" (his second wife Elisabeth of Bavaria) were pale yellow.

This is where the two perspectives of the park meet: across to the drive leading to the **Royal Gates**, and along the route running from St-Germain and the Seine Valley up to the **Grand Mirror** fountains and the green "carpet" of lawn.

The present grounds are suggestive of old Marly, with its terraces, fountains and hornbeam arbours. Further information can be obtained from the museum (🕭 *see below*) in the outbuilding near the Grille Royale.

Grille Royale

Louis XIV would use this entrance when he arrived from Versailles. Admire the perspective of the steep road climbing up the hillside and its continuation on the opposite slope, slicing its way through the trees.

Musée-Promenade de Marly-le-Roi-Louveciennes

♿ 🕐 *Open Thu–Sun 2–6.30pm.*
♺*3.50€.* 📞*01 39 69 06 26.*
www.musee-promenade.fr.

This museum contains precious material on the 13 pavilions and the garden statues which no longer exist. The plans drawn up in 1753 and a miniature model of the whole project give a fair idea of what the king's country residence looked like. The interior decoration of the royal pavilion is represented by Van der Meulen's *Capture of Gray* and

ties whose wit and charm would enliven the King's stays.

The formal etiquette of Versailles was dropped at Marly. The King shared his meals with his guests, with whom he conversed in a free, casual manner. Hunts, forest walks, outdoor games, card games, games of chance, balls and concerts were a regular feature of life here. The standard of comfort at the place, however, left something to be desired; in summer the guests caught fever, in winter they shivered with cold or choked with smoke because it was too damp to start a fire. Louis XIV, who personally undertook to tackle the heating problem, introduced new systems every year, in vain.

The end of Marly – On 9 August 1715, the King suffered a bout of exhaustion after following the hunt in his carriage. He was taken to Versailles, where he died on 1 September, aged 77.

Louis XV and **Louis XVI** stayed in Marly from time to time. The costly Grande Cascade was abandoned in favour of the present "green carpet." The furniture was sold during the Revolution.

In 1800, an industrialist bought the estate and set up a mill there. Having failed in business, he offered **Napoleon** the opportunity to buy Marly, but he was turned down. He then proceeded to demolish the château and sell the building materials. A year later, Napoleon retrieved the estate which has since been the property of the French State.

by Mme Vigée-Lebrun's *Summer* and *Autumn* which were hung at Marly. Admire one of Desportes' hunting scenes.

The Louis XV period features *Aeneas's Apotheosis* commissioned from Boucher for the King's bedroom; chests of drawers (Mondon, De Loose); a number of items including Pajou's statue of *Loyalty* concern Mme du Barry. The collection also presents religious works from St-Vigor Church, in particular a *Lamentation* (1516) and a St-John-the-Baptist from the School of Caravaggio. Before leaving the museum, visit the small room presenting the "Machine of Marly" (drawings and plans, together with a model).

Abreuvoir

After a steep descent – known as Côte du Cœur-Volant – D 386 leads to the **horse-pond,** once used as a spillway for the waters of Marly park. From here, the water was conveyed back to the Seine by a system of pipes and drains. The terrace flanked by yew trees above the pond used to display Coysevox' *Winged Horses* and at a later date, Guillaume Coustou's *Rearing Horses.* Two replicas stand in their place. The original statues once adorned place de la Concorde in Paris and have now been moved to the Louvre.

ADDRESSES

⏺ EAT

◒◒◒ *Le Village – 3 Grande Rue, 78 160 Marly-le-Roi. ℘01 39 16 28 14. Closed Aug 3–24, Sat lunch, Sun dinner and Mon.* Appealing restaurant-inn in Old Marly. The Japanese chef skilfully mixes flavours from the Land of the Rising Sun with French classics.

EXCURSIONS
Château de Monte-Cristo★

Located in Port-Marly. ◐Open Apr–end Nov daily (except Mon) 10am–12.30pm, 2–6pm, Sat–Sun and holidays 10am–6pm. Nov– end Mar Sun only 2–5pm. ◐Closed Jan 1 and Dec 25. ◒5€. (Sun pm ◒6.50€ by guided tour only). ℘01 39 16 49 49. www.chateau-monte-cristo.com.

Built in 1846 on a hill overlooking the Seine Valley, this extravagant folly expressed the eccentricity of **Alexandre Dumas** through a wonderfully eclectic combination of Gothic, Renaissance and Moorish styles. After holding sumptuous receptions for the fashionable Paris set when his works *The Count of Monte-Cristo* and *The Three Musketeers* were enjoying great success, Dumas ran up enormous debts and was finally forced to sell up. The delightful building, which houses a library and information centre, is decorated with medallions representing the famous writer and the great minds whom he particularly admired, Homer, Aeschylus, Sophocles.

Some of the rooms contain portraits and documents.

Visitors can also see the great man's study and the splendid **Moorish drawing room★** in which the exuberance of the carvings and brilliant stained glass is equalled only by the furniture.

A few yards from the château is the little **Château d'If**, a pseudo-Gothic construction designed by Dumas as a place to which he could retire for peace and quiet. Note the titles of his works engraved on the freestone walls.

After being abandoned for many years, the **park** has now been exceptionally well preserved and again provides a charming setting with its grottoes and man-made features. The many natural springs have been skilfully channelled to form tiny waterfalls cascading into the basins and ponds.

Louveciennes★

This small residential town on the edge of Marly Forest still features several large estates. Many famous people were attracted by this charming place: the portrait painter Élisabeth Vigée-Lebrun (1755–1842); the poet André Chénier (1762–94); the sculptor Emmanuel Frémiet (1824–1910); and above all, several Impressionist painters such as Renoir.

🖝 Two itineraries guide you in the footsteps of the Impressionists and help you discover the town's history: the "Chemin des Impressionnistes" (4km/

The Machine of Marly

One of the greatest scientific invention of its time, this massive contraption was designed to divert the waters of the Seine River to supply the fountains of Marly and, subsequently, those of Versailles. Colbert succeeded in finding a Belgian engineer, **Arnold Deville**, and a master carpenter, **Rennequin Sualem**, who agreed to take on the daring project of raising the water 150m/493ft above the level of the river.

The work started in 1681, took three years and involved a considerable amount of equipment: 14 hydraulic wheels with a diameter of 12m/40ft operated some 225 pumps arranged on three levels, by which the water was conveyed from the water tower – 163m/535ft above the Seine – to the Louveciennes reservoirs via an aqueduct with a capacity of 5 000m³/176 575cu ft per day. From there, the water was channelled to Marly or Versailles.

Plagued by constant breakdowns, this hydraulic Titan required constant costly repairs. It functioned for 133 years before being demolished in 1817. Since the 19C, several pumping devices have occupied the site; the last disappeared in 1967.

2.5mi starting from the town hall) and the "Liaison Verte" (6km/3.7mi starting from the Musée-promenade at Marly-le-Roi).

The **church** (12C–13C) on the village square retains a Romanesque look, but the polygonal bell-tower is 19C. The interior boasts a fine collection of stone piscinae, resting against the east end. Walk through the public gardens, along rue de l'Étang and down rue du Pont for a pleasant view of the 16C **Château du Pont** (private), the groves of trees and the rippling waters of the moat.

Follow rue du Général-Leclerc to the town hall, opposite which stand arches of the disused aqueduct which convey ed the waters of the Seine to Versailles thanks to the "Machine of Marly."

Return to the church and walk along rue du Professeur-Tuffier, then follow the signposts to reach **Field Marshal Joffre's Tomb**. Known as the "Victor of the Marne", this World War I hero was extremely fond of Louveciennes and insisted on being buried here rather than at the Invalides in Paris. He died in 1931, and this rotunda-shaped temple was his last resting place.

Bougival★

4km/2.5mi .

In the 19C, Bougival was a centre of art, fêtes and bohemian life. Bizet, Corot, Meissonier and Renoir lived here. The **boaters** – fun-loving, young Parisian men and women – who flocked to the dances at **La Grenouillère** had their carefree lives evoked by Maupassant in his novels and short stories, and captured on canvas by Impressionists (Renoir, Berthe Morisot, Monet).

Musée Tourgueniev

16 rue Ivan-Tourgueniev.
Access on foot via a small alleyway off N 13, near the Holiday Inn Hotel.
Open Apr–Oct Sun 10am–6pm.
5.50€. 01 45 77 87 12.
www.tourgueniev.fr.

Built on the heights, the house where **Ivan Turgueniev** (1818–1883) lived during his exile was part of the property owned by his friends Louis Viardot and his wife Pauline, a singer like her sister La Malibran. On the ground floor are some of the writer's documents, photographs of family and friends, engravings, and his piano. His works are evoked through extracts from novels and essays, among them the Récits d'un Chasseur published in 1852, in which he predicted the abolition of serfdom in Russia.

On the first floor, the writer's study and the room where he died on 3 September 1883 have been re-created. His body was taken to St Petersburg on 1 October: a photograph captures Ernest Renan giving a speech at the Gare du Nord in Paris (Adieu Paris); another shows the funeral procession in St Petersburg.

The Machine of Marly

(♿ see sidebar p154)

The **Île de la Loge** road bridge affords a good view of the buildings *(quai Rennequin-Sualem at Bougival)* which contained the Machine of Marly, and the pipes lining the hillside.

From up there, one can see a white lodge in the distance: this was **Madame du Barry's Music Pavilion**. Designed by Claude-Nicolas Ledoux, the pavilion was inaugurated on 2 September 1771, during a sumptuous banquet attended by Louis XV.

Forêt de Marly

Once royal hunting grounds, jealously guarded by high walls, this State forest covers a rough but picturesque plateau planted with oaks, beeches and chestnut trees. The total area is estimated at 2 000ha/5 000 acres.

The thicker groves, featuring some beautiful trees, lie west of the road from St-Germain to St-Nom-la-Bretèche, particularly between Étoile des Dames and Étoile de Joyenval.

Meudon★

From this residential town, nestled on the slopes of a plateau covered by the Meudon Forest, the Seine valley unfolds at your feet, with Paris on the horizon. In clear weather, you may even see some of the Capital's most emblematic landmark monuments, such as the Eiffel Tower and the Sacré-Coeur... A breathtaking sight that Rodin certainly enjoyed as he created some of his most famous works from his beloved retreat.

> ▶ **Population:** 43 663
> ♿ **Michelin Local Map:**
> 305: E-8, map 101 folds 23–24 or 106 fold 18.
> 🛈 **Info:** Mairie de Meudon, 6 av. Le Corbeiller, 92195. ☎01 41 14 80 00. www.ville-meudon.fr.
> ◗ **Location:** From Paris, SNCF rail link from Gare Montparnasse (Bellevue) or RER C5/C7 (Meudon–Val-Fleury).

A BIT OF HISTORY

There is a long and complicated story behind what is called the **Domaine national de Meudon**.

Around 1540, Anne de Pisseleu, **Duchess of Étampes** and a favourite of François I, had a Renaissance-style manor house built at the edge of what is known today as Meudon's Terrace (♿*see below*).

The estate was purchased in 1552 by Charles de Guise, **Cardinal de Lorraine**. In 1654, it was sold to Abel Servien, **Marquis de Sablé** and Minister of Finance. Servien commissioned **Le Vau** to renovate the château at great expense and gave orders to build the terrace, a large-scale project.

When he died in 1659, his son sold the estate to **Louvois**, the lord of Chaville. The new owner renewed the decoration and embellished the park, asking **Trivaux** to create the perspective and entrusting the plans of the gardens to **Le Nôtre**, then to **Mansart**.

After Louvois' death, the estate went to Louis XIV's son, the **Grand Dauphin,** who made considerable changes in the interior decoration and layout of the **Château-Vieux**, and who even had an addition built: the **Château-Neuf**. Upon his death in 1711, the estate came into the hands of **Louis XV** who didn't show much interest in it. Meudon further declined under **Louis XVI,** and was emptied out during the French Revolution. A devastating fire in 1795 resulted in the **demolition** of the Château-Vieux eight years later. Relatively spared, the refurbished Château-Neuf was used during the **First**, then **Second Empire,** but the **Franco-Prussian War** of 1870 was to be fatal. Occupied by the Prussian forces who used Meudon's terrace as a prime defensive spot, the Château-Neuf

Bellevue

In the mid 18C, **Madame de Pompadour**, King Louis XV's favourite, acquired the Bellevue estate and had a château built on the property. Purchased by the king in 1757, the château became home to his two unmarried daughters, aunts of Louis XVI. They added a botanical garden and a charming hamlet. The estate was pillaged during the Revolution and sold as State property. All that remains of the former estate is part of the terrace and its balustrade at the junction of rue Marcel-Allégot and avenue du 11-Novembre.

was set on fire at the end of the conflict in 1871. The fire left only a few walls standing, which now house the city's famous observatory.

SIGHTS
Avenue du Château

This stately avenue is lined with four rows of lime trees. Halfway down the street, a plaque on the left marks the little house *(no 27)* where **Richard Wagner** composed the score for the *Flying Dutchman* in 1841.

Terrace★

Meudon's famous terrace (450m/1480ft long and 136m/ 447ft wide) is planted with handsome trees and sweeping lawns. It commands a **panoramic view★** of the city, the Seine Valley and Paris.
The far end of the esplanade rests on the foundations of the **orangeries** of the Château-Vieux. From here, visitors may discover Le Nôtre's beautiful perspective, with the modern complex of Meudon-la-Forêt in the far distance.

Observatoire

(ⓒ*Guided tour once a month on a Sat at 2.30pm. Call for details and reservations.* ⊛6€. ℘*01 45 07 75 30.*
Founded in 1876 by astronomer **Jules Janssen**, this observatory now houses the astrophysics section of the Paris Observatory. It is also a leading aerospace research centre in France. A large **revolving dome** with a diameter of 18.5m/60ft crowns the central block of the Château-Neuf.

Musée d'Art et d'Histoire

11 rue des Pierres, at the foot of the terrace. ⦿*Museum closed until 2010, but the gardens remain open.*
℘*01 46 23 87 13.*
The house that **Molière**'s widow **Armande Béjart** bought in 1676, three years after the writer's death, has been turned into a museum. Partly dedicated to the history of Meudon, it also features a fine collection of works by 20C sculptors, including names such as Rodin or César. The French **gardens** are dotted with sculptures by Jean Arp, Bourdelle and Stahly.

Musée Rodin

19 avenue Auguste-Rodin. ⓒ*Open Apr–end Sept Fri –Sun 1–6pm (last admission 5.15pm).* ⓒ*Closed May 1 and Dec 25.* ⊛4€. ℘*01 41 14 35 00.*
www.musee-rodin.fr.
An indispensable complement to the world-famous Rodin Museum in Paris, this Rodin museum stands next to the **Villa des Brillants**, Rodin's residence and studio from 1895.
The 17C façade of the old château at Issy-les-Moulineaux, that Rodin had purchased after the castle was set on fire and reasssembled in his garden, has been integrated to the museum's building.
You will see moulds, drawings and rough sketches by the great sculptor, together with a number of original plaster casts *(The Gates of Hell, Balzac, The Burghers of Calais)*. Rodin died in 1917 and his grave was laid out in front of the museum, a cast of the world-famous *Thinker* sitting pensively on his tombstone.

Montmorency★

Ancient fief of the Montmorency family, one of the most distinguished lines of the French nobility, this wealthy suburb of Paris and its beautiful forest once attracted artists, politicians, socialites and writers fleeing Paris, the "Town of noises, of mud and smoke". Among these was 18C celebrated author and social theorist Jean-Jacques Rousseau who came here, closer to nature, to write some of his greatest works.

▶ **Population:** 20 599.
> **Michelin Local Map:** 305: E, F-7, map 101 fold 5 or 106 fold 19.
> **Info:** Office du tourisme de Montmorency, 1 av. Foch, 95160. ℘01 39 64 42 94. www.ville-montmorency.
> **Location:** North of Paris, between St-Denis and Sarcelles, on D 301. From Paris, SNCF rail link from Gare du Nord (Enghien-les-Bains), then bus 13 (Mairie-de-Montmorency).

A BIT OF HISTORY

The First Christian Barons – The Bouchard family, who held the lordship of Montmorency, had the reputation of being difficult vassals, and it was only after the 12C that they served the French court loyally. Over a period of 500 years, the **Montmorency family** produced six constables, 12 marshals and four admirals. They had connections with every ruler in Europe and chose to call themselves the "first Christian barons".

The oldest branch of the family died out in 1632 when the constable's grandson **Henri II de Montmorency**, governor of Languedoc, was beheaded at the age of 37 for having plotted against **Cardinal Richelieu**. Although the duchy passed into the hands of Henri de Bourbon-Condé, King Louis XIV decided that the prestigious title of Duke of Montmorency should remain in the **Montmorency-Boutteville** family.

Jean-Jacques Rousseau's Literary Retreat – Rousseau (1712–18) lived in Montmorency from 1756 to 1762. Invited by **Mme d'Épinay**, a society woman who moved in literary circles, the 44-year-old author took up residence in the **Ermitage,** a small garden pavilion which has since been taken down. He was living with **Thérèse Levasseur**, a linen maid whom he later married, but fell passionately in love with his hostess' sister-in-law **Mme d'Houdetot**, who was nearly 20 years his junior.

His romantic involvements caused him to fall out with Mme d'Épinay in 1757, at which point he moved to the **maison du Mont-Louis**, a house in the village, where he completed The New Eloisa and published Emilius and Sophia and A Treatise on the Social Contract. These were his three major works.

In 1762, Emilius and Sophia was qualified as subversive literature by the Parlement de Paris and a warrant was issued for Rousseau's arrest. Fortunately, the author was forewarned. He fled Mont-Louis with the help of **Marshal de Montmorency-Luxembourg**, an influential figure who had taken the writer under his wing, and sought refuge in Switzerland.

SIGHTS
Collégiale St-Martin★

Started in the 16C by **Guillaume de Montmorency** and completed by his son **Constable Anne**, this collegiate church is characteristic of the Flamboyant Gothic style. It was originally designed to be the mausoleum of the Montmorency family.

The chapel was intended to receive the remains of the Montmorency family and, in the 18C, the tombs of several members of the Condé family. The tombs were destroyed during the Revolution. Some were salvaged and moved to the Louvre, including those of Constable Anne and his wife Madeleine. The others have disappeared, save for the funeral slab of Guillaume de Montmorency and his wife Anne Pot, of the famous Burgundian family; it has been placed at the top of the south aisle.

Stained-glass windows★ – The 14 windows that adorn the apse and the five nearest right-hand bays of the chancel provide fine examples of Renaissance decoration, tastefully restored in the 19C. The family connections of the Montmorency are illustrated by the effigies of their ancestors, the brightly coloured coats of arms and the saints they worshipped. The other windows in the nave – executed in the 19C – harmonise well with the earlier Renaissance windows.

Polish connection – In the chancel, you may be surprised to see a copy of the statue of **Our Lady of Czestochowa**, patron saint of Poland. This is a reminder that the Polish elite, exiled after the failed insurrection of 1830–1831 against the Russian rule, had settled in Montmorency in the 19C.

Musée Jean-Jacques-Rousseau
5 rue Jean-Jacques-Rousseau.
Guided tours (1hr) Tue–Sun 2–6pm. *Closed May 1, Dec 20–Jan 3.* *4€.* *01 39 64 80 13. www.ville-montmorency.fr.*
This is the Mont-Louis House where French writer **Jean-Jacques Rousseau** lived from 1757 to 1762, and where he wrote his major works. Partly reconstituted with period furniture, the interior evokes the daily life of Rousseau and his wife. The old part of the house affords a good **view** of the valley.
A little arbour, planted with lime trees, leads through to the small garden pavilion Rousseau used as a **study**, which he sardonically called his "keep".
In the modern part of the house, the exhibition hall and audio-visual room present particular aspects of Rousseau's life and work. On the edge of the grounds, a 18C house called the "maison des Commères" (House of Gossips) contains a library with numerous studies on Rousseau, and houses the town's historic research centre.

EXCURSION
Forêt de Montmorency
Extending over an area of 2 000ha/4 942 acres north of the River Seine, the Montmorency Forest covers the highest hill (195m/640ft) in the Paris region. The area west of Domont and N 309 is the most interesting section of the forest, with deep wooded vales and patches of moist undergrowth. Oaks, planted in vast quantities in the 18C, and chestnut trees are the dominant species, but you will also see ash trees and the occasional coniferous tree.

The forest boasts several footpaths (GR1, various hiking trails) for long and shorts rambles; a road known as the **Route du Faîte**, opened to both cyclists and walkers, which cuts through the forest; and the Caesar's Camp recreational area.

Château de la Chasse – *30min on foot from N 309 (green gate on the left, 2km/1.2mi beyond Montlignon Church).* The oddly shaped castle (12C), flanked with truncated towers, stands in a picturesque setting, on the edge of a pond.

ADDRESSES

⊉ EAT
Au Cœur de la Forêt – *Av. du Repos de Diane. Access via a forest lane. 01 39 64 99 19. www.aucoeurdelaforet.com. Closed Aug 15–25, Thu dinner, Sun dinner and Mon.* A welcoming decor in two rustic rooms, one of which is very spacious with rafters and a fireplace. Shaded summer terrace. Simple, traditional menu in tune with the seasons.

St-Cloud★

Situated on the west bank of the Seine River, right across the Bois de Boulogne, this hillside residential community is particularly renowned for its park, a popular Sunday afternoon destination for Parisians and suburbanites alike.

A BIT OF HISTORY

Clodoald – Unlike his unfortunate brothers, Clodoald, the grandson of **Clovis** and Clotilda, escaped murder and became a disciple of the hermit **Severin**. He founded a monastery, where he died in 560. His tomb soon became a place of pilgrimage and the town of Nogent, which surrounded it, was subsequently renamed St-Cloud. The saint bequeathed his seigniorial rights to the bishops of Paris who, until 1839, held the title of dukes of St-Cloud and peers of France.

The assassination of Henri III – In 1589 Henri III laid seige to Paris, which had fallen into the hands of the **Catholic League**. This religious alliance between members of the French nobility (led by the Guise and Montmorency families) and Spain had been formed in order to gain military and political power during a time of weak monarchy in France. Following the King's alliance with his cousin, the Protestant Henri of Navarre, a vengeful young Jacobin friar called **Jacques Clément** gained admission to the King's presence and stabbed him in the abdomen. Henri III died two days later.

Monsieur's Castle – In 1658, the episcopal building became the property of Louis XIV's brother, known to all as "Monsieur." His first wife Henrietta of England died there in 1670. The Sun King's brother later married Charlotte-Elisabeth of Bavaria. He extended the grounds to 590ha/1 460 acres and asked **Jules Hardouin-Mansart** to draw up the plans for a series of beautiful buildings. The park and its impressive cascade were designed by **Le Nôtre** between

▶ **Population:** 28 157.
🚲 **Michelin Local Map:** 311: J-2, map 101 folds 14, 24 or 106 fold 18.
ℹ️ **Info:** Hôtel de ville, 13 place Charles- de-Gaulle, 92210. 𝒫01 47 71 53 00. www. ville-saint-cloud.fr.
◐ **Location:** From Paris, Metro Line 10 (Boulogne-Pont-de-St-Cloud) or Tramway T2 or SNCF rail link from Gare St-Lazare.

1690 and 1695. **Marie-Antoinette** bought the estate in 1785, but it became State property during the Revolution.

The 18 Brumaire – When General **Bonaparte** returned from his campaign in Egypt, the army troops and the French people saw him as the leader who would restore peace and order. On 18 Brumaire of the year VIII in the new French calendar (9 November 1799), the **seat of the Consulate** was moved to St-Cloud. The following day, the Five Hundred held a meeting at the orangery, presided over by Napoleon's brother **Lucien Bonaparte**. The General was greatly disconcerted by the hostile reception he got, and was saved only by the swift intervention of his brother who had the assembly room cleared by Murat. The Directoire was abolished.

St-Cloud during the Empire – In 1802, Bonaparte was appointed consul for life, and St-Cloud became his favourite official residence. He celebrated his civil wedding with Marie-Louise on the estate and followed it with a religious ceremony in the Square Salon of the Louvre (1810).
Later, in 1814, the Prussian **Marshal Gebhard Blücher** took up residence at the château. In an act of vengeance, he cut the silk hangings to ribbons, and wrecked both the bedroom and the library.
It was at St-Cloud that **Charles X** signed the **Ordinances of July 1830**, which abolished the charter and precipitated

his downfall. It was also from St-Cloud that he went into exile.

On 1 December 1852, the Prince-President **Louis-Napoleon** was made Emperor. A meeting was held at the Château de St-Cloud on 15 July 1870, during which it was decided to declare **war on Prussia**. The building was badly damaged in a fire three months later. It was finally razed to the ground in 1891.

DOMAINE NATIONAL DE SAINT-CLOUD★★

⏱*Open daily Mar–Apr and Sept–Oct 7.30am–9pm. May–Aug 7.30am–10pm. Nov–Feb .30am– 8pm. ◉4€ per car, no charge for pedestrians. ☏01 41 12 02 90. www.saint-cloud.monuments-nationaux.fr.*

The 450ha/1,112-acre national estate of St-Cloud spreads from the slopes of the Seine Valley to the Garches plateau. It may no longer boast a château, but still offers beautiful expanses of gardens, park and woodland which have retained most of the original classical layout designed by Le Nôtre.

Musée historique

⏱*Open daily (except Mon and Tue) 10am–1pm and 2–6pm. ◉2. 50€. ☏01 41 12 02 90.*

Housed In the former stables where the private suite of **Richard Mique** (1728–1794), Marie-Antoinette's architect, used to be located, this museum tells the story of the estate of St-Cloud, its gardens and its now defunct château.

St-Cloud porcelain

Founded by **Pierre Chicaneau** in 1677, the porcelain manufacture functioned for almost a century. The delicate, translucent porcelain objects are characterised by blue-monochrome lambrequin motifs enhanced by gold decorations. Some items are adorned with oriental motifs. The trademark is a **blue sun**.

Jardin du Trocadéro★

These gardens were laid out on the site of the former château. They date from the Restoration period. This beautiful landscaped garden features a charming pond and an aviary.

The far end of the terrace commands a **view** of Paris. In the foreground, note the Pavillon d'Artois, part of which was built in the 17C.

Grande Perspective

Terrase du château – A cluster of yew trees and a marble layout mark the former site of the château, which was also the start of the Grande Perspective, a succession of parterres, lawns and ponds and their continuation, the allée de Marnes, stretching over a distance of 2km/1.2mi. The private gardens used to spread on either side. The terrace offers a superb **panorama**★★ of Paris, stretching from the Bois de Boulogne to the woods at Clamart and Meudon.

Terrasse de l'Orangerie – Some 50 orange trees and oleanders spend the summer months here from May to October. In winter they take shelter inside the orangery in Meudon

Tapis vert – Running from the Grande Gerbe to Rond-Point des 24 Jets, these lawns command a lovely view of the flower beds and the city of Paris.

Rond-Point de la Balustrade

On this site, Napoleon erected a monument surmounted by a lantern which was lit when the Emperor was staying at the château. It was based on a model from ancient Greece, which is why the Parisians called it Demosthene's lantern. It was blown up by the Prussians in 1870.

Bas-Parc

Grande Cascade★ – Designed in the 17C by Lepautre, these impressive falls were later enlarged by Jules Hardouin-Mansart. Dominated by allegorical statues of the Seine and the Marne, the waters of the cascade flow into a series of basins and troughs before reaching the lower falls, from where they are channelled down to the edge

Pont de St-Cloud

In the 8C, a bridge was built across the River Seine. According to tradition, no king was to set foot on it, or he would die a sudden death. Until the middle of the 16C, French rulers would cross the river in a boat. However, when François I died in Rambouillet, it was decided that the funeral procession would cross the famous bridge. No ill omens were feared as the King was already deceased.

This put an end to the long-standing tradition. François' son Henri II replaced the old wooden bridge with a magnificent stone construction featuring 14 arches. The local people were astonished by such a massive display of stonework, which they claimed was the Devil's work, and the bridge had to be exorcised.

of the park. The whole works are about 90m/296ft long.

The **Grandes Eaux**★★ fountain display, staged every Sunday in June, is quite remarkable.

Grand Jet – Nestling in greenery near the Great Cascade, this is the most powerful fountain in the park, rising to a height of 42m/138ft.

Pavillon de Breteuil – This 18C pavilion – St-Cloud's former Trianon – houses the **Bureau International des Poids et Mesures** (World Centre for Scientific Measurement). The Bureau still has the old standard metre.

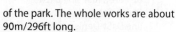 Ferme pédagogique du Piqueur

ⓉOpen to general public Sat–Sun and holidays 10am– noon, 1.30–5.30pm. ⬢2€. Guided tours and workshops available. ☏01 46 02 24 53. www.lafermedupiqueur.fr.
One may not expect to find a pedagogical farm, complete with its orchard, its vegetable garden and the usual barnyard animals, right at the gates of Paris! Tucked away in the heart of the Domaine national de St-Cloud, on a 2ha/4.9-acre site, this child-friendly place is housed in Napoleon III's former stud farm. It introduces young visitors to farm life through a variety of workshops and agricultural activities.

TOWN

Overlooked by the spire of the **Église St-Clodoald** (1865), the steep, narrow streets of the old town wind their way up the hillsides of the Seine Valley.

Église Stella-Matutina★

Place Henri-Chrétien, along avenue du Maréchal-Foch.
This modern church (1965) is shaped like a huge circular tent made of wood, metal and glass. It is fixed to a concrete base by nine pivots and fronted by a porch roof in the shape of a helm. The converging lines of the copper roofing and the pine timbering create an impression of loftiness and soaring height, further emphasised by the concentric rows of pews round the altar.

ADDRESSES

⏦/ EAT

⬤⬤⬤ **Le Garde-Manger** – *21 r. d'Orléans. ☏01 46 02 03 66. www.legardemanger.com. Closed Mon on holidays and Sun.* After a temporary move, this establishment has regained its original address and a brand new decor. Find a generous bistro cuisine and tempting wine list.

HORSE RACES

Hippodrome de Saint-Cloud – *1 r. du Camp-Canadien. ☏01 47 71 69 26.* The Saint-Cloud racetrack is well known among enthusiasts. Situated at the foot of Mont Valérien, it spreads over 75 ha and has a rather unexpected golf course in the middle. Several renowned events take place here, including the Grand Prix de Saint-Cloud and La Journée de l'Élégance.

St-Denis★★

North of Paris, right outside the Périphérique, St-Denis may not be the prettiest of Parisian suburbs, but don't let appearance deceive you. In the heart of this working-class neighbourhood stands the very first masterpiece of Gothic art, sheltering the amazing necropolis of the kings of France… A stark contrast with the futuristic architecture of neighbouring Stade de France, inaugurated for the 1998 Football World Cup.

A BIT OF HISTORY

The beginnings – A Roman town called **Catolacus** had stood on the site of St-Denis since the 1C AD, as it was possible to keep watch over the Paris-Beauvais road and the river from this spot. In AD 475, the first large church was built. **Dagobert I** had it rebuilt in AD 630 and set up a Benedictine community there with orders to take charge of the pilgrimage. The building we see today dates mainly from the 12C and 13C.

The burial ground of kings – For 1 200 years from Dagobert to Louis XVIII, almost all the kings of France were buried here. In 1793, Barrère asked the Convention for permission to destroy the tombs. The bodies were thrown into communal graves. **Alexandre Lenoir** saved the most precious tombs by taking them to Paris, storing them in the Petits-Augustins which was to become

---

"Monsieur Saint Denis"

Saint Denis was a preacher, and the first **Bishop of Lutetia**. Legend has it that, after being beheaded in **Montmartre**, he picked up his head and walked away. He finally died in the country and was buried by a pious woman. An abbey was built over the grave of the man popularly known as "Monsieur Saint Denis", and soon attracted large crowds of pilgrims.

▶ **Population:** 85 832.
◔ **Michelin LocalMap:** 305: F-7, map 101 fold 16 or 106 folds 19, 20.
ℹ **Info:** Office du tourisme de St-Denis-Plaine commune, 1 r. de la République, 93200. ☎01 55 87 08 70. www.saint-denis-tourisme.com.
◑ **Location:** From Paris. Metro line 13 (Basilique de St-Denis or St-Denis Porte de Paris), RER line B (La Plaine-Stade de France) or line D (St-Denis or Stade de France-St-Denis).

---

the Musée des Monuments Français. In 1816, Louis XVIII returned the tombs to the basilica.

Abbot Suger – Suger is the outstanding figure in the history of St-Denis. He came from a poor family and was "given" to the abbey at the age of 10. His exceptional gifts gave him immense power over his fellow pupil, the son of Louis VI the Fat, who became a close friend of the young monk, summoned him to the royal court and consulted him on every possible subject. Suger was elected Abbot of St-Denis in 1122 and drew the plans of the present minster himself.

BASILICA★★★

◷*Open Apr–end Sept 10am–6.15pm (Sun and holidays, noon–6.15pm). Oct–end Mar 10am–5.15pm (Sun and holidays, noon–5.15pm). Last admission 30min before closing.* ☙ *Guided tours daily 10.30am (Sun 12.15pm) and 3pm.* ◷*Closed Jan 1, May 1, Dec 25.* ◉*7€, no charge on 1st Sun of the month Nov–Mar.* ☎01 48 09 83 54.
Widely considered as the first major monument showing evidence of Gothic style in its design, Saint-Denis holds a place of prime importance in the history of architecture. It provided inspiration for the architects of countless late-12C cathedrals such as the ones in Chartres, Senlis and Meaux.

Fête des Loges

This annual event, which goes back to the **Saint-Louis** period, takes place in the **St-Germain Forest** on a site known as **Les Loges**. It is a convivial funfair which lasts for seven weeks from the end of June to the Sunday following 15 August. The numerous attractions and stands appeal to around 3 million visitors who also enjoy the roast chickens, sauerkraut and beer on offer.

In later years, the basilica was poorly maintained, and the **French Revolution** brought with it further damage. Napoleon had the most urgent repairs carried out and returned the basilica to the Church in 1806.

The architect **François Debret** (1777–1850) renovated the church in 1813, but he knew little or nothing about medieval architecture, and his work raised public indignation. He began to work on the magnificent spire, but used materials that were too heavy and the delicate balance was destroyed. In 1846, the spire threatened collapse and had to be removed.

Replacing Debret in 1847, **Eugène Viollet-le-Duc** (1774–1879) gathered up documents that enabled him to restore the building to its original condition. From 1858 until his death in 1879, he undertook a considerable amount of work, and the church we contemplate now is largely to his efforts.

Today, Saint-Denis Basilica is surrounded by gardens laid out on the site of medieval buildings which have disappeared.

Exterior

The absence of the north tower mars the harmony of the **west front**. In the Middle Ages, the building was fortified and some crenellations are still visible at the base of the towers. The tympanum on the **central doorway** represents the Last Judgment, that on the right doorway (it has been re-carved) depicts the Last Communion of Saint Denis and on the left, the Death of Saint Denis and his companions Rusticus and Eleutherus (also re-carved). The **door jambs** feature the Wise and Foolish Virgins (*centre*), the labours of the months (*right*) and the signs of the Zodiac (*left*).

Interior

The cathedral is 108m/354ft long, 39m/128ft wide in the transept and 29m/95ft high, making it slightly smaller than Notre-Dame in Paris.

The elegant nave is attributed to **Pierre de Montreuil**. The bays in the triforium open onto the exterior (one of the first examples of such arrangements). The stained-glass windows in the nave are modern.

Tombs and recumbent effigies★★★ – St-Denis houses the tombs of 46 kings, 32 queens, 63 royal children, and 10 leading personalities who served the French court, such as **Bertrand du Guesclin** (**1**). These tombs have been empty since the French Revolution.

Up to the Renaissance, the only sculpture adorning tombs were recumbent figures. Note the tombs of **Clovis** (**2**) and **Frédégonde** (**3**), featuring a copper cloisonné mosaic made in the 12C for St-Germain-des-Prés Church.

Basilique St-Denis

Jacass/MICHELIN

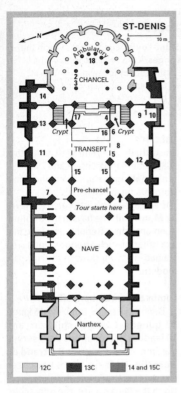

ST-DENIS

Around 1260, Saint-Louis commissioned a series of effigies of all the rulers who had preceded him since the 7C. Their idealised figures were purely symbolic, but they provide a telling example of how royalty was portrayed toward the mid-13C. They include the imposing tomb of **Dagobert** (**4**), with its lively, spirited scenes, the recumbent effigies of **Charles Martel** (**5**) and **Pépin the Bref** (**6**), and a female effigy carved in Tournai marble (**7**).

The tomb of **Isabelle of Aragon** and of **Philippe III le Hardi** (**8**), who died in 1285, shows an early concern for accurate portraiture.

From the 14C on, it became customary to remove the heart and viscera from the bodies of kings before embalming them. The inner organs, the heart and the body were all buried in different places, but the bodies stayed in St-Denis. Representative of the mid-14C period, the effigies of **Charles V** (**9**) by Beauneveu, and those **Charles VI** and

Isabelle de Bavière (**10**) are life-like portrayal of them.

During the Renaissance era, the **mausoleums** took on monumental proportions and were lavishly decorated. The upper level featured the king and his queen, kneeling in full regalia. On the lower level, the deceased were pictured lying down as naked cadavers. Admire the twin monuments built for **Louis XII** and **Anne de Bretagne** (**11**), and that of **François I** and **Claude de France** (**12**), sculpted by Philibert Delorme and Pierre Bontemps.

Catherine de' Medici, who survived her husband Henri II by 30 years, gave orders to build the royal tomb. When she saw how she had been portrayed according to tradition, she fainted in horror and ordered a new effigy which substituted sleep for death. Both works are on display in the cathedral. Their making was supervised by Primaticcio (**13**), and Germain Pilon (**14**), respectively.

Chancel – The beautiful pre-Renaissance **stalls** (**15**) in the forward part of the chancel and the carved wooden door inside the basilica, leading to the south-side necropolis, were taken from the Norman Castle in Gaillon.

On the right stands a splendid 12C Romanesque **Virgin Mary**★ in painted wood (**16**), brought from St-Martin-des-Champs.

The **bishop's throne** opposite (**17**) is a replica of Dagobert's royal throne *(the original is in the Medals and Antiquities Gallery at the Bibliothèque Nationale in Paris)*. At the end, the modern **reliquary** (**18**) of the saints Denis, Rusticus and Eleutherius flanks Suger's **ambulatory**★, characterised by wide arches and slender columns.

Crypt★★ – The lower ambulatory was built in the Romanesque style by Suger (12C) and restored by Viollet-le-Duc (capitals with plant motifs). In the centre stands a vaulted chapel known as **Hilduin's Chapel** (after the abbot who had it built in the 9C).

Beneath the pavement lies the burial vault of the Bourbon family, which

Effigies of Louis XVI and Marie-Antoinette

houses the remains of Louis XVI, Marie-Antoinette and Louis XVIII.

In 1817, the remains of the kings and queens, royal highnesses, princes of the blood, Merovingians, Capetians and members of the Orléans and Valois dynasties which had beed taken from the tombs and thrown together during the French Revolution, were reburied in a common **ossuary** *(in the north transept),* since they could not be sorted out anymore.

ADDITIONAL SIGHTS
Musée d'Art et d'Histoire

22 bis rue Gabriel-Péri. Open daily *(except Tue) 10am–5.30pm, Thu 10am–8pm, Sat–Sun 2–6.30pm.* Closed *holidays.* 5€. 01 42 43 05 10. *www.musee-saint-denis.fr.*

This museum was set up in the former **Carmelite convent** (1625) which managed to escape the wrecking ball in the 1970s, when most of St-Denis run-down historic centre had to be razed and rebuilt.

In the refectory and the kitchen, **archaeological exhibits** feature various artefacts unearthed in St-Denis: Romanesque sculptures, fragments of medieval potteries etc. Many of the items on display come from the **hôtel-Dieu** hospital, including a superb reconstruction of an **apothecary**'s shop, with

17C and 18C ceramic phials and jars. The cells on the first floor, with mystical adages inscribed on the walls, contain many pieces of religious art evoking the daily life of the Carmelite nuns, and a room devoted to post-impressionist painter **Albert André** (1869–1954).

On the second floor, once reserved for the King Louis XV when he visited his Carmelite daughter Louise de France, numerous drawings, paintings and documents relate to the Paris Commune of 1871. The former Louis XV pavilion houses an exhibition of the works of **Paul Éluard**, with a collection of personal memorabilia.

Maison d'éducation de la Légion d'honneur

5 rue Légion d'Honneur. Closed to *the public, except during the Journées du Patrimoine. For more details, call tourist office at* 01 55 87 08 70.

To the South of St-Denis Basilica, surrounded by large grounds in the very heart of town, the old **royal abbey buildings** house the Légion d'Honneur National School. This unusual boarding institution, with a student population of approximately 400, was founded by Napoleon I in 1809 for the daughters of holders of the **Légion d'Honneur**.

Built as early as the 7C, this magnificient architectural ensemble was rehandled in the 18C by prestigious architects such as Robert de Cotte, Jacques Gabriel, Charles Bonhomme, François Franque, Jacques Wailly. It has managed to retain the solemn atmosphere of the original abbey, where the court would stay during the funeral processions which took place at the nearby basilica.

The **cloister** – incidentally the largest one in France – boasts a superb wrought-iron **gate★** attributed to Frère Denis, a famous craftman of the Louis XIV period. Also note, in the refectory, the monumental *Martyre de saint Denis, de saint Eleuthère et de saint Rustique* painted by Gaspar de Crayer in the 17C.

Stade de France★

⏱*Guided tours daily 10.30am, noon, 1.30pm, 3pm, 4.30pm (during sports event, schedules may vary).* ✆*12€.* ✆*01 55 93 00 00. www.stadefrance.com.*
The **1998 World Football Cup** was the force that generated the stadium, now the biggest multifunction Olympic-sized stadium in the world.

Designed by architects Zubléna, Macary, Regembal and Constantini, the elliptic structure is 270m/295yd long, 230m/240yd wide, 35m/115ft high and covers an area of 17ha/42 acres. Thanks to its variable capacity, it can host all kinds of sporting and entertainment events. The circle of stands (25 000 seats) nearest the track can be reconfigured to accommodate athletics competitions. The middle stand has a capacity of 30 000 and the upper stand 25 000. When the field is used for concerts, the total capacity reaches 100 000.

SURROUNDS
Parc de la Courneuve
2.5km/1.5mi east along rue de Strasbourg and N 301 (on the right).
This 350ha/865-acre stretch of greenery features a cycling track, bridlepath, a ski jump, a little train, sports facilities, and playgrounds for children. Rowing boats and pedaloes may be hired to explore the 12ha/30-acre lake *(bathing prohibited).*

St-Germain-en-Laye★★

Nestled on a loop of the Seine River, amidst a forest of oaks, this residential suburb west of Paris was once an important royal town. A great number of monarchs made it their residence, including the Sun King who was born in its castle, grew up and lived there for many years until he and the court left for Versailles in the last quarter of the 17C. Very popular among the locals, St-Germain's famous stone terrace, designed by Le Nôtre, unfolds sweeping views of the Capital, some 20km/12.4mi away.

▶ **Population:** 40 162.
‌◔ **Michelin Local Map:** 311: I-2, map 101 fold 12 or 106 folds 17, 18.
▌ **Info:** Office du tourisme de St-Germain-en-Laye, Maison Claude Debussy, 38 r. au Pain, 78100. ✆01 34 51 05 12. www.ot-saint germainenlaye.fr.
▶ **Location:** From Paris, access via the A 14 and N 13, or RER line A 1 (terminus).

A BIT OF HISTORY
The old castle (château Vieux) – In the 12C, **Louis VI le Gros**, eager to exploit the strategic position of the St-Germain hillside, built a fortified stronghold on the site of the present château. The fortress was destroyed during the **Hundred Years War** and restored by **Charles V** around 1368. In 1514, **Louis XII** married his daughter Claude de France to the Duc d'Angoulême, who became **François I** the following year. The young ruler was acquainted with Italian culture, and the ancient

Château de St-Germain-en-Laye

H. Le Gac/ MICHELIN

citadel was hardly suited to his taste for palatial comfort and luxury. In 1539, he had the whole building razed with the exception of Charles V's keep and the chapel built by **Saint-Louis**.

The new château (château Neuf) – Even the new building presented itself as a fortified structure equipped with machicolations and defended by a garrison numbering 3 000. **Henri II**, who wanted a real country house, commissioned **Philibert Delorme** to draw up plans for a new château on the edge of the plateau. The château became famous on account of its fantastic location and the terraces built along the slopes overlooking the River Seine.

The area beneath the foundation arches was arranged into artificial grottoes where hydraulically propelled automatons re-enacted mythological scenes: Orpheus playing the viola and attracting animals who came to listen, Neptune's chariot in full motion etc.

Chronology of court events – The court occupied both the new château and the old castle, which were used as a palatial residence, or a safe retreat when riots broke out in Paris. Henri II, **Charles IX** and **Louis XIV** were all born at St-Germain. **Louis XIII** died here. **Mary Queen of Scots** lived here between the ages of 6 and 16. In 1558, she married the Dauphin François, aged only 15, and

was crowned Queen of France the following year.

Mansart's improvements – Louis XIV, who was christened and brought up at St-Germain, grew fond of the château. As king, he paid frequent visits to the estate. The apartments of the old castle had become too cramped for Louis' liking, and he commissioned **Jules Hardouin-Mansart** to build five large pavilions as a replacement for the five corner turrets adjoining the outer walls. **Le Nôtre** drew up the plans for the park, the terrace and the forest. In 1665, the grounds were replanted with five and a half million trees. In 1682, the court moved from St-Germain to Versailles. In 1689, the deposed King of England **James II** came to stay at the old castle, where he died in great financial straits in 1701, a well-loved figure (funeral monument in St-Germain Church, facing the château).

Final developments – In 1776, the badly dilapidated new château was ceded to the Comte d'Artois by his brother **Louis XVI**. The future king **Charles X** had the building demolished, except for the Henri IV pavilion on the terrace and the Sully Pavilion, in Le Pecq. The remains, together with the park, were sold during the Revolution. The old castle was stripped of its furniture. Under **Napoleon I**, it was the seat of a

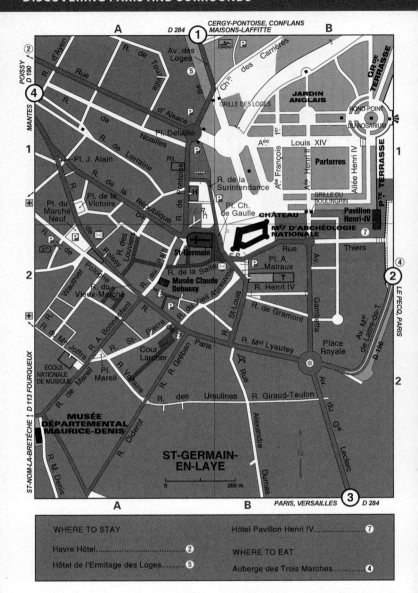

CERGY-PONTOISE, CONFLANS
MAISONS-LAFFITTE

POISSY
D 190

MANTES

JARDIN
ANGLAIS

GRILLE DES LOGES

Av. des
Loges

R. de Tourville

R. d'Avon

Rue

R.

d' Alsace

Pl. Detaillé

R. de
Noailles

R. de Lorraine

Pl. J. Alain

R. de la
République

PBL

R. de
Poissy

R. de Pontoise

R. de la
Surintendance

Pl. Ch.
de Gaulle

Louis XIV

Parterres

ROND-POINT
DU ROSARIUM

Allée Henri II

Allée Henri IV

GRILLE DU
BOULINGRIN

Pavillon
Henri-IV

CHÂTEAU

Mée D'ARCHÉOLOGIE
NATIONALE

Thiers

Pl. du
Marché
Neuf

Pl. de la
Victoire

St-Germain

R. des
Louviers

R. de la Salle

Musée Claude
Debussy

Pl. A.
Malraux

R. Henri IV

R. de Gramont

Rue

Av.

Gambetta

Place
Royale

Wauthier

R. du
Vieux-Marché

R. A. Bonnenfant

Pierre de

Paris

R. Mal Lyautey

Rue

Av. Mal
de-Lattre-de-T.

Cour
Larcher

Pl.
Mareil

R. de Mareil

R. Diderot

R. des

Ursulines

R. Giraud-Teulon

ÉCOLE
NATIONALE
DE MUSIQUE

MUSÉE
DÉPARTEMENTAL
MAURICE-DENIS

ST-GERMAIN-
EN-LAYE

Alexandre

Dumas

Av. du Gal. Leclerc

0   200 m

PARIS, VERSAILLES   D 284

ST-NOM-LA-BRETÊCHE | D 113 FOURQUEUX

LE PECQ, PARIS

D 190

WHERE TO STAY

Havre Hôtel..........................②

Hôtel de l'Ermitage des Loges..........⑤

Hôtel Pavillon Henri IV....................⑦

WHERE TO EAT

Auberge des Trois Marches............④

cavalry college. Under **Louis-Philippe**, it housed a military penitentiary, but **Napoleon III** ordered its closure in 1855. It was then entirely restored under the guidance of the architect **Millet**, succeeded by **Daumet**.

In 1862, Napoleon III inaugurated the National Museum of French Antiquities which he had set up on the premises. The signing of the 1919 **peace treaty** with Austria took place in the château at St-Germain.

CASTLE AND SURROUNDS

The most striking approach to the château is from the north, along the road from Les Loges. The tour starts from the square beside the château, **place Charles-de-Gaulle**.

Château★

The château is the shape of an imperfect pentagon. The feudal foundations are distinguishable together with the covered watch-path and a series of machicolations restored by Daumet. The roof, laid out as a terrace edged with vases and a balustrade and dominated by tall chimneys, was an innovative idea.

The royal suites were on the first floor; the king and the dauphin lived in the wing facing the parterres, the queen's suite looked toward Paris, and the children's rooms were in the wing which now faces rue Thiers. Under Henri IV, 12 of the 14 royal infants, born to five different mothers, romped noisily in these quarters.

Ste-Chapelle★ –Built by Saint-Louis from 1230 to 1238, this chapel precedes the Ste-Chapelle in Paris by some 10 years. It was probably designed by the same architect, **Pierre de Montreuil,** but its tall windows do not have the stained glass that gives such dazzling splendour to its counterpart in Paris. Within the thickness of the keystones are carvings of figures thought to represent Saint- Louis, his mother Blanche of Castille, his wife, and other people close to him. If this is true, it would make these precious images the oldest pictures of royal families in existence.

Musée d'Archéologie nationale★★

Place Charles-de-Gaulle. &. ○*Open daily (except Tue) year-round 10am– 5.15pm.* ○*Closed Jan 1 and Dec 25.* ◎*4.50€.* ℘*01 39 10 13 00.* *www.musee-archeologienationale.fr.* Particularly famous for its collection of carved or engraved prehistoric artefacts, the French National Archaeology Museum displays an amazing array of antiquities ranging from the early settlements of France to the reign of Charlemagne.

– Toolmaking techniques of the **Palaeolithic Age** (from the origins till around 8000 BC) were characterized by the use of materials such as stone (flint), quartz, bone and antlers. The major works of art dating from that period are surprisingly small, as illustrated by world-famous **Lady of Brassempouy** (3.6cm/1.44in high), the oldest representation of a human face found to date (c. 21 000 BC).

– During the **Neolithic Age** (6000 BC– 3000 BC), man developed farming and cattle rearing, community life in huts and the use of ceramics. He produced arms and tools by polishing very hard stones. Found in Bernon (Britany), a set of 16 large polished axe blades (15–18cm/5.9–7.1in) dating from around 5000 BC is a fine illustration of this.

– The discovery of an alloy combining copper and tin led to the early stages of metallurgy, called the **Bronze Age** (2000 BC–c. 800 BC). Gold too was widely used, and the museum displays several objects and pieces of jewellery made of solid gold or gold leaf. Also note numerous weapons (daggers, axes with curved blades), metal necklaces and other decorative objects.

– Roughly ending with the Roman conquest, the **Iron Age** (750 BC–1C AD) is marked by profound mutations in the traditional rural society, and by the rise of fortified *oppida*. One of the highlights of this section is the remains of a chariot burial from c. 400 BC excavated at La Gorge-Meillet in the Marne region.

– In **Roman Gaule** (1C–5C AD), the lengthy period of Roman peace, the indulgence of the victors and the deeply rooted religious feeling for indigenous gods gave rise to a flourishing industry of mythological and funeral sculpture. Ceramic pieces played an important role in domestic life. The museum offers a fairly comprehensive presentation of "sigillate" ceramics, decorated with stamped motifs, made in workshops at Lezoux, La Graufesenque etc.

– Gaul progressively became France with the **Merovingians** (5C–8C AD) whose heritage mainly consists of burial places rich in arms – swords with damascene blades – and items of finery: heavy flat buckles for belts, S-shaped clasps etc.

Grounds

Parterres – Enter the gardens through the gate on place Charles-de-Gaulle and skirt the château. Built into the façade is the loggia opening onto the inner main staircase. The moat contains restored megalithic monuments and replicas of Roman statues.

The Last Judicial Duel

Now the site of a pillbox, St-Germain castle's east esplanade was the scene of the last judicial duel during which the will of God was invoked. The duel between **Jarnacc** and **La Châtaigneraie** was attended by **Henri II**, accompanied by his retinue of courtiers. La Châtaigneraie, one of the finest swordsmen in Europe, was confident about the outcome of the battle. Jarnac, however, had learnt a new tactic: he severed the left hamstring of his adversary, who collapsed and slowly died.

Pavillon Henri-IV – This brick pavilion was built on the very edge of the escarpment. It is crowned by a dome, and, together with the **Sully Pavilion** set lower down on the hillside at Le Pecq, is all that remains of the new château. It contains the Louis XIII **oratory** where Louis XIV was baptised on 5 September 1638, the day he was born.

The **hotel** (&see Addresses on opposite page) which opened in this historic building in 1836 became an important meeting place for 19C writers, artists and politicians. Alexandre Dumas wrote *The Three Musketeers* and *The Count of Monte Cristo* while he was staying here, Offenbach composed *The Drum Major's Daughter* and Léo Delibes produced the ballet *Sylvia*. The statesman and president Thiers died here in 1877.

Terraces★★ – The **Small Terrace** starts beside the hotel and extends to the Rosarium roundabout. There, a worn Touring Club of France viewing table is a reminder of past views toward the western suburbs of Paris.

The **Grand Terrace** extends beyond the roundabout. Completed in 1673 after four years of large-scale construction work, this is one of **Le Nôtre**'s finest accomplishments. Lined with stately lime trees, it is also one of the most famous promenades around Paris (400m/8 000ft long). The **vista★** from the terrace being the same all the way along, visitors pressed for time may return to their car through the lovely **English-style garden★**.

ADDITIONAL SIGHTS
Musée Claude Debussy

38 rue au Pain. ⚲*Open Mar–Oct Tue–Fri 2.30–5.45pm, Sat 10am–12.30pm, 2.30–5.45pm. Nov–Feb Tue–Fri 3–5pm, Sat 10.30am–12.30pm, 3–5pm.* ⚲*Closed holidays.* ☎*01 34 51 05 12.*
This restored building was the birthplace of **Claude Debussy** (1862–1918). It features mementoes of the composer and houses the tourist office.

Musée départemental Maurice-Denis★

2 bis, rue Maurice-Denis. ⚲*Open Tue–Fri 10am–5.30pm (1st Thu of the month 9pm). Sat–Sun and holidays 10am–6.30pm.* ⚲*Closed Jan 1, May 1, Dec 25.* ⚙*4.50€ (no charge 1st Sun of the month).* ☎*01 39 73 77 87. www.musee-mauricedenis.fr.*
Founded in 1678 by Mme de Montespan as a royal hospital, this old **priory** became the property of the painter **Maurice Denis** (1870–1943), who moved here with his large family and freely entertained his friends of the **Nabis movement**.

The museum explains the origin of this group of post-Impressionist artists, founded by **Paul Sérusier** in 1888, which became very influential in the field of graphic art, rejecting Realism and Naturalism, and claiming the necessity to put feeling at the centre of every work of art.

The collections assembled in the Priory feature *Eternal Spring*, a set of ten panels by Maurice Denis, depicting women bathing, near a fountain or in a garden, gathered together for the sake of music or conversation.

ADDRESSES

🏨 STAY 🍴 EAT

⊜⊜ **Havre Hôtel** – *92 r. Léon-Desoyer. ✆01 34 51 41 05. 10 rooms. ⊇7€.* Outside of the historical centre, this small, colourful hotel has simple, pleasant rooms. A good, dependable address in town.

⊜⊜⊜ **Auberge des Trois Marches** – *15 r. J. Laurent (pl. de l'Eglise), 78110 Le Vésinet. ✆01 39 176 10 30. 15 rooms. ⊇11€. Restaurant ⊜⊜.* Quiet guesthouse in an area with a village atmosphere. Functional, impeccably-maintained rooms and a friendly welcome. A fresco recalling scenes from the 1930s decorates the dining room.

⊜⊜⊜⊜ **Ermitage des Loges** – *11 av. Loges. ✆01 39 21 50 90. www.ermitage-des-loges. 56 rooms. ⊇13€. Restaurant ⊜⊜⊜.* Hotel made up of two buildings on the edge of the St Germain forest. The main building dates from the 19C. Rooms in the more modern annexe have views over the garden.

⊜⊜⊜⊜ **Pavillon Henri IV** – *21 r. Thiers. ✆01 39 10 15 15. www.pavillon henri4.fr. 42 rooms. ⊇17€. Restaurant ⊜⊜⊜⊜.* This building (1604) was the birthplace of Louis XIV. High-class atmosphere in the nicely refurbished lounges and rooms. The comfortable dining room has superb views over the River Seine valley and Paris.

Sceaux★

The town of Sceaux, in the southern suburbs of Paris, boasts many parks and gardens that are popular with families at the weekend. The grounds of the picturesque château are host to a classical music festival in the summer and are laid out with formal terraces, dotted with fountains and criss-crossed with shaded alleyways.

> ▶ **Population:** 19 494.
> 🚗 **Michelin Local Map:** 312: C-3, map 101 fold 25 or 106 fold 31.
> 🅸 **Info:** Office du tourisme de Sceaux, 70 r. Houdan, 92330. ✆01 46 61 19 03. www.sceaux-tourisme.fr.
> ◐ **Location:** From Paris, RER line B 2 (Sceaux) or B 4 (Parc-de-Sceaux).

A BIT OF HISTORY

Colbert's Sceaux – In 1670 Louis XIV's superintendent of buildings **Jean-Baptiste Colbert** commissioned **Claude Perrault**, **Le Brun**, **Girardon** and **Coysevox** to build a superb residence in Sceaux. The two groups of sculptures flanking the entrance pavilion were created by Coysevox: the dog and the unicorn, representing loyalty and honesty, were Colbert's emblems.

The canal, basins and fountains were supplied by the waters diverted from the hillsides of Le Plessis-Robinson. The château was inaugurated in 1677 at a lavish reception attended by the Sun King in person; one of the many attractions that night was the performance of Jean Racine's famous tragedy *Phaedra*.

Sceaux under the Duke of Maine – In 1700, the estate became the property of the Duc du Maine, the legitimised son of Louis XIV and Mme de Montespan. The King often came to stay with his favourite son. The **Duchess of Maine**, the Great Condé's granddaughter, surrounded herself with a large court of brilliant personalities. She entertained on a grand scale, providing opera, ballet, comedy and tragedy for her many guests. The dazzling **Nights of Sceaux**, enhanced by superb displays of fireworks and twinkling lights, were the talk of all Paris and Versailles.

On the eve of the Revolution, the estate of Sceaux belonged to the **Duke of Penthièvre**, the Duke of Maine's nephew,

Grandes Cascades

M.O. Bernard/ MICHELIN

Orangerie
Designed by **Jules Hardouin-Mansart** in 1685, this conservatory (60m/196ft long) is decorated with a series of carved pediments. Today, it is a venue for conferences, exhibitions and concerts.

Grandes Cascades★
The waters spring out of masks carved out by **Rodin** and stumble down a series of 10 terraces before flowing into the **Octagonal Basin**.

Grand Canal★
As long as Versailles' Petit Canal (1030m/3380ft), it is flanked by a double row of Lombardy poplars.

Musée de l'Île-de-France★
 Open Nov–end Mar daily (except Tue) 10am–1pm, 2–5pm. Apr–end Oct 10am–1pm, 2–6pm (Sun 6.30pm). Closed Jan 1, May 1, Jul 14, Aug 15, Nov 1, Dec 25. 3€ (no charge 1st Sunday of the month). 01 41 87 29 50. www.chateau-sceaux.fr
Housed in the **château** that once belonged to the Duke of Trévise, the museum's collections are laid out around four major themes: Sceaux, the estate and its owners; ceramics from the Paris Basin; royal and princely residences; and scenery in the Paris Basin from the 18C to the 20C.
The museum boasts the largest existing collection of **Sceaux faience**. It also features 17C–18C porcelain (Bourg-La-Reine, Vincennes, Sèvres, St-Cloud), fine 19C faience, and works by Art Nouveau ceramist **Pierre-Adrien Dalpayrat** (1844–1910). The luxurious residences built in the vicinity are illustrated with etchings by Rigaud, oils including the *Château de St-Cloud* by C Troyon, and furniture by Riesenburg and the Jacob brothers.
The variety of landscapes in the Paris Basin has provided much inspiration for 18C–20C artists such as Utrillo, Luce, A Dunoyer de Ségonzac, Chaplain-Midy, Foujita, J Fautrier, etc. Among the highlights, do not miss *Un dimanche aux prés St-Gervais* by Auguste Lepère and J Veber's *La Foire à St-Cloud*.

for whom the fabulist Florian acted as librarian. The domain was confiscated and subsequently sold to a tradesman who had the château razed to the ground and the park turned into arable land.

Sceaux today – In 1856, the **Duke of Trévise**, who inherited the estate through his wife's family, built the château that stands today. The grounds gradually slipped into a state of neglect. **Alain-Fournier** found inspiration there for his novel *Le Grand Meaulnes*. In 1923 the château was bought by the Seine *département*, which undertook to restore both the building and its park. The Île-de-France Museum was installed in 1936. The estate now belongs to the Hauts-de-Seine dé-partement.
The famous physicists **Pierre** (1859–1906) and **Marie** (1867–1934) **Curie** and their daughter **Irène Joliot-Curie** (1897–1956) lived in Sceaux. Their remains were transferred to the Panthéon in Paris in 1995.

CHÂTEAU AND PARK★★
 Park open from 7am at the earliest till 10pm at the latest, depending on the season. 01 41 87 28 60.

Main Entrance
Designed for Colbert, the two entrance pavilions with sculpted pediments are flanked by two small lodges surmounted by **Coysevox**'s groups of statues.

Sèvres★

A suburb of Paris situated between the Parc de St-Cloud and Meudon Forest, Sèvres is famous throughout the world for the Manufacture Nationale de Porcelaine (National Porcelain Factory) established here in the 18C.

MUSÉE NATIONAL DE LA CÉRAMIQUE★★

&. ⓞOpen daily (except Tue) 10am–5pm. ⓞClosed Jan 1, May 1, Dec 25. ⬮4.50€ (no charge 1st Sun of the month). ☎01 41 14 04 20. www.musee-ceramique-sevres.fr.

Founded in 1824 by **Alexandre Brongniart**, director of the Sèvres porcelain manufacture from 1800 to 1847, the museum has an outstanding collection of pottery, faience, and porcelain classified by origin and by historical period. Collections on the ground floor include a rich variety of Islamic, Chinese, Japanese, Korean and American pieces from various periods, some of them very rare and very ancient. It also features apothecary's jars and superb Renaissance works by **Bernard Palissy** (1510–1590) and from the **Della Robia** workshop.

The collections on the first floor illustrate the gradual changes in the use of materials and the evolution of decorative techniques, not only in Sèvres, but in Europe and worldwide. Some rooms focus on soft-paste porcelain (18C–20C). French works are well represented through Chantilly, St-Cloud, Vincennes and Sèvres. Note the various background colours (green, purple, blue). The 19C collection includes the industrial arts service painted by Develly from 1820 onwards. It is representative of the Sèvres porcelain which, unlike others, must include gold.

Others room are dedicated to the history of 18C French and European porcelain, with some splendid pieces. The decoration can be in a range of blues, like the porcelain from Rouen or Marseille, but much of the high-fired porcelain has multicoloured decoration, as illustrated

▸ **Population:** 22 534.
Ⓒ **Michelin Local Map:** 305: E-8, map 101 fold 24 or 106 fold 18.
▯ **Info:** Hôtel de Ville, 54 Grande Rue, 92311. ☎01 41 14 10 10. www.ville-sevres.fr.
◖ **Location:** From Paris, Metro line 9 (Pont de Sèvres) or Tramway T2 (Musée de Sèvres) or SNCF rail link from Gare St-Lazare (Sèvres/Ville d'Avray) or SNCF rail link from Montparnasse (Sèvres-Rive Gauche).

by some magnificent pieces from the Moustiers and Strasbourg manufactures, to name a few. Some rooms also feature Nevers and Delft pieces.

ADDITIONAL SIGHT
Maison des Jardies

14 av. Gambetta. ⓞOpen Thu–Sun 2.30–6.30pm. ⓞClosed Jan 1, May 1, Dec 25. ⬮5€. ☎01 45 34 61 22.

This modest gardener's lodge was once part of the Jardies estate, where **Honoré de Balzac** (1799–1850) settled in 1838 and attempted to cultivate pineapples, unsuccessfully. **Corot** also stayed here, and this is where **Gambetta** died on 31 December 1882. Several of the politician's mementoes have been kept and are on show to the public.

ⓨ EAT

⬤⬤⬤ **Auberge Garden** –
24 rte du Pavé des Gardes. ☎01 46 26 50 50. Closed first 3 weeks Aug, Sat lunch, Sun evening and Mon. This former inn perched on the heights of Sèvres is gradually being refurbished by its current owners. The menu is highly attractive and made with delicious produce. Traditional dining room with movable partitions and a piano. Terrace for the sunny days.

Château de
Versailles★★★

Who could have guessed that a humble hunting lodge would some day become the seat of government and the political centre of France, the outmost symbol of royal absolutism and one of the greatest achievements of 18C classical French art? The French Revolution and the ensuing fall of the monarchy could have proved fatal for Versailles, as furnishings were being dispersed and the park turned into farmland... But somehow, the worst was avoided and today, as night falls over this World Heritage site, subtly enhancing the elegance of its design, one may still feel the spirit of the Grand Siècle and its foremost icon Lous XIV, the Sun King.

A BIT OF HISTORY

Louis XIII's hunting lodge – In the 17C, the locality of Versailles was the seat of a medieval castle perched on a hillock. At the foot laid the village, surrounded by marshes and woodland abounding in game. **Louis XIII** used to come hunting here often, and in 1624 he bought the lordship of Versailles from the **Gondi family** and commissioned a small château built of brick, stone and slate. The castle was completed in 1634.

Taming nature – The year 1661 marked **Louis XIV**'s accession to power. The King hired the various artists, builders, designers and landscape architects who had produced **Vaux-le-Vicomte** and entrusted them with an even more challenging task.

Louis was wary of settling in Paris following the Fronde uprisings, and so searched for a site on the outskirts of the capital. He chose **Versailles** as he had spent many happy days there as a boy and, moreover, he was fond of hunting. It was by no means an ideal site, the mound being too narrow to allow Louis XIII's château to be enlarged.

Michelin Local Map: 311: I-3, map 101 folds 22, 23 or 106 folds 17, 18.

Location: 18km/11mi west of the Capital. From Paris, A 13 motorway toward Rouen (exit Versailles-Château), RER line C (Versailles-Rive-Gauche), SNCF rail link from Gare St-Lazare (Versailles-Rive-Droite) or SNCF rail link from Gare Montparnasse (Versailles-Chantiers).

If you plan on enjoying Versailles gardens and Marie-Antoinette's Estate after you have visited the royal apartments, note that a little train departing from the château's North Terrace provides a convenient shuttle service between the palace, both Trianons and the Grand Canal (see Addresses p200 for more details).

Don't Miss: The King's Bedroom, where everyday, Louis XIV would submit himself to the rising and retiring ceremonies in front of the courtiers; the Baroque decor of his parade apartment, a seven-room prestigious enfilade full of allegorical compositions; the unforgettable Hall of Mirrors, which lent splendour to formal receptions and celebrations; the interior apartments, where sovereigns could retire away from the Court to enjoy moments of relative privacy.

Timing: Versailles is definitely worth a full day's visit, not only for a peek at its refined interior, but also for an overview of the park, with the Trianon Palaces, Marie-Antoinette's Estate and the fabulous gardens.

Grille d'Honneur – the main entrance to the Palace

Ph. Gajic/MICHELIN

An ambitious project – It took 50 years to complete the structural work on the palace at Versailles. In the early stages **(1662–1668)**, various alterations were made to the old structure and the gardens to accommodate festivities. During the second building campaign **(1669–1672)**, a stone "envelope" reminiscent of Italian architecture was built around the old château by **Louis Le Vau**, providing new lodgings for Louis XIV and its immediate circle. **Jules Hardouin-Mansart** was appointed head architect in 1678. This started the third, most important phase of construction **(1678–1684)**, which actually gave Versailles the look it has today. **Charles Le Brun** supervised a team of accomplished painters, sculptors, carvers and interior decorators, while **Le Nôtre** applied himself to the embellishment of the grounds; when designing the waterworks, he joined forces with the **Francines**, a family of Italian engineers. A last building campaign **(1688–1697)** would give Versailles its final touch: the royal chapel.

It was necessary to build a **hill** to accommodate the entire length of the new palace (680m/2 230ft). Whole **forests** were transplanted, and the King's gardeners produced 150 000 new flowering plants every year.

The problem of **water supply** was of great concern. The waters of Clagny Pond proved insufficient, and the builders were forced to divert the course of the Bièvre and drain the Saclay plateau. The famous **Machine of Marly** (&see p154) conveyed the waters pumped from the River Seine.

Life at Court – When the King and his entourage moved to Versailles, the palace and the adjacent outbuildings were required to lodge at least **3 000 people**. The Fronde movement had been a humiliating experience for the King, who had witnessed many intrigues involving men in high places. Consequently, his main concern was to keep the aristocracy with him at court, in an attempt to stifle opposition that might threaten the stability of the throne. The lavish entertainments suited his extravagant tastes and served to keep the nobility under his thumb. For the first time in French history, the royal suites in the palace were given fixed, **permanent furnishings**. Thanks to Colbert's efforts to encourage the production of **luxury goods** (tapestries, furniture, lace etc) on a national scale, the palace – which remained open to the public – offered a standing exhibition of arts and crafts in France. Strict **etiquette** governed

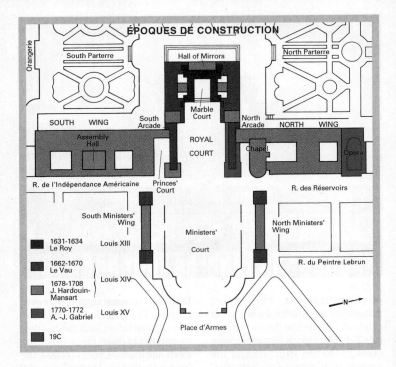

ÉPOQUES DE CONSTRUCTION

Orangerie

South Parterre | Hall of Mirrors | North Parterre

Marble Court

SOUTH WING | South Arcade | North Arcade | NORTH WING

Assembly Hall | ROYAL COURT | Chapel | Opera

R. de l'Indépendance Américaine | Princes' Court | R. des Réservoirs

South Ministers' Wing | Ministers' Court | North Ministers' Wing

R. du Peintre Lebrun

- 1631-1634 Le Roy — Louis XIII
- 1662-1670 Le Vau
- 1678-1708 J. Hardouin-Mansart — Louis XIV
- 1770-1772 A.-J. Gabriel — Louis XV
- 19C

Place d'Armes

N→

the visits that the French people would pay to Versailles. The famous chronicler **Saint-Simon** described a day at court as a "clockwork ceremony" consisting of a series of banquets, audiences and entertainments.

Versailles in the 18C – When Louis XIV died in 1715, his successor was still a young boy. The Regent **Philippe d'Orléans** administered the King's affairs from the Palais-Royal in Paris. During this time, the court left Versailles and moved to the **Tuileries**.

In 1722, **Louis XV**, aged 12, decided to settle at Versailles. In order that royal etiquette might not interfere with his private life, he gave orders to convert several of the private apartments. He dreamed of having the front of the palace remodelled, a task he entrusted to **Jacques-Anges Gabriel**. Unfortunately, no major alterations could be carried out owing to insufficient funds, but the **Petit Trianon** was built.

Louis XVI commissioned no major works. However, he gave Marie-Antoi-nette the Petit Trianon, completed by Gabriel in 1768, and had the **hamlet** designed for her in 1774. On 6 October 1789, the national insurrection forced the royal family to return to Paris. After that date, Versailles ceased to be a place of residence for the kings of France.

To the Glory of France – After the storming of the Tuileries and the fall of the monarchy on 10 August 1792, most of the furniture was removed and auctioned. The major works of art – paintings, carpets, tapestries and a few items of furniture – were kept for the art museum which opened in the Louvre in August 1793. After the renovation work undertaken by **Napoleon** and **Louis XVIII**, Versailles was threatened once more. It was spared demolition by **Louis-Philippe**, who contributed a large part of his personal fortune to turn it into a museum of French history in 1837.

More recently, Versailles was restored following World War I, thanks to the generosity of the Academy of Fine Arts and the handsome contributions made by a number of wealthy patrons, including the American JD Rockefeller.

The 1952–1980 period witnessed some major **restoration projects** such as the Royal Opera, the King's Bedroom and the Hall of Mirrors (both restored to their 18C splendour). It also saw the completion of various refurnishing and maintenance projects, including the installation of central heating and electric lighting.

Launched in 2003, an ambitious renovation project called **Grand Versailles** should be completed around 2020.

THE PALACE AND ITS SURROUNDS★★★

🕐*Open daily (except Mon) Apr–end Oct 9am–6.30pm. Nov–end Mar 9am–5.30pm.* 🎫*13.50€ ("Billet Château" including the most famous places in the palace). Last admission 30min before closing time.* 🕐*Closed Jan 1, May 1, Dec 25.* 📞*01 30 83 78 00. www.chateauversailles.fr.*

♿*As soon as you arrive, proceed to the "Aile sud des Ministres" (South Ministers' Wing) to purchase your ticket, then go the visitors' entrance (A access). If you already have your ticket (online ticket sale service available at www.chateauversailles.fr), directly proceed to the A access.*

Cour de Marbre

©Terraxplorer/iStockphoto.com

Commissioned by Louis-Philippe in the 19C, Versailles's emblematic **equestrian statue** of Louis XIV was in 2006 removed from its original location (near the newly-installed royal gate) to undergo a much-needed renovation. Since June 2009, it stands proudly on the **Place d'Armes**, facing the Avenue de Paris, where it greets visitors as they enter the royal compound.

Courtyards★★

The wrought-iron railings date from the reign of Louis XVIII. Beyond them stretches a series of three courtyards.

Louis XIV's artistic taste

Louis XIV, whose education was neglected owing to the rebellion known as the **Fronde**, inherited from his mother, **Anne of Austria**, an inclination for politeness and refinement and acquired from **Mazarin** a collector's passion. The festivities organised at Vaux-le-Vicomte showed him how splendid garden entertainment and fountains could be. The King, who spoke Italian and Spanish fluently, made his court the melting pot of his own aesthetic values reflected by festivities, balls, games and fashion. Until 1671, the King performed on stage (dressed as the Sun in the *Ballet de la Nuit* in 1653), playing the roles of gods or mythological heroes, Roman emperors, even Alexander the Great.

He particularly liked music and had a good ear. He often played the guitar, "better than a master" according to Palatine, and learned to play the harpsichord which he appreciated at the end of his life thanks to **Couperin**; he kept himself informed of **Delalande**'s compositions and **Lully**'s operas, attended rehearsals and sang arias. Evolved from a hunting lodge, Versailles was thus designed for music, with the chapel as its temple.

Garden façade viewed from Apollo Basin

S. Sauvignier/MICHELIN

– The forecourt or **Cour des Ministres** is flanked by two long wings linking the four pavilions in which the King's ministers were accommodated.

– Since 2008, the **Cour royale** is separated from the outer courtyard by a replica of the Baroque-style **royal gate** by Jules Hardouin-Mansart, which had disappeared during the French Revolution. Only persons of high rank (peers, princes of the blood, noblemen etc) could pass in carriages through this gate. The two wings lining this court were originally separate from the palace and used as outbuildings. They were joined to the main building and fronted by a set of colonnades under Louis XV and Louis XVIII.

– Paved with slabs of black and white marble, the **Cour de Marbre★★** has been raised to its original level. It is surrounded by Louis XIII's old château, the façades of which were altered and greatly improved by Louis Le Vau and Jules Hardouin-Mansart: balustrades, busts, statues, vases etc. On the first floor of the central pavilion, the three arched windows belonging to the King's bedroom are fronted by a gilded balcony resting upon eight marble columns.

Garden Façade★★★

Walk under the North Arcade, skirt the main part of the palace and step back to get a good view of this entirely renovated façade.

The huge building occupies a total length of 680m/2 230ft and yet, its general appearance is not monotonous.

The central body stands proud from the wings, and the length of the façade is articulated with intermittent rows of sculpted columns and pillars to break the rigidity of the horizontal lines. The flat roof, built in the Italian style, is concealed by a balustrade bearing ornamental trophies and vases.

The statues of Apollo and Diana, surrounded by the Months of the Year, surmount the central body which housed the Royal Suite. Certain members of the royal family, including several of the King's children, stayed in the South Wing.

The terrace extending in front of the château commands an extensive view of the park and its many perspectives. It bears two **giant vases★**, one at each end. The one to the north was executed by **Coysevox** and symbolises War, while the south vase, attributed to **Tuby**, is a representation of Peace. They are appropriately placed outside the bay windows of the Salon de la Guerre and the Salon de la Paix respectively.

At the foot of the main building lies a row of four sculptures, the very first to be cast by the Keller brothers who drew inspiration from a classical model: Bacchus, Apollo, Antinoüs and Silenus.

The terrace offers a general **view★** of the grounds and their distinctive features: in the foreground, the Water Gardens (*Parterres d'Eau*), with a sweeping perspective as far as the Grand Canal: on the left, the South Parterre (*Parterre du Midi*); on the right, the North Parterre (*Parterre du Nord*) and groves (*Bosquets du Nord*), cut across by another canal leading to the Neptune Basin.

Return to the Cour de Marbre through the South Arcade in the south wing.

GRANDS APPARTEMENTS
Grand Appartement
du Roi★★★

The King's formal apartment consists of six salons, built by **Le Vau** in 1668 and decorated by **Le Brun**, running from the Salon d'Hercule, dedicated to a man endowed with divine powers, to the Salon d'Apollon, built in honour of the son of Jupiter and Latona.

In former times, the apartment was approached from the Royal Court by means of the Ambassadors' Staircase (destroyed in 1752). It provides a splendid example of early Louis XIV decoration. The Grand Appartement symbolised the solar myth to which Louis XIV claimed to belong. Most of the time, it was sparsely furnished with a few stools, folding chairs, pedestal and console tables. Three times a week, the King held court in the Grand Appartement. The ceremony was enhanced by dancing and gaming.

Salon d'Hercule★★★ – This drawing room stands on the site formerly occupied by the fourth and penultimate chapel of the original château.

The room boasts two splendid compositions by Veronese. **Christ at the House of Simon the Pharisee★** was a present to Louis XIV from the Venetian Republic.

On the ceiling, note the **Apotheosis of Hercules★** by François Lemoyne.

Salon de l'Abondance (a) – At the time of Louis XIV, on the days when the King held court, this reception room contained three buffets: one for hot drinks, and two for cold drinks such as wine, eaux-de-vie, sorbets and fruit juice. The walls are hung with the winter furnishings, made of embossed velvet in deep emerald tones.

Salon de Vénus (b) – The ceiling of this salon and those of the following rooms were painted by Houasse. It features decorated panels framed by heavy gilt stucco.

Salon de Diane (c) – This used to be the billiard room under Louis XIV. Observe the **bust of Louis XIV** by Bernini (1665), a remarkable piece of Baroque workmanship. The room displays several paintings by De Lafosse and Blanchard.

Salon de Mars (d) – The lavish decoration (wall hangings) is a reminder that this room once belonged to the royal suite (guard-room). Louis XIV subsequently used it for dances, games and concerts. The two galleries which housed the musicians were placed on either side

©Bertrand RIEGER/hemis.fr/Photoshot

Apotheosis of Hercules by François Lemoyne on the ceiling and Christ at the House of Simon the Pharisee by Veronese on the wall of Salon d'Hercule

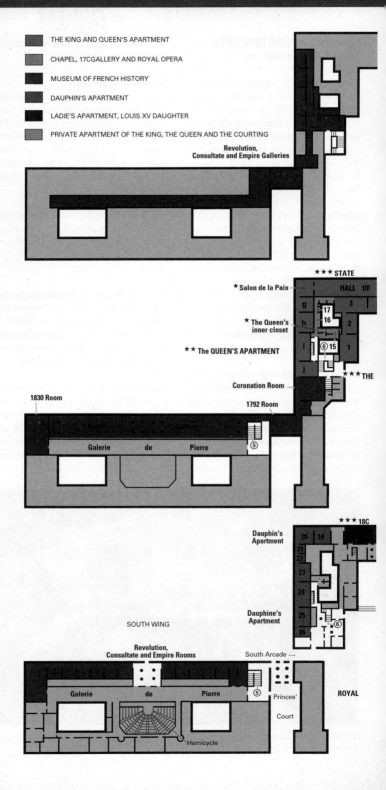

THE KING AND QUEEN'S APARTMENT

CHAPEL, 17C GALLERY AND ROYAL OPERA

MUSEUM OF FRENCH HISTORY

DAUPHIN'S APARTMENT

LADIE'S APARTMENT, LOUIS XV DAUGHTER

PRIVATE APARTMENT OF THE KING, THE QUEEN AND THE COURTING

Revolution,
Consultate and Empire Galleries

★★★ STATE

★ Salon de la Paix

HALL OF

g

17
16

3

★ The Queen's
inner closet

h

2

★★ The QUEEN'S APARTMENT

i

⑥ 15

1

j

★★★ THE

Coronation Room

1830 Room

1792 Room

Galerie   de   Pierre

⑤

Dauphin's
Apartment

★★★ 18C

20 19

21
22

23

24

Dauphine's
Apartment

25

26

⑥

SOUTH WING

Revolution,
Consultate and Empire Rooms

South Arcade

Galerie   de   Pierre

⑤

Princes'

ROYAL

Court

Hemicycle

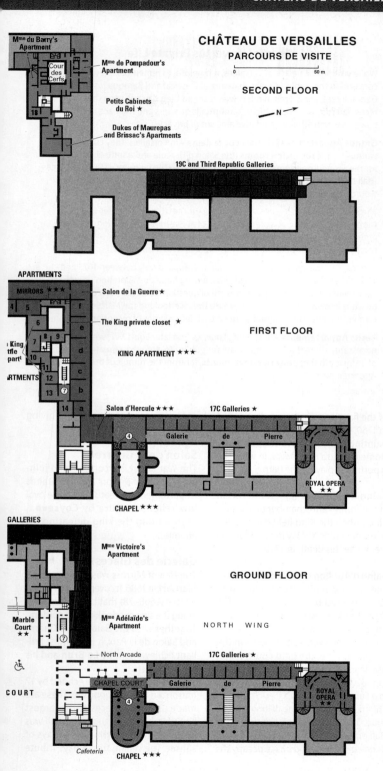

CHÂTEAU DE VERSAILLES
PARCOURS DE VISITE

0   50 m

SECOND FLOOR

N →

Mme du Barry's Apartment

Cour des Cerfs

Mme de Pompadour's Apartment

Petits Cabinets du Roi ★

18

Dukes of Maurepas and Brissac's Apartments

19C and Third Republic Galleries

APARTMENTS

MIRRORS ★★★

Salon de la Guerre ★

4   5   f

6   e

The King private closet ★

FIRST FLOOR

King tfle part

7   8   9   d

KING APARTMENT ★★★

10

RTMENTS

11

12   c

13   ⑦   b

14   a

Salon d'Hercule ★★★

17C Galleries ★

④   Galerie   de   Pierre

ROYAL OPERA ★★

CHAPEL ★★★

GALLERIES

Mme Victoire's Apartment

GROUND FLOOR

Marble Court ★★

⑦

Mme Adélaïde's Apartment

NORTH   WING

♿

COURT

North Arcade

CHAPEL COURT

17C Galleries ★

Galerie   de   Pierre

④

ROYAL OPERA ★★

Cafeteria

CHAPEL ★★★

Public Life versus Private Life

While visiting the palace of Versailles, it is helpful to remember a few facts concerning the layout of great châteaux of Classical and Baroque inspiration. Generally speaking, French rulers would spend their day between the ornate reception rooms of their official, semi-public quarters and their actual living quarters which afforded a relative amount of privacy.

Grands Appartements du Roi et de la Reine – In Versailles, they consisted of various formal **reception rooms** (the Salon d'Hercule and a suite of six rooms for the Grand Appartement du Roi), together with the famous Galerie des Glaces (Hall of Mirrors), and also included the **royal suites** where the King and Queen would appear in public.

The King and Queen's suites were placed **symmetrically** on either side of the central pavilion. Each suite consisted of at least one guard-room, several antechambers, the bedroom, the grand cabinet and a number of private drawing rooms (it was through these that the two royal suites connected).

At Versailles, this symmetrical disposition was applied only between 1673 and 1682. When Marie-Thérèse died in 1683, having Mme de Maintenon occupy the apartments of the former queen was out of question. Louis XIV moved into new quarters known as the **Appartement du Roi**, overlooking the Marble Court. His former suite was transformed, at great cost, into a series of reception rooms.

Petits Appartements – In the 18C, Louis XV and later Louis XVI , who did not necessarily share the Sun King's taste for public life, enjoyed a greater degree of intimacy in these **interior apartments**, far from the tumult of the Grands Appartements.

of the fireplace. They were dismantled in 1750. One of the Sun King's favourite paintings hangs above the fireplace: Domenichino's *King David*, in which he is portrayed playing the harp.

Salon de Mercure (e) – A fire was lit in this former antechamber on the evenings when the King held court. It was here that Louis XIV lay in state for one week after his death in 1715.

Salon d'Apollon or Salle du trône (f) – The throne was placed on a central platform covered by a large canopy. The three hooks to which the canopy was attached still remain.

The King received ambassadors in this chamber. When he held court, it was used for dances and concerts. The ceiling sports a fresco by De Lafosse: *Apollo in a Sun Chariot*.

This room marks the end of King's formal suite. Set at a perpendicular angle, the Hall of Mirrors and the adjacent rooms dedicated to war and peace occupy the

entire length of the main front giving onto the palace gardens.

Salon de la Guerre★

The War Salon is a corner room joining the Hall of Mirrors and the Grands Appartements. it features a huge oval low-relief sculpture by **Coysevox**, representing the king defeating his enemies.

Galerie des Glaces★★★

The Hall of Mirrors was completed by **Mansart** in 1686. It covered a short-lived terrace (1668–78) that Le Vau had built along the side overlooking the gardens. Together with the Salon de la Guerre and Salon de la Paix, it is the most brilliant achievement by **Le Brun** and his team of artists.

The 17 large windows are echoed by 17 mirrors on the wall opposite. These are made up of 578 pieces of the largest size possible at the time. This hall was designed to catch the golden rays of sunset. The ceiling fresco pays tribute

Galerie des Glaces

©World Illustrated/Photoshot

to the early reign of Louis XIV (from 1661 to 1678, up to the Treaty of Nijmegen). The Hall of Mirrors was used for court receptions, formal ceremonies and diplomatic encounters. On these occasions, the throne was placed under the arch leading into the Salon de la Paix.

It is easier to picture the hall during court festivities, when it was thronged with elegant visitors in formal attire, brightly lit by the thousands of flickering candles reflected in the mirrors. The tubs bearing the orange trees, as well as the chandeliers and other furnishings, were made of solid silver in Louis XIV's time.

In 1980, the Hall of Mirrors was restored to its former glory. With its crystal chandeliers and new set of candelabra – cast after the six surviving originals – it presents the same dazzling appearance as in 1770 when Marie-Antoinette was married to the Dauphin, the future King Louis XVI.

It was here that the German Empire was proclaimed on 18 January 1871, and that the **Treaty of Versailles** was signed on 28 June 1919.

The central windows offer a splendid **view★★★** of the Grand Perspective.

Salon de la Paix★

Placed at the southern end of the Hall of Mirrors, the Peace Salon counterbalances the War Salon.

Originally designed as an extension of the great gallery, it was made into an annex of the Queen's Suite toward the end of Louis XIV's reign; it communicated with the Hall of Mirrors by means of a movable partition.

Above the mantelpiece hangs *Louis XV Bringing Peace to Europe*, a painting by François Lemoyne.

Appartement du Roi★★★

Louis XIV's more private suite is arranged around the Cour de Marbre. It was designed by **Jules Hardouin-Mansart** and set up in Louis XIII's château between 1682 and 1701. The style shows a marked change in the Louis XIV period. The ceilings are no longer coffered but painted white, the marble tiling has been replaced by white and gold panelling, and large mirrors adorn the stately fireplaces.

The **salle des Gardes** or Guard-Room(**1**) and a **first antechamber** (**2**) lead to the a second, most famous antichamber.

Salon de l'Œil-de-Bœuf (**3**) – The Bulls'-Eye Chamber was originally two rooms: the King's bedchamber between 1684 and 1701 – the part nearest to the two windows looking onto the Cour de Marbre – and a small study. The two were united under the supervision of Mansart and Robert de Cotte. Lightness

and elegance are the principal characteristics of this charming drawing room, which contrasts sharply with the earlier achievements of Louis' reign. Level with the famous bull's-eye – echoed by a mirror on the opposite wall – runs a frieze depicting children at play. Note Coysevox' bust of Louis XIV. It was in this antechamber that the courtiers assembled before witnessing the rising and retiring ceremonies of the King.

Chambre du Roi (4) – This became Louis XIV's formal bedroom in 1701. At the centre of the palace, this bedroom, which looks onto the Cour de Marbre, faces in the direction of the rising sun. Louis XIV, suffering from a gangrenous knee, died here on 1 September 1715. The ritual rising and retiring ceremonies (*see sidebar below*) took place in this room from 1701 to 1789.

Daytime visitors were requested to make a small bow when passing in front of the bed, which symbolised the divine right of the monarchy.

The King's bedroom is hung with its summer furnishings of 1722 – Louis XV's second year at the palace. Beyond the beautifully restored gilded balustrade is a raised four-poster bed, complete with canopy and curtains.

Salle du Conseil (5) – Like the Salon de l'Œil-de-Bœuf, this originally consisted of two rooms: the Cabinet des Termes and the Cabinet des Perruques. The

decoration of the present room – created under Louis XV – was entrusted to **Gabriel**. The mirrors dating from Louis XIV's reign were replaced with wainscoting by **Rousseau**, who produced a splendid Rococo interior. Over a period of 100 years, many grave decisions affecting the destiny of France were taken in this council chamber, including that of France's involvement in the **American War of Independence** in 1775.

Grand appartement de la Reine★★

The Queen's suite was originally created for Louis XIV's wife **Marie-Thérèse**, who died here in 1683.

Chambre de la Reine (g) – In 1975, after a restoration programme lasting 30 years, this room regained its summer furnishings of 1787. Originally designed for **Marie-Thérèse**, the bedchamber was later occupied by the wife of the Grand Dauphin, the King's son; by the Duchesse de Bourgogne, wife of the Sun King's grandson, who gave birth to Louis XV here; by Marie Leszczynska, wife of Louis XV (for 43 years); and by Louis XVI's wife **Marie-Antoinette**. Nineteen children belonging to French royalty – among them Louis XV and Philippe V of Spain – were born in this bedroom.

A long-standing tradition ruled that the delivery of royal infants should be made in public. Even the proud Marie-Antoinette had to comply with this custom, surrounded by curious onlookers.

Note the magnificent silk hangings and furnishings decorated with flowers, ribbons and peacock tails, which were rewoven to the original pattern in Lyon.

Salon des Nobles de la Reine (h) – The official presentations to the Queen took place in this former antechamber. It was also here that the queens and dauphins of France used to lie in state prior to the burial ceremony. The original fresco on the ceiling, attributed to Michel Corneille, has been preserved.

The rest of the decoration was considered staid and old-fashioned by Marie-Antoi-

---

The rising ceremony

The Sun King was woken up at 7am by his first valet. The first visit he received was that of his **doctor**. Next came the **grandes entrées** (important guests including members of his family and those who held an office), then the **secondes entrées** (less important guests) and finally the **nobility**. **Breakfast** was followed by the **dressing ceremony**, then the king left his apartments to hear **Mass** in the Chapel.

nette, who had it entirely refurbished by the architect **Richard Mique** (1785). Furnished with commodes and corner cupboards by **Riesener** and embellished with magnificent green silk hangings, the salon looks very much as it would have done on the eve of the French Revolution in 1789.

Antichambre du Grand Couvert (i) – This chamber was used as a guard-room under Marie-Thérèse. It was here that Louis XV and Marie Leszczynska – and later Louis XVI and Marie-Antoinette – would dine in full view of the public. A family portrait of Marie-Antoinette and her children (1787) by Mme Vigée-Lebrun hangs here.

Salle des gardes de la Reine (j) – The decoration was the work of Le Brun and N Coypel. It was moved from its original setting – the Salon de Jupiter – when the Hall of Mirrors was completed in 1687. The Salon de Jupiter was subsequently renamed the Salon de la Guerre. On 6 October 1789, several of the queen's guards were stabbed to death by a group of dedicated revolutionaries.

Escalier de la Reine – Towards the end of the Ancien Régime, the Queen's Staircase was the official entrance to the royal apartments. The decoration of the staircase is extremely ornate; from the top landing, admire the elegant display of multicoloured marble designed by Le Brun. The huge *trompe-l'œil* painting is jointly attributed to Meusnier, Poerson and Belin de Fontenay.

CHAPELLE, GALERIES DU 17C, OPÉRA ROYAL★★

Chapelle★★★
Only in 1710 was the chapel finished, by which time Louis XIV was 72. Dedicated to **Saint-Louis** (Louis IX), it is an elegant display of stonework decorated in white and gold tones.
This masterpiece is the work of **Mansart** and was completed by his brother-in-law **Robert de Cotte** in 1710. The pillars and arches bear exquisite bas-reliefs

by, among others, Van Clève, Le Lorrain, Coustou.
As the usual place for an organ is occupied by the royal gallery, it stands instead at the east end in the gallery, a splendid piece of craftsmanship by **Clicquot**, enhanced by fine carvings based on studies by Robert de Cotte.
While the members of the royal family were seated in the gallery, the courtiers stood in the nave.
The ceiling, representing Hercules entering the Kingdom of the Gods, was painted by **François Lemoyne**. His work met with widespread acclaim, but the following year the artist suffered a nervous breakdown and committed suicide (1737).

Galeries du 17C★
These small rooms – occupying the greater part of the north wing – feature a charming selection of paintings and portraits, also busts and console tables.

Ground Floor – The vestibule by the chapel leads to this suite of 11 rooms. The first six were once occupied by the Duc de Maine, the son of Louis XIV and Mme de Montespan, while the last four housed the apartments of the Princes of Bourbon-Conti. The series of portraits includes Henri IV, who enjoyed visiting

Chapelle Royale
©Sarah Dusautoir/iStockphoto.com

The King's valets

The Sun King had 28 valets who served and assisted him according to a very precise timetable. What were their privileges? They were close to him daily and could, if the need arose, request a favour from him. In addition, their office automatically made them members of the aristocracy, exempted them from paying the *taille*, a royal tax and provided them with a substantial income. The best known of the King's valets was undoubtedly **Marie Du Bois** (a man, despite his name), who left a diary, but the most renowned was **Alexandre Bontemps**, an important member of the court for nearly 60 years, whom Louis XIV trusted implicitly.

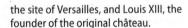

modern looking. The court engineer **Arnoult** designed the sophisticated machinery required for the new opera house. For banquets and formal receptions, the floor of the stalls and of the circle could be raised level with the stage.
Ithough initially reserved for members of the court, the opera house at Versailles was later used for lavish receptions organised on the occasion of official visits. A number of foreign rulers were received at the palace, including the **King of Sweden** (1784), Marie-Antoinette's brother the **Emperor Joseph II** (1777 and 1781) and **Queen Victoria** (1855). The sessions of the **National Assembly** were held in the Royal Opera between 1871 and 1875. It was here that the **Wallon Amendment** was voted on 30 January 1875, laying the foundation stone of the Third Republic. The latest restoration ended in 1957 and was marked by an official reception in honour of **Queen Elizabeth II** and **Prince Philip**.

the site of Versailles, and Louis XIII, the founder of the original château.

First Floor – Portraits of the royal family, Mme de Maintenon, Louis XIV's legitimised children and the celebrated figures of the King's reign, painted by Le Brun, Mignard Van der Meulen, Coypel, Rigaud Largillière etc, bring these rooms to life. Note the set of portraits of famous men (Colbert, Racine, Molière, La Fontaine, Le Nôtre and Couperin) and the vast battle scenes by Van der Meulen, characterised by attention to detail and a true love of nature.

Opéra Royal★★

Entirely made of wood, the Royal Opera House enjoys excellent acoustics and can seat 700. After two years of restoration and maintenance work on the building (2007–2009), it is once again open to the repertoires of Classical and Baroque music, dance and theatre.
Gabriel started work on the Royal Opera House in 1768 and completed it in time for the wedding ceremony of **Marie-Antoinette** and the future **King Louis XVI** in 1770. It was the first oval-shaped opera house in France. **Pajou**'s decorative work, inspired by the classical models of Antiquity, remains surprisingly

APPARTEMENTS DU DAUPHIN, PRINCE HÉRITIER

The apartments of the Crown Prince and his wife have partially retained or regained their 18C ornamentation and have been redecorated and sometimes refurnished. The entrance is through the **Salle des Gardes**, decorated with splendid Gobelins tapestries. A second antechamber completes the first by exhibiting portraits of Louis XV's daughters by Nattier.

Chambre du Dauphin (19) – Occupied from 1684, first of all by Louis XIV's son and then by subsequent heirs to the throne until 1789 (the last occupant was Louis XVI's son), this has retained its original 1747 décor: wardrobe with lacquered panels (Bernard Van Rysenburgh – BVRB), commode by Boudin and an 18C embroidered canopied bed.

Grand Cabinet du Dauphin (20) – This room houses portraits of Mesdames Adélaïde, Louise, Sophie and Victoire by Nattier, as well as some beautiful pieces of furniture by Jacob, taken from Louis

Daily life at Versailles

The court included some 4 000 to 5 000 people altogether, and up to 10 000 on crowded days according to Mme de Sévigné. The **Grand Maître de la Maison du Roi** (Grand Master of the King's Household), a post held since 1641 by the Prince de Condé, was in charge of food supplies. Suppliers were keen financiers who advanced the necessary funds and paid themselves back through advantages bestowed by the King. The remains of royal feasts were sold by all those who ordered, prepared and served the dishes. This was a very lucrative business. Meat and fish were sold to the town's shopkeepers through the château's Swiss guards; drinks, coffee and chocolate were sold from kiosks made of plaster or wood, located near the access ramps or the gates. Courtiers had no kitchens and had to be content with warming up dishes bought in this way. Improvised kitchens, dish-warmers and coal shops caused the upper and lower galleries to stink. If you add to this the continuous flow of visitors and lawyers who, provided they were properly dressed (men could hire swords at the castle entrance), mingled with the courtiers hoping to catch a glimpse of the King on his way to the chapel through the Grands Appartements, you can well imagine the crowds.

XVI's gaming room at St-Cloud. The amazing globe was commissioned by Louis XVI for his son's education.

Bibliothèque (21) – The library boasts magnificent wooden panelling in deep amber tones, enhanced by turquoise relief work. Admire Vernet's delicate seascapes above the doors. This room leads to the Dauphine's apartments which are visited in reverse order.

Cabinet Intérieur de la Dauphine (22) – This room features Vernis Martin wainscoting as in the Dauphin's library. Note Gaudreaux' commode and a writing desk by Bernard Van Rysenburgh (BVRB). The back rooms were refurbished under Louis XVIII for the Duchesse d'Angoulême, the daughter of Louis XVI: couch formerly belonging to the Comtesse de Provence, antechamber, study-library and servant's quarters.

Chambre de la Dauphine (23) – The bedroom contains a Polish-style bed and a magnificent set of six armchairs by Heurtaut. Note Nattier's two portraits of Mme Henriette and Mme Adélaïde, portrayed respectively as Flora and Diana.

Grand Cabinet de la Dauphine (24) – This room evokes the marriage of Marie Leszczynska to Louis XV. It also presents Lemaire's sculpted barometer, offered on

the occasion of Marie-Antoinette's marriage to the Dauphin, and several corner cupboards by Bernard Van Rysenburgh (BVRB). If one compares the Savonnerie tapestry with that of the next room, one notices that the fleur-de-lis motifs have been replaced by stars (Revolution).

Deuxième antichambre (25) – The fireplace, adorned with a bust of the Regent, was taken from the Queen's Bedroom at the time of Marie Leszczynska. Savonnerie tapestry.

Première antichambre (26) – This houses a number of pictures representing the rulers who succeeded the Sun King: portrait of the five-year-old Louis XV by Alexis Belle (1723), *Cavalcade of the King (Louis XV) after His Coronation on 22 October 1722* by Pierre-Denis Martin.

APPARTEMENTS DE MESDAMES, FILLES DE LOUIS XV

Symmetrical to the Appartements du Dauphin, these were the private suites of Louis XV's two unmarried daughters who lived here until the French Revolution.

Galerie basse – Divided into apartments under Louis XVI and partly restored under Louis-Philippe, the gallery now stands as it did under Louis XIV. From 1782 to 1789 the rooms in this gallery were used by Marie-Antoinette and her children.

Appartement de Mme Victoire – The Sun King's former bathroom and its two marble piscinae underwent several alterations before being used as the antechamber to this suite, occupied by the fourth daughter of Louis XV.
The **Grand Cabinet** (**27**) is an exquisite corner room with a delightful carved cornice and panelling by Verberckt. It has retained its original fireplace.
Mme Victoire's former **bedroom** (**28**) has been furnished with some outstanding pieces, set off by the newly restored summer hangings.

Appartement de Mme Adélaïde – These rooms housed the second suite of Mme de Pompadour, who died here in 1764. Five years later, Mme Adélaïde moved into the suite.
The **Salle des Hocquetons** (**29**) was an annex adjoining the former Ambassadors' Staircase, destroyed in 1752. The stately proportions of this room give an idea of how magnificent the flight of stairs once looked. Note the huge **clock★** by Passement and Roque with bronze ornamentation by Germain; it dates from 1754 and illustrates the creation of the world.

APPARTEMENTS PRIVÉS DU ROI, DE LA REINE, DES FAVORITES ET DES COURTISANS★

These were the private apartments of the King, Queen, favourites and courtiers.

Petit Appartement du Roi

This suite of rooms, with its superb wainscoting by Gabriel, provides a delightful feast for the eyes. The fine Rococo carvings are the work of Verberckt.

Chambre à coucher (**6**) – The absence of furniture makes it difficult to picture this room in its original state. Owing to the constraints of court etiquette, Louis XV (after 1738) and then Louis XVI (up to the end of the Ancien Régime) daily had to leave this room and slip away to the formal bedroom, where they "performed" the rising and retiring ceremonies. It was here that Louis XV died of smallpox on 10 May 1774.

Cabinet de la Pendule (**7**) – This was a games room until 1769. Passemant and Dauthiau's **astronomical clock★★★** was installed here in 1754. A copper line running across the floor indicates the Versailles meridian. In the centre of the room stands the equestrian statue of Louis XV by Vassé. It is a replica of Bouchardon's sculpture which initially adorned place Louis XV – now called place de la Concorde – in Paris and which was destroyed in 1792.

Antichambre des Chiens (**8**) – A charming passageway off the king's private staircase (known as *degré du Roi*). The decoration features Louis XIV panelling, in sharp contrast to the adjoining rooms.

Salle à manger dite des Retours de chasse (**9**) – Between 1750 and 1769 hunts were organised every other day in the forests surrounding Versailles. Louis XV and a few privileged fellow hunters would come here to sup after their exertions.

Cabinet intérieur du Roi (**10**) – This masterpiece of 18C French ornamental art was commissioned by Louis XV. Gabriel and the accomplished cabinetmaker Verberckt were responsible for the stunning Rococo décor. The celebrated **roll-top desk★★★** by Oeben and Riesener (1769) was among the few prestigious works of art to be spared in 1792. The **medal cabinet** attributed to the cabinetmaker Gaudreaux (1738) is heavily decorated with gilded bronze: it bears the 1783 candelabra commemorating the role played by France in the American War of Independence, flanked by two Sèvres vases (bronzes by Thomire).
Two corner cupboards made by Joubert in 1755 to house Louis XV's ever-increasing collections were added subsequently, as was a set of chairs attributed to Foliot (1774).

In 1785 the room was the scene of a formal encounter attended by Marie-Antoinette, at which the King informed **Cardinal de Rohan** that he would shortly be arrested for his involvement in the **Diamond Necklace Affair**.

The Corner Room leads through to the study where Louis XV and Louis XVI kept all confidential documents relating to State affairs, and where they granted private audiences.

Cabinet de Mme Adélaïde (11) – This was one of the first "new rooms" laid out at the instigation of Louis XV. It overlooks the Royal Court and was designed by Louis XV for his favourite daughter Mme Adélaïde (1752). The ornate decoration features delightful Rococo wainscoting and gilded panelling embellished with musical instruments, as well as fishing and floral motifs: the room was used as a music room by the King's daughter. It is believed that the young Mozart performed on the harpsichord before the royal family in this very room, during the winter of 1763–64. Louis XVI later made the room his "jewel cabinet."

Bibliothèque de Louis XVI (12) – Designed by the ageing Gabriel and executed by the wood carver Antoine Rousseau, this extremely refined library is a perfect example of the Louis XVI style (1774). The austere appearance of the bookcases, in which the door panels are concealed by a set of false decorative backs, is countered by the gay Chinese motifs on the upholstery and the curtains. Next to Riesener's flat-top desk stands the vast mahogany table where the King spent many enjoyable hours correcting geographical maps.

Salon des Porcelaines (13) – This room was used as the Hunters' Dining Hall under Louis XV, and from 1769 to 1789 under Louis XVI. It houses numerous exhibits of Sèvres porcelain, painted after drawings by Oudry.

Salon des Jeux de Louis XVI (14) – From the doorway admire the full effect of this perfect vignette of 18C furniture and ornamental art: corner cupboards by Riesener (1774), set of chairs by Boulard, curtains and upholstery in rich crimson and gold brocade.

Cabinets Intérieurs de la Reine★

Also called "Appartements de Marie-Antoinette" who brought her own touch to them, these cramped interior apartments, looking onto two inner courtyards, were used as a daytime retreat by the queens of France who, unlike kings, were not allowed to live anywhere but in their Grands Appartements.

Cabinet doré (15) – The panelling by the **Rousseau brothers** marks the revival of Antique motifs: frieze with rosettes, sphinx, trivets, small censers. A lovely chandelier features among the magnificent bronze works. The commode was made by **Riesener**. Naderman's harp reminds visitors that the Queen was an enthusiastic musician in her spare time; she would often play with Grétry, Gluck or even his rival Piccinni.

Bibliothèque (16) – Note the drawer handles in the shape of a two-headed eagle, the emblem of the House of Hapsburg.

Méridienne (17) – This little octagonal boudoir was used for resting by Marie-Antoinette. It was designed in 1781 by the Queen's architect Mique in honour of the birth of the first dauphin. The decoration evokes romance and the period leading up to the dauphin's birth: lilies, hearts pierced with arrows and the famous dolphin.

Petits Cabinets du Roi★

These were originally Louis XV's interior apartments, where he could retire away from it all, quietly read or have dinner, and receive his relatives, close friends and mistresses. Over the years, the rooms changed many times of occupants and had various functions.

Appartement de Mme de Pompadour – This was the first suite occupied by Louis XV's mistress between 1745 and 1750. The Grand Cabinet features splendid carved woodwork by Verberckt.

Appartement de Mme du Barry – The wooden panelling has been meticulously restored to its original colours. The suite looks out onto the Cour des Cerfs and the Cour au Marbre. It consists of a bathroom, a bedroom, a library and a corner **drawing room (18)** which was one of Louis XV's favourite haunts; he would enjoy sitting here and gazing out at the town of Versailles, nestled among wooded slopes.

Appartements des ducs de Maurepas et Brissac– These apartments were occupied by two ministers of Louis XVI. Most of the furniture was donated by the Duke and Duchess of Windsor.

GALERIES DE L'HISTOIRE DE FRANCE

Little known by the general public, the collections of paintings and sculptures of the old **Musée de l'Histoire de France** at Versailles, set up by King Louis-Philippe in 1837, occupy several halls and galleries throughout the palace.

They include the rooms described below, which are open to the public and which you may want to see after having visited the Grands Appartements. They also feature other galleries, such as the Salles de la **Révolution**, du **Consulat** et de l'**Empire** and the Salles de la **Restauration**, de la **Monarchie de Juillet**, du **Second Empire** et de la **IIIᵉ République**, which can only be visited by guided tour. *For more details, call* ℘*01 30 83 78 00.*

Galerie des batailles★

Created in 1837 on the site of the princes' suite in the south wing, this gallery caused quite a stir because of its huge dimensions (120m/394ft by 13m/43ft). It was designed to house the 33 paintings of **France's major victories** under the Ancien Régime, the Empire and the Republic, from Tolbiac *(first on the left when entering)* to Wagram *(first on the right)* by Horace Vernet, Louis-Philippe's favourite painter (who also painted Iéna, Fontenoy, Bouvines and Friedland), and including works by Eugène Delacroix (Taillebourg) and Baron Gérard (Austerlitz).

Salle de 1792

This large, unfurnished room lies at the junction of the south wing and the main central pavilion. The walls are hung with portraits of soldiers, paintings of famous battles and war scenes. Cogniet's work *The Paris National Guard* shows Louis-Philippe proudly sporting his Lieutenant-General's uniform.

Salle de 1830

Commissioned by Louis-Philippe, this room is devoted to the last king of France, who was known as the 'Citizen-king'.

Salle du sacre

The Coronation Room room was initially used as a chapel between 1676 and 1682. The **Parlement of Paris** used to hold its sessions in this former guard room. It was altered by Louis-Philippe in order to accommodate several huge paintings depicting the Emperor's coronation. David's second *Coronation of Napoleon* – painted between 1808 and 1822 – lies to the left of the entrance. The original is exhibited in the Louvre Museum (Salle Mollien). On the opposite wall hang David's *Distribution of Eagles on the Champ de Mars* and a painting by Gros representing *Murat at the Battle of Aboukir* (1806).

Parc du château de
Versailles★★★

For over a century, Versailles provided Europe with a model of the ideal royal residence. This included its gardens and park, born from the Sun King's determination to transform the marshland surrounding his château into a true masterpiece. The colossal undertaking will forever be associated with the name André Le Nôtre, whose refined sense of balance between symmetry and fantasy, combined with a skilful play on shadow and light, and abundant use of water effects, created what is widely considered to be the most beautiful example of 17C landscape architecture.

A BIT OF HISTORY

The palace of Versailles was built on top of a small hillock consolidated by vast loads of earth. The terrace rises above the **Latona Basin** by a height of 10.5m/35ft, the **Apollo Basin** by 30m/98.4ft, the Grand Canal by 32m/105ft and the **Orangery** by 17m/56ft.

Before the French Revolution, the park was surrounded by a 43km/27mi-long wall, punctuated by 22 royal gates. Beyond the actual **gardens** of the Château (93ha/230 acres), the Versailles estate used to incorporate the **Petit Parc** (which included the Grand Canal and the Trianon), and the **Grand Parc**, a vast hunting reserve dotted with villages. Under the Second Empire, the area of the park shrank to around 815ha/2 014 acres. Today, the distance between the palace and its perimeter is about 950m/1 040yd.

THE GARDENS★★★

Open Apr–Oct daily 7am–8.30pm; Nov–Mar Tue–Sun 8 am–6 pm. 8€ entrance fee only required during the Grand Musical Fountain Display season (see Addresses). 01 30 83 78 00. www.chateauversailles.fr.

Michelin Local Map: 311: I-3, map 101 folds 22, 23 or 106 folds 17, 18.

Info: www.chateau versailles.fr and www.chateau versaillesspectacles.fr.

Location: The park lies northwest both of the town of Versailles and the château. If you plan on visiting the royal apartments prior to discovering the park and its major highlights, note that a little train departing from the château's North Terrace provides a convenient shuttle service between the palace, both Trianons and the Grand Canal (*see Addresses*).

Don't Miss: Walking through Versailles' beautiful gardens to the sound of Baroque music, during the enchanting Grand Musical Fountain Displays (*see Addresses*); Marie-Antoinette's delicate, bucolic retreat at the Queen's Hamlet.

Timing: If you only have a few hours to spare, treating yourself to a Segway tour of this large park (*see Addresses*) will enable you get a good overview of it in record time.

The terrace and *parterres* provide a perfect balance to the monumental front of the palace, which screens the town of Versailles.

Lower down, the lawns and the Grand Canal cut across the middle of the grounds, creating a sweeping **perspective★★★** that extends into the far distance. Numerous groves and straight paths are laid out on either side of this central axis. The 300 sculptures which adorn the park make it one of the biggest open-air museums of classical sculpture. In order to return to Le Nôtre's original layout, Versaille's gardeners brought down the chestnut trees lining the Allée royale and replanted this stretch framed by six groves so as to re-create the decor, which Louis XIV was so fond of: clipped box trees, high hornbeam hedges and a generous use of trellis work.

AXE DU SOLEIL

Here are some major highlights along the east–west axis of the gardens.

Parterre d'eau★★

The Water Parterres are two huge basins which front the stately palace and constitute a sort of aquatic esplanade where the three main perspectives meet: the central view and the line along the North and South Parterres.

Bassin et parterre de Latone★

An imposing flight of steps known as Latona Staircase, flanked by two fountains and a double ramp flanked with yew trees and replicas of antique statues, lead from the Parterre d'Eau down to the Bassin de Latone (&see below).

The two fountains – Three allegorical statues decorate each of the two fountains (1687) which were originally called *Combats des animaux* (Animal Combats). Particulaly noteworthy, **Le Point du Jour** (**1**) by Gaspard Marsy, features Dawn with his head crowned by a star, while Desjardins statue of **L'Heure du Soir ★** (**2**) portrays the hunting goddess Diana.

Bassin de Latone★ – This composition by Marsy was the first marble sculpture in the gardens of Versailles (1670). It tells the story of Latona, mother of Apollo and Diana, who was showered with insults by the peasants of Lycea and prevented from quenching her thirst. She appealed to Jupiter, the father of her children, who avenged the offence by turning the culprits into aquatic animals. Originally, the statue of Latona looked toward the palace, a clear indication of how the

King viewed the public or private insults concerning his love life. At the foot of the steps lies the **Nymphe à la coquille** (**3**), a replica of Coysevox' statue, featuring a nymph with a shell. The original work, inspired by the statues of Antiquity, was moved to the Louvre.

Allée royale

The Royal Walk is run down the middle by the **Tapis Vert**, a long stretch of lawn replanted according to Le Nôtre's plans. It is lined with a superb collection of ornamental **vases** and **statues**.

A stroll along the Allée du Midi leads to the **Vénus de Richelieu** (**4**), sculpted by Le Gros after an Antique bust which featured among the Cardinal's private collections.

BOSQUETS DU MIDI

You will find below some of the south groves' main sights.

Bosquet de la Girandole

This is one of the oldest groves in Versailles. Its sculptures were commissioned by Nicolas Fouquet for his splendid castle in Vaux-le-Vicomte (&see p291).

Bosquet de la Salle de Bal★ (5)

This elegant Ballroom Grove, also known as the Rocaille Grove, was used as an outdoor theatre for performances given by members of the court or for dancing. It was part of Le Nôtre's original plans and his last creation (1682). Shaped as a circular stage, it is surrounded by gentle slopes, grassy banks and tiered rockeries where small cascades tumble down.

Bassins des Saisons

Dedicated to the seasons, four fountains were laid out to plans by Le Brun along paths parallel to the Tapis Vert. Their lead figures were re-gilded and decorated in natural tones. They are *Bacchus or Autumn* (**6**) designed by Marsy, *Saturn or Winter* (**9**) by Girardon, *Flora or Spring* (**13**) by Tuby, *Ceres or Summer* (**14**) by Regnaudin.

"Ten thousand trees for Versailles"

The park was severely damaged by storms, which hit the Île-de-France region in December 1999, when thousands of trees, particularly old, tall ones, were brought down. However, the devastating action of the storm had one very positive effect: the renovation programme launched in 1990 was brought forward with the invaluable help of numerous patrons, among them Americans, Koreans, Canadians and a village in Switzerland. And today, quite a few sections of the park have been restored to their original condition.

Bosquet de la Reine (7)

The Queen's Grove lies on the site of a former maze and was created in 1775, at the time of the great replanting campaign. In its centre stand a number of busts and bronze statues cast after Antique models: Aphrodite, a Fighting Gladiator, etc. The maple groves are a magnificent sight in autumn.

Bassin du Miroir (8)

Of the two fountains circling the Allée royale, the larger one began to silt up and Louis XVIII replaced it by a landscape garden, known as the Jardin du Roi. The only one to survive is the Mirror Fountain, adorned handsomely with statues.

Jardin du Roi★

A dazzling sight in summer, when all the flowers are in full bloom, the King's Garden is a welcome change from the formal groves of Versailles.

The Colonnade★★

This grove boasts a magniificient peristyle with 32 marble columns, built by **Mansart** in 1685. In its centre, note the statue of *Proserpine Ravished by Pluto* attributed to Girardon.

Bassin d'Apollon★

This whole composition, created by Tuby after drawings by Le Brun, portrays Apollo the Sun God seated in his chariot, surrounded by marine monsters, rising from the ocean waters to bring Light to the Earth. From the Apollo Fountain, an esplanade bordered by statues (parts of which are genuine antiquities) leads to the Grand Canal.

BOSQUETS DU NORD

The north groves' major highlights are as follows.

Bosquet des Dômes (10)

The Grove of Domes was named after two pavilions crowned by domes which were designed by **Mansart**. They were demolished in 1820. A series of low-relief sculptures adorns the edge of the fountain, representing the weapons used in different countries. It has the elegant touch of Girardon. Among the statues feature two works by Tuby, *Acis* and *Galatea*.

Bosquet de l'Encelade★★ (11)

The stark realism of this Baroque composition by Marsy contrasts sharply with the other groups dotted around the gardens. A head and two arms is all that is visible of the Titan Enceladus, being dragged down towards the bowels of the earth by the rocks of Mount Olympus by which the Titan had hoped to reach the sky (a clear warning to Fouquet).

Bassin de l'Obélisque (12)

Designed by Mansart, this raised fountain is surrounded by a flight of stone steps and several lawns. When the fountains are in operation, the central sculpture lets out a gigantic spray of water, which resembles a liquid obelisk.

Bosquet des Bains d'Apollon★★ (15)

Only open during the Grand Musical Fountain Display (&see Addresses). Designed by Hubert Robert in 1776, the Grove of Apollo's Baths heralded the Anglo-Chinese style, which Marie-

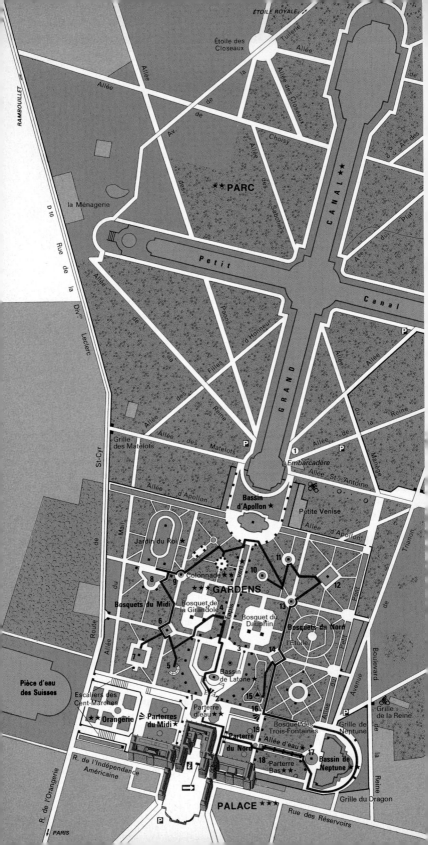

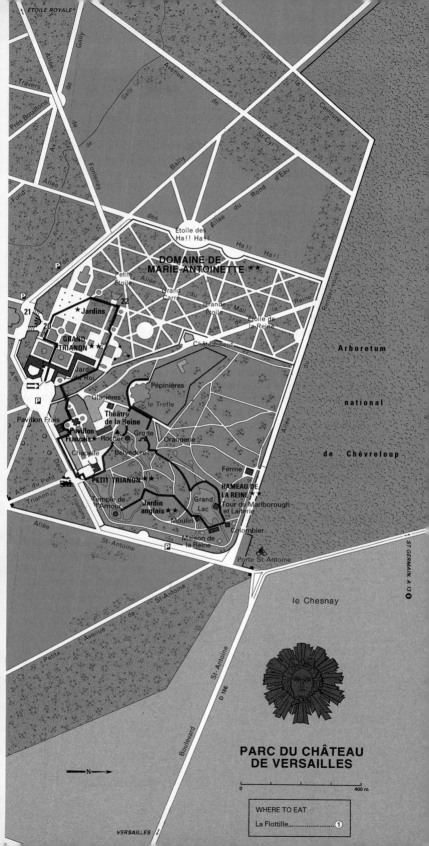

ÉTOILE ROYALE

Allée de Bailly

Allée des

Prés Bouillons

Travers

Fond

Allée

Allée de Gally

Avenue de Gally

St-Cyr

Ax de Fontenay

Bailly

Allée du Rond d'Eau

Etoile des Ha!! Ha!!

Ha!! Ha!!

Allée de la Ceinture

Rendez-vous

DOMAINE DE MARIE-ANTOINETTE ★★

Petite Étoile

Allée

Grand Carré

Grand du Étoile

Grande Étoile

Grande Mail

Allée de la Reine

★ **Jardins**

21   22

20

GRAND TRIANON ★★

Jardin du Roi

Châteauneuf

Étoile de la Reine

Arboretum

national

Glacières

Pépinières

le Trèfle

Allée du

de   Chèvreloup

Pavillon Frais

Théâtre de la Reine ★

Pavillon Français ★

Rocher ▲ Grotte

Orangerie

Allée du Petit

Chapelle

Belvédère

Allée des Deux Trianons

PETIT TRIANON ★ ★

Ferme

Allée du Petit Trianon

HAMEAU DE LA REINE ★★

Temple de l'Amour

Jardin anglais ★★

Grand Lac

Tour de Marlborough et Laiterie

Moulin

Trianon

Maison de la Reine

Colombier

Allée St-Antoine

P

Porte St-Antoine

le Chesnay

Avenue de St-Antoine

Petite

Rue St-Antoine

D 186

ST GERMAIN A 13 ⑩

PARC DU CHÂTEAU DE VERSAILLES

Boulevard

→ N

0   400 m

VERSAILLES

WHERE TO EAT

La Flottille..........................①

Antoinette later adopted for the Trianon park. On the edge of a small lake, a charming artificial grotto houses the **Apollo Group★**.

Its lush setting is a far cry from the austere 17C Versailles. The Sun God, tired by the day's exertions, is portrayed resting, waited upon by a group of nymphs (Girardon and Regnaudin).

Carrefour des Philosophes (16)

Flanked by impressive statues, the Philosophers' Crossroad offers an interesting sideways **view★★** of the palace (northwest corner).

BASSINS DE NEPTUNE ET DU DRAGON – ALLÉE D'EAU
Bassin de Neptune★★

The Neptune Fountain was designed by **Le Nôtre**, but acquired its present appearance in 1741, during the reign of Louis XV. It is by far the largest fountain in Versailles. Its proportions are wildly extravagant by classical standards, and it extends northwards beyond the rectangle formed by the gardens.

Bassin du Dragon (17)

This allegorical sculpture evoking the victory over deep-sea monsters is an allusion to the crushing of the Fronde Revolt, symbolised by a wounded dragon.

Allée d'Eau★

The Water Walk is a double row of 22 small white-marble fountains bearing bronze groups of three children, each holding pink marble vessels.

PARTERRES – ORANGERIE
Parterre du Nord

The very first royal suite looked out onto the North Parterre, a 'terrace of greenery' created in 1668.

Bassin des Nymphes de Diane (18)

The cascade known as the Bath of Diana's Nymphs is surrounded by fine **low-relief carvings★** by Girardon, which inspired 18C and 19C painters such as Renoir.

Parterre Bas★★

Close to the groves, this terrace is flanked along its northern and western boundaries by bronze statues representing the four Continents, four Poems, four Seasons and four Temperaments. The lead **Pyramid Fountain★** (**19**), made by Girardon from a study by Le Brun, combines grace with originality: dolphins, crayfish and tritons. At the top of the steps leading to the Parterres d'Eau, note **Le Rémouleur** (the Knife-grinder), a bronze replica of a Classical statue. Coysevox' **Vénus à la tortue** (Venus on a tortoise), is a bronze cast, also inspired by Antique sculpture.

Parterres du Midi★

The flower beds of the South Parterre, with their vivid blossoms and pretty boxwood patterns, were laid out in front of the Queen's apartments.

The terrace running along the Orangery offers a good **view★** of the octagonal **Pièce d'Eau des Suisses**. Designed to embellish the north–south axis of the gardens, the 700m/2 275ft-long Swiss Ornamental Lake was named after the Swiss guards who built it in 1678.

Orangerie★★

One of **Mansart**'s creations (1684), the south-facing Orangery has retained its original double glazing. It extends south by means of two corner pavilions set at right angles which support the colossal **Escalier des Cent-Marches**, a flight of 100 steps. At the time of Louis XIV, the Orangery housed 3 000 rare trees in tubs; 2 000 of these were orange trees. The Orangery looks splendid during the summer season, when its 1 055 orange trees, palm trees, oleanders and others are brought outside and arranged around the restored flower beds.

THE PARK★★

⏰Open Apr–Oct daily 7am–8.30pm. Nov–Mar Tue–Sun 8 am–6pm. ⊛No charge for pedestrians; 5€/car (restricted parking areas; access from boulevard de la Reine or Grille St-Antoine). ✆01 30 83 78 00. www.chateauversailles.fr.

Relaxing by the Grand Canal

©Alexandre Fagundes De Fagundes/Dreamstime.com

Grand Canal★★

Built from 1668 to 1679, the Grand Canal was designed by **Le Nôtre** in the shape of a large cross: the long canal is 1 670m/5 480ft long by 62m/204ft wide; the shorter one measures 1 070m/3 500ft long by 80m/263ft wide. Years ago, the 1 872 trees lining the Grand Canal were clipped back to a height of 15m/49ft in order to return to the initial perspective.

DOMAINE DE MARIE-ANTOINETTE★★

○*Open Tue–Sun Apr–Oct noon–6.30pm; ⊚10€. Nov–Mar noon–5.30pm; ⊚6€. Ticket includes access to both Trianon Palaces, the Queen's Hamlet, the French and English Gardens, the French Pavilion, the Temple of Love and the Belvedere. ℘01 30 83 78 00. www.chateauversailles.fr.*

Formed by the **Petit Trianon** and its **gardens** and **hamlet**, the area called Marie-Antoinette's Estate has been returned to its former arrangement. This is where Louis XVI's wife would retire, away from the Court's rigorous etiquette expected from a woman of her rank.

PETIT TRIANON★★

Louis XV's love of gardening and farming prompted the construction of the Petit Trianon. **Gabriel** completed the project in 1768, shortly before Louis XV's reign ended. Mme de Pompadour, the woman behind the initial project, never saw the château. Louis XVI gave the Petit Trianon to his wife **Marie-Antoinette** in 1774. The Queen would often come here with her children and her sister-in-law, relieved to get away from the pomp of Versailles and its court intrigues.

Exterior – Overlooking the formal gardens, the somewhat austere façade facing the courtyard is a perfect example of Gabriel's talent. The four regularly spaced columns are crowned by a balustrade and two fine flights of steps lead down to the gardens.

Interior – This masterpiece of the Louis XVI style offers many highlights. Among these, Guibert's craftsmanship is particularly evident in the superb **panelling★★** of the dining room and drawing room. In the dining room, the decoration presents fruit, flower and foliage motifs, set off against a pale green background, a welcome change from the "Trianon grey" prevalent throughout the 19C. The drawing room, partly refurnished by Empress Eugénie in the 19C, houses one of **Riesener**'s greatest achievements, the famous astronomical writing desk (1771).

GARDENS AND HAMLET★★
Pavillon français★

Built in 1750 by Gabriel for Louis XV and Mme de Pompadour, this pavilion features a refined interior comprising a circular room, a boudoir and a kitchen.

197

Note the cornice and its sculpted frieze representing the farm animals that were raised on the estate. The pavilion is surrounded by **French gardens**.

Orangerie de Jussieu

Louis XV commissioned **Claude Richard** to design this experimental greenhouse (1759) which was entrusted to the famous botanist **Bernard de Jussieu**.

Petit théâtre de Marie-Antoinette

As the queen loved acting, a small theatre, accommodating a hundred spectators, was designed for her by **Mique** in 1780. The machinery used for the scenery changes has been preserved.

Hameau de la Reine★★

Reminiscent of a Norman village, this bucolic composition, which forms the Queen's Hamlet, was built in 1783. The grounds around the lake (Grand Lac) are dotted with pretty cottages featuring cob walls and thatched or tiled roofs: the **Queen's House**, the Boudoir, the Malborough Tower, the Mill, the Warming Room, the Refreshments Dairy, the Dovecote, the Guards' Room, and last but not least, the Farm, the products of which actually supplied Versailles' kitchens.

Jardin anglais★★

In 1774, Louis XV's former **botanical garden** was torn down to give way to this English Garden, often known as landscape gardens. Created between 1777 and 1787 by **Richard Mique** with the help of the painter **Hubert Robert**, this succession of artificial landscape scenes includes the Belvedere (a bandstand decorated with statues by Deschamps), the Rock and the Grotto (affording pleasant views of the garden) and the **Temple of Love**, a fine Neoclassical building out of marble housing a replica of Bouchardon's *Cupid cutting his bow from the Club of Hercules*.

GRAND TRIANON★★

Known as the **Trianon de Porcelaine**, the first pavilion (1670) built on this site, faced with blue-and-white Delft tiling, was a quiet, secluded meeting place for Louis XIV and his favourite, Mme de Montespan. When she fell from favour, the pavilion deteriorated and was taken down in 1687. In six months, **Jules Hardouin-Mansart** completed the **Trianon de Marbre**, a retreat built by Louis XIV for the royal family.

Château★★

This "pink marble and porphyry palace with delightful gardens", as Mansart described it, is widely regarded as the most refined set of buildings within the Versailles compound. Walk past the low railings and enter the semicircular court-

Hameau de la Reine

S. Sauvignier/MICHELIN

Peristyle of the Grand Trianon

S. Sauvignier/MICHELIN

yard to discover two buildings with a flat terrace roof, joined by a **peristyle**.

Interior – The austere interior decoration has changed very little since the days of Louis XIV. The apartments were occupied by **Napoleon, Louis-Philippe** and their families. The furniture is either Empire, Restoration or Louis-Philippe, and the paintings are by 17C French artists. Here are just a few highlights, but there is a lot more to see.

In the left pavilion, the **Salon des Glaces** was used as a council chamber. Admire the splendid Empire furniture and the lavish silk hangings, rewoven according to the original pattern ordered by Marie-Antoinette. The **bedroom** contains the bed Napoleon commissioned for his apartments at the Tuileries; it was later altered for Louis-Philippe's use.

The **reception rooms** in the right wing were remodelled by Louis-Philippe, who gave them a more personal touch. The salons are enhanced by a collection of 17C paintings dedicated to mythological subjects. The **Salon des Malachites** owes its name to various objects encrusted with malachite given to Napoleon by Tsar Alexander I.

The north-facing **drawing room** houses paintings representing the early days of Versailles. The two filing cabinets (1810) and the console table (1806) were made by Jacob Desmalter from a drawing by Charles Percier. The **Salon des Sources**,

used by Napoleon as a topographical study, leads to the Imperial suite.

Placed at a right angle, the **Galerie des Cotelle★** houses a precious collection of 21 paintings by Cotelle. They conjure up a vivid picture of the palace and its stately grounds at the time of Louis XIV. The lovely Empire chandeliers were manufactured in the town of Le Creusot. At the end of the gallery, the luminous **Salon des Jardins** features a fine set of chairs from the Château de Meudon.

Gardens★

These derive their simple charm from the displays of flower beds and the absence of allegorical meanings. Some of the flowers in fashion during the 17C and 18C have been reintroduced. The terrace of the **Jardin Bas** or Lower Gardens **(20)** commands a good view of the **Bassin Bas** or Lower Basin **(21)**, which is reached via a horseshoe staircase, and of the Grand Canal beyond, seen from the side. Beyond the *parterres* lies a charming wood featuring fine avenues, rows of stately trees and several small ponds. The only sculpture with a mythological theme is Mansart's **Buffet d'Eau (22)**, a fountain completed in 1703.

Skirt **Trianon-sous-Bois** and walk through what was once the King's private garden. It is flanked by two square pavilions that housed the apartments of Mme de Maintenon and Louis XIV toward the end of the Sun King's reign.

ADDRESSES

⏹ EAT

⊜⊜ **La Flotille** – *Parc du Château de Versailles. ℘01 39 51 41 58. www.la flotille.fr. Closed evenings except during evening events. Reservations required Sun.* On the edge of the Grand Canal, in the château's park, there's a small, late 19C house brightened by a glass roof. This *guinguette*-like establishment offers three options: restaurant, brasserie and tearoom. The food is nothing to write home about, but the summer terrace is utterly delightful!

GRAND FOUNTAIN DISPLAYS AT VERSAILLES

☺ You may purchase your ticket for either of the following events on the day you come *(at the entrance of the Gardens)* or in advance, by using the online reservation service at www. chateauversaillesspectacles.fr or by calling ℘01 30 83 78 89.

Les Grandes Eaux musicales – *Apr– end Oct Sat–Sun and holidays (except 1 May). Fountains 11am–noon, 3.30–5.30pm. Grand Perspective 11am–noon. Ballroom, Colonnade Groves and Mirror Fountain 11.15–11.45am. Grand Perspective, all Groves and Fountains 3.30–5pm. Finale at the Fountain of Neptune 5.20–5.30pm. 8€.* The Grand Musical Fountain Display takes the spectator back to the magical fountains and groves of 17C Versailles to the sound of Baroque music. A brochure describing the itinerary is given out. Spectators await the beginning of the displays above the Bassin de Latone. As soon as the Bassin de Latone fountain begins gushing, follow the plan without dawdling, and make sure not to miss the *bosquets* (groves) that are only open for these events, especially La Salle de Bal and the Bosquet d'Apollon (invisible from the alleys). The end – and climax – of the show *(at 5.20pm, lasting 10mn)* takes place in the Bassin de Neptune and the Bassin du Dragon: 99 jets, with one of the latter's reaching 28m/92ft high.

Les Grandes Eaux nocturnes – *End Jun–mid-Aug Sat 9pm–11.30pm. 20€.* On summer evenings, visitors will discover yet another enchanting sight of musical fountains and illuminated groves and terraces. Beautiful fireworks over the Grand Canal add a stunning final touch to the Grand Evening Fountain Display.

VERSAILLES FROM ANOTHER ANGLE

Petits trains de Versailles – *Daily year round. Schedules and frequency of trains vary depending on the season: they run from 10am a the earliest to 6.15pm at the latest, every 10 to 25mn. Optional audio-commentary. 6€ round trip (children 4.50€). These tickets are not valid for Versailles visits. ℘01 39 54 22 00. www.train-versailles.com.* From the château's North Terrace, this little train takes you to the **Petit Trianon** *(from, there, you can walk to the Queen's Hamlet)*, to the **Grand Trianon** and the **Grand Canal**. This 5km/3.1mi tour lasts 50mn. You may get off at any stop and take the next train with the same ticket.

Bicycle rentals – *Parc du Château de Versailles. ℘01 39 66 97 66. Open daily (weather permitting) Feb–Nov 10am– 5.30pm to 7pm (depending on the season). 6.50€ (1hr), 15€ (4hr), 17€ (8hr).* There are three rental points within the park: Petite Venise, Grille St-Antoine (on boulevard St-Antoine) and Grille de la Reine (on Boulevard de la Reine).

Grand Canal Boat rentals – *Parc du Château de Versailles. ℘01 39 66 97 66. Open daily Mar–Oct 10am (at the earliest) –7.30pm (at the latest); opening hours vary depending on the season. 15€ (1hr) or 11€ (30min) for 4-person boats.* Rental point near La Flotille restaurant.

Segway Tours – *℘06 59 69 74 21. www.versaillesevents.fr. 45€ (1hr) 69€ (2hr) . Reservations required 24hrs in advance.* What about using this self-balancing electric vehicle for an original guided tour of the royal park? It will allow you to see its major highlights, including the gardens and Marie-Antoinette's Estate, in record time!

Ville de
Versailles★★

The steady stream of visitors to Versailles too often overlook this charming town. Originally home to courtiers of the King, the Royal City has retained a certain austere character with its three avenues converging on the Château, its private mansions, imposing churches and narrow cobbled streets.

A BIT OF HISTORY

Royal city – In 1671, Louis XIV decided that plots of land in Versailles would be granted to those citizens who put in a request, in exchange for a levy of five sous for each arpent (3 194sq m/ 3 833sq yd). The new buildings had to conform to the rules laid down by the **Service des Bâtiments du Roi**, a building commission answerable to the court. The purpose of these measures was to achieve architectural unity. Moreover, in order that the palace might continue to dominate the area, the roofs of the village houses were not to exceed the height of the Cour de Marbre.

Today very little remains of these 17C buildings. Most of the old town was completed in the 18C, enlarged and renovated in the 19C.

Parliamentary town – France's defeat in the 1870–71 Franco-Prussian War enabled Versailles to regain its political role as the seat of the French government. The population rose from 40 000 to 150 000 in a matter of days. Ministers, senators and members of the **National Assembly** who were unable to find lodgings in town, occupied the palace which also housed the **Banque de France** and other official institutions. A **Salle du Congrès** was built in the middle of the castle's south wing to house the Parliament, but in 1879, the Parliament returned to the capital.

However, during the 3rd and 4th Republics, presidential elections were held here. And today, when the French Constitution needs to be amended, the

▶ **Population:** 85 726.
◔ **Michelin Local Map:** 311: I-3, map 101 fold 23 or 106 folds 17, 18 .
▯ **Info:** Office du tourisme de Versailles, 2bis av. de Paris, 78000. ℘01 39 24 88 88. www.versailles-tourisme.com.
◗ **Location:** From Paris: RER C (Versailles-Rive-Gauche), SNCF rail link from Gare Montparnasse (Versailles-Chantiers) or from Gare St-Lazare (Versailles-Rive-Droite).

Senate and the National Assembly are both required to meet here.

Versailles today – More than 200 years after the end of absolute monarchy in France, there are very few 17C houses left in Versailles: most of the old town dates from the 18C with 19C alterations. Having long suffered from being too close to Paris, Versailles has nevertheless managed to develop its own cultural programme and to enhance its exceptional site by restoring its beautiful façades in Quartier St-Louis, for instance.

The pedestrianised rue Satory, in the heart of the old town, has become as lively as **Quartier Notre-Dame** where antique dealers and outdoor cafés abound.

DISCOVERING VERSAILLES
AROUND THE CHÂTEAU
Place d'Armes★★

This huge square was the junction of the three wide avenues leading to Paris, St-Cloud and Sceaux, separated by the **Écuries royales★**, the stables built by Jules Hardouin-Mansart in 1683. Identical in size, the Grande and Petite Écuries were so named for reasons of convenience.

These imposing buildings housed some 600 horses, as well as riders, grooms, musicians and page boys.

Grande Écurie★

To the right of the square as you look towards the Château.

This is where the dressage of saddle horses for the use of the kings and princes took place. Beside its striking architecture, there are two good reasons to visit this impressive compound.

Musée des Carosses – ○*Only open on certain dates. Call ℘01 30 83 78 00 (château de Versailles) for details. www.chateauversailles.fr.*

Various sedan chairs and carriages can be seen (carriages used for Napoleon's wedding, Charles X's coronation, presidential elections under the 3rd Republic, etc.).

Académie du Spectacle équestre★ – ○*Only open on certain dates. Call ℘0 892 681 891. www.acadequestre.fr.*

Visitors will get to watch dressage shows and workout sessions at the Academy of Equestrian Arts, directed by Bartabas They will also enjoy beautifully choreographed equestrian performances.

Petite Écurie

To the left of the square as you look towards the Château.

This was used for carriages and carriage-horses. Today, it houses a school of architecture and workshops specialising in restoration work.

Rue de l'Indépendance-Américaine

In the 18C this street housed many buildings occupied by ministries and public services, in particular the **Grand Commun**, built by Mansart in 1684, which lodged a total of 1 500 officials, cooks etc.

At n° 5 stands the former **Ministry of the Navy and Foreign Affairs** (1761), fronted by a magnificent gate crowned by statues of Peace and War. It was here that an alliance was signedin 1762 between France and the American *insurrectionaries*, acting as a prelude to the 1783 treaties granting the independence of the United States. The mansion has been made into a public library.

QUARTIER ST-LOUIS★

Rue du Vieux-Versailles, lined with carftsmen's workshops, leads to **rue Satory**: General Hoche's birthplace is at n° 18, near the Petite Écurie where his father took care of the horses; note the fine wrought-iron work (*not open to the public*).

The St-Louis district boasts a wealth of **historic mansions** built during the reign of Louis XV, and the Jeu de Paume (♿*see below*) where the National Assembly took their famous oath on 20 June 1789. Also note the Potager du Roi or King's Vegetable Garden (♿ *see p375*) which stretches its chequered layout at the foot of the Château

Cathédrale St-Louis★

St Louis' Cathedral was built in 1754 to serve the "Old Versailles" and the Parc aux Cerfs. It lies close to the King's Vegetable Garden. The west front with its two towers, and the dome above the transept crossing are reminiscent of the great Classical churches.

Carrés St-Louis

Louis XV gave orders to create a "shopping area" near St Louis' Church, along the streets presently named **rue Royale** and **rue d'Anjou** (1755). The **market,** dating back to Louis XV's reign, has been beautifully restored. The shops – featuring mansard roofs – were arranged around four small squares known as *carrés*: Carré au Puits, Carré à l'Avoine, Carré à la Fontaine, Carré à la Terre.

Salle du Jeu de Paume

By guided tour only Sat 3pm. Call tourist office on ℘01 39 24 88 88 for details.

This is one of the only remaining courts where people used to play *Jeu de Paume*, a predecessor of modern lawn tennis. Built for the Court in 1686, it became famous on 20 June 1789 when the Members of the Tiers État (representing the people) and of the lower clergy gathered here after having been excluded from the Hôtel des Menus-Plaisirs where the States General were being held. They then swore that their assembly would not be dissolved until they had given a constitution to the French people.

Potager du Roi★

10 rue du Mar.-Joffre. & ⏱*Open Jan–end Mar Tue and Thu 10am–6pm. Apr–end Oct Tue–Sun 10am–6pm (guided tours Sat, Sun and holidays at 11am, 2.30 and 4pm).* ≋*4.50€ (6.50€ Sat–Sun and holidays).* ✆*01 39 24 62 62. www.potager-du-roi.fr.*

The King's Vegetable Garden was commissioned by Louis XIV from **J-B La Quintinie** (1624–88) to supply the king's table with a variety of fruit and vegetables, many of which have become quite rare. The kitchen garden, which now houses the **École nationale supérieure du paysage**, has survived and its produce is sold in a shop on the grounds. The garden is divided into sixteen vegetable plots where some 50 different species grow. These plots are surrounded by a dozen orchards planted with 5 000 fruit trees lovingly cared for (there are 130 varieties of apple and pear!).

QUARTIER NOTRE-DAME★

The Notre-Dame district features the oldest church in Versailles and a few houses built under Louis XIV, situated near the Notre-Dame marketplace.

Église Notre-Dame★

The church built in rue Dauphine (renamed rue Hoche) by **Jules Hardouin-Mansart** in 1686 was the parish church to the King and his court. The King would attend Solemn Masses such as Corpus Christi here. The requirements of the Service des Bâtiments du Roi (⏱*see p201*) explain why the church presents a flattened front flanked by truncated towers.

A large openwork dome graces the church interior, characterised by Doric embellishments. The nave is surrounded by 12 carved medallions representing Apostles and figures from the New Testament; these were the works presented by the new entrants to the Académie Royale de Sculpture et de Peinture between 1657 and 1689. The 19C axial chapel (called the chapel of the Blessed

Sacrament) houses the *Assumption*, a 16C painting by Michel Corneille.

Hôtel du Baillage

On the corner of rue de la Pourvoierie. Built by **Gabriel** in 1724, this mansion served as the bailiff's tribunal and municipal prison until it was restored and turned into a residence in 1844. The ground floor houses antique dealers.

Follow rue de la Paroisse to the **Marché Notre-Dame**, a group of four covered market halls surrounded by picturesque streets such as **rue des Deux-Portes** lined with shops and restaurants.

You could end this stroll by walking along rue Rameau, then turning right onto boulevard de la Reine towards the Musée Lambinet.

Musée Lambinet★

54 boulevard de la Reine. & ⏱*Open Tue, Thu and Sat–Sun 2–6pm, Wed 1–6pm, Fri 2–5pm.* ⏱*Closed major holidays.* ≋*5.50€.* ✆*01 39 50 30. www.musee-lambinet.fr.*

This museum is housed in the wood-panelled drawing rooms of the charming **Hôtel Lambinet** built in 1750 for Joseph-Barnabé Porchon, building contractor to the King, whose initials can be seen in the wrought ironwork on the balcony in the middle of the pleasing façade.

Place Hoche in the Quartier Notre-Dame

A. de Valroger/MICHELIN

The atmosphere of an 18C town house is re-created by the period furniture, paintings and sculptures (Pajou, Houdon). At the same time, the museum illustrates the history of Versailles through numerous pieces of furniture and objects, including a collection of French ceramics, watches, miniatures, snuff-boxes, silverware, engraved copper plates used to print the calico known as *toile de Jouy*, and works by local artists, such as the busts of Rousseau and Voltaire by Houdon, the bust of Louis XVI by Pajou or the *Maréchal de Saxe* by Jean-Baptiste Lemoyne.

The first floor houses an extensive collection of items related to Revolutionary events and figures: **Marat**'s murder; **Charlotte de Corday**'s arrest; events in Versailles during 1789 with, in particular, the Declaration of Human Rights; Général Hoche, one of Versailles' most famous sons. One room is devoted to the **Manufacture d'armes de Versailles**, created in 1793. The factory enjoyed an excellent reputation during the days of the Empire for the quality of the workmanship. This is evident in the collection of ceremonial arms (sabres, rifles) and the very fine boxed pistols with accessories said to have belonged to Général Scherer.

On the second floor, the museum features a section devoted to **sacred art**★, with beautiful pieces from the abbeys of Maubuisson and Le Lys, and displays works by 19C landscape painters (Corot, Eugène Isabey, Charles-Émile Lambinet) as well as genre painting by Louis-Léopold Boilly.

The Orientalist painter André Suréda, the Nabis painter Jean Lacombe and the landscape painter Henri Le Sidaner are also among the artists represented.

QUARTIER DE MONTREUIL
Orangerie de Mme Élisabeth

Impasse Champ-Lagarde.

The Orangery formed part of the estate offered to Mme Élisabeth in 1783 by her brother, Louis XVI. The building de-signed by **La Brière**, Louis XVI's architect, consists of a vast rectangular south-facing room. The house was later turned into a residence which implied the addition of many windows.

In 1997, it was bought by the Conseil général des Yvelines and refurbished to house temporary exhibitions of contemporary art. The garden, which was also remodelled, has retained the original atmosphere of the place.

SURROUNDS
Arboretum National de Chèvreloup

30 route de Versailles, in Rocquencourt. Via boulevard St-Antoine NW on the town plan opposite the Parly II shopping centre. ○*Open Mon, Wed, Sat–Sun and holidays 10am–6pm.* ⊗*2.50€.* ✆*01 39 55 53 80. www2.mnhn.fr/adc.*

In 1924, a plot of land formerly belonging to the Grand Parc (& *see Parc du château de Versailles)* was offered to the Natural History Museum of Paris so that the Botanical Gardens could enrich their collection of tree species. The first steps were to set up a Tree Centre.

The arboretum houses 2 500 species and varieties from temperate or cold regions (from China to the Caucasus and the United States). An alleyway lined with blue cedar trees from the Atlas mountain range separates conifers from broad-leaved trees.

The **Maison de l'arbre** provides valuable information about the arboretum and the development of trees: temporary exhibitions, films.

Haras de Jardy

2km/1.2mi northeast along N 182. Leave Versailles by avenue de St-Cloud towards Paris.

This huge stud farm, a horse-lover's paradise, forms part of an important complex of leisure activities (tennis, golf, riding, show jumping). The vast park offers fine walks and is the site of numerous show jumping competitions.

ADDRESSES

🏨 STAY

🛏🍽 **Ibis** – *4 av. Gén. de Gaulle.*
℘*01 39 53 03 30. www.ibishotel.com.*
85 rooms. 🍽*8€.* Recently refurbished
hotel near the château and town hall,
offering the chain's latest standards of
comfort. Poppy red rooms, which are
functional and attractive.

🛏🍽 **Mercure** – *19 r. Ph. de Dangeau.*
℘*01 39 50 44 10. www.mercure.com.*
60 rooms. 🍽*10€.* In a quiet area, an
establishment with particularly practical
rooms. Well-furnished lobby giving on
to a pleasant breakfast room.

🛏🍽🍽 **Novotel Château de
Versailles** – *4 bd St-Antoine, 78152
Le Chesnay.* ℘*01 39 54 96 96. www.
novotel.com. 105 rooms.* 🍽*14€.
Restaurant*🛏🍽. Hotel at the entrance to
the town, on the place de la Loi. Functional rooms lead off an atrium made
into a lounge (numerous green plants).
Restaurant with modern, bistro-style
interior and traditional menu.

🛏🍽🍽🍽 **Hôtel Le Versailles** –
7 r. Ste-Anne, Petite Place. ℘*01 39 5064
65. www.hotel-le-versailles.fr. 46 rooms.*
🍽*14€.* This renovated hotel is situated
in a quiet side street not far from the
château. The Art Deco style rooms are
spacious, bright and elegant. Cosy bar-
lounge and terrace where breakfast is
served in summer.

🛏🍽🍽🍽 **La Résidence du Berry** –
14 r. d'Anjou. ℘*01 39 49 07 07.
www.hotel-berry.com. 38 rooms.* 🍽*14€.*
Located in the Saint-Louis quarter, this
18C edifice has been entirely restored
by Les Bâtiments de France. Comfort
and top-quality materials await you in
rooms with time-worn beams overhead.
In summer breakfast is taken on a
veranda that opens onto the patio.

🛏🍽🍽🍽 **Trianon Palace** – *1 bd de la
Reine.* ℘*01 30 84 50 00. www.trianon
palace.com. 199 rooms.* 🍽*38€.
Restaurant*🛏🍽🍽🍽. This classical
style luxury hotel standing on the
edge of the grounds of the château has
very comfortable, contemporary-style
guestrooms. Excellent spa. Up-to-date
menu and summer terrace at the
Veranda.

🍽 EAT

Place du Marché – This agreeable
square is marked out by bars, crêperies,
pizzerias and restaurants, with outdoor
tables in summer.

🍽🍽 **La Brasserie du Théâtre** – *15 r.
des Réservoirs.* ℘*01 39 50 03 21.
www.flobrasseries.com. Closed 25 Dec,
1 May. Reservations advisable evenings.*
The walls of this 1895 brasserie situated
next to the theatre, as its name would
suggest, are covered with photos of
artists who have frequented it over the
years. 1930s style décor, covered terrace
and traditional cuisine.

🍽🍽 **Le Bœuf à la Mode** – *4 r. au Pain (Pl.
du Marché Notre-Dame).* ℘*01 39 50 31 99.
www.leboeufalamode-versailles.com.*
A typical 1930s bistro with a convivial,
relaxed atmosphere. The decor – red
wall-seats, knick-knacks, posters, mirrors
– is a hit and the regional specialities are
delicious. Very busy on market days.

🍽🍽🍽 **Au Chapeau Gris** – *7 r. Hoche.*
℘*01 39 50 10 81. www.auchapeaugris.com.
Closed Tue eve, Wed. Reservations required.*
This restaurant, said to date back
to the 18C, is a veritable institution
hereabouts. Quintessential Versailles
ambience and décor are the setting for
appetising, traditional cuisine.

🍽🍽🍽 **Le Potager du Roy** –
1 Mar.-Joffre. ℘*01 39 50 35 34. Closed
Sun–Mon.* Delightfully retro setting and
meat and fish dishes with vegetables
in pride of place. Hardly surprising as
the name refers to the nearby King's
Vegetable Garden !

🍽🍽🍽 **Le Valmont** – *20 r. au Pain* –
℘*01 39 51 39 00. www.levalmont.com.
Closed Sun eve, Mon.* This nicely restored
old house on the Place des Halles is
bound to catch your eye. Venture inside
and appreciate the first-rate reception,
charming decoration, modern colours,
elegant tables and succulent cookery.
A meal to look forward to!

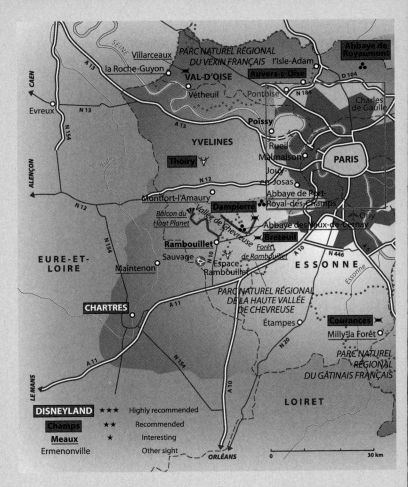

Île de France is the vast, fertile region surrounding Paris. Despite a population of just over ten million, most residential areas are tightly concentrated, particularly close to the capital, giving much of the region the look and feel of rural countryside with its farms and forests. Hidden amongst these dense woodlands and ploughed fields are some of the most impressive royal châteaux and ancient abbeys in the country. Within an hour of leaving the French capital, discover medieval villages, charming towns straddling sleepy rivers, and some of the favourite haunts of writers and artists.

The Landscape

Many of the towns in the Île-de-France grew around the Seine river and its tributaries, such as the Marne, the Oise, the Loing, the Essonne and the Eure. Today, many new towns have been created on the outskirts of the Île-de-France, as regional councils work to maintain the balance of historic monuments and rural industries with much-needed modernisation and development.

Immediately outside Paris, the ring of administrative *départements* known as the Petit Couronne (Little Crown) is home to heavily populated suburbs, international airports and industrial zones. The larger *départements* beyond, called the Grand Couronne (Big Crown), are the farmlands where a

Highlights

1 Attend a Gregorian music concert at **Chartres Cathedral** (p214)

2 Enjoy the horse stunts at **Buffalo Bill's Wild West Show** (p230)

3 Sample the best Brie cheeses in **Meaux** (p259)

4 Tour the manufacturing centre at **PSA Peugeot-Citroën** (p271)

5 Go on a romantic candlelight tour of **Vaux-le-Vicomte** (p291)

and writers looking for inspiration, peace and quiet, or simply a bit of fresh air, made their home in towns like Barbizon, Moret-sur-Loing, Auvers-sur-Oise, Milly-la-Forêt, Jouy-en-Josas and L'Isle-Adam. Their contributions are remembered in the museums, galleries, and the very landscape of these towns.

Châteaux such as Fontainebleau, Rambouillet and Vaux-le-Vicomte host seasonal festivals of music, dance and open-air theatre, while Chartres Cathedral and the Abbey of Pont-Royal-des-Champs are known for their religious music concerts. Far from the crowds of the capital, these cultural outings are a great way to mingle with the locals as well.

lot of the region's food is still produced, livestock reared and the famous Brie cheeses made. In addition to the more industrialised producers, small family farms can still be found along the country roads, often with signs advertising fresh eggs, free range chickens, or pick-your-own-fruit.

At the weekend Parisians sometimes escape the hustle and bustle of the city to one of several important forests in the area (Fontainebleau, Rambouillet, Auvers-sur-Oise), where you can cycle or hike in the great outdoors.

The Culture

Landed gentry and religious devotees weren't the only ones who wished to escape the crowded city: many artists

Touring the Region by Car

Southwest: visit Chartres then Rambouillet with its château, forest and elegant town; side trips can be made to Dampierre, Maintenon and Breteuil châteaux, Montfort-l'Amaury and Port-Royal-des-Champs.

Northwest: Thoiry, Poissy, Malmaison and La Roche-Guyon can all be visited from Auvers-sur-Oise and the charming l'Isle-Adam.

Southeast: Provins and Fontainebleau deserve a full day, with excursions to Vaux-le-Vicomte, Moret-sur-Loing, Barbizon or Milly-la-Forêt worth an extra day trip.

East: Disneyland; add an extra day if you want to visit Meaux and the Château de Ferrières.

Auvers-Sur-Oise★★

In the early 19C, this pleasant river village just outside Paris became the favoured stomping ground for a new generation of painters known as the 'Impressionists' (&see Introduction), who came here to stay and paint, including Monet, Van Gogh and Corot. An old walking trail, now a series of narrow streets, still carries the memory of the artists who brought it fame. Here and there, panels indicate the scenes portrayed by Impressionist painters, while the district around the church is a favourite 'place of pilgrimage' for art lovers.

IN VAN GOGH'S FOOTSTEPS

During his stay in Auvers, Vincent Van Gogh was extremely active. The restful countryside, where he hoped to find peace after his internment in Provence, encouraged his quest for freedom and his frantic need to work. He completed over 70 paintings in a very short time.

Auberge Ravoux★

Place de la Mairie. ©*Open Mar–Oct Wed–Sun 10am–6pm.* ☜*5€.* ✆*01 30 36 60 60. www.maisondevangogh.fr.*
Known as the **Maison de Van Gogh**, this is the inn where Van Gogh stayed for two months before his tragic death. Feeling guilt towards his brother Theo, upon whom he was entirely dependent, Van Gogh shot himself in the chest while he was out in a field; he died two days later

Auberge Ravoux

D. Pazery/MICHELIN

- ▶ **Population:** 6 956
- ⚙ **Michelin Local Map:** 305: E-6 or map 106 fold 6.
- 🛈 **Info:** Manoir des Colombières, Rue de la Sansonne, 95430 Auvers-sur-Oise, ✆01 30 36 10 06. www.auvers-sur-oise.com.
- ▶ **Location:** Auvers-sur-Oise lies just 32km/20mi northwest of Paris, along the A 115. SNCF depart from Gare du Nord or Gare St-Lazare, changing at Pontoise.
- ✎ **Don't Miss:** Use the map available at the tourist office to locate the various sites with ease.
- 👪 **Kids:** The 17C Château d'Auvers.
- ⏱ **Timing:** Spend a full day here to have a look at the home of Dr Gachet and the Maison du Pendu.

in his room. He was 37 years old.
The inn has been carefully restored and has retained its interior decoration and restaurant. Outside are panels describing the artist's eventful life. The small garret he occupied has remained unchanged and, despite the absence of furniture, gives an insight into the ascetic conditions in which he lived. The tour ends with an audiovisual presentation of Van Gogh's stay in Auvers.

▶ *Follow rue des Colombières past the museum and studio of Charles-François Daubigny (& see Additional Sights).*

A path to the right leads to a cemetery set among the corn fields that Van Gogh loved to paint.

Vincent and Theo Van Gogh's Graves

Rue Émile-Bernard.
The famous Dutch painter's tomb stands against the left-hand wall. His brother Theo, who supported him and who died soon after him, rests by his side.

ADDITIONAL SIGHTS
Musée de l'Absinthe
44 rue Alphonse Callé. ⒸOpen mid-Jun–mid-Sept Wed–Fri 1.30–6pm, Sat–Sun 11am–6pm; mid-Sept–mid-Jun Sat–Sun 11am–6pm. *5€.* ℘01 30 36 83 26. www.musee-absinthe.com.

The famous green liqueur reached the peak of its popularity in the cafés of the 19C. It was often described as the **green fairy** and was closely linked to the life of the artists of the day who spent a great deal of time in cafés. The documents, posters and objects displayed in the museum bring back to life the history of a drink, which had a profound social influence until it was banned in 1915.

Musée Daubigny
Rue de la Sansonne. ⒸOpen Apr–Oct Wed–Fri 2–6pm, Sat–Sun 10.30am–12.30pm, 2–6pm; Nov–mid-Dec and mid-Jan–Mar Wed–Fri 2–5pm, Sat–Sun 2–5.30pm). *4€.* ℘01 30 36 80 20. www.musee-daubigny.com.

Housed in the Manoir des Colombières, this museum displays a collection of 19C paintings, water colours, drawings and engravings illustrating the birth of Impressionism: works by Daubigny and Goeneutte, an engraver and painter who portrayed elegant Parisian women. There are also contemporary works of art.

Maison-Atelier de Daubigny★
61 Rue Daubigny ⒸOpen Apr–Oct Thur–Sun 2–6.30pm. *5.50€.* ℘01 34 48 03 03. www.atelier-daubigny.com.
Charles-François Daubigny (1817–78), a landscape painter, settled in Auvers on the advice of his friend, Camille Corot. He had a studio-house built in 1861 and asked his family and friends to take part in the interior decoration.

Charles, his son Karl and his daughter Cécile, as well as Corot and Daumier, left their marks of artistic inspiration on the walls and doors. Daubigny loved to paint on the River Oise, aboard a small, specially designed boat.

Later on, Monet followed his example. In 1890, Van Gogh painted Daubigny's garden; in his last letter to his brother Theo, he gives details about the colours he chose for the painting and asks his advice.

▲⁑ Château d'Auvers
50 rue de Léry ⚐ *Audio tours (1hr30min); last admission 1hr30min before closing.* ⒸOpen Apr–Sept Tue–Sun 10.30am–6pm; Oct–Mar Tue–Sun 10.30am–4.30pm. *12€ (children 7.90€).* ℘01 34 48 48 40. www.chateau-auvers.fr.

This 17C château, which has been restored and laid out with extensive use of audiovisual presentations, offers visitors a chance to enjoy a **Journey Back to the Days of the Impressionists★** and gain some insight into the wonderful adventure that was Art in the 19C. Using reconstructions of interiors and the projection of some 600 works, it brings to life the Paris of the time, a city undergoing immense change thanks to the work of Baron Haussmann, and a city where the wealthy middle classes led a bustling, frivolous life with little appreciation of the new style of painting.

Although some of the artists fed on the capital's atmosphere for their works (Degas, Toulouse-Lautrec), most of them preferred to travel on the brand-new railway from Paris to the seaside in search of new sources of inspiration. They found it in the open-air bars *(guinguettes)* in Asnières and Chatou, along the banks of the Seine and the Oise (Argenteuil, Vétheuil, Auvers-sur-Oise, etc.), in the lush countryside of the Paris basin (haystacks by Monet and Thornley), in the sea, the harbours (Le Havre), the cliffs (Étretat) and the beaches.

ADDRESSES

⍭/EAT

⊝⊜⊜ **Auberge Ravoux** – *Opposite the town hall.* ℘01 30 36 60 60. www.maisondevangogh.fr. Closed Mon–Tue, Fri–Sat lunches, Nov–Feb. Reservations required. This old artists' café, with its late 19C decor, was Van Gogh's last home. Very pleasant, history-rich atmosphere, a pretty serving counter and large tables of solid wood. Traditional cuisine and wine from small vintners.

Barbizon★★

Lying on the edge of the Fontainebleau Forest, the village of Barbizon, which was part of Chailly until 1903, was a popular spot with landscape painters (👁️*see Introduction: Landscape Painting*) and still carries memories of the artists who made it famous. The Bas-Bréau coppices nearby are reminders of a time when, according to the Goncourt brothers, "every tree was like an artist's model surrounded by a circle of paint-boxes."

A BIT OF HISTORY
The Barbizon School

Breaking the rules of studio work and official art, the Barbizon artists were landscape painters who perfected the technique of working directly from nature after two great masters: **Théodore Rousseau** (1812–67) and **Jean-François Millet** (1814–75).

The local people were happy to welcome these nature-loving artists, who rose at dawn and whose genius and mischievous nature enlivened local weddings and banquets. Next came the writers, seduced by the beauty of the forest and the congenial atmosphere of this small, international community: George Sand, Henri Murger, the Goncourt brothers and Taine, for example. Thereafter, Barbizon remained a fashionable spot.

> ▶ **Population:** 1 571
> ♿ **Michelin Local Map:** 312: E-5 or map 106 fold 45.
> ❐ **Location:** 10km/6mi northwest of Fontainebleau – Local map, *see Forêt de FONTAINEBLEAU.*
> 🛈 **Info:** 55 Grande-Rue, 77630 Barbizon. ☎01 60 66 41 87. www.barbizon-tourisme.com.

Millet, a patriarch with nine children, died after a life of hard work, his eyes forever riveted on the landscapes of the Bière plain. Like Rousseau, he was buried at **Chailly Cemetery** *(2km/1mi north along D 64; plan of graveyard at entrance).*

SIGHTS
La Grande Rue

This long high street (Grande Rue) is lined with galleries, restaurants and villas. Many of these buildings bear commemorative plaques to the artists who stayed there.

Auberge du Père Ganne★

92 Grande Rue. 🕐*Open Wed–Mon 10am–12.30pm, 2–5.30pm.* 🎟️*5€.* ☎*01 60 66 22 27.*
This was a popular meeting-place for artists, many of whom had rooms here. The inn is now the **Musée Municipal**

Auberge du Père Ganne

Ph. Gajic/MICHELIN

de l'École de Barbizon. A lively educational audiovisual display describes 'Ganne's painters', who revolutionised art and brought life and laughter to the inn through their tricks. On the ground floor, three restored rooms are representative of their habit of decorating all the wood panelling in the inn as a means of paying for their keep. They decorated cupboards, doors, the sideboard, the fireplace, in fact any flat surface, all of them ideal as supports for the talents of the artists.

On the first floor the museum has numerous paintings indicating the influence of Barbizon on Impressionists through the 'Back to Nature' theme: works by Camille Corot, Charles Jacque, Jules Dupré, Ferdinand Chaigneau, Georges Gassies and Eugène Lavieille.

Maison de Rousseau (55 Grande-Rue). The home of Théodore Rousseau is behind the war memorial.

Maison-atelier de Jean-François Millet
27 Grande-Rue. Open Mon and Wed–Sat 9.30am–12.30pm, 2–5.30pm. 3€. 01 60 66 21 55.

Millet's home and studio for 25 years contains etchings of some of Millet's most famous paintings: *The Angelus*, *The Gleaners* and others. In the dining room, there are drawings and engravings by Millet. The living room is reserved for exhibitions of contemporary works.

Monument de Rousseau et Millet
A bronze medal embedded in the rock is the work of Henri Chapu. Behind this monument, a plaque set into another rock commemorates the centenary of the setting up of the first artistic reserve in 1853 at the instigation of Rousseau.

ADDRESSES

STAY
La Ferme des Vosves (Bed and Breakfast) – *155 r. de Boissise, 77190 Village de Vosves, 10km/6mi N. 01 64 39 22 28. 2 rooms. www.fermedevosves.com.* Take your time and enjoy the pretty gardens of this old farm nestled in the heart of a village overlooking the Seine. The bedrooms are simply furnished, and the quietness, the hospitable welcome and modest prices make this an excellent place to stay.

EAT
Le Relais de Barbizon – *2 av. du Gén-de-Gaulle. 01 60 66 40 28. Closed 2 weeks in Aug, mid-Dec–mid-Jan, Tue eve, Wed.* A modest little inn at the village entrance. Enjoyable dining room with a section set aside for family gatherings. Cuisine made from fresh ingredients; a variety of fixed-price menus.

L'Angelus – *31 Grande-Rue. 01 60 66 40 30. http://angelusbarbizon. monsite.wanadoo.fr. Closed mid-Jan– mid-Feb, Mon–Tue.* This rustic inn takes its name from one of the works of Millet, painted at Barbizon. You're sure to appreciate the relaxing atmosphere and traditional cuisine.

NIGHTLIFE
Bizon's Club – *1 Grande Rue. 01 60 66 40 01. Closed Mon–Wed.* The Forest of Fontainebleau's foremost discotheque manages to be hip, selective and convivial... the perfect balance! The younger crowd congregates on the big dance floor with techno music; other patrons prefer the small club downstairs with music from the 1980s.

SHOPPING
Verrerie d'Art – *Le Moulin des Noues, 91840 Soisy-sur-École, 13km/8.5mi NW of Barbizon. 01 64 98 00 03. http://verrerie-soisy.fr. Hours vary for boutique and workshops, call ahead.* Set in a pretty park with a river, this glassmaker's atelier has opened its doors so that you can learn how glass is blown and hand-crafted. A short film, an exhibition and a boutique round off the visit.

Musée de l'Air et de l'Espace du

Bourget★★

Le Bourget airfield was created in 1914 and rapidly became an important airport and military air base. It was from here that Nungesser and Coli set off in their *White Bird* on 8 May 1927 in a doomed attempt to reach the American coast. Thirteen days later, in the early hours of 22 May, Lindbergh successfully landed his *Spirit of St Louis* in Paris, after achieving the first ever non-stop solo flight across the Atlantic. Costes and Bellonte were the first to accomplish this feat in the opposite direction when *Question Mark* landed on 1 September 1930.

Visit

👫 ♿🕐*Open Tue–Sun 10am–6pm (Oct–Mar until 5pm).* ⊛*6€ (children 4€) to see the planes and exhibitions; entry to permanent museum collection free.* 📞*01 49 92 70 62. www.mae.org.*
The museum has been laid out in the former terminal building at Le Bourget and it boasts some extraordinary collections, retelling the history of the conquest of the skies. The adventure began with **hot air balloons★** after the experiment carried out by Pilâtre de Rozier and Arlandes in 1783; a model of their balloon can be seen in the museum. This first success resulted in the rapid expansion of ballooning. Later, balloons were to prove very useful in military operations or as a means of transport during the Franco-Prussian War of 1870–71.

Grande Galerie★★ – This gallery traces the early years of aviation and has the largest collection in the world dealing with this period. Some of the aircraft were inspired by bionics, among them Clément Ader's strange *Éole*, which was designed after observing a bat. Among the earliest aircraft, note Farman's *Voisin* (first round trip, 1km/0.6mi, in Issy-les-Moulineaux, 1907), the elegant and

♿ **Michelin Local Map:** 305: F-7, map 101 folds 7, 17 or 106 fold 20.

popular *Levasseur Antoinette* (1908), the *Blériot-XI*, which succeeded in flying across the Channel, etc. With the outbreak of World War I, aviation underwent rapid progress. Aircraft structures and power were increased and the skies became the setting for the first aerial battles.

▶ *Proceed in chronological order via the Hall de l'Espace to the Hall de l'Aviation légère et sportive.*

Hall de l'Aviation légère et sportive – This hall contains the famous *Potez-53* (which achieved average speeds of 322kph/200mph over a distance of 2 000km/1 243mi in 1933), the very powerful *Caudron 714R* (900hp) and the *Breguet XIX* 'Nungesser-Coli', in which Costes and Le Brix made the first successful crossing of the South Atlantic in 1927.

Hall des Prototypes français★ – This hall presents the history of the French Air Force since 1945 and contains some amazing prototypes with thermopropulsion, such as the *Leduc-016*.

Hall du Concorde★★ – Fearsome fighters of World War II are represented here such as the *Spitfire MK-16*, used by the Free French Airforce, or the enormous *P-47 Thunderbolt* (a 2 000hp fighter bomber). However, the star is the prototype of *Concorde 001*, the retired supersonic aircraft.

▶ *Retrace your steps via the Hall des Prototypes.*

Hall de l'Espace★ – The conquest of space is represented by launchers and space capsules (the famous **Sputnik** was the Earth's first artificial satellite); in 1965, France became the third power to conquer space after the United States and the USSR through its *Diamant* launcher, replaced later by the famous *Ariane* launcher.

Château de
Breteuil★★

Breteuil is one of the most charming châteaux in the Île-de-France region, owned by the Le Tonnelier de Breteuil family since 1712. The estate has several attractive features: its architecture, fine furniture, souvenirs of a family of famous diplomats, a pleasant park and, as a special treat for children, well-known fairytale characters.

VISIT

Guided tours (45min) Mon–Sat 2.30–5.30pm, Sun and holidays 11.30am, 2.30–5.30pm. Grounds open at 10am. ☜12.50€ (children 9.50€). ℘01 30 52 05 02. www.breteuil.fr.

The château is built in the Louis XIII style in brick and stone. It consists of a main building flanked by two low wings.

On the first floor, waxwork figures bring to life a few historical events. Louis XVI is shown with Louis-Auguste de Breteuil and Marie-Antoinette, signing the arrest warrant for the Cardinal de Rohan who was implicated in the affair of the Queen's necklace.

In the smoking room, the figures represent Henri de Breteuil, Gambetta and

Michelin Local Map:
311: I-3, map 101 fold 32 or 106 fold 29

the future Edward VII laying down in 1881 the basis of the Entente Cordiale.

The château's most outstanding exhibit remains the **Teschen table★★★**, inlaid with stones, gems and petrified wood, given to Louis-Auguste de Breteuil (1730–1807) by Empress Maria Teresa of Austria after successfully mediating the Treaty of Teschen (1779), which put an end to a serious regional conflict between the Empire and Prussia.

The Park★★

The 75ha/185-acre park, where deer roam freely, provides some beautiful views and diverse landscapes. Near the château are the **formal French gardens**, created by the Duchênes (father and son) in accordance with Le Nôtre's principles. They include a lake, a 16C dovecote, statues and topiary. The **Princes' Garden** is coloured with flowering cherries, roses and some outstanding peonies. A box **maze** occupies one of the terraces of the orangery. Two ponds lower down form an ideal setting for a romantic stroll.

Château de Breteuil in spring

Michel André/Château de Breteuil

Chartres★★★

Chartres is the capital of Beauce, France's famous corn belt, but for visitors the town is known mainly for the Cathedral of Our Lady, a magnificent edifice, now a UNESCO World Heritage Site, which reigns supreme over a picturesque setting of monuments and old streets.

A BIT OF HISTORY
A Town with a Destiny
Since ancient times Chartres has had a strong influence over religious matters. It is believed that a Gallo-Roman well on the Chartres plateau was the object of a pagan cult and that in the 4C this was transformed into a Christian cult by the first evangelists. Adventius, the first known bishop of Chartres, lived during the middle of the 4C. A document from the 7C mentions a bishop Béthaire kneeling in front of Notre-Dame, which points to the existence of a Marian cult.

In 876 the chemise said to belong to the Virgin Mary was given to the cathedral by Charles the Bald, confirming that Chartres was already a place of pilgrimage. Up to the 14C the town of Chartres continued to flourish.

The Pilgrimage
Chartres Cathedral was consecrated to the Assumption of the Virgin Mary in 1260; in the Middle Ages it attracted many pilgrims.

In 1912 and 1913 the writer and poet **Charles Péguy** (1873–1914) visited the cathedral. The strong influence it had on his work inspired a small group of enthusiasts after World War I to follow suit and led, in 1935, to the establishment of the 'Students' Pilgrimage' (during Whitsun).

An exceptional man
In the **Église St-Jean-Baptiste** in the Rechèvres district to the north of the town lies the body of the abbot **Franz Stock**. This German priest, chaplain to the prisons of Paris from 1940 to 1944, refused to retreat with the Wehrmacht and was taken prisoner. At the Morancez

▶ **Population:** 40 022
Michelin Local Map: 311: E-5 or map 106 folds 37 and 38.
Info: Place de la Cathédrale, 28000 Chartres. ℘02 37 18 26 26. www.chartres-tourisme.com.
Location: Chartres lies off the A11, southeast of Paris. The town is situated on a knoll on the left bank of the River Eure, in the heart of the Beauce. The cathedral dominates the Old Town, known as the Quartier St-André.
Parking: There is a large underground car park at Le Bouef Couronne, and street parking (fee) along the boulevard de la Résistance and the boulevard Maurice Violette.
Don't Miss: For a bird's-eye view of the cathedral, stand behind the Monument aux Aviateurs Militaires, a memorial to the French Air Force high above the east bank of the river. The view is impressive.
Timing: Allow 1.5–2hr to visit the cathedral and at least 4hr to visit the Old Town.

prison camp near Chartres he founded a seminary for prisoners of war and was the Superior there for two years. He died in February 1948, at the age of 43.

CATHÉDRALE★★★
Allow 1hr30min. ⏰*Open daily 8.30am–7pm.* ℘*02 37 21 75 02.* ⊛*Free entry.*
The 4 000 carved figures and the 5 000 characters portrayed by the stained-glass windows demanded a lifelong commitment from the specialists who studied them.

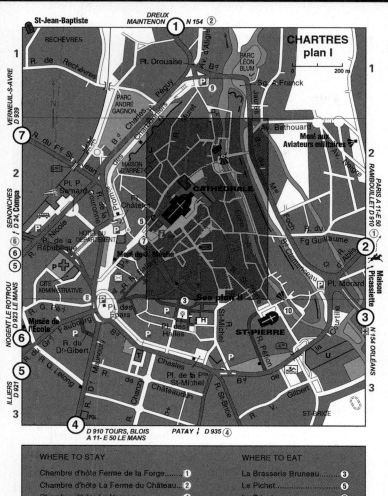

CHARTRES plan I

WHERE TO STAY	
Chambre d'hôte Ferme de la Forge	①
Chambre d'hôte La Ferme du Château	②
Chambre d'hôte La Varenne	④
Chambre d'hôte L'Établais	⑥
Hôtel Le Grand Monarque	⑧
Ibis Centre Hôtel	⑨

WHERE TO EAT	
La Brasserie Bruneau	③
Le Pichet	⑤
Le Tripot	⑦
Saint-Hilaire	⑩

A Swift Construction

The building rests upon the Romanesque cathedral erected by Bishop Fulbert in the 11C and 12C. There remain the crypt, the towers and the foundations of the west front, including the Royal Doorway, and fragments of the Notre-Dame-de-la-Belle-Verrière stained-glass window. The remaining sections of the cathedral were built in the wake of the Great Fire of 1194; princes and dignitaries contributed generously to the work, while the poor offered their labour.

These efforts made it possible to com-plete the cathedral in 25 years, and to add on the north and south porches 20 years later, with the result that the architecture and decoration of Notre-Dame form a harmonious composition almost unparalleled in the history of Gothic art. By some miracle, the Wars of Religion, the French Revolution and the two World Wars spared the famous cathedral, which Rodin referred to as 'the Acropolis of France' on account of its aesthetic and spiritual value. Only the cathedral's 'forest' – the superb roof tim-bers – were destroyed by flames in 1836,

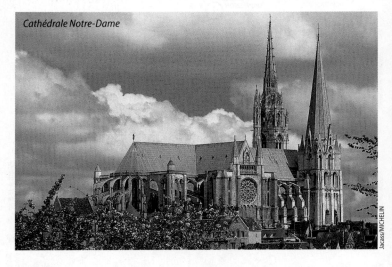

Cathédrale Notre-Dame

Jacass/MICHELIN

and subsequently replaced by a metal framework.

Beneath the cathedral close, archaeological excavations covering around 1.2sq km/0.46sq mi are currently in progress. The remains of two 13C houses have so far been uncovered.

Exterior
West front

The two tall spires and the Royals Doorway form one of the most perfect compositions encountered in French religious art. The New Bell Tower on the left was built first; the lower part dates back to 1134. Its present name dates from the 16C, when Jehan de Beauce erected a stone spire (115m /377ft high) to replace the wooden steeple, which had burned down in 1506. The Old Bell Tower (c. 1145–64), rising 106m/384ft, is a masterpiece of Romanesque art, forming a stark contrast to the ornate Gothic construction. The Royal Doorway and the three large windows above date from the 12C. Everything above this ensemble was built at a later date: the rose window (13C), the 14C gable and the king's gallery featuring the kings of Judah, the ancestors of the Virgin Mary. On the gable, the Virgin Mary is depicted presenting her son to the Beauce area.

The **Royal Doorway**★★★ (Portail Royal), a splendid example of Late Romanesque architecture (1145–70), represents the life and triumph of the Saviour. The Christ in Majesty on the central tympanum and the statue-columns are famous throughout the world. The elongated features of the biblical kings and queens, prophets, priests and patriarchs study the visitors from the embrasures. While the faces are animated, the bodies remain rigid, in deliberate contrast to the figures adorning the arches and the capitals. The statues were primarily designed to be columns, not human beings.

North porch and doorway

Leave the west front on your left and walk round the cathedral, stepping back to get a clear view of its lines. The nave is extremely high and unusually wide. The problem of how to support it was brilliantly resolved with the construction of three-tiered flying buttresses (*see Introduction*); the lower two arcs were joined together by colonnettes.

The elegant Pavillon de l'Horloge near the New Bell Tower is the work of Jehan de Beauce (1520).

The ornamentation of the north porch is similar to that of the doorway, executed at an earlier date. Treated more freely than those on the Royal Doorway, the characters are elegant and extremely lively, illustrating a new, more realistic approach to religious art. The statue of St Modesta, a local martyr, who is pictured gazing up at the New Bell Tower, is extremely graceful.

Once again, the decoration of the three doors refers to the Old Testament. The right door pays tribute to the biblical heroes who exercised the virtues recommended in the teachings of Christ. The central panel shows the Virgin Mary and the Prophets who foretold the coming of the Messiah. The door on the left presents the Annunciation, Visitation and Nativity, together with the Vices and Virtues.

In the bishop's garden, the raised terrace commands a view of the town below lying on the banks of the lower River Eure. Before reaching the garden gate, look left and note the archway straddling a narrow street: it used to open into the Notre-Dame cloisters.

East end

The complexity of the double-course flying buttresses – reinforced here with an intermediate pier as they cross over the chapels – and the succession of radiating chapels, chancel and arms of the transept are stunning. The 14C St Piat Chapel, originally separate, was joined to Notre-Dame by a stately staircase.

South porch and doorway

Here, the upper stonework is concealed by a constellation of colonnettes. The perspective of these planes, stretching from the arches of the porch to the gables, confers to this arm of the transept a sense of unity that is lacking in the north transept.

The theme is the Church of Christ and the Last Judgment. In the Middle Ages, these scenes would usually be reserved for the west portal, but in this case the Royal Doorway already featured ornamentation. Consequently, the scenes portraying the Coming of a New World, prepared by the martyrs, were destined for the left-door embrasures, while those of the Confessors (witnesses of Christ who have not yet been made martyrs) adorn the right door.

Christ reigns supreme on the central tympanum. He is also present on the pier, framed by the double row of the 12 Apostles with their lean, ascetic faces,

draped in long, gently folded robes.

Among the martyrs, note the statues standing in the foreground: St George and St Theodore, both admirable 13C representations of knights in armour. These figures are quite separate from the columns – the feet are flat and no longer slanted – and are there for purely decorative purposes.

The most delightful feature of the sculpted porch is the display of medallions, grouped in sets of six and placed on the recessed arches of the three doorways: the lives of the martyrs, the Vices and Virtues, etc.

Returning to the west front, note the Old Bell Tower and its ironical statue of a donkey playing the fiddle, symbolising man's desire to share in celestial music. At the corner of the building, stop briefly to admire the tall figure of the sundial Angel.

Access to the Bell Tower★

Open Sept–Apr Mon–Sat 9.30am–12.30pm, 2–5pm, Sun 2–5pm; May–Aug 9.30am–12.30pm, 2–6pm, Sun 2–6pm; last ascent 30min before closure.
Closed holidays. 7€. 02 37 21 22 07. www.monum.fr.

The tour (*195 steps*) leads round the north side and up to the lower platform of the New Bell Tower. Seen from a height of 70m/230ft, the buttresses, flying buttresses, statues, gargoyles and

Royal Doorway of the west front

B. Kaufmann/ MICHELIN

Old Bell Tower are most impressive. It is still possible to recognise the former Notre-Dame cloisters thanks to the old pointed roof. Enclosed by a wall right up to the 19C, this area was frequented by clerics, especially canons.

Interior

The nave (16m/52ft) is wider than any other in France (Notre-Dame in Paris 40ft; Notre-Dame in Amiens 46ft), though it has single aisles. The vaulting reaches a height of 37m/121ft and the interior is 130m/427ft long. This nave is 13C, built in the style known as early or lancet Gothic. There is no gallery; instead, there is a blind triforium (*see illustration in the Introduction: Religious Architecture*). In a place of pilgrimage of this importance, the chancel and the transept had to accommodate large-scale ceremonies; they were therefore wider than the nave. In Chartres, the chancel, its double ambulatory and the transept form an ensemble 64m/210ft wide between the north and south doorways.

Note the gentle slope of the floor, rising slightly towards the chancel; this made it easier to wash down the church when the pilgrims had stayed overnight.

The striking state of semi-darkness in the nave creates an element of mystery which was not intentional: it is due to the gradual dimming of the stained glass over the centuries.

Stained-glass windows★★★

The 12C and 13C stained-glass windows of Notre-Dame constitute, together with those of Bourges, the largest collection in France. The Virgin and Child and the Annunciation and Visitation scenes in the clerestory at the far end of the chancel produce a striking impression.

West front

These three 12C windows used to throw light on Fulbert's Romanesque cathedral and the dark, low nave that stood behind, which explains why they are so long.

The scenes *(bottom to top)* illustrate the fulfilment of the prophecies: *(right)* the Tree of Jesse; *(centre)* the childhood

and life of Jesus (Incarnation cycle); and *(left)* Passion and Resurrection (Redemption cycle).

You can feast your eyes on the famous 12C 'Chartres blue', with its clear, deep tones enhanced by reddish tinges, especially radiant in the rays of the setting sun. For many years, people believed that this particular shade of blue was a long-lost trade secret. Modern laboratories have now established that the sodium compounds and silica in the glass made it more resistant to dirt and corrosion than the panes made with other materials and in other times. The large 13C rose window on the west front depicts the Last Judgment.

Transept

This ensemble consists of two 13C rose windows, to which were added a number of lancet windows featuring tall figures. The themes are the same as those on the corresponding carved doorway: Old Testament (north), the End of the World (south).

The north rose *(rose de France)* was a present from Blanche of Castille, mother of St Louis and Regent of France, and portrays a Virgin and Child. It is characterised by the fleur-de-lis motif on the shield under the central lancet and by the alternating Castile towers and fleurs-de-lis pictured on the small corner lancets. The larger lancets depict St Anne holding the infant Virgin Mary, framed by four kings or high priests: Melchizedek and David stand on the left, Solomon and Aaron on the right.

The centre roundel of the south rose shows the risen Christ, surrounded by the Old Men of the Apocalypse, forming two rings of 12 medallions. The yellow and blue chequered quatrefoils represent the coat of arms of the benefactors, the Comte de Dreux Pierre Mauclerc and his wife, who are also featured at the bottom of the lancets.

The lancets on either side of the Virgin and Child depict four striking figures – the Great Prophets Isaiah, Jeremiah, Ezekiel and Daniel – with the four Evangelists seated on their shoulders.

The morality of the scene is simple:

although they are weak and lacking dignity, the Evangelists can see farther than the giants of the Old Testament thanks to the Holy Spirit.

Notre-Dame-de-la-Belle-Verrière★ (1)

See Illustration in the Introduction.
This is a very famous stained-glass window. The Virgin and Child, a fragment of the window spared by the fire of 1194, has been mounted in 13C stained glass. The range of blues is quite superb.

Other stained-glass windows – The aisles of the nave and the chapels around the ambulatory are lit by a number of celebrated stained-glass windows from the 13C verging on the sombre side. On the east side, the arms of the transept have received two works of recent making, in perfect harmony with the early fenestration: St Fulbert's window *(south transept)* (2), donated by the American Association of Architects (from the François Lorin workshop, 1954),

and the window of Peace *(north transept)* (3), a present from a group of German admirers (1971).

The Vendôme Chapel (4) features a particularly radiant 15C stained-glass window. It illustrates the development of this art, which eventually led to the lighter panes of the 17C and 18C.

Parclose ★★

The screen was started by Jehan de Beauce in 1514 and finished in the 18C. This fine work consists of 41 sculpted compositions depicting the lives of Christ and the Virgin Mary. These Renaissance medallions, evoking biblical history, local history and mythology, contrast sharply with the Gothic statues of the doorways.

Chancel

The marble facing, the Assumption group above the high altar and the low-relief carvings separating the columns were added in the 18C.

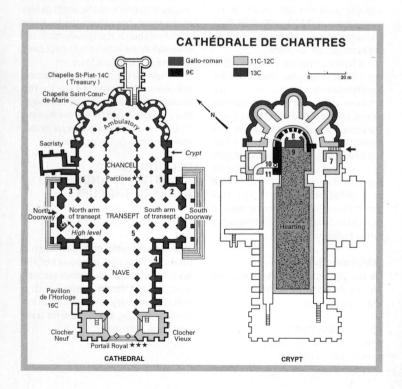

CATHÉDRALE DE CHARTRES

Organ (5)

The case dates from the 16C.

Vierge du Pilier (6)

This wooden statue (c 1510) stood against the rood screen, now sadly disappeared. The richly clothed Virgin is the object of an annual procession.

Treasury

🔒 Closed to the public.

Chapelle St-Piat has been built to house the cathedral treasury. It is linked to the east end of the cathedral by a Renaissance staircase.

Chapelle des Martyrs

This chapel has been refurbished and now contains the **Virgin Mary's Veil**, laid out in a beautiful glass-fronted reliquary. Pilgrims used to pray to this veil, calling it a tunic or 'Holy Chemise'.

Crypt★

🔦 Guided tours (30min) Apr–Oct Mon–Sat 11am, 2pm, 3.30pm, 4.30pm; Sun 2pm, 3.30pm, 4.30pm; rest of year call for hours. ⊛2.70€. 𝄐02 37 21 75 02. The entrance is outside the cathedral, on the south side (𝄐see plan).

This is France's longest crypt (220m/722ft long). It dates largely from the 11C and features Romanesque groined vaulting. It is a curious shape; the two long galleries joined by the ambulatory pass under the chancel and the aisles and give onto seven chapels. The central area, which has been filled in, remains unexplored. Of the seven radiating chapels, only three are Romanesque. The other four were added by the master architect of the Gothic cathedral to serve as foundations for the chancel and the apse of the future building.

St Martin's Chapel (7)

Located by the south gallery, this chapel houses the originals of the statues on the Royal Doorway.

▷ A staircase, starting from the ambulatory, leads down to a lower crypt.

Crypt St-Lubin (8)

This crypt served as the foundations of the 9C church. A thick, circular column with a visible base backs onto a Gallo-Roman wall (**9**), its bond easily recognisable by the alternating bricks and mortar. The crypt was a safe place that protected the cathedral treasures in times of social unrest or natural disaster. Thus, the chemise of the Virgin Mary survived the Great Fire of 1194.

Puits des Saints-Forts (10)

The lower part of this 33m/108ft deep shaft has a square section characteristic of Gallo-Roman wells. The coping is contemporary. The name dates back to 858; it is believed that several Christian martyrs from Chartres were murdered during a Norman attack, and their bodies thrown down the well.

Chapelle Notre-Dame-de-Sous-Terre (11)

A sacred retreat where pilgrims indulge in fervent praying. Since the 17C the chapel, together with the north gallery of the crypt, has played the part of a miniature church. It originally consisted of a small alcove where the faithful came to venerate the Virgin Mary.

The interior of the chapel and its decoration were refurbished in 1976. On this occasion, the 19C statue of the Virgin Mary was replaced by a more hieratic figure, based on the Romanesque model, enhanced by a Gobelins tapestry.

OLD TOWN★ (QUARTIER ST-ANDRÉ AND BANKS OF THE EURE)

▷ Follow the route on the plan.

This pleasant walk leads past the picturesque hilly site, the banks of the River Eure, an ancient district recently restored and the cathedral which is visible from every street corner. In the summer season, a small **tourist train** circles the old town.

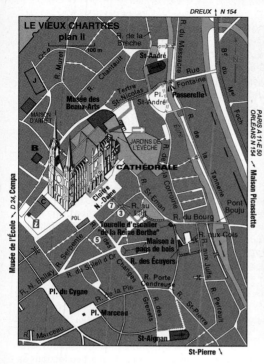

LE VIEUX CHARTRES
plan II

WHERE TO EAT

La Vieille Maison............❸

Le Café des Arts............❺

Le Serpente................❼

Centre international
du Vitrail.................**B**

Église St-André

🚫 *Closed temporarily for restoration.*
📞 *02 37 21 03 69.*

This Romanesque church *(deconsecrated)* was the place of worship of one of the most active and densely populated districts in town. Most of the trades were closely related to the river: millers, dyers, curriers, cobblers, tanners, drapers, fullers, tawers, serge makers, etc. The church was enlarged in the 13C, and in the 16C and 17C it received a chancel and an axial chapel resting on arches that straddled the River Eure and Rue du Massacre. Unfortunately, both these structures disappeared in 1827 leaving a much less picturesque church.

▷ *Cross the Eure by a metal footbridge.*

There is a good **view**★ of the old humpback bridges. At the foot of the shortened nave of St Andrew's lie the remains of the arch that once supported the chancel.

▷ *Wander upstream.*

The washhouses and races of former mills have been prettily restored. **Rue aux Juifs** leads through an ancient district that has recently been renovated, featuring cobbled streets bordered by gable-ended houses and old-fashioned street lamps.

Rue des Écuyers – This is one of the most successful restoration schemes of the old town. At nos 17 and 19 the houses have 17C doorways with rusticated surrounds, surmounted by a bull's-eye window. Stroll along the street to rue aux Cois. The corner building is a delightful half-timbered villa, with an overhang in the shape of a prow. Opposite stands Queen Bertha's stair turret, a 16C structure, also half-timbered.

CENTRAL DISTRICT
Place du Cygne

The street has been widened into a little square planted with trees and shrubs *(flower market on Tuesdays, Thursdays and Saturdays)* and is at present an oasis of calm in this lively shopping district in the town centre.

At the end of rue du Cygne, on place Marceau, a monument celebrates the memory of the young local general who died at Altenkirchen (1796) at the age of 27. His ashes have been shared among Chartres (funeral urn under the statue on place des Épars), the Panthéon and the Dome Church of the Invalides in Paris.

Église St-Pierre★

This 12C and 13C Gothic church used to belong to the Benedictine abbey of St-Père-en-Vallée. The belfry porch dates from pre-Romanesque times. The **Gothic stained-glass windows★** can be traced back to the late 13C and early 14C, before the widespread introduction of yellow staining.

The oldest stained glass is in the south bays of the chancel, portraying tall, hieratic figures from the Old Testament.

Monument de Jean Moulin

Jean Moulin was *préfet* (chief administrator) of Chartres during the German invasion. On 8 June 1940, despite having been tortured, he resisted the enemy and refused to sign a document claiming that the French troops had committed a series of atrocities. As he was afraid of being unable to withstand further torture, he attempted to commit suicide. Moulin was dismissed by the Vichy government in November 1940 and, from then on, he planned and coordinated underground resistance, working in close collaboration with General de Gaulle. Arrested in Lyon on 21 June 1943, he did not survive the harsh treatment he received from the Gestapo.

Grenier de Loëns

From the 12C onwards, this half-timbered barn with treble gables in the courtyard of the old chapter house was used to store the wine and cereals offered to the clergy as a tithe. Renovated to house the **Centre international du Vitrail** (& ⏰ open Mon–Fri 9.30am–12.30pm, 1.30–6pm, Sat 10am–12.30pm, 2.30–6pm, Sun and public holidays 2.30–6pm; ⇒4€; ℘02 37 21 65 72; www.centre-

vitrail.org), which organises stained-glass exhibitions, the building now features a large hall with beautifully restored roof timbering and a magnificent 12C cellar with three aisles.

Musée des Beaux-Arts

🕐*Open Wed–Sat 10am–noon, 2–5pm (May–Oct 6pm).* 🕐*Closed holidays, Sun morning.* ⇒3€ *(ticket combined with the Maison Picassiette 7€).* ℘02 37 36 41 39. www.ville-chartres.fr.

The museum is housed in the old bishop's palace and occupies the first terrace of the bishopric's gardens. The large, handsome edifice, which was built over four centuries consists of a 15C section arranged around an interior courtyard, a 17C and 18C façade, and an early 18C wing overlooking the garden.

The old sacristy, close to the chapel, houses 12 unusually large **enamels★** representing the Apostles, by Léonard Limousin.

The museum's new rooms house the permanent modern art collections as well as temporary exhibitions. There are several works by Vlaminck (*The House in Auvers, Red Bouquet with Anemones*) and J Guérin *(Flower Woman with the Poplar).* The South Sea Island collection and works by master glass-painter Navarre are also on show.

Le COMPA: Conservatoire du Machinisme et des Pratiques Agricoles

West of the town by D 24. & ☞ *Guided tours (1hr30min).* 🕐*Open Tue–Fri 9am–12.30pm, 1.30–6pm, Sat–Sun 10am–12.30pm, 1.30–7pm).* ⇒3.80€. ℘02 37 84 15 00. www.lecompa.com.

The museum is located in a converted, semicircular former railway shed. The spacious, modern building, has a good view of Chartres and the cathedral, and gleaming old machines and tools.

Tools and machines – At the museum's core stands machines, grouped according to function: seeders, binder-harvesters, combine-harvesters.

Land, men and methods – A comparison of two farming concerns in different regions of France, in 1860 and today, provides an understanding of rural life. Ploughs from around the world illustrate the diverse methods used on the land.

Galerie des inventeurs et des inventions – The 80m/262ft-long gallery introduces the figures responsible for major agricultural developments over the centuries. The ideas and innovations of Pliny the Elder, Olivier de Serres, Henri de Vilmorin, and Ferguson and the national agricultural research centre (INRA) are explained through information panels and interactive displays.

Salle des tracteurs – The tour ends with an exhibition of tractors, the oldest dating from 1816, the most recent from 1954.

Musée de l'École

&. ☉*Open Mon–Fri 10am–noon, 2–6pm; last admission 4.30pm.* ∞*3.50€.* ☏*02 37 30 07 69.*

A classroom of the old teacher training college houses teaching aids and furniture, evoking the schools of yesteryear: abacuses, magic lanterns using paraffin, books advocating humanist ethics, a collective money-bank with a separate compartment for each pupil, etc.

Maison Picassiette

22 rue du Repos. ☉*Open Wed–Sun 10am–noon, 2–5pm (May–Oct 6pm).* ☉*Closed holidays, Sun morning.* ∞*4.50€ (ticket combined with the musée des Beaux-Arts 7€).* ☏*02 37 34 10 78. www.ville-chartres.fr.*

Built and decorated by Raymond Isidore (1900–64), this house offers an amazing medley of naive art. Numerous monuments and religious scenes are suggested by mosaic compositions made with diverse materials.

ADDRESSES

🏠 STAY

⊜⊜ **L'Érablais (Bed and Breakfast)** – *38 r. Jean-Moulin, 28300 Chazay, 10km/ 6mi W by D 24 and D 121.* ☏*02 37 32 80 53. www.erablais.com. 3 rooms.* A converted 19C farm in a small hamlet near Chartres, with three bedrooms in the former cowshed (two with mansard roofs). Peaceful garden and bike hire available.

⊜⊜ **Ibis Centre Hôtel** – *14 Pl. Drouaise.* ☏*02 37 36 06 36. www.accor.com. 79 rooms.* ⊗*8€. Meals*⊜. This elegant Beauce farm offers functional, well-kept rooms. The restaurant terrace is very nice in fine weather.

⊜⊜ **La Ferme du Château (Bed and Breakfast)** – *In Levesville, 28300 Bailleau-l'Évêque, 8km/5mi NW via N 154 and D 134.* ☏*02 37 22 97 02. www.ferme-levesville.com.* ✍. *3 rooms. Meals*⊜⊜. This elegant Beauce farm offers pretty, comfortable rooms that have been decorated with a light hand. Neighbouring a small château, the farm is very quiet and its kind, hospitable owners very discreet.

⊜⊜ **Ferme de la Forge (Bed and Breakfast)** – *2 r. des Prunus, at Cherville, 28700 Oinvill-sous-Auneau, 17.5km/11mi E by D 910 and D 19.* ☏*02 37 31 72 80. www.cherville.com.* ✍. *4 rooms.* A 19C farmhouse with a friendly owner ready to welcome you to a mansarded room decorated with rustic period furnishings.

⊜⊜ **La Varenne (Bed and Breakfast)** – *20 r. de Tachainville, La Varenne, 28630 Ver-lès-Chartres, 6km/3.7mi S by D 935 and D 114.* ☏*02 37 26 45 32. http://la varenne28.free.fr.* ✍. *4 rooms.* In the middle of wheat fields, this renovated home has four rooms on the ground floor, simple yet elegant in style. Heated indoor pool and contemporary kitchen.

⊜⊜⊜⊜ **Hôtel Le Grand Monarque** – *22 Pl. des Épars.* ☏*02 37 18 15 15. www. bw-grand-monarque.com. 50 rooms.* ⊗ *14€. Restaurant*⊜⊜⊜⊜. A 16C coaching inn at the heart of the city. The comfortable rooms have a personal touch; some are embellished with cheerfully flowered patterns and canopies while others are more sober. Snug dining room with ornamental wood carvings and works of art.

EAT

Le Pichet – *19 r. du Cheval-Blanc. 02 37 21 08 35. Closed Tue eve, Wed.* Just down the street from the cathedral, a very friendly little bistro. Inside, there is a pleasant jumble of bric-a-brac decor; the food is traditional French cuisine.

Café des Arts – *45 r. des Changes. 02 37 21 07 05. Closed Sun in winter.* A trendy bar next to the cathedral with decor inspired by the owner's travels in the Sahara. Cocktails, theme nights and brasserie dishes and tartine sandwiches make it a lively place, day and night. Nice terrace in summer.

La Brasserie Bruneau – *4 r. du Mar.-de-Lattre-de-Tassigny. 02 37 21 80 99. Closed Jan–May, Sat lunch, Sun.* A 1930s style brasserie just outside the Hôtel de Ville, with traditional dishes and young, laid-back atmosphere.

Le Café Serpente – *2 r. du Cloître Notre-Dame. 02 37 21 68 81. Reservations requested in winter.* A bicycle on the ceiling, posters on the walls and enamelled plaques in the stairwell comprise the decor of this thoroughly genial old café opposite the cathedral. On your plates: appetizing salads, brasserie fare and authentic cuisine at all hours.

Le Tripot – *11 Pl. Jean-Moulin. 02 37 36 60 11. Closed last 2 weeks in Aug, Mon, Wed eve, Sun eve.* This house built in 1553 used to accommodate a real tennis court called 'Le Tripot'. Well-preserved rustic interior and contemporary cuisine.

Saint-Hilaire – *11 r. du Pont-St-Hilaire. 02 37 30 97 57. Closed 3 weeks in Aug and Dec, Sat lunch, Sun–Mon.* This old 16C house has two tiny dining rooms with exposed wooden beams, clay tile floors and traditional French cuisine inspired by the seasons.

La Vieille Maison – *5 r. Au-Lait. 02 37 34 10 67. www.lavieillemaison.fr. Closed Sun eve, Mon, Tue lunch.* Exposed stone walls, a fireplace and wooden beams give this ancient restaurant a rustic feel. Traditional French cuisine with a gourmet touch.

Château de Dampierre★★

Dampierre is closely associated with two distinguished families, the Luynes and the Chevreuse, who still own it today. From 1675 to 1683 Jules Hardouin-Mansart rebuilt the Château de Dampierre for Colbert's son-in-law the Duke of Chevreuse, a former student at Port-Royal and the mentor of the Duke of Burgundy. The castle and its park, laid out by Le Nôtre, form one of the rare well-preserved estates close to Paris.

Michelin Local Map: Michelin Local map 311: H-3, map 101 fold 31 or 106 fold 29.

Info: 01 30 52 53 24. www.chateau-de-dampierre.fr.

Location: Situated in the narrow upper part of the Chevreuse Valley, 43.4km/27mi southwest of Paris; accessible by the A 12.

Timing: You should allow half a day to get the best out of your visit.

VISIT

Château★★

Open Apr–Sept Mon–Sat 11am–6.30pm, Sun, public holidays, 11am–noon, 2–6.30pm. 10€; grounds only, 6.5€. 01 30 52 53 24.

The main body of the château, surrounded by a moat, opens onto a courtyard flanked by stables and outbuildings. In front of it are two buildings with arcades. The pinkish tones of the brick harmonise with the sober stone string courses and columns, contrasting sharply with the darker hues of the park.

On the ground floor, visitors may admire Cavelier's statue of Penelope (1848) in the hall leading to the drawing rooms embellished with Louis XV wainscoting, the suite occupied by Marie Leszczynska, and an imposing dining room decorated with Louis XIV panelling.

The first floor houses the **Royal Suite**, which accommodated Louis XIV, Louis XV and Louis XVI. The splendid 17C and 18C furnishings are beautifully preserved and reminiscent of the King's suite at Versailles. Note the furniture, portraits, wainscoting, medallions and overdoor panels by old masters.

The most amazing achievement stands at the top of the great staircase.

The Salle de la Minerve is a formal reception room dating from the 19C when the castle was restored by Duban. Ingres was commissioned to paint a fresco representing the Golden Age; it was never completed. The Duc Honoré de Luynes, who conceived the whole project, ordered a colourful 3m/9.8ft statue of Minerva, a miniature replica of the legendary gold and ivory Minerva of the Parthenon executed by Phidias in the 5C BC.

Park★

A walk round the castle starting from the right will lead you to a large ornamental pond, the favourite spot of many anglers. Water is omnipresent in this vast romantic park: canals, fountains and waterfalls embellish this green open space in the heart of the forest, in the middle of the picturesque Chevreuse Valley. The park and the castle form one of the rare protected estates near the capital.

EXCURSION
Vaux de Cernay

4km/2.5mi south by D 91 to Cernay-la-Ville, then right onto D 24 (🚶 30min–2hr).

The road weaves up the wooded narrow valley, past a restaurant and across a brook by a mill, Moulin des Roches.

▶ *Park near the Chalet des Cascades.*

Étang de Cernay

The pond was created by the monks of the local abbey to stock fish. A memorial to the 19C landscape painter Léon-Germain Pelouse stands at the top of the embankment, near a stately oak tree.

The walk may be continued for another 30min or 1hr by following the wide path, which veers right and leads straight up to the wooded plateau. From the edge of the plateau turn back, bear right and return along the cliff path that skirts the promontory.

Abbaye des Vaux-de-Cernay★

Now a hotel, the abbey was founded in the early 12C. It came under Cistercian rule and reached its heyday in the 13C, but in the 14C it suffered from epidemics of plague and successive wars and started to decline. In 1791 it was abandoned by its last 12 monks and sold. The Rothschild family who bought the abbey in 1873 restored and preserved it until World War II. On the **grounds**, the ruins of the abbey church may be seen (late-12C façade with rose window), and the monk's building, now a concert hall.

ADDRESSES

🛏 STAY

🍴🛏🛏🛏 **Abbaye des Vaux de Cernay** – *78720 Cernay-la-Ville, 2.5km/ 1.5mi W. ☎01 34 85 23 00. www.abbaye decernay.com. 57 rooms. ⊒16€. Restaurant🍴🛏🛏.* To fall asleep in the superb Cistercian abbey and awake to the monastic quietude of its magnificent park: heavenly! The spacious rooms are a successful blend of modern comfort and antique materials. Restaurant and tea room.

🍴 EAT

🍴🛏🛏 **Auberge Saint-Pierre** – *1 r. de Chevreuse, 78720 Dampierre-en-Yvelines. ☎01 30 52 53 53. Closed Sun eve, Mon, Tue eve.* A traditional French country inn in the heart of the Chevreuse Valley, the perfect place to eat a hearty meal after a day of hiking. Rustic decor and a menu of traditional cuisine with a modern twist.

Disneyland Resort Paris★★★

Disneyland is a place to relive your childhood dreams. Not far from the hotels, the main entertainment centre called Disney Village re-creates the American way of life with shops, restaurants and entertainment. A short distance from the complex lies Golf Disneyland Paris, with its 27-hole course.

A BIT OF HISTORY
A Magician called Walt Disney

Walt Disney's name is linked to innumerable animated cartoons that have entertained children throughout the world. No one can forget the heroes of his creations (Mickey Mouse, Minnie, Donald, Pluto, Pinocchio, Snow White, and others).

Born **Walter Elias Disney** in Chicago in 1901, Walt soon showed great ability at drawing. After World War I, in which he served as an ambulance driver in France, he returned to the US where, in Kansas City, he met a young Dutchman called Ub Iwerks. In 1923 the pair produced in Hollywood a series of short films called *Alice Comedies*. In 1928 Mickey Mouse, the future international star, was created. There next followed the era of the Oscar-winning, full-length animated cartoon films: *The Three Little Pigs* (1933), *Snow White and the Seven Dwarfs* (1937), and *Dumbo* (1941).

Disney also produced films starring real people, such as *Treasure Island* (1950) and *20 000 Leagues Under the Sea* (1954). In 1966 the man who had spent his life trying to bring dreams to life died, but Walt Disney Studios continued to make films, remaining faithful to Walt's ideas.

▲ DISNEYLAND PARK★★★

🕐*Opening times are announced biannually; please check before entry.*
Disneyland: *daily mid-Jul–Aug 9am–11pm; Sept–mid-Apr 10am–7pm,*

- 🕭 **Michelin Local Map:** 312: F-2 or map 106 fold 22.
- ▋ **Info:** ✆08448 008 898 (in UK), ✆01 60 30 60 53 (from outside France), ✆0825 82 51 00 (in France). www.disneylandparis.com.
- ▶ **Location:** The resort is 32km/20mi east of Paris, with excellent transport links. On arrival, find the information desk in City Hall (Disneyland Park) where a programme of the attractions is provided.
- 🅿 **Parking:** There is parking available in the northeast portion of the park, but with both train and bus terminals, Disneyland Paris is easily accessible by public transport.
- 🕐 **Timing:** To avoid long queues, visit popular attractions during the parade, at the end of the day or with a Fast Pass *(free)* issued by machines at the entrance to attractions; this ticket bears a time slot of one hour during which time you may have access to the attraction within a few minutes.

Sat–Sun and public holidays 10am–10pm; mid-Apr–mid-Jul 10am–8pm, Sat 9am–8pm. www.dlrpmagic.com.
Disney Studios: *high season 9am–6pm, low season 10am–7pm.*
🐾*Guided tours: contact the City Hall (Disneyland Park) on Town Square in Main Street, or the Studio Services in Walt Disney Studios.* 🎫*1 day/1 park 50€ (child 42€); 2 days 60€ (child 52€); 3 days 108€ (child 92€).*
Disneyland Passport *(Passeport Annuel) 300 days 89€, 335 days 129€, 365 days 189€. Passports allow total freedom of movement between both Parks.*
The large Disneyland Paris site (over 55ha/135 acres) comprises five territo-

ries or 'lands', each with a different theme.

As well as the spectacular shows featuring amazing automatons in particularly detailed settings, each region has shops, ice cream vendors, restaurants and self-service restaurants.

Every day, the **Disney Parade★★**, a procession of floats carrying all the favourite Disney cartoon characters, takes place. On some evenings and throughout the summer the **Main Street Electrical Parade★★** adds extra illuminations to the fairytale setting.

Main Street USA

The main street of an American town at the turn of the 20C, lined with shops and restaurants with Victorian-style fronts, is brought to life as though by magic. Horse-drawn street cars, limousines, fire engines and Black Marias transport visitors from Town Square to Central Plaza while colourful musicians play favourite ragtime, jazz and Dixieland tunes. On either side of the road are **Discovery Arcade** and **Liberty Arcade** (exhibition and diorama on the famous Statue of Liberty).

From Main Street station a small steam train, the **Disneyland Railroad★**, travels across the park and through the **Grand Canyon Diorama**, stopping at the station in each land.

Frontierland

The conquest of the West, the gold rush and the Wild West with its legends and folklore are brought together in Thunder Mesa, a typical western town. The waters here are plied by two handsome **steamboats★**, the *Mark Twain* and the *Molly Brown*.

Big Thunder Mountain★★★

In the mountain, there's an old gold mine. On the banks of the lake, in the buildings belonging to a mining company, are crowds of travellers patiently waiting to board the **Mine Train**. The trip in the hurtling carriages racing down the track at top speed includes explosions and risks of falling rocks.

Phantom Manor★★★

A dilapidated manor house stands high above the Rivers of the Far West. Inside, strange things happen: the walls stretch and shrink. The tour through the rooms and basement continues in small black 'haunted' chairs. When you leave, take a stroll to the **Boot Hill** cemetery and have a look at the strange tombstones.

Adventureland

Adventureland conjures up pictures of exotic adventures, travel to far-distant lands, treasure island, and pirates.

Visionaries

Leonardo da Vinci (1452–1512): as early as the 15C, he had conceived the parachute and the helicopter. Jules Verne (1828–1905) used to state: "Everything a man can imagine other men can realise". His science fiction novels show how right he was. Herbert George Wells (1866–1946): this master of fantasy shook the Americans with his novel entitled *War of the Worlds*, which Orson Welles interpreted on radio in 1938.

How old is Mickey?

The famous young mouse has not got a single wrinkle, yet he was born in 1928 thanks to Disney and the cartoonist of Dutch origin, Ub Iwerks. Mickey first appeared in a small film entitled *Plane Crazy*, based on Charles Lindbergh's achievement. However, it was on 18 November of the same year that he made his debut as a star, together with the delightful Minnie, in the first silent cartoon film entitled *Steamboat Willie*. One small detail: age has caused Mickey to lose not his hair, but his tail!

Pirates of the Caribbean★★★

This fortress is easy to spot – the skull and crossbones fly at the top of its walls. Cross the underground passages which reserve a few surprises then board a small boat and watch the attack and ransacking of a Spanish harbour town by pirates.

Indiana Jones et le Temple du Péril … à l'envers★★★

In the jungle lies a ruined temple; courageous archaeologists in wagons enter it in reverse and defy the laws of gravity. This is not for the faint-hearted.

La Cabane des Robinson★★

The Swiss Family Robinson survived a shipwreck and were able to salvage a few objects and building materials that enabled them to build a tree house in a giant banyan tree (an Indian fig). A staircase leads up to the various rooms with their wonderful furniture.

Fantasyland

The land of fairytales, Sleeping Beauty's Castle and all of your favourite Disney characters 'in the flesh': Mickey, Minnie, Donald, Goofy and Pluto are ready to pose for photos.

Le Château de la Belle au bois dormant★★ (Sleeping Beauty's Castle)

On the upper floor, stained-glass windows and Aubusson tapestries recount episodes from this famous fairy story. Below, in the depths of the castle, a huge scaly dragon appears to be sleeping. A magnificent view from the ramparts.

It's a Small World★★

A 'cruise' takes visitors past dolls dressed in national costume, singing and dancing in sets that represent their home countries.

Alice's Curious Labyrinth★

An episode from *Alice in Wonderland* in which the path to the Queen of Heart's castle is full of surprises.

Peter Pan's Flight★★

Like the flight of Peter Pan, the boy who never grew up, the trip takes visitors over the rooftops of London and Never-Never Land, and past episodes of Peter Pan, all in small boats.

Blanche-Neige et les Sept Nains★ (Snow White and the Seven Dwarfs)

In the mysterious forest crossed by small wagons is the wicked witch who cast a spell on Snow White.

Discoveryland

A fascinating land dedicated to the future, paying homage to the world of inventions and Science Fiction.

Space Mountain★★★ – Mission 2

This superb attraction was inspired by Jules Verne's novel *From the Earth to the Moon*. A huge copper and bronze mountain encompassing a gigantic cannon pointing skywards awaits the most audacious visitors. After being catapulted toward the cosmos, you experience a mind-bending, and highly acrobatic, intergalactic trip.

Star Tours★★★

A breathtaking trip on a spaceship. Based on George Lucas' famous film *Star Wars*. A stopover at the **Astroport Services Interstellaires** is highly recommended. · Use the **Photomorph** to change your looks (laughter guaranteed) and have your photo taken.

Chérie, j'ai rétréci le public★★★ (Honey, I've shrunk the audience)

An extraordinary experience awaits you in the hall of the Imagination Institute: the famous professor Wayne Szalinski is giving a public demonstration of his shrinking machine. Are you volunteering? If so, hang on: the settings may not be spot on!

Buzz Lightyear Laserblast

Save the universe of toys using your lasergun to target in on the pesky Emporer Zurg and win points.

WALT DISNEY STUDIOS PARK★★★

Inaugurated on 16 March 2002, this park is entirely dedicated to the wonders of cinema. It offers its guests a chance to take a trip backstage and discover some of the secrets of filming, of animation techniques and of television.

Front Lot

The park entrance is overlooked by a 33m/108ft-high water tower, a traditional landmark in film studios. In the centre of the Spanish-style courtyard, planted with palm trees, stands a fountain dedicated to Mickey.

Disney Studio 1 is the reconstruction of a famous Hollywood film set, Hollywood Boulevard, lined with restaurants and boutiques.

Toon Studio

Disney contributed much to the development of 20C animation.

Animagique★★★

This attraction celebrates Disney's full-length animation films; spectators find themselves at the centre of a 3D cartoon, next to Mickey, Donald Duck, Dumbo's pink elephants, Pinocchio.

Art of Disney Animation★★

An interactive discovery of the secrets of animation.

Flying Carpets★★

Guests wait backstage for instructions which direct them to the main film set where Aladdin's Genie guides them onto flying carpets!

Sleeping Beauty's Castle ©Disney

MAKING THE MOST OF THE THEME PARKS

To avoid long queues at popular attractions, visit these attractions during the parade, at the end of the day or, better still, get a **Fast Pass**, issued by distributors outside the most popular attractions in both parks; this ticket bears a time slot of one hour during which time you may have access to the attraction within a few minutes.

Disneyland Park

Indiana Jones (Adventureland); Peter Pan's Flight (Fantasyland); Big Thunder Mountain (Frontierland); Space Mountain and Star Tours (Discoveryland).

Walt Disney Studios Park

Rock 'n' Roller Coaster (Backlot); Flying Carpets (Animation Courtyard); Studio Tram Tour (Production Courtyard).

GENERAL INFORMATION

Booking a show – Entertainment programmes and booking facilities can be found at City Hall, in Town Square, just inside Disneyland Park.

Currency exchange – Facilities are available at the main entrance to the park.

Visitors with Disabilities – A guide detailing special services available can be obtained from City Hall (Disneyland Park) or from the information desk inside Walt Disney Studios Park.

Storage areas – Near the main entrance, beneath Main Street Station.

Animals – These are not allowed in the theme parks, in Disney Village or in the hotels. The Animal Care Centre is located near the visitors' car park.

Baby Care Centre, Meeting Place for Lost Children, First Aid – Near the Plaza Gardens Restaurant (Disneyland Park) or in Front Lot (Walt Disney Studios Park).

Production Courtyard

Here spectators are allowed to see what happens behind-the-scenes of cinema and television studios: how film sets and special effects are created.

Cinémagique★★★

When fiction meets reality, spectators literally go through the screen and become the actors and heroes of the film.

Famous Fairytale Writers

Charles Perrault (1628–1703): *Sleeping Beauty*; Charles Lutwidge Dodgson, better known as Lewis Carroll (1832–98): *Alice in Wonderland*; the Grimm Brothers: *Snow White and the Seven Dwarfs*; anthology of German fairy tales; Carlo Collodi: *Pinocchio*; Hans Christian Andersen (1805–1875): *The Little Mermaid*; James Matthew Barrie (1860–1937): *Peter Pan*.

Television Production Tour★★

You are offered a guided tour of Disney Channel France and the possibility to watch the live filming of *Zapping Zone*.

Studio Tram Tour★★

Sit back and enjoy this guided tour aboard a small tramway through amazing film sets, until you reach **Catastrophe Canyon★★★**!

The Twilight Zone Tower of Terror

A terrifying visit to the fourth dimension as you ride the elevator of an old Hollywood hotel, which plunges 13 floors to the ground!

BackLot

This is here the action is! Fasten your seatbelts…

Armageddon★★

The Russian space station is threatened by meteorites, a gripping (and particularly loud) experience!

Rock'n Roller Coaster★★★

A unique 'musical' experience awaits you inside a recording studio; be prepared to be propelled at full speed on a breathtaking journey…(not for the faint-hearted!).

Moteurs… Action!★★★

A hero chasing some villains through a village in the south of France, an occasion to see some superb stunts.

DISNEY VILLAGE★

The main street of this American town offers continuous entertainment and a convivial atmosphere, particularly once the theme parks are closed for the night. Shops, restaurants and bars are crowded. In the street. Night-owls can then go on to the discotheque **Hurricanes**. The quality of the shows, the increasing number of cinemas, and the reputation of establishments such as **Planet Hollywood** have ensured the success of this 'village', which attracts a growing number of visitors from the Île-de-France region.

Buffalo Bill's Wild West Show★★

The famous adventures of pioneer William Frederick Cody (1846–1917), alias Buffalo Bill, inspired this dinner-show, which, complete with horses, bison, cowboys and Indians, evokes the epic days of the Wild West. The Texas-style meal is served on tin plates.
Why the name Buffalo Bill? William Cody became famous for his skill as a marksman and for hunting buffaloes during the building of the Kansas Pacific Railroad.

ADDRESSES

🏨 STAY

For the total Disney experience, you can choose your accommodation among the park's hotels. All managed by Disney, their decor is inspired by different regions of the United States.

⊖ **Camping Base de Loisirs de Jablines-Annet** – 77450 Jablines, 6km/ 3.7mi N. ✆01 60 26 09 37. www.camping-jablines.com. Closed Nov–Mar. Reservations advisable. 150 sites. Offering water sports, camping and bungalow rentals, the Île-de-France's biggest beach is spread before you while Disneyland is right around the corner. Large, paved alleys give onto pretty views of the surrounding landscapes.

⊖ **Domaine de Bellevue Bed and Breakfast** – 77610 Neufmoutiers-en-Brie,10km/6mi S. Take A 4, D 231 then D 96. ✆01 64 07 11 05. www.domaine-de-bellevue.net. 7 rooms. Don't turn around when you see the modern buildings, you'd be sorry. Nestled in an attractive garden, this residence is most pleasant: both simple and elegant, close to Paris and Disneyland, it is a charming stopover in the heart of the Brie region.

⊖⊖ **Les Hauts de Montguillon** – 22 r. de St-Quentin, in Montguillon, 77860 St-Germain-sur-Morin, 3km/1.8mi NE. ✆01 60 04 45 53. www.les-hauts-de-montguillon.com. Reservations required. 🚭. 5 rooms. Meals ⊖⊖.
This recently restored farmhouse located a few minutes from Disneyland is an opportune, comfortable halt. Bedrooms are a successful blend of old and new; bathrooms are stylish and ultra-modern. Cottage sleeps four.

⊖⊖⊖ **Hôtel Santa Fé** – In Disneyland. ✆01 60 45 78 00. 1 000 rooms. Welcome to New Mexico! A larger than life poster of Clint Eastwood, straight out of *The Good, The Bad and The Ugly*, welcomes you on your way to rooms cooled by ceiling fans. The Tex-Mex restaurant is enlivened by *mariachi* bands.

⊖⊖⊖⊖ **Hôtel Cheyenne** – In Disneyland. ✆01 60 45 62 00. 1 000 rooms. Come play cowboys and Indians with your kids in this reconstructed Far West town! Simple rooms designed for family visits; restaurant with a self-service menu and costumed service staff who put on a Western-style show.

⊖⊖⊖⊖ **Newport Bay Club** – In Disneyland. ✆01 60 45 55 00. 1 093 rooms. On the shores of Lake Disney, discover the charm of an early 20C New England coast resort, complete with rocking chairs on the veranda. Two restaurants: the Cape Cod, serving buffet meals, and the Yacht Club, featuring seafood.

ⵏ/ EAT

INSIDE DISNEYLAND

For a quick snack or a leisurely meal, a multitude of restaurants awaits you. Here's a sampling:

⊖ For a nibble, take a quick trip to Italy via la **Bella Notte**, have a seat on **Colonel Hathi's** terrace, or enjoy the buffet at the **Plaza Gardens**. If you have more time, you might opt for one of the restaurants – you'll enjoy a fine meal in original surroundings. Remember to reserve your table by phone (℘01 64 74 28 82) or at the City Hall, just left of the park entrance.

⊖⊜ **Auberge de Cendrillon** – *Fantasyland*. Once upon a time, Cinderella's Inn stood at the foot of a lovely castle. A beautiful girl in glass slippers would come by coach – so the legend goes – to savour the tenderly simmered dishes served in front of the big fireplace or on the flowered terrace in summer.

⊖⊜ **Silver Spur Steakhouse** – *Frontierland. Closed Mon-Tue*. You can leave your horse at the entrance of this Far West saloon. While you probably won't run into cowboys or rich cattle farmers, you will be able to savour grilled meat prepared ranch-style.

⊖⊜ **Walt's Restaurant** – *Main Street. Closed Wed–Thu*. After having climbed the sweeping staircase of this handsome Victorian mansion on Main Street and admired the photos of Mr. Disney that line the walls, choose a table in one of the cosy salons of this comfortable restaurant. Our favourite dining areas are Discoveryland and the Library

⊖⊜⊜ **Blue Lagoon Restaurant** – *Adventureland*. Tropical moonlight and Caribbean ambience among luxurious greenery, where island specialities include seafood, *accras de morue* (cod fritters), West Indian *boudin* (blood pudding) and the Creole *rougail de poisson*. Have a seat along the Pirate of the Caribbean's river and tuck in.

IN DISNEY STUDIOS PARK

⊖⊜ **Rendez-vous des Stars Restaurant** – *Production Courtyard*. This buffet restaurant in the Art Deco style is where Hollywood's greatest stars convene. The walls are covered with portraits of the most famous celebrities of the Big Screen.

OUTSIDE THE THEME PARKS

⊖ **Annette's Diner** – *Disney Village*. ℘01 60 45 70 37. Interested in experiencing a blast from the past, as seen in the 1950s-era film *American Graffiti*? Come in and order true-to-life hamburgers, hot dogs, milk shakes… Waiters and waitresses leave their posts every now and again and start dancing!

⊖⊜ **L'Ermitage** – *allée Jean-de-la-Fontaine, Ecluse de Chalifert, 77144 Chalifert, 6km/3.7mi N. ℘01 60 43 41 43. www.notrermitage.com. Closed 29 Jul–29 Aug. Reservations required*. The oldest guinguette on the banks of the Marne, founded in 1860, is still packed every weekend. Patrons of all ages come here to enjoy the unique festive atmosphere during dinner or a *thé-dansant*. Dancing Fridays, cabaret Saturdays and retro Sundays.

⊖⊜ **Rainforest Café** – *Disney Village*. ℘01 60 43 65 53 – www.rainforest cafe.com. You'll need to cross a shop, not an ocean, to get to this Amazonian rain forest. Gorillas, elephants and other exotic beasts observe you as you dine on mildly spicy dishes served in a sensational equatorial decor.

⊖⊜ **The Steakhouse** – *Disney Village*. ℘01 60 45 70 45. Closed Sat lunch*. Connoisseurs of juicy steaks and fine wines: this place is for you. Before your meal arrives, enjoy the superb decor inspired by Prohibition-era Chicago. If you have children with you, don't miss Sunday brunch in the company of Disney heroes.

Château de
Ferrières★

The shooting parties on Ferrières estate, the luxurious furnishings of the château and the precious collections gathered by the members of the Rothschild dynasty were the talk of the town for over a century. The landscape park, created at the same time as the Bois de Boulogne, is extremely attractive, especially in the vicinity of the lake. The nearby town got its name from iron ore *(fer)* extracted in great quantities during the 16C and 17C.

A BIT OF HISTORY
A Challenge to Tradition

In 1829 James de Rothschild, founder of the French line of the family, acquired 7 500 acres of hunting grounds formerly belonging to Fouché, with a view to building a villa, which would accommodate his invaluable collections.

The baron did not choose a professional architect; he broke with tradition and hired **Joseph Paxton**, the English glasshouse and garden designer with a penchant for modern materials such as iron and glass. Already famed for the Crystal Palace in London *(destroyed by fire in 1936)*, Paxton erected a rectangular building flanked by square towers, with a central hall equipped with zenithal lighting. Construction work was completed in 1859. The decoration, left in the hands of the baroness,

⏱ **Michelin Local Map:**
312: F-3, map 101 fold
30 or 106 folds 21, 22

🔲 **Info:** ☎01 64 66 31 25.
www.chateaudeferrieres.
sorbonne.fr.

was entrusted to the French specialist Eugène Lami.

On 16 December 1862, Napoleon III paid an official visit to the Rothschilds in their new residence. Delighted by the splendid apartments and the 800 head of game for his day's shoot, the Emperor planted a sequoia tree as a commemorative gesture.

Less than ten years later, Jules Favre – in charge of Foreign Affairs in the new National Defence government – turned up at the gates of the château on 19 September 1870. In his capacity as Minister, Favre came to see Kaiser Bismarck, who was staying at Ferrières with Kaiser Wilhelm I of Prussia, to ask him to agree to an armistice.

The chancellor however made this conditional on the surrender of Strasbourg, Toul and Bitche, and further implied that the cession of Alsace and part of Lorraine was inevitable. Jules Favre left the premises the following morning. On 28 January 1871, Paris fell to the hands of the enemy.

In 1977 Baron Guy de Rothschild and his wife Marie-Hélène donated their château and part of the estate to the Confederation of Paris Universities.

Château de Ferrières

B. Kaufmann/ MICHELIN

VISIT
Exterior
The castle's architecture reflects the various styles of the Renaissance period, including the odd eccentricity that was acceptable in the 19C. Although balusters, galleries and colonnades reigned supreme, the façades were each different. The most striking and the most typically English is the main front overlooking the lake, with its centrepiece flanked by turrets and its display of superimposed galleries. Step back to take in the tall decorative stone chimneys, reminiscent of the Château de Chambord.

Interior
🕐 *Open daily May–Sept 2–7pm; Oct–Apr 2–5pm.* 🎟8€. 📞 *01 64 66 31 25.*
A pavilion sporting a large clock is fronted by the main entrance porch which bears the baron's monogram (JR) and the family coat of arms (the five Rothschild arrows).
The main staircase leads to the central hall – 40m/130ft wide and 12m/40ft high under the glass ceiling – now stripped of its paintings and tapestries. Above the main door, a row of telamones and caryatids in bronze and black marble support a musicians' gallery. The use of such statues was a popular decorative feature in the mid-19C. The Salon Bleu, overlooking the park, has busts of the Empress Eugénie and Bettina de Rothschild, the first proprietress of the château. The Louis XVI salon is the most typical example of Eugène Lami's work: it features off-white wainscoting with pinkish hues, a painted ceiling inspired by Boucher and reproduction Louis XVI furniture. Opposite is the Salon Rouge, in which the 1870 negotiations took place. It now presents an exhibition on the history of the estate.

Musée de l'Imaginaire
🕐 *Open May–Sept Sun and holidays 2–6pm; Oct–Apr 2–5pm.* 🎟5€ *(includes Park entrance).* 📞 *01 64 66 31 25. http://castledream.free.fr.*
This small museum housed on the second floor showcases a changing collection of paintings and sculptures by an international group of contemporary artists who express their extravagant visions in the style known as Fantastic Realism. The works are shown here before being offered for public sale.

Park★
🕐 *Same hours as château.* 🎟5€ *(includes Museum visit).* 📞 *01 64 66 31 25.*
The park designed by Paxton boasts a number of superb compositions, mainly consisting of ornamental coniferous trees: cedars of Lebanon, numerous Atlas cedars – including the highly decorative blue form – and sequoias, introduced into France around 1850.
Several individual trees also deserve a mention: a Lebanese cedar with unusually long, spread-eagled branches, swamp cypresses with twigs which turn deep russet and drop off in winter, copper beeches, groves of plane trees and, on the far side of the lake, feathery weeping species, adding an autumnal touch to the tableau.
Outside the park, the allée des Lions presents an imposing driveway of stately sequoias.

Forêt de Ferrières
In 1973, the Île-de-France region acquired the forest surrounding the castle and covering 2 800ha/ 6 919 acres. The forest now includes parking and picnic areas, as well as numerous footpaths and cycle paths accessible all year round. The Étang de la Planchette is an angler's paradise (🎣 *fishing permits delivered on the spot*).

ADDRESSES

🏨 STAY
🍽🛏 **Hôtel St-Rémy** – *77164 Ferrières-en-Brie.* 📞*01 64 76 74 00. 25 rooms.* 🍴*8€. Restaurant*🍽🛏🛏. Located right behind the church, this late-19C house has given up most of its original features following a total overhaul. Note the upstairs ballroom, originally decorated by the Rothschild family.

Fontainebleau ★★★

The area owes its name to a spring at the heart of a forest abounding in game, which was known as the 'Fontaine de Bliaut' or 'Blaut', probably after a former owner. However, Fontainebleau essentially owes its fame to the castle and the park named on UNESCO's World Heritage list. It was not until the 19C that Fontainebleau started to develop, owing to the growing popularity of country residences and the general appreciation of its unspoilt forest.

A BIT OF HISTORY

The **Palais de Fontainebleau** owes its origins to royalty's passion for hunting; it owes its development and decoration to the kings' delight in amassing works of art and displaying them in their 'family home'. This palace has an extremely distinguished past; from the last of the Capetians up to Napoleon III, it was occupied by French rulers.

A hunting lodge – A spring – called Bliaut or Blaut fountain in the middle of a forest abounding in game – prompted the kings of France to build a mansion here. The exact date is not known but it was probably before 1137 as a charter exists issued under Louis VII from Fontainebleau, dating from that year. Philip Augustus celebrated the return of the Third Crusade here during the Christmas festivities of 1191 and St Louis founded a Trinitarian convent, whose members were called Mathurins. Philip the Fair was born here in 1268; unfortunately, he also died here following a serious riding accident.

The Renaissance – Under François I almost all the medieval buildings were pulled down and replaced by two main edifices, erected under the supervision of Gilles Le Breton. The oval-shaped east pavilion – built on the former foundations – was linked to the west block by a long gallery. To decorate the palace, François I hired many artists; he dreamed

- ▶ **Population:** 15 942
- ⌚ **Michelin Local Map:** 312: F-5 or map 106 folds 45, 46
- **Info:** Office du tourisme du pays de Fontainebleau-Avon, 4, r. Royale, 77300 Fontainebleau. ☎01 60 74 99 99. www.fontaine bleau-tourisme.com.
- ▷ **Location:** Fontainebleau is 60km/37mi from Paris, via the A 6, and then the N 37. Access from Paris: SNCF rail link from Gare de Lyon.
- **Don't Miss:** The Renaissance features of the castle, especially its famous horseshoe staircase.
- ○ **Timing:** Take a whole day, including 1hr for the palace.

of creating a 'New Rome' furnished with replicas of Classical statues.

The actual building consisted of rubble-work as the sandstone taken from the forest was too difficult to work into regular freestones. The harled façades are enlivened by string-courses of brick or massive sandstone blocks.

Henri II's château – Henri II pursued the efforts undertaken by his father. He gave orders to complete and decorate the ballroom, which remains one of the splendours of Fontainebleau Palace. The monograms – consisting of the royal H and the two intertwined Cs of Catherine de' Medici – were legion. In a form of ambiguity that was generally accepted in its day, the two Cs placed immediately beside the H form a double D, the monogram of the King's mistress Diane de Poitiers.

When Henri II was killed in a tournament, his widow Catherine de' Medici sent her rival to Chaumont-sur-Loire (⌚see The Green Guide CHÂTEAUX OF THE LOIRE) and dismissed the architect in charge of the building work, Philibert

Central façade of the Château de Fontainebleau

Ph. Gajic/MICHELIN

Delorme, who was Diane's protégé. He was replaced by the Italian Primaticcio; those working under him, including Niccolo dell'Abbate, favoured light, cheerful colours.

Henri IV's palace – 17C – Henri IV, who adored Fontainebleau, had the palace enlarged quite significantly. The irregular contours of the Oval Court were corrected and the Kitchen Court and the Real Tennis Court (Jeu de Paume) built. These he had decorated by a new group of artists of largely Flemish, not Italian, inspiration: frescoes were replaced by oil paintings on plaster or canvas. In the same way, the plain wood panelling highlighted with gilding gave way to painted wainscot. This was the Sec-ond Fontainebleau School, whose representatives moved in Parisian circles.

The House of Eternity – Louis XIV, XV and XVI undertook numerous renovations aimed at embellishing their apartments. The Revolution spared the château but emptied it of its precious furniture. Napoleon, who became consul, then emperor, thoroughly enjoyed staying at the palace. He preferred Fontainebleau to Versailles, where he felt haunted by a phantom rival. He called the palace 'The House of Eternity' and left his mark by commissioning further refurbishments. The last rulers of France also took up residence in this historic palace. It was eventually turned into a museum under the Republic.

Military and Equestrian Tradition

Throughout French history, whether under monarchic or republican rule, independent units have been posted to Fontainebleau. Tradition, it seems, favoured the cavalry, present in the 17C with the king's bodyguard. A number of racecourses and riding schools were created under Napoleon III; the Centre National des Sports Équestres perpetuates this tradition (*see Calendar of Events*), while the forest caters to riding enthusiasts.

The history of the town has been marked by several military organisations, notably the École Spéciale Militaire (1803–1808, before St-Cyr), the polygon-shaped École d'Application d'Artillerie et du Génie (1871–1914) and the SHAPE (Supreme Headquarters, Allied Powers, Europe) headquarters of NATO, which gave the town a cosmopolitan touch from 1947 to 1967.

The Farewell

On 20 April 1814, Emperor Napoleon Bonaparte appeared at the top of the horseshoe staircase; it was 1pm. The foreign army commissioners in charge of escorting him away were waiting in their carriages at the foot of the steps. Napoleon started to walk down the staircase with great dignity, his hand resting on the stone balustrade, his face white with contained emotion. He stopped for a moment while contemplating his guards standing to attention, then moved forward to the group of officers surrounding the Eagle, led by General Petit. His farewell speech, deeply moving, was both an appeal to the spirit of patriotism and a parting tribute to those who had followed him throughout his career. After embracing the general, Bonaparte kissed the flag, threw himself into one of the carriages and was whisked away amid the tearful shouts of his soldiers.

THE PALACE★★★
Exterior
Cour du Cheval Blanc or des Adieux★★
– This former bailey was used only by domestics, but its generous size soon earmarked it for official parades and tournaments. It was sometimes called the White Horse Court after the day Charles IX set up a plaster cast of the equestrian statue of Marcus Aurelius in Rome; a small slab in the central alley marks its former location.

The golden eagles hover above the pillars of the main gate reminding visitors that the Emperor had this made into his main courtyard. He gave orders to raze the Renaissance buildings that lay to the west of the court, but kept the end pavilions. The right wing – which boasted the Ulysses Gallery decorated under the supervision of Primaticcio – was

dismantled by Louis XV and rebuilt by Jacques-Ange Gabriel.

The façades show a certain unity of style. The large horizontal planes of the blue slating are broken by the white façades, the trapezoidal roofs and the tall chimneys of the five pavilions.

The celebrated horseshoe staircase executed by Jean du Cerceau during the reign of Louis XIII is a harmoniously curved, extravagant composition showing clearly royalty's taste for splendour.

Cour de la Fontaine★ – The fountain at the edge of the pond *(Étang des Carpes)* used to yield remarkably clear water. This was kept exclusively for the king's use and to that end the spring was guarded by two sentinels both night and day. The present fountain dates back to 1812 and is crowned by a statue of Ulysses.

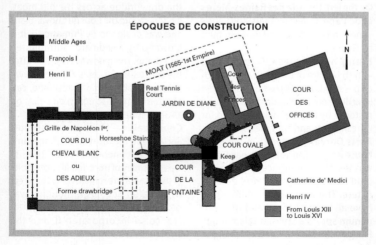

ÉPOQUES DE CONSTRUCTION

Middle Ages
François I
Henri II

MOAT (1565-1st Empire)

Real Tennis Court
JARDIN DE DIANE

Cour des Princes

COUR DES OFFICES

Grille de Napoléon Ier
COUR DU CHEVAL BLANC
ou
DES ADIEUX

Horseshoe Stairca

COUR OVALE
Keep

COUR DE LA FONTAINE

Forme drawbridge

Catherine de' Medici
Henri IV
From Louis XIII to Louis XVI

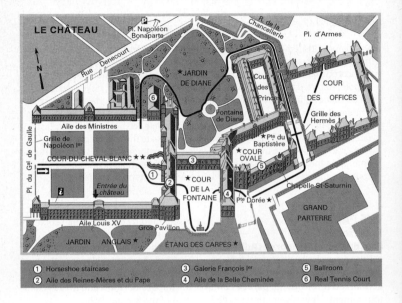

LE CHÂTEAU

① Horseshoe staircase   ③ Galerie François Ier   ⑤ Ballroom
② Aile des Reines-Mères et du Pape   ④ Aile de la Belle Cheminée   ⑥ Real Tennis Court

The **Aile de la Belle cheminée** on the right was built by Primaticcio around 1565. The name originated from the fireplace that adorned the vast first-floor hall until the 18C. At that point in history Louis XV – who had turned the room into a theatre and rechristened it Aile de l'Ancienne Comédie – dismantled the fireplace, and the low-relief carvings were scattered. The monumental external steps consist of a dog-legged staircase with two straight flights in the Italian style.

On the left, the **Aile des Reines-Mères et du Pape** (Queen Mothers' and Pope's wing) ends in the Grand Pavilion built by Gabriel.

Étang des Carpes★ (Carp Pond) – In the centre of the pond – alive with carp – stands a small pavilion built under Henri IV, renovated under Louis XIV and restored by Napoleon. It was used for refreshments and light meals.

Porte Dorée★ – Dated 1528, this gatehouse is part of an imposing pavilion. It was the official entrance to the palace until Henri IV built the Porte du Baptistère. The paintings by Primaticcio have all been restored and the tympanum sports a stylised salamander, François I's emblem. On the two upper levels are Italian-style loggias. The first floor – its loggia sealed off by large bay windows – used to house Mme de Maintenon's suite.

The ballroom is flanked by an avenue of lime trees. The view from the bay windows is splendid. The east end of the two-storeyed chapel dedicated to St Saturnin can be seen in the distance.

Porte du Baptistère★ – The gateway opens onto the Oval Court. The base of the gateway is the rustic entrance with decorative sandstone that once held the drawbridge across the old moat. It opened onto the Cour du Cheval-Blanc and was designed by Primaticcio. It is crowned by a wide arch surmounted by a dome. The gateway is named after the christening of Louis XIII and his two sisters, Élisabeth and Chrétienne, celebrated with great pomp on a dais on 14 September 1606.

Cour Ovale★ – This is by far the most ancient and the most interesting courtyard of Fontainebleau Palace. The site was the bailey of the original stronghold; of the latter there remains only the keep, named after St Louis, although it was probably built prior to his reign.

François I incorporated it into the structure he had erected on the foundations of the old castle, shaped like an oval or rather a polygon with rounded corners. Under Henri IV, the courtyard lost its shape, though not its name; the east side was enlarged, and the wings were aligned and squared by two new pavilions framing the new Porte du Baptistère. The general layout of the palace was preserved.

Cour des Offices – The entrance faces the Porte du Baptistère and is guarded by two arresting sandstone heads depicting Hermes, sculpted by Gilles Guérin in 1640. The Cour des Offices was built by Henri IV in 1609; it is a huge oblong, sealed off on three sides by austere buildings alternating with low pavilions. With its imposing porch executed in the style of city gates, it bears a strong resemblance to a square. Walk through the gate and admire its architecture from place d'Armes; the sandstone front presents rusticated work and has a large niche as its centrepiece.

Jardin de Diane★ – The queen's formal garden created by Catherine de' Medici was designed by Henri IV and bordered by an orangery on its northern side. In the 19C the orangery was torn down and the park turned into a landscape garden. Diana's fountain, an elegant display of stonework dated 1603, has survived in the middle of the grounds. It has now resumed its original appearance; the four bronze dogs formerly exhibited in the Louvre Museum sit obediently at the feet of their mistress, the hunting goddess.

Grands Appartements★★★

&⊙Open Wed–Mon Jun–Sept 9.30am–6pm; Oct–May 9.30am–5pm; last admission 45min before closing. ⊜8€ (children and Paris Museum Pass holders no charge); no charge 1st Sun in the month. ℘01 60 71 50 60. www.musee-chateau-fontainebleau.fr. The main apartments are reached by the stucco staircase **(a)**, the Galerie des Fastes **(b)** and the Galerie des Assiettes **(c)**, which features 128 beautifully decorated pieces of Sèvres porcelain.

Chapelle de la Trinité★ – The chapel takes its name from the Trinitarian church set up on the premises by St Louis. Henri IV had the sanctuary reinforced by vaulting and then decorated. Martin Fréminet (1567–1619), one of the lesser-known followers of Michelangelo, painted the arches with strong, vigorous scenes representing the mystery of the Redemption and figures from the Old Testament.

It was in this chapel that Louis XV was wedded to Marie Leszczynska in 1725 and that Louis Napoleon, later to be Napoleon III, was christened in 1810.

Galerie de François I★★★ – This gallery was built from 1528 to 1530 and was originally open on both sides, resembling a covered passageway. When Louis XVI enlarged it in 1786, he filled in the windows looking onto Diana's garden. A set of false French windows was fitted for reasons of symmetry. The greater part of the decoration – closely combining fresco and stucco work – was supervised by Rosso, while the wood panelling was entrusted to an Italian master carpenter. François I's monogram and his emblem the salamander were widely represented.

The scenes are difficult to interpret (there are no explanatory documents), though they seem to split into two groups, one on either side of the central bay which is adorned with an oval painting depicting two figures: Danaë by Primaticcio and *The Nymph of Fontainebleau* (1860) after Rosso.

The east side, near a bust of François I, features mostly violent scenes, perhaps referring to the recent misfortunes of the French king (the defeat of Pavia, the king's captivity in Madrid), the inescapable nature of war and death (the battle between the Centaurs and the Lapiths, Youth and Old Age, the Destruction of the Greek fleet). Beneath the vignette depicting Venus and Love at the edge of a pond, note the miniature picture set in a tablet, representing the château around 1540 with both the gallery and the Porte Dorée clearly visible.

On the west side, near the entrance, the decor exemplifies the sacred qualities of

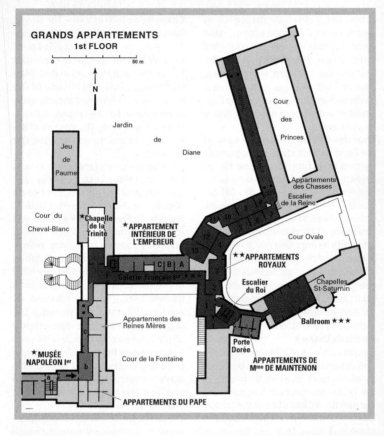

GRANDS APPARTEMENTS
1st FLOOR

0   50 m

N

Jardin   de   Diane

Jeu de Paume

Cour du Cheval-Blanc

★ Chapelle de la Trinité

★ APPARTEMENT INTÉRIEUR DE L'EMPEREUR

Galerie François Iᵉʳ ★★★

Appartements des Reines Mères

★ MUSÉE NAPOLÉON Iᵉʳ

Cour de la Fontaine

APPARTEMENTS DU PAPE

Cour des Princes

Appartements des Chasses

Escalier de la Reine

Cour Ovale

★★ APPARTEMENTS ROYAUX

Escalier du Roi

Chapelles St-Saturnin

Ballroom ★★★

Porte Dorée

APPARTEMENTS DE Mᵐᵉ DE MAINTENON

---

the royal function – Sacrifice, the Unity of the State – and the concept of filial piety, in the old-fashioned sense of the word (the twins Cleobis and Biton): the king, his mother Louise of Savoy and his sister Marguerite d'Angoulême were devoted to one another.

The most striking scene is the portrait of an elephant whose caparison bears the royal monogram; the pachyderm no doubt symbolises the perennity of the monarchy.

Escalier du Roi★★ – The staircase was built in 1749, under Louis XV, in what was once the bedchamber of the Duchess of Étampes, François I's favourite. The murals – the history of Alexander the Great – are by Primaticcio (note Alexander taming Bucephalus above the door) and dell'Abbate (Alexander placing Homer's books in a chest, on the far wall). Primaticcio's stucco work is highly

original; the upper frieze is punctuated by caryatids with elongated bodies.

Salle de Bal★★★ (Ballroom) – This room (30m/98.4ft long and 10m/33ft wide) was traditionally reserved for banquets and formal receptions. It was begun under François I and completed by Philibert Delorme under Henri II. A thorough restoration programme has revived the dazzling frescoes and paintings by Primaticcio and his pupil dell'Abbate. The marquetry of the parquet floor, completed under Louis-Philippe, echoes the splendid coffered ceiling, richly highlighted with silver and gold. The monumental fireplace features two telamones, cast after Antique statues in the Capitol Museum in Rome.

Chapelles St-Saturnin – *Access via Cour Ovale* – Completed in 1546 under François I and situated behind the ballroom, this chapel is divided into two levels, the upper chapel and lower chapel. The organ tribune was designed by Philibert Delorme, and the stained glass made from cartoons by Marie d'Orléans.

Appartements de Mme de Maintenon – Note the delicate wainscoting in the Grand Salon, most of which was executed in the 17C.

Appartements royaux★★ – At the time of François I, Fontainebleau featured a single suite of apartments laid out around the Oval Court. Towards 1565, the regent Catherine de' Medici gave orders to double the curved building between the Oval Court and Diana's Garden. Subsequently, the royal bedrooms, closets and private salons overlooked Diana's Garden. The original suite now houses antechambers, guard rooms and reception rooms where the king used to entertain his guests.

Salle des Gardes (1) – Late 16C ceiling and frieze.

A wide arch leads from the **Salle du Buffet (2)** to a chamber in the oldest tower of the castle.

Salle du Donjon (3) – Until the reign of Henri IV this sombre room was occupied by French kings, who used it as a bedroom, hence its other name, the St Louis Bedroom. The equestrian low-relief sculpture (c. 1600) portraying Henri IV on the fireplace came from the 'Belle Cheminée'.

Salon Louis XIII (4) – It was here that Louis XIII was born on 27 September 1601. His birth is evoked by the coffered ceiling which depicts Cupid riding a dolphin (the word *dauphin* means both dolphin and heir to the throne). The panel with painted wainscoting is crowned by a set of 11 pictures by Ambroise Dubois; the Romance between Theagenes and Chariclea, works dating from c. 1610.

Salon François I (5) – Of Primaticcio's work there remains only the fireplace.

Salon des Tapisseries (6) – This room, having been the queen's chamber, the guard room and the queen's first antechamber, became the empress's principal drawing room in 1804, the guard room once more in 1814 and finally the Tapestry Salon in 1837.

The fireplace dates from 1731 and the Renaissance ceiling in pine wood is the work of Poncet (1835). The furniture was made during the Second Empire (mid-19C). The tapestries telling the story of Psyche were manufactured in Paris in the first half of the 17C.

Antichambre de l'Impératrice (7) – Formerly the queen's guard room, this chamber was built on the site of the old royal staircase; the ceiling and panelling are both dated 1835. The Gobelins tapestries, executed after cartoons by Le Brun, illustrate the four seasons. The Second Empire furniture features a console, a carved-oak writ-

Ballroom

Ph. Gajic/MICHELIN

Throne Room

Ph. Gajic/MICHELIN

ing desk (Fourdinois, 1865) and a set of armchairs of English inspiration. Note the two Indian-style enamel vases produced by the Sèvres factory.

Galerie de Diane – This long, gilt passageway (80m/263ft) was decorated during the Restoration and turned into a library under the Second Empire.

Salon blanc- Petit salon de la Reine (8) – In 1835 the room was decorated with furnishings from an earlier period: Louis XV wainscoting, Louis XVI fireplace inlaid with bronze, etc. The furniture is Empire: chairs in gilt wood by Jacob Frères, settee, armchairs and chairs from St-Cloud, mahogany console and heads of fantastic animals in bronzed, gilt wood (Jacob Desmalter).

Grand Salon de l'Impératrice (9) – This drawing room, formerly the queen's gaming room, features a ceiling painted by Berthélemy; the scene is Minerva crowning the Muses.

The furniture dates from the reign of Louis XVI (chests by Stöckel and Beneman, seats upholstered with painted satin, a carpet made by the Savonnerie works) or from the First Empire (seats and chests by Jacob Desmalter, the so-called 'Seasons Table' made of Sèvres porcelain and painted by Georget in 1806–7, and a carpet rewoven to an old design). The two sets of furniture are displayed in turn.

Chambre de l'Impératrice (10) – This used to be the queen's bedroom. The greater part of the ceiling was designed for Anne of Austria in 1644; the wood panelling, the fireplace and the top of the alcove were created for Marie Leszczynska in 1747 and the doors with arabesque motifs were installed for Marie-Antoinette in 1787. Among the furniture note Marie-Antoinette's bed, designed in 1787 by Hauré, Sené and Laurent, a set of armchairs attributed to Jacob Frères and several commodes by Stöckel and Beneman (1786). The vases are Sèvres porcelain.

Boudoir de la Reine (11) – This delightful room was designed by Marie-Antoinette. The wainscoting was painted by Bourgois and Touzé after sketches by the architect Rousseau. The ceiling – representing sunrise – is the work of Berthélemy. The roll-top writing desk and the work table were made by Riesener in 1786.

Salle du Trône (12) – This was the king's bedroom from Henri IV to Louis XVI; Napoleon converted it into the throne room. The ornate mural paintings, dating from several periods, were harmonised in the 18C. Above the fireplace is a full-length portrait of Louis XIII, painted in Philippe de Champaigne's studio.

Salle du Conseil (13) – This room was given a semicircular extension in 1773. The ceiling and panelling are splendid examples of Louis XV decoration.

Five pictures by Boucher adorn the ceiling, representing the four seasons and Apollo, conqueror of Night. The wainscoting presents an alternation of allegorical figures painted in blue or pink monochrome by Van Loo and Jean-Baptiste Pierre.

Appartement Intérieur de l'Empereur★
– Visit included in the tour of the Grands Appartements. **Napoleon** had his suite installed in the wing built by Louis XVI, on the garden side running parallel with the François I Gallery.

Chambre de Napoléon (A) – Most of the decoration – dating from the Louis XVI period – has survived. The furniture is typically Empire.

Petite chambre à coucher (B) – A little private study which Bonaparte furnished with a day bed in gilded iron.

Salon de l'Abdication (C) – This is the room in which the famous abdication document was signed on 6 April 1814. The Empire furniture in this drawing room is from that momentous time.

The François I Gallery leads to the Vestibule du Fer-à-cheval, at the top of the curved steps of the same name. This was the official entrance to the palace from the late 17C onwards.

Appartements du Pape – First floor of the Gros Pavillon – This part of the château is named for Poe Pie VII, who stayed here twice during the First Empire. It consists of a string of rooms created under the Renaissance in a pavillion constructed by Gabriel. The Henri II bedroom retained its sculpted wood ceiling, that of Anne of Austria its painted ceiling, and stamped leather wall coverings from the Second Empire. The ensemble of Second Empire furnishings and decor were restored in 1970.

Musée Chinois★ – ♿ ⏰Open intermittently, check the information each day. Jun–Sept Wed–Mon 9.30am-6pm; Oct–May 9.30am–5pm. Admission included in the ticket for the visit to the Grands Appartements. ✆01 60 71 50 60.

This small museum, commissioned by Empress Eugénie on the ground floor of the Gros Pavillon, comes as a surprise because of the contrast between the comfortable, heavy furniture and the slender elegance of the objects on show. The collection was originally the booty captured during the Franco-British conflict with China in 1860. The following year, a delegation of Siamese ambassadors completed the collection with a number of opulent presents, an event which was faithfully recorded in a painting by Gérôme.

The tour begins in the **antechamber** decorated with two luxurious Siamese palanquins. The **nouveaux salons** beyond are decorated with crimson wall hangings, padded armchairs, ebony furniture and objects from China and Siam. Most of the collection, however, is to be seen in the **cabinet de laque** decorated with 15 panels from an 18C Chinese fan. Note the four large tapestries on the ceiling and the huge glass-fronted cabinet filled to the brim with objects, including a copy of the Siamese royal crown.

Musée Napoléon I★

The **museum** (♿ ☜ guided tours (1hr15min) daily 10.30am, call in the morning to reserve; ⊜12.50€; ✆01 60 71 50 60) is dedicated to the Emperor and his family; it occupies 15 rooms on the ground level and first floor of the Louis XV wing and is only accessible through the guided tour. Exhibits include portraits (paintings and sculptures), silverware, arms, medals, ceramics (Imperial service), clothing (coronation robes, uniforms) and personal memorabilia.

The rooms on the first floor evoke the Coronation (paintings by François Gérard), the Emperor's various military campaigns, his daily life (remarkable folding desk by Jacob Desmalter), the Empress Marie-Louise in formal attire or painting the Emperor's portrait (picture by Alexandre Menjaud) and the birth of Napoleon's son, the future King of Rome (cradles).

The ground floor presents the Emperor's close relations. Each of the seven rooms is devoted to a member of the family: Napoleon's mother, his brothers Joseph, Louis and Jérôme and his sisters Elisa, Pauline and Caroline.

Petits Appartements et Galerie des Cerfs

☜Guided tours (1hr15min) daily 2.30pm; call in the morning to reserve. ⊜12.50€. ✆01 60 71 50 60.

These rooms, on the ground floor below the François I Gallery and the Royal Suite, are only accessible on the guided tour.

Petits Appartements de Napoléon I – This suite comprises François I's former bathroom suite, and the ground floor of the new Louis XVI wing, situated under the Imperial Suite. The rooms opening onto the garden have been decorated with Louis XV wainscoting and Empire furniture.

Appartements de l'Impératrice Joséphine★ – This suite of rooms adorned with Louis XV panelling was designed for Joséphine in 1808. It lies beneath the grand royal suite.

The study, with its large rotunda, is located beneath the Council Chamber (*first floor*). The Empire furniture here has a feminine touch: Marie-Louise's tambour frame, her easel, etc. The Salon Jaune constitutes one of the palace's most perfect examples of Empire decoration. The gold-coloured wall hangings provide an elegant setting for Jacob Desmalter's choice furniture set off by a large Aubusson carpet with a white background.

Galerie des Cerfs★ – The gallery is decorated with numerous deer heads (only the antlers are genuine). The mural paintings were renovated under Napoleon III; they show palatial residences at the time of Henri IV, seen in perspective. It was in this gallery that Queen Christina of Sweden had her favourite, Monaldeschi, assassinated in 1657. The original casts used to make Primaticcio's 1540 replicas of Antique statues are on display in the gallery.

GARDENS★

🕐*Open daily Nov–Feb 9am–5pm; Mar, Apr and Oct 9am–6pm; May–Sept 9am–7pm. The Jardin anglais closes 1hr before the rest.* 🕐*Closed 25 Dec, 1 Jan.* 📞*01 60 71 50 70. www.musee-chateau-fontainebleau.fr.*

These comprise the Jardin de Diane, the Landscape Garden (*Jardin anglais*), the *Grand Parterre* and the park.

▶ *Follow the route on the map below.*

Grotte du Jardin des Pins★

This rare ornamental composition carved in sandstone reveals the popular taste, copied from the Italians, for ponds, man-made features and bucolic landscapes in vogue toward the end of François I's reign. The rusticated arches are supported by giant telamones. The frescoes have disappeared.

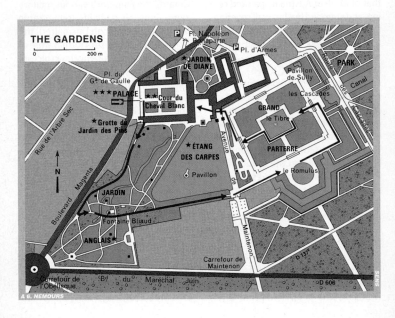

Jardin anglais★

The garden was created in 1812 on the site of former gardens (featuring a pine grove) redesigned under Louis XIV and abandoned during the Revolution. The Bliaut or Blaut fountain, which gave its name to the palace, plays in a small octagonal basin in the middle of the garden.

Park

The park was created by Henri IV, who filled the canal (in 1609) and had the grounds planted with elms, pines and fruit trees. Sixty years before the installation of the Grand Canal at Versailles, this dazzling sight was a great novelty for the *Ancien Régime*, as were the aquatic displays.

Forêt de
Fontainbleau
★★★

This lovely (25 000ha/62 000 acres) forest surrounding Fontainebleau is largely State-owned and has always provided magnificent hunting grounds. It is immensely popular with ramblers and climbing enthusiasts. The forest was damaged in several places by the violent storm of December 1999, but conscientous management of replanting over a decade has restored the most damaged areas.

GEOLOGY OF THE FOREST

Geological formation – The relief of the forested area comprises a series of parallel sandstone ridges thought to be the result of a tropical spell during the Tertiary Era, when strong winds gradually accumulated sand deposits. The sand dunes subsequently solidified into a hard sandstone matrix and then buried beneath deposits of Beauce limestone, resulting in the preservation of the area's rolling landscape.

Where the limestone has eroded revealing the sandstone, the resultant rocky areas are known locally as **platières**. These **moorlands** covered with heather and other shrubs are often cracked and dotted with ponds. When the sandstone layer has many crevices and holes, water seeps through and starts to wash away the underlying sands. The upper sandstone stratum is no longer supported and crumbles as a result, producing

⚲	**Michelin Local Map:** 312: F-5 or map 106 folds 44, 45 and 46.
🄸	**Info:** Office du tourisme du pays de Fontainebleau-Avon, 4 r. Royale, 77300 Fontainebleau. ☏01 60 74 99 99. www.fontainebleau-tourisme.com.
▶	**Location:** Fontainebleau is 60km/37mi from Paris, via the A 6, and then the N 37.
🅿	**Parking:** There are few designated parking areas in the forest, but ample opportunity to pull off the road (leave no valuables in the car).
⚐	**Don't Miss:** The chance to take a walk in the woodlands
🕐	**Timing:** Allow as much time as you want; the area is excellent for walking. So, take a picnic and make a day of it.

picturesque rocky clusters, the famous Fontainebleau **rochers**. **Vales** or **plains** averaging 40–80m/130–260ft in height are found where the sandstone layer has been eroded away, exposing the sand or the Brie marl and limestone beneath. The planting of conifers fertilises the soil, making it possible to grow beeches. These produce humus and are eventually replaced by oaks, the ideal tree species for a forest.

Forest Layout – The forest is divided into 747 plots and consists of copses and

🦉 Driving in the Forest 🦉

Some of the roads running through the forest carry heavy traffic and turning left onto minor forest roads is often forbidden; for this reason, it is advisable, when planning a sightseeing tour of the forest, to avoid N 6, N 7 and route Ronde between the Table-du-Roi and Grand-Veneur crossroads.

thickets, moorland and rock. Sessile oak covers 8 000ha/19 768 acres, Norway pines 7 500ha/18 532 acres, and beeches 1 500ha/3 706 acres. The other species (hornbeam, birch, maritime and Corsican pine, larch, chestnut, acacia and service trees) are reminders of earlier attempts at acclimatisation. Some 416ha/1 433 acres constitute a biological reserve.

Denecourt-Colinet Footpaths

Footpaths laid out by the 'two Sylvains' (Denecourt and Colinet) take you to the most famous spots in the forest. Sylvain Denecourt served with Napoleon's Grande Armée. He removed rocks and boulders from caves, cleared the finest beauty spots, and laid out 150km/93mi of footpaths. On carefully selected trees (see the guide book entitled *Guide des arbres remarquables de la forêt de Fontainebleau*, by l'Association des Amis de la Forêt) or rocks, discreet blue lines topped by numbers (1 to 16) indicate the main paths. Blue letters (also explained in the guide) and stars are also used as markings on specific sights. Colinet, once a civil servant with the Ponts et Chaussées (Ministry of Public Buildings and Works) continued where his predecessor had left off. The markings were completed, after 1975, by the inclusion of white enamelled signposts bordered in green at all the main junctions.

'Bleau' and 'Bleausards'

By 1910, a few climbing enthusiasts from the Club Alpin Français had already begun to train at Fontainebleau. In the inter-war years, the idea of a rock climbing school became commonplace among climbers in France. Fontainebleau was the ideal spot for climbers

living in Paris. The compact sandstone in the forest provides a challenge and a few valuable examples of potential difficulties.

There are more than 100 climbs marked out with arrows on the rocks. Each of them is a succession of climbs, descents and, in some cases, jumps; there are never any walks along paths.

🚶 HIKING TOURS

① GORGES DE FRANCHARD★★

🚶 *30min–2hr round trip.*

From the Croix de Franchard crossroads, drive to the spacious shady esplanade at the Ermitage de Franchard, a very popular spot at weekends. However, do not expect to find waterfalls here – no river, not even a stream runs through this gorge. Among the different species of trees, note cedar trees from the Atlas mountain range (North Africa), pine trees from Vancouver (Canada) and horse-chestnut trees.

Ancien Ermitage de Franchard – A hermitage developed here in the 12C, and in the 13C a community moved in to look after the pilgrims. By the 19C, the pilgrimage had become a country fête held on the Tuesday after Whitsun. Today only the chapel walls remain, incorporated into the forest warden's house.

Grand Point de vue★ – 🚶 *30min round trip.* Beyond the warden's garden skirt the sandy track on the left and climb towards the rocks without changing direction. This leads to a very sandy road *(route de Tavannes)*; after 300m/330yd a mushroom-shaped rock will appear ahead. At the plateau turn right and on reaching the rock bear left to a bench overlooking the ravine. The view of the gorge is breathtaking.

▶ *To return to the hermitage, walk down three steps and bear left. This path returns to the route de Tavannes.*

Circuit des Druides★★ – 🚶 *2hr* – Beyond the Grand Point de Vue shown on the map, go down three steps and turn right. Follow the blue markings indicating Denecourt-Colinet path 7 which wends its way through a labyrinth of half-splintered boulders, some of them forming overhangs. At the bottom of the 'gorge', cross a sandy road beside an isolated oak tree and climb back up among the rocks (follow the "÷" signs) to the 'second belvedere' marked by a star.

Remain on the edge of the plateau. There is a wonderful view of the gorge and across the **Belvédère des Druides** (marked 'P'). Go down to the easterly footpath and, at the bottom of the gorge, join the *route Amédée*. Turn right. At the first crossroads, turn left onto the route de la Roche-qui-Pleure which climbs back up the hill and through a gap in the side of the plateau to the hermitage. *Do not follow the path with the blue signs; it zigzags its way up through the rocks on the left.*

Gorges de Franchard

J.-L. Gallo/MICHELIN

2 GORGES D'APREMONT★

🚶 *10km/6mi round trip – about 4hr.*
Leave Barbizon by allée aux Vaches, the continuation of Grande Rue, a magnificent tree-lined avenue that was so well known to artists. This road leads to the carrefour du Bas-Bréau, an intersection near a cluster of trees now protected by a preservation order spearheaded by a group of artists.

Chaos d'Apremont★ – 🚶 *45min round trip from the crossroads.*
Follow the path marked in blue left of the refreshment chalet *(buvette)* and continue up amid the rocks; at the top bear right and follow the edge of the plateau. Views are over the wooded slopes of the gorge and the Bière plain. The path veers left: a clump of acacia and pine trees marks the entrance to the **Caverne des Brigands** (*take a torch with you*).

▶ *Return to the car. Take the Sully road through the woods to the bare plateau high above the distant ravines.*

Grand Belvédère d'Apremont★ – 🚶 *15min.* About 1.7km/1mi from the crossroads called Le Bas-Bréau, park at the junction with the 'road' to Le Cul-de-

Chaudron. Progress along the plateau and turn left onto the path with blue markings. At a crossroads with a Denecourt-Colinet sign, turn right.

The path runs downhill past boulders and rocks. Bear left, remaining above the rocks. Below is the 'gorge', its slopes strewn with blocks of stone. To the west is the Plaine de Bière.

▶ *Return to the car and to carrefour du Bas-Bréau.*

Circuit du Désert★★ – 🚶 *3hr30min.* This part of the forest is famous for its barren and desert-like appearance that was so well known to artists and, later, to film directors.

Take the old road from Barbizon to Fontainebleau; after 1.6km/1mi turn south onto the road to Le Clair Bois. Take the first lane on the right, route de la Chouette, over a pass and down to the Désert d'Apremont, a valley dotted with oddly shaped boulders. Bear left onto path no 6 marked in blue. On reaching the rock resembling an animal with two snouts (trail marker N), bear right. At the carrefour du Désert take the blue-marked

path that lies between route du Clair-Bois and route de Milan; it leads to a ravine framed by boulders, then along a rocky ledge.

Immediately after the Grotte des Dryades, marked with a star, bear left and walk down path '6-6' and up the far side of the valley to the raised platform; the pond called Mare aux Sangliers lies to the left.

The prominent part of the plateau offers a good **view** of the Désert d'Apremont and the Bière plain.

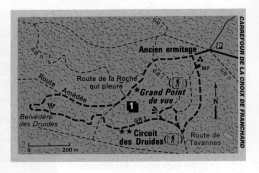

○ *Return to the car via carrefour du Désert and route de Clair-Bois.*

5 LE LONG ROCHER

1.5km/0.9mi – then 2hr30min round trip. From route Ronde, branch off towards Bourron-Marlotte (D 58).
Start from carrefour de Marlotte. After 1km/0.6mi, before reaching a steep slope, turn left onto route du Long Rocher, a sandy forest lane (ONF board: 'Zone de Silence de la Malmontagne').

○ *Park at the next crossroads (barrier). Take route des Étroitures (first turning on the right). After 100m/110yd, turn right onto path no 11, marked in blue.*

Belvédère des Étroitures – ⓜ *Trail marker U.* Admire the view of Marlotte and the Loing Valley.

○ *Turn round and follow the blue-marked path, which soon begins to wend its way between the boulders in the shade of the pine trees.*
It then winds here and there along a seemingly aimless route until it reaches the top of the plateau, the 'Restant du Long-Rocher'.

Restant du Long Rocher★★ – ⓜ The edge of the plateau, strewn with boulders, offers several good views of the southern and northern areas of the forest. Return to the blue path and

continue in an easterly direction. Leave the plateau via the steep slope which includes Grotte Béatrix. Walk past a series of boulders used for exercise by mountaineering schools *(red arrows)*. Further along, the path rises slightly; branch off left and take the steep, clearly marked track down. This leads back to route du Long Rocher; bear left to return to the starting point.

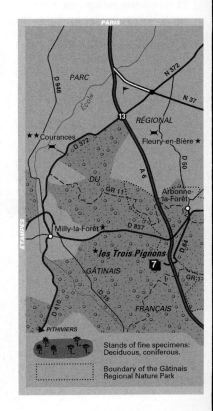

Stands of fine specimens:
Deciduous, coniferous.

Boundary of the Gâtinais
Regional Nature Park

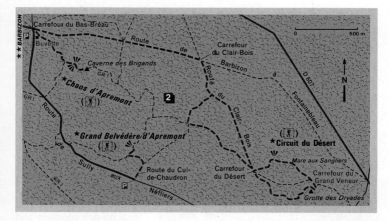

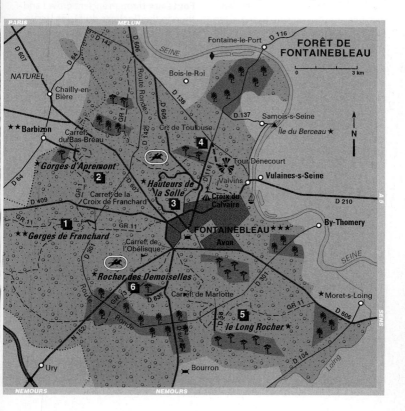

7 **LES TROIS PIGNONS★**
2.5km/1.5mi – then 3hr round trip.

● Leave from the southern end of Arbonne (junction of the Fontaine-bleau-Milly road). Take the Milly road but immediately turn left onto the Achères-la-Forêt road (D 64). After 1.6km/1mi the road veers towards the motorway; turn right under it. Park the car.

Les Trois Pignons massif is an unusual extension of Fontainebleau Forest: it is a stony, barren site, unique in Île-de-France, with dry valleys, eroded peaks and other peculiarities, which are com-

tinues southeast and then south, crossing a sandy, rocky area cleared of trees.

Point de vue de la Vallée Close★★ –  The edge of the plateau offers a good **view★★** of the uplands. In the foreground, a monument crowned by a cross of Lorraine honours the local Resistance network.

The blue path then turns north and descends eastward, avoiding the wide sandy track previously explored to lead through oak coppices and heather back to the starting point.

Suggestions for Additional Tours:

♦ North of Fontainebleau ③ **Hauteurs de la Solle★** along **route Louis-Philippe★** and **route du Gros-Fouteau★** through ancient groves and then to the **Rochers du Mont Ussy★** where a pleasant path leads through pine trees;

♦ A round trip northeast of the town ④ taking in **Tour Dénecourt**, a 19C tower offering **panoramic views★**, and **Samois-sur-Seine**, an attractive and once-important town on the banks of the river;

♦ To the southwest ⑥, pleasant rambles through the Cirque des Demoiselles and to the **Rocher des Demoiselles★**.

mon to sandstone landscapes.

From the car park go straight ahead and follow the road past two houses on the right. At the corner of the fencing, bear right and walk to the edge of a sandy depression, to the starting point of the Denecourt-Colinet path (no 16).

On the other side of the depression, directly opposite the plaque, is the first blue mark. The path crosses a flat stretch of land dotted with boulders and leads past the platform of the old Noisy telegraph transmitter to the plateau.

The path follows the recesses of the impressive Gorge aux Chats and con-

Rocher du Bilboquet in the massif des Trois Pignons

ADDRESSES

🏨 STAY

🍽🛏 Hôtel du Pavillon Royal – *40 av. Gallieni, 77590 Bois-le-Roi, 10km/6mi N of Fontainebleau via N 6, D 116 and D 137. ℘01 64 10 41 00. 26 rooms. ⛶7€.* Located next to the Hydraulic Institute, this modern hotel receives many foreign visitors in its well-soundproofed, spacious rooms. You'll enjoy taking strolls in the garden and dips in the pool.

🍽 EAT

🍽🛏 Auberge de la Treille – *5 r. Grande, 77210 Samoreau, 6km/3.7mi E of Fontaine bleau via D 210. ℘01 64 23 71 22. Closed Thu eve, Sun eve.* An ancient grape vine covers the façade of this attractive country inn. The dining room is prolonged by a quiet garden terrace, to be enjoyed without moderation as soon as the sun comes out. Fixed-price menus proposing traditional cuisine.

🍽🛏 La Marine – *52 quai Olivier-Metra, at l'Écluse (the lock), 77590 Bois-le-Roi, 10km/6mi N of Fontainebleau via N 6, D 116 and D 137. ℘01 60 69 61 38. Closed 2 weeks in Feb, 15 Sept–1 Oct, Mon–Tue.* On the banks of the Seine, just opposite the lock gate, here's an engaging restaurant whose terrace resembles the prow of a barge. Dining room with exposed beams; traditional cuisine.

🍽🛏🛏 Hostellerie du Cheval Noir – *47 av. J.- Jaurès, 77250 Moret-sur-Loing, 11km/7mi SE of Fontainebleau via N6. ℘01 60 70 80 20. www.chevalnoir77.com.* Built opposite one of the city gates, here's an 18C coaching inn-cum-restaurant featuring a luminous dining room-veranda. Decorated with Alfred Sisley prints, it sets the stage for a meal of creative cooking that tends toward the sweet and spicy. A few guest rooms named after famous artists.

DISCOVERING THE FOREST

Caution! The fragile ecosystem of this forest must be respected. Making fires, leaving litter behind, gathering plants, cutting branches off trees and wandering off the trails are all prohibited!

Rambles – Over time, an increasing number of paths have been cleared. Their markings sometimes overlap, making orientation difficult.

Grande Randonnée (GR): Red and white.

Petite Randonnée (PR): Yellow.

Tour du Massif de Fontainebleau (TMF): Green and white (vertical lines).

Denecourt and Colinet's original trail markers (blue), much older than the current ones, have been maintained on certain trails.

The *Guide des Sentiers de Promenade dans le Massif Forestier de Fontainebleau* (A Guide to the Fontainebleau Forest's Hiking Trails) is published by the *Association des Amis de la Forêt de Fontainebleau.* It may be purchased in the Office de Tourisme or in bookshops.

Cycling – The asphalt roads criss-crossing the forest, many of which are open to bicycles and closed to cars, are much appreciated by cyclists. A map is available at the Office National des Forêts. Trailbikes are also permitted on certain trails. For organised outings and cycle hire contact Top Loisirs *(10 passage Ronsin, 77300 Fontainebleau; ℘01 60 74 08 50 (by reservation); www.toploisirs.fr).*

Centre équestre de Recloses-Fontainebleau – *Chemin Clos de la Bonne, 77760 Recloses. ℘01 64 24 21 10. www.centre-equestre77.com.* Horse riding.

Club Alpin Français, Île-de-France – *24 av. Laumière, 75019 Paris. ℘01 53 72 88 00. www.ffcam.fr.* Mountaineering.

Club Alpin Français, Fontainebleau – *6 r. du Mont Ussy, 77300 Fontainebleau. ℘01 64 22 67 18. http://caf77.free.fr.* Rock climbing.

Orienteering – *77300 Fontainebleau. ℘01 60 74 08 50. www.toploisirs.fr.* Guidance and equipment rentals at Top Loisirs (🌢*see Cycling, above).*

Fitness trail (Parcours de santé) – *77300 Fontainebleau.* In the Forêt de Fontainebleau at the Faisanderie, near the Carrefour du Coq.

L'Isle-Adam

In 1014 a castle built on one of the islands in the River Oise was ceded to Adam de Villiers by Robert II the Pious, Hugh Capet's son. Honoré de Balzac was a regular visitor and set several of his novels in the area. In the 19C, Villiers de L'Isle-Adam, the author of *Cruel Tales*, was to become one of the great names of French literature. Today l'Isle-Adam has one of France's largest inland beaches, with a popular water sports centre for sailing, rowing and canoeing. The old bridges – in particular Cabouillet Bridge, a 16C stone construction with three arches – command a pleasant view of the Oise, which is still frequented by traditional rowing boats *(boat hire office on the beach)*.

> ▶ **Population:** 11 231
> 👢 **Michelin Local Map:** 305: E-6 or map 106 fold 6.
> 🗐 **Info:** 46 Grande-Rue, 95290 L'Isle-Adam. ✆01 34 69 41 99. www.ville-isle-adam.fr.
> ◐ **Location:** Situated north of Paris along the Oise Valley
> 🅿 **Parking:** There are plenty of free parking areas.

SIGHTS
Musée d'art et d'histoire Louis-Senlecq

46 Grande-Rue. ⊙*Changing exhibitions; reserve in advance.* ✆*01 34 69 45 38. www.musee.ville-isle-adam.fr.*
Housed in a former 17C school, this art and history museum displays the town's collections gathered since 1939. The painting gallery contains the works of Émile Boggio, Jules-Romain Joyant, Jules Dupré, and Vlaminck.

Centre d'Art Jacques-Henri-Lartigue

31 Grande-Rue. &⊙*Open Wed–Mon 2–6pm.* ⊜*3.20 € (no charge Sun).* ✆*01 34 69 45 44. www.musee.ville-isle-adam.fr.*
Jacques-Henri Lartigue (1894–1986) was a famous photographer and a prolific painter: 300 of his paintings are exhibited in rotation. His vigorous brushstrokes and bright colours are easily recognisable. The centre also organises exhibitions of contemporary artists.

Pavillon Chinois de Cassan

Follow rue de Beaumont. Enter through the main gateway of the former park.
This quaint pavilion overlooking a lake was built to adorn the landscaped park of Cassan by the financier Bergeret (1715–85), an enthusiastic art lover and patron; the rest of the estate is now a residential area. The pagoda, brightly decorated in red, green and saffron tones, stands on a stone base resting upon arches that house the spillway for the waters of the park. The roof conceals the elaborate network of overlapping domes that act as a lantern and, inside, crown the room, decorated with paintings.

Forêt de L'Isle-Adam

This State-owned forest, which covers an area of 1 500ha/3 800 acres, is separated from the Forêt de Carnelle by the Presles Valley. Oak trees make up two-thirds of the thickets and copses; the remainder of the forest is beech, chestnut, hornbeam, birch and lime. It is crossed by a network of roads fanning out from the remarkable star-shaped crossroads known as **Le Poteau La Tour**.
The forest was very carefully enclosed and maintained for hunting by the Princes de Conti until 1783. Nowadays, several major roads cut through it, including the D 64 to Paris and N 184.

ADDRESSES

ⵋ EAT

⊜⊜ **Le Cabouillet** – *5 quai de l'Oise.* ✆*01 34 69 00 90. www.lecabouillet.com. Closed Feb school holidays, Sun eve, Mon. Reservations Sat–Sun.* Very popular 200-year-old establishment. The setting is as refined as the cuisine. Tables upstairs overlook the River Oise; those on the terrace are popular in summer.

Abbaye de
Jouarre★

Jouarre stands on a hilltop high above the River Petit Morin before it flows into the Marne. The town already had two abbeys in the 7C. The monastery was short-lived, but the convent adopted the Benedictine rule and survived, soon acquiring a prestigious reputation. The great ladies of France, among them Madeleine d'Orléans, François I's half-sister, were flattered to receive the title of abbess. In 1572, during the Wars of Religion, one of the abbesses, *Charlotte de Bourbon*, attracted by the new Calvinist ideas, renounced the Catholic religion and later married William of Nassau, the founder of the Dutch Republic. Badly damaged during the Hundred Years' War, the abbey was rebuilt several times, particularly in the 18C. When the abbey was seized during the Revolution, it was the residence of a fervent, united religious community, close observers of monastic rules. The monastery resumed its activity in 1837.

VISIT

○*Open Wed–Mon 9.45am–12.15pm, 2.30–6pm (5.30pm in winter), Sun and public holidays 10.15am–12.15pm, 2.30–6pm.* ✆*4.50 €.* ✆*01 60 22 06 11.*

Tower

Only the tower remains from the old medieval sanctuary; it once served as bell tower and porch to the 12C Romanesque church.
The interior has been carefully restored: three vaulted rooms, furnished by Madeleine d'Orléans in the 16C, house abbey memorabilia (note the armorial bosses) and temporary exhibitions.

Crypt★

⚜ *Guided tours (30min) Apr–Sept Wed–Mon 10.15, 11.15am, 2.15pm, 3.15pm, 4.15pm, 5.15pm; Nov–Mar Wed–Sun 10.15am, 11.15am, 2.15pm,*

⚜ **Michelin Local Map:** 312: H-2 or map 106 fold 24.
🛈 **Info:** ✆01 60 22 06 11. www.abbayejouarre.org.
▶ **Location:** Just under 1hr from Paris via the autoroute A4 (leave at the exit for St Jean les deux Jumeaux) -then take the RN3 (direction La Ferté sous Jouarre), and then D 402.
○ **Timing:** Allow 2hr.

3.15pm, 4.15pm. ○*Closed holidays.* ✆*4.50€.* ✆*01 60 22 64 54.* www.tourisme-jouarre.com.
The crypt lies behind the parish church, at the end of place St-Paul. The square presents an imposing 13C cross resting on a stone base with the Virgin and Child in the centre of a four-lobed medallion. The crypt consists of two formerly underground chapels which were linked in the 17C.
Crypte St-Paul, the mausoleum of the founding family, is considered to be one of the oldest religious monuments in France. The crypt is divided into three aisles by two rows of three columns dating from Gallo-Roman times, made of marble, porphyry or limestone. The famous Merovingian wall near the entrance presents a primitive stone mosaic with geometric motifs (oblongs, squares, diamonds, etc.).
The most striking sarcophagus is the Tomb of St Agilbert, Bishop of Dorchester and later of Paris, the brother of Abbess Theodechilde; Christ sits enthroned, surrounded by the Chosen Few with upraised arms. One of the galleries affords a good view of the bas-relief at the head: Christ circled by the four Evangelists' symbols (man, lion, bull, eagle). The tomb of St Osanne – an Irish princess who allegedly died in Jouarre – presents a 13C recumbent figure. The most elaborate decoration is that of the sarcophagus of Theodechilde, the first abbess of Jouarre. A display of large cockleshells adorns a Latin inscription in honour of the wise Virgins.

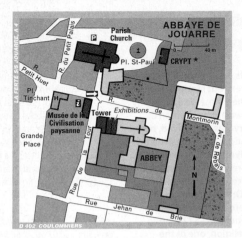

The **crypte St-Ébrégésile** is a small Romanesque church beyond the first crypt. An archaeological dig carried out in 1989 revealed that it had been built between Merovingian walls. The capitals in the crypt are also Merovingian, as is Bishop Ebrégésile's sarcophagus, which was discovered in 1985 to the left of the altar.

Recent excavations have revealed the nave of the modest St-Ébrégesile Church, along with several Merovingian sarcophagi.

Musée de la Civilisation Paysanne-Briard

Rue de la Tour. ○ *Open Wed–Mon morning and afternoon.* ∞*2.50€.* *℘01 60 22 64 54.*

This museum displays exhibits relating to regional folklore, customs and history: costumes, tools, paintings, etc.

ADDRESSES

🏨 STAY

⊜⊜ **Plat d'Étain** – *77260 La Ferté-sous-Jouarre, 4.5km/3mi N of the abbey via D 402. ℘01 60 22 06 07. www.le-plat-d-etain.com. Closed 1–12 Oct, 17–31 Dec, Sun eve, Fri eve. 18 rooms.* ⊐*8€* *Restaurant*⊜. While this inn, a stone's throw from the abbey, was built in 1840, its rooms are modern. A pewter plate *(plat d'étain)* adorns the wall of the charming, faintly outmoded dining room. Traditional fare.

Église Paroissiale

Enter by the south transept (&see plan) at the end of the cul-de-sac.

This was rebuilt after the Hundred Years' War and completed in the early 16C. The north arm of the transept features a 16C Entombment, a 15C *Pietà* and two reliquaries (12C and 13C) covered in silver-gilt with enamels, cabochons and filigree work. The south aisle contains a 16C statue of Our Lady of Jouarre.

EXCURSION
Doue

10km/6mi southeast of Jouarre.
Doue hill (181m/594ft) offers a view of the Plateau de la Brie des Morins in the distance. The squat nave of the **Église St-Martin** contrasts with its lofty Gothic chancel and transept. Inside, note the luminosity of the chancel with its open-work design, characteristic of the Early Gothic style (13C).

⍩ EAT

⊜⊜ **Le Bec Fin** – *1 quai des Anglais, 77260 La Ferté-sous-Jouarre. ℘01 60 22 01 27. www.restaurant-lebecfin.fr. Closed Sun eve, Mon–Tue, Wed eve.*
Reservations advisable Sat–Sun.
This restaurant, ideally located near the River Marne is popular with the locals. The delightfully 'retro' decor and excellent reception accompany traditional cuisine with an accent on seafood.

Jouy-en-Josas

This town has retained a noble appearance owing to the neat, tidy houses and the substantial estates. The village was once a secluded spot favoured by the writer Victor Hugo. In the street bearing his name, a plaque indicates the small house rented by the poet for his mistress Juliette Drouet in 1835. His stay here inspired the writing of *Olympio*. The former French President Léon Blum and the bacteriologist Professor Albert Calmette, who discovered the tuberculosis vaccine, are buried in Jouy cemetery. But the town is most famous for its *toile de Jouy* fabrics.

▶ **Population:** 8 055
⚏ **Michelin Local Map:**
  311: J-3 or map 106 fold 30.
🛈 **Info:** 29 bis av. Jean-Jaurès, 78350 Jouy-en-Josas.
  ☏01 39 56 62 69.
  www.jouy-en-josas.fr.
◗ **Location:** 6km/3.7mi southeast of Versailles.
🅿 **Parking:** Limited parking opportunity in town centre *(fee)*.
◈ **Don't Miss:** The Musée Français de la Photographie.
◔ **Timing:** Allow an hour or so for each museum.

A BIT OF HISTORY
A textile centre

In the 17C, printed cotton was imported from India. A year after Louis XIV lifted a ban on printed material in 1759, at the age of 22, **Christophe-Philippe Oberkampf** founded his first textile workshop, specialising in a type of printed calico known as *toile de Jouy*. In 1783 the factory became the Royal Works, and business prospered. Oberkampf recruited his first skilled workers in Switzerland, and they in turn trained new apprentices.

Showing a great interest in scientific advancement and modern machinery, this gifted manufacturer employed up to 1 300 workers, a remarkable number for the time. However, the Napoleonic wars, foreign invasions and competition dealt a deathblow to the Royal Works. In 1843 the company filed for bankruptcy and the factory was demolished 20 years later.

SIGHTS
Musée de la Toile de Jouy★

♿ *54 rue Charles-de-Gaulle.* ◷*Open Tue–Sun 11am–6pm.* ▦*5€.* ☏*01 39 56 48 64. www.museedelatoiledejouy.fr.* The museum is housed in the 19C Château de l'Églantine, close to the former manufacture. The rooms on the ground floor contain displays explaining the his-

tory and the techniques used to make the famous fabrics. Copper plates and cylinders or blocks of wood were used to print the pattern on the fabric. The Salon d'Oberkampf has been reconstructed with waxwork figures, Jouy hangings and family portraits. There are also some superb pieces of furniture stamped with the name of the cabinetmaker (Jacob). On the first floor are showcases of dresses, shawls and panels from the 18C and 19C. Note the various sets of bedclothes. Floral motifs and pastoral scenes were the first to become fashionable, then came antique motifs. The shop sells reproductions of the original patterns.

Marc Walter pour le musée de la toile de Jouy

L'escarpolette (1783–1789),
Musée de la toile de Jouy

A Great Statesman

Léon Blum (1872–1950) was not only the first Socialist Prime Minister of France, but also the first Jewish one. He studied law at the Sorbonne before becoming a young leader of the Socialist movement. He was arrested and sent to a concentration camp during World War II and afterwards served as provisional president of France from Dec 1946–Jan 1947.

Eglise Saint-Martin

11 rue Bonnard. ○*Open daily 9am–6pm, except during services.* ℘*01 39 56 42 64. http://jouysm-catholique-yvelines.cef.fr.*
The oldest vestiges of St-Martin date back to the 13C, but by the 15C the church fell into ruin after the Hundred Years' War and the Plague. It was rebuilt in 1549, the date inscribed on the plaque to the right of the entrance. In 1960 the interior walls, 16C carved wood choir, and the 19C organ were cleaned and restored. Don't miss the gorgeous 17C marble statue of St-Sébastien.

Maison de Jeanne et Léon Blum

4 rue Léon-Blum. ○*Open May–Jun and Sept–Oct Sun 2–5pm.* ✎*4€.* ℘*01 30 70 68 46.*
This was the home that the former French president acquired in 1945 and in which he lived until his death in 1950 with his wife Jeanne (whom he had married in 1943 in Buchenwald concentration camp). Several of the rooms contain documents relating to his early days, his literary works (essays, reviews) and his role in both the Socialist movement and French current affairs. The main room houses his writing desk and most of his private collection of books.

EXCURSION
Bièvres

Lying in the valley of the River Bièvre, the town of Bièvres has retained memories of Victor Hugo, a frequent visitor.

Maison littéraire de Victor Hugo

45 rue de Vauboyen. ♿ ◗*Guided tours Mar–Nov Sat–Sun 2.306.30pm.* ✎*4€.* ℘*01 69 41 82 84. www.maison litterairedevictorhugo.net.*
The Château des Roches belonged to the director of a newspaper, the *Journal des Débats*, who held a literary salon and was a friend of Victor Hugo. The museum founded in 1991 by a patron of the arts, Daisaku Ikeda, has been carefully restored in its original romantic style to house mementoes of the poet: letters written by Victor Hugo himself and by some of his contemporaries, hastily scribbled drafts, annotated proofs of *Les Misérables* and *Les Contemplations* and photos. Regular temporary exhibitions.

Musée Français de la Photographie★

78 rue de Paris, in the direction of Le Petit Clamart. ○*Open Wed–Mon 9.30am–12.30pm, 1.30–5.30pm.* ○*Closed public holidays.* ✎*3€.* ℘*01 69 35 16 50. www.museedelaphoto.fr.*
A history of photography from technical and artistic viewpoints. Some 15 000 items, including 300 Kodak cameras, and about a million photographs are on show. Exhibits range from Da Vinci's studies to the very latest equipment, relying on sophisticated technology. The crucial discoveries of Nicéphore Niepce, who took the first photograph on 5 May 1816, are explained, as are Daguerre and his photographic process, the advent of amateur photography in 1888, the invention of the miniature camera (Leica) in 1925, etc.
The museum highlights the continuous quest for technical advancement, and craftsmanship; the large-format cameras are masterpieces of cabinetmaking and leatherwork. The first aerial photograph was taken in 1858 by Félix Tournachon, known as Nadar (1820–1910), from a hot-air balloon hovering over Bièvres. A stele, erected at the intersection of RN 118 and A 86, recalls his achievement. Every year Bièvres hosts an internationally renowned photography fair on the first weekend in June.

Maintenon★

This charming town on the banks of the River Eure is renowned for its château, irrevocably linked to the incredible destiny of **Françoise d'Aubigné**. Born in 1635 to a family with Calvinist views, she was orphaned at the age of 12, became the widow of the burlesque poet Paul Scarron at the age of 25, the clandestine governess of Mme de Montespan's children by the age of 34 and, in a secret ceremony, the wife of Louis XIV at the age of 48.

▶ **Population:** 4 427
🜨 **Michelin Local Map:** 311: F-4 or map 106 fold 26.
🛈 **Info:** Mairie, pl. Aristide-Briand, 28130 Maintenon. ✆02 37 23 05 04. www.mairie-maintenon.fr.
▶ **Location:** 80km/50mi from Paris, along the A 10. Access from Paris: SNCF rail link from Gare Montparnasse.
🕐 **Timing:** Allow 1–2hr to visit the château.

A BIT OF HISTORY

The corridors of power – When her clandestine charge, the Duc de Maine, was legitimised, Françoise Scarron made a public appearance at court. Thereafter Louis XIV, who was extremely fond of his son, used to see her every day. Initially, he found her a trifle pedantic, but soon revised his opinion of 'the Scarron widow' and succumbed to her charm, intelligence and strong temperament. After the Queen's death, Louis XIV secretly married Mme de Maintenon in the winter of 1683–84. The morganatic queen acceded to the rank of peer and marquise in 1688 – a privilege bestowed on her directly by the King – and from then on she became an extremely powerful figure in the country's political life.

A Herculean task – Between 1685 and 1688, the area around Maintenon saw one of the century's most ambitious projects: the diverting of the waters of the River Eure to the fountains of Versailles. François Louvois acted as supervisor; he left Sébastien Vauban in charge of the plans and entrusted him with the construction of an 80km/50mi-long aqueduct linking Pontgouin *(Michelin Local Map 311 C 5)* to the Étang de la Tour. The Maintenon aqueduct was a colossal enterprise, 4 600m/15 000ft in length with three superimposed rows of arches, placed 72m/237ft above the level of the River Eure. In fact, it was only possible to fit in one row of arches.

The construction was carried out like a military campaign. Over 20 000 soldiers took part in the excavation work,

Château de Maintenon

A. de Valroger/MICHELIN

in addition to 10 000 skilled workers from remote villages and local peasants who helped cart the materials. The River Voise and River Drouette were canalised and used to convey the freestone and sandstone rubble from the Gallardon and Épernon quarries. In 1689, the wars triggered off by the Augsburg League interrupted the work. The French troops, in poor physical condition, were sent off to the borders to defend their country. The work was never resumed.

SIGHTS
Château★

◷*Open Wed–Mon mid-May–mid-Sept 10.30–6pm; mid-Sept–mid-Dec and mid-Feb–Apr 2–5pm; last admission 45min before closing.* ⊜*6.50€ (children 3€).* ✆*02 37 23 00 09.*

The present château occupies the site of a former stronghold, circled by the waters of the Eure. The construction work was undertaken by Jean Cottereau, Minister of Finance to Louis XII, François I and Henri II, and completed around 1509 in the Renaissance style.

The estate passed to the d'Angennes family until Louis XIV bought it In 1674 and gave it to the future Marquise de Maintenon. The Marquise left it to her niece, who was married to the Duke of Ayen, son of the first Maréchal de Noailles. The château has remained in this family ever since.

The archway flanked by two protruding turrets and bearing Jean Cottereau's coat of arms (three lizards) leads to the inner court which is the starting-point for tours. The square 12C keep, now crowned with an elegant roof, is all that remains of the original stronghold.

The adjoining wing was built by Mme de Maintenon and the narrow door in the tower still sports the Marquise's emblem, a griffin's head. A door depicting St Michael and bearing the lizard emblem gives onto a staircase leads to Mme de Maintenon's suite, consisting of an antechamber, bedroom – where Charles X spent the night on 3 August 1830 when he fled Rambouillet – and a small cabinet.

After leaving the central building, visitors are shown round the first floor of the Renaissance wing, redesigned to accommodate the apartments of Mme de Montespan and her royal charges.

The tour ends with the reception rooms furnished by the Noailles family in the 19C. The Grand Salon bears portraits of the two royal rivals, Mme de Montespan and Mme de Maintenon. In the Portrait Gallery, a collection of paintings represents the illustrious members of the family.

ADDRESSES

🏠 STAY

⊜⊜ **Les Chandelles (Bed and Breakfast)** – *19 r. des Sablons, in Les Chandelles village, 28130 Villiers-le-Morhier, 8km/5mi N of Maintenon via D 116, dir. Coulomb.* ✆*02 37 82 71 59. www.chandelles-golf.com. 5 rooms.* A large gate guards the entrance to this pretty farm built in 1840 and surrounded by a garden where horses graze. The bedrooms are decorated in bright colours, and their bathrooms are very nicely fitted out. Activities proposed include horse riding, fishing and especially golf – the owner, a former golf pro, now teaches the sport and can point you towards the best courses.

⊜⊜ **Ferme du Château (Bed and Breakfast)** – *Levesville, 28300 Bailleau l'Evêque, 15km/9mi SW.* ✆*02 37 22 97 02. www.ferme-levesville.com. 3 rooms. Restaurant* ⊜⊜. Peace and quiet in the countryside at this 19C farmhouse. Spacious rooms overlook the gardens, and local French country cuisine served in the restaurant.

♥/ EAT

⊜⊜ **Relais des Remparts** – *2 Place du Marché aux Légumes, 28210 Nogent-Le-Roi, via D983.* ✆*02 37 51 40 47. www. relais-des-remparts.com. Closed Aug, Feb holidays, Sun–Tue eves, Wed.* This historic inn serves traditional French cuisine in a bright and cosy country-style dining room. Meals served in the gardens during summer.

Meaux★

Nestling inside a deep bend of the River Marne, Meaux lies at the intersection of several main roads. It's known for the famous Brie de Meaux cheese. In the summer months, a **Son et Lumière (sound and light) performance** featuring a cast of more than 2 000 re-enacts Meaux's moments of glory in the charming setting of the Episcopal Precinct.

EPISCOPAL PRECINCT
Cathédrale St-Étienne★

Exterior – The construction of the church continued from the late 12C to the 16C, covering the entire gamut of Gothic architecture. The façade (14C–16C) is pure Flamboyant. The limestone used for the stonework has crumbled in several places and the exterior decoration is badly damaged. The Wars of Religion brought further destruction.

The south transept façade is an elegant example of Radiant Gothic. In poor condition, the south doorway is dedicated to St Stephen. Only the left tower (68m/223ft) was completed. The one on the right, a plain bell tower, is called the Black Tower on account of its dark-coloured shingles.

▶ **Population:** 48 842
🚗 **Michelin Local Map:** 312: G-2 or map 106 folds 22, 23.
ℹ **Info:** 1 pl. Doumer, 77100 Meaux. ☎01 64 33 02 26. www.ville-meaux.fr.
◗ **Location:** In Île de France, 55km/34mi east of Paris, along the A 4. Access from Paris: SNCF rail link from Gare de l'Est.
🅿 **Parking:** Limited town centre parking.
🕐 **Timing:** Allow 1–2hr to visit the cathedral and episcopal palace.

Interior – Last restored in the 18C, the interior of the cathedral contrasts sharply with the badly weathered exterior. The lofty, well-lit nave is an impressive sight. The two bays of the nave next to the transept date from the early 13C. The transept are superb examples of 14C architecture. Below the huge stained-glass window runs an openwork triforium so fine that it allows a full view of the lancets.

Note the pretty 15C Maugarni doorway to the left. A walk round the ambulatory leads to Bossuet's tomb, marked by a

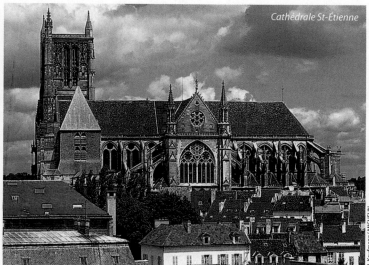
Cathédrale St-Étienne

B. Kaufmann/ MICHELIN

slab of black marble in the south part of the chancel.

Ancien palais épiscopal

⊙*Open Apr–Sept Wed-Mon 10am–noon, 2–6pm. Oct–Mar Wed–Sat 10am–noon, 2–5pm, Sun 2–5pm.* ⊗3€, *no charge Wed.* ✆*01 64 34 84 45.*

The old palace houses a **museum** largely dedicated to the bishop Bossuet. The building was completed in the 12C and altered in the 17C. The two magnificent **Gothic rooms** facing the park on the ground floor, the lower and the upper chapel are the oldest parts of the palace. The amazing brick ramp leading to the first floor was designed by Bishop Briçonnet in the 16C to enable the mules loaded with grain to reach the attics.

Musée des Beaux-Arts

The Salle du Synode and the Grands Appartements have been made into a Fine Arts Museum (15C–19C). Artists featured include Boullogne, De Troy, Bouchardon, Courbet, Senelle, Coypel and Van Loo. The Petits Appartements in the west wing house 19C works by Orientalist painters Gérôme and Decamps and landscape artists Daubigny and Millet.

Appartement de Bossuet

Located in the east wing, Bossuet's apartment has retained its original layout but the decoration was renewed in the Louis XV style. Admire Mignard's portrait of the bishop and a splendid Cressent commode (early 18C).

Anciens remparts

🐾 *The ramparts are only accessible during the guided tours of the town.*

At the top of the steps stands the humble 17C pavilion which Bossuet used as a study. The bishop would retire here to collect his thoughts or to write in the peaceful hours of the night.

The centre of the terrace affords a good **view**★ of the gardens, the Bishop's Palace and the cathedral.

EXCURSION
Château de Montceaux

8.5km/5mi east. Leave Meaux by N 3 (east). Beyond Trilport, in Montceaux Forest, turn right onto D 19 (signposted Montceaux-les-Meaux).

Montceaux was known as the Château of the Queens. Catherine de' Medici had it built and Philibert Delorme almost certainly worked on it between 1547 and 1559. On the death of the woman who was 'almost Queen', the king gave the château to his bride Marie de Medici who entrusted the works to Salomon de Brosse. The château then fell into disrepair and after 1650 became uninhabitable. Handsome ruins lurk among the trees, and from the roofless entrance pavilion there is an especially good view of a section of wall with gaping windows.

ADDRESSES

♀/ EAT

⊜⊜ **Le Cep** – *36 r. du Tan.* ✆*01 64 34 20 33. Closed Sun eve, Mon. Reservations advised Sat–Sun.* Despite the no-frills decor – walls of mimosa-yellow wood panelling and white tablecloths – connoisseurs file in for perfectly prepared traditional meals. The house specialities, Brie de Meaux pané (breaded and cooked) and salmon in pastry, are simply divine.

🛒 SHOPPING

Fromagerie de Meaux – *4 r. du Gén.-Leclerc.* ✆*01 64 34 22 82. Closed Mon.* This shop is known for its Brie de Meaux, of course, but also Brie de Melun, coulommiers camemberts, goat cheeses and roquefort.

BOATING

Marne Loisirs – *quai Jacques-Prévert.* ✆*01 64 34 97 97. www.marne-loisirs.fr. Closed Nov–Mar.* Small boat rentals, no special permit required.

Milly-La-Forêt★

This charming village developed around the old covered market, Les Halles. Milly has been a long-standing centre for the growing of medicinal plants, including one variety still considered a local speciality: peppermint. As part of the *Parc Naturel Régional du Gâtinais Français,* it is now an important starting-point for many of the forest lanes crisscrossing the wooded uplands of Les Trois Pignons and Coquibus. A few activities intended for visitors are organised (horse-drawn carriages are used to encourage the discovery of the region's traditional heritage) and a guide is available in the park to help and advise tourists.

SIGHTS
Halles

Located on the town square, the market building, made entirely of oak and chestnut wood, dates back to 1479. The imposing roof structure resting on 48 pillars slopes almost down to the ground.

Rue Jean-Cocteau leads to rue du Lau, a no-through road, which ends in front of a Romanesque doorway flanked by two turrets; these are in turn linked to the Louis XIII-style former Governor's residence where Jean Cocteau lived from 1947 to his death in 1963 (⊶*closed to the public*).

▶ **Population:** 4 728
🌼 **Michelin Local Map:** 312: D-5 or map 106 fold 44
🚹 **Info:** 60 r. Jean-Cocteau, 91490 Milly-la-Forêt. ℘01 64 98 83 17. www.milly-la-foret.fr.
◐ **Location:** Milly-la-Forêt lies 64km/40mi south of Paris, via the A6.

Espace culturel Paul-Bédu

8 bis rue Farnault. & ⊘*Open Wed–Sun Apr–Oct 2–6pm; rest of year 2–5pm.* ∞*Free entry.* ℘*01 64 98 75 52.*
Situated opposite the town hall, this cultural centre stages temporary exhibitions and houses late-19C to early 20C objets d'art and small paintings collected by Paul Bédu, a native of Milly; a collection of lithographs, drawings and ceramics by Cocteau is also on display.

Conservatoire National des Plantes Médicinales Aromatiques et Industrielles

Route de Nemours. & ⊘*Open Apr–Oct daily 10am–6pm; Mar and Nov Sat–Sun 10am–5pm.* ∞*7€.* ℘*01 64 98 83 77.* *www.cnpmai.net.*
2ha/5 acres on the edge of the forest have been set aside for the preservation of over 1 200 species of plants: culinary and medicinal herbs as well as plants used for dyeing such as woad and madder and a selection of exotic plants. An herb

Elaborate grill-work and the garden façade of Château de Courances

Ph. Gajic/ MICHELIN

market is held in the market building at the beginning of June.

EXCURSIONS
Le Cyclop
👁‍🗨 *Guided tours only (45min) May–Oct Sat 2–5pm, Sun 11am–5.45pm.* ♿*Note: children under 10 are not allowed inside the sculpture.* ✆7€. 📞01 64 98 95 18. www.lecyclop.com. *Leave Milly on the Étampes road (D 837); follow the signs.*

This monumental sculpture was donated to the French government in 1987 by artists Jean Tinguely and Niki de Sainte-Phalle. Its enormous head 22.5m/73ft high is made with 300t of steel.

The face sparkles, whereas inside the head there is a strange world of disorder and utopia. On the top of the piece is a vast water-filled basin dedicated to France's most innovative post-war artist Yves Klein (1928–62), noted for his use of a rich ultramarine commonly referred to as Yves Klein blue. Works by other artists are also displayed.

ADDRESSES

🛏 STAY
😴 **M. Lenoir (Bed and Breakfast)** – *9 r. du Souvenir, 91490 Moigny-sur-École, 3.5 km/2mi N of Milly-la-Forêt.* 📞01 64 98 47 84. www.compagnie-des-clos.com. 📠. *4 rooms. Meals* 😴. High protective walls ensure the privacy of this handsome stone house and its heterogeneous garden. The rooms, tastefully decorated, are extremely peaceful. Breakfast room housed in the former chicken coop, pool in summer.

🍴 EAT
😋 **La Truffière** – *14 Route de Boutigny (dir. Ferté-Alais).* 📞01 64 98 70 27. *Closed Sun eve, Tue.* The warm welcome and attentive service are among the main assets of this restaurant situated in the old Milly railway station. The play area and chicken coop behind the restaurant, just next to the pleasant terrace, are very popular with the youngsters.

Château de Courances★★
Rue du Château, 5km/3mi north of Milly-la-Forêt via D372. 👁‍🗨*Guided tours (40min) Apr–Oct Sat–Sun and holidays 2.30–6pm.* 🕐*Gardens open Apr–Oct Sat–Sun and holidays 2pm–sunset; Wed 10am–6pm.* ✆9€ *(7€ for gardens only; children under 13 free).* 📞01 64 98 07 36 or 01 64 98 41 18. www.courances.net.

This 16C castle on the edge of the Fontainebleau forest was the residence of the royal secretary to the king and his heirs. Its Louis XIII architecture was completely restored in the 19C.

It served as a field hospital in World War I, and in World War II it was occupied by the Germans then Field Marshal Montgomery from 1947–1954. It's best known for its amazing **French formal gardens**★★ and Grand Canal, considered among the best in Europe.

🛒 SHOPPING
L'Herbier de Milly – *16 Place du Marché.* 📞01 64 98 92 39. *Open Tue-Sun 9.30am–12.30pm, 2.30–7.30pm.* Come discover this herbalist's shop, run by the same family for four generations, where you can sample regional specialities such as Milly peppermint and several kinds of honey. Beginning in May, a visit to the shop's medicinal garden is well worth the detour.

PARC NATUREL RÉGIONAL DU GÂTINAIS FRANÇAIS
Created in 1999, the Natural Park of the Gâtinais Region protects and develops the natural and cultural heritage of this area, promotes economic development while respecting the environment (farming is the local main-stay), improve the quality of life, and revitalise the villages. Some tourist activities, such as tours of the region's attractions in horse and wagon, and a tourist brochure covering park territory, are available. *Maison du Parc, Place de la République.* 📞01 64 98 73 93.

Montfort-l'Amaury★

This old town is built on the side of a hill dominated by castle ruins. Before the French Revolution, Montfort was an important county town enjoying far more power than nearby Rambouillet. The composer Maurice Ravel and Jean Monnet, one of the founders of the European Union, were among the town's distinguished residents. Today, Montfort-l'Amaury is an elegant holiday resort of antique shops and small 'country' restaurants.

▷ **Population:** 3 076
⚲ **Michelin Local Map:** 311: G-3 or map 106 north of folds 27, 28.
🅸 **Info:** 6 r. Amaury, 78490 Montfort-l'Amaury. ☏01 34 86 87 96. www.ville-montfort-l-amaury.fr.
◑ **Location:** 48km/30mi almost due west of Paris, via the A 12/N 12.

A BIT OF HISTORY

The district was founded and fortified in the 11C by the builder Amaury de Montfort. The most famous descendant of this illustrious family was Simon IV, the leader of the Albigensian Crusade against the heretical Cathars of Languedoc.

A Breton outpost in Île-de-France – In 1312 the marriage of the Breton Duke Arthur to one of the Montfort daughters made this citadel a part of Brittany. Subsequently, when Anne of Brittany, Comtesse de Montfort married Charles VIII and then Louis XII, Montfort-l'Amaury became a French fief. The duchy became Crown property after the accession of Henri II, the son of François I and Claude de France.

SIGHTS
Église St-Pierre★

The rebuilding of the church was commissioned by Anne of Brittany in the late 15C. The decoration work continued through the Renaissance and was completed in the early 17C; the nave was uniformly elevated and the bell tower and the façade were both remodelled. Walk round the church, surrounded by quaint old houses. Observe the striking gargoyles that adorn the walls of the apse and the high flying buttresses supporting the chancel. The pretty doorway on the south front bears medallions portraying the benefactors André de Foix

and his wife, whose generosity made it possible to carry out the renovation work in the Renaissance. The interior features a superb set of Renaissance **stained-glass windows★** in the ambulatory and around the aisles.

Ancien charnier

This old cemetery is enclosed within an arcaded gallery surmounted by splendid timbered roofing in the shape of an upturned ship. The left gallery is 16C, the other two date from the 17C. In accordance with medieval tradition, these galleries were intended to receive the bones of the dead when there was a lack of space in the graveyard.

Castle ruins

Take the narrow, twisting road to the top of the hill. Two sections of wall overgrown with ivy are all that remain of

Ancien charnier

S. Sauvignier/MICHELIN

the 11C keep. The stone and brick turret belonged to the building commissioned by Anne of Brittany. The summit offers a good **view**★ of the town, the old-fashioned roofs and the edge of the forest.

Musée Maurice-Ravel★

5 rue Maurice-Ravel. 👄 *Guided tours by reservation only, Wed–Fri 2.30pm, 3.30pm, 4.30pm, Sat–Sun 10am, 11am, 2.30pm, 3.30pm, 4.30pm.* ⊗7€. ☏*01 34 86 00 89. www.ville-montfort-l-amaury.fr.*

In 1920 the French composer **Ravel** bought a tiny villa in Montfort-l'Amaury. It was in this house – called Le Belvédère – that he wrote most of his music: *L'Enfant et les Sortilèges, Boléro, Daphnis et Chloé*, etc. The composer developed a brain tumour and was forced to move back to Paris in 1937, where he died soon afterwards.

The rooms are somewhat cramped and Ravel – who was a short man – had several of them made even smaller. The interior decoration has remained intact; much of the painting was done by Ravel himself and featured dark, sombre tones. The museum exhibits include the composer's piano, his gramophone and numerous mementoes reflecting his taste for refinement.

Jardin zen – Ravel had spent a fortune on his tiny garden (300sq m/359sq yd). It has now been relaid in the Japanese style the composer liked so much: bamboos and azaleas, irises and small trees with gnarled branches.

EXCURSIONS
Musée International d'Art Naïf

4km/2.5mi north along D 76. ♿ 🕐*Open Tue–Sun 10am–6pm.* ⊗5.50€. ☏*01 34 86 06 22. www.midan.org.*

This museum devoted to the world of fantasy contains the Max-Fourny collection – more than 1 500 works displayed in rotation with temporary exhibitions.

La Queue-les-Yvelines, La Serre aux Papillons

4.5km/3mi NW. Leave Montfort by D 155 to La Queue-les-Yvelines. ♿ 🕐 *Open end Mar–early Nov 9.30am–12.30pm,*

2.30–7pm. ⊗7€ *(children 5€).* ☏*01 34 86 42 99. www.serreauxpapillons.com.*
The butterfly house is part of the Jardinerie Poullain. More than 500 butterflies live in it, in tropical conditions.

Maison Jean-Monnet (Centre d'information sur l'Europe)

In Houjarray, 4.5km/3mi east of Montfort via D 13. 🕐 *Open Mon–Fri 10am–5pm, Sat 1–6pm, Sun and public holidays 9am–6pm.* ☏*01 34 86 12 43. www.jean-monnet.net.*

Jean Monnet (1888–1979), the political economist and diplomat, bought this country retreat in 1945; it has a thatched roof and a large, gently sloping garden which overlooks the surrounding countryside.

The text of the declaration regarding the Schuman Plan of 1950 (embodied in a treaty that same year) was conceived and written here; it led to the creation of the European Coal and Steel Community (ECSC).

Monnet would return to this haven of peace after his frequent trips around the world, and had man famous figures and heads of state to stay. He retired here in 1975, writing his memoirs until his death.

Some of the original furnishings remain, together with various possessions: Monnet's *Memoirs*, letters from Schuman, Roosevelt, Adenauer and de Gaulle, various publications with Monnet on the cover, paintings by his wife Sylvia, a bust of Marianne (1945) by the sculptor Paul Belmondo. Display panels recount important moments of his career.

ADDRESSES

🍴 EAT

😋😋 **Hostellerie des Tours** – *Pl. de l'Église.* ☏*01 34 86 00 43. Closed Tue eve, Wed. Reservations advisable.* A two-storey 19C hostel: on the ground floor, you'll find a pleasant dining room decorated with copper cookware and a 1930s style bar, while in the cellar there's a picturesque vaulted cave. Traditional fare and Provençal specialities.

Moret-Sur-Loing★

Moret is a fortified medieval town perched at the confluence of the Loing and Seine river. The 19C artist Alfred Sisley immortalised the charming scenery in his paintings.

A BIT OF HISTORY
A fortified town and a royal residence

Situated near the Champagne border, Moret and its fortified castle defended the king's territory from the reign of Louis VII up to Philip the Fair's marriage to Jeanne of Navarre, the daughter of the Comte de Champagne (1284), which put an end to the feud between the two families. Its keep and curtain wall – the two gates still stand – lost their strategic value, and Fontainebleau became the official place of residence for French rulers. The fortifications remained until the mid-19C and the part of town traversed by the River Loing kept its secluded character.

The history of Moret was marked by a number of famous women, including Jacqueline de Bueil (1588–1651), one of the last loves of Henri IV, who founded the Notre-Dame-des-Anges hospital and convent. Marie Leszczynska was greeted in Moret by Louis XV on 4 September 1725; a commemorative obelisk marks the place where the betrothed met (at the top of the rise along N 5). The following day they were married in Fontainebleau, 16km/10mi northwest.

SIGHTS
The river banks★

Branch off the road to St-Mammès and proceed towards the Pré de Pin, which runs along the east bank of the Loing. Admire the **view** of the lake, the shaded islets, the fishermen, the church and the ancient keep.

This view provided inspiration for the Impressionist, Alfred Sisley, who chose Moret and the surrounding area as the theme for some 400 of his paintings.

▶ **Population:** 4 478
Michelin Local Map: 312: F-5 or map 106 fold 46.
Info: Pl. de Samois, 77250 Moret-sur-Loing. ✆01 60 70 41 66.
Location: Near Fontainebleau, 80km/50mi south of Paris via the A 6/N 6. Access from Paris: SNCF rail link from Gare de Lyon.

Bridge over the Loing

One of the oldest bridges in the Île-de-France, this was probably built around the same time as the town fortifications but was frequently torn down and then widened. On the approach to the Porte de Bourgogne the ramparts and several houses with overhangs – one of which rises out of the Loing waters – come into view.

Église Notre-Dame

The **chancel** is believed to have been consecrated in 1166. The original elevation is visible in the apse and on the south side; the main arches resting on round columns are crowned by a gallery opening onto triple arching, surmounted by clerestory windows. The arches and the bays on the north side were walled up to offer greater support to the structurally unsound bell tower erected in the 15C.

Ancien hospice

The corner post at rue de Grez bears an effigy of St James. A few steps along rue de Grez a modern cartouche bears the foundation date of the hospital (1638). The place became famous for the Moret barley sugar sweets made by the nuns. This tradition was continued by the town's confectioners.

Maison de Sisley

Alfred Sisley (1839–99), the Impressionist painter of English parentage, spent the latter part of his life in Moret. His studio was at no 19 rue Montmartre (*private*). He turned his back on a life in commerce to paint, and belonged to the Impressionist group but never achieved fame in his lifetime and was continually beset by financial difficulties. A pure landscape painter, Sisley delighted in the scenery of the Île-de-France and showed feeling for portraying water, light and air.

Rue Grande

At no 24 a commemorative plaque marks the house where Napoleon spent part of the night on his way back from Elba (19 to 20 March 1815).

ADDRESSES

🛏 STAY

🍴 **M. Gicquel (Bed and Breakfast)** – *46 r. René-Montgermont, 77690 Montigny-sur-Loing, 7km/4.3mi SW via D 104. ℘01 64 45 87 92. 2 rooms. ⊇ 10€.* These imposing stables and their paved courtyard, nestled in the heart of a tiny village, offer upper-floor bedrooms with sloped ceilings, exposed beams and furniture of days gone by. Restaurant overlooking river.

🍴🍴 **Auberge de la Terrasse** – *40 Rue de la Pêcherie. ℘01 60 70 51 03. www.auberge-terrasse.com. Closed mid-Oct–early Nov. 17 rooms. ⊇8.90€.* Enjoy the view of the river from the dining room of this very nicely situated hotel along the Loing. Families will be particularly pleased: the well-fitted, comfortable rooms are free for children under ten, and a children's meal is offered for two adult meals taken.

🍴 EAT

🍴 **Le Refuge** – *8 r. de l'Église. ℘01 60 70 86 65. Closed Sun eve, Mon.* Be sure to reserve a table in advance in this tiny, charming restaurant with the traditional French favourites prepared by the young chef.

🍴🍴🍴 **Relais de Pont-Loup** – *14 r. Peintre-Sisley. ℘01 60 70 43 05. Closed Sun evening, Mon. Reservations required Sat–Sun.* Exposed bricks, wooden beams and rotisserie in an open fireplace serves as the decor of this laid-back restaurant. The outdoor terrace overlooks the Loing River.

Maison François I

Walk through the town hall porch and into the small courtyard.
Note the extravagant Renaissance decoration of the gallery, and the door crowned by a salamander.

Porte de Samois

Also known as the Paris Gate. A statue of the Virgin Mary adorns the inner façade. Note the old-fashioned royal milestone that once marked out the highway leading from Lyon to Paris (now N 5).

🛒 SHOPPING

Sucre d'orge des Religieuses de Moret – *5 r. du Puits-du-four. ℘01 60 70 35 63. Closed Feb.* The Nuns of Moret have been making barley sugar since 1638 and this family museum tells their story. A collection of sweets boxes and antique objects complements the video describing the main aspects of small-scale barley sugar manufacturing. One may sample the wares and buy some to take home.

BOATING

Bâteaux du Confluent – *6 quai de Seine, 77670 St-Mammès. ℘01 64 23 25 59. Oct–Mar Mon, Wed and Fri afternoons or mornings by appointment; May–Sept Mon–Fri afternoons, Sat–Sun all day.* This boat rental company is well situated at the convergence of the Loing and the Seine. Different boats (no special licence necessary) are available depending on the length of your journey, (from one hour to one week). Navigational equipment and souvenirs.

Larguez les Amarres – *55 r. Gambetta, 77670 St-Mammès. ℘01 64 23 16 24. Closed Nov–Mar.* Cruises along the Loing River from the old locks at St-Mammès to Samois, from 13€.

Vallée de l'Ourcq

Beyond La Ferté-Milon, the River Ourcq follows a winding course through the Marne Valley. **Canal cruises** along the Ourcq are available in season. The poet Charles Péguy was one of the many French soldiers killed in the famous Battle of the Marne (1914).

BATTLE OF THE MARNE

The first Battle of the Marne originated with the Battle of the Ourcq, which in fact took place on the heights of the Multien plateau and not in the valley itself. The outcome of this battle did much to secure the success of the general offensive launched between Nanteuil-le-Haudouin, north of Meaux, and Révigny, northwest of Bar-le-Duc.

It is little known that this battle began – on both sides – with the engagement of large reserve units (55th and 56th French Divisions, 4th German Corps). Owing to the hazards of drafting and the movement of retreat, many of the French soldiers were in fact defending their native territory.

🚗 DRIVING TOUR

THE BATTLEFIELD AND THE OURCQ VALLEY

Round trip starting from Meaux

96km/58mi – allow 4hr – local map, see overleaf.

Meaux★
See MEAUX.

▶ *From Meaux take N 3 (west) towards Paris. After 6.5km/4mi, a memorial paying tribute to Gallieni stands on the left-hand side of the road. Turn right onto D 27, towards Iverny, then right again towards Chauconin-Neufmontiers.*

🔹 **Michelin Local Map:**
   312: G-1 to H-2 or map
   106 folds 12, 23, 24

Mémorial de Villeroy

This stands on the site of the early operations of 5 September 1914.

The funeral vault houses the remains of 133 officers and soldiers who died in the fields nearby.

The 19th Company of the 276th Regiment was called in to relieve the Moroccan Brigade who accompanied them and who were dangerously engaged in battle near Penchard. It launched an attack towards Monthyon, under the fire of the enemy, sheltered in the valley around the Rutel brook. **Charles Péguy** (1873–1914) was the only surviving officer. He told his men to lie down and was inspecting the German positions when he was struck by a bullet.

Péguy was buried with his comrades-in-arms belonging to the 276th Infantry Regiment (reserve). Their collective grave lies to the right of the vault. The cross celebrating the memory of the writer, philosopher and social reformer has been moved to the intersection of D 27 and D 129.

▶ *At the next crossroads, turn left towards Chauconin-Neufmontiers. Drive through Penchard and follow directions to Chambry. Drive through the village.*

The bell tower of Barcy is visible to the left.

Cimetière National de Chambry

Most of the soldiers buried here died during the fighting that took place on 6, 7 and 8 September when they were defending the village of Chambry, which was taken, lost and re-taken several times.

Along the road there is a view of the Chambry-Barcy Plateau covered in war graves that seem to mark out the progression of the Allied troops beneath the fire from the lines of German defence.

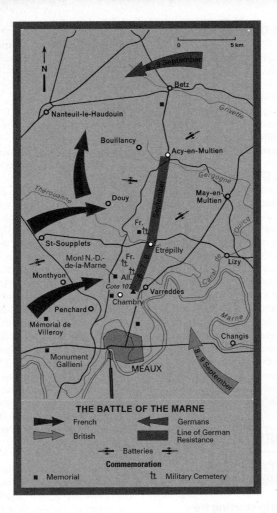

THE BATTLE OF THE MARNE

French	Germans
British	Line of German Resistance

Batteries ⊢⊣

Commemoration

■ Memorial   ♰♰ Military Cemetery

Located 500m/500yd east of the cross-roads, the German military cemetery marks the place where the main German line – which roughly follows the dirt track – crossed the road to Varreddes.

◐ *Turn back, towards Barcy.*

Monument Notre-Dame-de-la-Marne

This was erected in response to a vow made by Monseigneur Marbeau, Bishop of Meaux, in 1914 and dominates the whole battlefield.

◐ *Turn to the north for a good view of the Multien plateau in the far distance.*

Proceed towards Puisieux. At the crossroads after the old factory, turn right to Étrépilly. In the centre of the village, 200m/220yd before reaching the church, turn left towards Vincy and Acy-en-Multien.

Étrépilly

The small national cemetery and the memorial evoke the fighting that took place during the night of 7–8 September, reaching a climax near the village graveyard.

Acy-en-Multien

This village nestling in the Gergogne Valley was the scene of intensive warfare on

7 September 1914. The winding alleys, the hillsides planted with small spinneys and the estate walls of the château provided many opportunities for close combat, often ending in tragic death.

▶ *Take the left-hand fork out of Acy towards Nanteuil-le-Haudouin.*

Église de Bouillancy
Located in the lower part of the village. In the quiet valley – rural life is concentrated in the village on the plateau – lies an early Gothic church (12C–13C) with harmonious proportions.

▶ *Turn back to Acy and take D 18 up to the plateau.*

Enjoy the view of **Acy** and the elegant village spire. Beyond Étavigny, the road moves away from the battlefield.

▶ *Just before Thury-en-Valois take D 922 to the right.*

The road leads to **Mareuil-sur-Ourcq**, marking the start of the canal.

▶ *Cross Varinfroy to Crouy-sur-Ourcq.*

Crouy-sur-Ourcq
Just after the level crossing, the road skirts the ruins of the **Château Fort de Houssoy**. In order to see the **keep**, which has remained separate, park the car in the station car park and walk to the courtyard gates. From the top of the tower, there is a fine view of the surrounding area.
Crouy Church *(visits by arrangement;* ☎*01 64 35 63 02)* features a Gothic interior with two 16C aisles. Admire the beautifully crafted panelling (1670) in the chancel.

▶ *Turn back, and after the bridge turn left towards May.*

The twisting, hilly road affords extensive **views** of the surrounding landscape.

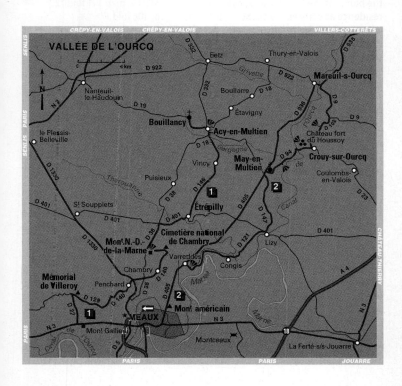

May-en-Multien

The village is well situated 100m/330ft above the River Ourcq. It is visible from afar on account of its church tower.

◯ *Drive down to Lizy. Do not cross the canal bridge but go up the hill on |the north bank along the road to Congis (D 121).*

View of the last loop of the Ourcq, overgrown with greenery.

◯ *Cross Congis and Varreddes and join D 405, south.*

On the left stands the huge **American monument** that pays homage to the Marne combatants. The road dips and leads straight down to Meaux.

Poissy

The town of Poissy, situated on the banks of the Seine, was a royal residence as early as the 5C. St Louis was christened here in 1214; the king's private correspondence was even signed Louis de Poissy. The castle used to stand on place Meissonnier but it was demolished by Charles V. Up to the middle of the last century, Poissy was the main Paris cattle market. Today, it is the site of a large automobile plant (Peugeot).

SIGHTS
Collégiale Notre-Dame★
👁 *Guided tours Sun 3–6pm.*
📞*01 39 65 08 03.*
The greater part of the collegiate church is Romanesque, dating from the 11C and 12C. The front tower built in the Romanesque style once served as a belfry-porch. The square base of the tower develops to an octagonal section on the highest level, ending in a stone spire. The central tower is eight-sided and ends in a timberwork spire.
Interior – The nave is a rare example of transitional style. The capitals of the south columns in the first two bays were

ADDRESSES

🍴 EAT

🍽🍽 **L'Assiette du Marché** – *1 Pl. du Marché, 77840 Crouy-sur-Ourcq, 5km/3mi E of May-en-Multien by D 94.* 📞*01 64 35 67 41. Closed Sat lunch, Tue.* This city residence on the market square houses a small yet delightful restaurant. The tiny dining room, with its neat decoration, reminiscent of a tea shop, offers simple cuisine noted for its original flavours salads, daily specials and meat or fish dishes.

CANAL CRUISING
Boat trips, with or without lunch on board, are organised along the Canal de l'Ourcq. *Information and bookings,* 📞*0800 95 21 21 or 01 60 01 13 65.*

▶ **Population:** 35 860
🗺 **Michelin Local Map:** 311: I-2, map 101 fold 12 or 106 fold 17.
🅱 **Info:** 132 r. du Gén.-de-Gaulle, 78300 Poissy. 📞*01 30 74 60 65.* www.ville-poissy.fr.
◯ **Location:** A little over 32km/20mi from the centre of Paris, on the Seine. Access from Paris: RER line A 5 or SNCF rail link from Gare St-Lazare.
👪 **Kids:** Musée du Jouet.
🕐 **Timing:** Half a day.

---

recarved in the 17C. The other capitals feature interlacing monsters and foliage motifs. Some of them are thought to be older than this building and were probably taken from another church. The nave is very well lit owing to the installation of a triforium by Viollet-le-Duc in the three bays nearest to the chancel which is circled by an ambulatory with groined vaulting. The side chapels – added in the 15C – pay homage to the various trade guilds: butchers, fishermen, etc.

The first chapel to the right of the doorway contains fragments of the font used for St Louis' christening. For many centuries, the faithful would scrape the stone sides of the font, dissolve the dust in a glass of water and drink the potion as a remedy for high fever. This explains why the font is in such bad condition.

The most impressive furnishings are in the first chapel on the right: majestic 15C statues of John the Baptist and St Barbara, and a superb 16C Entombment (see below) portraying Mary, John, Mary Magdalene, the Holy Women, Nicodemus and Joseph of Arimathea.

Musée d'Art et d'Histoire

12 rue St-Louis. ⚬━ *Closed temporarily for refurbishment.*

The history of Poissy from Merovingian times (sarcophagi) up to the late 1940s (automobile industry) is presented here. There are numerous seals dating back to the 12C, and a painting by Meissonnier of summer bathers in the Seine a splendid 16C painted wooden statue taken from the Church of Our Lady, etc.

⚋ Musée du Jouet

1 enclos de l'Abbaye. ⏰*Open Tue–Sun 9.30am–noon, 2–5.30pm.* ⚬4€ *(children 3€).* ☎*01 39 65 06 06.*

The toy museum is housed in the building flanked by two towers that used to be the entrance to the abbey. The toys and games exhibited in the museum cover the period from 1850 to 1960. There are a large number of dolls showing the changes in fashion over a century. On the first floor, there is a display case full of clockwork toys, another filled with teddy bears and yet another with lead and paper soldiers dating from the 19C. On the top floor are collections of cars and trains, some clockwork, others powered by steam. An electric train track from the 1930s operates automatically as visitors approach.

Villa Savoye★

82 Rue de Villiers. ⏰ *Open Tue–Sun May–Aug 10am–6pm; Mar–Apr and Sept–Oct 10am–5pm; Nov–Feb 10am–1pm, 2–5pm.* ⚬7€. *01 39 65 01 06.*

www.monuments-nationaux.fr.
This masterpiece of modern architecture was designed in 1929 by **Le Corbusier** and **Pierre Jeanneret** for the industrialist Savoye. The use of cylindrical piles made it possible to do away with load-bearing walls and introduce huge glass surfaces. The main rooms are located on the first floor, at a height of 3.5m/12ft, arranged around a large terrace which opens onto the countryside. A solarium occupies the top level of the house.

Centre de Production Peugeot

45 Rue J.-P.-Timbaud. ⚬*Guided tours by appointment one month in advance.* ☎*01 30 19 56 97.*

PSA Peugeot-Citroën is the second margest car maker in Europe. The Peugeot brand roots go back to the 19C when it was making coffee and bicycles. In 1974, Peugeot took over Citroën, although both brands have maintained their identity. The group then bought Chrysler's European subsidiaries, including Talbot. Just like the Renault factory in Flins, the PSA Peugeot Citroën factory in Poissy has contributed to shape the Seine Valley. Today, this ultra-modern car plant has a large number of industrial robots producing over 1 200 cars every day.

ADDRESSES

ᵞ/ EAT

⊜❺ **Le Bon Vivant** – *30 av. Émile-Zola.* ℘*01 39 65 02 14. Closed 23 Feb–1 Mar, Aug, Sun eve, Mon.* This Belle Epoque guinguette on the banks of a branch of the Seine is perfect for a weekend getaway. Two agreeable dining rooms – one of which is adorned with hunting trophies – and a terrace are the setting for traditional cuisine.

⊜❺ **Saint-Martin**– *2 r. Galande, 78510 Triel-sur-Seine.* ℘*01 39 70 32 00. Closed Aug, Wed, Sun.* A tiny yet cosy restaurant near a 13C gothic church, with a loyal local following for its home-made bread and creative mix of old and new French specialties.

Abbaye de **Port-Royal-des-Champs**★

Little remains of this famous abbey, which was the scene of a serious religious dispute for more than 100 years of French history.

A BIT OF HISTORY
An abbess aged eleven

In 1204 a Cistercian convent was founded in Porrois, a town later known as Port-Royal. Although this order was supposed to be strict, the rules grew extremely lax over a period of five centuries and by the turn of the 17C, the ten nuns and six novices who resided at the abbey were leading a most unsaintly life; the cloisters had become a promenade, fasting was a bygone practice and the vows of poverty were hardly compatible with the entertaining carried out at the abbey, including Carnival celebrations. In 1602 **Angélique Arnauld**, the 11-year-old daughter of an influential family of lawyers was passed off as 17 and appointed Abbess of Port-Royal.

⇘ SHOPPING

Noyau de Poissy – *105 r. du Gén.-de-Gaulle.* ℘*01 39 65 20 59. www.noyau depoissy.com. Boutique closed Mon. Tours available through the tourism office.* ℘*01 30 74 60 65.* Come and visit this hundred year-old distillery to learn how the famous Noyau de Poissy liqueurs are made. Enjoy the guided tour and then stop in the attached shop, a most practical place for stocking up on delicacies to take home.

Ⓒ **Michelin Local Map:** 311: I-3, map 101 fold 22 or 106 fold 29.

🛈 **Info:** ℘01 30 43 74 93. www.port-royal-des-champs.eu.

A reformer without mercy

Recovering from a bout of ill health, Mother Angélique began a series of reforms at the convent, reinstating the enclosure and imposing Cistercian rule, meditation and manual labour. From 1648 the growing community split its time between Port-Royal-des-Champs and Paris.

Theological battles

Over the course of the 17C, Port-Royal-des-Champs became a hotbed of theological controversy as the 'Petites Ecoles' at the abbey produced some of the greatest minds of the day, promoting **Jansenism** to the great indignation of the Jesuits. The monastery buildings were razed to the ground in 1710 by order of Louis XIV. Ongoing renovations have renewed several buildings, the orchards and meadows.

Racine at Port-Royal

Jean Racine (1639–99) lived at Port-Royal from age 16 to 19. He was taught Greek, Latin, French versification, diction and rhetoric. The French poet soon became an outstanding reader. Louis XIV was spellbound by his beautiful voice and Racine's advice was sought by many an actor.

A 7km/4.3mi footpath dedicated to Racine starts from the Granges de Port-Royal, with his poems about the natural beauty of the area inscribed on panels along the way. The path crosses D 91, runs through the hamlet of La Lorioterie, past the Fauveau mill, then across the Roi de Rome and Madeleine crossroads and ends at the church in Chevreuse.

RUINS AND MUSEUMS

A tour of Port-Royal estate comprises a pilgrimage to the abbey ruins and a visit to the park. The Little Schools building is situated on a plateau, surrounded by shaded grounds. It now houses a national museum, containing documents on the former colleges.

Ruins and Abbey Museum

Open Sat–Sun 10.30am–6pm. Closed 22 Dec–4 Jan. 5€. 01 39 30 72 72. www.port-royal-des-champs.eu.

Avenues of lime tree mark the site of the former cloisters. The graveyard where the Cistercian nuns were buried after 1204 has been planted with grass. The church adjoined the cloisters, whose original level was restored and the base of the pillars and the walls of the first building discovered. Next to the dovecote, a 17C barn houses a collection of paintings, engravings and memorabilia.

Les Granges, where the Solitaires lodged, lies above the valley on the north side screened by tree, connected to the Abbey by the Hundred Stairs.

Musée National des Granges de Port-Royal

Open Apr–Oct Mon–Fri 10.30am–12.30pm, 2–6pm, Sat–Sun 10.30am–6.30pm; rest of year Mon and Wed–Fri 10am–noon, 2–5.30pm, Sat–Sun 10.30am–6pm. Closed 22 Dec–4 Jan. 5€. 01 39 30 72 72. www.port-royal-des-champs.eu.

The building was specially designed for the Little Schools (established by the Messieurs at the Abbey to provide religious education) in 1651–52 and presents a suitably austere front. In the 19C a Louis XIII-style wing was added. Most of the rooms have been restored and contain books, engravings and drawings on the history of the abbey and the Jansenist movement.

The exhibition hall dedicated to Philippe de Champaigne (two paintings, *Ecce Homo* and *Mater Dolorosa*) reminds visitors of the strong ties that linked this painter to the abbey.

Blaise Pascal came here on a retreat to write his *Mystery of Jesus* in 1655. His knowledge of mathematics came in useful at the abbey when he produced calculations for a new winch for the well: this enabled the nuns to draw a huge bucket as big as nine ordinary buckets from a depth of 60m/197ft with no extra effort.

Musée National des Granges de Port-Royal

S. Sauvignier/MICHELIN

Provins★★

Whether approaching Provins from the Brie plateau to the west or from Champagne and the Voulzie Valley, this medieval town presents the eye-catching and distinctive outlines of the Tour César and of the dome of St-Quiriace Church. The splendid ramparts contribute to the town's medieval atmosphere and the rose gardens add to its visual appeal. The lower town, a lively shopping centre, sits at the foot of the promontory and extends along the River Voulzie and the River Durteint. The town, which boasts 58 historic monuments, is now a UNESCO World Heritage Site.

A BIT OF HISTORY
The Provins fairs

In the 10C Provins became one of the economic capitals of the Champagne region, thanks to its two annual fairs which, with those of Troyes, were among the largest in the region. Traders from the north and from the Mediterranean came here with their linens, silks, spices from the Orient and wine, attracting people from many walks of life: money agents and merchants among the hard-working bourgeoisie of the region. These fairs were prosperous until the early 14C, when the political and economic weight shifted to Paris, eclipsing the Champagne region.

Roses

According to tradition it was **Thibaud IV** the Troubadour who brought roses back from Syria and grew them successfully

> ▶ **Population:** 11 871
> ċ **Michelin Local Map:** 312: I-4
> 🛈 **Info:** Chemin de Villecran, 77160 Provins. ℘01 64 60 26 26. www.provins.net.
> ◗ **Location:** In the Île de France, 87km/54mi southeast of Paris via the A 4 and then D 231. Access from Paris: SNCF rail link from Gare de l'Est.
> 🅿 **Parking:** Place Honore de Balzac, the rue Vieille Notre-Dame or the rue de Temple. Or park near Porte St-Jean, near the tourist office.
> ⊛ **Don't Miss:** A tour of the ramparts and the upper town. If you are staying for a few days, consider buying a Provins Pass (*Office du Tourisme*); it can save you money.
> ◷ **Timing:** Allow at least half a day, or more, to get the most from your visit.

here in Provins. Edmund Lancaster (1245–96), brother of the King of England, married Blanche of Artois and was for a while suzerain of Provins, at which time he introduced the red rose into his coat of arms.

🐾 WALKING TOUR

UPPER TOWN★★

It is advisable to park in the car park near Porte St-Jean, location of the tourist office and departure point for the tourist train.

Porte St-Jean

St John's Gateway was built in the 13C. This stocky construction is flanked by two projecting towers which are partially hidden by the buttresses that were added in the 14C to support the drawbridge.

Guided tour of the city

Provins, an official City of Art and History, offers two-hour discovery tours led by guides certified by the Ministry of Culture and Communication. For information, contact the Office du Tourisme ℘01 64 60 26 26 or visit www.provins.net.

▷ *Follow allée des Remparts which overlooks the old moat.*

Remparts★★

The town walls were built in the 12C and 13C along an existing line of defence, then altered on several occasions. They constitute a very fine example of medieval military architecture. A house straddling the curtain wall was the home of the Provins executioners. The last one to live here was Charles-Henri Sanson who executed Louis XVI. The most interesting part of the ramparts runs between Porte St-Jean and Porte de Jouy. The Tour aux Engins, on the corner, links the two curtain walls; it derives its name from a barn nearby in which engines of war were housed.

In summer, on a space behind this tower, within the ramparts, the falconers of the 'Aigles de Provins' company put on a show of birds of prey; other birds of prey are displayed in shelters.

Beyond the 12C Porte de Jouy take Rue de Jouy, which is lined by picturesque low houses with long tiled roofs or an overhanging upper storey.

Place du Châtel

This vast, peaceful square, rectangular in shape, is bordered by attractive old houses: the 15C Maison des Quatre Pignons (southwest corner), the 13C Maison des Petits-Plaids (northwest corner), and the Hôtel de la Coquille to the north.

The remains of Église St-Thibault (12C) stand on the northeast corner.

Walk past the **Musée de Provins et du Provinois** (&*see Additional Sights*), housed in one of the town's oldest buildings, the 'Maison Romane' (Romanesque house).

Tour César (Caesar's Tower)★★

ⓘ*Open Apr–Oct 10am–6pm; Nov–Mar 2–5pm.* ⊕*3.50€.* ℘*01 64 60 26 26.*

This superb 12C keep, 44m/144ft high and flanked by four turrets, is the emblem of the town. It was once part of the walls of the upper town. The pyramidal roof was built in the 16C.

The guard-room on the first floor is octagonal and 11m/36ft high; it is topped by vaulting formed of four arcades of pointed arches ending in a dome and pierced by an orifice through which the soldiers on the floor above were passed supplies. The gallery encircling the keep at turret-level was originally roofed over. The view★ extends over the town and the surrounding countryside.

▷ *Return to Porte St-Jean via place du Châtel, then rue St-Jean on the left.*

ADDITIONAL SIGHTS
Grange aux Dîmes★

Rue St-Jean. ⓘ*Open Apr–Aug 10am–6pm; Sept–Oct Mon–Fri 2–6pm, Sat–Sun 10am–6pm; rest of year Sat–Sun 2–5pm.*

Tour César

M. Gaspar/MICHELIN

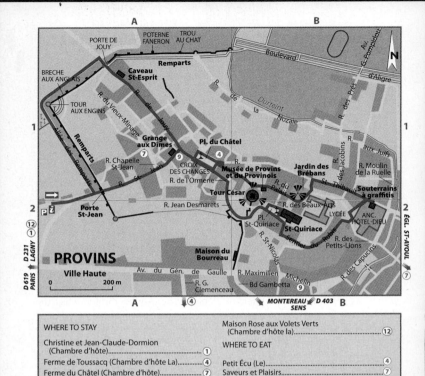

A   B

PROVINS
Ville Haute
0   200 m

MONTEREAU ⇒ D 403
SENS

WHERE TO STAY		Maison Rose aux Volets Verts (Chambre d'hôte la)............ ⑫
Christine et Jean-Claude-Dormion (Chambre d'hôte)............ ①		**WHERE TO EAT**
Ferme de Toussacq (Chambre d'hôte La)............ ④		Petit Écu (Le)............ ④
Ferme du Châtel (Chambre d'hôte)............ ⑦		Saveurs et Plaisirs............ ⑦
Ibis (Hôtel)............ ⑨		Table St-Jean (La)............ ⑨

⊚*3.50€.* ℘*01 64 60 26 26.*
www.provins.net.
This massive 13C building belonged to
the canons of St-Quiriace, who hired
out the space to merchants during the
major fairs. When the fairs went into
decline the barn became a store for the
tithes *(dîmes)* levied on the harvests of
the peasants.
The vast hall on the ground floor houses
a permanent exhibition (audio-guided
tour) re-creating the atmosphere of the
town's famous fairs: scenes and dum-
mies evoke craftsmen and shopkeepers
of bygone days.

Musée de Provins et du Provinois

🕐*Open Apr–mid-Jun noon–5.30pm.*
Mid-Jun–mid-Sept 11am–6.30pm; mid-
Sept–Oct noon–5.30pm; rest of year
Sat–Sun noon–5.30pm. ⊚*3€.*
℘*01 64 01 40 19. www.provins.net.*
On the ground floor are displayed **the
sculpture and ceramic collections**★,

valuable works of local medieval and
Renaissance art.
Exploiting the underground clay quarries enabled potters to produce pieces
now noted for their remarkable variety
and timelessness.

Souterrains à graffiti

*Entrance in rue St-Thibault, left of the
doorway to the Ancien Hôtel-Dieu.*
🔦 *Guided tours (45min): hours vary
throughout the year, call for times*
⊚*3.80€.* ℘*01 64 60 26 26.*
www.provins.net.
A substantial network of underground
passages lies beneath Provins, some
marked with ancient graffiti. The section that is open to the public runs
through a layer of tufa that lies parallel to the base of the spur on which the
Upper Town stands. The public entrance
is through a low-roofed chamber with
ribbed vaulting in the old hospice. Note
that the tunnels can be chilly, even in
summertime.

ADDRESSES

STAY

⊖ **Christine and Jean-Claude Dormion (Bed and Breakfast)** – *2 r. des Glycines, 77650 Lizines, 15km/9mi SW of Provins.* ☎*01 60 67 32 56.* 🖼 *5 rooms.* Agriculture is still the mainstay of this 300 year-old farm offering perfectly maintained, rustic bedrooms, each equipped with a kitchenette corner. Garden and orchard.

⊖⊜ **Ferme du Chatel (Bed and Breakfast)** – *5 r. de la Chapelle-St-Jean.* ☎*01 64 00 10 73.* 🖼 *5 rooms.* This farm, built between the 12C–18C, is in the heart of the medieval town. The rooms, with exposed timberwork, are quiet and impeccably maintained. A vast garden planted with fruit trees.

⊖⊜ **La Ferme de Toussacq** – *In the Toussacq hamlet, along the Seine, 77480 Grisy-sur-Seine, 20km/12.4mi S.* ☎*01 64 01 82 90. http://hameau-de-toussacq.com. 5 rooms.* Amidst a bucolic setting on the banks of the Seine, come discover this group of 17-19C edifices offering simple bedrooms in the château's out-buildings. Meals, featuring long-simmered dishes made from farm produce, occasionally include vegetarian fare.

⊖⊜ **Hôtel Ibis** – *77 av. du Gén.-de-Gaulle.* ☎*01 60 67 66 67. www.accor.com. 51 rooms. Restaurant⊖.* In a calm district, with a medieval architectural style and contemporary styled rooms. Neo-rustic restaurant.

⊖⊜ **La Maison Rose aux Volets Verts (Bed and Breakfast)** – *3 & 5 r. Maximilien-Michelin.* ☎*01 64 08 92 95/06 81 13 58 06. 5 rooms.* At the foot of the medieval city, these two 19C houses provide modern comforts and historic charm. Rooms are lovingly decorated, some overlooking the pretty gardens.

EAT

⊖ **Le Petit Écu** – *9 Pl. du Châtel (upper town).* ☎*01 64 08 95 00.* Located on the charming Place du Châtel in the heart of old Provins, this fine half-timbered house offers a weekend special in season that includes a country buffet.

⊖⊜ **Saveurs et Plaisirs** – *6 Pl. St-Ayoul.* ☎*01 60 58 41 70. Closed Mon eve, Sun.* A contemporary restaurant with a dedicated, self-taught chef, with a choice between traditional or 'creative' menus, heavy on fish dishes.

⊖⊜ **La Table Saint-Jean** – *1 r. St-Jean, (upper town).* ☎*01 64 08 96 77 Closed Sun evening in winter, Tue eve, Wed.* Located in the upper town, opposite the grange aux dîmes (tithes barn), this half-timbered house purportedly dates from the 11C. Depending on the season, you may dine in the decidedly rustic décor of the dining room or on the terrace set up in a pretty, flower-filled courtyard.

ENTERTAINMENT

👥 **À l'Assaut des Remparts – War Machines** – ☎*01 64 60 26 26. www.provins.net. Closed winter. Tickets and schedule at the Office de tourisme. 6.50€ (children 4.50€).* Near the Porte Saint-Jean towards the back of the moat, you'll be transported into the Middle Ages thanks to a faultlessly realistic performance demonstrating the use of long-gone military equipment and defensive weapons.

👥 **Les Aigles des Remparts (Eagles of the Ramparts)** – ☎*01 60 58 80 32. www.provins.net. Closed early Nov–late Mar. Tickets and timetable at the Office de Tourisme. 9€ (children 6€).* One of the nobility's favourite pastimes during the Middle Ages was watching birds of prey swoop through the skies. After the show, the falconers will invite you to visit the aviary.

👥 **La Légende des chevaliers** – ☎*01 64 60 26 26. www.provins.net. Closed late Aug–late Jun. Tickets and schedule at the Office de tourisme. 10.50€ (children 7.50€).* From within the rampart ditches, witness a jousting match featuring knights on horseback, battling with lances and swords, and on foot, fighting with studded flails and battleaxes.

SHOPPING

Gaufillier – *2 av. Victor-Garnier.* ☎*01 64 00 03 71. Closed Mon.* For over ten years, this chocolatier-confectioner-pastry chef has been pampering customers with rose-flavoured treats: jam, ice cream, sweets, fruit pastes, nougat, tea, caramels and syrup.

Rambouillet

The combination of an attractive château, park and forest makes Rambouillet one of the main sights in the Île-de-France. Since 1883 it has been the official summer residence of the President of the French Republic. Distinguished guests include Hosni Mubarak (Egypt, August 1998), Nelson Mandela (South Africa, July 1996), Boris Yeltsin (Russia, October 1995), George Bush (United States, July 1991) and Mikhail Gorbachev (USSR, October 1990).

CHÂTEAU

Guided tours (30min). ○*Open Wed–Mon 10am–noon, 2–5pm (Apr–Sept 6pm).* ○*Closed during presidential visits.* ○*5€; no charge first Sun in the month from Oct–May.* ☎*01 34 83 00 25. www.monuments-nationaux.fr.*

Leave from place de la Libération, the site of the town hall *(if the car park is full, leave the car in the park Château's park).* The château presents a triangular shape after Napoleon dismantled the left wing. The large round tower, where François I is believed to have died, belonged to the 14C fortress. It is difficult to distinguish

> ▶ **Population:** 25 661
> ⚲ **Michelin Local Map:** 311: G-4 or map 106 fold 28.
> 🛈 **Info:** Hôtel de Ville, pl. de la Libération, 78120 Rambouillet. ☎01 34 83 21 21. www.rambouillet-tourisme.fr.
> ◑ **Location:** 53km/33mi SW of Paris, via the A 13 and A 12. Access from Paris: SNCF rail link from Gare Montparnasse.
> 🅿 **Parking:** Near the château or on the place Jeanne d'Arc (charge).
> ◉ **Don't Miss:** Visit the deer observation points in the Forêt des Cerfs.
> 👥 **Kids:** Espace Rambouillet, shows. The toy train collection (Musée Rambolitrain).
> ◕ **Timing:** The château itself will not take more than an hour.

because of the numerous additions made by the Comte de Toulouse. The façades are essentially 19C.

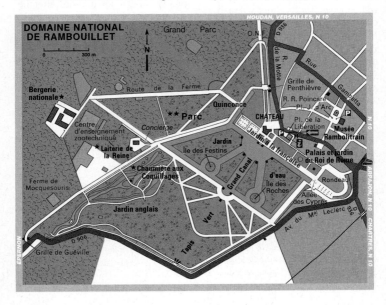

International meetings in Rambouillet

Let to various persons after the abdication of Charles X, Rambouillet Château came back into State ownership on the fall of the Second Empire. In 1897, it became one of the official country residences of the presidents of the Republic. De Gaulle organised hunting parties on the estate.

On the initiative of Valéry Giscard d'Estaing, the château was the venue of the first summit meeting of industrialised countries, which began as an informal get-together of six western heads of state. More recently, the Rambouillet conference of March 1999 attempted to find a solution to the Kosovo problem, unfortunately without success.

Mezzanine

The reception rooms commissioned by the Comte de Toulouse are embellished with superb Rococo **wainscoting★**. Note the charming boudoir designed for the Comte's wife.

The corridor adjoining the François I tower leads through to the Imperial bathroom suite, adorned with Pompeian frescoes. This opens onto the Emperor's Bedchamber, where he spent the night of 29 June 1815, and the study. It was in the dining room – the former ballroom – that Charles X signed the abdication document. The view of the park is stunning.

PARK★

&.❍*Open daily May–Sept 8am–7pm (Jun–Aug 7.30pm); Feb–Apr 8am–6pm; Nov–Jan 8am–5pm.* ✆*01 34 94 28 79.*

The château is set in a pleasant park, renowned for the variety of its gardens remodelled throughout the 17C and 18C, which reflect the evolution of taste during that period, from the formal parterres to the winding alleyways lined with exotic trees.

Jardin à la française

Walking back towards the château, one goes through the 'petit bosquet' (small copse), the 'miroir' (mirror) and the 'grand bosquet' (large copse) forming a French-style garden.

Quinconce

This quincunx, situated to the east of the château and created in 1710, comprises a group of lime trees from Holland planted according to a chequered pattern known as a 'quinconce'. In its centre stands *La Barque* solaire, a bronze sculpture by Karel, inaugurated in 1993.

Jardin à l'anglaise

In 1779, Hubert Robert designed an English-style garden beyond the green carpet of lawn. It is essentially planted with exotic species. The **Grotte des Amants** (Lovers' grotto) was named after a couple of lovers who took refuge inside during a thunderstorm. Canals crisscross the park, forming small islands: Île des Festins, Îles des Roches etc. 18C follies are scattered among the greenery.

Chaumière des Coquillages★

❍*Open same hours as château.* *Guided tours only (45min).* ✆*3€.* ✆*01 34 94 28 79. http://chaumiere-laiterie-rambouillet.monuments-nationaux.fr/en.*

The **landscape garden** in the park features a charming cottage built for the Princesse de Lamballe. The walls of the rooms are encrusted with a variety of sea shells, chips of marble and mother-of-pearl. A small boudoir with painted panelling adjoins the main room.

Laiterie de la Reine★

❍*Open same hours as château.* *Guided tours only (45min).* ✆*3€.* ✆*01 34 94 28 79. http://chaumiere-laiterie-rambouillet.monuments-nationaux.fr/en.*

Louis XVI had the Dairy built in 1785 to amuse his wife Marie-Antoinette. The small sandstone pavilion resembling a neo-Classical temple consists of two rooms. The first – which houses the actual dairy – features marble paving and a marble table from the First Empire.

The room at the back was designed as an artificial grotto adorned with luxuriant vegetation. It includes a marble composition by Pierre Julien depicting a nymph and the she-goat Amalthea (1787).

ADDITIONAL SIGHTS
Palais du Roi de Rome
◷*Open during exhibitions only: Wed–Sun 2–6pm.* ✆*01 30 88 77 77. www.rambouillet-tourisme.fr.*
This mansion was built in 1813 at the request of Napoleon who intended to give it to his son the king of Rome. It was only very briefly used before he left for Austria with his mother, Maria-Louise. The right-hand wing stages themed exhibitions.

Musée du Jeu de l'Oie
◷*Open Tue–Sun 2–6pm.* ✆*2.50€.* ✆*01 30 88 73 73. www.rambouillet-tourisme.fr*
The left-hand wing houses Pierre Dietsch's collection including 80 games of snakes and ladders from the 17C to the 20C.

Jardin
◷*Open daily 2–7pm.*
Laid out according to its original plan, this romantic garden covering 5 000sq m/ 5 980sq yd contains a stele erected in memory of the 'young king of Rome'.

♣♣ Musée Rambolitrain
4 place Jeanne-d'Arc. ◷*Open Wed–Sun 10am–noon, 2–5.30pm.* ◷*Closed 1 Jan, 25 Dec.* ✆*3.50€.* ✆*01 34 83 15 93. www.rambolitrain.com.*
An astounding collection of more than 4 000 toy trains and models explains the history of the railway from its early beginnings to the present day.

Bergerie Nationale★
&. ◷*Open Wed and Sat–Sun 2–5.30pm.* ◷*Closed 24 Dec–mid-Jan.* ✆*4.50€.* ✆*01 61 08 68 00. www.bergerie nationale.educagri.fr.*
In 1785, Louis XVI added Spanish merino sheep, Angora goats and Swiss cows to his experimental farm to produce wool. The sheep buildings were completed during the Second Empire.

Forêt de
Rambouillet★

This vast forest has some delightful footpaths for those who enjoy walking, as well as 60km/37mi of cycle tracks, 20 or more lakes with picturesque banks, and a number of villages with old houses.
The forest is home to a thriving game population.

A BIT OF HISTORY
Rambouillet is part of the ancient Yveline Forest, which in Gallo-Roman times stretched as far as the outskirts of Nogent-le-Roi, Houdan, Cernay-la-Ville and Etampes. A large part of it is now included in the Parc Naturel Régional de la Haute Vallée de Chevreuse.
Of the total 20 000ha/49 421 acres, 14 000ha/34 595 acres are State owned. They cover a clay plateau with an altitude

♻	**Michelin Local Map:** 312: A-4 to B-4 or map 106 fold 28.
🛈	**Info:** Hôtel de Ville, pl. de la Libération, 78120 Rambouillet. ✆01 34 83 21 21.
▶	**Location:** 53km/33mi southwest of the centre of Paris, Rambouillet is reached via the A 13 and A 12. Access from Paris: SNCF rail link from Gare Montparnasse.
♣♣	**Kids:** Espace Rambouillet.
◷	**Timing:** 1 day.

of between 110m/358ft and 180m/585ft, crisscrossed by sandy valleys. In the Middle Ages, wide-scale deforestation took place and the vast clearances now divide it into three main areas of woodland: St-Léger and Rambouillet itself, the most popular areas with tourists situated north of Rambouillet, and Yvelines to the south, which is rather more divided up into private estates.

Flora and fauna

The forest around Rambouillet is damper and has more rivers, lakes and ponds than the one at Fontainebleau. From time immemorial it has been particularly well stocked with game such as deer, roe-deer and wild boar – and it remains so today.

♟ VISIT

Espace Rambouillet

⏱*Open Feb–Nov daily 10am–6pm (call ahead for demonstration schedule).* ⌖*10€ (children 7€).* ☎*01 34 83 05 00. www.onf.fr/espaceramb. Visitors centre 500m/540yd SW of the Rambouillet-Clairefontaine road (D 27).*

This 250ha/625-acre wildlife park has been divided into various areas (binoculars are recommended):

Forêt des Cerfs, where observation hides provide a view of deer, stags, and wild oxen.

Forêt Sauvage, a 180ha/450-acre site in which the animals roam free.

Forêt des Aigles, with more than 100 birds of prey in aviaries. Free flight shows.

Coin des Fourmis, where young children can get acquainted with these industrious insects (ants).

HIKES AND TOURS

The **GR 1** trail runs through the forest from north to south between Montfort-l'Amaury and Rambouillet. The **GR 22** trail runs in a northwest/southwest direction from Gambaiseuil to St-Léger-en-Yvelines.

Rochers d'Angennes

8.5km/5.3mi from Rambouillet via D 936 then D 107. Leave from the parking area of the 'Zone de Silence des Rabières'. Walk 100m/110yd through the village up the steeper slope of the valley to find the right path leading to the summit.

🚶 Go past an arena-shaped shelf circled by boulders to reach the crest: **view** of the Guesle Valley and Angennes Lake,

bordered by bulrushes, reeds and other aquatic plants.

Balcon du Haut Planet★

12km/7.4mi from Rambouillet along D 936 to Carrefour du Haut-Planet, then turn right onto the unsurfaced road which crosses rough, hilly ground and leave your vehicle in the car park at La Croix Pater.

🚶 After passing the Blue Fountain spring on the right, the lane reaches a shaded terrace on the edge of the plateau, unfolding the most spectacular panorama of the whole massif: to the north, the **view** extends across the Vesgre Valley and the Château du Planet.

Étangs de Hollande

8km/5mi from Rambouillet along N 10 then D 191 to St-Hubert; leave the car near the Étang de St-Hubert. For information on regulations for fishing in the ponds, contact the Fédération des Yvelines pour la Pêche et la Protection du Milieu Aquatique, 19 r. du Docteur-Roux, 78520 Limay. ☎*01 34 77 58 90.*

🚶 *4hr there and back.*

The ponds were part of one of Vauban's projects to create reservoirs for Versailles' water requirements. A series of six ponds separated by paths was laid out near the **Étangs de Hollande**. Only the two end basins are filled with water. In summer, the ponds offer **swimming** and **fishing** facilities.

Head west out of St-Hubert, follow the Corbet forest track, cross the Villarceau alleyway, and walk to the Petites-Yvelines crossroads then the Malmaison

Hikers on the GR1 trail, Forêt de Rambouillet

D. Hée/MICHELIN

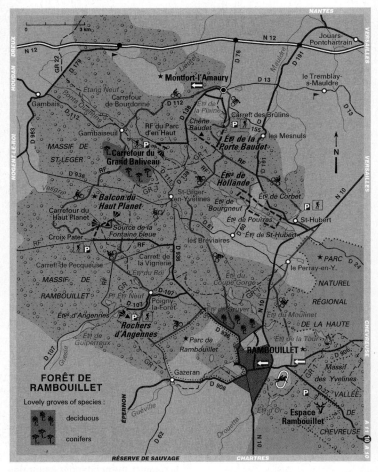

FORÊT DE
RAMBOUILLET

Lovely groves of species :

deciduous

conifers

crossroads. Turn left towards the Bourg-neuf crossroads and, to the southeast, the Route des Étangs which skirts the north shore of the **Bourgneuf** pond. Follow D 60 to the south shore of the **Corbet** pond. Walk past the sluice-gate which separates it from the **Pourras** pond and skirt the Pourras woods to Croix Vaudin. A path on the left runs through the woods to the Pont Napoléon; on the right lies the **St-Hubert** pond. This leads back to the Corbet forest track.

Carrefour du Grand Baliveau

8km/5mi from Montfort-l'Amaury via D 138. *At the crossroads, follow the path to the right of the panel marked 'Route forestière du Parc-d'en-Haut'. 30min there and back.*

The path offers a charming walk through a lovely green glade. One of the clearings affords a good **view★** of a secluded valley.

Étang de la Porte Baudet ou des Maurus

4km/2.5mi from Montfort by D 112 and D 13: go past the turning to Gambais (right) and turn left onto rue du Vert-Galant. Follow the plateau along the winding road.

Starting point: parking des Brûlins; 45min there and back.

This is one of the finest sites in the forest; farther on, Route Belsédène then Route Goron lead (1km/0.6mi) to Chêne Baudet, a splendid 550-year-old oak tree with an impressive girth.

La Roche-Guyon★

This village developed at the foot of an old stronghold; its crumbling keep still dominates the steep, rocky ledge. Life at La Roche-Guyon has resumed its peaceful character since the bombings of July 1944 and the Battle of Normandy, when Marshal Rommel established his headquarters in the castle.
The village has retained some of its cave dwellings and fine old houses.

A BIT OF HISTORY
The La Rochefoucauld estate
In the 13C, a residential château was erected at the foot of the cliff not far from the fortress; it was linked to the keep by a flight of steps carved in the rock. François I and his numerous retinue took up residence here in 1546. La Roche-Guyon was made a duchy peerage in 1621. In 1659, the title came into the hands of **François de La Rochefoucauld**, who wrote many of his famous *Maximes* at the château.

SIGHTS
The banks of the Seine★
The quayside promenade commands a good **view**★ of the sleepy countryside and the meandering river. Behind, the two castles stand side by side. The abutment pier of the former suspension bridge (dismantled in the 19C) provides a good observation point.

Château★
⊙*Open Mar–Oct 10am–6pm, Sat–Sun and public holidays 10am–7pm. Feb–Apr and Nov 10am–5pm.* ⊛*7.50€.* ℘*01 34 79 74 42. www.chateaudela rocheguyon.fr.*
The superb wrought-iron gates bearing the La Rochefoucauld crest open onto the courtyard and 18C stables, which now house the reception desk and temporary exhibitions. The house still has some 13C features, such as the towers flanking the main apartments. Built in the 16C, they stand on a terrace

- **Population:** 550
- **Michelin Local Map:** 305: A-6 or map 106 fold 2.
- **Info:** 8 rue du Général Leclerc, 95780 La Roche-Guyon. ℘01 34 79 70 55. www.larocheguyon.fr.
- **Location:** Between the Seine and the Vexin plateau, 80km/50mi west of Paris, via the A 13.
- **Parking:** Large free car park at west side of the village.
- **Don't Miss:** A visit to see the troglodyte caves along the Route des Crêtes.
- **Timing:** This tranquil village will consume more than the 1–2hr needed to see the château.

supported by arcaded foundations. The parapet walkway and 'southeast' tower provide some wonderful panoramic views of the Seine Valley. A newly restored corridor leads to the three chapels. The main one is dedicated to Our Lady of the Snows. During the German Occupation, numerous pillboxes were built into the cliffs. They now house a retrospective look at Rommel's stay at the château. The remainder of the buildings in the cliffs, including the orangery, are now used as the backdrop for a sound and light show on regional art, entitled **Parcours de lumière en Vallée de Seine**.

EXCURSIONS
Route des Crêtes★
Round trip of 4km/2.5mi.
Take the road to Gasny which passes the entrance to the famous troglodyte caves or stables called **boves**, carved in the chalk. On reaching the pass, turn right onto D 100, also known as *Route des Crêtes*. When the estates no longer conceal the view of the river, park the car on a belvedere near a spinney of pine trees.
There is a **view**★★ of the meander of the Seine carpeted with the trees of the

Château de La Roche-Guyon

Jacass/MICHELIN

Forêt de Moisson and, further along the promontory, of the spurs of the Haute-Isle cliffs. Note, in the foreground, down below, the truncated **keep** of the Château de La Roche-Guyon.

Continue along D 100. At the first junction, turn right onto Charrière des Bois, which leads back to the starting point. The road follows a steep downward slope and passes under the 18C aqueduct that supplies water to the village and the château.

Arboretum de La Roche
On D 37 towards Amenucourt.

The arboretum, which spreads over 12ha/29 acres, has been planted to reproduce the geography of the Île-de-France area. Each *département* is distinguished by a different species: oak for Seine-et-Marne, maple for Essonne, hornbeam for Val-de-Marne, ash for Val-d'Oise, cherry for Seine-Saint-Denis, lime for Les Hauts-de-Seine, and beech for

Yvelines. The plane trees in the middle represent Paris. They are all young trees, apart from the 20-year-old Lebanese cedar at the central roundabout.

Vétheuil
6km/3.7mi east along D 913.

This former wine-growing village has a lovely riverside setting on the steep banks of one of the Seine's meanders. The village houses – built with a fine pale-yellow stone – are characteristic of the French Vexin region. The small town was made famous by the Impressionists, in particular Claude Monet who lived here for three years.

Domaine de Villarceaux
10km/6.2mi NE. From Chaussy, follow D 71 towards Magny-en-Vexin. Follow signposted road 'La Comté'. A little further on the right, a new access road leads to a vast parking area. ☉*Open Apr–Aug Tue–Sun 2–5pm; Sept Wed and Sat–Sun 2–5pm. ℘01 53 85 72 10 or 01 34 67 74 33. http://www.iledefrance. fr/villarceaux.*

Villarceaux estate is graced by a magnificent setting and two châteaux: a 15C-16C manor house which belonged to the celebrated beauty Ninon de Lenclos, and a Louis XV château. Approaching the estate from the south, the road from Villers-en-Arthies offers a glimpse of a third edifice, the Château du Couvent surrounded by a golf course.

Prolonged by vast outbuildings forming a courtyard, the Manoir de Ninon replaced a former fortified house now reduced to the Tour St-Nicolas. Ninon's

The Duke and the young Romantic writers

In 1816 Louis-François Auguste, **Duc de Rohan-Chabot**, acquired the estate. He lost his wife in 1819 and took holy orders at the age of 31. Then he continued to entertain at the château, combining acts of charity with the fashionable manners of pre-Revolutionary France. Among the guests were fellow students at St-Sulpice Seminary and the young Romantic authors Victor Hugo, Alphonse de Lamartine, Hugues Lamennais, Henri Lacordaire and Father Dupanloup.

They delighted in the grand services celebrated in the underground chapel to the strains of a superb Italian organ. In 1829 the duke was appointed Archbishop of Besançon, and then Cardinal, and sold the château and its grounds to François de la Rochefoucauld-Liancourt. La Roche-Guyon has remained in this family ever since.

pavilion ends with a tower which houses a charming Italian closet and an intriguing hideout dimly lit by a loophole.
Gardens★ – These illustrate the evolution of gardens through the centuries. The former Renaissance terraces on the left of the entrance are overlooked by the unusual St-Nicolas Tower, known as

the 'tower of the condemned' because witches were hanged there. The tour of the large pond leads past Ninon's pool, supplied by an Italian waterfall, and reveals a **view★** of the south front of the Louis XV castle. he other façade of the 18C castle overlooks the open Vexin countryside

ADDRESSES

🏠 STAY

😊😊 **Prieuré Maïalen** – *4 allée du Jamburee, 78840 Moisson, 2km/1mi E of La Roche-Guyon via D 124.* ℘*01 34 79 37 20. www.prieuremaialen.com.* 📧. *5 rooms. Meal* 😊😊. In the heart of a village dear to Monet, here's an old 16C priory, entirely refurbished, where each bedroom has been carefully decorated. Large swimming pool and restaurant

🍽 EAT

😊😊 **Les Bords de Seine** – *21 r. du Dr-Duval, 95780 La Roche-Guyon.* ℘*01 30 98 32 52. www.bords-de-seine.fr. Reservations advisable.* This big house with blue shutters is very nicely situated along the Seine. Gourmet dining on traditional French country dishes, with a good selection of meat and fish. The sparkling clean rooms, the restaurant's maritime decor and the delightful terraces add up to a lovely stay. Children's menu available.

Abbaye de Royaumont★★

Royaumont Abbey is an impressive symbol of the wealth that often accrued to the great French abbeys of the Middle Ages. Founded in 1228 and completed in 1235, the abbey was occupied by members of the Cistercian order. Six of St Louis' relatives – three children, a brother and two grandsons – were buried in the abbey. Their remains have since been moved to St-Denis.
In 1793 Royaumont was sold as State property and the church dismantled. In 1964 the last owners Isabel and Henri Gouïn (1900–77) created the Royaumont Foundation for the Advancement of Human Science, to which they donated the estate.

VISIT

♿🕐*Open daily 10am–6pm (Nov–Feb 5.30pm).* 🚶 *Guided tours Sat, 2.30pm, 3.30pm, 4.30pm, Sun and public holidays 11.45am, 2.30pm, 3.45pm, 5pm*

- ♿ **Michelin Local Map:** 305: F-6 or map 106 fold 7.
- 🛈 **Info:** ℘01 30 35 59 91. www.royaumont.com.
- ▶ **Location:** Located 35.4km/22mi north of Paris, 27km/17mi from Paris CDG Airport and the Roissy TGV train station. The Abbey is easy to reach by the A1 and A16 autoroutes.
- 🕐 **Timing:** Allow yourself 1hr to tour the abbey.

(Nov–Feb 11.45am, 2.30pm, 3.30pm, 4.30pm). 😊6€ *(children 4.50€).*

Church ruins
♿*See plan.* Royaumont Church, consecrated in 1235, is, unlike traditional Cistercian churches, an unusually large edifice (101m/330ft long) in keeping with its royal origins. The chancel and its radiating chapels break with Cistercian tradition in that they have no flat east end. A corner turret (**1**) belonging

Abbaye de Royaumont

H. Champollion/ MICHELIN

to the former north transept gives an idea of its elevation (the keystone was 28m/91ft above ground).

Cloisters

These surround a garden. The west gallery *(opposite the entrance)* is paralleled, at the back, by a narrow, uncovered passageway. It was built for the lay brothers to have access to their wing and church without passing through the cloisters, habitually reserved for the monks.

Refectory

This spacious dining hall is a masterpiece of Gothic architecture. It could accommodate 60 monks without difficulty. St Louis would take his turn serving the monks at table while they sat in silence listening to the reader who stood in a pulpit carved out of the thick stone wall.

Former kitchen quarters

The kitchens house a statue of the Virgin of Royaumont (**2**), carved in the 14C. The strange building resting on 31 semicircular arches astride the canal is the **latrines and machinery building**. In former times, the water reached a higher level and activated the machinery in the workshops. One of the water wheels has remained intact.

Abbot's Residence (Palais Abbatial)

Built on the eve of the Revolution for the last commendatory abbot of Royaumont, this white cubic construction is reminiscent of an Italian villa. The façade facing the road to Chantilly is reflected in the waters of a charming pond.

ABBAYE DE ROYAUMONT

CHANTILLY
Abbey ★★
P
PARIS
0   200 m
0   100 m
CHURCH
Ruelle des Convers
Cloisters
Sacristy
Exhibition hall
ABBEY ★★
Canal
P
Former kitchen quarters
Medieval Garden
Hostelry
Latrines and machinery building
Refectory
Canal
Canal
Non-existant parts

Rueil-Malmaison★★

The town of Rueil is famed for Malmaison, the delightful estate that remains firmly attached to the name of Napoleon Bonaparte.

A BIT OF HISTORY

Malmaison during the Consulate

Marie-Joseph-Rose Tascher de la Pagerie, born in Martinique in 1763, the widow of Général de Beauharnais, married General **Bonaparte** in 1796. Three years later, while Napoleon was away on campaign, she bought Malmaison and the 260ha/640 acres surrounding the château.

When Napoleon was First Consul he lived at the Tuileries, which he found 'grand and boring'. He decided to spend the end of each 10-day 'week' at Malmaison. These were the happiest moments of his married life. Elegant, lively **Josephine** – she had 600 dresses and would change five or six times a day – was the life of the party at Malmaison. Life was carefree and formal protocol was dropped.

Malmaison in Imperial times

Crowned Emperor in 1804, **Napoleon** had no alternative but to stay at St-Cloud, Fontainebleau and the Tuileries, which were the official places of residence. Visits to Malmaison were too rare for the Empress' liking; she began to miss her splendid botanical and rose gardens, unparalleled in France. Josephine was a generous person with expensive tastes, who spent money unstintingly. When she ran into debt, her husband would complain bitterly but invariably give in.

Malmaison after the divorce

Josephine returned here after her divorce in 1809. Napoleon had given her Malmaison, the Élysée and a château near Évreux. She fled the estate in 1814, but the Allied powers persuaded her to return, entertaining the Russian Tsar and the King of Prussia. She caught cold while staying with her daughter Hort-

- ▶ **Population:** 76 700
- ⚲ **Michelin Local Map:** 311: J-2, map 101 folds 13, 14 or 106 fold 18
- ⓘ **Info:** 160 av. Paul-Doumer, 92500 Rueil-Malmaison. ℘01 47 32 35 75. www.rueil-tourisme.com.
- ▶ **Location:** On the edge of Paris, 15km/9mi from the centre, in a loop in the Seine. Take the N 13. **Access from Paris:** *RER line A 1.*
- ☺ **Don't Miss:** A walk in the forest.
- ◷ **Timing:** If you want to see all the museums you will need most of a day.

ense at the Château de St Leu and died on 29 May 1814, at the age of 51. The debts she left behind were estimated at 3 million francs.

The farewell to Malmaison

Ten months after Josephine's death, Napoleon escaped from Elba and revisited Malmaison. At the end of the Hundred Days he returned to the estate and stayed with Hortense, who had married Napoleon's brother, Louis, and was to give birth to Napoleon III. On 29 June 1815 the Emperor paid a last visit to the

Josephine's Chamber

©Massimo Listri/Corbis

château and his family before leaving for Rochefort and St Helena.

A succession of owners

After Josephine's death, the Château de Malmaison and its 726ha/1 800 acres of land passed to her son Prince Eugène, who died in 1824. The château changed hands several times until it was bought by Napoleon III for the sum of one million francs. The Emperor undertook to restore the architecture and interior decoration to its former glory.

By 1877 the château was in a sorry state and the grounds reduced to a mere 60ha/148 acres. Malmaison was sold as State property and saw yet another succession of owners. The last proprietor, a Mr Osiris, acquired the estate – by now reduced to 6ha/15 acres – in 1896, restored the château and gave it to the State in 1904.

The site of the Mausoleum of the Imperial Prince was bequeathed to Malmaison by Prince Victor-Napoleon. Mr and Mrs Edward Tuck, an American couple who owned Bois-Préau Château, also gave their residence and its 19ha/47-acre park, formerly part of Josephine's private gardens.

SIGHTS

Museum

○*Open Wed–Mon Apr–Sept 10am– 12.30pm, 1.30pm–5.45pm (Sat–Sun 6.15pm); Oct–Mar 10am–12.30pm, 1.30pm–5.15pm (Sat–Sun 5.45pm); last admission 45min before closing.* ☞*6€, 8€ during expositions; no charge first Sun in the month or students under 25.* ☏*01 41 29 05 55. www.chateau-malmaison.fr.*

When Josephine bought it in 1799, the **château**, built around 1622, featured the central block and two jutting pavilions dating from the 18C. The museum was founded in 1906. It houses many exhibits which were purchased, donated or taken from either Malmaison, St-Cloud and the Tuileries, or from other national palaces connected with the Imperial family.

Pavilions

The **Pavillon Osiris** contains all the collections that have been donated over the years: the works of art and Antique pieces belonging to Mr Osiris, a remarkable selection of snuff boxes, glass objects and caskets relating to the Napoleonic legend. The central area is dominated by Gérard's full-length portrait of Tsar Alexander I. The **Pavillon des Voitures** displays several Imperial carriages, including the landau that Blücher captured at Waterloo in June 1815.

Musée d'Histoire Locale

6 Avenue Paul-Vaillant-Couturier, inside the former town hall. ○*Open Mon–Sat 2.306pm.* ☏*01 47 32 66 50. www.rueil-tourisme.com.*

This museum, housed in the old town hall, offers an interesting overview of Rueil's history and of the town's main economic activities in the past: wine-growing, laundering. One room on the first floor is devoted to the Consulate and Empire periods (impressive collection of tin soldiers representing Napoleon's Grande Armée led by the Emperor himself). Another room illustrates the importance of Rueil at the beginning of the 20C (postcard-printing).

Musée des Gardes suisses

5 place du Mar.-Leclerc. ○*Open Sept–Jun Thu 2.30–6pm; by request on other days.* ☞*2€.* ☏*01 47 32 66 50.*

Documents, weapons, personal objects and uniforms illustrate the lifestyle of the Swiss guards stationed in the Rueil barracks over a period of 200 years.

ADDRESSES

⑪/ EAT

☺☺☺ **Le Bonheur de Chine** – *6 allée A.-Maillol.* ☏*01 47 49 88 88. www. bonheurdechine.com. Closed Mon.* The sculpted wooden façade and decorative fixtures shipped back from the Far East add to the ambiance. Everything here is extravagant, ranging from the marble reception area and its giant fish-tank to the dining halls and even the menu.

Château et Parc de
Thoiry★

Thoiry is a vast estate comprising a large Renaissance château and 250ha/ 625 acres of gardens and park. The family who has owned it for the past 400 years or more has undertaken a considerable amount of work to turn it into a magical spot where history and nature merge.

SIGHTS
Château

♿ 🕐 *Open Feb–mid-Nov daily, hours vary considerably. See website or call for details.* ☞*Combined tickets for château, gardens, labyrinthe, wildlife park, etc. 25€ (children 18€).* ✆ *01 34 87 53 76. www.thoiry.net.*

The 16C Renaissance château de Thoiry, which has remained in the La Panouse family for 16 generations, was built on a small hill by the Henri II's treasurer and alchemist Raoul Moreau, renowned for his passionate interest in alchemy and esoterics. It was he who had this 'solar house' built on a magnetic fault, to designs using the Golden Section. This outstanding position on a hilltop enables the château to act as a solar instrument, with spectacular sights such as the sunrise or sunset in line with the façade at the solstices.

The house is also a 'time machine', which has come down to us through the centuries and now gives an insight into an eventful history. The ancestors conversing from their picture frames in the portrait gallery, and the tales uncovered in the 50 trunks full of family archives, are all rather unconventional means of taking a look at history.

👥 Zoological Gardens

♿ 🕐*Open daily, hours vary. See website for details.* ☞*Combined tickets for château, gardens, labyrinth, wildlife park, etc. 25€ (children 18€).* ✆ *01 34 87 53 76. www.thoiry.net.*

▶ **Population:** 1 120
🚗 **Michelin Local Map:** 311: G-2. or map 106 folds 15, 16.
🖥 **Info:** www.thoiry.net.
📍 **Location:** 53km/33mi west of Paris. By car, take A 13 then A 12 to St-Quentin-en-Yvelines. Leave the motorway at the Bois d'Arcy exit towards Dreux and follow N 12 to Pontchartrain, then turn onto D 11 to Thoiry.
👥 **Kids:** All of it, but especially the African wildlife park.
🕐 **Timing:** Make a day of it.

The area of park adjacent to the château has been laid out as a zoo, with numerous special events. The most impressive section is the tiger enclosure which visitors cross on a concrete footbridge among the trees. It is also possible to see the animals from the glass tunnel in which only the armoured glass separates visitors from the claws and teeth of these wild beasts.

Various trails pass the elegant but fearsome black panthers, the emus and cassowaries, the mandrill island, and a tribe of lemurs running free. There are demonstrations of birds of prey in flight. The trees, too, speak to visitors about the natural environment. Do not miss the impressive Asian dragons (5m/16ft long) and become familiar with the ecosystem of European rivers (otters).

👥 Safari

♿ 🕐*See Château for details.*

The château's 1 200 acres are home to an African wildlife zoo, vast botanical gardens and forested trails. The château is richly decorated with antique furnishings, including a magnificent Gobelins tapestry. The wildlife park is visited by car only (windows closed) as the animals roam freely.

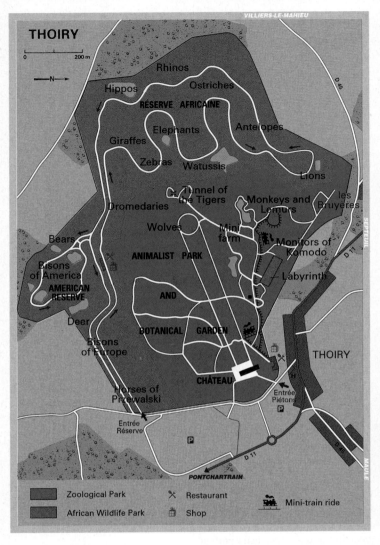

THOIRY

VILLIERS-LE-MAHIEU

0 —— 200 m

N →

Rhinos

Hippos

Ostriches

RÉSERVE AFRICAINE

Elephants

Antelopes

Giraffes

Zebras

Watussis

Lions

Tunnel of
the Tigers

Dromedaries

Monkeys and
Lemurs

les
Bruyères

Wolves

Mini
farm

Monitors of
Komodo

Bears

ANIMALIST PARK

Labyrinth

Bisons
of America

AMERICAN
RESERVE

AND

Deer

BOTANICAL   GARDEN

Bisons
of Europe

THOIRY

CHÂTEAU

Horses of
Przewalski

Entrée
Piétons
P

Entrée
Réserve

P

PONTCHARTRAIN

D 11

	Zoological Park	✕ Restaurant	Mini-train ride
	African Wildlife Park	🏠 Shop	

Allow an entire day to visit Thoiry. The park is so huge that many species of African, North American, and European wildlife are able to live together quite happily. There are over 1000 animals throughout the park. The road, which covers a distance of 10km/6mi, allows you to see antelopes, bison, giraffes, zebras, elephants, rhinos, hippos, and much more. A drive through two high-security enclosures provides a close-up view of lions and bears.

The botanical gardens can be visited on foot, and include a children's play area, a giant hedge labyrinth, petting zoo for children, a lake, and komodo dragon enclosure, the only one of its kind in France.

From February to October at 4.15pm, visitors can watch the zookeepers feed the tigers in the Tunnel des Tigres.

There are also regular events at the château and gardens, including summer and winter solstice festivals. A gift shop and self-service restaurant are also on site.

Château de Vaux-le-Vicomte★★★

This château, built by Fouquet, foreshadowed the splendour of Versailles and remains one of the greatest masterpieces of the 17C. A walk through the gardens laid out by Le Nôtre offers an unforgettable experience, as does a tour of the château by candlelight.

- ♿ **Michelin Local Map:** 312: F-4 or map 106 folds 45, 46
- 🈯 **Info:** ℘01 64 14 41 90. www.vaux-le-vicomte.com
- ▶ **Location:** 6km/3.7mi northeast of Melun, and 57km/36mi south of Paris via the D 51 and then A 5.
- 🅿 **Parking:** On site.
- 🕓 **Timing:** Allow half a day.

A BIT OF HISTORY

The rise of Nicolas Fouquet

Born to a family of magistrates, Fouquet became a member of the Parlement of Paris by the age of 20. He was made Procureur Général of this respectable assembly and was appointed Superintendent of Finances under Mazarin. Intoxicated with success, Fouquet chose a squirrel as his emblem – in Anjou patois *fouquet* means a squirrel – and decreed his motto would be *Quo non ascendam* (To what heights can I not rise?).

In 1656 Fouquet decided to grace his own seignory of Vaux with a château worthy of his social standing. He showed excellent taste when it came to choosing his future 'collaborators': the architect **Louis Le Vau**, the decorator **Charles Le Brun** and the landscape gardener **André Le Nôtre**. He was equally discerning in

other matters; the famous chef Vatel was hired as his majordomo and La Fontaine as close adviser.

The builders were given carte blanche. A total of 18 000 workers took part in the project, which involved the demolition of three villages. Le Brun created a tapestry works at Maincy to fulfil his commission. After Fouquet's fall it was moved to Paris, where it became the Manufacture Royale des Gobelins. The whole operation took five years to complete and the result was a masterpiece that Louis XIV wished to surpass with the construction of Versailles.

An invitation to royal vexation

On 17 August 1661 Fouquet organised a fête for the King and his court, who were staying at Fontainebleau. The reception was one of dazzling splen-

Château de Vaux-le-Vicomte

Julien Valle/Château de Vaux-le-Vicomte

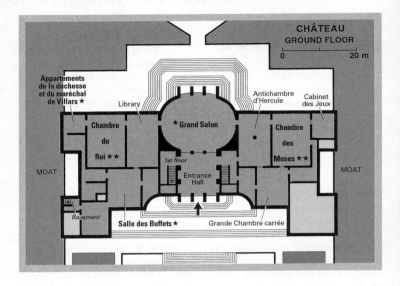

CHÂTEAU
GROUND FLOOR

0   20 m

Appartements
de la duchesse
et du maréchal
de Villars ★

Library

★ Grand Salon

Antichambre
d'Hercule

Cabinet
des Jeux

Chambre
du
Roi ★★

Chambre
des
Muses ★★

1st floor

MOAT

Entrance
Hall

MOAT

Basement

Salle des Buffets ★   Grande Chambre carrée

dour. The King's table featured a service in solid gold; this detail annoyed him intensely as his own tableware had been sent back to the smelting works to meet the expenses incurred by the Thirty Years' War.

After a banquet at which Vatel surpassed himself, the guests feasted their eyes on the garden entertainments, enhanced by 1 200 fountains and cascades. The programme included country ballets, concerts, aquatic tournaments and lottery games in which all the tickets won prizes. It also included the première of *Les Fâcheux*, a comedy ballet by Molière, performed by the author and his troupe against a delightful backdrop of greenery.

The King was vexed by such an extravagant display of pomp and luxury, unparalleled at his own royal court. His first impulse was to have Fouquet arrested immediately but Anne of Austria managed to dissuade him.

The fall of Nicolas Fouquet
Nineteen days later, the Superintendent of Finances was sent to jail and all his belongings sequestrated. The artists who had designed and built Vaux entered the King's service and were later to produce the Palace of Versailles. At the end of a three-year trial, Fouquet was banished from court, but this sentence was altered by the King to perpetual imprisonment.

It changed hands several times and survived the Revolution without suffering too much damage. In 1875, Vaux was bought by a wealthy industrialist Mr Sommier, who restored and refurnished the château and grounds.

VISIT
L'Écureuil Restaurant, a boutique, 4-seater electric cars and 'nautils' (animal-shaped boats to glide along the canal).

Château★★
🕐*Open mid-Mar–mid-Nov 10am–6pm; May–mid-Oct candlelight visit Sat 8pm–midnight (Jul and Aug Fri–Sat); mid-Dec–3 Jan 11am–6.30pm.* 🕐*Closed Wed except Jul–Aug.* ✆*14–16€; (gardens only 8€; candlelight visit 17–19€). ✆01 64 14 41 90. www.vaux-le-vicomte.com.*
The château stands on a terrace surrounded by a moat. The impressive approach leads towards the château's imposing northern front, with its tall windows indicating the *piano nobile* on a raised ground floor.
The first floor is occupied by the **suites of Mr and Mme Fouquet**.

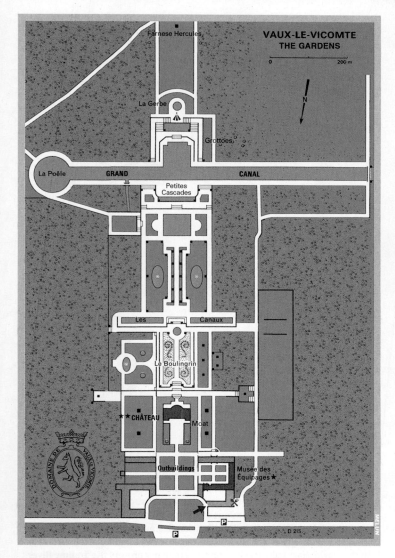

VAUX-LE-VICOMTE
THE GARDENS

Farnese Hercules

La Gerbe

Grottoes

La Poêle GRAND CANAL

Petites
Cascades

Les Canaux

Le Boulingrin

★★ CHÂTEAU Moat

Outbuildings Musée des
Équipages ★

P P P D 215

ADDRESSES

🏠 STAY 🍴 EAT

Labordière (Bed and Breakfast) –
*16 r. Grande, La Borde hamlet, 77820
Châtillon-la-Borde, 12km/7.4mi SE of Vaux-
le-Vicomte via D 215, D 47 and D 47E.
℘01 60 66 60 54. Closed Nov. 🚭. 2 rooms.
Meal ☺☺.* This smallholding dating
from 1850 adjoins the Borde town hall.
Enjoy the serenity of the large, leafy
garden and discover regional produce
fresh from the farms during your table

d'hôte meal. The bedrooms are somewhat old-fashioned; the largest has
a sloping roof.

☺☺ La Ferme du Couvent – *77720
Bréau, 14.5/8.8mi east of Vaux-le-Vicomte
via D 408 Rte de Provins & D 227. ℘01 64
38 75 15. www.lafermeducouvent.com. 🚭.
9 rooms.* A relaxing sojourn is guaranteed
in this 18C Briard farm set in a verdant
7ha/17-acre park. The rooms, with
sloping roofs, are all decorated with
creamy colours and modern furniture.
Tennis courts available.

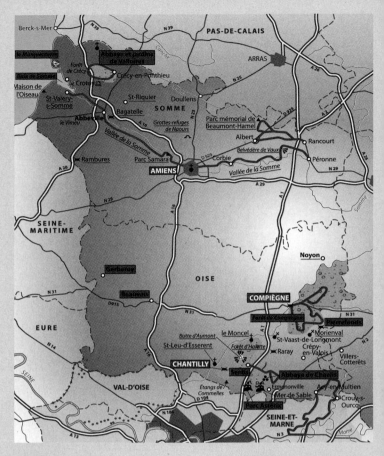

The Picardy region actually owes its names to its inhabitants who, back in the Middle Ages, where dubbed as "picards" (meaning "axe" or "pike" wielders) by their neighbours. Best known for being the cradle of Gothic architecture, Picardy still retains a wealth of medieval treasures such as the magnificent World Heritage cathedral of Amiens or the fortified town of Laon. A crossroad between Belgium, England and the Parisian Basin, the region was a strategic prize in many struggles and the setting of some decisive battles, the scars left by both World Wars still attesting to it, particularly around the Somme River Valley. Yet, the region's dynamic spirit and lively culture has always prevailed.

History

In earlier times Picardy included all of the Somme, northern Oise and Aisne, as well as the coastal Pas-de-Calais.

In the 5C, the region of Somme stood as frontier land between the Frankish Kingdom and the last remnant of Roman Gaul. Following defeat at the **Battle of Soissons** (486), the region was invaded by the Franks, and Soissons became the capital of the **Frankish Kingdom**.

In 843, Picardy was incorporated to the Kingdom of France, by effect of the **Treaty of Verdun**. Northern Picardy then became a possession of **Burgundy**, then a **Spanish territory**.

Up to the 17C, Picardy was a place of bloody battles and invasions, especially during the **Hundred Years War** (14C) and the **Thirty Years War** (17C). Only in 1667, with Louis XIV capturing Lille, did that situation change.

The two **World Wars** have left their marks on Picardy, an obvious strategic target for the invading German troops. Today, places like the battlefields of the Somme or the Chemin des Dames are much visited heritage sites.

Environment

Picardy includes three French *départements*: **Aisne**, **Oise** and **Somme**. It has a **temperate** climate and its northwestern coastline faces the English Channel. The estuary of the Somme River, known as the **Baie de Somme**, is one of Europe's largest stopover areas for **migrating water birds**, as well as a wintering and nesting area for many other species. About half of the Baie has been turned into a **natural preserve** and the place is a paradise for bird watchers, especially in the spring. Over a hundred

Highlights

1. Take to **Amiens'** picturesque water gardens by boat *(p303)*.
2. Follow the **Chemin des Dames**, a tribute to WW I soldiers *(p328)*.
3. Discover the amazing refuge-caves of **Naours** *(p353)*.
4. At lowtide on **Baie de Somme** natural preserve, try to spot a harbour seal basking in the sun *(p368)*.

harbour seals also live in the Baie, the largest colony in France.

To the south of the region, endless **plateaus** link up Picardy with the North of the Parisian Basin. Rich **agricultural grounds** are found there, as well as vast forests (Compiègne, Senlis).

Chalk plains and **cliffs** lie to the north of Picardy, while the northeast exhibits beautiful **farmland landscapes**.

Lying across the country like a scar, the **Oise River Valley** is the most important passageway of the region.

Economy

The region has a wealth of open plains cultures: peas and sugar beetroot, potatoes, endives and wheat. Over 70% of the regional territory is dedicated to **agriculture**. **Food processing** naturally plays an important role locally, with groups like Nestlé and Bonduelle.

Located halfway between Île-de-France and the heavy industry centres of the Nord-Pas-de-Calais, Picardy has developed a powerful **manufacturing industry**: plastics, rubber, glass (Saint-Gobain), metallurgy etc. It has also benefited from relocation of plants from the Parisian Basin that have become sources of regional employment in the automotive or chemical industry.

The region hosts **research centres**, well rated **universities** like the Technology University in Compiègne (UTC), and two Silicon Valley-like competitiveness plants. Its **road**, **railway** and **canal** networks have significantly densified over the years to transform Picardy into one of the best connected areas of Europe.

Abbeville

Abbeville (pronounced Abb'ville) is the capital of the Ponthieu region and stands on the edge of the River Somme, about 20km/12mi from the sea. In the 19C artists flocked to its medieval streets overlooked by the towers of the Collégiale St-Vulfran. Since WW II, the city has taken on a more modern aspect.

▶ **Population:** 24 567
⊙ **Michelin Local Map:** 301: E-7
ℹ **Info:** Office du tourisme d'Abbeville, 1 pl. Amiral-Courbet, 80100. ℘03 22 24 27 92. www.ot-abbeville.fr.

A BIT OF HISTORY
Medieval Conflicts
Abbeville (from the Latin *Abbatis Villa*) originally developed around the country house of the abbot of St-Riquier. From the 13C to the 15C, the town became the property of the English, the Burgundians and the French, depending on the outcome of the struggles for possession of the Somme Valley. It finally became French under Louis XI in the 15C.

SIGHTS
Collégiale St-Vulfran
1 pl. de l'Amiral-Courbet. ⊙*Open Apr–end Oct 10am–noon, 2–6pm (Sun, Mon & holidays 2–6pm). Rest of the year Sun 2–5pm.*
Celebrated by Victor Hugo, this collegiate church is a stunning example of the lavish Flamboyant Gothic style. Its construction began in 1488, but was interrupted in 1539 owing to lack of funds. As a result, the neo-Gothic chancel was not completed until the 17C.
Note the soaring twin towers, over 55m/180ft high. Harmoniously blending with the elegant **façade★**, the beautiful Renaissance panels of the **central doorway** are also quite remarkable. Take time

Collégiale St. Vulfran

S. Sauvignier/ MICHELIN

to admire the figures of the Evangelists framed by St Peter (*left*) and St Paul (*right*). Inside, the abstract stained-glass windows were designed by an American artist: William Epstein.

Musée Boucher-de-Perthes★
24 rue Gontier Patin. ⊙*Open daily except Tue, 2–6pm.* ⊙*Closed Jan 1, May 1, Jul 14, Nov 1, Dec 25.* ℘*03 22 24 08 49.* ⊗*1€.*
This museum spreads across three buildings: one of the oldest belfries in France (13C), the former Mint (15C), and a modern building at the back. Of particular interest, its **archaeology section** showcases the Boucher de Perthes prehistoric collections (including paleolithic and neolithic tools), a mammoth tooth discovered on Ault beach, and various Gallic, Gallo-Roman and Merovingian findings excavated around Abbeville. Medieval sculpture, ceramics and tapestries, paintings from the 16C to the 18C and 17C furniture from Picardy are also on exhibit. Do not miss a sculpture by French artist Camille Claudel (1864–1943) and a superb silver Virgin and Child (1568).

Église du St-Sépulcre
Place St-Sépulcre. ⊙*Open Apr–end Oct 10am–noon, 2–6pm (Sun, Mon & holidays 2–6pm). Rest of the year Sun Mon 2–5pm.*
Little remains of the original 15C building, as the church underwent extensive Flamboyant Gothic remodeling in the 19C, and was partially destroyed in 1940. Its outstanding contemporary **stained-glass windows★★** by Alfred Manessier (1911–1993), a major non-figurative painter, represent *The Passion* and the *Resurrection of Christ*.

SURROUNDS
Château de Bagatelle★

133 rte de Paris. Visit of the interior by guided tour only. Self-guided tour of the grounds. ⊗*8€ (combination ticket). For opening hours call the Abbeville Tourist Office.*

Restored in 2000, this elegant "Folly" was originally built c. 1740 as a country home for textile industrialist Abraham Van Robais. In spite of successive additions, it managed to keep harmonious proportions and a unity of style.

Interior – Reception rooms: Rococo decoration, 18C furniture, delicately paint-ed panelling. A graceful double staircase with a wrought-iron balustrade was ingeniously adapted to fit the hall, to give access to the low-ceilinged first-floor rooms.

Grounds★ – Beautiful **French garden** adorned with statues and **English-style park** containing a large collection of plants, including some rare species.

Monts de Caubert

5km/3mi west of Abbeville.

At the first sharp bend before a road junction, turn left onto the narrow road running along the crest of the rise. Some 1.5km/1mi farther on is a wayside cross

from which there is a good **view** over the Somme Valley, Abbeville and the plains of Ponthieu beyond.

The Vimeu Region

Between the River Somme and River Bresle, the Vimeu region of Picardy, gets its name from a tributary of the latter. It seems like an isolated plateau, grooved by green valleys with hedged meadows full of apple trees.

This farming country also contains many châteaux and villages hidden among the trees. Making locks and wrought-iron-work have been traditional occupations of the area since the 17C.

Musée des Industries du Vimeu

Friville-Escarbotin, 20km/12.4mi west of Abbeville. Place Adéodat Gilson, ○ *Open Mar–end Oct Tue and Wed 2.30–4.30pm (Sun 2.30–6.30pm).* ⊗*3.50€* ✆*03 22 26 42 37.*

This museum traces the history of small-scale metalwork: locksmithery, taps and fittings, ironmongery, ship chandlery etc. The ground floor displays 19C machines and reconstructed work-shops. Note the impressive display of padlocks, the smallest of which is made from a gold coin.

Albert

The town, which was originally called Ancre for the river which flows through it, was the seat of a marquess; the title was acquired in 1610 by Marie de Medici's favourite, Concino Concini. Following his tragic death in 1617, Louis XIII offered Ancre to Charles d'Albert, Duc de Luynes, who gave it his name. Albert was almost totally destroyed during the Battle of the Somme in 1916 and the Battle of Picardy in 1918 *(see Introduction: History)*. Today it is a well-planned, modern town boasting 250 Art Deco façades. Méaulte, a large suburb to the south, is the home of aircraft factories founded by Potez, but now run by Aérospatiale.

▶ **Population:** 10 065
🚗 **Michelin Local Map:** 301: I-8
ℹ **Info:** Office du tourisme d'Albert, 9 r. Gambetta, 80300. ✆03 22 75 16 42. www.ville-albert.fr.

SIGHTS
Musée des Abris 'Somme 1916'

○*Open daily Feb–mid Dec 9am–noon, 2–6pm (Jun–Sept 9am–6pm).* ○*Closed Jan 1 and Dec 25.* ⊗*5€* ✆*03 22 75 16 17.* *www.musee-somme-1916.org.*

A 13C underground tunnel turned into an air-raid shelter in 1938 houses a moving exhibition of wartime memorabilia illustrating the daily life of French, British and German soldiers, and the evolution of weaponry during WW I.

BATTLEFIELDS

Round trip of 34km/21mi – 1hr.
East and north of Albert, the **Poppy Route** (circuit du Souvenir) commemorates the British and South African soldiers under Douglas Haig who fell during the Allied attack in the summer of 1916 (Battle of the Somme). For more details, visit the Historial de la Grande Guerre in Péronne (*see PÉRONNE*).

Mémorial de Thiepval

Open daily Mar–end Oct 10am–6pm. Nov–end Feb 9am–5pm. Closed Christmas holidays. 03 22 75 60 47.
Overlooking the Ancre Valley, this triumphal arch is the largest and one of the most moving memorials to the missing from any war in which British soldiers have died. It was built in the village of Thiepval which was turned into an underground fortress by the Germans during the summer of 1916, and was besieged by the British for 116 days.

Parc-mémorial de Beaumont-Hamel★

Open daily May–end Oct 10am–6pm. Nov–end Apr 9am–5pm. Closed Christmas holidays. Guided tours in French and English. 03 22 76 70 86.
This wind-swept plateau was the site of a bloody battle fought by the Royal Newfoundland Regiment in July 1916, on the opening day of the Battle of the Somme. Topped by a bronze cariboo, the memorial includes a platform affording impressive **views** over the battlefield.

Mémorial de Pozières

The village of Pozières, which has a namesake in far away Queensland, was barring the way to Thiepval hill. Because of its strategical importance, it was taken by Australian and Canadian forces. The names of some 14 690 fallen men are engraved on the Australian memorial.

Mémorial de Longueval

Open Apr –mid-Oct, 10am–5.45pm. Rest of the year 10am–3.45pm. Closed Mon, mid-Nov–Feb & holidays. 03 22 85 02 17.
In July 1916, the Germans dropped shells containing tear gas on the South African positions who endured five days of fierce fighting to regain what was subsequently named "Devil's Wood." Out of the 3 153 men who engaged in combat, only 780 survived. The memorial and the museum commemorate South African soldiers who lost their lives during both World Wars.

Rancourt

Three war cemeteries (French, British and German) are located here. The sole and only memorial to French soldiers killed during the Battle of the Somme bears some 8 566 names.

Parc-mémorial de Beaumont-Hamel

©Band Photo/UPPA/Photoshot

Amiens★★

The historic capital of Picardy is an important communications centre and the setting for the largest Gothic cathedral in France. Rebuilt in the aftermath of the bombardments which devastated its core during the two World Wars, it still shelters the precious remains of its past in picturesque areas, its floating gardens right in the centre giving the city a special character. Amiens will also surprise you with its gastronomic specialities such as chocolate tiles, macaroons, savoury pancakes *(ficelles picardes)* and duck pâtés in pastry *(pâtés de canard en croûte)*.

A BIT OF HISTORY

In Gallo-Roman times Amiens was the capital of a Belgian tribe, the Ambiani. In the 4C the town was converted to Christianity by Firmin and his companions. In 1218 the Romanesque church on the site was destroyed by fire. Bishop Evrard de Fouilloy and the people of Amiens decided to build a replacement, something exceptional, worthy of sheltering the "head of John the Baptist," the precious relic, albeit a fragment, brought back in 1206 from the fourth crusade by Wallon de Sarton, canon of Picquigny.

Steely Assaults

The valleys of the River Somme and River Aisne were major obstacles to invaders from the north, and being the bridgehead, Amiens suffered many attacks. In 1918, during the Battle of Picardy, the town was attacked by Ludendorff and bombarded with 12 000 shells. It was set ablaze in 1940 during the Battle of the Somme. In 1944 its prison was the target of a dangerous aerial attack aimed at helping the imprisoned Resistance members to escape (Operation Jericho).

Local Heroes

Amiens' great legend is that of a Roman soldier who, passing near Amiens, sliced his cloak in two and gave half to a wretched beggar; he later became

- ▶ **Population:** 136 000
- **Michelin Local Map:** 301: G-8
- **Info:** Office de tourisme d'Amiens Métropole. 6 bis r. Dusevel, 80000. ℘03 22 71 60 50. www.amiens-tourisme.com.
- ▶ **Location:** The majority of the city's attractions sit on the south bank of the Somme River, some clustered around the cathedral, others a little farther west and southwest. Consider taking an art and history tour for an overview of the city *(see Addresses)*. Good shopping areas are rue du Hocquet and place du Don. Cross the River Somme to explore the Quartier St-Leu.
- **Parking:** There are several parking areas near the cathedral and on the perimeter roads enclosing the cathedral district.
- **Don't Miss:** The cathedral, of course, but also the marvellous Picardy Museum and the lovely Hortillonnages (gardens).
- **Timing:** Allow 1hr–2hr to see the cathedral. The walking tour requires 1hr, as does the Picardy Museum.
- **Kids:** Enjoy the Marionnette Theatre featuring puppet shows for children (*see Addresses).
- **Also See:** Corbie, the Parc Samara, and the Cité souterraine de Naours.

known as **Saint Martin**, patron saint of France. The city was also home to famous writers such as **Choderlos de Laclos** (1741–1803), **Jules Verne** (1828–1905), **Paul Bourget** (1852–1925), **Roland Dorgelès** (1885–1973), and to physicist **Edouard Branly** (1844–1940).

CATHÉDRALE NOTRE-DAME★★★

⊙Open daily Apr–end Sept 8.30am–6.30pm; Oct–Mar 8.30am–5.30pm.
☛Guided tours available. ⊛5.50€.
✆03 22 71 60 50.

A UNESCO World Heritage SIte, Amiens Cathedral is the largest Gothic building in France (145m/475ft long with vaults 42.5m/139ft high). Its plans were entrusted to **Robert de Luzarches** who was succeeded by Thomas de Cormont and then his son Renaud.

The cathedral was begun in 1220 and the speed with which it was built explains the remarkable unity of style, though the towers remained uncrowned until the beginning of the 15C.

Restored by Viollet-le-Duc in the 19C, the cathedral was miraculously unscathed after the bombardments which devastated the city in 1944.

Exterior

The superbly restored **west front** (👈 see illustration p77) of Amiens Cathedral is one of its most remarkable features. Note the three doorways; the **Kings' Gallery** supporting colossal effigies; the great Flamboyant rose-window (16C) framed by twinned open bays; and the small **Bell-ringers' Gallery** topped by light arcading between the towers. Elegant sculptures further enhance the ensemble.

The **central doorway** is framed by the Wise and Foolish Virgins who, together with the Apostles and the Prophets on the piers, escort from a respectable distance the famous **Beau Dieu**, a noble and serene Christ standing on lavender and basil. He is the focal point of this enormous carved Bible. The tympanum portrays the Last Judgment presided over by a more archaic and severe God.

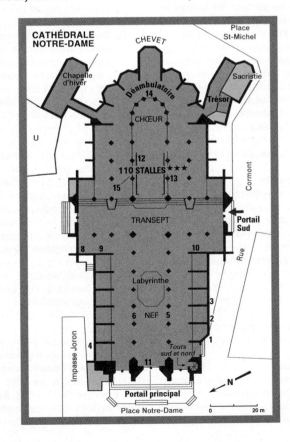

CATHÉDRALE NOTRE-DAME

CHEVET
Place St-Michel
Chapelle d'hiver
Déambulatoire
Sacristie
Trésor
14
CHŒUR
U
12
110 STALLES ★★★
13
15
Cormont
TRANSEPT
Portail Sud
8   9
10
Rue
Labyrinthe
3
6   NEF   5
2
Impasse Joron
4
1
Tours sud et nord
11
N
Portail principal
Place Notre-Dame
0   20 m

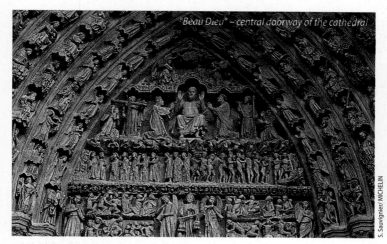
"Beau Dieu" – central doorway of the cathedral

S. Sauvignier/ MICHELIN

The **left doorway** is dedicated to **St Firmin**, the evangelist of Amiens and to the Picardy region. The quatrefoils on the base enclose representations of a **Calendar** symbolised by the signs of the Zodiac and the Labours of the Months. The **right doorway** is dedicated to the **Mother of God**.

▷ *Walk along impasse Voron.*

On the north side, note the statue of Charles V (**4**) on the 14th buttress supporting the tower.
Go round the cathedral to the right, passing a giant St Christopher (**1**), an Annunciation (**2**), and, between the 3rd and 4th chapels, a pair of woad merchants with their sack (**3**).

▷ *Follow rue Cormont to place St-Michel.*

From here there is a fine view of the **east end** with its pierced flying buttresses, and the soaring lead-covered chestnut **spire** (112.70m/370ft high).

▷ *Retrace your steps and enter the cathedral through the south doorway.*

The **south doorway**, known as the Golden Virgin Doorway because of the statue which used to adorn the pier, is dedicated to St Honoré who was bishop of Amiens. Visitors can mount the 307 steps to the top of the **north tower** *(via the South tower and Rose gallery)*, for a close up view of the spires and statuary atop the cathedral, and a wide-angle view of the city below.

Interior

The sheer size and the amount of light inside the cathedral are striking. The **nave** is the highest in France, reaching 42.50m/139ft. Its elevation consists of large and exceptionally high arcades surmounted by a band of finely detailed foliage, a blind triforium and a clerestory; 13C recumbent **bronze effigies**★ of the cathedral's founding bishops lie in the third bay: Evrard de Fouilloy (**5**) and Geoffroy d'Eu (**6**); the latter faces towards St-Saulve Chapel which contains a figure of Christ in a long gold robe.
In the center of the nave, note the striking black and white pattern of the **labyrinth**, a 19C replica of the original one, built in 1288 and damaged during the French Revolution. In medieval times, the faithful would follow its meandering lines on their knees, as a Way of the Cross. The **north transept** is adorned with a 14C rose-window with star-shaped central tracery. The font (**8**), to the left of the door, dates from 1180 and was originally used to wash the dead. On the west wall, a painted sculpture in four parts represents Christ and the money lenders in the Temple (**9**) (1520).

The **south transept**, which is illuminated through a Flamboyant rose-window, bears on its west wall four scenes in relief (**10**) portraying the conversion of the magician Hermogene by St James the Great (1511).

The perspective back down the nave reveals its elegance and the boldness of the organ loft supporting the **great organ (11)** (1442) with its delicate golden arabesques, crowned by the majestic rose-window at the west end.

The chancel is enclosed within a beautiful 18C choir screen, wrought by Jean Veyren. Stunning works of art, the 110 Flamboyant **stalls★★★ (12)** were created between 1508 and 1519 by the master cabinet-makers Arnould Boulin, Antoine Avernier and Alexandre Huet. They are arranged in two rows and surmounted by wooden tracery, and are presided over by two master-stalls destined for the king and the dean of the chapter. Over 4 000 figures realistically and spiritedly evoke Genesis and Exodus, the life of the Virgin Mary, and scenes of 16C life in Amiens. One worker carved himself holding his mallet and inscribed his name: Jehan Turpin.

In the **ambulatory** on the right, on the choir screen above two recumbent effigies, eight remarkable carved and coloured stone groups (1488) under delicate Gothic canopies evoke the life of **St Firmin (13)**, his martyrdom and his

---

Confrérie du Puy Notre-Dame

This literary and religious society devoted to the glorification of the Virgin Mary was founded in Amiens in 1389. The master of the brotherhood was elected on an annual basis and used to recite his "royal hymn" from a podium or *puy*. The refrain or *palinode* was unusual in that it was a play on words based on the name of the donor who from 1450 onwards was required to offer to the cathedral a votive painting referring to the theme of the *palinode*.

---

exhumation by St Saul three centuries later. The highly expressive figures are wearing 15C dress: the nobles in sumptuous attire, the humble poorly dressed and the executioner in curious breeches. Behind the main altar, facing the central chapel containing a 19C gilded statue of the Virgin Mary, are the tomb of Cardinal de la Grange (1402) and the much larger tomb of Canon Guislan Lucas, famous for its **Weeping Angel (14)**, carved by Nicolas Blasset in 1628 (the angel became a popular postcard for allied soldiers during World War I). In the apsidal chapels vestiges of the 13C stained-glass windows remain.

The choir screen north of the chancel bears scenes from the **life of St John (15)** (1531) *(read from right to left)*.

ꞈ WALKING TOUR

▶ *Start near the cathedral, and cross the river via the Dodane bridge.*

Quartier St-Leu★

Several arms of the Somme flow through this district, which has undergone widescale renovation in an effort to preserve its special charm. Craft and antique shops, trendy cafés and restaurants now occupy the spaces where tanners, millers, weavers and dyers once worked. A flea market takes place on the second Sunday of every month on place Parmentier.

From the bridge known as **Pont de la Dodane**, there is a fine **view** of the cathedral. A stroll through the streets (rue Bélu, rue des Majots, rue Motte, rue d'Engoulvent) lined with small colourful half-timbered houses gives a feel of the area's discreet charm.

Do not miss the **église-halle St-Leu**, a 15C hall-church with three aisles and a 16C Flamboyant Gothic bell-tower, and the nearby **Théâtre des Marionnettes** 👥👤 (🕭 *see Addresses*).

▶ *Return to place Notre-Dame and walk along the south side of the cathedral which is best viewed from the pedestrian street leading to place Aguesseau.*

Puppets

Famous for its string puppets dating back to about 1785, Amiens now boasts its own puppet theatre. Known in the Picardy dialect as *cabotans*, the puppets are about 50cm/19in in height, carved out of wood and operated from above. The king of St-Leu (a district that existed in medieval times) is **Lafleur**. He is the leader of the *cabotans* and is undoubtedly the most expressive embodiment of the spirit and character of the Picardy people.

Since the 19C, but arguably from an earlier date, this mythical, truculent, bold, irreverent, and brave character with a fiery temper has expressed plain common sense and described the nobility and pride of the province in the language of his ancestors. Wherever he is, wherever he comes from, and however far away he is, he is always recognisable for his impressive height, his characteristic gait, and most of all, his 18C valet's livery of beautiful red Amiens velvet. He is often accompanied by his wife Sandrine and his friend Tchot Blaise.
His motto is "Drink, eat and do nothing."

On the corner of the law courts, a low-relief sculpture by J. Samson (1830) depicts the story of St Martin's Cloak.

Maison du Sagittaire et Logis du Roi

The **Sagittarius House** (1593), with its Renaissance front, owes its name to the sign of the Zodiac embellishing its two arches. The adjacent **King's Lodging** (1565), featuring a pointed-arch door decorated with a Virgin with a Rose, is the seat of the **Rosati** of Picardy, a society with the motto "Tradition, Art and Literature."

Old Theatre

The Louis XVI façade was the work of Rousseau in 1780; the building now houses a bank. Three large windows are framed by elegant low-relief sculptures depicting garlands, medallions, muses and lyres.

Bailliage

The restored front is all that remains of the bailiff's residence built under François I in 1541, presenting mullioned windows, Flamboyant gables and Renaissance medallions. On the right, note the "fool" wearing a hood with bells.

Bell-tower

Guided tours available.
Call ℰ03 22 22 58 97 for more details.

Located on place au Fil, this enormous bell-tower consists of a square 15C base and an 18C belfry surmounted by a dome.

Looking down rue Chapeau-des-Violettes, you will see the **Église St-Germain**, built in Flamboyant Gothic style in the 15C, with its tower leans slightly.

On your way back to the cathedral, stop by the Dewailly clock and the statue of *Marie sans chemise*, a half-naked little nymph symbolising spring, carved by Albert Roze (1861–1952).

Hortillonnages★

Maison des Hortillonnages, 54 bd Beauvillé. ⚌⚌ ⊙Guided boat tours (45mn) Apr–end Sept daily 2pm onwards. ⚌ 5.50€. ⊙ Closed Jan 1, Nov 1 & 11, Dec 25. ℰ03 22 92 12 18.

Emblematic of Amiens, these "floating gardens" are exclusively accessible by boat. They are small vegetable gardens known as *aires* which have been cultivated since the Middle Ages by market gardeners or *hortillons* (from the Latin *hortus* meaning garden) who supplied the local population with fruits and vegetables. The gardens stretch over an area of 300ha/740 acres amid a network of canals or *rieux* fed by the many arms of the River Somme and River Arve. Today, fruit trees and flowers tend to replace

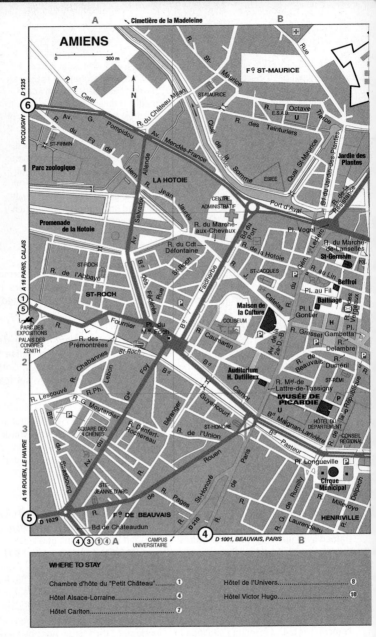

AMIENS

Cimetière de la Madeleine

0 ——— 300 m

N

WHERE TO STAY

Chambre d'hôte du "Petit Château".............①

Hôtel Alsace-Lorraine.................................④

Hôtel Carlton..⑦

Hôtel de l'Univers.......................................⑧

Hôtel Victor Hugo......................................⑩

vegetables while gardeners' huts are becoming weekend holiday homes. Note in your diary that a **water market** to which the *hortillons*, dressed in traditional costumes, come to sell their produce, is held every year on the third Sunday in June!

ADDITIONAL SIGHTS
Musée de Picardie★★

48 rue de la République.

♿ ⊶*Closed for restoration until Nov 2009, then will partially reopen.* ⊙*Open daily 10am–12.30pm, 2–6pm.* ⊙ *Closed Mon, Jan 1, May 1 and 8, Jul 14, Nov 1. and 11, Dec 25.* ⊷*5€ (no charge 1st Sun*

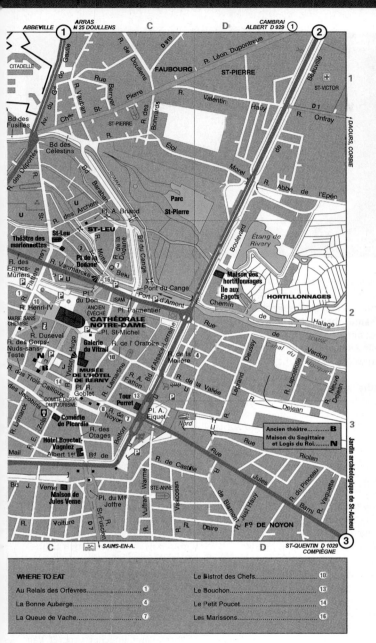

ABBEVILLE ① ARRAS N 25 DOULLENS

CAMBRAI ALBERT D 929 ① ②

CITADELLE

Bd des Fusillés

FAUBOURG ST-PIERRE

ST-VICTOR

Parc St-Pierre

Bd des Célestins

Théâtre des marionnettes

St-Leu

ST-LEU

Maison des hortillonnages

Île aux Fagots

HORTILLONNAGES

Étang de Rivery

Pt de la Douane

Pont du Cange

Port D'Amont

CATHÉDRALE NOTRE-DAME

Galerie du Vitrail

MUSÉE DE L'HÔTEL DE BERNY

Tour Perret

Comédie de Picardie

Hôtel Bouctel-Vagniez

Maison de Jules Verne

Ancien théâtre	**B**
Maison du Sagittaire et Logis du Roi	**N**

DE NOYON

ST-QUENTIN D 1029 COMPIÈGNE ③

WHERE TO EAT			
Au Relais des Orfèvres	①	Le Bistrot des Chefs	⑩
La Bonne Auberge	④	Le Bouchon	⑬
La Queue de Vache	⑦	Le Petit Poucet	⑭
		Les Marissons	⑯

in the month). ✆ 03 22 97 14 00.
The museum's significant collections of archaeology, medieval art and fine arts are housed in a Napoleon III building constructed between 1855 and 1867 for the Picardy Society of Antiquaries. Upon entering the central hall, visitors will not miss the rotunda and its a colour-ful mural (1992) created by American artist Sol LeWitt (1928–2007).

Archaeology
Lower level.
In addition to Egyptian and Greek antiquities, most of the collection is dedicated to regional prehistory and protohis-

Hortillonnages

Y. Tierny/MICHELIN

tory. It includes relics excavated from sites in and around Amiens. A gallo-roman section gives special emphasis to **Samarobriva** (Amiens), one of the most important cities of Belgian Gaul, while a smaller section illustrates the Merovingian period.

Medieval Art
Ground level.
This remarkable collection showcases 9C–13Cpieces of **religious statuary** which formerly adorned the Amiens cathedral and local churches and abbeys now disappeared. It also presents a variety of 14C religious statues along with finely ciseled medieval pieces made of ivory, enamel or silver. Finally, 15C and 16C examples of votive sculpture and funerary statuary from Picardy give an insight into the late Gothic period.

Fine Arts
Ground and upper levels.
The museum's collection of **sculptures** includes 17C and 18C classic and baroque pieces, as well 19C Romantic and Realist works. Note the beautiful *Christ Triumphant* by Nicolas Blasset (1600–1659) and the *Head of an Old Woman from Picardy* from another local artist: Albert Roze (1861–1952).
Painting definitely holds a place of choice in this museum. The Grand Salon contains huge historical paintings (18C–19C) by Van Loo and Vernet. Enor-

mous murals by **Puvis de Chavannes** (1824–1898) adorn the main stairway and first-floor rooms.

The Notre-Dame du Puy Gallery and part of the following room house the works of art of the **Confrérie du Puy Notre-Dame d'Amiens** (& *see sidebar p302*). You will recognise François I in the Renaissance panel (1518) entitled *Au juste poids, véritable balance* ("For just weight, true scales"), and Henri IV under the Gothic canopy bearing the poem entitled *Terre d'où prit la vérité naissance* ("Land where Truth was born") (1601). Take time to admire the remarkable *Virgin with Palm Tree* (1520), with Amiens Cathedral in the background.

The Nieuwerkerke Gallery presents 17C paintings from the Spanish School (Ribera and El Greco), the Dutch School (Frans Hals) and the French School (Simon Vouet).

Subsequent rooms exhibit 18C French painting including works by Oudry, Chardin, Fragonard and Quentin de La Tour, as well as the nine *Chasses en pays étrangers* ("Hunts in Foreign Lands") by Parrocel, Pater, Boucher, Lancret, Van Loo and De Troy for Louis XV's small apartments at Versailles. Italian masters (Guardi, Tiepolo) express the charm of Venetian painting.

The Charles-Dufour gallery is dedicated to 19C French landscape painters and in particular to the Barbizon School (Millet, Isabey, Corot, Rousseau). Modern art is represented by Balthus, Masson, Fautrier, Dubuffet, Picasso and Picabia.

Maison de Jules Verne

2 rue Charles Dubois &. ○*Open Mid Apr–Mid Oct Mon–Fri 10am–12.30pm, 2–6.30pm (Tue 2–6.30pm), Sat–Sun 11am–6.30pm. Rest of year daily (except Tue) 10am–12.30pm, 2–6pm (Sat–Sun 2–6pm).* ○*Closed Jan 1, May 1, Dec 25.* ◎*5€.* ☎*03 22 45 45 75.*

Jules Verne (1828–1905) was born in Nantes but spent much of his life in Amiens where he wrote masterpieces such as *Around the World in Eighty Days* and *Michel Strogoff*. He played an active part in local life and was a town councillor. With more than 20 000 documents and various personal effects, this house, where he lived from 1882 to 1900, provides a vast amount of information about the writer and his works. Do not miss the smallest room in the house, a replica of his study where he used to write his novels... Also take a look at the area dedicated to **Pierre-Jules Hetzel**, the famous editor who presented Jules Verne's books in magnificient, highly collectable cardboard bindings.

≗≗ Jardin archéologique de St-Acheul

10, rue Raymond Gourdain. &. ○*Open year-round 9am–12.30pm, 2pm–5pm. School spring and summer holidays 9am–noon, 2–7pm.* ○*Closed Jan 1, Dec 25.* ◎*No charge, but guided tour available by appointment 6€.* ☎*03 22 47 82 57.*

St-Acheul, one of the suburbs of Amiens, has, since 1872, given its name to a Palaeolithic period, the **Acheulian**. This is actually where sharpened tools were found for the first time along with the fossils of large, extinct animals. The garden of St-Acheul extends across a former gravel quarry in a pleasant rural setting which has not altered the character of the original site.

A long alleyway known as the **Fil du temps** (time line), dotted with panels, lists the most important dates in Man's evolution. It takes you on a journey back in time and space to 450 000 BC

and leads to the entrance of the garden where a **geological cross section** shows the successive layers of sediment accumulated since that time.

A footbridge leads to an **observation tower** (19m/62ft) revealing a **panoramic view** of the site, the Somme Valley and Amiens.

≗≗ Parc zoologique d'Amiens

139 r. du Fbg-de-Hem. ○*Open Apr–Sept 10am–6pm (Sun and holidays 10am–7pm). Oct–Mar Wed, Sat, Sun and holidays 2–5pm (Dec–Jan Sun 2–5pm).* ○*Closed Jan 1, Dec 24–25 and 31.* ◎*5€.* ☎*03 22 69 61 12.*

Bordering the Promenade de la Hotoie (18C) and its lake, the zoo was redesigned within a pleasant landscaped park crisscrossed by several arms of the River Selle, home to swans, pelicans and cranes. The zoo is committed to the protection of endangered species such as the red panda or the maned woolf, and not one of its 300 inmates was captured in its natural environment.

🚗 DRIVING TOURS

As a natural barrier, the **Somme River** was the site of numerous encounters and gave its name to two major battles, one in 1916, the other in 1940. Its source is upstream of St-Quentin, at an altitude of 97m/318ft; from there, it flows 245km/152mi westward.

The gentleness of this descent, together with the absorbent quality of the peat through which the river meanders, largely explains the lazy pace of its waters. They often burst their banks to spill into silvery ponds or dark peat bogs, and have formed the wide, lush **Somme Valley** in Picardy's chalky plateau.

The two following driving tours will introduce you to these restful landscapes.

From Amiens to Péronne

63km/38mi – about 1h 30min.

▷ *Take D 1 (east) out of Amiens.*

Look behind you for fine views of Amiens, dominated by its world-famous cathedral and by the 26-storeys of the **Perret Tower**, a symbol of the city's reconstruction after World War II.

▷ *At Daours, turn left at traffic light, then take a right towards La Neuville.*

The road passes through an area where watercress is grown, then rises up a hill. Nice **views** over the valley and Corbie with its imposing abbey church.

Corbie and La Neuville
♿ *See CORBIE*

▷ *From Corbie to Chipilly, follow the banks of the Somme River.*

The drive takes you through the middle of two landscapes : lakes and ponds, sometimes hidden in the fronds of forest ferns on one side, and steep cliffs on the other. **View** of the towers of Corbie in the horizon at certain bends in the road.

▷ *From Etinehem, follow D 1^F to Bray-sur-Somme.*

Bray-sur-Somme
With the nearby river, Somme Canal and neighboring ponds, this old port has a strong fishing tradition. Its lovely **church** is noteworthy, with its big square bell tower and Romanesque chancel. ⏱*Open daily (except Wed and Sun afternoon) 9.30am–5pm. Guided tours available upon request.* ✆*03 22 76 11 38.*

▷ *Take D 329 (south) until you reach Froissy, on the Somme Canal.*

Froissy
From this hamlet, visitors can ride to Dompierre *(7km/4.3mi)* aboard the **P'tit train de la Haute Somme** which used to supply the trenches during the World War I. Froissy's old covered market houses the **musée des Chemins de fer militaires et industriels** which showcases an interesting collection of renovated

locomotives and wagons. 👥 ⏱*For museum's opening hours and train timetable (mainly operates Jul–Aug daily except Mon, and May, Jun and Sept on Sun), check* www.appeva.org *or call* ✆*03 22 83 11 89.* ⊚*9€ (museum and train ride).*

▷ *Drive back to Bray-sur-Somme, then take D 1 towards Cappy.*

Cappy
This former river port is now an attractive marina. The 12C Romanesque **Église St-Nicolas**, remodelled in the 16C, has a massive square tower surmounted by a turreted steeple.

▷ *Take the road to Éclusier-Vaux, on your left. It crosses the Somme River and the village of Vaux, then winds up towards the plateau.*

Belvédère de Vaux★
This platform along the road is a good place to enjoy the **panorama★** over the meanders of the River Curlu and the red rooftops of the hamlet of Vaux. On a clear day, you will see Péronne in the distance.

▷ *Upon entering the village of Maricourt, take a right onto D 938.*

As you drive along the plateau, you will see the valley below. The road crosses the motorway, passing the **Étangs de la Haute-Somme** near **Cléry**, then crosses the Canal du Nord before reaching **Péronne**.

From Amiens to Abbeville
58km/36mi – about 3hr

▷ *Leave Amiens on N 235 (west) toward Picquigny. Follow the road parallel to the Paris-Calais railway line.*

Ailly-sur-Somme
This market town is overlooked by the sober lines of its modern church whose unusual design comprises a great slanting roof like the sail of a boat.

▶ *Cross to the north bank of the Somme River and turn left toward La Chaussée-Tirancourt.*

Parc Samara★

♛☨ ⊙*Open Mar–end Jun and Sep–end Oct 9.30am–5.30pm (Sat–Sun 6pm). Jul–Aug 10am–6.30pm.* ⊙ *Closed Nov–Mar.* ⊛*7–9€ depending on the package.* ℘*03 22 51 82 83. www.samara.fr.*

This park (25ha/62 acres) lies at the foot of a Celtic settlement overlooking the River Somme (known as the Samara in the days of the Gauls). Footpaths lead to an **arboretum**, a **botanical garden**, the marshes at the bottom of the valley and **reconstructions** of dwellings from the Neolithic, Bronze and Iron Ages.

The working of flint, wood and pottery is brought to life by **demonstrations** of prehistoric techniques, while various ecosystems such as the peat bog are cultivated and explained.

Daily life in Picardy from the Palaeolithic era to the Gallo-Roman period is evoked in the **Exhibition Pavilion.**

Follow the path leading to the Chaussée-Tirancourt's **Roman Oppidum**. From this vantage point, you will enjoy a nice **view** over the Somme Valley.

▶ *Take D 3 (north-west) out of Picquigny.*

Hangest-sur-Somme

Guided tours daily (except Sat–Sun) by request at town hall. ℘*03 22 51 12 37.*
The village specialises in growing watercress. Its 12C–16C **church** contains 18C furniture from the Abbaye du Gard. In 1940 the German 7th Tank Division commanded by **Rommel** crossed the River Somme between Hangest and **Condé-Folie** (large French military cemetery using the only railway bridge that had not been blown up.

Longpré-les-Corps-Saints

The town derives its name from the relics which the **church** founder, Aléaume de Fontaine, sent from Constantinople during the Crusades.

▶ *1km/0.5mi beyond Longpré, turn right at Le Catelet onto D 32 toward Long.*

The road crosses the floor of the valley, dotted here with ponds, offering a lovely view of the Château de Long.

Long

The great Gothic **church** in this pretty hillside village was rebuilt in the 19C, but retained its original 16C spire. Nice Cavaillé-Coll organ inside.

The elegant Louis XV **château** (⊶ *not open to the public*) has a slate mansard roof and red brick and white stone. Note the unusual, rounded wings and the graceful openings surmounted by keystones carved with masks and other ornamentation.

▶ *Cross the Somme River and follow D 3.*

Église de Liercourt

The charming **church** of Flamboyant Gothic style, with its gable tower, stands just before the village. The fine basket-handled doorway is surmounted by the arms of France and a recess containing a statue of Saint Riquier.

▶ *Turn right onto D 901, crossing the Paris-Calais railway line.*

Château de Pont-Remy

This château was built on an island near Pont-Remy in the 15C, but it was rebuilt in 1837 in the Gothic Troubadour style. It has a fine landscaped park.

▶ *Return to D 3.*

The road runs along the bottom of the hillside, skirting ponds and meadows, and approaches the Monts de Caubert.

▶ *Turn right to Abbeville.*

Abbeville
♿*See ABBEVILLE*

ADDRESSES

🛏 STAY

Hôtel Alsace-Lorraine – *18 r. de la Morlière. ℘03 22 91 35 71. 14 rooms. ⊡7€.* This comfortable, likeable little hotel hides behind an imposing carriage entrance a five-minute walk from the town centre and train station. Bedrooms, brightened with colourful fabrics, give onto the charming inner courtyard.

Hôtel Victor Hugo – *2 r. de l'Oratoire. ℘03 22 91 57 91. www.hotel-a-amiens.com. 10 rooms. ⊡6€.* Small family hotel a stone's throw away from the Gothic cathedral and its famous Crying Angel. Lovely wooden staircase leads up to simple and well-kept rooms.

Chambre d'hôte Le Petit Château – *2 r. Grimaux, Dury. 6km/3.6mi S of Amiens via N 1 dir. Beauvais. ℘03 22 95 29 52. www.le-petit-chateau.fr. 4 rooms.* In the countryside, 10min from central Amiens, a massive 19C residence whose comfortable guest rooms are housed in an outbuilding. The owner is happy to show his collection of old automobiles.

Grand Hôtel de l'Univers – *2 r. Noyon. ℘03 22 91 52 51. www.hotel univers-amiens.com. 41 rooms. ⊡11€.* A period building with a renovated façade situated along a busy road. Smart entrance hall and fine glass-roofed stairwell leading to comfortable rooms.

Le Saint-Louis – *24 r. des Otages. ℘03 22 91 76 03. www.le-saintlouis.com. 15 rooms. ⊡8€. Restaurant ⊜⊜.* A warm welcome awaits you in this charming establishment on the town's doorstep. Very well-kept, cosy rooms. An attractive pastel colour scheme adorns the bright dining room serving traditional cuisine.

All Seasons Cathédrale – *17 pl. au Feurre. ℘03 22 22 00 20. www.allseasons.com. 47 rooms.* This hotel is set in a magnificent, town centre, 18C post house. It offers recently spruced up, well-appointed rooms, some of which are ideal for families.

Hôtel Carlton – *42 r. de Noyon. ℘03 22 97 72 22. www.lecarlton.fr. 24 rooms. ⊡8.50€.* Behind the attractive 19C façade, discover a modern, plush interior. Every room features waxed furniture and murals. Their simple restaurant, Le Bistrot, serves grilled meats.

🍴 EAT

La Queue de Vache – *51 quai Bélu. ℘03 22 91 38 91. Closed Mon. ⊡7.50/15.80€.* On the ground floor, a convivial wine bar with a few tables. Upstairs, the cosy dining room, hung with old posters and advertisements, features a fireplace for winter warmth. Terrace overlooking the Somme. Simple fare. Jazz concert on the first Tuesday of every month.

Le Bouchon – *10 r. Alexandre Fatton. ℘03 22 92 14 32. www.lebouchon.fr. Closed Sun eve.* A Parisian-style bistro near the railway station specialising in typically Lyonnais dishes and traditional cuisine of the region; a relaxed, "no fuss" atmosphere.

Le Petit Poucet – *52 r. des Trois-Cailloux. ℘03 22 91 42 32. Closed Mon.* This attractive establishment is very popular with the people of Amiens who come for a slice of quiche, a *ficelle picarde* (baked crepes, stuffed and rolled), or a mixed salad for lunch, a delectable chocolate for tea, or a box of divine pastries to enjoy at home.

Au Relais des Orfèvres – *14 r. des Orfèvres. ℘03 22 92 36 01. Closed 10 –31 Aug, Feb holidays, Sat lunch, Sun and Mon.* Take a seat in this attractive blue, modern dining room, to enjoy reasonably-priced, up-to-date cuisine, after visiting the magnificent cathedral.

La Bonne Auberge – *63 rte Nationale, 80480 Dury. ℘03 22 95 03 33. Closed Jul 12–Aug 11, Sun dinner, Mon and Tue.* The smart regional façade is covered with flowers in summer. In the recently decorated dining room you will be offered contemporary cuisine.

Le Bistrot des Chefs – *12 r. Flatters. ℘03 22 92 75 46. Closed 16 Apr– 2 May, 6–21 Aug, 24 Dec–6 Jan Sun and Mon.* Chefs' jackets, kitchen utensils and menus hang on the walls of this contemporary bistro: the pleasant décor celebrates the art of cooking. Look at the boards for a selection of dishes.

🍽🍽🍽 **Les Marissons** – *Pont de la Dodane, Quartier St.-Leu.* 📞*03 22 92 96 66. www.les-marissons.fr. Closed Wed & Sat for lunch and Sun.* The place to be in the Saint-Leu quarter is this old marine workshop transformed into a restaurant. The flowery mini-garden becomes a terrace in summer, while in winter diners sit under the sloping wooden frame in a pleasant décor of handsome beams and round tables.

GUIDED TOURS

City Tours – Contact the tourist office at 📞*03 22 71 60 50* for guided tours of Amiens (in French) several times daily.

Barge Tours – 📞*03 22 76 12 12.* Explore the canals of St-Leu in traditional style. Depart from chemin du port Cappy.

🎭 NIGHTLIFE

After dark, the Quai Belu canalside area in the St-Leu quarter is the place for pubs, discos and nightlife.

Texas Café – *13 r. des Francs-Mûriers, Quartier St.-Leu.* 📞*03 22 72 19 79.* This enormous Confederate-themed 'saloon' of brick and wood is always crowded and popular. Before midnight, drink beer and cocktails), dance and sing karaoke). After midnight, it's a disco and dance venue.

🎭 SHOWTIME AND ART

"The cathedral in living colour" – 📞*03 22 22 58 90. www.amiens.fr/ decouvrir/cathedrale.* The artist Skertzò uses lighting to highlight the colourful entrance on the cathedral's west side. The presentation is held mid-Jun–Sept at dusk, and from during December at 7pm. Commentary in French and then English.

Comédie de Picardie – *62 r. des Jacobins.* 📞*03 22 22 20 20. www. comdepic.com.* This venerable old manor, entirely restored, houses a very pretty 400-seat theatre. The region's creative and dramatic hub, it produces 15 different shows for a total of 250 performances per season.

Maison de la Culture d'Amiens – *pl. Léon-Gontier.* 📞*03 22 97 79 79. www.maisondelaculture-amiens.com.* Two halls (1 070 and 300 seats), a movie theatre devoted to art and experimental films and two exhibition rooms. This complex offers an unusually interesting and eclectic selection of events.

🎭 Théâtre de Marionnettes – *Chés Cabotans d'Amiens, 31 r. Édouard-David, quartier St-Leu.* 📞*03 22 22 30 90. www.ches-cabotans-damiens.com.* This fascinating family-orientated show, established in 1933, takes place in a veritable miniature theatre with a beautifully designed set. The puppets all have their own history and language (French or Picard) plus remarkably expressive faces that can also be admired in the ground-floor exhibition.

🛒 SHOPPING

Atelier de Jean-Pierre Facquier – *67 r. du Don.* 📞*03 22 92 49 52.* Transforming them into traditional and invented wooden Picardy puppets, Monsieur Facquier carves life into pieces of wood before your eyes. Madame Facquier sews their clothes using fabric chosen with care. Each unique character is a genuine work of art.

Jean Trogneux – *1 r. Delambre & 2nd branch at Parvis de la Cathédrale.* 📞*03 22 71 17 17. www.trogneux.fr.* The city's speciality since the 16C, the Amiens macaroon, with its blend of almonds and honey, is ever popular. The Trogneux family, confectioners and chocolatiers for five generations, sell more than two million of them every year! The shop also carries a nice selection of local products.

Marché des Hortillons – The local market gardeners, who grow their produce in canal-bordered wetlands *(hortillonnages)*, come to market Saturday mornings at **Place Parmentier**. Once a year, on 3rd Sunday in June, a market is held as in years gone by: the gardeners, wearing traditional attire, come in flat-bottomed punts and unload their produce onto the docks.

Parc Astérix★★

Astérix the Gaul, comical hero of the famous cartoon strip by Goscinny and Uderzo known throughout the world and translated into several languages, provides the theme for this 50ha/123 acre fun park which opened in 1989. It is a fantasy world for all ages that offers a madcap journey into the past. The Gauls, and in particular Astérix's friends, the mighty Obelix who follows him everywhere, Panoramix (Getafix) who prepares magic potions, Assurancetourix (Cacofonix) the bard and Abraracourcix (Vitalstatistix) the chief of the tribe are the heroes, but beware the Romans are never very far away!

👥 VISIT

🕐 Open Apr–end Aug daily 10am–6pm, Sep–Oct Sat–Sun, and Christmas holidays season. Rest of the year, opening hours vary. 💶39€ (under-11 29€, child under-3 free). 📞0826 30 10 40 (0.15€/min). www.parcasterix.fr.

The park is basically divided into five "historical" sections, complete with various attractions, shows, and a choice of snacks and meals. To explore this enchanting world, start at **Via Antiqua**, a "street" lined with stalls symbolising Asterix's journeys across Europe.

Gaul

At the very heart of the park, Astérix's **Village Gaulois★** consists of huts where visitors can meet the little hero and his fellow characters. A tour of the **Forêt des Druides** will attract young and not-so-young visitors alike. Nearby, the atmosphere is much damper at the **Grand Splatch★**. But perhaps the most popular site is a Stone Age village built on piles, where an ingenious delivery system called **Menhir Express★★** takes anybody who dares on a trip through a network of canals bristling with surprises! You will also love the ride known as the **Trace du Hourra★★★** aboard a small train racing along a bobsleigh track at 60kph/37mph.

🎯 **Michelin Local Map:** 312: G-6 or map 106 fold 9. 30km/18.6mi north of Paris.

▶ **Location:** By **car**: 30min from central Paris on autoroute A1; by **Métro/RER** train: line B3 from Châtelet or Gare du Nord stations (alight at Roissy-Charles de Gaulle 1 station); by **coach**: from Roissy coach station with Courriers Île-de-France (CIF; www.cif-bus.com).

👥 **Kids:** Camp de Petitbonum, La Ronde des Rondins, Les Petits Drakkars, La Forêt des Druides, Au Pied du Grand Huit, La Petite Tempête, Les Petits Chars Tamponneurs.

Roman Empire

In the arena, witness a charming young Gallic spy become the heroine of acrobatic fights in a show called **La Légion recrute★★**. Now you are inspired, and you want to find out what is going on in the Gallic village? Then, join the **Espions de César★** who have devised a very efficient surveillance system above ground level. And if you are really serious about a spy career, go through intensive spy training and meet the four challenges of the **Défi de César**. Unless you prefer to brave a tumultuous river on board buoys. In this case, the **Romus et Rapidus** attraction is definitely the one for you...

Greece

The entrance to this part of the park is marked by the colonnade from the Temple of Zeus. The **Vol d'Icare** (Icarus' flight) takes you out of Daedalus' labyrinth, but you still have to defeat the terrible **Hydre de Lerne**. Now that you are safe and sound, you may want to embark on a daring journey aboard a giant roller coaster called **Tonnerre de Zeus★★**, with the angry god watching you from atop Mount Olympus! After so much action, relax and enjoy a wonderful **spectacle of dolphins**★★ at the Theatre of Poséidon or a trip down the **Elis River**.

Vikings

The hiighlights of this section of the park include **Goudurix**★★, a gigantic roller coaster taking visitors through a succession of vertiginous drops, swooping round corners, and going into spins and loops, all at breathtaking speed; **La Galère**, a funny swing in the shape of a boat; and for your little ones, **Les Petits Drakkars** (boats slipping on water) and **Les Petites Chaises Volantes** (flying chairs).

Across Time

A long journey in time takes place along **Avenue de Paris**★★. Ten centuries of history are illustrated here, each period represented by people in costume, typical shops and the avenue's own special atmosphere. The Middle Ages live again with street entertainers and **artisans**★ working in dark, mysterious streets. Going on holiday has not always been plain sailing as you can see from the

numerous adventures to be encountered along the **Nationale 7** main road to the south of France.

However, it may not be necessary to leave for the country as the **Oxygénarium**★★ has been specially designed to offer city dwellers the combined benefits of water and fresh mountain air: guaranteed thrills!

This trip through time ends in 1930, in **Main basse sur la Joconde**★★, a splendid enactment of a historical detective story during which a gang of thieves attempts to steal the *Mona Lisa*.

ADDRESSES

🖾 STAY

⊖🏠🏠🏠 **Hôtel des Trois Hiboux** – *Parc Astérix, 60128 Plailly. 96 rooms. Restaurant ⊖🏠. ℘03 44 62 68 00.* According to legend, each of the three forests surrounding the amusement park used to be the territory of one owl (hibou). Perhaps you'll fall asleep to the lullaby of their songs in one of the cosy bedrooms of this hotel where they are said to convene. Sweet dreams!

Beauvais★★

At the heart of the hills of Beauvaisis, the capital of the Oise region is a dynamic, entrepreneurial town, shaped by the likes of fashion designer Givenchy, aviator Marcel Dassault and Jean-Claude Decaux, king of urban property. Beauvais' cultural heritage, which reflects the richness of its past, survived the terrible bombardments of World War II, as attested by its magnificent cathedral, an architectural masterpiece almost defying the laws of gravity.

A BIT OF HISTORY

Bishops and Burghers

Beauvais, the capital of the Belgian tribe the **Bellovaci**, became a Gallo-Roman city enclosed within walls during the 3C.

▶ **Population:** 59 003
🜨 **Michelin Local Map:** 305: D-4
🚩 **Info:** Office du tourisme de Beauvais, 1 r. Beauregard, 60000. ℘03 44 15 30 30. www.beauvaistourisme.fr.

From the 11C the city had as its lord a bishop, who was often in conflict with the town's wealthy merchants and jealous of their franchises.

One of the bishops, **Pierre Cauchon**, has a dubious claim to fame: while the town wanted to surrender to Charles VII, Cauchon rallied to the English. Chased out of Beauvais in 1429 by the burghers, he took refuge in Rouen where, on 30 May 1431, he sent **Joan of Arc** to the stake.

Jeanne Hachette

On 27 June 1472, Beauvais was besieged by Charles the Bold, Duke of Burgundy, who was marching on Paris with 80 000 men. The town had no troops so men and women ran to the ramparts and watched in horror as ladders were laid against the fortifications.

Jeanne Laîné, the daughter of a humble craftsman, saw an assailant appear at the top of the wall, a standard in hand. She threw herself on him, tore away his banner and struck him with a hatchet, sending him flying into the moat below. This example fired the courage of the others; the resistance gained momentum, giving time for reinforcements to arrive. Charles lifted the siege on 22 July. Each year, at the end of June, Beauvais honours Jeanne "Hachette".

Tapestries

In 1664, Louis XIV founded the **Manufacture Royale de Tapisserie**.

The artisans worked on horizontal looms producing low-warp tapestries in wool and silk which are noted for being extremely fine; they were usually used as upholstery. The Manufacture Royale changed its name to Manufacture Nationale in 1804. The workshops, which were evacuated to Aubusson in 1939, were unable to return to Beauvais after the buildings were destroyed in 1940. The looms were relocated to the Gobelins Works in Paris and remained there until Beauvais could welcome them back in 1989.

Ceramics and stained glass

Pottery making has been going on in the area since Gallo-Roman times. Glazed earthenware and stoneware, manufactured locally since the 15C, have made the Beauvais region one of the great ceramic centres of France.

Around 1850, pottery workshops were replaced by ceramic and tile factories which in turn attracted fine pottery workshops in their vicinity. Beauvais' 16C stained glass is also famous, particularly that by the Leprince family.

👣 WALKING TOUR
Bishop's Palace and Surrounds

Place Jeanne-Hachette

There is a fine **statue** of the local heroine opposite the town hall with its beautifully restored 18C façade.

▷ *Take the rue de la Frette.*
Turn right on rue Beauregard, then left on rue St-Pierre.

Ruins

On the corner, you will see traces of the **Collégiale St-Barthélémy** and, opposite, behind the Galerie Nationale de la Tapisserie, the ruins of **Gallo-Roman town walls**.

▷ *Turn right on rue du Musée, then follow the rue de l'Abbé-Gelée.*

Ancien Palais Épiscopal

The former bishop's palace was restored in 2000. Flanked by two large **towers** with pepper-pot roofs, the 14C **fortified doorway** was built by Bishop Simon de Clermont de Nesle with 8 000 livres of fines that the town had to pay after a riot in 1306 during which the bishopric was pillaged. At the far end of the courtyard stands the main body of the palace; set ablaze in 1472 by the Burgundians, it was rebuilt around 1500 and retains an elegant Renaissance façade. The buildings house the Musée Départemental de l'Oise *(see p316)*.

15C House

The oldest house in Beauvais (15C) was dismantled from rue Oudry to be rebuilt rue de l'Abbé-Gelée (number 16). Dedicated to the preservation of rural traditional habitat, an association called **Maisons paysannes de l'Oise** proposes various temporary exhibits. ◐*Open Mon 2–6pm, Tue–Sat 10am–6pm.* ℘*03 44 48 77 74. http://maisonspaysannesoise. wifeo.com.*

▷ *To return to place J.-Hachette, turn right on rue J.-Racine, then right again on rue Carnot.*

SIGHTS
Cathédrale St-Pierre★★★

R. St-Pierre. ⏱*Open daily Nov–Apr 9am–12.15pm, 2–5.30pm.May–Jun and Sept–Oct 9am–12.15pm, 2–6.15pm. Jul–Aug 9am–6.15pm.* ☎*03 44 48 11 60. www.cathedrale-beauvais.fr.*

During the Carolingian period (751–987), a small cathedral, known as the **Basse-Œuvre**, was erected. In 949, another cathedral was begun, but it was destroyed by two fires.

Subsequently, in 1225, the bishop and chapter decided to erect the biggest church of its day, a **Nouvel-Œuvre** (New Work) dedicated to Saint Peter. Started in 1238, the construction of the chancel proved to be a real challenge for the architects. The height to the vault's keystone was to be slightly above 48m/158ft, making the roof (68m/223ft high) about the height of the towers of Notre-Dame in Paris. But the pillars were too widely spaced and the buttresses on the piers too weak. In 1284, the chancel collapsed: 40 more years of work went into saving it. The three large arches of the chancel's right bays were reinforced by the addition of intermediary piers, the flying buttresses multiplied, the abutments strengthened.

The Hundred Years War interrupted the project. In 1500, work resumed on the cathedral. The construction of the transept was entrusted to **Martin Chambiges** (c. 1460–1532),and in 1550, the transept was finally completed. Unfortunately, instead of building the nave next, it was decided to erect an openwork tower over the transept crossing, surmounted by a spire. The cross at the top of the spire was positioned in 1569, at a height of 153m/502ft. But as there was no nave to counterbalance the thrusts, the piers gave way on Ascension Day in 1573, just as the procession had left the church. Despite tremendous efforts and sacrifices, the clergy and people of Beauvais were able to restore only the chancel and the transept. The unfinished cathedral would never again have a spire, and would never have a nave!

Chevet★

♿ *See illustration in the Introduction.*
The chancel dates from the 13C. Like the Flamboyant transept arms, it is shored up by flying buttresses with high piers which rise up to the roof. The transept arms were to have been very long and framed by towers.

South transept façade

Richly decorated, it bears two high turrets flanking the **Portail de St-Pierre** (St Peter's Doorway), the embrasures, tympanum and arching of which are adorned with niches beneath openwork canopies. The doorway is surmounted by a rose-window with delicate tracery.

Interior★★★

The dizzying height of the vaults (almost 48m/157ft high) is immediately apparent. The generous transept is almost 58m/190ft long, and the chancel is extremely elegant. There is an open triforium and the clerestory is 18m/59ft high. Seven chapels open off the ambulatory. Most of the 16C **Stained-glass windows**★★ are to be found in the transept, including the **Roncherolles** stained glass (**1**) dating 1522. Also admire the rose-window (1551) featuring the Eternal Father in the central medallion. Underneath, 10 Prophets and 10 Apostles or Doctors stand in two rows.

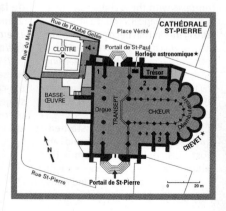

In a side chapel on the right side of the chancel, note a 16C polychrome **altarpiece** (**3**).

Set in a Roman Byzantine style case, the monumental **Astronomical Clock★** was made by engineer Louis-Auguste Vérité from 1865 to 1868. In the glazed openings, 52 dials show the positions of the planets, the seasons etc. Several times a day, 68 automats re-enact a scene from the Last Judgement. *Display at 40min past the hour May–end Oct 10.40–11.40am, 2.40–4.40pm (Jul–end Aug additional display at 12.40pm and 5.40pm), Sat–Sun 5.40pm. Nov–end Apr 11.40am, 2.40–3.40pm, Sat–Sun 10.40am and 4.40pm.* ⊛4€. ℘03 44 48 11 60.

To the right of the astronomical clock is possibly the world's oldest surviving **chiming clock** (14C) (**2**) which plays psalms corresponding to the different periods of the year.

Located on the eastern wing of the **cloister**, the chapter house (**4**) is also noteworthy.

Basse-Œuvre

Traces remain of the original 10C cathedral built from salvaged Gallo-Roman quarry stones known as *pastoureaux*. It served as the parish church until the 1789 Revolution.

Église St-Étienne★

The nave and the transept of the church dedicated to St Stephen are Romanesque. Their restraint, softened by the "Beauvais-style" bracketed cornices, contrasts with the architectural richness of the chancel, rebuilt a little after 1500 in a refined Flamboyant style. The chancel, which is higher than the nave, is encircled by chapels. The tower flanking the west front served as the town belfry. The left aisle gives on to a Romanesque doorway with a finely carved tympanum and arching.

The chancel's Renaissance **stained-glass windows★★**, by Engrand, are most beautiful; among them is the extraordinary **Tree of Jesse★★★** with its stunning design, colours and translucency.

Musée Départemental de l'Oise★

1 rue du Musée, in the Ancien Palais Episcopal. Some collections may not be visible because of ongoing renovation works. ☉*Open daily (except Tue) year-round 10am–noon, 2–6pm (Jul–Sept 10am–6pm).* ☉*Closed Jan 1, Easter, Mon, May 1, Whit Mon and Dec 25.* ℘*03 44 11 43 83. http://www.oise.fr.*

The museum houses a rich collection of medieval **woodcarvings** from churches and abbeys and **sculpted fragments** from some of the old Beauvais' timber-framed houses. Visitors will also enjoy the **Fine Arts** collections (mainly paintings), with pieces from the 16C to the 20C: 16C French School (*Résurrection du Christ* by Antoine Caron) and 17C and 18C Italian and French Schools. The 19C and 20C section includes works by Paul Huet *(Le Retour du Grognard),* Thomas Couture and Ingres, to name a few. **Art Nouveau furniture** by Gustave Serrurier-Bovy and **ceramics** by Auguste Delaherche should also be mentioned.

Manufacture nationale de la tapisserie

24 rue Henri Brispot. ☛*Guided tours only available for groups.* ℘*03 44 15 30 30.*

The national tapestry works have, since 1989, been housed in the former slaughterhouses. Today the factory contains about a dozen looms. The entire production is reserved for the State.

Galerie nationale de la Tapisserie

22 rue Saint-Pierre. ☉*Open daily except Mon 9.30am–12.30pm, 2–5pm.* ☉*Closed Jan 1, May 1, Dec. 25.* ℘*03 44 15 39 10.*

Housed in a low-roofed building beyond the cathedral's east end, the gallery stages **temporary exhibits** giving an overview of French tapestry from the 15C to present day.

🚗 DRIVING TOUR

Le Pays de Bray
58km/36mi – allow 2hr

Carved liked a buttonhole into the chalk of the Paris basin, the landscape of the Bray is one of wide panoramas, of farmland planted with apple orchards, and gently curving valleys. It is also renowned as the place where Swiss-born Charles Gervais 'invented' the soft cheese known as "Petit Suisse".

▶ *Leave Beauvais along avenue J.-Mermoz. Turn left towards Gisors (D 981). 5km/3mi beyond Auneuil, turn right (D 129). Cross Le Vauroux. At Lalandelle, follow signs for « Table d'orientation » from which there is a fine view over the countryside of Bray. Turn right onto the D 22 at the start of the descent.*

At the first turning to the right, you can see a hollow where the strata of the underlying chalk is clearly visible.

▶ *Retrace your route to the crossroads and continue along the D 574.*

You pass through the village of Coudray-St-Germer, then descend, with a nice **view★** of Gournay.

St-Germer-de-Fly
Saint Germer founded an abbey here in the 7C. Its huge **church★** was built between 1150 and 1175.
Ongoing renovations. Contact tourist office for information 📞*03 44 82 62 74.*

▶ *Take the D 109 towards Cuigy-en-Bray and Espaubourg, and the narrow road along the foot of the steep slopes of the Bray. At St-Aubin-en-Bray, turn left. Cross the RN to Fontainettes.*

Les Fontainettes
Garden pottery manufacture and sandstone piping. This very undulating and wooded region, is the cradle of Beauvais ceramics and pottery.

Lachapelle-aux-Pots
Le **musée de la Poterie** exhibits the work by local potters such as Delaherche and Klingsor.
🕐*Open Apr–Oct daily (except Mon), 2–6pm, Sat–Sun and holidays, 2.30–6.30pm.* 🕐*Closed Nov–Mar and the Mon of holidays.* 💶*2€.* 📞*03 44 04 50 72.*

Savignies
This charming village, a stronghold of pottery was surplanted in the 19C by Lachapelle. But you can still find traces of this industry such as chimneys and walls, and a few artists who maintain the tradition.

ADDRESSES

🛏 STAY
Hôtel du Cygne – *24 r. Carnot.* 📞*03 44 48 68 40. 21 rooms.* 🍴*8€.*
A conveniently located hotel in the heart of old Beauvais. The rooms are simple and well-kept; those looking onto the back are quieter. The breakfast room is of spruce.

Hostellerie St-Vincent – *241 r. de Clermont.* 📞*03 44 05 49 99. 79 rooms.* 🍴*10€. Restaurant.*
A recently-built hotel near main roads and the motorway slip road, offering redecorated, functional rooms. Traditional menus completed by blackboard specials.

🍴 EAT
La Baie d'Halong – *32 r. de Clermont. Closed Apr 20–May 4, Jul 14–Aug 15, Dec 21–Jan 2.* 📞*03 44 45 39 83.*
Exclusive Vietnamese cuisine combining fresh ingredients with a delicate use of spices. Paintings depicting the Bay of Halong adorn the dining room.

La Maison Haute – *128 r. de Paris. Closed Jul 21–Aug 17, Dec 24–Jan 4, Sat lunch, Sun–Mon.* 📞*03 44 02 61 60.*
In a residential district, this restaurant with a contemporary setting is in perfect keeping with its modern cuisine.

Abbaye de
Chaalis★★

👤 **Michelin Local Map:** 305: H-6 or map 106 fold 9

This estate lies on the edge of Ermenonville Forest, near the Mer de Sable theme park (👤 *see Excursion*). During the 19C, it evoked the gentle, romantic charm suggested by religious contemplation. Later, and up to 1912, Chaalis inspired its last owners to collect works of art and to entertain some of the most notable personalities of their time.

A BIT OF HISTORY
A Royal Abbey

Chaalis was a Cistercian abbey built on the site of a former priory in 1136 by Louis the Fat. The monks led a pious and modest country life, husbanding the land, cultivating vines, keeping bees and fishing in the lakes.

During the 16C the abbey was held *in commendam* and the abbots were appointed by the king. The first was Cardinal Ippolito d'Este, son of Alfonso d'Este and Lucrezia Borgia. Known as **Cardinal of Ferrara**, this enthusiastic art lover had his private chapel decorated with murals and commissioned fine gardens.

In the 18C the ninth abbot, one of the Great Condé's grandsons, attempted to restore the abbey to plans by **Jean Aubert**, the architect who designed the Great Stables at Chantilly. It was a disaster; after only one side of the building had been completed (1739, currently the Château-Museum), work stopped owing to lack of funds. This financial crisis prompted Louis XVI to close down the abbey in 1785. During the upheaval of the French Revolution, Chaalis was badly pillaged and the greater part of the building destroyed.

The estate frequently changed hands. In 1850, the highly distinguished **Mme de Vatry** bought the abbey ruins. She converted the 18C building into a château, had the park refurbished and entertained lavishly. Later on, a couple of art lovers (👤 *see sidebar p319*) would

make of Chaalis the wonderful museum that it is today.

VISIT *1hr*

🕐 *Park, rose garden and church: open daily year-round 10am–6pm. Museum: Mar–Mid Nov daily 11am–6pm; rest of year, Sun and holidays 10.30am–12.30pm, 1.30pm– 5.30pm.* 🕐 *Closed Dec 25.* ⊛*6.50 € (museum, park and rose garden).* ☎*03 44 54 04 02. www.chaalis.fr.*

Church ruins★

Consecrated in 1219, Chaalis was the first Cistercian church built in the Gothic style. Of the original buildings there remain a staircase turret, the northern transept arm surrounded by radiating chapels, part of the chancel and the altar.

Chapelle Ste-Marie de l'abbé★

Built around 1250, the chapel is a fine example of Gothic splendour from the time of the Sainte-Chapelle in Paris. Note the extraordinary cycle of murals by 16C Italian master **Francesco Primaticcio** (1504–1570) and the bronze bust of Nélie André by Denis Puech (1972).

Rose garden and park

Beyond the chapel, a strange 16C crenellated wall with asymmetrical merlons sets the boundaries of the rose garden. Above the heavy archway, the coat of arms of Cardinal Louis d'Este, nephew of Cardinal of Ferrara, is displayed. From north of the château, there is a fine perspective of the park with its flowerbeds and dazzling lake, restored in the 19C.

Château-Musée★★

The **Salle des Moines** houses many marvels, including Italian 15C Gothic furniture, two panels from an altarpiece painted by Jean de Bellegambe, religious statues (14C–16C French) and above all, the famous Giotto's **painted panels★★**, depicting St John the Evangelist and

St Lawrence. Do not miss Nélie André's **private appartments,** and the **Jean-jacques Rousseau Gallery**, with some exceptional documents and personal effects.

EXCURSION
Ermenonville
3km/1mi south on N 330.

In May 1778, **Jean-Jacques Rousseau** was invited to stay at the Château d'Ermenonville (*private*) by the Marquis de Girardin, who had acquired the estate in 1763, and it is here that Rousseau rekindled his passion for nature; he walked, daydreamed in the park and taught music to his host's children.

The **Parc Jean-Jacques Rousseau** was transformed by the marquess from sandy, swampy land into a superb landscaped garden in the French style with shaded paths, graceful vistas, elegant rockeries and follies. (call for current information at 03 44 54 01 58).

Mer de Sable★
0.5km/0.25mi south on N 330.
Open mid-Apr–end Sept 10am–6pm (call or check website for details as opening days vary). 19.50€ *(children 3–11 16.50€).* 0 825 252 060 *(0.15€/min). www.merdesable.fr.*

This family theme park has been set in the middle of the Ermenonville forest, in a sandy clearing dating from the Tertiary Era, at the end of the Ice Age when

Ph. Gajic/MICHELIN

St. Lawrence, by Giotto

this region was probably one vast sandy moor covered with wild heather. The park evokes three worlds to explore: the **Wild West**, the **Sahara** and the great **Jungle**. Ride through the desert aboard the little **Train des Sables** and expect lots of shows (re-enactments of Western movies) and attractions (thrill seeker rides, pony rides, toboggan, Merry Go Round, Ferris wheel, canoe rides, etc).

Patrons of the arts

Of humble origin, **Nélie Jacquemart** (1841–1912) stayed for long periods, during her childhood, at Mme de Vatry's who considered her almost as her daughter. She became acquainted with members of the aristocracy and the upper middle-class who were very useful to her in the pursuit of her career as a fashionable portrait painter, having studied with Léon Cogniet. In 1872, **Édouard André**, the heir to one of the largest fortunes in banking, commissioned a portrait from her, which still hangs in the private apartments of his Parisian mansion, and they met for the first time on this occasion. In 1881 they got married and their union was a happy one. Having no children, the couple devoted their efforts to collecting beautiful things, mainly from Italy, in the sumptuous mansion on boulevard Haussmann. Nélie André completed this collection after the death of her husband. In 1902, she realised one of her dreams: going to India; however she gave up the idea of a world tour when she learned that the Chaalis estate was for sale. She acquired it and devoted the last years of her life to it.

Château de
Chantilly★★★

"Chantilly" brings to mind a forest, a fine porcelain, a delicate lace, a famous racetrack... and of course, an impressive Neo-Renaissance castle with a canal twice as big as Versailles. Because of its remarkable setting, its beautiful park and the outstanding collections of its museum, the former residence of the Duke of Aumale, son of King Louis-Philippe, definitely deserves to be considered one of the major sights in France.

A BIT OF HISTORY

From Cantilius to the Montmorency – Over the past 2 000 years, five castles have occupied this part of the Nonette Valley. Above the ponds and marshes of the area rose a rocky island where a native of Roman Gaul called **Cantilius** built the first fortified dwelling. His name gave birth to Chantilly. In the Middle Ages the building became a fortress belonging to the **Bouteiller**, named after the hereditary duties he carried out at the court of the Capetians (originally in charge of the royal cellars, the Bouteiller was one of the king's close advisers). In 1386, the land was bought by **Chancellor d'Orgemont**,

> **Ġ Michelin Local Map:** 305: F-5 or map 106 fold 8
> **ℹ Info:** Office du tourisme de Chantilly, 60 av. du Mar. Joffre, 60631. ℘03 44 67 37 37. www.chantilly-tourisme.com.

who had the castle rebuilt. The feudal foundations bore the three subsequent constructions. In 1450, the last descendant of the Orgemont married one of the **Barons of Montmorency** and Chantilly became the property of this illustrious family. It remained in their possession for 200 years.

Constable Anne, Duc de Montmorency – Anne de Montmorency was a devoted servant to a succession of six French kings from Louis XII to Charles IX. This formidable character gained a reputation as warrior, statesman, diplomat and patron of the arts. For 40 years, he remained the leading noble of the land, second to the king. Childhood friend and companion-in-arms to François I, close adviser to Henri II, he even had some influence over Catherine de' Medici. .

In 1528, the feudal castle of the Orgemont was demolished and the architect **Pierre Chambiges** replaced it with the **Grand Château**, a palace built in the French Renaissance style. On a nearby island,

Château de Chantilly

D. Pazery/MICHELIN

Jean Bullant erected a charming château which still stands today: the **Petit Château**. It was separated from the Grand Château by a moat (now filled in) which was spanned by two superimposed bridges. New gardens were designed, the best artists were called to decorate both castles, and Chantilly became one of the most prestigious estates in the kingdom of France.

Constable Anne died in 1567, during the second of the Wars of Religion.

The last love of Henri IV – Henri IV often stayed at Chantilly, with his companion-in-arms **Henri I de Montmorency**, the son of Constable Anne.

At the age of 54, the king fell in love with his host's ravishing daughter Charlotte, aged only 15. He arranged for her to marry Henri II de Bourbon-Condé, a shy and gauche young man, whom the king hoped would prove an accommodating husband. The day after the wedding, however, Condé left the capital with his wife. Henri IV ordered them to return to Paris. The young couple fled to Brussels, where they stayed under the protection of the king of Spain. Henri IV raged, implored, threatened and went as far as to ask the Pope to intervene. Only when he was murdered by Ravaillac did the two fugitives return to France.

Henri de Montmorency – Encouraged by Louis XIII's brother, the scheming Gaston d'Orléans, **Henri II de Montmorency** plotted against Richelieu. He was defeated at Castelnaudary near Toulouse and made a prisoner after receiving 18 wounds. By way of an apology, he bequeathed to Cardinal Richelieu the two *Slave* statues by Michelangelo, now in the Louvre; those at Chantilly and Écouen are replicas.

The Great Condé – Charlotte de Montmorency and her husband the Prince of Condé – the couple persecuted by Henri IV – inherited Chantilly in 1643 and the château remained family property until 1830. Descendants of Charles de Bourbon, like Henri IV, the Princes of Condé were of royal blood and the heir apparent to the title was called the Duke of Enghien.

Statue of Henri IV

S. Sauvignier/ MICHELIN

The Great Condé was the son of Charlotte and Henri II. He applied himself to renovating the Château de Chantilly with the same energy and efficiency he had shown in military operations. In 1662 he commissioned **Le Nôtre** to redesign the park and the forest. The fountains at Chantilly were considered the most elegant in France and Louis XIV made a point of outclassing them at Versailles. The work lasted 20 years and the result was a splendid achievement, part of which still stands today.

The Last of the Condés –The Prince of Condé died at Fontainebleau in 1686, to the king's great dismay. During the religious ceremony preceding the burial, Bossuet delivered a funeral oration which became famous.

The great-grandson of the Great Condé, **Louis-Henri de Bourbon**, alias "Monsieur le Duc", was an artist with a taste for splendour, who gave Chantilly a new lease on life. He asked **Jean Aubert** to build the Grandes Écuries, a masterpiece of the 18C, and set up a porcelain factory which closed down in 1870.

The **Château d'Enghien** was built on the estate by **Louis-Joseph de Condé** in 1769. His grandson the Duke of Enghien, who had just been born, was its first occupant. The father of the newly born baby was 16, his grandfather 36. The young prince died tragically in 1804; he was seized by the French police in the margravate of Baden and shot outside the fortress of Vincennes on the orders of Bonaparte.

During the **French Revolution**, the main building was razed to the ground, though the Petit Château was spared.

Louis-Joseph was 78 when he returned from exile. His son accompanied him back to Chantilly and the two of them were dismayed: their beloved château was in ruins and the park in a shambles. They decided to renovate the estate. They bought back the plots of their former land, restored the Petit Château, redesigned and refurbished the grounds.

The prince died in 1818, but the duke continued the work. He was an enthusiastic hunter and at the age of 70 he still hunted daily. Thanks to his efforts, Chantilly became the lively, fashionable place it had been in the years preceding the Revolution. As in former times, the receptions and hunting parties attracted crowds of elegant visitors. The renovation and restoration work was a source of income for the local population.

The duke was worried by the Revolution of 1830, which raised his cousin Louis-Philippe to the throne, and considered returning to England. A few days later, he was found hanging from a window at his castle in St-Leu. He was the last descendant of the Condé.

The Duke of Aumale – The Duke of Bourbon had left Chantilly to his great-nephew and godson the Duke of Aumale, the fourth son of Louis-Philippe. This prince gained recognition in Africa when he captured Abd el-Kader and his numerous relations. The Revolution of 1848 forced him to go into exile and he returned only in 1870; in 1873 he presided over the court martial which sentenced Marshal Bazaine.

From 1875 to 1881, the duke commissioned **Daumet** to build the Grand Château in the Renaissance style. This castle, the fifth, still stands today. Back in exile between 1883 and 1889, he died in 1897 and the Institute of France inherited his estate at Chantilly, together with the superb collections that constitute the Condé Museum.

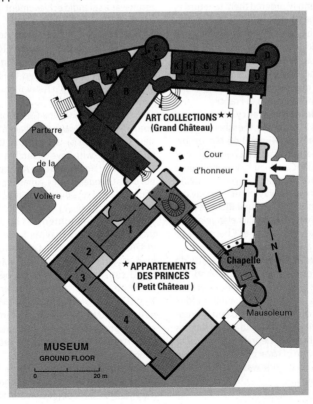

MUSEUM
GROUND FLOOR

CHÂTEAU★★★

🕐*Open daily except Tue Apr–Nov 10.30am–6pm. Rest of the year 10am–5pm.* 🎫*11€ (château and park).* 📞*03 44 27 31 80. www.chateaude chantilly.com.*

Try to picture the Château de Chantilly at the time of the Condé, when the two main buildings were still divided by an arm of water: the 16C Petit Château (or barbican) and the Grand Château, for which Daumet used the foundations of the former stronghold.

Cross the constable's terrace, which bears the equestrian statue of Anne de Montmorency, and enter the main courtyard through the gateway flanked by the two copies of Michelangelo's *Slaves*.

The Duke of Aumale never intended to create a museum for educational purposes; he merely wanted to build up a fine art collection. He therefore hung the works in chronological order of purchase though favourite ones were sometimes placed in a separate room. The curators have respected his layout.

According to the terms of the duke's legacy, the Institute must agree "to make no changes to the interior and exterior architecture of the château." Moreover, it is not allowed to lend any of the exhibits.

🎧 *The reception hall is the starting point for guided tours* 🔊 *of the chapel and various apartments as well as for unaccompanied tours of the collections. if a group has already formed, it is best to join it . It is advisable to interrupt a visit to the collections if the custodians announce a guided tour of the apartments.*

Appartements des Princes★ (Petit Château)

♿The **Grands Appartements,** occupied by the Great Condé and his descendants, were embellished with Regency and Rococo **wainscoting★★**, especially in the 18C thanks to the Duke of Bourbon.

The Duke of Aumale took up residence in the **Petits Appartements** on the ground floor, and had them designed

Library

D. Pazery/ MICHELIN

and decorated by painter Eugène Lami specially for his marriage in 1844.

Discover below some highlights of the Petit Château, but there is a lot more to see.

Cabinet des Livres★ (Library) **(1)** 🕐*Open Mon–Fri 9.15am–5pm. Reservations only.* 📞*03 44 62 62 69.* –This contains a splendid collection of manuscripts, including **The Rich Hours of the Duke of Berry** (*Les Très Riches Heures du duc de Berry*) with 15C illuminations by the Limbourg brothers. This extremely fragile document is not permanently exhibited, but visitors may see a facsimile by Faksimile Verlag of Luzern. Another interesting reproduction is the psalter of Queen Ingeburge of Denmark. Among the ornamental motifs feature the monogram of the Duke of Aumale (H O for Henri d'Orléans) and the Condé coat of arms (France's "broken" coat of arms with a diagonal line symbolising the younger branch of the family).

Chambre de Monsieur le Prince (2) –This title referred to the reigning Condé Prince, in this instance the Duke of Bourbon (1692–1740), who installed a wainscot at the far end of the room, into which were embedded panels painted by C Huet in 1735. The famous Louis XVI commode was designed by Riesener and made by Hervieu.

Salon des Singes (3) –This collection of monkey scenes *(singeries)* dating from the early 18C is a masterpiece by an anonymous draughtsman; note the fire screen depicting the monkeys' reading lesson.

Galerie de Monsieur le Prince (4) –The Great Condé had ordered his own battle gallery, which he never saw completed (1692). The sequence was interrupted from 1652 to 1659 during his years of rebellion. A painting conceived by the hero's son portrays him stopping a Fame from publishing a list of his treacherous deeds and asking another Fame to issue a formal apology.

Chapelle

An **altar**★ attributed to Jean Goujon and some 16C wainscoting and stained-glass windows from the chapel at Écouen were brought here by the Duke of Aumale. The apse contains the **mausoleum** of Henri II de Condé (bronze statues by J Sarrazin taken from the Jesuit Church of St-Paul-St-Louis in Paris) and the stone urn which received the hearts of the Condé princes.

Up to the Revolution, the Condé necropolis was at Vallery in Burgundy, where another sepulchral monument celebrating Henri II still stands.

The Collections★★ (Grand Château)

As you cross the **Galerie des Cerfs (A)**, dedicated to hunting themes, note 17C Gobelins tapestries.

Galerie de Peinture (B) – The variety of paintings reflects the eclectic tastes of the Duke of Aumale. Military events are illustrated on huge canvases (*Battle on the Railway Line* by Neuville, Meissonnier's *The Cuirassiers of 1805*). Orientalism is well represented with Gros' work, *The Plague Victims* of Jaffa, H Vernet's *Arab Sheikhs holding Council*, and *The Falcon Hunt* by Fromentin. Note, too, the famous portrait of *Gabrielle d'Estrées in her Bath* (16C French school), the portraits of Cardinals Richelieu and Mazarin by Philippe de Champaigne, and *The Massacre of the Holy Innocents* by Poussin.

Rotonde (C) – The *Loreto Madonna* by **Raphael, Piero di Cosimo's** portrait of the ravishing Simonetta Vespucci, who is believed to have been Botticelli's model for his *Birth of Venus*, and Chapu's kneeling statue of Joan of Arc listening to voices are exhibited here.

Salle de la Smalah and Salle de la Minerve (D) – Family portraits of the Orléans (17C, 18C and 19C) and of Louis-

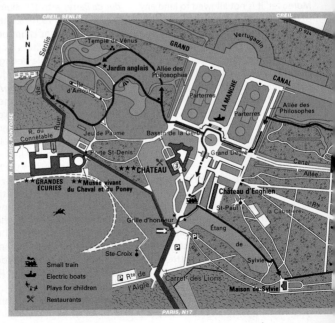

Philippe's relations in particular: Bonnat's picture of the Duke of Aumale at the age of 68.

Cabinet de Giotto (E) – A room devoted to Italian Primitives: *Angels Dancing in the Sun* (Italian School, 15C).

Salle Isabelle (F) – Numerous 19C paintings including *Moroccan Guards* by Delacroix, *Horse Leaving the Stables* by Géricault, and *Françoise de Rimini* by Ingres.

Salon d'Orléans (G) – The glass cabinets contain **soft-paste Chantilly porcelain** manufactured in the workshops founded in 1725 by the Duke de Bourbon (armorial service bearing the Condé coat of arms or the Duke of Orléans' monogram).

Salle Caroline (H) – 18C painting has pride of place here, with portraits by Largillière and Greuze, *Young Woman Playing with Children* by Van Loo, *The Worried Lover* and *The Serenade Player* by Watteau, or *Snowstorm* by Everdingen.

Salle Clouet (K) – A precious collection of small and extremely rare **paintings★★** executed by the **Clouets**, Corneille de Lyon, etc portraying François I, Marguerite de Navarre (stroking a little dog) and Henri II as a child etc.

Galerie de Psyché (L) – The 44 **stained-glass windows** (16C) that tell the story of the loves of Psyche and Cupid came from Constable Anne's other family home, Château d'Écouen.

Santuario★★★ (N) – This houses the museum's most precious exhibits: **Raphael**'s *Orléans Madonna*, and *The Three Ages of Womanhood*, also known as *The Three Graces*, by the same artist; *Esther and Ahasuerus*, the panel of a wedding chest painted by **Filippino Lippi**; and 40 miniature works by **Jean Fouquet**, cut out of Estienne Chevalier's book of hours, a splendid example of French 15C art.

Cabinet des Gemmes (P) – This contains jewels of stunning beauty. The Pink Diamond, alias the Great Condé (*a copy of which is permanently on show*), was stolen in 1926 and subsequently found in an apple where the thieves had hidden it. The room also boasts an outstanding collection of enamels and miniatures.

Tribune (R) – Above the cornice of this polygonal room are painted panels representing episodes from the life of the Duke of Aumale and the house of Orléans. The paintings include *Autumn* by **Botticelli**, *Love Disarmed* and *Pastoral Pleasures* by **Watteau**, a portrait of Molière by **Mignard**, and on the "Ecouen Wall", three superb works by **Ingres**: a self-portrait, *Madame Devaucay* and *Venus*.

PARK★★

🕐*Open daily except Tue Apr–Nov 10.am–8pm. Rest of the year 10.30am–6pm.* ⊘6€ *(park only).* 📞*03 44 27 31 80. www.chateaudechantilly.com.*
Take a stroll in this huge park (115ha) designed at the end of the 17C by Le Nôtre at the request of the Grand Condé, and discover some of its highlights.

Maison de Sylvie – This charming 18C house was named after the duchess of Montmorency whom French poet Théophile de Viau had nicknamed "Sylvie".

♣♣ Enclos des kangourous – Finding kangourous in the park may seem a bit surprising, but it is a reminder of the Princes de Condé's former *ménagerie*,

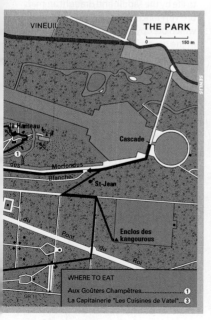

VINEUIL

THE PARK

0   150 m

SENLIS

la Hameau

Cascade

des

Mortlondus

Blanche

St-Jean

du

Pont

du

Roi

Enclos des
▲ kangourous

WHERE TO EAT
Aux Goûters Champêtres.....................❶
La Capitainerie "Les Cuisines de Vatel"..❸

which was destroyed during the French Revolution.

Chapelle St-Jean – This chapel was erected on the estate by Constable Anne in 1538, with six other chapels, in memory of the seven churches of Rome he had visited in order to gain the indulgences granted to those who undertook this pilgrimage. Two other chapels still stand on the estate: **Ste-Croix**, on the lawns of the racecourse, and **St-Paul**, located behind the **Château d'Enghien**, which was built in 1769 by Jean-François Leroy to house the Princes of Condé's numerous guests.

Cascade – These tiered waterfalls mark the start of the **Grand Canal** that Le Nôtre created in 1671–1673 by canalizing the waters of the Nonette River.

Hameau – Nestled in the Anglo-Chinese part of the park, this charming miniature village (1775) was renovated in 2008. The mill and a few half-timbered buildings used to accommodate a kitchen, a dining room and a billiard room. The barn provided a drawing room that was restored by the Duke of Aumale. All the big parties included supper in this pleasant spot in the park.

Parterres à la française – Completed in 2009, the renovation of these French gardens, which included the restoration of Le Nôtre's ingenious **hydraulic system**, has given them a new lease of life. Both parterres are framed by the **Allée des Philosophes**, named after the great writers who visited Chantilly and used to pace up and down the shaded avenue, exchanging their views and ideas. The circular Vertugadin lawns lie along the line of **La Manche**, flanked by delightful stretches of water. Between La Manche and the round **Bassin de la Gerbe** stands Coysevox's statue of the Great Condé, framed by the effigies of La Bruyère and Bossuet (statues of Molière and Le Nôtre, seated, may be seen in the near distance). The **Grand Degré** is a monumental stairway leading from the parterres up to the terrace; on either side of these imposing steps are grottoes, their carved decoration representing rivers.

Jardin anglais★ – Designed by **Victor Dubois** in 1819 for Prince Louis-Joseph de Condé, this lovely landscaped English-style garden was laid out on the surviving relics of Le Nôtre's park. Its charm derives from the pleasant groves (plane trees, swamp cypresses, weeping willows) rather than from its symbolic monuments: remains of the **Temple de Vénus** and **Île d'Amour**.

ADDITIONAL SIGHTS
Grandes écuries★★

⛓ *Ongoing restoration works in parts of the Grand Stables. Museum rooms closed until 2011.* 🕐*Stables, dome, "Galerie des disciplines" open to the public, and equestrian shows and horse training sessions going on. For more details, call* ☎*03 44 27 31 80. www.museevivantducheval.fr.*

Designed by **Jean Aubert** for Louis-Henri de Bourbon, the Great Stables constitute the most stunning piece of 18C architecture in Chantilly. The St-Denis Gateway, built astride the road leading to town, marks the site of an uncompleted pavilion. The most attractive façade of the stables overlooks the racetrack.

Musée Vivant du Cheval et du Poney★★ – This museum is brought to life by the saddle and draught animals bred in France or in the Iberian Peninsula which occupy the stalls and boxes built in the days of the Duke of Aumale.

Le Potager des Princes

17 r. de la Faisanderie. 🕐*Open daily (except Tue) end Mar–end Oct, 2–7pm.* 🎫*7.50€.* ☎ *03 44 57 39 66. www.potagerdesprinces.com.*

Originally designed in 1682 by André Le Nôtre and Jean-Baptiste de la Quintinie for the Grand Condé's **pheasantry**, this garden includes an area reserved for farmyard animals, an orchard, a rose garden and a vegetable garden where medicinal and culinary herbs grow next to traditional vegetables.

SURROUNDS
Forêt de Chantilly

Managed by the Office National des Forêts, this vast wooded area (6 300 ha) shelters deers, wild boars and other animals, and offers a network of paths particularly suitable for country walks. Its light soil also favours riding activities (horse training sessions take place at carrefour du Petit Couvert every morning). Hikers will appreciate nature walks around **Coye-la-Forêt**, **Orry-la-Ville** and **Pontarmé**.

Étangs de Commelles – Located near the village of Coye-la-Forêt, this 19C recreational site (40 ha/98.8 acre) features four ponds fed by the Thève River: the étang de Commelles, the étang Chapron, the étang Neuf and the étang de la Loge. These were built in the 13C by monks from the Chaalis Abbey (*see p318*) who used them as fishponds.

Château de la Reine Blanche – The ponds of Commelles are home to this former watermill restored in the Troubadour Style in 1825 by the last of the Condés, the Duke of Bourbon, who used it as a hunting lodge. It stands on the site of a legendary château believed to have been built by Queen Blanche of Navarre, wife of Philippe VI of Valois, after her husband's death around 1350. Part of the lodge is now occupied by a pancake house. An avenue of age-old beeches completes this delightful **site**★.

ADDRESSES

STAY

Pavillon St-Hubert – *In Toutevoie, on the banks of the Oise, 60270 Gouvieux. 3.5km/2mi W of Chantilly via D 909. 03 44 57 07 04. 18 rooms. 9€. Restaurant*. A former hunting lodge and its lovely garden by the Oise offering small rooms reminiscent of the inns of yore. The dining room, furnished in the Louis XIII style, is adorned with hunting trophies. Terrace in the shade of sycamore trees, with the Oise River in the background.

Château de la Tour – *60270 Gouvieux. 3.5km/2mi W of Chantilly via D 909. 03 44 62 38 38. Closed Christmas period. 41 rooms. Restaurant*. This early 20C domain, formerly belonging to a famous banker, overlooks a spacious park that can be contemplated from the terrace. There are modern and old-fashioned bedrooms available for the asking; elegant dining rooms with a Louis XIII flair.

EAT

Aux Goûters Champêtres – *In the Château de Chantilly. 03 44 57 46 21. Open daily except Tue lunch–6pm. Closed mid-Nov to early Mar.* In a décor of thatched roofs, half-timbering and greenery, you will enjoy a typical local "goûter" (teatime snack): confit of duck, foie gras, deer pâté, cider, jams or honey from the region or from Picardy, orange-flavoured gingerbread, delicious apple and strawberry tarts...

La Capitainerie "Les Cuisines de Vatel" – *Château de Chantilly. 03 44 57 15 89. www.restaurantfp-chantilly.com. Closed Tue and evenings. Reservations advisable.* One would be hard put to find a more prestigious setting for a restaurant than this one, located under the ancestral arches of kitchens once governed by the illustrious chef Vatel. The inviting decor features copper ware, porcelain, old ovens, the original brick fireplace and leather chairs. The menu changes with the seasons.

ON THE CANAL

L'hydrophile – *Château de Chantilly. 03 44 527 31 80. Late Mar–late Oct daily, weather permitting.* The hydrophile takes you on a twenty-minute electric boat ride on the Grand Canal and in the moats of the château, amidst native aquatic fauna.

Chemin des Dames

Michelin Local Map: 306: C-6 to F-6

The Chemin des Dames is a path running along the ridge which separates the Aisne from the Ailette River. It owes its name to the daughters of Louis XV, known as "Mesdames", who followed this route on their way to the Château de La Bove, home of their friend the Duchess of Narbonne. A charming name for a moving site which still bears the marks of the bitter fighting which took place here during World War I.

A BIT OF HISTORY

Nivelle Offensive

In 1914, after the Battle of the Marne, the retreating Germans stopped here, having realised that the location was an excellent defensive spot which they fortified by making use of the quarries (*boves* or *creuttes*), hollowed out of the ridge. **General Nivelle**, commander of the French armies from December 1916, searched for a way of penetrating their defence along Chemin des Dames. In spite of the difficult terrain, riddled with machine gun nests, on 16 April 1917 he sent an army under **General Mangin** to attack the German positions. The French troops occupied the ridges following the first assault, but the Germans clung onto the slopes of the **Ailette Valley**: the terrible French losses that ensued, together with the failure of the venture, caused a crisis of morale which provoked

mutinies in parts of the French army. General Nivelle and General Mangin were dismissed. **Marshal Pétain** (then a general) took over and suppressed the rebellion.

FROM SOISSONS TO BERRY-AU-BAC

▶ *From Soissons, take N 2 toward Laon, then turn right onto D 18.*

The **Carrefour du Moulin de Laffaux** marks the western extremity of the Chemin des Dames. Signs along the itinerary below lead you to through 8 major historic sites, each of them with informative panels explaining the stakes at hand:
Fort de la Malmaison (**1**); Royère viewpoint (**2**); Cerny-en-Laonnois (**3**); Caverne du Dragon (**4**); Monument des Basques (**5**); Plateau de Californie (**6**); Craonne (**7**); Berry-au-Bac (**8**).

Do not miss the memorial musem of the **Caverne du Dragon★**, as it presents harrowing testimonies of both German and French presence in underground galleries located below the first lines of the front during WW I. ⏱*Open Feb–Apr and Oct–Dec Tue–Sun 10am–6pm. May, Jun, Sept daily 10am–6pm. Jul–Aug 10am–7pm.* ⬡5€ *(1hr 30min guided tour only).* ☎03 23 25 14 18.

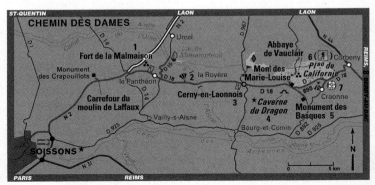

Compiègne★★★

Bordered by one of the most beautiful forests in Europe for walking and hiking, Compiègne was a royal residence long before it hosted the brilliant parties and receptions of the Second Empire. It long played an important strategic military role, and it was there that the armistices of November 11 1918 and June 22 1940 were signed. Today, the city boasts many monuments that bear testimony to its prestigious history.

A BIT OF HISTORY

Origins – The city of Compiègne developed around the palace that **Charles the Bald** had built in 9C to resemble Charlemagne's in Aix-la-Chapelle, and the abbey that he had founded to preserve the relics of Saint Cornelius. This abbey did precede St-Denis (& see p162) as the royal necropolis and centre of culture.

Joan of Arc Imprisoned – In May 1430, the Burgundians and the English were camping beneath Compiègne's town walls, on the north side of the River Oise. Joan of Arc came to examine the enemy position and returned on the 23rd, entering the town from the south. That same evening, she attempted an assault, crossing the river and chasing the Burgundian vanguard. However, reinforcements came to the aid of the Burgundians, while the English attacked from the rear. The 'Maid of Orléans' covered the retreat with a handful of men. She reached the moat just as the commanding officer in Compiègne gave the order to raise the drawbridge, fearing the enemy would slip inside with the last of the French soldiers. A short skirmish ensued. A Picardy archer toppled Joan of Arc from her horse and she was taken prisoner. The place of capture is located near place du 54e-Régiment-d'Infanterie, where Frémiet's **equestrian statue** of Joan of Arc stands.

A Castle of Many Owners – All the kings of France enjoyed staying in Compiègne,

▶ **Population:** 108 234

⚅ **Michelin Local Map:** 305: H-4 or map 106 fold 10

ℹ **Info:** Office du tourisme de Compègne, pl. de l'Hôtel-de-Ville, 60200. ℘03 44 40 01 00. www.compiegne-tourisme.fr.

◖ **Location:** Most of the city occupies the left bank of the Oise River. The Palace dominates Place du General de Gaulle. Three blocks south in the centre of town stands the city hall which houses the tourist office.

🅿 **Parking:** Parking places around the Palace, near St-Jacques Church, on Cours Guynemer, and at at the train station (on the opposite side of the river).

☺ **Don't Miss:** The Palace, with its royal and imperial private apartments, and two outstanding museums; the forest surrounding the town, for its its beauty and for the famous Clairière de l'Armistice where two major treaties were signed, icluding the one which put a end to World War I.

🕐 **Timing:** Allow at least 2hr for the palace, more if you'd like to explore the grounds. And if you want to discover the highlights of the forêt de Compiègne, note that the driving tours we suggest require 1hr to 1hr30min each.

👫 **Kids:** Kids should find a visit to the Cité des Bateliers, in Longueil-Annel, quite interesting, as they will get to take a look at a barge hold, walk along a canal and learn how a lock works.

⚅ **Also See:** Longueil-Annel; Ourscamps; Pierrefonds.

which they often visited. Yet, with four main buildings haphazardly arranged around a central courtyard, the château was not an obvious royal residence. **Louis XIV** said, "At Versailles, I am lodged like a king; at Fontainebleau, like a prince; and at Compiègne, like a peasant." He had new apartments built facing the forest. His 75 visits here were marked by sumptuous feasts and great military camps.

When **Louis XV** ordered the complete reconstruction of the palace in 1738, he was less interested in outdoing his predecessor than in having a place where he could reside with his court and ministers. His master plan of 1751 was brought to a halt by the Seven Years War. **Louis XVI** continued the project and achieved a great deal, but left it unfinished.

He was only able to occupy the royal apartments in 1785. A great terrace was built in front of the palace's façade, which looked out onto a park. This terrace was connected to the gardens by a monumental central flight of steps, replacing the moat that had formerly been part of Charles V's fortifications.

After the Revolution, the palace served first as a military school, then as an engineering college. In 1806, it became an Imperial residence and **Napoleon I** had the place entirely restored by the architect Berthaut, the painter Girodet and the decorators Redouté and the Dubois brothers.

A Wedding Palace – It was in the Compiègne Forest that, on May 14 1770, the future Louis XVI was introduced to **Marie-Antoinette of Austria** for the first time. On 27 March 1810, the great-niece of Marie-Antoinette, **Marie-Louise of Austria**, was to arrive in Compiègne. She had married Napoleon I by proxy and the Emperor couldn't wait meeting his bride. The dinner planned in Soissons was cancelled and instead the couple had supper at Compiègne. Some days later, the wedding ceremonies were celebrated at St-Cloud, serving only as the consecration of a union imposed at Vienna and willingly accepted in Compiègne. In 1832, **Louis-Philippe**, who transformed the tennis court into a theatre, married his daughter Louise-Marie to the first king of Belgium, Leopold of Saxe-Coburg.

The Second Empire "Series" – Compiègne was the favourite residence of **Napoleon III** and **Empress Eugénie**. They came every autumn for several weeks to enjoy the hunting season. They also received the celebrities of the time, arranged in five "series" of about 80 people, grouped by "affinities". Lodging the guests often posed great difficulties and

Palace of Compiègne

Ph. Gajic/ MICHELIN

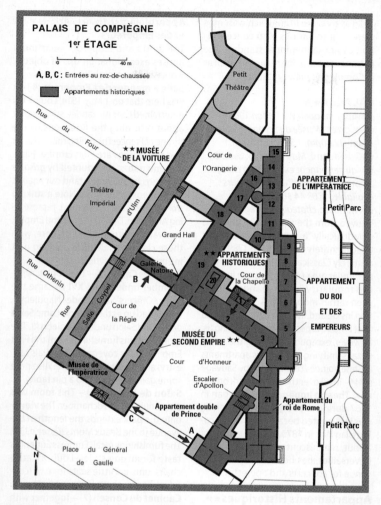

PALAIS DE COMPIÈGNE
1ᵉʳ ÉTAGE

0 _____ 40 m

A, B, C : Entrées au rez-de-chaussée

Appartements historiques

Petit Théâtre

Rue du Four

★★ **MUSÉE DE LA VOITURE**

Cour de l'Orangerie

Théâtre Impérial

Rue d'Ulm

15
14
16
13
17
12
18
11
10

APPARTEMENT DE L'IMPÉRATRICE

Petit Parc

Grand Hall

Rue Othenin

Galerie Natoire

★★ **APPARTEMENTS HISTORIQUES**

9
8
7
6
5

19

20

Cour de la Chapelle

APPARTEMENT DU ROI ET DES EMPEREURS

Rue

Salle Coypel

Cour de la Régie

B

1
2
3
4

MUSÉE DU SECOND EMPIRE ★★

Cour d'Honneur

Musée de l'Impératrice

Escalier d'Apollon

21

Appartement du roi de Rome

Petit Parc

C

Appartement double de Prince

A

N

Place du Général de Gaulle

---

many distinguished individuals had to content themselves with rooms under the eaves. The hunts, theatrical evenings and balls left the guests with little free time. Romantic and political intrigue mixed freely. To amuse the Imperial couple and their guests, the writer **Mérimée** composed his famous dictation, comprising the words with the greatest spelling difficulties in the French language. The Empress made the highest number of mistakes. Pauline Sandoz, Metternich's daughter-in-law, had the least. The luxuries and endless frivolities intoxicated the courtiers, who delighted in waltzes and long forest outings. The events of 1870 interrupted this joyous life and the work

on the new theatre. During the Emperor's long periods of residence at Compiègne most of the First Empire furniture was replaced.

The World Wars – From 1917 to 1918 the palace was the headquarters of general **Nivelle** and then **Pétain**. The armistice of 11 November 1918 (between the Allies and Germany) was signed in the Compiègne forest. Later, on 22 June 1940, another treaty (between Germany and France) would be signed in the same place (see p338).

Compiègne suffered heavy bombing during World War II. **Royallieu**, a district south of the town, served from 1941 to

1944 as a centre from which prisoners were sent to various Nazi concentration camps (a memorial stands at the entrance to the military camp as well as in Compiègne railway station).

PALACE★★★

⏱*Museums open Wed–Mon 10am–6pm, except Musée du Second-Empire 10am–12.30pm, 1.30pm– 5.15pm.* ⏱*Closed Jan 1, May 1, Dec 25.* ✺*6.50€ (for all permanent exhibits); no charge 1st Sun of month.* *Guided tours available.* ✆*03 44 38 47 02. www.musee-chateaucompiegne.fr.*

Viewed from the square, the palace is paradoxically "a Louis XV château built almost entirely from 1751 to 1789". This austerely Classical château covers a vast triangular area (3ha/7.5 acres); indeed, the regularity of its arrangement is even rather monotonous. The decoration inside and the collection of 18C and First Empire tapestries and furnishings is, however, exceptional. Among the many details unifying the various apartments are fine *trompe-l'œil* paintings by Sauvage (1744–1818) over the doors. Work on the new **Théâtre Impérial**, which began in 1867 during the reign of Napoleon III, was interrupted because of the Franco-Prussian War in 1870. Today, its interior layout, reminiscent of the opera house in Versailles, has become popular as a venue for concerts and operettas.

Appartements Historiques★★

The Historic Apartments of the palace begin with rooms devoted to its history; beyond them rises the Queen's Grand Staircase (or Apollo Staircase), which led directly to the Queen's apartment. Farther still is the entrance hall or Gallery of Columns which precedes the **Grand Staircase** (**1**). Climb the staircase with its beautiful 18C wrought-iron balustrade to the landing where a great Gallo-Roman sarcophagus lies; it once served as the font in the abbey church of St Cornelius and is a relic of very early Compiègne. The first-floor **Guard-room** (1785) (**2**) leads into the antechamber or **Ushers' Salon** (**3**), which gave access to both the King's apartment (*left*) and the Queen's (*right*).

Appartement du Roi et des Empereurs

The King's and Emperors' apartment houses exceptional groups of objects, works and memorabilia.

Salle à manger de l'Empereur (**4**)– It was here that on 1 May 1814, Louis XVIII entertained Czar Alexander, still hesitant about returning the Bourbons to the throne of France. The dining room's decor and furnishings are First Empire. Pilasters and doors, surmounted by *grisaille* paintings by Sauvage, stand out against the fake rose-pink onyx. Note a striking *trompe-l'œil*, also by Sauvage, representing Anacreon. During the Second Empire, a private theatre was set up here, with those close to the empress taking part in charades and revues.

Salon des Cartes (**5**) – The Nobles' Antechamber under Louis XVI became the Senior Officers' Salon under Napoleon I, and ended up as the Aide-de-Camp Salon or the Card Salon under Napoleon III. The room contains furnishings from the First Empire (chairs covered in Beauvais tapestry) and the Second Empire. Also note some games (quoits and a pin table).

Salon de Famille (**6**) – This room was once Louis XVI's bedchamber. The **view**★ onto the park extends the length of the avenue to the Beaux Monts (⏱*see p337*). The furnishings recall Empress Eugénie's taste for mixing styles: Louis XV armchairs, unusual little seats for two (*confidents*) or for three (*indiscrets*) etc.

Cabinet du Conseil (**7**) – Together with Versailles and Fontainebleau, Compiègne was one of the three châteaux where the king held counsel. Representatives of the Republics of Genoa and of the Kingdom of France signed two successive treaties here (1756 and 1764) which accorded France the right to garrison troops in the maritime citadels of Corsica. An immense tapestry illustrates the Crossing of the Rhine by Louis XIV.

Chambre de l'Empereur (**8**) – The Emperor's bedchamber was restored to its appearance during the First Empire, with Jacob-Desmalter furnishings and friezes representing eagles.

Bibliothèque (**9**) – This room was used as a library during the First Empire. The bookcase and furnishings are by Jacob Desmalter, while the *Minerve entre Apollon et Mercure* painted on the ceiling is the work of Girodet. A secret door used lead to the Empress's apartment.

Appartement de l'Impératrice

These rooms comprised the queen's principal apartments, the only ones in which Marie-Antoinette ever stayed. Later, they were particularly favoured by Empresses Marie-Louise and Eugénie.

Salon du Déjeuner (10) – The delightful breakfast room, with pale blue and yellow silk hangings, was prepared for Marie-Louise in 1809.

Salon de Musique (11) – This was one of Empress Eugénie's favourite rooms. The Louis XVI pieces, from the apartment of Marie-Antoinette at St-Cloud, recall that the last sovereign consort of France kept the memory of the unfortunate queen alive.

Chambre de l'Impératrice (12) – The majestic tester bed is enclosed by white silk curtains and gold-embroidered muslin. Paintings by Girodet represent the seasons, and the Morning Star appears in the centre of the ceiling. The round boudoir leading to the bedchamber served as a dressing-room and for taking baths. The last three of these interconnecting rooms form a decorative First Empire ensemble. Seats are arranged formally around a couch in the **Grand Salon (13)**; the **Salon des Fleurs (14)** owes its name to the eight panels painted with lily-like flowers, after Redouté; the **Salon Bleu (15)** strikingly contrasts blue walls and seats with a red marble fireplace and console tables. These rooms belonged to the imperial prince at the end of the Second Empire.

Salle à manger de l'Impératrice (16) – The walls of this modestly sized room are lined with stucco-marble, of a caramel colour more elegantly known as "antique yellow". It was here that the Archduchess Marie-Louise dined with the Emperor for the first time.

Galerie des Chasses de Louis XV (17) – The room is hung with Gobelins tapestries, which were woven as early as 1735 in accordance with sketches by

Oudry. One represents a hunt along the River Oise and includes the silhouettes of Compiègne and the old Royallieu Abbey. The series continues in the **Galerie des Cerfs (18)**, formerly the Queen's Guardroom, then the Empress' Guard-room.

Galerie du Bal (19) – The room (39×13m/ 128×43ft) was constructed within a few months for Marie-Louise's arrival, by gutting two floors of small apartments. The ceiling paintings glorify the Emperor's victories; the mythological scenes at the end of the room are by Girodet. Throughout the Second Empire the gallery served as a dining room at the time of the "series", the sovereigns presiding from the centre of an immense table set up for the occasion.

Galerie Natoire and Salle Coypel – These were built by Napoleon III to lead to the imperial theatre. Their decoration illustrates the Story of Don Quixote. **Tapestry drawings★** by Natoire (1700–77).

Chapel (20) – The First Empire chapel is surprisingly small for such a vast château, as the great chapel planned by Gabriel was never built. It was here, on 9 August 1832, that the marriage took place between Princess Louise-Marie, eldest daughter of Louis-Philippe, and Leopold I, King of Belgium. Princess Marie of Orléans, the French king's second daughter, designed the stained-glass window.

Appartement double de Prince – Napoleon I had this apartment arranged to receive a foreign sovereign and his or her consort. This excellent group of Empire rooms comprises a dining room, four salons and a great bedchamber.

Appartement du roi de Rome – This apartment has been restored to its appearance in 1811, when Napoleon I's son (five months old at the time) stayed in it for one month. All the original furnishings adorn the salon-boudoir, bathroom, boudoir, bedchamber and main drawing room. In the middle of the apartment, a room (21) has been restored to appear as it did at the end of the 18C, when it was used as Queen Marie-Antoinette's games room.

Musée du Second Empire★★

The museum is located in a series of small, quiet drawing rooms and presents life at Court and in the outside world, and the arts, during the Second Empire.

Beyond the first room, displaying **Daumier**'s humorous drawings, a space is devoted to the "beauties" of the period. **Princess Mathilde** (1820–1904), one of the reign's great figures, has pride of place here. She was for a brief time the fiancée of Louis Napoléon, her close cousin. After her Spanish marriage, she devoted herself entirely to her salon in rue de Courcelles, which was much frequented by important writers and artists of the day, some of them hostile to the power in place, and to her château in St-Gratien.

The museum owns the famous painting *The Empress with her Ladies-in-Waiting* by **Winterhalter** (1855). Among the many sculptures by **Carpeaux** in the last rooms, note the bust of **Napoléon**, aged by the fall of the Empire, and the statue of the Imperial Prince with his dog.

Musée de l'Impératrice – This collection includes memorabilia of official life and life in exile, as well as popular objects associated with Empress Eugénie. Among the more moving items are those evoking the Empress and her son, the Imperial Prince, who was massacred by the Zulus.

Musée de la voiture et du tourisme★★

Created in 1927 on the initiative of the Touring Club of France, this museum is dedicated to the history of locomotion, from the origins of horse-drawn vehicles to the early years of the automobile. Its fascinating collection includes 18C–19C carriages, cycles, early electric and steam vehicles and cars up to World War I.

Grand Hall – Antique carriages are on display in what was formerly the kitchen courtyard, now covered over: the oldest, a travelling berlin coach, which belonged to the kings of Spain, dating from c 1740; the berlin coach used by the Pope in Bologna, and the one in which Bonaparte made his entrance to the town in 1796. Also on show are 18C and 19C travelling carriages, a mail-coach, charabancs, a Madeleine-Bastille omnibus and Orsay broughams. The 1924 Citroën from the Croisière Noire (first trans-African car expedition) and the imperial train carriage used by Napoleon III for his trips between Paris and Compiègne are among the finest exhibits.

Kitchens and Outbuildings – The evolution of the two-wheeler, starting with the heavy ancestors of the bicycle, hobbies (1817) which the rider set in motion by pushing off, can be seen. Pedals appeared with the 1863 Michaux velocipede. Around 1880, the penny-farthing, built out of iron tubing, had an unusually large front wheel to increase its speed. Developments such as the invention of the chain belt, which first appeared on the English tricycle, rendered wheels of disproportionate size unnecessary. The true bicycle became possible in about 1890. The army took advantage of the idea by developing a folding velocipede just before World War I.

First Floor – These rooms are devoted to foreign vehicles and their accessories: Dutch and Italian cabriolets, a Sicilian

---

The Motorcar's "first steps"

Vehicles of note include the **Panhard** No 2, the first car equipped with a four-stroke **Daimler** engine; the 1895 **vis-à-vis** by **Bollée & Son** which was one of the entrants in the race from Paris to Marseille-en-Beauvaisis (north of Beauvais); the **De Dion-Bouton** series, the large 1897 break belonging to the Duchess of Uzès, the first woman driver; the 1899 **Never-satisfied** on **Michelin** tyres, which was the first car to attain speeds of 100kph/62mph; and the 1900 4-CV **Renault**, the first saloon car. Steam, combustion and electric motors are also exhibited, showing the various ideas of the researchers and creators of the automobile industry.

cart, palanquin, sleighs, coachmen's clothes etc.

Petit Parc

The "Petit Parc" refers to the gardens (the "Grand Parc" surrounding the gardens and being part of the forest).

The Emperor's guiding idea was *"to link the château as soon as possible to the forest, which is the true garden and the real beauty of this residence"*. The enclosing wall which blocked the view of the woods was taken down and replaced by iron railings. Beyond, the openness of avenue des Beaux-Monts creates a magnificent linear perspective (4km/6mi long).

Impatient to reach the forest without having to go through the town, Napoleon I had a central ramp built for carriages between the terrace and the park; this was unfortunately at the expense of the glorious flight of steps by Gabriel. From then on, the Petit Parc was redesigned as a formal English garden by **Berthault** and lost its importance. The present layout dates from the Second Empire.

ADDITIONAL SIGHTS
Hôtel de ville

This remarkable building was constructed under Louis XII in the late-Gothic style. It was restored during the 19C and the façade statues date from this period. They represent, from left to right around the central equestrian statue of Louis XII: Saint Denis, Saint-Louis, Charles the Bald, Joan of Arc, Cardinal Pierre d'Ailly who was born in Compiègne, and Charlemagne.

The belfry, which consists of two floors and a slate-covered spire flanked by four pinnacled turrets, houses a communal bell melted and reshaped in 1303. At the base of the spire, three figures, called **picantins** and dressed as Swiss foot-soldiers from the period of François I, ring the hours and the quarter-hours.

♣♣ Musée de la Figurine historique★

In the Hôtel de la Cloche, to the right of the Hôtel de Ville. ♿ ◷*Open Mar–end Oct 9am–noon, 2–6pm. Nov–end Feb 9am–noon, 2–5pm.* ◷*Closed Mon and*

Sun morning, Jan 1, May 1, Jul 14, Nov 1, Dec 25 . ☞*3€ (no charge 1st Sun of the month).* ☏*03 44 40 72 55.*

This museum houses an amazing collection of over 100 000 model figures in tin, lead, wood, plastic, paper and cardboard, sculpted wholly or partly in the round, or flat. Sophisticated **dioramas**, composed of up to 12 000 figurines, recount various episodes of the military and civilian history of France, some of them directly related to the history of Compiègne.

For instance, the scene describing the arrival of Empress Marie-Louise at the château de Compiègne, gives a detailed insight into how extravagant receptions must have been at the imperial palace in those times.

Historical reconstitutions of Napoleonian wars and World War I are also noteworthy.

Église St-Jacques

The church features a 15C tower, the highest in the town, at one of the corners of its west front. This was the parish church of the king and the court, hence funds provided for the chancel to be reworked in marble in the 18C and for the addition of carved-wood panels at the base of the nave's pillars. The harmony of the Gothic style at the time of Saint-Louis is particularly evident in the chancel with its narrow, clerestory lit triforium and the 13C transept.

Hôtel de Ville

A. de Valroger/ MICHELIN

An ambulatory was added in the 16C. The 13C stone Virgin and Child in the north transept, known as "Our Lady of the Silver Feet" (*Notre-Dame aux pieds d'argent*), is the subject of much veneration. A chapel in the north aisle houses three 15C painted wooden statues.

Vieille Cassine
From place St-Jacques, cross rue Magenta to reach rue des Lombards. This half-timbered house (number 10) dates from the 15C. This is where the "Maîtres du Pont" used to live. They controlled the boat traffic on the Oise River, particularly treacherous around the Saint-Louis bridge.

Musée Antoine-Vivenel
⊙*Mar–fin Oct 9am–noon, 2–6pm. Nov–end Feb 9am–noon, 2–5pm.* ⊙*Mon and Sun morning, Jan 1, May 1, Jul 14, Nov 1, Dec 25.* ⊚3€ *(no charge 1st Sun of month).* ℘*03 44 20 26 04.*
This municipal museum is located in the **Hôtel de Songeons** (late 18C), whose gardens were turned into a public park. Focusing on antiquities from Picardy and the Mediterranean, the archaeological collections present artefacts and art pieces from Prehistory to the end of the Gallo-Roman period. Note three bronze helmets dating from c 600 BC, as well as Greek and Roman marbles and bronzes. But he highlight of the museum is undoubtedly its remarkable group of **Greek vases**★★ discovered in Etruria and Southern Italy.
The first-floor rooms have preserved their Directoire wainscoting. They house a collection of paintings, including a large altarpiece representing the Passion by Wolgemut (Dürer's teacher), ceramics (pitchers in "Flemish stoneware," Italian majolicas), ivories and Limousin enamels.

EXCURSION
Longueil-Annel
6km/3.7mi northeast along N 32.
This village lies on the banks of the River Oise and of the canal running alongside it. The **Cité des Bateliers**, which offers visitors a journey on the theme

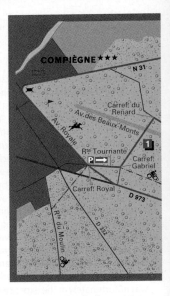

of inland waterways, includes a visit to a former boatmen's café turned into a small museum, a look at the *Freycinet* barge hold, a stroll along the banks of the canal and a tour of the Janville lock. ♿👤 ⊙*Mid-Apr–Mid-Oct daily except Mon 10am–7pm. Mid-Oct–Mid-Apr Tue– Fri 1pm–6pm, Sat–Sun 10am– 6pm.* ⊙*Jan and Dec 25 .* ⊚*5.30€.* ℘*03 44 96 05 55. www.citedesbateliers.com.*

🚗 DRIVING TOURS

FORÊT DE COMPIÈGNE★★
The State forest of Compiègne (14 500ha/ 35 800 acres) is a remnant of the immense **Cuise Forest** which extended from the edge of the Île-de-France to the Ardennes. It embraces delightful beech groves, magnificent avenues, valleys, ponds and villages, and occupies a sort of hollow with the valleys of the River Oise and River Aisne on two sides.
A series of hills and promontories sketches a sharply defined crescent to the north, east and south. These peaks rise on average 80m/262ft above the sandy base of the hollow, which is grooved with numerous rivulets.
The largest of these, the **Ru de Berne**, links a series of ponds.

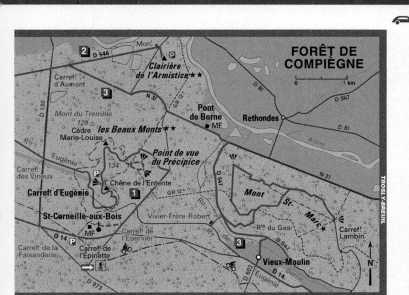

FORÊT DE COMPIÈGNE

●← The forest is criss-crossed by 1 500km/ 930mi of roads and footpaths. François I first cut great rides through the trees, with Louis XIV and Louis XV later contributing to extend this network in order to create an ideal place for hunting.

1 Beaux Monts★★

18km/11mi – about 1hr

▶ *Leave Compiègne by avenue Royale. At carrefour Royal, turn left onto route Tournante. At carrefour du Renard, take a right on route Eugénie.*

Carrefour d'Eugénie

Some of the forest's oldest **oak trees**★ stand around this junction. The most ancient ones date from the time of François I.

▶ *Take the winding road on the left which climbs to the Beaux Monts.*

Beaux Monts★★

Stop at the summit, near the Beaux Monts viewpoint. From here, the **view**★ stretches along the straight line of the avenue des Beaux-Monts through the forest all the way to the palace, barely visible 4km/ 2.5mi away. This magnificient linear perspective had been drawn to remind the Emperor's young bride of

the castle of Schönbrunn near Vienna, Austria.

▶ *Keep on going. Drive by the "Cèdre Marie-Louise", and park your car as you come across a dirt road on your right.*

Point de vue du Précipice

The Precipice Viewpoint offers an extensive **view**★ over the woody stretches of the valley of the Berne River and Mont St-Marc.

▶ *Return to your car and keep going.*

The road runs through a magnificent grove of oak and beech to a junction.

▶ *Take a right, cross route Eugénie and park your car as you come across the first dirt road to your right.*

Chapelle St-Corneille-aux-Bois

A chapel, attached to the abbey of St-Corneille in Compiègne, was originally built here in 1164 to welcome pilgrims and travellers. What stands today is a 13C Gothic structure with a 15C peculiar roof frame shaped like an upturned ship. The 16C **pavilion** built next to the chapel for François I's hunting staff unfortunately lost its original appearance during some 19C renovation works.

▷ *Return to your car. Continue to D 14 and turn right toward Compiègne.*

② Clairière de l'Armistice★★

6km/3.5mi northeast

▷ *Leave Compiègne by N 31 (east). Go straight across carrefour d'Aumont and carry straight on (D 546) to carrefour du Francport and the car park.*

The **First Armistice** was signed by the Allies and the Germans on 11 November 1918, hereby ending the Great War. The event took place in a clearing of the Compiègne Forest, near the village of **Rethondes**. A site where a network of tracks existed for heavy artillery installations, was cleared to make room for the **private train** of the allied forces' commander-in-chief, Field-Marshal Foch, and for that of the German plenipotentiaries. The tracks were linked to the Compiègne-Soissons line at Rethondes train station.

Twenty two years later, on 22 June 1940, Nazi Germany would force the French to sign, in the very same Pullman, the **Second Armistice** which established a German occupation zone in Northern France.

Today, rails and flagstones, marking the site of the former railway carriages, surround a memorial commemorating this important page in history..

Wagon du maréchal Foch

⊙*Open mid-Oct–end Mar 9am–noon, 2–5.30pm. Apr–mid-Oct 9am–12.30pm, 2–6pm.* ∞*4€.* ℘*03 44 85 14 18.*

The original dining-car, which was converted into an office for Field Marshal Foch, was exhibited in the courtyard of the Invalides in Paris from 1921 to 1927, then returned to the forest clearing and placed in a shelter built for the purpose. Transported to Berlin as a trophy in 1940, it was destroyed in the Thuringia Forest in April 1945. In 1950, it was replaced by another railway car from a similar series.

Housed in a little museum, the replica of the carriage was refurbished to its condition at the time of the First Armistice, and shows the original artefacts (which had been safely put aside) used by the delegates during the meeting.

Display rooms devoted to both armistices include contemporary newspapers, maps, photographs, military uniforms, and a few striking 3D shots of the Great War.

③ Mont Saint-Marc and ponds★

26km/16mi – about 1hr 30min

▷ *Leave Compiègne by N 31 (east).*

Pont de Berne

This is where the Dauphin, the future Louis XVI, met Marie-Antoinette for the first time; the future queen had just arrived from Vienna.

▷ *Turn right toward Pierrefonds (D 547). At Vivier-Frère-Robert, turn left onto route du Geai.*

Mont St-Marc★

The slopes of this long rise are covered with beeches. On reaching the plateau, turn left onto the forest road that follows the edge; there are good views of the valleys of the Berne and Aisne Rivers, Rethondes and Laigue Forest. The road follows the northern promontory of the hill. Some 2.5km/1.5mi farther along, **Carrefour Lambin** offers a particularly fine **view** of the Aisne Valley.

▷ *Return by the same road and fork left onto the first road suitable for vehicles. Drive down Route du Geai and continue toward Pierrefonds. Turn right and continue along the main street in Vieux-Moulin.*

Vieux-Moulin

This former woodcutters' village later became a wealthy holiday resort. The little church was rebuilt in 1860 at Napoleon III's expense.

▷ *Turn left at the junction with the war memorial and take route Eugénie to Étang de l'Étot.*

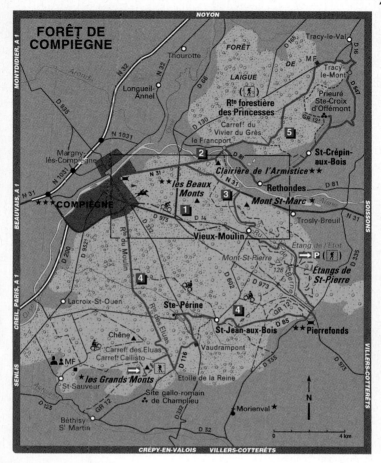

Étangs de St-Pierre

These ponds were created to stock fish; they were dug by members of the Celestine community from the priory of Mont-St-Pierre, to the west. Empress Eugénie's former chalet is now a forest warden's house.

◐ *About 1km/0.5mi beyond the last pond, at a fork near the edge of the forest, take the small road left that climbs up to the hilltop districts of Pierrefonds.*

4 Grands Monts★

27km/17mi – about 1hr 30min

Château de Pierrefonds★★
◐ *See PIERREFONDS*

◐ *Leave Pierrefonds by D 85, heading west.*

The road first rises to a wooded plateau, where the beautiful beech groves were largely destroyed during storms in 1984; it then descends into St-Jean-aux-Bois.

St-Jean-aux-Bois

This charming village was appropriately renamed "Solitude" in 1794. The 12C monastic buildings which were at the heart of the village can be seen along one side of it, marked by a moat filled with water. The Benedictine nuns left their abbey for Royallieu (on the outskirts of Compiègne) in 1634 as the forest was no longer safe; for a while Augustine canons took their place but in 1761, St-Jean was abandoned by its religious inhabitants.

The old fortified gate leads to the esplanade and the last vestiges of the abbey: the church, the chapterhouse and the doorway to the "Small Courtyard" (formerly farm buildings). The architectural purity of the 13C **church★** is remarkable. Inside, the sober harmony of the transept and chancel create an impression of grandeur. The slenderness of the columns separating each transept arm into two bays emphasises the church's height. The arrangement here, that was common later in the 16C, is the only example in the region from that period. The grisailles recall the luminous atmosphere of the nave in the 13C. The oldest part of the church, on the south side, is the **chapter house** (c.1150), used as a chapel.

Ste-Périne

The pond surrounded by plane trees and poplars, and the woodland house in an old priory form an attractive sight. The nuns of Ste-Périne occupied this hermitage from 1285 to 1626. Fear for their safety forced them to move first to Compiègne, then to Paris, then La Villette, Chaillot and finally Auteuil.

▶ *Turn around. Take a right onto the main road to Crépy-en-Valois and at Vaudrampont, turn right onto D 116. At Étoile de la Reine roundabout, turn sharp right onto route des Éluas and first left onto an unpaved road that leads to carrefour Callisto. Park your car.*

Grands Monts★

🚶This southern part of the forest is divided into the plateau and the swamps. The short trip described below (*30min round trip*), along an overhanging path shaded by beech groves, introduces some of the area's characteristics. Walk down route des Princesses; immediately after the barrier, turn left onto the path marked with yellow indicators which goes around the promontory.

Turn back when the path becomes less accessible and reaches the bottom of the gully.

▶ *Return to route des Éluas, and return to Compiègne via route du Moulin.*

Another itinerary (no 5) might take in the **village of Rethondes**, the church at **St-Crépin-aux-Bois**, and the 16C ruins of the church of the old **Prieuré Ste-Croix-d'Offémont**. The route des Princesses is a popular starting point for rambles.

ADDRESSES

🏠 STAY

⊖⊖ **Auberge de la Vieille Ferme** – *58 r. de la République, Meux. ✆ 03 44 41 58 54. www.aubergedelavieilleferme. abcsalles.com. 14 rooms. ⮂9.50€. Restaurant⊖⊖🍽.* This old farmhouse built of Oise Valley brick offers rooms that are simple but well-kept and practical. The restaurant sports exposed beams, rustic furniture, a tile floor and gleaming copperware. The menu offers traditional and regional cuisine.

⊖⊖🍽 **Hôtel des Beaux Arts** – *33 cours Guynemer. ✆03 44 92 26 26. www.bestwestern.com. 50 rooms. ⮂10€.* Located along the Oise waterfront, here's a contemporary hotel whose modern, well-soundproofed rooms have been furnished in teak or laminated wood. Some are larger and have a kitchenette.

🍴 EAT

⊖⊖ **Le Bistrot des Arts** – *33 cours Guynemer. ✆ 03 44 20 10 10. Closed Sat lunch and Sun.* Located on the ground floor of the Hôtel des Beaux-Arts, an appealing, authentic bistro decorated with various objects and etchings. In the kitchen, the chef concocts appetizing dishes using market-fresh produce.

⊖⊖ **Auberge du Buissonnet** – *825 r. Vineux, Choisy-au-Bac. 5km/3mi NE of Compiègne via N 31 and D 66. ✆03 44 40 17 41. www.aubergedu buissonnet. com. Closed Sun eve, Tue eve and Mon. Reservations recommended.* Ask for a table near the bay windows of the dining room or on the terrace, weather permitting, and watch ducks and swans glide peacefully over the pond, then shake themselves off and waddle proudly toward the garden.

Corbie

Corbie lies in the Somme Valley, at the confluence of the Ancre River. It developed around a powerful Benedictine abbey, renowned for its library and scriptorium, whose influence spread all over Europe and which was granted the rare privilege of minting coins.

▶ **Population:** 6 317
◔ **Michelin Local Map:** 301: I-8
❚ **Info:** Office du tourisme de Corbie, 28-30 pl. de la République, 80800. ✆03 22 96 95 76.

A BIT OF HISTORY

A Cradle for Saints – A monastery was founded here between 657 and 661 under the patronage of **Saint Bathild**, widow of the Frankish king Clovis II.

In Carolingian times, it became a centre of Christian civilization under the direction of **Saint Adalard**, Charlemagne's cousin. More than 300 monks took part in the constant worship of the Lord, and apostolic activity developed around **Saint Paschase Radbert** who wrote the first theological treatise on the Eucharist.

The abbey spread to **Corvey** in Westphalia, which became the main centre of evangelism in northern Europe under the impetus of **Saint Anschaire**, born in Corbie in 801. In the 11C, **Saint Gerard**, a monk from Corbie, retreated to the area between the Garonne and the Dordogne, founding the monastery of La Sauve Majeure.

Saint Colette (1381–1447), the daughter of a local carpenter, favoured with numerous visions, establish several convents of Poor Clares.

SIGHTS
Museum

◔*Daily (except Mon) Jul– end Sept 2.30–5.30pm. ✆03 22 96 43 37.*
Essentially dedicated to the history of the abbey, it contains pieces from the Merovingian (7C), Carolingian (8C), Viking (9C–10C) and Romanesque (11C–13C) periods: statues and various stone carvings, pottery, seals, coins etc. Also note a relief map of the 1636 **siege of Corbie** (then occupied by the Spaniards) by the army of Louis XIII.

From the vast place de la République, go through the 18C **monumental gateway** to the abbey. The cloisters and convent buildings were razed during the French Revolution.

Abbatiale St-Pierre

◔*2.50€ (guided tours), 0.50€ (unaccompanied). Call tourist office on ✆03 22 96 95 76 for more details.*
The construction of the former abbey church lasted from the 16C to the 18C, but in 1815, the transept and chancel were knocked down, since they were by then in a state of collapse.

Somme Valley, Corbie

S. Sauvignier/ MICHELIN

The stylistic unity of the remaining buildings is due to the architects' continued use of the Gothic style throughout the Renaissance and Classical periods: this accounts for the ribbed vaults in the three aisles, the rose-window, the twin towers pierced by twin bays, and the west front featuring three doorways with broken arches, all following the style of Gothic cathedrals. The **interior**, which used to be 117m/384ft long, is now only about 36m/118ft long. To the right of the altar is **Saint Bathild** an example of majestic 14C statuary, and on a pillar in the north aisle is a 13C head of **Saint Peter**.

Chapelle Ste-Colette

The chapel was built in 1959 on the site of the house in which Saint Colette was born, and contains a 16C statue of the saint kneeling.

SURROUNDS
Église de La Neuville

2km/1mi west, on the right bank of the River Ancre.
Above the doorway of the early-16C church is a large, interesting **high-relief carving**★ showing Christ's entry into Jerusalem on Palm Sunday. The relief is remarkable for its clarity and wealth of detail: spectators perched in the trees, in the background a miller wearing a cotton bonnet at the window of his mill.

Australian Memorial

3km/2mi south. Leave Corbie by D 1 (toward Amiens) and in Fouilloy, turn left onto D 23 toward Villers-Bretonneux.
In spring 1918, the hills around **Villers-Bretonneux** were fiercely fought over by the Germans and the Australians, following the German offensive on Picardy. More than 10 000 Australian men lost their lives. A memorial and a cemetery recall their sacrifice. Extended **view** towards the Somme River and Amiens.

ADDRESSES

♈ EAT

☕ **L'Abbatiale** – *Pl. Jean-Catelas* – 𝄡 *03 22 48 40 48. Closed Sun.*
☕☕ *7 rooms.* This down-to-earth family establishment facing the St-Pierre church welcomes guests with benevolence and simplicity. Two menus await diners: a brasserie-type formula and the traditional restaurant fare; a few rooms are available. Very affordable prices.

Coucy-Le-Château-Aufrique★

Coucy extends along a promontory overlooking the Ailette Valley on an impressive defensive **site**★, further sheltered by ramparts. Today, the remains of what was one of the biggest fortresses in Europe, dismantled in the 17C, consolidated in the 19C, then seriously damaged during World War I, still bear witness to the power of medieval lords.

A BIT OF HISTORY

The Lord of Coucy – "Neither king nor prince am I: I am the Lord of Coucy!"

- ▶ **Population:** 995
- 🜨 **Michelin Local Map:** 306: B-5
- 🄘 **Info:** Office du tourisme de Coucy-le-Château, 8 r. des Vivants, 02380. 𝄡 03 23 52 44 55. www.coucy.com.
- ▶ **Location:** 12 miles north of Soissons, and reached by the D 1, D 934 or the D 13.
- 😊 **Don't Miss:** The view of the port of Soissons; the medieval sound and light show in July.
- 🕐 **Timing:** Two hours to explore the ramparts, and one more for the museum.
- 🜨 **Also See:** The forest of Saint-Gobain, and Soissons.

was the proud boast of **Enguerrand III** (1192–1242), the castle's owner. Related to Louis IX of France, he fought loyally and valiantly at the **Battle of Bouvines.**

Although he sought to take possession of the French throne during **Blanche of Castille**'s regency, he eventually returned to the royal favour.

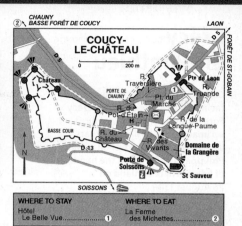

WHERE TO STAY
Hôtel
Le Belle Vue..................①

WHERE TO EAT
La Ferme
des Michettes...............②

SIGHTS

Château

🕐*Open daily May–end Aug 10am–1pm, 2–6.30pm. Rest of the year 10am–1pm, 2–5.30pm.* 🚫*Closed Jan 1, May 1, Dec. 25* ⊚*5€ (no charge first Sun of month Nov–May).* 📞*03 23 52 71 28.*

Visitors enter a **bailey** before the castle proper. To the right of the bailey entrance the **Guard-room** (Salle des Gardes) contains a model and documents relating to Coucy.

The foundations of a Romanesque **chapel** are visible on the approach to the castle, which stands as an irregular quadrilateral at the end of the promontory. The great round **towers**, built with hoardings that used to surround the castle, were over 30m/98ft high and the **keep**, destroyed by the Germans in 1917, reached a height of 54m/177ft.

The dwellings were rebuilt by Enguerrand VII at the end of the 14C, then completed at the end of the 15C by Louis of Orléans, Charles VI's brother. Remains of two large **chambers** (Salle des Preuses and Salle des Preux) still exist, with a **cellar** underneath. From the west tower, good **view** over the valleys of the Ailette and Oise Rivers.

Porte de Soissons

This gate, which was built in the 13C, is reinforced by the Coucy tower and now houses the **Tour musée**. Models of the town and its castle are among the exhibits, together with engravings and old photographs, and figures dressed in period costumes.

In the upper part of the tower, a platform affords good **views** over the Ailette

Valley. 🕐*Open Thu–Sun 2–6pm. For more details call the tourist office at* 📞*03 23 52 44 55.*

Eglise St-Sauveur

Built against the ramparts, this church with a Romanesque façade and Gothic naves (12C–14C) was almost entirely rebuilt after World War I.

Porte de Laon

Located at the base of the promontory, this gate (13C) played a major defensive role. It was guarded by two huge round towers, with walls 8m/26ft thick at their base.

Domaine de la Grangère

This garden was once part of the Governor's estate where the legitimized son of Henri IV and Gabrielle d'Estrées: **César, Duke of Vendôme,** was born in 1594. Note the lip of the well, made from a keystone from the castle keep.

ADDRESSES

🛏 STAY

⊖ **Hôtel Le Belle Vue** – *In the Upper Town.* 📞*03 23 52 69 70. Closed 1 week at Christmas. 7 rooms.* ⊆*5€. Restaurant*⊖. Ask for a room on the second floor and enjoy an unbeatable view of the Château and the plain beyond. The rather old-fashioned dining room serves traditional fare.

Crécy-en-Ponthieu

Crécy is a peaceful little town facing the plateau on which Crécy Forest stands. Its name conjures up images of the Hundred Years War, particularly the defeat of King Philippe VI of France at the hands of Edward III of England on 26 August 1346.

▸ **Population:** 1 611
⚲ **Michelin Local Map:** 301: E-6
🛈 **Info:** Office du tourisme de Crécy-en-Ponthieu, 32 r. Mar. Leclerc-de-Hauteclocque, 80150. ℘03 22 23 93 84. www.crecyen ponthieu.com.

A BIT OF HISTORY
The Battle of Crécy
Crécy was the site of the bitter defeat inflicted on **Philippe VI** of France by Edward III of England at the beginning of the Hundred Years War. **Edward III** had landed in Normandy with 3 900 knights, 11 000 longbow men and 5 000 armed Welshmen; they rampaged through Normandy as far as Poissy and took up a defensive position at Crécy. Philip VI advanced with 1 200 knights, 6 000 Genoese archers and 20 000 men-at-arms.

An attack was then launched by the French cavalry, in a spirited but ill-planned move. The assault disintegrated under the hail from the English archers, reinforced for the first time in European history by bombardments; in the resulting carnage, 11 princes, 1 542 knights and 10 000 soldiers fell on the battlefield.

SIGHTS
Eglise Saint-Séverin
Inside this 14C–15C church, four paintings attributed to Nicolas Poussin School illustrate the life of Moïse.

"Croix du Bourg"
Erected in the lower part of town, this monument (c13C) remains a mystery. It may have been dedicated to Aliénor of Castille, beloved wife of Edward I.

Moulin Edouard III
1km/0.5mi north on D 111.
This hillock is the site of the windmill from where the King of England directed the Battle of Crécy.

From the top, **view** over the undulating plain (*viewing table*).

"Croix de Bohême"
On D 56 southeast of Crécy.
This cross marks the spot where Philip VI's ally **John the Blind**, the old king of Bohemia, was killed while being carried to his badly wounded son at the heart of the battle.

🚗 DRIVING TOUR
29km/18mi round trip – about 1hr

Natural habitat of deers, wild boars and pheasants, the **Forêt de Crécy** (4 300ha/10 625 acres) lies on a plateau to the south of the Maye River. It is carpeted with lily-of-the-valley in springtime. Viewing tables have been set out on the edge of the forest in **Forêt-Montiers** and **Forêt-l'Abbaye**.
The forest has been laid out for tourism, with lay-bys and picnic areas, 10 footpaths and 47 km of bridlepaths where cyclists are allowed.

▷ *From Crécy, take the Forêt-l'Abbaye road (D 111) to the crossroads at Le Monument, then turn right onto the Forest-Montiers road.*

The road runs past some superb beech and oak copses.

▷ *Continue to Le Poteau de Nouvion, then turn right onto the forest road called Le Chevreuil, to the crossroads at La Hutte-des-Grands-Hêtres.*

Hutte des Grands-Hêtres

This part of the forest, crossed by a footpath called Sentier des Deux-Huttes, is absolutely outstanding.

▶ *Return to Poteau de Nouvion and turn right towards N 1 and Forêt-Montiers.*

Forêt-Montiers

It was here that Saint Riquier founded his hermitage. It was also here that François I's son, Charles, died of plague at the age of 23.

▶ *Take N 1 in a northerly direction.*

Bernay-en-Ponthieu

This village, lying on the south-facing slopes of the Maye Valley, has retained its old **posting house** opposite the church. The street façade of the former **coaching inn** dates from the 15C: the corbelled upper floor rests on a beam carved with garlands and grotesques.

Laon★★

Former capital of France in the Carolingian era, Laon occupies a dramatic **site★★** along a narrow, hilly ridge (100m/328ft high) overlooking wide plains. Located on the borders of Picardy, the Paris Basin and the Champagne region, it is a celebrated tourist destination, with its Gothic cathedral, one the oldest in the country, its picturesque old houses stretching along narrow streets, its mysterious network of underground galleries running under the citadel, and its medieval ramparts facing a vast horizon.

A BIT OF HISTORY

Carolingian Capital – Ancient **Laudunum** was the capital of France during the Carolingian period (9C–10C). Berthe au Grand Pied, Charlemagne's mother, was born northeast of Laon, while Charles the Bald, Charles the Simple, Louis IV d'Outremer, Lothar and Louis V all lived on "Mount Laon" in a palace near the Ardon Gate. The reign of

▶ *Turn right onto D 938 and return to Crécy-en-Ponthieu.*

The road overlooks the wide **Maye Valley** with its alternating fields of crops, meadows and thickets. The southern slopes are topped by the Crécy Forest.

ADDRESSES

⍩ EAT

⊖⊜ **Hôtel La Maye** – *13 r. de Saint-Riquier. ℘03 22 23 54 35. Closed Sun dinner and Mon except hols from Sept to Jun. 11 rooms. Restaurant⊖⊜.*
The atmosphere is warm and convivial in this restaurant which offers a brasserie-style formula at lunchtime and a gastronomic menu including such specialities as warm lobster and foie gras salad. Upstairs there are 11 pleasant rooms with comfortable beds and TV. Large car park and attractive riverside garden.

▶ **Population:** 26 265
♿ **Michelin Local Map:** 306: D-5
🛈 **Info:** Office du tourisme de Laon, pl. duParvis-Gautier-de-Mortagne, 02000. ℘03 23 20 28 62. www.tourisme-paysdelaon.com.
▶ **Location:** Laon is 130km from Paris via the N 2, and 50km from Reims by the N 44.
🅿 **Parking:** Parking is very limited in the Upper Town; leave your car in the Lower Town *(underground parking, Place de la Gare)*, then travel to the Upper Town via the cable-drawn mini-metro *(♿see p346).*
👁 **Don't Miss:** The nave of Cathédrale Notre-Dame, reaching to an amazing height; the collections of the Musée d'Art et d'Archéologie.

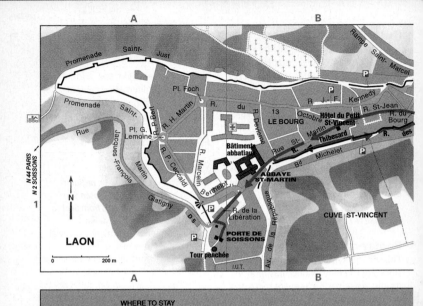

WHERE TO STAY

Hostellerie Les Chevaliers...①

the Carolingians finally came to an end with the arrival of **Hugues Capet**, who took Laon by treachery. Charlemagne's descendants were driven out and Capet established himself in Paris.

From the Carolingian period on, Laon became a renowned religious and intellectual centre under the impetus of **Scot Erigène** and **Martin Scot** (9C); **Anselme** and **Raoul de Laon** (11C); and Bishop **Gautier de Mortagne** (12C), who had the cathedral built. In the 13C the town was surrounded with new ramparts, and from the 16C, Laon was a powerful military stronghold, besieged on several occasions, including once by Henri IV in 1594. In 1870 the munitions magazine exploded, killing or injuring over 500 people were.

👣 WALKING TOUR
VILLE-HAUTE

Laon is divided into two sectors. The Upper Town or **Ville-Haute** is Laon's true historical core, whose highlights are described below.

The Lower Town or **Ville-Basse**, was severely damaged by both World Wars, and does not particularly lend itself to tourism. Driving can be very tricky in the

Upper Town, and parking is extremely limited there.

Visitors are advised to leave their car in the Lower Town and travel to the Upper Town via a cable-drawn railway called the **Poma.** ⊙Open Mon–Sat 7am–8pm (Jul–Aug Sun 2.30pm–7pm). ⊙Closed holidays. ≈1.10€ (round trip). ℘03 23 79 07 59 (SNCF train station). www.tul-laon.net.

Palais épiscopal

Contiguous to the cathedral, the former Bishop's Palace now houses the court house. It is preceded by a courtyard offering a view of the east end of the cathedral.

The 13C building on the left rests on a gallery of pointed arches, its capitals decorated with plant motifs.

Upstairs, the **Grande Salle du Duché** (over 30m/98ft long) houses the Assize Court. In the building at the far end (17C) were the bishop's apartments which lead directly to the two-storey 12C chapel.

The lower chapel was reserved for servants while the upper chapel, in the form of a Greek cross, served for religious ceremonies in the bishop's presence.

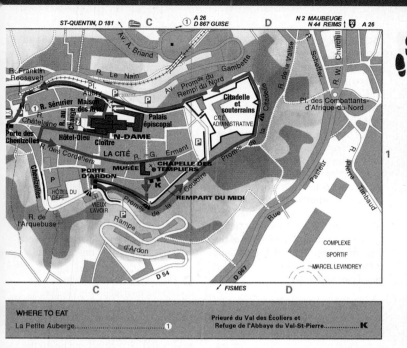

WHERE TO EAT

La Petite Auberge.......................................❶

Prieuré du Val des Écoliers et
Refuge de l'Abbaye du Val-St-Pierre.................**K**

Facing the palace, the **Maison des Arts et Loisirs** stands on the site of the third hospital founded in the 13C. The hall of this municipal theatre houses contemporary art exhibits. ◷*Open Tue–Fri 1–7pm, Sat 1–6pm daily.* ◷*Closed from mid Jul–Aug and holidays.* ✆*03 23 22 86 86.*

In **rue Sérurier**, no 53 has a 15C entrance and no 33 bis incorporates the 18C door of the old town hall. The 16C–17C Dauphin Inn, at no 7–11 **rue au Change**, still has its original wooden gallery.

Cathédrale Notre-Dame★★

This is one of the oldest Gothic cathedrals in France, its construction began in the 12C and was completed around 1230. The cathedral originally had seven towers: two on the west front, one over the transept crossing and four on the transept arms, two of which lost their spire during the Revolution.

The lovely, unusual **west front**, which boasts three finely decorated porches (rehandled in the 19C), is framed by two famous towers (56m/184ft tall), attributed to **Villard de Honnecourt**. Imposing yet harmonious, these are pierced by

large bays and framed by slender turrets, and they bear great oxen on their corners. Built on the same model, the two towers of the transept arms reach a height of 60m/196ft and 75m/246ft.

Interior – Its dimensions are amazing: 110m/360ft long, 30m/98ft wide and 24m/78ft high (Notre-Dame de Paris: 130m/426ft, 45m/147ft, 35m/114ft). Roofed with sexpartite vaulting, the **nave★★★** rises to a magnificent height through four levels: great arches, galleries, a blind triforium and a clerestory. Beyond the nave, the wide chancel terminates in a flat east end, as in Cistercian churches. The transept crossing offers a good view of the nave, chancel, transept arms and the Norman-style lantern tower (40m/131ft high).

Beautiful 13C **stained-glass windows** grace the apse's lancet bays and rose window, dedicated to the Glorification of the Church. The rose window in the north transept also contains 13C stained glass representing the Liberal Arts. Note the chancel railings and the organ dating from the 17C.

▶ *Leave the cathedral by the south transept and follow the outer wall of the cloisters, decorated with a frieze of sculpted foliage. On the corner is an Angel with a sundial.*

Hôtel-Dieu

One of the few surviving medieval hospitals in France, this 12C–13C building used to open onto the street, but its bays and wide tierce-point arches have been walled up. On the lower level, the **Salle gothique Bernard de Clairvaux** *(open to the public)* attended to the needs of pilgrims and passers-by.Now occupied by the tourist office, the great **Hall of the Sick**, on the upper level, has retained some interesting elements, including mural paintings from the 15C.

▶ *Follow rue Châtelaine, then one of the two lanes on the left leading to rue des Cordeliers. Cross place des Frères-Le Nain and continue along rue G.-Ermant.*

Musée d'Art et d'Archéologie de Laon★

🕐*Open daily (except Mon) Jun–end Sept 11am–6pm. Oct–end May 2–6pm.* 🕐*Closed Jan 1, May 1, Jul 14, Dec 25* 🎫*3.60€.* ✆*03 23 22 87 00. http:// pagesperso-orange.fr/jpjcg/index.htm.* Part of the museum's section dedicated to Mediterranean archaeology, the collection of **Greek art** consists of some 17 000 pieces: vases, terracotta, figurines and sculptures, including a striking head of Alexander the Great (3C BC).

The section on regional archaeology displays local finds such as tools, jewellery, weapons, figurines and pottery from the Gallo-Roman and Merovingian periods. Finally, the Beaux-Arts section includes paintings by the Master of the Rohan Hours (15C), the **Le Nain** brothers (17C), Desportes (17C) and Berthélemy (18C). It also showcases 18C Sinceny faïence pieces, and some furniture and sculpture from the Middle Age to the 19C

Chapelle des Templiers★

Located in the Museum's courtyard. Same opening hours as for the Museum. ✆*03 23 20 19 87.*

Half way between the cathedral and Laon's first medieval castle, the Temple commandery founded here in the 12C was a recruiting center for the warrior-monks. After the order was suppressed, the building passed on to the Knights of St John of Jerusalem.

A peaceful flower garden has replaced the Knights Templar's cemetery, but the Romanesque, octogonal chapel has been preserved. Note its gabled bell tower and small chancel with a semicircular apse. The porch and the gallery were added in the 13C and 14C. The interior houses two remarkable **statue-columns** of prophets removed from the west front of the cathedral.

▶ *On leaving, turn right onto rue G.- Ermant, then follow rue Vinchon.*

The street is lined with old houses: no 44 was the 13C Val des Écoliers Priory (15C chapel and 18C portal) and no 40 the Val-St-Pierre Abbey refuge (15C–16C).

Rempart du Midi and Porte d'Ardon★

The 13C Porte d'Ardon or Porte Royée (belonging to the roi, the king in French), stands at the end of the south ramparts, flanked by watchtowers with pepper-pot roofs. The gate overlooks a picturesque old public wash-house and drinking trough. The south ramparts end in a **citadel** built for Henri IV by Jean Errard. Walk round it along Promenade de la Citadelle which offers views of the plain dotted with other, small Tertiary Age hillocks.

▶ *Continue to the St-Rémi rampart, and turn left toward place du Général-Leclerc. Walk along rue du Bourg, rue St-Jean and rue St-Martin.*

Hôtel du Petit St-Vincent

This building was constructed in the first half of the 16C as the town refuge for St Vincent's Abbey, which was outside the ramparts. The main body of the Gothic building by the road is surrounded by turrets and flanked with an entrance vault surmounted by a chapel.

A later wing set at right angles overlooks the courtyard.

Abbaye St-Martin★

🕐*Open daily (except Sat afternoon) Jan–Jul and Sept–end Dec, 5.30–6.30pm. Jul–end Aug daily 2–5pm.* 👣 *Guided tours (30mn).* 📞*03 23 20 28 62.* Restored after the fire of 1944, this 12C–13C former Premonstratensian abbey church is a beautiful example of the Early Gothic style. The square offers a good general view of the building. Note the long, Romanesque-looking nave, the height (35m/114ft) and arrangement of the two towers at the corner of the nave and the transept (Rhenish influence), and the tall south transept with its rose window and arcades.

The west front soars up, pierced by a great bay; its gable is decorated with a high-relief carving of Saint Martin sharing his cloak with a pauper. The tympana over the side doors depict the Decapitation of John the Baptist (*right*) and the Martyrdom of Saint Lawrence, who was roasted alive (*left*).

Interior – The chancel and the transept chapels have flat east ends, following Cistercian custom. Recumbent figures lie near the entrance: Raoul de Coucy, a Laon Knight (late 12C) and Jeanne de Flandre, his sister-in-law, abbess of Sauvoir-sous-Laon (14C). The wooden panels in the nave are in the Louis XV style and those in the chancel Louis XIII. A 16C Christ of Compassion stands to the right of the Chapelle St-Eloi, separated from the church by a Renaissance stone screen.

Abbey buildings – The restored 18C section, visible from the cloisters, houses the municipal library. A fine elliptical stone staircase leads to the first floor.

Porte de Soissons★

The gate was built in the 13C from quarried stone and reinforced with round towers. It stands in a park containing a monument to **Jacques Marquette** (1637–75), a Jesuit from Laon who discovered the Mississippi River. A curtain wall links the gate to the great **Tour Penchée** or leaning tower, so-named following subsidence.

Rue Thibesard follows the sentry path along the ramparts, offering unusual **views**★ of the cathedral. Its towers rise above the old slate roofs with their red-brick chimneys.

Continue along the ramparts and **rue des Chenizelles**, an old, cobbled street, to the 13C **Porte de Chenizelles**. The two towers create a narrow passageway through to rue du Bourg.

ADDRESSES

🏠 STAY

🛏 **Hostellerie Les Chevaliers** – *3 r. Sérurier.* 📞*03 23 27 17 50.* The stones, bricks, beams, cosy décor and hospitable welcome give this skilfully restored medieval house the charm of a homely guesthouse.

🛏 **Hôtel du Commerce** – *11 pl. des Droits-de-l'Homme.* 📞*03 23 79 57 16. www.hotel-commerce-laon.com. 24 rooms.* ⊒*5€.* Conveniently located a stone's throw from the train station, this unpretentious establishment offers simply furnished, well maintained, rooms, and a garage.

🛏🍽 **Hostellerie Saint-Vincent** – *Av. Charles-de-Gaulle.* 📞*03 23 23 42 43. www.stvincent-laon.com. Closed Christmas period. 47 rooms.* ⊒*7.50. Restaurant*🍽🍽. A modern motel at the base of the upper town. Spacious rooms, and restaurant serving Alsacienne cuisine.

🍴 EAT

🍽🍽 **La Petite Auberge** – *45 bd Brossolette.* 📞*03 23 23 02 38. Closed last day of Feb–4 Mar, 24 Apr–1 May, 7–20 Aug, Sat lunch, Mon dinner and Sun except hols.* This regional-style building has been converted to house two dining areas: the Bistrot Le Saint-Amour which offers simple menus and the main dining room where one can enjoy fine dishes successfully marrying traditional and modern cuisine.

Parc du
Marquenterre ★★

The Marquenterre area is an alluvial plain reclaimed from the sea, which lies between the Authie and Somme estuaries. Its name derives from *mer qui entre en terre* (sea which enters the land). The stretches of land are made up of briny marshes, salt-pastures and sand dunes secured to the land by vegetation.

Today this reserve is home to 344 species of birds (the continent of Europe has 650 species in all), 265 species of plants, and 27 species of mammals living both on land and in the water, including a large colony of seals; the most inquisitive of them are sometimes spotted at high tide near the quayside at St Valéry-en-Somme and Le Crotoy.

A BIT OF HISTORY

Reclaimed from the sea – The process of reclaiming the land was started in the 12C by monks from **St-Riquier** and **Valloires** who erected the first dikes and attempted to canalise the rivers. Many drainage canals were built. Perched on a hill, **Rue**, the future capital of the Marquenterre area, ceased to be an island in the 18C. During the 19C, dikes and beaches were strengthened, which allowed the development of vegetable and cereal growing. In 1923, the industrialist **Henri Jeanson** bought an area of marshland along the coast, which his successors drained and diked using Dutch methods, so that it was eventu-

- ♣ **Michelin Local Map:** 301: C-6
- **Info:** Comité Départemental du Tourisme de La Somme, 21 r. Ernest-Cauvin, 80000 Amiens. ℴ03 22 71 22 71. www.somme-tourisme.com.
- **Location:** The Park is accessible from Abbeville via the D 940, direction Crotoy.
- **Don't Miss:** The pleasure of moving silently across dunes, forests and marshes to observe migratory birds, concealed behind observation blinds .
- **Timing:** There are three different paths around the park that will take you from 45mn for the shortest one to 2hrs for a more in-depth tour.
- **Kids:** The red discovery trail is just tailored for them!
- **Also See:** The bay of the Somme; Le Crotoy, and St-Valery-sur-Somme.

ally possible to grow bulbs. At the same time, trees were planted. But the plans failed, and gave rise to the idea of a bird sanctuary.

The birth of the bird sanctuary – The Marquenterre lands have always been an important habitat for migratory and sedentary birds. Alas, it was also a

---

The Henson horse breed

This small robust horse is a cross between a French saddle horse and a Norwegian Fjord pony. Its coat varies from light yellow to brown, and its mane is a mixture of black and gold. This breed was developed in 1978 in a small village of the Baie de Somme area, thanks to the determination of **Doctor Berquin**. Hensons show remarkable endurance; they can remain out in the fields all year round and cover great distances without getting tired. Their docile and affectionate behaviour make them ideal companions for children and long-distance riders. They also fare very well in team competitions and horse shows generally.

MAKING THE MOST OF THE PARK
WHEN TO GO

Each season is interesting and enables visitors to watch different species.

Spring is the nesting season for many species such as storks, small waders (avocets, oystercatchers, plovers), grey lag geese, shelduck. The herons' nesting place is particularly spectacular since five species of large waders, including spoonbills, nest at the top of pine trees.

Summer is the migrating season for black storks; it is also the time when small waders gather at high tide and when large gatherings of spoonbills, cormorants and egrets can be seen.

Autumn sees the mass arrival of many species of ducks coming to spend the winter in the park (up to 6 000 birds, some of them arriving from Russia and Finland, can be observed). The park is the most important wader ringing centre in France, and studies on migration are carried out in cooperation with the Natonal Natural History Museum in Paris.

WHAT TO TAKE WITH YOU

Solid walking shoes, a wind-waterproof coat, and a pair of binoculars (*also available for rent at the park*).

RIDING TOURS 🐎

Espaces Equestres Henson – *34 chemin des Garennes, 80120 St-Quentin-en-Tourmont. 03 22 25 03 06. www.henson.fr.* The Henson horse riding centre organises guided riding tours for all levels of ability, including beginners and children.

---

paradise for hunters who brought many species close to extinction.

As a result, the Hunting Commission created in 1968 a reserve on the maritime land, to ensure the protection of the birds along 5km/3mi of coastline.

The owners of the Marquenterre estate next to the reserve decided to set up a bird sanctuary within it to allow the public to watch bird life in a natural habitat. Thirteen years later, the site became the property of the Office of Coastal Preservation. in 1994, it was granted the status of "protected nature reserve."

DISCOVERING THE BIRD SANCTUARY

🕐*Open daily Apr–end Sept 10am–7.30pm. Oct–Mid-Nov and Mid-Feb–Apr 10am–6pm. Mid-Nov–Mid-Feb 10am–5pm. Last admission 2h before closing. Closed Jan 1, Dec 25. 9.90€. 03 22 25 68 99. www.parcdumarquenterre. com. It is advisable to visit on a rising tide when the birds leave the stretches of the Baie de Somme or during the spring and autumn migration periods.*

The Bird Sanctuary covers 250ha/618acres on the edge of the reserve and houses numerous species of birds, including the red-beaked sheldduck, geese, tern, avocet, gulls, herons, sandpipers and spoonbill. Three marked **trails** and trained guides will help you discover the riches of the park at your own pace:

Red discovery trail – *1.5km/0.9mi.* This introductory tour of the park will offer you a close-up view of the birds that live here permanently: ducks, seagulls, geese and herons. Their calls attract wild birds of the same species. A few familiar mammals can be seen on the way: Henson horses, weasels and hares, as well as amphibians such as toads and insects such as dragonflies.

Blue observation trail – *4km/2.5mi.* This walk follows a path through the dunes to various observation hides.

Green extended observation trail – *5km/3.1mi.* An additional path shows the reserve from a completely different angle, allowing an in-depth discovery of its fauna and flora.

Morienval★

Nestled in the peaceful valley of the Automne River, on the edge of the forest, this small village shelters one of the earliest expressions of Gothic architecture in France: Notre-Dame de Morienval, a late Romanesque abbey church, beautifully set off by the trees, and a truly remarkable building as its bridges stylistic periods and illustrates the transition from Romanesque to Gothic.

▶ **Population:** 1 048
⚭ **Michelin Local Map:** 305: I-5 or map 106 fold 11
◗ **Location:** 72.4km/45mi northeast of Paris, and south of Compiègne.

ÉGLISE NOTRE-DAME★

🕓*Open 9am–7pm by prior arrangement only.* ℘*03 44 88 66 36.*

Notre-Dame church depended on a nunnery said to have been founded by **King Dagobert** in the 7C, and which was destroyed in 885 by the Vikings. The reconstruction of the nunnery and its church started in the 11C. Little has changed since the 12C, except for the reconstruction of the clerestory in the chancel. The narrow bays visible today date from the last restoration project (1878–1912).

Exterior – The abbey church has a distinctive silhouette, with its three towers, one adjoining the west front and two flanking the chancel; the north tower is marginally shorter and slimmer than the south tower. Go northward around the church to the apse; note the ambulatory which was squeezed onto the semicircle of the chancel at the beginning of the 12C, to give it extra strength.

Interior – The extremely narrow ambulatory is the most unusual part of the church. Its arches, dating from about 1125, are some of the oldest in France. Here for the first time ogee arches have been used in the curved part of a building; however, they are an integral part of the areas of vaulting that they support. The transition from groined vaulting to quadripartite vaulting can be seen.

A large number of memorial stones stand along the wall of the north aisle; one commemorates the great abbess Anne II Foucault (1596–1635). Farther along the same wall, past the northern arm of the transept, is a statue of **Our Lady of Morienval** (17C).

On the wall of the opposite aisle, 19C engravings show the church as it was before the last restoration. In the southern arm of the transept stands a 16C Crucifixion group once mounted on a rood beam, and a large 17C terracotta Saint Christopher stands on the same side in the nave near the main doorway.

🚗 DRIVING TOUR

If you have a half day to spare, you may want to drive through the pleasant **Automne River Valley**, making some interesting stops along the way: the Gallo-Roman theatre and baths of **Champlieu**; the 16C **Lieu-Restauré Abbey**; the medieval village of **Vez★**, complete with its castle and dungeon; François I's residence at **Villers-Cotterêts**; and finally, the impressive ruins of Cistercian **Longpont Abbaye★**.

Église Notre-Dame

S. Sauvignier/MICHELIN

Grottes-Refuges de
Naours★

Below the surface of the plateau near the old village of Naours lies an amazing number of refuge-caves dug out of limestone. There are many in Picardy and parts of Artois, known as *creuttes*, *boves* or, in Naours, *muches*. During times of trouble, the men of the village would hide there. Today, 33m/98ft below ground level, you will get to discover the largest underground hideaway in France.

A BIT OF HISTORY

Human occupation of the caves of Naours goes back to the 9C and the **Norman invasions**, although the caves are mentioned in documents only from the 14C. They were much used during the **Wars of Religion** and the **Thirty Years War**. In the 18C **salt-smugglers** used them to avoid the collectors of the hated salt tax.

Forgotten for a while, they were rediscovered in 1887 by Abbot Danicourt, the local priest, who explored and cleared them with the help of the villagers. In 1905 treasure was found: 20 gold coins from the 15C, 16C and 17C. During **World War II**, the caves were occupied by the Germans.

CAVES

▲♨ 🕐*Guided tour (45min) daily May–end Aug 9.30am–6.30pm. Feb–end Apr and Sept–end Nov 10am–noon, 2–5pm.* 🕐*Closed Dec–Jan.* ☜*10€ (park only 5€).* ✆*03 22 93 71 78 .*

These 28 underground galleries form a town which could shelter 3 000 people in its 2km/1.25mi of streets and squares, its 300 rooms, three chapels, cattle sheds and stables, bakery with ovens, storerooms etc. Chimneys link the passages to the surface of the plateau. During the tour, the different layers of the soil are revealed: chalk, clay in fissures and pockets, flint in parallel bands. Housed in a few of the chambers, the

- 🚻 **Michelin Local**
  Map: 301: G-7
- 🈳 **Info:** ✆03 22 93 71 78.
  www.grottesdenaours.com.
- ▶ **Location:** On a limestone plateau, 13km/8mi north of Amiens.
- 🕐 **Timing:** Tours take about 45min.
- 🅿 **Parking:** On site (free).
- 🚻 **Also See:** Amiens, the château of Bertangles.

small **Musée des métiers picards** evokes some traditional Picardian crafts, and ends the visit. Back on the surface, you may want to climb to the top of the ridge, to the two reconstructed wooden Picardy **post-mills**. From this vantage point, you will enjoy a nice bird's eye **view** of the site of Naours.

ADDRESESS

☝/ EAT

🍴 **La Chèvrerie de Canaples** – *172 r. de Fieffes, 80670 Canaples. 6km/3.6mi N of Naours via D 60 and D 933.* ✆*03 22 52 93 06. Closed Nov–Mar, Sun and holidays. Reserv required.* An original way to round off your tour of the caves. This farm serves mid-afternoon refreshments, farm-style, to groups of at least 10, or lets visitors sample their cheeses *(closed lunchtime – noon to 2pm)* and discover their goat farm and shop selling regional products.

Grottes-Refuges de Naours

Noyon★

Noyon lies in the heart of a picturesque area, locally known as the "Petite Suisse" (small Switzerland). Overshadowed by its imposing cathedral, which witnessed the coronation of two early kings of France, birthplace of yet another major figure, namely Calvin, the town's identity was truly forged by history and religion.

A BIT OF HISTORY

Originally Gallo-Roman, Noyon was elevated by **Saint Medard** to a bishopric linked to Tournai in 581. A century later, **Saint Eligius** was one of its bishops. The town witnessed the splendour of two coronations, **Charlemagne**'s in 768 as King of the Franks, and **Hugues Capet**'s in 987 as King of France. Noyon was one of the first French cities to obtain its own charter, in 1108.

CATHEDRAL★★

⏱*Open daily Apr–end Oct 9am–noon, 2–6pm. Nov–end Mar 10am–noon, 2–5pm.* 👥 *Possibility of guided visit by arrangement with the Tourist Office.* ✆*03 44 21 88.*

Noyon's cathedral is a remarkable example of the **Early Gothic style,** skilfully combining the typically sober, solid appearance of Romanesque architecture with the breadth and harmony indica-

> ▶ **Population:** 14 471
> ⛪ **Michelin Local Map:** 305: i, j-3
> 🛈 **Info:** Office du tourisme de Noyon, 1 pl. Bertrand-Labarre, 60400. ✆03 44 44 21 88. www.noyon-tourisme.com.
> ◐ **Location:** 24km/15mi northeast of Compiègne by the N 32.
> 👁 **Don't Miss:** The early Gothic cathedral; the Musée du Noyonnais.
> 🕐 **Timing:** A good time to visit is the first weekend of July, for the fruit festival.

tive of the Gothic Style. Four buildings preceded the present cathedral, whose construction began with the chancel in 1145, and ended with the west front in 1235. The cathedral was restored after the First World War.

Exterior – The sparse front is preceded by an early-13C porch with three bays. It was reinforced in the 14C with two flying buttresses decorated with small gables. The **north tower** is one of the loveliest types of bell tower built in northern France in the 14C; it is discreetly decorated with fine mouldings and twists of foliage on the gallery arcades, and foliate friezes under the upper shoulders of the buttresses. Compare it with the older (1220), more austere south tower.

The square in front of the cathedral, called the **Place du Parvis**, is edged with a semicircle of canons' residences, where each entrance is surmounted by a representation of a canon's hat. It has kept its old charm, despite the fact that most of these buildings were rebuilt after 1918.

To the north stands the old **chapter library** *(may only be visited in the summer)*, a fine 16C timbered building. One of the library rooms containing blacklisted works was known as "Hell."

Interior★★ – Both the nave and the chancel are extremely well proportioned. The nave has five double bays.

Red-Fruit Festival

The area around Noyon is the main red-fruit producing region in France, 90% of the production being destined for the manufacture of **sorbets**. In July, when the **Marché aux Fruits Rouges** is on *(first Sunday of the month)*, the square in front of the cathedral is dotted with punnets of mouth-watering strawberries, red currants, cherries and black currants. Popular activities include pastry tasting and competitions of fruit-stone throwing.

Chapter library

B. Kaufmann/ MICHELIN

The elevation rises through four storeys: great arches, large and elegant galleries with double arcading which are particularly striking when viewed from the transept crossing, shallow triforium and clerestory.

The chancel vault is as high as the nave's. The eight ribs of the apse radiate from a central keystone and develop into a cluster of small columns. Nine chapels open onto the ambulatory. The lack of stained glasses accentuates the severity of the transept.

Among the furnishings, the Louis XVI high altar shaped liked a temple is of particular interest, as are some largely 18C wrought-iron gates that enclose the chancel and the chapels in the nave.

Today only a single gallery remains of the **old cloisters** (*north aisle*); the bays with beautiful radiating tracery overlook the garden. The opposite wall is pierced with wide pointed arch windows and a door giving access to the 13C **chapter-house**. The pointed arches rest on a series of columns.

ADDITIONAL SIGHTS
Musée du Noyonnais
🕐*Open daily (except Mon) Apr–end Oct 10am–noon, 2–6pm. Nov–end Mar 10am–noon, 2–5pm.* 🕐*Closed Jan 1, Nov 11, Dec 25.* 🎫*3€.* 📞*03 44 09 43 41.*
Mostly dedicated to local history, the museum's collections are housed in a brick and stone Renaissance building (a remnant of the old bishop's palace) and a 17C wing which was rebuilt after World War I. Many artefacts on display were discovered during excavations in Noyon and the surrounding area (Cuts, Béhéri-

court). They include 12C chess pieces, a cache of Gallo-Roman coins, and various funeral objects and ceramics. Also note 12C and 13C beautiful oak **chests** from the cathedral, and a collection of works by orientalist painter Joseph-Félix Bouchor (1853–1937).

Musée Jean-Calvin
🕐*Open daily (except Mon) Apr–end Oct 10am–noon, 2–6pm. Nov–end Mar 10am–noon, 2–5pm.* 🕐*Closed Jan 1, Nov 11, Dec 25.* 🎫*3€.* 📞*03 44 44 03 59.*
Located on the site of **Jean Calvin**'s birth house (destroyed during World War I's bombings), this museum is dedicated to the work of the French great reformer (1509–1564) and to the early history of French protestantism. Numerous, portraits, engravings and documents together with manuscript letters give visitors an overview of the religious movement that swept across the continent of Europe in the 16C. Among other exhibits are 16C French Bibles, including the famous Olivetan Bible and the Lefèvre d'Étaples Bible, models of a 16C printing works and of the round Paradise temple in Lyon (1564) as well as writings by Calvin and his contemporaries. The library also holds 1 200 books dating from the 16C to the 20C.

ADDRESSES

🛏 STAY
🍽🍽 **Le Cèdre** – *8 r. de l'Évêché.* 📞*03 44 44 23 24. www.hotel-lecedre.com. 35 rooms.* 🛏*8€.* This hotel built of red brick blends in perfectly with the surrounding cité. The rooms are best described as practical; most give onto the cathedral.

🍴 EAT
🍽🍽 **Dame Journe** – *2 bd Mony.* 📞*03 44 44 01 33. www.damejourne.fr. Closed Sept 7–20, Jan 5–12. Also closed on Mon and for Sun, Tue, Wed and Thu dinners.* This restaurant with a regular clientele has a warm, well-cared-for setting: Louis XVI-style armchairs and wood panelling. Good choice of menus offering traditional cuisine.

Péronne

This old fortified town of the Upper Somme Valley stretches between fish-filled ponds and "hardines", cultivated marshlands similar to Amiens' famous water gardens. It was marked by centuries of territorial struggles for power, then largely destroyed by German troops during WW I. Today, the area around Péronne has become popular for eel, carp and pike fishing, as reflected in the local gastronomy which includes specialities such as smoked eel, stuffed pike and Colvert beer, brewed in Péronne.

> ▶ **Population:** 9 000.
> ⚆ **Michelin Local Map:** 301: K-8.
> 🛈 **Info:** Office du tourisme de Péronne, 16 pl. André-Oudi-not, 80200. ℘03 22 84 42. www.ville-peronne.fr.

A BIT OF HISTORY

The Meeting in Péronne – In 1468, **Charles the Bold** (Duke of Burgundy) invited **Louis XI** (King of France) in Péronne, then part of the Burgundian state, in an attempt to clear up some of their territorial issues. Both men had an eye on the strategic region of Picardy. Louis, who had supported the uprising of the town of **Liège** against Charles, was imprisoned by his rival for a few days. To be released, he had to sign a humiliating treaty which forced him to assist in quelling the revolt in Liège. Louis XI, who never forgot this affront, ended up bringing Péronne under French control after Charles the Bold's death in 1477.

Miseries of War – In 1536, the Spanish army of **Charles V** undertook the siege of Péronne, but was forced to retire. In 1870, the town was besieged by the **Prussians** who bombarded the town for 13 days. Finally, during **World War I**, Péronne was occupied by the Germans and virtually destroyed.

SIGHTS
Historial de la Grande Guerre★★

Place André-Oudinot. � ⊙*Open daily 10am–6pm.* ⊙*Closed mid-Dec–mid-Jan.* ⊜*7.50€.* ℘*03 22 83 14 18.* *www.historial.org.*
Right behind the 13C **castle**, a Le Corbusier-inspired structure (Henri-Edouard Ciriani, 1992) built on stilts by a pond houses the Museum of the Great War. It offers an international view of a conflict which involved combatants and civilians from over 20 nations, and attempts to provide keys for understanding the roots of the hostilities. A series of 50 etchings by German artist Otto Dix invites visitors to reflect on the horror of war. Displayed in shallow **marble pits** evoking the trenches, weapons, military gear and personal belongings illustrate life on the front. Video monitors and a 30-minute film entitled *En Somme* also feature archival footage of the period.

Hôtel de Ville

Place du Cdt-Daudré. Behind the distinctive Neo-Renaissance façade of the town hall (looted and destroyed during WW I, then rebuilt in the 1920s), stands the **Musée Alfred-Danicourt.** Particularly renowned for its collection of **Gallic coins,** one of the richest in France, it also exhibits some prehistoric tools as well as Greco-Roman, Merovingian and Carolingians artefacts. ⊙*Open daily (except Sun and Mon) 2–5.30pm, Sat 9am–noon, 2–4.30pm.* ⊙*Closed public holidays, 3 weeks in May, and Christmas to New Year.* ℘*03 22 73 3110.*

Porte de Bretagne

Off rue St-Sauveur. Marking the frontier between the kingdom of France and the Flanders, this gateway (1602) was one of two entrances giving access through the town walls (destroyed before WW I). It is now a free-standing brick pavilion with a slate roof, adorned with the emblem of Péronne. Beyond the moat, walk through the gate of the demilune and follow the old brick **ramparts** with stone courses (16C–17C) for an attractive **view** over the lakes and the "hardines".

Château de
Pierrefonds★★

Complete with its large crenellated towers, soaring walls, drawbridge and walkways, this impressive fairy-tale castle dominates the pretty lakeside village of Pierrefonds. In the 19C, the original 15C fortress was deeply altered and transformed into an imperial residence for Napoleon III. Crowning achievement of architect Viollet-le-Duc, who created here an idealized portrayal of what medieval architecture should be, the restored castle still emanates a genuine, masterful presence which has earned it the privilege of being the setting of many films.

A BIT OF HISTORY

Louis of Orléans' Castle – In 1406, King **Charles VI** elevated to a duchy the **Valois Earldom** which he had bestowed on his younger brother, **Louis I of Orléans.** It consisted of Béthisy, Crépy and La Ferté-Milon, together with **Pierrefonds** where a castle had stood since the 12C. Louis of Orléans assumed the regency during the episodic fits of madness of his brother, but was assassinated in 1407 by his cousin John the Fearless, Duke of Burgundy. However, before his death, he had constructed a **chain of fortresses** on his Valois lands, of which Pierrefonds was the linchpin. He had the original castle rebuilt by Charles VI's architect, and Pierrefonds triumphantly withstood sieges by the English, the Burgundians and the royal troops.

In the 16C, the castle passed to Antoine d'Estrées, Marquess of Coeuvres and father of **Gabrielle d'Estrées**, mistress of Henri IV. On the death of the King, the Marquess took sides with the Prince of Condé against the young Louis XIII. Besieged once again by the royal forces, Pierrefonds castle was finally seized and dismantled.

Viollet-le-Duc's Castle – In 1813 Napoleon I bought the castle ruins for

- **Michelin Local Map:** 305: I-4. Also see map under Forêt de Compègne.
- **Info:** Office du tourisme de Pierrefonds, pl. de l'Hôtel-de-Ville, 60350. ℘03 44 42 81 44. www.pierrefonds-tourisme.net.
- **Location:** Southeast of Compiègne, reached by the D 973.
- **Parking:** Free parking on rue Sabatier, a 10min walk from the castle.
- **Also See:** The town of Compiègne, its forest and the Armistice Clearing.

a little under 3 000 francs. Napoleon III, an enthusiastic archaeologist, entrusted its restoration in 1857 to **Viollet-le-Duc**. It was only a matter of returning parts of it (the keep and annexes) to a habitable condition, leaving the curtain walls and towers as "picturesque ruins". At the end of 1861, however, the programme of works took on an altogether different, larger dimension; Pierrefonds was to be transformed into an Imperial residence. Work lasted until 1884. Fascinated by medieval life and Gothic architecture in particular, Viollet-le-Duc set about a complete, much criticized reconstruction of the castle, following the basic shapes that were already outlined by the numerous walls and fragments remaining at the time, and letting his imagination work.

VISIT

Open May–Sept daily 9.30am–6pm. Sept–end Apr Tue–Sun 10am–1pm, 2–5.30pm. Last admission 45min before closing. 1 hr guided tours available. Closed Jan 1, May 1, Dec 25. ∞7€. ℘03 44 42 72 72. http://pierrefonds. monuments-nationaux.fr.

Exterior

The quadrangular castle (103m/337ft long, 88m/288ft wide) has a large defensive tower at each corner and in

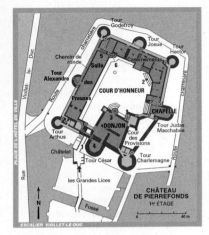

Tour Godefroy
Tour Josué
Tour Hector
Chemin de ronde
5
Salle
Casernements
6
Tour Alexandre
des
Preuses
2
COUR D'HONNEUR
CHAPELLE
3
DONJON
Cour des Provisions
Tour Judas Macchabée
Tour Arthus
Châtelet
4
Tour César
Tour Charlemagne
les Grandes Lices
Fossé

CHÂTEAU DE PIERREFONDS
1er ÉTAGE

N
0   40 m

ESCALIER VIOLLET-LE-DUC

Viollet-le-Duc
Route
PLACE DE L'HÔTEL DE VILLE
Rue
Charretière
Charretière
Route

Interior

A permanent exhibition in the barracks celebrates Viollet-le-Duc and his work (engravings, paintings, photographs of the ruins, history of the castle etc). Another exhibition, devoted to the **Monduit workshops**, displays a collection of works of art in lead, including the lion weathervane of the Arras belfry, the Cupid of Amiens Cathedral and some of the gargoyles decorating Notre-Dame Cathedral in Paris. The exhibits are authentic since they were made in the Monduit workshops at the same time as the commissioned items. They were used to illustrate the workshops' skills on the occasion of world exhibitions.

The **main front** appears with its basket-handled arcading forming a covered shelter, surmounted by a gallery. Neither of these existed in the original castle, but were created by Viollet-le-Duc, freely inspired by the courtyard at the Château de Blois. The **equestrian statue** of Louis of Orléans (**2**) by Frémiet (1868) stands before the monumental stairway.

The inside of the **chapel**, heightened by Viollet-le-Duc, presents a bold elevation with a vaulted gallery above the apse, which was another of the architect's inventions. The doorway pier incorporates a figure of St James the Great with Viollet-le-Duc's features.

The **keep**, where the lord had his living quarters, stands between the chapel and the entrance. Viollet-le-Duc accentuated its residential function by giving

the middle of the walls. On three sides, it overlooks the village, almost vertically; to the south a deep moat separates the castle from the plateau.

The walls have two **sentry walks**, one above the other: the covered lower one is dressed with machicolations. The **towers** (38m/124ft high with 5–6m/16–20ft thick walls) are crowned with two storeys of defences; from the cart track (*route charretière*), they are a formidable sight. Eight statues of named military heroes adorn them, indicating the building's political significance.

Having walked along the esplanade, cross the first moat to the forecourt known as Les Grandes Lices. A double **drawbridge (1)** – one lane for pedestrians, the other for vehicles – leads to the castle doorway which opens into the **main courtyard**.

Château de Pierrefonds

S. Sauvignier/ MICHELIN

it an elegant open stairway. It is flanked by three towers. The two on the outside are round whereas the one on the inside is square.

The **provisions courtyard**, between the keep and the chapel, communicates with the main courtyard by means of a postern gate and with the outside world by another postern, 10m/30ft above the foot of the castle walls.

To introduce food and other supplies into the fortress, a steeply inclined wooden ramp was lowered, and provisions dragged up.

Logis au donjon

Reaching the first floor of the keep, the tour leads through the **Imperial couple's rooms**: the **salle des Blasons** or Grande Salle (**3**), with woodwork and a few, rare pieces of furniture designed by Viollet-le-Duc. Among the symbolic decorative motifs, notice the Napoleonic eagle, the thistle (Empress Eugénie's emblem) and on the chimney-piece the heraldic arms of Louis of Orléans (the "broken" arms of France) and another family emblem, a knotted staff.

Beyond the **Emperor's bedroom** (**4**), which enjoys a view down over the fortified entrance, the tour leads to the Salle des Preuses, leaving the keep.

Salle des Preuses – Dedicated to the Worthies, this timber-ceilinged former courtroom (52×9m/170×29ft) was created by Viollet-le-Duc. The roof is shaped like an upturned ship. The mantelpiece of the double **fireplace** (**5**) is decorated with statues of nine worthy women, heroines from tales of chivalry. The central figure of Semiramis has the features of the Empress whereas the others are portraits of ladies of the court.

Tour d'Alexandre and Chemin de Ronde Nord – The original walls on this side of the ruins still stand 22m/72ft high; note the different colour of the stones. Along the **sentry walk**, Viollet-le-Duc highlighted the last step forward in defence systems before the

arrival of the cannon: level walkways without steps or narrow doorways, which allowed the defenders (housed in nearby barracks) to muster quickly at critical points without blundering into obstacles. The view extends over Pierrefonds Valley.

Salle des Gardes – A double spiral **staircase** (**6**) leads down to this **guard-room** (also called **Salle des Mercenaires**) which now houses lapidary fragments: remains of the original 15C statues of the heroic figures on each tower. The tour ends at the model of the castle.

ADDRESSES

🛏 STAY

👓🍽 **Domaine du Bois d'Aucourt** – *1.1km/0.7mi W of Pierrefonds via D 85, dir. St-Jean-aux-Bois.* ✆*03 44 42 80 34. 11 rooms.* ⬚*9€.* No two rooms are alike in this quiet 19C manor house in the heart of the Compiègne forest. Depending on your fancy, you may rest in surroundings reminiscent of Scotland, Seville, Tuscany, a Zen meditation chamber or a tropical island.

👓🍽 **Relais Brunehaut** – *Chelles, 4.5km/2.8mi E of Pierrefonds by D 85. 3 r. de l'Eglise.* ✆*03 44 42 85 05. 11 rooms.* ⬚*9€. Restaurant*👓🍽🍽. The watermill with its large wheel, and the inn are set around an attractive, flower-decked courtyard. The mill houses pleasant rooms, while the inn offers a rustic dining room..

🍽 EAT

👓🍽 **Aux Blés d'Or** – *8 r. Jules-Michelet.* ✆*03 44 42 85 91. Closed Jan 3–6, Feb 19–27, Nov 29–Dec 12, Tue and Wed.* This inn is a pleasant, family-friendly stopover with recently fitted-out rooms that are simple, comfortable and well maintained. The impressive silhouette of the medieval château can be admired from the restaurant's terrace. Good choice of fixed-price menus with an accent on traditional fare.

Château-Fort de
Rambures★

Surrounded by an English-style park and a lovely arboretum, Rambures Castle is a fine example of 15C military architecture. During the Hundred Years War, it played a significant role as a French enclave in the middle of the English-occupied territories, and came to be called "the key to the Vimeu," a strategic region marking the boundary between Picardy and Normandy.

VISIT

◷ *Open Mar–Nov daily (except Wed) 10am–noon, 2–6pm. Nov–end Feb Sun and holidays at 2.30pm and 4pm (other days by arrangement only). Mid-Jul–end Aug daily (except Wed) 10am–6pm.* 🐾 *Visit of the castle by guided tour only (1hr). Self-guided visit of the grounds.* ◷ *Closed Jan 1, Dec 25.* ⊚7€ *(castle and grounds), 5.50€ (grounds only).* ✆*03 22 25 10 93.*

Castle

Exterior – In the 18C, Rambures was converted into a country residence, and the courtyard façade pierced with huge windows. However, with its enormous machicolated round towers and rounded curtain walls, its deep moat

- 🕭 **Michelin Local Map:** 301: D-8.
- 🔲 **Info:** www.chateaufort-rambures.com.
- ◑ **Location:** From Abbeville (24km/15 mi), take the D 928, then the D 180.

and tall watchtower, and its amazing brick walls (3–7m/10–23ft thick), the old fortress has managed to preserve its powerful, medieval architecture.

Interior –For many of the rooms, the only source of daylight is still through loopholes. The alterations begun in the 18C did allow for some level of comfort though, and you will see reception rooms decorated with woodwork and marble chimney-pieces. Do not miss the 15C watch-path; the library-billiards room with its collection of portraits; the kitchen, located in the old guard-room above the dungeons; the cellars, used to shelter the villagers during invasions; and generally speaking, beautiful Picardy-style furniture from 15C–17C.

Park and gardens

Designed in the 18C, Rambures' English-style park (40ha/99 acre) is planted with some rare trees.

Also note the **rose garden** (with 400 different species), the **garden of simples**, and the **fern collection**.

Château-Fort de Rambures

A. Cassaigne/MICHELIN

Senlis★★

A tributary of the Oise, the Nonette River runs through this picturesque medieval town surrounded by the rich cornfields of Valois and the wooded expanses of Ermenonville, Chantilly and Halatte forests. Strolling along the winding streets of the Old Quarter, paved with flagstones and lined with relics of its past, you may still feel the powerful presence of the Frankish rulers and cathedral builders who left behind an invaluable legacy for us to enjoy.

A BIT OF HISTORY

The election of Hugues Capet – The conquerors of Senlis built a massive stronghold over the first Gallo-Roman ramparts of the town. The kings of the first two **Frankish dynasties** would often take up residence here, lured by the game in the nearby forests. The Carolingian line died out when Louis V suffered a fatal hunting accident. In 987, the Archbishop of Reims called a meeting at Senlis Castle in which he and the local lords decided that **Hugues Capet**, then Duke of France, would be the next king. The last king of France to have stayed in Senlis was Henri IV. The ciity went out of fashion as a royal place of residence and was gradually replaced by Compiègne and Fontainebleau.

CATHÉDRALE NOTRE-DAME★★

🕐*Open daily (except during religious office) 9am–7pm.* 🖉*03 44 53 01 59.*
The construction of Senlis cathedral started in 1153 – 16 years after St-Denis and 10 years before Notre-Dame in Paris – but progressed at a slow pace due to insufficient funds. The cathedral was not consecrated until 1191. It was only toward the mid-13C that the right tower was crowned with the magnificent **spire★★** which was to have such a strong influence over religious architecture in the Valois area. The **main doorway★★** is strongly reminiscent of the doorways at Chartres, Notre-Dame in Paris, Amiens and Reims.

▶ **Population:** 16 327
🖉 **Michelin Local Map:** 305: G-5 or map 106 folds 8, 9
🛈 **Info:** Office du tourisme de Senlis, pl. du Parvis-Notre-Dame, 60300. 🖉03 44 53 06 40. www.senlis-tourisme.fr.
◑ **Location:** Access from Paris: by car, via the A 1 (51.5km/32mi); by train, from Gare du Nord to Chantilly, then bus link to Senlis.
🅿 **Parking:** The car park near the cathedral fills early in the day. Try those off the rue de la République.
👁 **Don't Miss:** Notre-Dame's magnificient spire; the view over the remains of the old ramparts from the Jardin du Roy; the Gallo-Roman and Merovingian collections of the Musée d'Art et d'Archéologie; St-Frambourg Royal Chapel and its stained-glass windows by Joan Miro.
🖉 **Also See:** Château de Chantilly, St-Leu-d'Esserent.

South front – Constructed by **Pierre Chambiges** (1509–1544) in the 16C, the **transept façade★★** contrasts sharply with the main façade. One may follow the evolution of Gothic architecture from the austere 12C to the 16C, when Late Flamboyant already showed signs of Renaissance influence, introduced after the Italian wars. The clerestory and its huge Flamboyant windows were also completed in the 16C.
The lower part (12C) of the east end and the radiating chapels are intact. The galleries – dating from Romanesque times – support the nave and chancel with the help of Gothic flying buttresses.

Interior – The church interior is 70m/230ft long, 19.2m/63ft wide and measures 24m/79ft to the keystone. Above

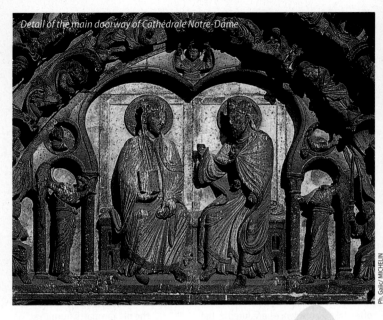

Detail of the main doorway of Cathédrale Notre-Dame

Ph. Gajic MICHELIN

the organ, the 12C vaulting which escaped the ravages of a fire in 1504 marks the original height of the church. The nave and the chancel, comparatively narrow in spite of their height, are graced with an airy lightness.

The first chapel to the right of the south doorway features superb vaulting with pendant keystones, a 14C stone Virgin Mary and a lovely set of stained-glass windows. These are the only original panes to have remained intact. A statue of St Louis from the 14C is placed in the south aisle of the ambulatory.

The north transept chapel houses a 16C Christ made of larch. The left-hand aisle features an elegant statue of St Barbara dating back to the late 16C-early 17C.

North side – The cathedral's setting on this side is much less solemn. It features several patches of greenery and is extremely picturesque.

Skirt the little garden that follows the east façade of what was once the bishop's palace. The building rests on the ruins of the old Gallo-Roman ramparts; the base of one tower remains. Lovely **view** of the cathedral's east end.

WALKING TOUR
OLD QUARTER
Jardin du Roy

These gardens occupy the former moat of the Gallo-Roman ramparts which, at their widest point, measured 312m/ 1 024ft across and at their narrowest 242m/794ft. Twenty-eight towers (7m/ 23ft high and 4m/14ft thick) defended the city walls; 16 remain today, some still intact, others badly damaged.

Place du Parvis★

This is a charming little square at the foot of the cathedral.

Eglise St-Pierre

Built in the 12C, heavily rehandled in the 17C, and deconsecrated during the French Revolution, this church now houses a centre for Romanesque, Gothic and Renaissance culture.

Ancien Château Royal

Before entering the courtyard of the old Royal Castle, take time to walk up rue du Châtel to see the original **fortified entrance** to the stronghold, now walled up. Adjoining the old doorway, the 16C **Hôtel des Trois Pots** proudly sports its old-fashioned sign.

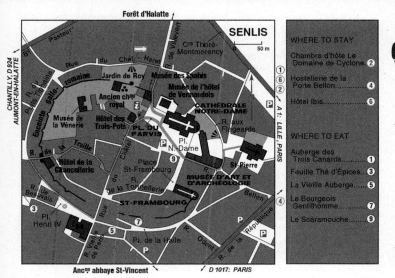

SENLIS
50 m

Forêt d'Halatte

CHANTILLY, D 924
AUMONT-EN-HALATTE

Jardin du Roy
Musée des Spahis
Musée de l'hôtel de Vermandois
Ancien château royal
CATHÉDRALE NOTRE-DAME
Musée de la Vénerie
Hôtel des Trois-Pots
PL. DU PARVIS
Pl. N. Dame
R. aux Flageards
A 1: LILLE, PARIS
Hôtel de la Chancellerie
Place St-Frambourg
St-Pierre
MUSÉE D'ART ET D'ARCHÉOLOGIE
Pl. Henri IV
ST-FRAMBOURG
Bellon
R. de la République
Pl. de la Halle

Anc.ne abbaye St-Vincent
D 1017: PARIS

WHERE TO STAY

Chambre d'hôte Le Domaine de Cyclone .... ②

Hostellerie de la Porte Bellon............. ④

Hôtel Ibis................ ⑥

WHERE TO EAT

Auberge des Trois Canards.......... ①

Feuille Thé d'Épices.... ③

La Vieille Auberge...... ⑤

Le Bourgeois Gentilhomme............ ⑦

Le Scaramouche........ ⑨

The medieval castle where Hugues Capet was proclaimed King of France in 987 was built on a site which had already been fortified under the Romans at the time of Emperor Claudius (AD 41–54). The castle was unfortunately taken apart bit by bit to the benefit of more comfortable residences such as Compiègne or Fontainebleau. Included within the compound, an old priory now houses the Musée de la Vénerie (& *see SIGHTS below*).

Old Streets★

Rue du Châtel used to be the main street through Senlis for those travelling from Paris to Flanders, until the opening of rue Neuve-de-Paris (now called rue de la République) in 1753. Its southern continuation, named rue Vieille-de-Paris, thus refers to the ancient thoroughfare.

Take the charming **rue de la Treille** and walk to the "Fausse Porte", which was the postern of the former Gallo-Roman ramparts. On the left stands the Hôtel de la Chancellerie, flanked by two towers.

The **town hall** (Hôtel de Ville), on place Henri-IV, was rebuilt in 1495.

The front bears a bust of Henri IV and an inscription recalling its benevolence towards the town of Senlis.

These date back to a visit by Charles X on his return from his coronation in Reims Cathedral (1825).

SIGHTS
Musée d'Art et d'Archéologie★

Place Notre-Dame. ⊶*Closed for restoration until 2010.* ℘*03 44 53 06 40. www.senlis-tourisme.fr.*

This museum is housed in the old bishop's palace (13C–18C buildings). It features a **bronze base★** dating from AD 48 and engraved with a dedication to Emperor Claudius, along with other Gallo-Roman artefacts, and Merovingian jewellery and glassware. Its medieval collection includes striking sculptures such as the **Head of a Bearded Man★** (early 13C), a majestic marble **Virgin and Child** (late 14C), and mid-12C stained-glass windows recounting the creation of Eve and the Temptation of Adam and Eve.

Paintings dating from the 17C to the 20C include the works of artists such as Philippe de Champaigne, Luca Giordano, Francesco Solimena, Corot, Boudin, Sérusier, and **Thomas Couture** (1815–79), a native of Senlis. Centring on pieces by Séraphine Louis, nicknamed Séraphine de Senlis, is a collection of works by 20C naïve artists.

Musée des Spahis

By the entrance to the old Royal Castle. ⊙*Open Mon, Thu–Fri 10am–noon, 2–6pm. Wed 2–6pm. Sat –Sun 11am–1pm, 2–6pm.* ⊙*Closed Jan 1,*

May 1, Dec 25. ≋2€. ℘*03 44 32 00 81. www.senlis-tourisme.fr.*

This **museum of the Algerian troopers** retraces 150 years of history of the North African cavalry, which held a special place in the French Army from 1780 to 1814 and from 1830 to 1964. It largely concentrates on the old **Spahis** (native Algerian horsemen), **Goumiers** (indigenous horsemen and foot soldiers), **Meharists** (dromedary riders) and **Saharans** (cameleers).

Musée de la Vénerie

ⓒOpen Mon, Thu–Fri 10am–noon, 2–6pm. Wed 2–6pm. Sat –Sun 11am–1pm, 2–6pm. ✒Guided tour of the upper floor every hour. ⓒClosed Jan 1, May 1, Dec 25. ≋2€. ℘*03 44 32 00 81. www.senlis-tourisme.fr.*

In the 13C, King Saint-Louis had a **priory** built next to the Royal Castle to keep the precious relics of Saint Maurice of Agaune. This priory now houses the city's **Hunting Museum**. The works presented here were chosen from among the many illustrations of stag hunts which have enriched French culture.

The walls are hung with numerous trophies and stags' heads. The display of historical **hunting gear** renders the exhibition particularly interesting. For instance, he hunting costume of the Condé – fawn and amaranth-purple – can be seen on a figure representing a Chantilly forest warden, and in the painting depicting the young Duc d'Enghien (1787).

Musée de l'Hôtel de Vermandois

o━ *Closed for restoration until end of 2009.* ℘*03 44 53 06 40.*

This small history museum is housed within a fine example of Romanesque civil architecture (12C). Visitors are being introduced to the history of Senlis and its cathedral through audio-visual accounts. Do not miss the rich **statuary collection** which includes the 12C head of an angel from one of the doorways of Notre-Dame, along with capitals and consoles from the cathedral and St-Maurice priory.

Chapelle Royale St-Frambourg★

ⓒ*Open May–Oct (except Jul 15–Aug 15) Sat–Sun 3–6.30pm. Nov–Apr (except Dec 12–Feb 15) Sun 3–5pm.* ≋*4.50€.* ℘*03 44 53 39 99.*

This chapel was founded before 990 by the wife of Hugues Capet, in order to conserve the relics of a solitary from Bas-Maine, Saint Fraimbault or Frambourg. Through the efforts of the pianist Georges Cziffra, the chapel was restored and turned into the **Franz Liszt auditorium** in which concerts and exhibitions are organised. Note the Gothic high church with beautiful **stained-glass windows★** by Joan Miro, and the archaeological crypt, with remnants of a sanctuary dating back to year 1000.

EXCURSIONS
Forêt d'Halatte★

✒ This large forest (4 300ha) north of Senlis includes beech groves, cherished by the Capetians, oaks, hornbeams, pine trees and other species of trees.

Pont-Ste-Maxence

11km/7mi north by D 1017.

Because of its old bridge spanning the Oise River, the town has always been an important staging post. .

East of the town stands the **Abbaye du Moncel★** that Philippe le Bel had built next to a royal castle, two towers of which still remain. The main façade still looks medieval and offers two imposing chimneys. The **courtyard★** is surrounded by three wings crowned with tall roofs of brown tiles. Other elements of note include one of the galleries from the 16C cloisters and the amazing 14C **timberwork★** above the nuns' dorter, made with oak from Halatte Forest. ⓒ✒ *Guided tours (1hr) Mar–Nov Tue–Sat 2.30pm and 4.30pm, Sun 10.30am, 11.30am, 2pm, 3.30pm, 5pm.* ≋*5€.* ℘*03 44 72 33 98*

Château de Raray

13km/8mi northeast by D 932ᴬ, D 26ᴱ and D 26.

Standing on the edge of a charming hamlet, the castle – now part of a golf club – is famous for the striking decoration of its main courtyard, particularly its **porticoes★**, used in Jean Cocteau's film *Beauty and the Beast*.

St-Vaast-de-Longmont
16km/10mi northeast by D 932^A.
Seen from the village cemetery, the Romanesque bell tower and its stone spire appear to be extremely ornate:

cornices with billet moulding, arcades resting on finely decorated columns. In nearby **Rhuis** (*west on D 123*), the 11C Romanesque **church** has an elegant bell tower with a double row of twinned windows. The tower is believed to be one of the oldest in Île-de-France. The interior features four bays and an apsidal chapel with no vaulting; it rests on small ornately decorated columns.

ADDRESSES

⌂ STAY

⊝⊟ Hostellerie de la Porte Bellon – *51 r. Bellon. ✆03 44 53 03 05. www.portebellon.com. Closed Dec 18– Jan 8. 16 rooms + 1 apartment. �8 €. Restaurant ⊝⊟.* A few paces from the city centre, this handsome manor – a former coaching inn – welcomes guests to pleasant, well fitted-out bedrooms. The splendid paved and shaded courtyard leads to the garden where breakfast may be taken when the weather allows. Pretty vaulted cellar.

⊝⊟ Hôtel Ibis – *2km via N 324 on D 1324. ✆03 44 53 70 50. www.ibishotel.com. 92 rooms. ⊡8€. Restaurant⊝.* Practical hotel just off the motorway. All the rooms in the main building and the annexe have been renovated in keeping with the chain's latest concept. Country-style decor (exposed beams, fireplace). Grilled meats the speciality.

⊝⊟⊟ Chambre d'hôte LeDomaine de Cyclone – *2 r. de la Gonesse, 60305 Baron. 9km NE of Ermenonville via D 922 and D 100. ✆06 08 98 05 50. 5 rooms. ⊡.* Joan of Arc is supposed to have slept in this castle. The guests now occupy very tasteful rooms, nearly all of which overlook the park. Pony trekking.

⸸ EAT

⊝ Feuille Thé d'Epices – *18 r. de Beauvais. ✆03 44 60 04 00. Closed Sun and Mon.* This tearoom located in the heart of Senlis offers a selection of teas and coffees as well as home-cooked lunch. Smart dining room and warm welcome. The small terrace is popular in summer.

⊝⊟ Auberge des Trois Canards – *3 pl. de l'Église, 60810 Ognon. 6km/3.6mi NE of Senlis via D 932^A. ✆03 44 54 41 21. www.troiscanards.fr. Closed 2 weeks in Feb, 3 weeks in Aug, Wed lunch, Mon and Tue. Reservations advisable weekends.* Decorated in shades of yellow and carmine, this venerable old inn has retained its country flavour. At the end of the terrace there's an enclosed garden with children's games.

⊝⊟⊟ Le Bourgeois Gentilhomme – *3 pl de la Halle. ✆03 44 53 13 22. www.bourgeois-gentilhomme.com. Closed 31 Jul–22 Aug, Sat lunch, Sun and Mon.* If the kings of France had not been so quick to abandon Senlis, Molière would no doubt have performed in the town... At any rate, in this place which is dedicated to him, you will find everything to your taste, including the personalised cuisine. Fine 12C cellar where the owner holds wine tastings.

⊝⊟⊟ Le Scaramouche – *4 pl Notre-Dame. ✆03 44 53 01 26. www.le-scaramouche.fr. Closed Aug 18–30.* Warm house with pretty painted wood exterior. Pleasant interior with paintings and tapestries. The attractive terrace overlooks the cathedral of Notre-Dame (12C).

⊝⊟ La Vieille Auberge – *8 r. Long-Filet. ✆03 44 60 95 50. www.lavieilleauberge-senlis.com. Closed Jan 1, Jul 7–25, Dec 3– Jan 7, Sun evening and Tue.* The Old Inn's name is particularly apt – construction commenced in 1588! The dining room, decorated in warm tones and English style furniture, serves contemporary cuisine. And for fine weather there's an agreeable terrace set up at the back.

Soissons★

The ancient capital of the first Merovingian kings rises in the midst of rich agricultural land, overlooked by the tall spires of what was one of the most flourishing monasteries of the medieval period. Largely rebuilt after the First World War, the city not only managed to retain its magnificent abbey, but also its cathedral, a masterpiece of Gothic art.

- ▶ **Population:** 29 453
- **Michelin Local Map:** 306: B-6
- **Info:** Office du tourisme de Soissons, 16 pl. Fernand-Marquigny, 02200. ℘03 23 53 17 37. www.ville-soissons.fr.
- **Location:** 100km/62mi from Paris by N 2. Accessed from St-Quentin and Coucy-le-Château-Auffrique by the D 1, and from Rouen, Beauvais or Reims by the N 31/E 46.

A BIT OF HISTORY

The Frankish capital – Soissons played an important role at the time of the Frankish monarchy. It was at the town's gates that Clovis defeated the Romans, ruining them for his own benefit. The famous story of the **Soissons Vase** took place after this battle: **Clovis** demanded that his booty include a vase which had been stolen from a church in Reims. A soldier angrily opposed him, broke the vase and cried "You will have nothing, O King, but that which Destiny gives you!" The following year, while Clovis was reviewing his troops, he stopped before the same soldier, raised his sword and split the soldier's skull, saying "Thus you did with the Soissons vase".

SIGHTS

Ancienne Abbaye de St-Jean-des-Vignes★★

◷*Open Apr–end Sept Mon–Fri 9am–noon, 2–6pm, Sat–Sun 2–7pm. Oct–end Mar Mon–Fri 9am–noon, 2–5pm, Sat–Sun 2–6pm.* ◷*Closed Jan 1 and Dec 25.* ℘03 23 53 42 40. www.musee-soissons.org. ☛*Guided tours available.* ℘03 23 53 17 37.

The old Abbey of St John of the Vines (1076) was one of the richest monasteries of the Middle Ages. In the 13C–14C, the generosity of the kings of France, bishops, great lords and burghers allowed the Augustinian monks to build a great abbey church. In 1805, however, an imperial decree approved by the Bishop of Soissons ordered its demolition, so that its materials could be used to repair the cathedral. The resulting outcry led to

the preservation of the west front, one of the city's most emblematic piece of architecture.

West front – The cusped portals are delicately cut and surmounted with late-13C gables. The rest of the front dates from the 14C, except for the two Flamboyant bell towers (15C), the **north tower** being larger and more ornate. An elegant openwork gallery separates the central portal from the great rose window, which has lost its tracery.

Refectory★ – It was built into the extension of the west front, at the back of the great cloister. The 13C construction has two naves with pointed vaulting. The transverse arches and ribs rest on seven slender columns with foliate capitals. Eight great lobed rose windows pierce the east and south walls.

Cloisters – All that remains of the **great cloister★** are two 14C galleries. The pointed arches separated by elaborate buttresses had a graceful blind arcade, remains of which can be seen in the south bays. The **small cloister** features two beautiful Renaissance bays.

Cathédrale St-Gervais-et-St-Protais★★

◷*Open daily Jul–Aug 9.30am–noon, 2–6.30pm. Sept–Jun 9.30am–noon, 2–4.30pm.* ☛*Guided tours available.* ℘03 23 53 17 37.

The purity of its lines and the simplicity of its design make this cathedral one of the most beautiful examples of Gothic art. Its construction began in the 12C with the south transept. The chancel, nave and side aisles rose date from the 13C. The north transept and the upper part of the façade were not completed until the early 14C.

The Hundred Years War brought work to a halt before the lone, north bell tower, inspired from the towers of Notre-Dame in Paris, was completely built. It was never to be finished.

The **interior★** is totally symmetrical, no extraneous detail breaking the harmony of this vast vault. Divided into four levels, the wonderfully graceful **south transept★★** ends in an apse. Note 13C–14C stained-glass windows in the **chancel**, and hung in the **north transept**, Ruben's *Adoration of the Shepherds*.

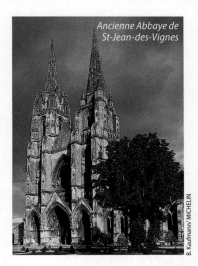

Ancienne Abbaye de St-Jean-des-Vignes

B. Kaufmann/ MICHELIN

ADDITIONAL SIGHT
Musée municipal de l'Ancienne Abbaye de St-Léger

⊙*Open Apr–end Sept Mon–Fri 9am– noon, 2–6pm, Sat–Sun 2–7pm. Oct–end Mar Mon–Fri 9am–noon, 2–5pm, Sat– Sun 2–6pm.* ⊙*Closed Jan 1 and Dec 25.* ☎*03 23 55 94 73. www.musee-soissons. org.* ⚫*Guided tours available.* ☎*03 23 53 17 37.*

Founded in 1139 , St Leger's Abbey was devastated in 1567 by Protestants who

also demolished the nave of the church. Today, the old monastery buildings house the permanent collections of the municipal museum.

The **archaeology** section is dedicated to the development of the Aisne Valley from the Neolithic period to the High Middle Ages. A skilful chronological presentation traces the **history** of Soissons from Gallo-Roman times to the post-war era.

Do not miss the museum's **fine arts** section, with a collection of Flemish, French and Italian paintings from the 16C–19C.

ADDRESSES

🏠 STAY

⊜☻**Chambre d'hôte Ferme de la Montagne** – *02290 Ressons-le-Long. 8km/5mi W of Soissons via N 31 et D 1160.* ☎*03 23 74 23 71. http://lafermedela montagne.free.fr. 5 rooms.* ☺. *Closed Jan–Feb.* This 13C farm is located on a plateau overlooking the Aisne Valley. Each guest room has its own entrance- way, a thoughtful touch indeed.

⊜☻**Hôtel Prime** – *Rond point de l'arche, along the RN2.* ☎*03 23 73 33 04. 42 rm.* ☺*8€. Restaurant*⊜. This hotel located on the outskirts of the town offers small functional rooms which can be useful on occasion. Stopover restaurant offering buffet meals.

🍴 EAT

⊜☻**L'Assiette Gourmande** – *16 av. de Coucy.* ☎*03 23 93 47 78. Closed Apr 12–20, Aug, Sat lunch, Sun dinner, dinner on holidays and Mon.* This establishment easily won the hearts of the inhabitants of Soissons, thanks to its elegant décor, low-key atmosphere and tasty, reinterpreted traditional cuisine.

⊜☻**Le Grenadin** – *19 rte de Fère-en- Tardenois, 02200 Belleu.* ☎*03 23 73 20 57. Closed Jan 15–31, Sun dinner, Mon and holidays.* A cherub keeps vigil over the façade of this charming establishment serving carefully prepared traditional cuisine. Country style and rustic rooms. In the summer, tables are set in the garden.

Baie de
Somme★★

Approximately 5km/3mi wide between the Pointe du Hourdel and the Pointe de St-Quentin, the Somme estuary offers open spaces, luminous landscapes and, at low tide, its endless stretches of sand and grass. The bay is a wonderful area for visitors who wish to relax while watching seals sprawled on the sand and migratory wild ducks, or riding on the charming little train which merrily whistles across the countryside.

A BIT OF HISTORY

Slow silting-up process – Like all bays, the Somme experiences the flow of water and silt which settles and tends to widen the sandbanks. These become covered with grass, creating the **mollières** or salt-pastures where lambs now graze.

The silting-up combined with a gradual increase in the size of boats in general has considerably affected the formerly active traffic here. The development of the **Somme canal** from 1786 to 1835 and the creation of a sheltered port at Le Hourdel merely slowed its decline.

It is worth noting, however, that during WW I, the bay served as a British base: in 1919, traffic reached an exceptional 125 000t.

Hunting and fishing –The bay's three fishing ports (St-Valery-sur-Somme, Le Crotoy and Le Hourdel) specialise in **shellfish** and **squid fishing**.

When the tide is out, fish are also caught in the channels, pools and ruts on the shore: cockles, mullet, eels and flatfish, either speared or just picked up by hand.

Wildfowl hunters lie in wait in special boats or in hides formed in grassy mounds pierced with firing holes, using domestic or artificial ducks as decoys.

Michelin Local Map:
301: C-6

Info: Office du tourisme du Crotoy, 1 r. Carnot, 80550 ℘03 22 27 05 25. www.tourisme-crotoy.com.

AROUND THE BAY
Chemin de fer de la Baie de Somme

👤👥🕐 *For detailed timetable and charges, call ℘03 22 26 96 96, check website www.chemin-fer-baie-somme. asso.fr or visit the tourist office.*

Superbly restored trains comprising old carriages with viewing platforms pulled by steam or diesel engines run between Le Crotoy, Noyelles, St-Valery, Lanchères-Pendé and Cayeux-sur-Mer, providing a pleasant journey of discovery through this lush area bordered by the River Somme's grassy sandbanks.

Parc du Marquenterre★★
See p350.

Le Crotoy

Back in 1430, **Joan of Arc** was imprisoned in the town's fortress before being taken to Rouen. Today, Le Crotoy is a popular seaside resort affording beautiful **views**★ of the bay. The port is used by small coastal fishing trawlers catching shrimps, flatfish and herrings. Casting on the Somme's bed brings in plaice and eel. The local **beach** lends itself to speedsailing, kite-flying and landsailing. Sailing enthusiasts will also find a wide choice of crafts (sailboards, sailing dinghies, catamarans etc).

St-Valery-sur-Somme★
See p375.

Maison de la baie de Somme et de l'Oiseau★

👤👥♿🕐*Open daily Jan–end Mar 10am–5pm. End Mar–end Jun 9.30am–6pm. End Jun–end Aug 9.30am–7pm. Sept–Mid-Oct 9.30m–6pm. Mid-Oct–end Dec 10am–5pm. 🕐Closed Jan*

Chinese cemetery in Noyelles

This is the largest Chinese cemetery in France. Situated along the road from **Sailly-Flibeaucourt** to the hamlet of **Nolette**, the cemetery includes more than 800 white tombstones engraved with Chinese characters. Following an agreement signed in 1916, thousands of Chinese nationals, most of them farmers from the north of China, undertook to serve in the British army in exchange for a salary. The first contingent landed in April 1917. Between 1917 and 1919, the camp welcomed 12 000 workers who worked in difficult conditions, were kept apart from the local population and could not come and go as they pleased. Some were killed in the fighting, but most succumbed to the epidemic of Spanish influenza which hit the area in the autumn of 1918. At the end of 1919, most of the workers went back home, although a few chose to remain in France.

1 and Dec 25. 6.90€ *(9.90€, bird-of-prey show included).* 03 22 26 93 93. *www.maisondeloiseau.com.*

This is the place to come to learn all about the distinctive fauna of the Somme's estuary. A superb collection of **naturalised birds** displayed in tasteful recreations of their natural settings (cliffs, sand and mudflats, dunes and gravel pits) gives visitors the rare opportunity to have a close view of their plumage, colours etc.

In a room dedicated to ducks, a reconstructed hide looks out over a pond behind the house where wild ducks, geese, waders and other fowl live. Videos, exhibitions, and a wide choice of guided excursions are also at your disposal to enhance your understanding of the estuary's environment.

Le Hourdel

The typical Picardy houses of this small fishing harbour and yachting marina stand at the tip of an offshore bar which begins at Onival.

The bar consists of pebbles which are crushed to make emery powders and filtering materials. With a good pair of binoculars, it may be possible to observe a colony of **harbour seals** sprawled on the sand lining the estuary, ready to flee at the first sign of danger.

A surveillance system has been set up to reduce human interference so that females can give birth without being disturbed.

Cayeux-sur-Mer

This resort is bordered by a promenade and a 2km/over 1mi-long wooden path lined with more than 400 cabins. The long beach of hard sand extends from the Hâble d'Ault to the Pointe de Hourde. Footpaths crisscross the woods of Brighton-les-Pins.

ADDRESSES

STAY

Logis Auberge de la Dune – *1352 r. de la Dune, 80550 Le Crotoy.* 03 22 25 01 88. *www.auberge-de-la-dune.com. 11 rooms. Restaurant.* A small, friendly inn located between Rue and Le Crotoy, in a countryside setting close to the ornithological park. Regional Picardy specialities and a range of fish dishes. Cosy, comfortable rooms, each individually decorated. Country-style dining room serving traditional cuisine and local specialities.

EAT

La Clé des Champs – *Place des Frères Caudron, 80120 Favières. 5km/3mi NW of Crotoy via D 940 and D 140.* 03 22 27 88 00. *Closed Jan 5–16, Feb 8–21, Aug 25 –Sept 2, Mon and Tue except holidays.* An epicurean address in the heart of a tiny village. Amidst a decor of copper plates and cooking ware, relax at one of the round tables set in this simple country inn and savour the fare proposed in the chef's carefully composed menus.

Forêt de
St-Gobain★★

Spread over 6 000ha/14 000 acres between the Oise and the Ailette Rivers, this beautiful forest covers a plateau pitted with quarries and furrowed with vales dotted with lakes. Deer-hunting, a tradition here since the time of Louis XV, still continues today. In season, the area also provides a rich crop of mushrooms and lily of the valley.

DRIVING TOUR

From St-Gobain and back
23km/14.3mi – about 2hr.

This itinerary takes you along charming roads winding through the forest, with several interesting stops along the way, from the birthplace of the Royal Glassworks to a series of old religious buildings nestled in lush valleys.

St-Gobain
This little town lies on the edge of a limestone ridge.

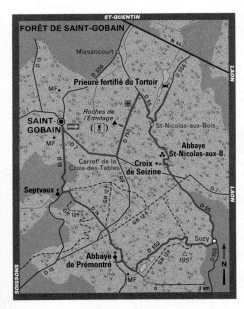

- **Michelin Local Map:** 306: C-5
- **Info:** Office du tourisme de Chauny, pl. du Marché-Couvert, 02300. ✆03 23 52 20 79. http://assoc.pagespro-orange.fr/tourisme-chauny.

It owes its name to an Irish hermit called **Goban** who had settled in a nearby forest in the 7C. St-Gobain is best-known for its **Manufacture royale des grandes glaces**, a prestigious factory of mirror glass founded by Louis XIV at Colbert's request, and established in 1692 in the ruins of the castle that had belonged to the Lords of Coucy. It was the first to use a method of casting which allowed the production of very large mirrors. The manufacturer, which closed its doors in 1993, initiated the long process which made today's **Saint-Gobain Group** a world leader in its category.

◖ *Take D 7 toward Laon. At the La Croix-des-Tables crossroads, turn left onto D 730.*

The picturesque **Roches de l'Ermitage** (*15min round trip*) are a starting point for various hiking trails.

◖ *Turn right onto D 55, then left onto D 556.*

Le Tortoir★
The walls of Le Tortoir, a 14C **fortified priory** and once a daughter-house of the abbey of St-Nicolas-aux-Bois, appear in a clearing surrounded by lakes where teal and moorhen are to be found.

◖ *Return to D 55 and continue south.*

Soon after the village of St-Nicolas-aux-Bois, you see the ruins of the abbey.

Abbaye St-Nicolas-aux-Bois★
Not open to the public.

The Benedictine abbey, the remains of which have been incorporated into a private property, occupied a delightful setting here on the floor of a valley.

The road first skirts the moat which protected the abbey walls, and then two ponds encircled by greenery, beyond which the 15C abbey buildings appear.

Croix Seizine
400m/440yd from D 55, on your right.
This expiatory monument was erected by Enguerrand IV, Lord of Coucy, who was condemned in 1256 by Saint-Louis for having executed students from St-Nicolas-aux-Bois who were caught hunting on his land.

◐ *In Suzy, take a right onto D 552.*

Abbaye de Prémontré★
◷*Open Apr–Oct 9am–7pm. Nov–Mar 9am–5pm.* ✆*03 23 23 66 66.*

Nestled in a wooded valley, this former abbey was founded by **Saint Norbert**. Born at the end of the 11C he lived a worldly life before retreating to Prémontré where he founded the abbey and the order which took its name.

Rebuilt in the 18C, the abbey was converted to a glassworks in 1802, then became a psychiatric hospital, which it still is today. For this reason, only the gardens, St-Norbert Chapel and the abbot's house are open to the public. The main body has a round outer porch with an unusual curved triangular pediment, with a cardinal's shield above.

◐ *Follow D 14 to Septvaux.*

Septvaux
This Romanesque church with its two belfries stands on a rise overlooking a lovely 12C wash-house *(on the road to Coucy).*

◐ *D 13 returns to St-Gobain.*

St-Leu-d'Esserent★

The Archbishop of Sens, Saint Leu, who died in 623, gave his name to several French localities, including this one. Located on the banks of the Oise River, St-Leu-d'Esserent boasts a magnificent church that the philosopher and historian Ernest Renan compared to a Greek temple on account of its harmonious lines.

ABBEY CHURCH★
The bridge over the Oise affords the best **view** of the church from a distance. Nearby quarries produced the lovely stone which was used for the construction of many other churches and cathedrals, as well as the palace at Versailles. The Germans converted these quarries into workshops for their V1 missiles. As a result, the town was repeatedly bombed and the church wrecked in 1944.

▸ **Population:** 4 867
Ⓖ **Michelin Local Map:** 305: F-5 or map 106 folds 7, 8
▤ **Info:** Office du tourisme de St-Leu-d'Esserent, 7 av. de la Gare, 60430. ✆03 44 56 38 10. www.saintleudesserent.fr.

Exterior – Significantly restored since the 19C, the façade is separate from the nave. It forms a Romanesque block (first half of the 12C) presenting a porch and, on the upper level, a gallery, each consisting of three bays. Two square towers frame the chancel.

Interior★ – The nave is filled with a golden light filtering through modern stained glass (1960). The chancel and the first two bays of the nave are Romanesque (12C) whereas the rest of the nave is 13C.

371

St-Quentin

Perched on a limestone hill riddled with caves and underground passages, St-Quentin overlooks the canalised Somme River which flows across the Isle marshlands. St-Quentin's waterways and railways link the city to the north European capitals and the Ruhr, making it a transportation centre between Paris, the English Channel, the countries north of France and the Champagne region.

▶ **Population:** 103 781
⚫ **Michelin Local Map:** 306: B-3
ℹ **Info:** Office du tourisme du St-Quentinois, 27 r. Victor-Basch, 02100. ☏03 23 67 05 00. www.tourisme-saintquentinois.fr.
◎ **Location:** 161km/100mi north of Paris, and mid-way between Cambrai and Laon.

🐾 WALKING TOUR

◎ *Walk from place de l'Hôtel-de-Ville to rue des Canonniers.*

Rue des Canonniers
The 18C **Hôtel Joly-de-Bammeville** *(no 9)*, which houses the town library, has a staircase with wrought-iron banisters. The entrance to the old **Hôtel des Canonniers** *(no 21)* has military trophies carved in low relief.

◎ *Return to place de l'Hôtel-de-Ville and follow rue des Toiles. Walk round the basilica, cross rue du Gouvernement near the east end of the basilica. Rue E.-Ovres leads to the Champs-Élysées Park.*

Champs-Élysées
The site of the original fortifications was turned into a pleasant **park** (10ha/24 acres) during the Restoration period: playgrounds, sports field, flower garden.

◎ *The Parc d'Isle Jacques-Braconnier is accessible via boulevard Gambetta and place du 8-Octobre leading to the quai Gayant bridge. Turn left after crossing the bridge.*

Parc d'Isle Jacques-Braconnier
The **Marais d'Isle** covers over 100ha/247 acres. It features fishing and water sports facilities, and also a **wetlands reserve** which lies along the route taken by migratory birds from Northern and Eastern Europe.

You will be able to see rare plant species like water hemlock (also known as dropwort or cowbane) or strange ones like bladderwort, a carnivorous plant. You will also observe numerous birds, particularly nest-building species (crested grebes) and overwintering species (ducks). Near the entrance to the park (av. Léo-Lagrange), the **Maison de l'environnement** features a permanent exhibition on renewable energies and the greenhouse effect. ♿ ◎*Open Mon–Fri 10am–noon, 2–5.30pm, Sat 10am–noon, 2–5pm, Sun 9.30am–noon, 2–5pm.* ☏03 23 05 06 50.

The Art Deco Trail

St-Quentin suffered extensive damage during WW I and was partially rebuilt in the 1920s by architect **Louis Guindez** (1890–1978). A walk through the town's streets reveals numerous house fronts decorated with bow windows, projecting balconies, floral or geometric motifs, coloured mosaics and wrought-iron work.
Among the most outstanding buildings are the **post office** *(r. de Lyon)*, the **council chamber** in the Hôtel de Ville (town hall), the **Carillon cinema** *(r. des Toiles)*, the **music school** *(47 r. d'Isle)*, the **buffet** in the railway station and, next to it, the **bridge** flanked by lantern towers.

St-Quentin Canal

Before the Canal du Nord was built, this was the busiest canal in France. It links the basins of the **Somme** and **Oise** to the **Escaut** (Scheldt), flowing for about 100km/62mi between **Chauny** and **Cambrai**. Napoleon considered it one of the period's greatest achievements. The canal is made up of two sections: the **Crozat Canal**, running between the Oise and the Somme, which was named after the financier who had it constructed, and the **St-Quentin Canal** proper, which crosses the plateau between the Somme and the Escaut partly through tunnels at **Tronquoy** (1km/0.5mi long) and **Riqueval**. It is the St-Quentin Canal which is used for regular shipments of sand, gravel and especially grain to the Paris region. The enlargement of the canal, which is part of a long-term project, will improve the town's links with Dunkirk.

SIGHTS
Hôtel de Ville★

Guided tours by prior arrangement with the tourist office. ℘03 23 67 05 00.
This is a gem of Late Gothic architecture (early 16C). The vigorous design of the façade includes ogival arches topped with pinnacles, mullioned windows and a traceried gallery beneath three gables. It is decorated with picturesque carvings in the Flamboyant Gothic style. Rebuilt in the 18C, the campanile houses a peal of 37 bells. Inside, the **wedding hall,** a mixture of medieval and Renaissance styles, and the beautiful Art déco **council chamber** are noteworthy.

Espace St-Jacques
14 rue de la Sellerie.
Built on the ruins of a 13C church, this gallery proposes temporary art exhibits and houses the **Musée des Papillons**, with the largest collection of butterflies and other insects in Europe.
👥 ⊙*Open daily (except Tue) 2–6pm.* ⊙*Closed Jan 1, May 1, Whitsun, Jul 14, Nov 1, Dec 25.* ⊛2.50€. ℘03 23 06 93 93.

Basilica★
Guided tours available.
Call tourist office at ℘03 23 67 05 00 for more details.
A masterpiece of Gothic architecture, St-Quentin Basilica began as a collegiate church dedicated to Saint Quentin, who worked as a missionary in the region and was martyred at the end of the 3C. It only became a basilica in 1876, and barely escaped destruction in 1918.

Exterior – The west front incorporates a massive belfry-porch; its lower part dates from the late 12C whereas the upper storeys were rebuilt in the 17C and the top after 1918. The spire dates from 1976 and reaches the height of the original one (82m/269ft).
Interior – The 15C nave (34m/111ft high) has a long maze (260m/284yd) traced on its floor, which the faithful followed on their knees. The sculpted Tree of Jesse, at the start of the south aisle, dates from the early 16C; the second chapel bears 16C mural paintings.
The impressively large 13C **chancel**★★ consists of a double transept, double aisles, an ambulatory and radiating chapels. The vaulting of the chapels right of the ambulatory rests on two columns, following the elegant arrangement of the Champagne region.

Musée Antoine-Lécuyer★
⊙*Open daily (except Tue) 10am–noon, 2–5pm (Sat 10am–noon, 2–6pm; Sun 2–6pm only).* ⊙*Closed Jan 1, May 1, Whitsun, Jul 14, Nov 1, Dec 25.* ⊛2.60€.
℘03 23 06 93 98. www.museeantoine lecuyer.fr.
The pride of the museum is its magnificent collection★★ of 78 **pastel portraits**★★ by **Quentin de La Tour** (1704–88), who was born and died in St-Quentin. La Tour, who painted all the important 18C society figures, is representative of an age marked by the importance of individuality. His works, both sensitive and honest, were said to be "incomparable illustrations of moral anatomy".

St-Riquier★

Set in the heart of the rolling Somme countryside, this ancient fortified town grew around a powerful Benedictine abbey which is the setting, in July, of a renowned classical music festival. It boasts an imposing Gothic church to rival many cathedrals and a magnificent turreted belfry with look-out posts.

▶ **Population:** 1 186
◔ **Michelin Local Map:** 301: E-7
▣ **Info:** Office du tourisme de St-Riquier, Le Beffroi, 80135. ℰ03 22 28 91 72. www.saint-riquier.com.

A BIT OF HISTORY

Formerly called Centule, the town owes its name to **Saint Riquier**, evangeliser of the Ponthieu region who died in 645 in Crécy Forest, near the village of Forest-Moutiers. After his death, his body was transported to Centule where it inspired many pilgrimages. A Benedictine monastery was founded as a result. In 790, Charlemagne gave it to his son-in-law, the poet **Angilbert**, who gave a new lease of life to the abbey and had the buildings rebuilt in the most precious materials.

SIGHTS
Abbey church★★

ᵹ ◔*Open end Mar–end Oct daily except Tue, Sat am, Sun pm and during Music Festival in Jul. ℰ03 22 28 20 20.* ☛ *Guided tours available (℘03 22 71 82 20). ⌾3€ (treasury included).*

Despite having been destroyed and rebuilt several times, the present, largely Flamboyant (15C–16C) church has retained some of its 13C architectural features, such as the lower parts of the transept and chancel.

Exterior – The west front is essentially made up of a large square tower (50m/164ft high) flanked by stair towers and covered in abundant, finely carved ornamentation. Above the central doorway, the gable bears a Holy Trinity surrounded by two abbots and the Apostles.

Interior★★ – The beauty, size and simplicity of the architecture are worth admiring. The two storeys of the large central nave (13m/42ft wide, 24m/78ft high, 96m/314ft long) are separated by a frieze and a balustrade. The chancel still has its 17C decoration and furniture: wrought-iron **gates★**, lectern and monks' stalls, marble screen surmounted by a large wooden Crucifix by Girardon. The **south transept** is unusual: its end is cut off by the sacristy and the treasury above it which occupy three bays of the cloister gallery. The wall of the treasury is decorated with fine sculptures and statues.

The **Lady Chapel** contains stellar vaulting with ribs running down to historiated corbels (Life of the Virgin Mary); at the entrance, *The Apparition of the Virgin to St Philomena* (1847) is by Ducornet, an artist who painted with his feet as he had no arms. In **Saint Angilbert's Chapel**, the five polychrome statues of saints are typical of 16C Picardy sculpture: they show (*left to right*) Veronica, Helen, Benedict, Vigor and Riquier.

Treasury – This was the abbot's private chapel. The walls of the beautiful early-16C vaulted chamber are decorated with murals from the same period; the best of them depicts the *Meeting of the Three Dead and the Three Living*, which symbolises the brevity of life. The treasury contains a 12C Byzantine Crucifix, 13C reliquaries, a 15C alabaster altarpiece and a curious 16C hand-warmer.

Abbey buildings

Rebuilt in the 17C during the d'Aligre abbacy, the old buildings now house the **Musée départemental de la Vie rurale en Picardie**, entirely dedicated to rural life and crafts in Picardy. ◔*Open end Mar–end Apr and Oct–midNov daily 2–6pm (Sat–Sun and holidays 10am–noon, 2–6pm). May–Oct daily 10am–6pm. Mid-Nov–mid-Dec Fri, Sat–Sun 2–6pm. ℰ03 22 28 20 20.*

St-Valery-sur-Somme★

Capital of the Vimeu region, St-Valery occupies a lush setting overlooking the peaceful countryside of the Bay of Somme. It consists of a walled upper town with half-timbered houses, and a lower town beside the port used by coasters, yachts and fishing boats. Every year, the coast around St-Valery becomes the playground of an important colony of harbour seals.

> ▶ **Population:** 2 686
> ⏱ **Michelin Local Map:**
> 301: C-6
> 🛈 **Info:** Office du tourisme de St-Valery-sur-Somme, 2 pl. Guillaume-le-Conquérant, 80230. ℘03 22 60 93 50. www.saint-valery-sur-somme.fr.

A BIT OF HISTORY

St-Valery (pronounced "Val'ry") began as an abbey founded in the 9C by **Walrick**, a monk from Luxeuil in Lorraine. In 1066, **William the Conqueror** rested here before invading England. In 1430, **Joan of Arc** passed through town as prisoner of the English. St-Valery prospered in the 18C through the import of salt from the Vendée region.

VILLE BASSE

The lower town extends for almost 2km/1.25mi, to the mouth of the Somme River where the port is located.

Digue-promenade★

This promenade leads to a sheltered beach and offers lovely **views** over the Bay to Le Crotoy and the headland at Le Hourdel. Villas set in gardens stand inland. Beyond the Relais Guillaume de Normandy (*see Addresses*) are the ramparts of the upper town, overlooked by St-Martin Church.

Écomusée Picarvie★

👥👤 ⏱*Open end Mar–end Sept Wed–Sun 10am–12.30pm, 1.30–6pm.* ⊜*5.90€.* ℘*03 22 26 94 90.*
This museum faithfully recreates regional life before the industrial age. Workshops and stalls show the work of basket weavers, cobblers, locksmiths, coopers, blacksmiths, joiners etc. There is also a village, complete with its school, café and barber's shop. An entire period farm has also been recreated, with the

bedroom, kitchen, cowshed, stable, cider-press and the barn.

VILLE HAUTE
Porte de Nevers

Named after the dukes of Nevers, who owned St-Valery in the 17C, this 14C gate was heightened in the 16C.

Porte Guillaume

The 12C gate stands between two majestic towers and offers an extensive **view** over the Bay of Somme.

Herbarium des Remparts

36 r. Brandt. ⏱*Open daily (except Mon) May–Oct 10am–5.30pm (weekends and holidays 10am–12.30pm, 3–6pm).* ⊜*5€.* ℘*03 22 26 69 37.*
A wonderful garden that once belonged to the nuns in charge of the hospital is being preserved by an association of local residents as an unspoilt natural area, overgrown with wild flowers.

Château abbatial and Chapelle des Marins

Beyond the Porte Guillaume, take rue de l'Abbaye. **St-Valery's Abbey** used to lie in the vale to your left. Its brick and stone **Bishop's castle** survives, with a carved 18C pediment.

▶ *From pl. de l'Ermitage, take the path up to the chapel (30min round trip).*

The chequered sandstone and flint **chapel** houses the tomb of Saint Valery. Overlooking the Bay of Somme, the chapel offers an extensive **view★** of the salt meadows, the estuary and the Marquenterre reserve in the distance.

ADDRESSES

🛏 STAY ☕ EAT

😋 **Du Port et des Bains** – *1 quai Balvet.* ℰ*03 22 60 80 09. Closed Nov 15– Dec 6 and Jan 2–25. 16 rooms.* ⌷*9€. Restaurant* 😋😋. Well located near the harbour, this hotel has lovely views of the bay. Bright colours and cane furniture in the rooms. Painting of St-Valéry in the early 20C decorate the restaurant. Traditional dishes and seafood.

😋😋 **Le Relais Guillaume de Normandy** – *43 quai Romerel.* ℰ*03 22 60 82 36. http://relaisguillaumedenormandy. akeonet.com. Closed Dec 14–Jan 10 and Tue (except Jul 14–Aug 18). 14 rooms.* ⌷*10€. Restaurant* 😋😋. This hotel was named after Guillaume (William) the Conqueror, who left St-Valéry to conquer England. It is a pretty brick manor facing the bay of Somme, which houses practical rooms, some renovated. A classic menu is served in the panoramic dining room, which offers a view of the sea and the pleasant covered terrace.

La Thiérache★

The Thiérache region forms a green patch in the bare, chalky plains of Picardy and Champagne. The relatively high altitude (250m/820ft in the east) provides greater rainfall which, combined with the terrain's lack of porousness, creates a well-watered area, devoted to forestry and grazing. Ideal country for hikers, the whole region, abounding in brick-and-stone fortified churches, is also paradise for history buffs.

🚗 DRIVING TOURS

FORTIFIED CHURCHES★

Until the reign of Louis XIV, the Thiérache region was a frontier and so repeatedly invaded – by 14C mercenaries led by Du Guesclin, by German foot soldiers and by vagabonds – particularly during the Hundred Years War, the Wars of Religion and the conflicts between France and Spain under Louis XIII and Louis XIV. From the late 16C and during the 17C, local inhabitants, lacking fortresses and ramparts, fortified their churches.
This accounts for the **watch-turrets**, **round towers** and **square keeps** pierced with **arrow slits** found on most of the 12C and 13C buildings, resulting in an uncomfortable **architectural mix** of **brick and stone**.

⚅ **Michelin Local Map:** 306: D-3 to G-4

ℹ **Info:** Office du tourisme de Vervins et du Vervinois, 1 pl. du Général- de- Gaulle, 02140. ℰ03 23 98 11 98. www.ot-vervins.com.

Other fortress-churches date entirely from the turn of the 17C. The two following driving tours will help you discover some of this most unusual architectural heritage.

1 From Vervins and back

79km/49mi – about 3hr.

Vervins
The charm of the region's capital lies in its ramparts, its cobbled streets and its houses with steeply pitched slate roofs and brick chimneys. **Notre-Dame Church** features a 13C chancel, 16C nave and imposing brick tower (34m/ 111ft tall).
Inside, 16C mural paintings adorn the piers and a composition by Jouvenet (1699) portrays *Supper in the House of Simon*. Also note a 18C organ case and pulpit.

◗ *Leave Vervins by D 372 (southeast). At Harcigny take D 37 east.*

Plomion

The 16C **church** features a west front flanked by two towers, and a square keep with a great hall leading up to the garret. A picturesque, large covered market stands in front of the church.

▶ *Take D 747 east toward Bancigny and Jeantes.*

Jeantes

The façade of the **church** is flanked by two towers. Inside, expressionist frescoes by Charles Van Eyck (1962) represent scenes from the *Life of Christ*, and a 12C font.

Dagny-Lambercy

This old village has preserved its cob houses and half-timbered houses with brick courses.

Morgny-en-Thiérache

The chancel and nave of the **church** date from the 13C. The chancel was raised by a storey to create an extra room for those seeking a safe refuge.

Dohis

There are many half-timbered and cob houses here. The **church** has a 12C nave and a porch-keep, added in the 17C.

▶ *From the village, follow the road to Parfondeval.*

Parfondeval

Perched on a hill, this is a lovely village, with a 16C Renaissance-style **church** standing like an indisputable fortress behind the rampart of neighboring houses.

▶ *Back at the entrance to the village take D 520 (west) to Archon.*

The road offers a **view** over Archon and the undulating countryside.

Archon

Cob-walled and brick houses surround the **church** guarded by two massive towers. Between the towers, the footbridge served as a look-out point.

The D 110 runs through **Renneval** (fortified churchl) and Vigneux-Hocquet.

▶ *Head for Montcornet along D 966.*

Montcornet

The Gothic **St-Martin Church**, believed to have been built by the Knights Templars in the 13C, boasts a chancel ending in a flat east end, which is almost as long as the nave. 16C additions include a Renaissance porch and eight bartizans with defensive loopholes.

▶ *Continue along D 966 toward Vigneux-Hocquet. Turn left onto D 58.*

Chaourse

Former vital centre for the area, this village gradually declined to the benefit of Montcornet. The 13C **church** (nave and tower) was fortified in the 16C. interesting **view** of the Serre Valley.

▶ *Turn around and get back on D 966 toward Hary.*

Hary

A 16C brick keep rises above the chancel and nave of this 12C **church**.

▶ *D 61 follows the Brune Valley.*

Burelles

The 16C–17C village **church** features a number of defences: arrow slits, a reinforced keep with watch-turret, barbicans and watch-turrets above the north transept, the chancel flanked by a turret. The upper floor of the transept was turned into a vast fortified room.

Prisces

The 12C chancel and nave of the **church** were given an enormous, square brick keep (25m/82ft tall) with two turrets on diagonally opposing corners.
The four floors inside allowed soldiers to take shelter with their arms and provisions.

▶ *Cross the Brune River and follow D 613 to Gronard.*

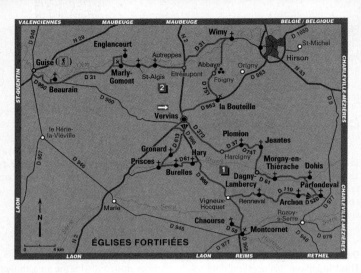

ÉGLISES FORTIFIÉES

Gronard
The **church** is partially hidden behind lime trees, its keep flanked by two round towers.

▶ *Return to Vervins along D 613 and D 966.*

The route offers a picturesque **view** of Vervins and its surrounding area.

2 From Vervins to Guise
51km/32mi – about 2hr.

This tour largely follows the **Oise Valley** which also features a number of fortified churches.

Vervins 🚶 *See above.*
▶ *From Vervins, follow D 963 to La Bouteille.*

La Bouteille
The church here has thick walls (over 1m/3ft) and is flanked by four turrets. It was built by Cistercians from the nearby **Abbaye de Foigny**, now in ruins.

▶ *D 751 and VC 10 lead to Foigny. Cross D 38 and take the little road which runs beside the abbey ruins, to Wimy.*

Wimy
The keep of the fortified church is flanked by two cylindrical towers. Inside, note

fireplaces, a bread oven and upstairs, a room for those seeking refuge.

D 31 crosses Etréaupont and continues through **Autreppes**. The road runs by its fortified church and continues past the village of **St-Algis**, overlooked by its church.

Marly-Gomont
Two great watch-turrets were added to the portal of this 13C–14C sandstone church. The large arrow slits near the base allowed crossbows to be used.

▶ *Take D 774 north to Englancourt.*

Englancourt
Overlooking the Oise River, the fortified **church** has a west front flanked by watch-turrets, a square keep in brick and a chancel with a flat east end reinforced by two round towers.

▶ *Return to D 31 via D 26.*

Beaurain
The **fortress-church** (16C) stands isolated on a hill that rises from lush surroundings. Its great square keep is flanked by towers, as is the chancel. A Romanesque font stands by the entrance.

Guise
🚶 *See Guise.*

Abbaye et Jardins de
Valloires★★

Located on a remote site in the heart of the Authie Valley, surrounded by woods and orchards, this beautiful abbey is a unique example of 18C Cistercian architecture in France, and its magnificent church "one of the last wonders from the Baroque period." Part of the abbey's gardens, the Jardin des "Îles" forms an ocean of greenery dotted with colourful islands while its rose garden offers thousands of sweet-smelling flowers.

A BIT OF HISTORY

The abbey of Valloires was founded in the 12C by **Guy II**, count of Ponthieu, and became a burial place for his family. In 1346, the bodies of knights killed at Crécy were transported here.
Ravaged by several fires in the 17C, the abbey was rebuilt in the 18C following plans by **Raoul Coignard**. The decoration is the work of Austrian sculptor **Simon Pfaff von Pfaffenhoffen** (1715–84).
Run by a charity since 1922, the abbey is now devoted to the care of children in difficulty and the elderly, but some 18C rooms welcome paying guests in a beautiful, peaceful setting (*see Addresses p380*).

ABBEY★

By guided tour only (1h). Jun–Aug daily 10.30am–5.30pm. Apr–May and Sept daily 11.30am–4.30pm. Oct–mid-Nov daily 11.30am–3.30pm (Sat–Sun 4.30pm). 7.50€. 03 22 29 62 33. www.abbaye-valloires.com.
A curious mix of austere simplicity and exuberant Baroque and Rococo flamboyance would best describe the architecture at Valloires. Upon entering the vast courtyard, you will note a 16C **dovecote** to your left, and to your right, the **abbot's loggings**.
The reception hall, decorated with remarkable **wood panelling★**, portraits and a Louis XIV chandelier, is a fine example of 18C classic elegance,

Michelin Local Map:
301: D-5
Info: www.abbaye-valloires.com and www.jardinsdevalloires.com.
Location: Argoules is in the north of the department of the Somme, 35km/22mi north of Abbevile.

and a complete departure from the sober lines of the **cloister**, with its plain groined vaults. The east wing housed the old chapter-house and the refectory on the ground floor, while the abbot's rooms and the monk's cells were upstairs. Adjoining the church, the **vestry** boasts finely decorated wood panels by Pfaffenhoffen and paintings by Parrocel.

Church★ – Inside, note the **organ (1)**, supported by a **gallery★** carved by Pfaffenhoffen with musical instruments. The statues on each side symbolise Religion. The balustrade and small organ case are decorated with *putti* and cherub musicians.
The graceful **wrought-iron gates★★ (2)** which enclose the chancel are attributed to Jean-Baptiste Veyren (1704–1788) who also did some of the metal work for the Amiens Cathedral. The central part is surmounted by the Valloires arms and Moses' brazen serpent (prefiguration of the Crucifixion), framed by baskets of flowers.
Two angels in gilded lead by Pfaffenhoffen are located around the **high altar (3)**, dominated by a curious abbot's crook.
The south transept houses **recumbent effigies (4)** of a count and countess of Ponthieu. In the north transept, you can still see the window through which sick monks could follow services.
Carved religious emblems adorn the **stalls (5)**. Those reserved for the abbot and the prior stand on either side of the entrance to the apsidal chapel, which is decorated with wood panels by Pfaffenhoffen.

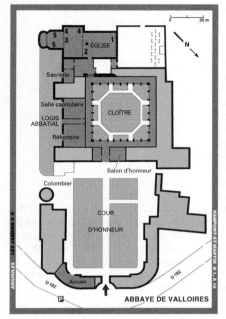

Map labels: 0 20 m, N, ÉGLISE, Sacristie, Salle capitulaire, LOGIS ABBATIAL, CLOÎTRE, Réfectoire, Salon d'honneur, Colombier, COUR D'HONNEUR, Accueil, D 192, D 192, NAMPONT-ST-MARTIN N 1, A 16, ARGOULES LES JARDINS ★★, P, ABBAYE DE VALLOIRES

GARDENS★★

🕐 *Open daily mid-Mar–mid-Sept 10am–6pm; mid-Sept–mid-Nov 10am–5pm.* 💶*5.90–7.80€.* 👣*1hr 30min guided tours available.* ☎*03 22 23 53 55. www.jardinsdevalloires.com.*
Landscaped by **Gilles Clément** in 1987, this 8ha/19.7-acre park contains 5 000 species of plants and trees, mostly from the northern hemisphere and Asia.

Jardin à la française – Laid out in the formal French style, this garden is somewhat reminiscent of Cistercian rigour. Yew trees evoking the pillars of the church surround the "plant cloister".

Jardin des îles – The colours of these island gardens, set on high ground within an English-style park, change with the seasons. The **winter** island displays the subtle hues of maple and birch tree. The **gold** island is home to elder and hazelnut bushes. The **shadow** island contains plants which do not favour sunlight. The **cherry-tree** grove, near the **lilac** island, showcases flowering varieties of prunus. The **silver** island, located next to the **viburnum** island, displays velvety white flowers. Other areas with evocative names include the **crimson-foliage** island, the **autumn** grove, the **butterfly** island and the island of **decorative fruit**, beautiful but sometimes poisonous, as well as the "**bizarretum**" where oddly shaped plants are gathered.

Espace Lamarck – Dedicated to the evolution of species, this garden was named after botanist **Jean-Baptiste Lamarck** (1744–1829) who outlined a theory of the evolution of living beings linked to the variations of their natural environment.

Jardin des 5 sens – 👥 You will discover a selection of plants and trees connected with the different senses: strawberries and apples (taste), thorny plants (touch), aspens with leaves that rustle with the breeze (hearing), colourful petunias (sight), jasmine, lily and mint (smell).

Roseraie – About 200 old and new different varieties of roses grow among aromatic plants and medicinal herbs, as it was customary in the Middle Ages. They include special specimens directly related to the site, such as the emblematic **Rose des Cisterciens** created in 1998 for the 900th anniversary of the Cistercian Order.

Jardin bleu – In this part of the gardens, trees and shrubs such as the evergreen oak, the indigo or the Hibiscus, bring a subtle touch of blue.

Jardin de marais – Lower down lies the wilder Marsh Garden with its artificial canal reminiscent of the arm of the Authie River which used to flow across the estate.

ADDRESSES

🛏 STAY

🍴🍴 **Hostellerie de l'Abbaye de Valloires** – *In Valloires Abbey.* ☎*03 22 29 62 33. Closed Nov 11–Apr 1. 17 rooms.* 🍽*6€.* Located at the very heart of the Cistercian abbey, this hostel is an exceptionally fine setting for a contemplative retreat. The rooms give onto the splendid gardens or the cloister.

Villers-Cotterêts

Almost entirely surrounded by the Retz Forest, Villers-Cotterêts is a peaceful little town which largely developed owing to King François I's passion for hunting. It was here, in 1539, that the monarch announced the famous Statute of Villers-Cotterêts, laying the foundations of the modern registry system. It was also here that was born one of the most widely read French writers of all times: Alexandre Dumas Senior, 19C prolific author of historic novels of high adventure.

↦ Population: 9 839
⚲ Michelin Local Map:
306: A-7
ℹ Info: Office de tourisme, pl. A.-Briand, Villers-Cotterêts 02600. ℘03 23 96 55 10. http://tourisme.cc-villers-cotterets.fr.

☙ IN THE FOOTSTEPS OF THE DUMAS

Several generations of Dumas have left their imprint on the streets of Villers-Cotterêts, and here are just a few examples. **Place du Docteur-Mouflier** (formerly place de la Fontaine) is mentioned in Dumas Senior's memoirs. His grandfather's **hotel** stood on the square, as did the **lawyer's office** where he was employed, and Madame Dumas' **tobacconist's shop**. The writer's **birthplace** is at 46 rue A.-Dumas. This street leads to the square of the same name where a **statue** of the writer by **Rodin** used to stand. It was unfortunately melted down by the Germans during the First World War; only his quill pen was saved and is now in the care of the museum.

Rue de Bapaume leads from this square to the cemetery where the **Dumas' family grave** is located. The other **statue** of Dumas by **Bourret** stands in the small public garden, on rue L.-Lagrange.

Musée Alexandre-Dumas

24 rue Demoustier. ⊙*Open year-round 2–5pm.* ⊙*Closed Tue, last Sun of the month and holidays.* ⊛*3.20€.* ℘*03 23 96 23 30.*
Three small rooms are dedicated to the famous "Three Dumas": letters, manuscripts, novels, paintings, satirical cartoons, busts and various objects including the uniform Dumas Junior wore as a member of the French Academy.

ADDITIONAL SIGHT
Château François I

⊙ ☙ *May– end Oct: guided tours daily (except Mon and May 1) at 11am and 3pm. Nov–end Apr: guided tours daily (except Sun and holidays) at 11am and 3pm.* ⊛*4€.* ℘*03 23 96 55 10.*
Within the courtyard, the east and west sides are bordered by buildings which retain Renaissance features. The **main staircase★** alone, with its spectacular double flight of stairs, is worth a visit. This true masterpiece (1535) dates from the period of François I. The carvings on the coffered ceiling are from the school of **Jean Goujon**. The same motifs are used in greater abundance in the State room, which was originally the chapel. The **King's staircase**, contemporary with the main staircase, has its original decoration of carved mythological scenes from *The Dream of Polyphyle*.
Outside, all that remains of **Le Nôtre's park** are the outlines of the parterre and the perspective of the Allée Royale.

The three Dumas

Grandfather: Thomas-Alexandre Dumas (1762–1806), general in Napoleon's army.

Father: Alexandre Dumas Senior (1802–1870), famous writer best known for his historical novels such as *The Three Musketeers*.

Son: Alexandre Dumas Junior (1824–1895), also author and dramatist, best known for *The Lady of the Camelias*.

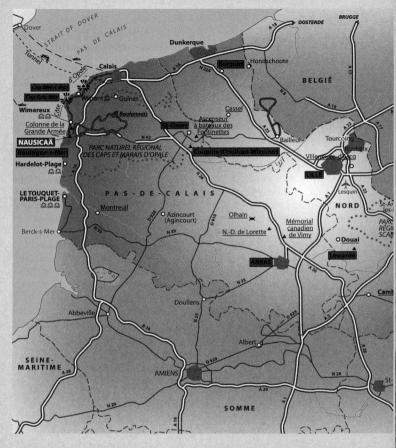

The Nord-Pas-de-Calais region has the Belgian border along the northeastern edge and the English Channel, or *La Manche*, to the northwest. This position at the crossroads of Europe has made it a highly prized possession, and the many military fortifications, trenches and memorials dedicated to the countless battles and sieges throughout the centuries bear witness to this. The historic procession of foreign conquerors has resulted in a colourful and cosmopolitan cultural, culinary and architectural heritage that gives this part of France its unique character. Today it is a major transportation and industrial hub, as well as a popular vacation spot for its beaches and natural parks.

Military History

The Pas-de-Calais region has been the arena for some of the most important military campaigns in history. After its Roman settlements, the French kings gave the lands to the Counts of Flanders in the 12C, but it was hotly-contested for its strategic location, and subsequently besieged, conquered or claimed by marriage by the English, the Spanish, the Hapsburgs, and the Burgundians.

Louis XIV brought it permanently into the French kingdom in the 17C and protected it with Vauban's imposing fortifications, but the region's proximity to England brought Napoléon's troops in the 19C, and considerable destruction and occupation by Germans during WW I and WW II. Today visitors can see the fortresses, bunkers, missile launch pads, memorials and museums of military history throughout the Pas-de-Calais.

NAUSICAÄ	★★★	Highly recommended
LILLE	★★	Recommended
Douai	★	Interesting
Bailleul		Other sight

Highlights

1 Catch a classical concert in Arras' **Abbaye St-Vaast** (p387).

2 Take a boat tour of the water ways in **St-Omer** (p454).

3 Tour the candy-making boutiques of **Cambrai** (p415).

4 Dance with the locals of Dunkirk at the annual **Carnival** (p428).

5 See the Les Miserables sound and light show in **Montreuil-sur-Mer** (p449).

For Nature Lovers

Many might turn up their noses at the industrialized stretch of coastline between Calais and Dunkirk, but the sandy beaches of the Nord-Pas-de-Calais known as the Opal Coast are the favoured holiday destination for Parisians and in-the-know British visitors who prefer the close proximity and relatively low prices compared to the French Riviera. This part of France is graced with three regional nature preserves, with scenic drives and lush forest trails for hiking, horseback riding, or cycling. You won't want to miss Boulogne-sur-Mer's Nausicaä, with the largest sea life aquariums in Europe.

Cosmopolitan Culture

There have been many different cultural influences on the towns and villages of the Pas-de-Calais throughout the centuries, which makes for a colourful mishmash of regional customs, folklore, and architectural styles. The area around the Belgian border, known as French Flanders, is recognizable by its distinctive architecture, windmills and culinary specialities with a decidedly Dutch influence (this region of Belgium was formerly part of the Low Countries).

A few words of the old French Flemish dialect have snuck into the French vocabulary such as the famous "estaminets" or café-bars. And, like their counterparts in Flemish Belgium, the carnivals in Pas-de-Calais towns often feature "giants", or paper-maché effigies of their local folk heroes.

A Dynamic Industrial Centre

After the widespread damage and destruction of the 20C wars, the cities of the Nord-Pas-de-Calais region slowly rebuilt themselves to become the economic and industrial powerhouses they are today. Boulogne-sur-Mer is the largest European fish processing industry, Dunkirk is an important petrochemical and steel port, Calais is still a major lace-producing centre, and Lille is an important business and manufacturing city, with a nod towards modern architecture with buildings by Rem Koolhaus, Christian de Portzampac, and Jean Nouvel. The region is an international transportation hub for Paris, Brussels, Antwerp, Amsterdam and London.

Arras★★

Arras, the capital of the Artois region, hides its little-known artistic beauties, the 18C Grand-Place and Place des Héros, behind a serious, reserved appearance. The city, a religious, military and administrative centre, is surrounded by boulevards that replaced the old Vauban-like fortifications. Chitterling sausages (*andouillettes*) and chocolate hearts are the local culinary specialities.

A BIT OF HISTORY

Influence in the Middle Ages – The Roman town of Nemetacum was founded on the slopes of Baudimont hill, which is still known today as La Cité. In the Middle Ages the town developed from a grain market around the Benedictine abbey of St Vaast into a centre of woollen cloth manufacture, and later became a centre for art, patronised by bankers and rich Arras burghers. The town is famous for its troubadours (*trouvères*) such as **Gautier d'Arras, Jean Bodel**, author of *Le Jeu de saint Nicolas*, and above all the 13C **Adam de la Halle** who brought dramatic art to Arras with his play **Le Jeu de la Feuillée**.

From 1384 the manufacture of high-warp tapestries, under the patronage of the dukes of Burgundy, brought Arras widespread fame – and the word *arras* passed into English to indicate a tapestry wall-hanging. After the Renaissance, this activity decreased as Beauvais and Antwerp took over.

Youth of "The Incorruptible" – **Maximilien de Robespierre**, whose father was an Artois Council barrister, was born in Arras in 1758. Orphaned at an early age, the young man became the protégé of the bishop and received a scholarship to attend school in Paris. Robespierre became a barrister on his return to Arras and was affiliated with the **Rosati** (an anagram of "Artois") poetic society. During this period the pale young man, later the spirited leader of the Revolution, courted young ladies with verse.

▶ **Population:** 124 206
⏱ **Michelin Local Map:** 301: J-6
ℹ **Info:** Hôtel de ville, pl. des Héros, 62000 Arras. ✆03 21 51 26 95. www.ot-arras.fr.
▶ **Location:** The centre of the town is marked by three large squares, the Grande Place, the Place des Héros, and the Petite Place. These are surrounded by many buildings restored to their pre-war WW I conditions, notably the Gothic town hall and the 19C cathedral.
P **Parking:** There are (paid) parking areas in and around the centre of Arras. Try the one near the tourist information office.
👁 **Don't Miss:** La Grande Place and the Place des Héros.
🕐 **Timing:** Start with a walk around the centre of town, which will give you a feel for the place. Allow about 1 hr.
👪 **Kids:** Cité Nature is a popular attraction
⏱ **Also See:** the hill on which stands Notre-Dame-de-Lorette; the Canadian War Memorial at Vimy.

In Arras, Robespierre knew **Joseph Lebon** (1765–95), a member of the Oratorian order who was mayor of the town during the Reign of Terror. During this time the former priest presided over the destruction of many churches and regularly sent aristocrats and rich farmers to the guillotine set up in place du Théâtre. Lebon himself was later guillotined.

Arras and the Battles of Artois – During the First World War, the front was close to Arras until 1917, so much of the area suffered heavy shelling. The most violent conflicts took place in the strategically important hills north of the town. After the Battle of the Marne the retreating Germans fought to hold on to them, clinging to Vimy Ridge and the slopes of Notre-Dame-de-Lorette Hill.

In the autumn of 1914 they attacked Arras, but were stopped after battles at Ablain-St-Nazaire, Carency and La Targette.

In May and June 1915 **General Foch**, in command of the French forces in the north, attempted to pierce the German ranks; his troops took Neuville St-Vaast and Notre-Dame-de-Lorette. The attack failed at Vimy however, which was won only in 1917 by the Canadians.

↝ WALKING TOUR
MAIN SQUARES
Grand'Place and place des Héros★★★

The two main squares in Arras, the theatrical Grand'Place and Place des Héros, joined by the short rue de la Taillerie, are quite impressive. They existed as early as the 11C, but have seen many transformations through the centuries.

Today's magnificent façades are fine examples of 17C and 18C Flemish architecture. The local council of the period was careful to control the town's development, permitting citizens to construct only "in stone or brick, with no projecting architectural elements."

The façades – formerly embellished with carved shop signs, of which a few remain – rest on monolith-columned arcades which protected market stallholders and customers alike from inclement weather. As evening comes the squares take on a different charm when the gables, discreetly floodlit, stand out against the night sky. The smaller and livelier of the two squares, **Place des Héros**, is surrounded by shops and overlooked by the belfry.

❯ *Stand facing the town hall and take rue D.-Delansorne, which starts in the left-hand corner of Place des Héros and leads to rue Paul-Doumer.*

On the corner of rue Doumer stands the **Palais de Justice** (Law Courts), the former seat of the Artois government (1701), embellished with Corinthian pilasters and its side entrance (1724) decorated with Regency shells.

❯ *From rue Doumer, follow the second or third side street on the left.*

Place du Théâtre

During the Revolution, the guillotine stood in this lively square. The **theatre** dates from 1784 (its façade has been restored). It was built where the fish market stood; it faces the **Ostel des Poissonniers** (1710), a narrow Baroque house carved with sea gods and mermaids. In rue des Jongleurs, note the majestic 18C Hôtel de Guines; no 9 rue

Grand'Place

Y. Tierny/ MICHELIN

Robespierre was the former residence of the famous revolutionary.

Maison Robespierre – Robespierre lived (1787–89) in this house. It has been turned into a **Musée du Compagnonnage** (crafts guild), which displays masterpieces by some of the best craftsmen in France (*Compagnons du Tour de France*).

◐ *Walk across the square and take rue St-Aubert on your right; place du Wetz-d'Amain is a little farther on the left.*

Place du Wetz-d'Amain

The square is graced by a pretty Renaissance house, to which a Classical stone porch was added later. It served as refuge to the monks of Mont St-Éloi.

◐ *Turn back, follow rue du Gén.-Barbot which crosses rue St-Aubert; turn left on rue A.-Briand; Église Notre-Dame-des-Ardents is on your left. One of the streets on the right leads to place V.-Hugo and the lower town.*

Église Notre-Dame-des-Ardents

Fragments of the Holy Taper, a miraculous candle entrusted by the Virgin Mary to two minstrels to cure ergotic poisoning in the 12C, are safeguarded. The silver reliquary is to the left of the high altar, in a latticed recess (*lighting below, to the right*).

◐ *Follow one of the streets on the right to reach place Victor-Hugo and the lower town.*

Basse-ville

This district lies between the town and the citadel. It is arranged around the lovely, octagonal **place Victor-Hugo**, built in 1756, where the cattle market used to be held.
Follow rue des Promenades towards the **Jardins du Gouverneur** and **Jardin des Allées**: a **stele** erected in honour of the Rosati depicts a marquess and a 20C man watching a procession of muses.
The **Citadel** (✆ *mid-Jun–mid-Sept, Sun 3.30pm, guided visits (2h); ∞4.60€;*

✆ *03 21 51 26 95*), a UNESCO World Heritage site, stands just across boulevard du Général-de-Gaulle; the octagonal stronghold designed by Vauban was built between 1668 and 1672.
It is composed of five bastions. A model of the fortifications is displayed in the entrance hall. The tour includes the arsenal and the Baroque Chapelle St-Louis. Avenue du Mémorial des Fusillés leads to the **Mur des Fusillés** where 217 members of the Resistance were executed during the Second World War.

◐ *Return to place V.-Hugo and walk to the Cité district via rue Victor-Hugo. Then take the cours de Verdun on the right; cross place du 33e and continue along rue de Châteaudun leading to rue d'Amiens.*

Cité

Place de la Préfecture was the heart of medieval Arras. Today the *préfecture* (county council) occupies the former bishop's palace, finished in 1780.
Opposite, the Église St-Nicolas-en-Cité (1839) stands on the site of Notre-Dame-de-la-Cité Cathedral, which was destroyed between 1798 and 1804. It houses a triptych depicting the *Climb to Calvary*, painted in 1577 by P Claessens of Bruges.
Follow rue Baudimont on the right for 135m/150yd to reach **place du Pont-de-Cité**. The name recalls the bridge on the River Crinchon (now flowing underground), which linked the Cité to the town when each had its own fortifications.

◐ *From the square, follow rue de Turenne which skirts the Jardin Minelle (on the left) and leads to quai du Rivage.*

The **Jardin Minelle**, which replaced the town's fortifications, is a haven of peace. **Place de l'Ancien-Rivage** is set back from the pleasant *quai du Rivage*. The square-turreted house on it was the former St-Éloi hospice, founded in 1635 by one of the town's goldsmiths. Until the 19C, the square formed a dock that was linked to the old harbour.

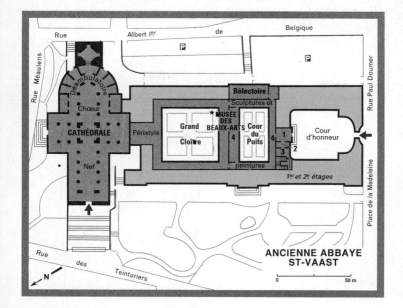

Rue Albert Ier de Belgique
Rue Méaulens
Déambulatoire
Chœur
CATHÉDRALE Péristyle
Nef
Réfectoire
Sculptures et
★ MUSÉE DES BEAUX-ARTS
Grand Cloître
Cour du Puits
Cour d'honneur
peintures
1er et 2e étages
Rue Paul Doumer
Place de la Madeleine
Rue des Teinturiers
N
ANCIENNE ABBAYE ST-VAAST
0   50 m

◗ *Return to the Grand'Place along rue du Mont-de-Piété, place G.-Mollet and rue Ste-Croix.*

ADDITIONAL SIGHTS
Ancienne Abbaye St-Vaast★★

The old abbey was founded in the 7C by St Aubert on the hill overlooking a tributary of the River Scarpe, and was entrusted with the relics of the first bishop of Arras, St Vaast. **Cardinal de Rohan**, commendatory abbot, began reconstructing the abbey buildings in 1746 in a style combining balance and elegance to produce an austere sense of beauty; they were deconsecrated during the Revolution, then restored after 1918.

Musée des Beaux-Arts★

22 rue Paul Doumer. ◷*Open Wed–Mon 9.30am–noon, 2–5.30pm.* ◷*Closed 1 Jan, 1–8 May, 14 Jul, 1–11 Nov, 25 Dec.* ⊜*4€ no charge 1st Wed and 1st Sun in the month.* ℘*03 21 71 26 43.*

The museum offers a splendid account of the town's history: archaeological finds, medieval sculpture, 15C tapestries, the cathedral treasury, 17C procelain and paintings (French and Dutch schools, large religious works) and pre-Impressionist paintings.

The **Italian Room (1)** decorated with the original lion from the belfry (1554) in Arras is used as a reception area. The tour begins in a series of small rooms on the left (**2** and **3**) containing the Gallo-Roman archaeology collection. The porphyry statue of Attis from a 2C–3C sanctuary in honour of Attis and Cybele bears witness to the influence of Near Eastern religions carried abroad by the army and merchants.

The **galleries around the small cloister (4)**, known as the Cour du Puits, contain some fine medieval sculptures and paintings: Virgin and Child by Pépin de Huy, tapestries made in Arras (legend of St Vaast); note in particular the 13C **Anges de Saudémont★** with their delicately rendered curly hair, almond-shaped eyes and faint smile. The 16C is illustrated by triptychs by **Bellegambe** (Adoration of the Christ Child) and an Entombment by Vermeyen.

Refectory – A tapestry bearing the arms of Cardinal de Rohan hangs above the great marble fireplace.

Grand cloître – The spacious main cloister, which used to lead through a

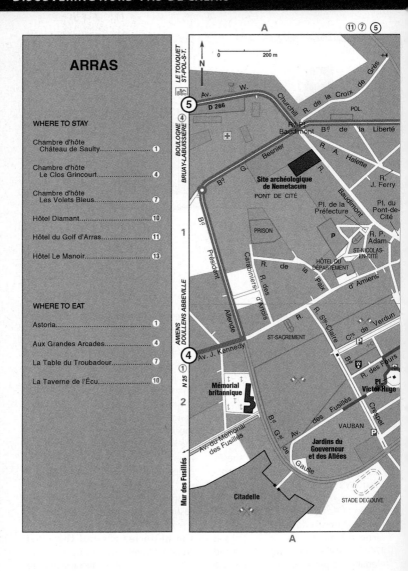

ARRAS

WHERE TO STAY

Chambre d'hôte
Château de Saulty...................... ①

Chambre d'hôte
Le Clos Grincourt...................... ④

Chambre d'hôte
Les Volets Bleus...................... ⑦

Hôtel Diamant............................. ⑩

Hôtel du Golf d'Arras................. ⑪

Hôtel Le Manoir.......................... ⑬

WHERE TO EAT

Astoria.. ①

Aux Grandes Arcades................. ④

La Table du Troubadour............. ⑦

La Taverne de l'Écu..................... ⑩

peristyle into the minster, contains capitals carved with garlands and rosettes. The **staircase** is decorated with a fine series of paintings by Giovanni Baglioni (1571–1644).
The **first floor** is given over to paintings from the 16C to 18C by the French School (Vignon, Nicolas de Largillière, Boullongne, Vien, Bouliar, Doncre) and the Dutch School (Brueghel the Younger, Adriaen Van Utrecht, Barent Fabritius, a student of Rembrandt, and Rubens). 17C and 18C sculpture.

The **Salle des Mays de Notre-Dame** owes its name to the works that were given to Notre-Dame Church in Paris every springtime between 1603 and 1707 by the guild of gold- and silversmiths. It contains huge works by La Hyre, Sébastien Bourdon, Louis de Boullongne, Philippe de Champaigne, Joseph Barrocel and Jouvenet.
On the **2nd floor**, the rooms on the front of the building contain the ceramics collections from the 16C to the 19C: Italian and glazed earthenware, and Arras and

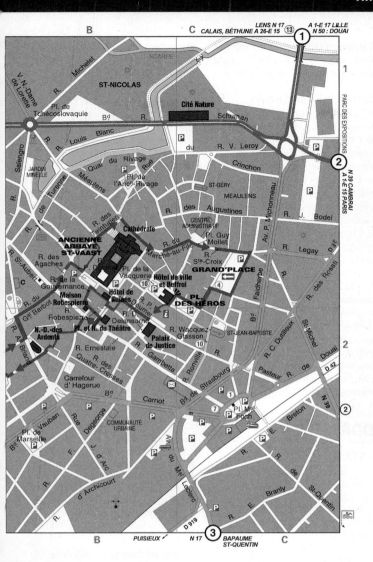

SCARPE

ST-NICOLAS

Cité Nature

Schuman

R. V. Leroy

②

N 39 CAMBRAI
A 1-E 15 PARIS

PARC DES EXPOSITIONS

V. N.-Dame de Lorette

Michelet

R.

Pl. de Tchécoslovaquie

Bd

R.

Louis Blanc

Salengro

JARDIN MINETTE

R. de Turenne

Quai du Rivage

Méaulens

Rue

Pl. de l'Anc.-Rivage

Crinchon

ST-GÉRY

MEAULENS

R. des Augustines

R. J. Bodel

Av. P. Michonneau

R. Legay

D 3 E

R. des Rosati

R. des Teinturiers

Cathédrale

CENTRE ADMINISTRATIF

Pl. Guy Mollet

R. du Marché-au-Filé

ANCIENNE ABBAYE ST-VAAST

R. des Agaches

R. St-Aubert

Pl. Daumer Pl. de la Vacquerie

Ste-Croix

GRAND'PLACE

Faidherbe

Hôtel de ville et Beffroi

Pl. de la Gouvernance

Maison Robespierre

Hôtel de Ruines

Pl. DES HÉROS

④

R. Gal Barbot

R. Robespierre

R. Daumer

R. D. Delansorne

N.-D.-des Ardents

Pl. et R. du Théâtre

Palais de Justice

R. Wacquez-Glasson

ST-JEAN-BAPTISTE

St-Michel

Douai

D 42

②

R. A. Briand

R. Ernestale

R. des Quatre-Crosses

Gambetta

R. Ronville

Pasteur

R. de

Carrefour d'Hagerue

Bd

Carnot

Bd de Strasbourg

N 39

Pl. de Vauban

Bd

Pl. de Marseille

Rue Degeorge

J. d'Arc

COMMUNAUTÉ URBAINE

Avd du Mal Leclerc

Pl. Mal Foch

⑦

E.

Breton

d'Archicourt

R.

R.

E.

Branly

St-Quentin

D 919

D 42

Tournai porcelain decorated with light, delicate motifs (note the "**Buffon bird dinner service**" commissioned by the Duc d'Orléans in 1787).

Around the small cloister are works by various schools of early-19C French landscape artists including Corot and Dutilleux. One spacious room is given over to large 19C works (**Delacroix, Chassériau**). Next to this room is the Salle Louise-Weiss containing 19C small paintings by Monticelli, Ribot and Ravier.

Cathédrale

🕙*Open May–Oct, Mon–Sat 10.30am–12.30pm & 2–6pm; Sun 2–6pm; rest of year Mon–Sat 2.30–5.30pm.* 📞*03 21 51 26 95. Entrance in rue des Teinturiers.*

The old abbey church of St Vaast was built beginning in the 18C. It was finished in 1833 and elevated to a cathedral, to replace Notre-Dame-de-la-Cité.

The Classical façade is graced by a monumental flight of steps. The luminous interior presents a line of lofty columns bearing Corinthian capitals. Enormous

19C statues of saints, from the Pantheon in Paris, adorn the side aisles. The right transept is decorated with frescoes.

Hôtel de Ville and Belfry

The City Pass Or tickets give admission to several sites including the Hotel de Ville, Cité Nature, the Belfry, the Musée des Beaux-Arts, and the underground Circuit des Souterrains are available from the Office de Tourisme 19€ (child, 10€). 03 21 51 26 95. www.ot-arras.fr. **Hotel de Ville:** *Guided visits (30min) Jul–Aug Wed & Sun 3pm. 2€.* **Belfry★:** *Open May–Sept Mon–Sat 9am–6.30pm, Sun, 10am–1pm & 2.30–6.30pm; Oct–Apr Tue–Sat 9am–noon, 2–6pm, Sun 10am–12.30pm & 2.30–6.30pm; Mon 10am–noon & 2–6pm). 2.70€.*
The town hall was destroyed in 1914 and rebuilt in the Flamboyant style. The beautiful front, with its uneven arches, stands on the western side of place des Héros, and the graceful 75m/246ft belfry, with its 40-bell peal, rises over the more severe-looking Renaissance wings. Downstairs, an audio-visual presentation on the history of Arras is an excellent introduction to the town.

Circuit des souterrains

Guided tours 45min-tour daily 10am–noon, 2–6pm (Sun and public holidays, 10am–12.30pm, 2.30–6.30pm. Closed 1 Jan and 25 Dec. 4.90€.
The 10C galleries, or *boves*, cut into the limestone bank on which the town stands, served as a refuge in wartime (during WW I the British set up a field hospital here for 24,000 troops) and above all as an enormous wine cellar; the caves (boves) are at the ideal temperature for storing wine.

Cité Nature

25 bd Schuman Open Tue–Fri 9am–7pm, Sat–Sun 2–6pm. 7€. 03 21 21 59 59. www.citenature.com.
An old warehouse renovated by Jean Nouvel in 2004 houses an interactive exposition on nature, ecology, and agriculture, with a green labyrinth in the gardens.

ADDRESSES

STAY

Le Clos Grincourt (Bed and Breakfast) – *18 Rue du Château, 62161 Duisans. 9km/5.4mi W of Arras via N 39 then D 56. 03 21 48 68 33. www.leclos grincourt.com. 3 rooms.* A tree-lined lane leads to a lovely bourgeois house that went into construction under Louis XIV, but was not completed until the days of Napoleon III. The rooms are like little apartments; all have views over the flower-filled garden. Hospitable, attentive reception.

Château de Saulty (Bed and Breakfast) – *82 Rue de la Gare, 62158 Saulty. 19km/11.5mi SW of Arras dir. Doullens via N 25. 03 21 48 24 76. Closed Jan. . 5 rooms.* This château, built in 1835, looks very fine in its 45ha/112 acre park at the village edge. After a cosy night spent in one of the smart, spacious guest rooms, your breakfast includes home-made jams and fresh juice.

Les Volets Bleus (Bed and Breakfast) – *47 Rue Briquet-Taillandier, 62223 Anzin-Saint-Aubin. 03 21 23 39 90. www.voletsbleus.com. 3 rooms. Restaurant .* Forget your diet at this pretty residence in a flowered garden facing the Gold d'Arras. The rooms are comfortable and functional, but the gourmet meals and buffet breakfasts are extraordinary.

Hôtel Diamant – *5 Place des Héros. 03 21 71 23 23. www.arras-hotel-diamant.com. 12 rooms. 9€.* This hotel enjoys a choice location on the Place des Héros at the foot of the belfry. The reception is very pleasant and the rather small rooms are impeccably maintained.

Hotel Le Manoir – *35 rte Nationale, 62580 Gavrelle. 11km/6.6mi NE of Arras via N 50 dir. Douai. 03 21 58 68 58. www.lemanoir62.net. Closed 3 wks in Aug, 2nd half of Dec, Sat lunch and Sun evening. 19 rooms. 8€. Restaurant .* One of the pleasures of staying in this bourgeois manor set in a park is that the windows open onto a picturesque view of the verdant countryside. Simple, clean rooms housed in the former stables. The restaurant serves traditional French cuisine.

⊜⊜⊜⊜ **Hôtel du Golf d'Arras**–
Rue Briquet-Tallandier, 62223 Anzin-Saint-Aubin, 5km/3mi NW of Arras on D 341. ℘*03 21 50 45 04, www.golf-arras.com.* *64 rooms. Restaurant ⊜⊜⊜.*
Located at the entrance to the Arras golf club, this elegant hotel with the Louisiana-inspired architecture has well-appointed rooms facing the greens, and a gourmet restaurant and bar.

♀/ EAT

⊜ **La Taverne de l'Écu** – *18–20 rue Wacquez-Glasson.* ℘*03 21 51 42 05.* Traditional brasserie fare and local specialities to satisfy appetites of all sizes! Located in a pedestrianised street, this tavern has been decorated with flair. Try the *écuflette*, a house recipe based on the *flammenküche*, a creamy Alsatian pizza-like delicacy.

⊜⊜ **Les Grandes Arcades** – *8–12 Grand'Place.* ℘*03 21 23 30 89.* Two formulas are available at this restaurant situated on the splendid Grand'Place: a brasserie menu and a proper restaurant menu. Don't forget to have a look at the magnificent 15C vaulted cellar below. A few renovated, personalized bedrooms are available.

⊜⊜⊜ **La Table du Troubadour** – *43 Blvd Carnot.* ℘*03 21 71 34 50. Closed 1st week in Aug, last week Dec, Mon evening & Sun.* The owner wants her restaurant to be unique – and it is! She has created a treasure trove of copper kettles, photos by Doisneau, old enamel stoves, a record player, dollies, a pram, and so on. The food is made from market-fresh ingredients and the dishes are worthy of a whisk-wielding French grandmother.

⊜⊜ **Astoria** – *12 pl. Foch.* ℘*03 21 71 08 14.* Sit comfortably on the terrace or in the warm dining-room of this brasserie-style restaurant. Traditional breakfast dishes and regional specialities are served here.

⇌ TAKE A BREAK

Pâtisserie Sébastien Thibaut – *50 Place des Héros.* ℘*03 21 71 53 20. Tue–Sun, 8am–7.30pm.* For the past 100 years, this pastry shop has been delighting gourmet palates with its *Cœur d'Arras* (a ginger-bread confection), *Petits Rats d'Arras*, waffles and other toothsome house recipes. In addition to sweetmeats and pastries, the tearoom serves salads and hot quiches.

☺ ON THE TOWN

Irish Pub – *7 Place des Héros.* ℘*03 21 71 46 08. Tue–Sun 11am–1am; Mon 3pm–1am.* The name tells the game: wooden tables, a waxed parquet, a good choice of beer and music with a Celtic accent transport patrons to the Emerald Isle. When the weather warms up, you may enjoy your mug of the frothy on the terrace. Theme evenings.

☗☗ SHOWTIME

Théâtre d'Arras – *Rue Paul Doumer.* ℘*03 21 71 66 16. Box office Tue–Sat, 2–7.15pm. Closed Jul–Aug.* This pretty *théâtre à l'italienne* seating 400 is listed as a historic building. The varied programming features music and drama. Events drawing larger crowds are held in the casino.

☗☗ SPORT

Stade d'eau vive (fresh water stadium) – Base nautique Robert-Pecqueur – *r. Laurent-Gers, 62223 St-Laurent-Blangy. 2km/1.2mi NE of Arras.* ℘*03 21 73 74 93. Mon–Fri, 8am–noon, 2pm–5pm; Sat–Sun by reservation.* Originally designed for the 2004 Olympic Games, this 300m/985ft long, 12m/40ft wide artificial torrent was excavated between the Scarpe lock and one of its overflow branches. Kayaks, rafts and canoes may be rented here at very reasonable prices.

⇲ SHOPPING

Markets – Traditional markets held at the Place des Héros on Wednesday, and the Grand'Place on Saturday mornings.

Avesnes-Sur-Helpe

This quiet town, which has preserved some of its Vauban-like fortifications, is the ideal starting point for drives through the patchwork of hedged-in meadows and slate-roofed hamlets of the Avesnois region. From here you can also explore the hiking trails of the Parc naturel régional de l'Avesnois.

☜ WALKING TOUR

Grand'Place
The town's narrow main square is surrounded by old houses with high slate roofs.

Hôtel de Ville
A double staircase with wrought-iron balustrades fronts the 18C Classical town hall in blue Tournai stone.

▷ Walk round the church and follow rue d'Albret.

Square de la Madeleine
Located on top of one of the bastions, this provides a bird's-eye view of the Helpe Valley.

EXCURSIONS
Cartignies
6km/3.7mi southwest along D 424.
The village boasts some 40 **blue-stone oratories.**

Pont-de-Sains
10km/6.2mi southeast along D 951.
Picturesque setting. The castle once belonged to Talleyrand, then to his niece, the Duchess of Dino.

Maroilles
12km/7.5mi west along D 962.
This place is famous for its cheeses, Maroilles and Dauphin, which used to be the speciality of the former Benedictine abbey (a few 17C buildings can still be seen). There's also a lovely watermill.

> ▶ **Population:** 5 003
> ⚲ **Michelin Local Map:** 302: L-7
> 🅸 **Info:** 41 pl. du Gén.-Leclerc, 59440 Avesnes-Sur-Helpe. ☏03 27 56 57 20. www.avesnes-sur-helpe.com
> ◖ **Location:** On the south bank of the River Helpe-Majeure close to the Belgian border, and closer to Brussels than to Paris.
> 🅿 **Parking:** On street parking (limited).
> ⊛ **Don't Miss:** Taste the local cheeses, Maroilles and Dauphin.

The **Maison du Parc Naturel Régional de l'Avesnois** *(Grange dîmière, 4 cour de l'Abbaye, 59550 Maroilles; ☏ 03 27 77 51 60. www.parc-naturel-avesnois.fr; ⊙ open Mon–Fri 9am–noon & 2–5pm; May–Sep Sun –Fri 3–7pm)* provides useful information about hiking tours in the area, the countryside with its hedged-in fields and the local cultural heritage.

🚗 DRIVING TOUR

Avesnois Region★★
Round-trip of 100km – Allow 2hr 30mins.

This region, which lies south of Maubeuge and extends along the Belgian border, is known for its undulating countryside of orchards, woodlands and pastures, through which meander the River Helpe-Majeure and River Helpe-Mineure, and for its pretty villages of brick, slate and stone. Of the many small bandstands, built on village squares by the foundries of the Sambre Valley, only about 20 have survived. The finest are in Beugnies, Floursies, Marbraix, Solre-le-Château, Avesnes, Cartignies, Dourlers and Trélon.

The vast forests and the cluster of lakes around Liessies and Trélon are traces of a period when the great abbeys – Maroilles, Liessies and St-Michel – domi-

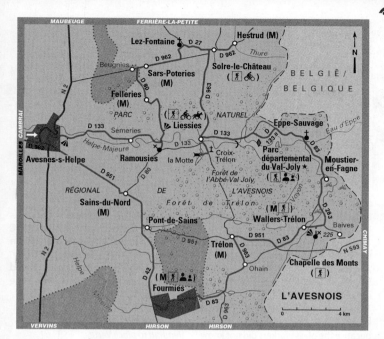

nated the region, constructing mills and forges on every river.

Many small industries developed in the 18C and 19C: glassmaking at Sars-Poteries, Trélon and Anor, wood turning at Felleries, spinning at Fourmies, marble quarrying at Cousoire etc. Converted into branches of the **Ecomusée de l'Avesnois** (*℘03 27 60 66 11, www. ecomusee-avesnois.fr*), museums at Sars-Poteries, Felleries, Trélon and Fourmies promote local economies and culture.

▶ *Leave Avesnes by D 133 (east) towards Liessies.*

Ramousies

The 16C **church** contains two beautiful Renaissance altarpieces from Antwerp workshops that once belonged to Liessies Abbey. One depicts the life of St Sulpice; the other represents the Passion. The 13C crucifix is from the oldest calvary in northern France.

▶ *Continue along D 80 to Felleries.*

Felleries

Since the 17C the town's inhabitants have specialised in bois-joli: turned

wood and cooperage. These workshops developed at the same time as the textile industry, the former making bobbins and spindles for the latter.

The Moulin des Bois-Jolis Museum (&. ⏰*Open Apr–Oct Mon–Fri 2–6pm, weekends and public holidays 2.30–6.30pm; ⏏3.50€; ℘03 27 59 03 46; www.ecomusee-avesnois.fr*), housed in a 16C watermill, brings together a wide variety of treen (wooden) items made in Felleries: butter moulds, salt boxes, spindles, tops etc.

Sars-Poteries

Since the 15C the earth around Sars has been used by potters, and many small pottery workshops exist locally while the larger factories specialising in pipes, ducts etc have all closed. In the 19C, two glassworks were set up specialising in dinner services and bottles. In 1900, they employed a work force of 800 but by 1938 the economic slump forced them to close.

The **Musée-Atelier du Verre★** (*1 rue du Général de Gaulle;* ⏰*open Wed – Mon 10am–12.30pm, 1.30–6pm; ⏏3€; ℘03 27 61 61 44*) is housed in the former home of the glassworks man-

Blue-stone Oratories

Blue-stone oratories have been built in the Avesnois and Thiérache regions since 1550; they are located in various places, mostly on the roadside, but also in fields, along ancient footpaths and even in woods or set in walls. These characteristic constructions consist of a narrow shaft surmounted by a fine recess, closed off by wire mesh as in Le Favril or Dimont, and a larger crowning piece. Each recess was intended to hold one or several polychrome statues carved by the clog makers of Mormal Forest. The oratories were erected for various reasons: in thanksgiving for a cure (as in Bérelles), to ask for a favour, to assert a certain social status, to abide by a family tradition. The Avesnois region is said to possess more than 700 blue-stone oratories including some 40 of them in the village of Cartignies alone.

ager, this museum boasts an unusual collection of popular glassware made by the workers for their own use.

The pieces were nicknamed *bousillés* (meaning "made after working hours") and they enabled the workers to make full use of their talent, artistry and imagination.

There are highly ornate engraved lamps, large dishes, "revenge inkwells" (so named because the glass workers did not know how to write, but they had the most beautiful inkwells), and strange "Passion bottles" containing representations of the instruments of Christ's Passion (these bottles were taken on pilgrimages to Notre-Dame de Liesse). As a result of local digs, the museum has built up a collection of grey-sandstone objects with glazed cobalt-blue decoration (17C and 18C).

In association with the glass workshop, the museum welcomes international artists.

The menhir, known as the **Pierre de Dessus-Bise**, stands on place du Vieux Marché. According to tradition, sterile women who sit on it become able to bear children.

The **watermill** north of the village was built in 1780 and still contains its great wheel and workings.

▶ *Take D 962 east, then turn left 3km/1.9mi farther on.*

Lez-Fontaine
In the 15C **church** the wooden vaults are decorated with paintings dating from 1531.

▶ *Follow D 27 to Solre-le-Château.*

Solre-le-Château
The seigniorial château no longer exists but there are still many 17C and 18C houses. The sober Renaissance **town hall** (late 16C) has an austere bell-tower. A covered market was held on the ground floor; note the Gothic writing on the keystones.

▶ *Walk through the archway leading to place Verte.*

The lovely 16C Gothic **church** is made of local blue stone. The powerful **belfry** was part of the fortifications; its base forms a most unusual porch, open on three sides. The mauve spire (1612) is crowned by a large bulb with openings where the watchman stood. Inside the church there is a double transept, wooden barrel-vaulting with carved tie-beams in the nave and diagonal vaulting in the chancel. The church also contains an 18C organ, 16C stained glass and Renaissance woodwork. The square is surrounded by fine 17C and 18C houses (*if the church is closed, ask at the town hall next door*).

▶ *Take D 962 towards Grandrieu.*

Hestrud
The **Musée de la Douane et des Frontières** (*Customs museum,* ○ *open mid-Jan –mid-Dec Wed–Sun 10am–7pm, Mon 10am–noon;* ⊚2€; ✆03 27 59 28 48) housed in the former customs building, illustrates the history of the borders of the Avesnois region since 1659: smuggled goods, customs officers' uniforms.

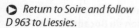

▶ *Return to Soire and follow D 963 to Liessies.*

Liessies

The village originated with an 8C Benedictine abbey which had exclusive use of the surrounding woods. The abbey prospered and by the 17C the abbots were powerful lords until the Revolution. The **Église St-Jean-et-Ste-Hiltrude** stands near the site of the old abbey. The **abbey park**, situated near the church, is open to the public. Several trails enable visitors to discover the local fauna and flora as well as former monastic buildings.

🔎 *Tours of the park ○Open Mon–Sat 9am–noon & 2–7pm, Sun 9.30am–1pm & 3–7pm. ○Closed Sun afternoons Jan–Feb and from mid-Jul–Aug. ℘03 27 61 81 66.*

The village is the starting point of an excursion to the 18C **Château de la Motte**, built of red brick, and to **l'Abbé-Val Joly Forest**. The 18C **Calvaire de la Croix-Trélon** stands to the east of the intersection of the Trélon road (D 963) and the Château de la Motte access road.

▶ *From Liessies follow D 133 along the Helpe Valley.*

The road becomes more winding, and the slopes are increasingly covered with thick woods.

Parc Départemental du Val-Joly★

The construction of the dam at Eppe-Sauvage on the Helpe-Majeure created a magnificent reservoir surrounded by the wooded banks of the River Helpe and its tributary, the Voyon.

The park has many leisure facilities including swimming, tennis, sailing, fishing, riding, hiking and mountain biking, and boating. There is also an aquarium (22 tanks). The park includes a camp site with bungalows for hire and shopping facilities.

Eppe-Sauvage

This village, close to the Belgian border, nestles in a pretty location where the River Helpe and River Eau d'Eppe meet. In the **Église St-Ursmar**, with its 16C chancel and transept, there are two remarkable 16C painted wood triptychs.

After Eppe-Sauvage, the valley opens out and becomes less wooded; the marshes here are called *fagnes*.

Moustier-en-Fagne

This small village derives its name from a 16C priory, or *moustier*. Olivetan Benedictines, who devote themselves to painting icons, live in the monks' quarters. They are near the **church** dedicated to St Dodon, the hermit invoked for back ailments, who was originally from this village. A handsome 1520 **manor house** is visible (left) on entering the village.

▶ *Continue south and, 2km/1mi beyond Moustier, fork left onto D 283, then turn right.*

The top of a knoll (225m/738ft high) affords a clear **view** of **Trélon Forest**.

Chapelle des Monts

🚶*15mins on foot.*

This 18C chapel is surrounded by lime trees.

Wallers-Trélon

Built entirely in blue stone, this beautiful village owes its unique appearance to the numerous quarries nearby. Nature trails allow visitors to discover the unusual flora of the **Monts de Baive**, which flourishes owing to the chalky soil.

To learn more about the blue stone in all its forms, take a tour of the exhibition in the **Maison de la fagne** (○*open Jul–Aug 2–6pm (weekends and public holidays 2.30–6.30pm); Apr–Jun and Sept–Oct weekends and public holidays, 2.30–6.30pm. ◎2.50€. ℘03 27 60 66 11).*

▶ *Take D 83 south; turn right onto D 951 to Trélon.*

Trélon

Formerly known for its glass industry, Trélon is today the location of the **Atelier-musée du verre** (rue Clavon; ♿ ○*open Apr–Oct Mon–Fri 9am–noon*

& 2–6pm; weekends and public holidays 2:30–6:30pm; ☺5.50€; ✆03 27 59 71 02, www.ecomusee-avesnois.fr), a branch of the Eco-musée. In the heart of the old hall of the 19C glassworks, which still contains two kilns from 1850 and 1920 together with their equipment, glass workers demonstrate the blowing and shaping of glass.

▶ *Follow D 963 then D 83 to Fourmies.*

ADDRESSES

🛏 STAY

☻ Les Prés de la Fagne (Bed and Breakfast) – *2 Rue Principale, 59132 Baives (1km/0.6mi E of Wallers-Trelon). ✆03 27 57 02 69. www.chambres-nord.fr. Closed Jan–Feb. ⌘. 5 rooms. Meals ☻.* A new gem in an antique setting. This tastefully restored 17C barn successfully blends different eras – some guest rooms even have a bathtub at the foot of the bed! Horse rides available for seasoned riders.

☻☻ Hôtel Les Paturelles – *21 Route d'Etroeungt (exit from the N 2, Route de Lacapelle). ✆03 27 61 22 22. www. lapentiere.com. 26 rooms. ⌷ 6€.* The oldest part of this hotel has classic decor, but the 9 newer rooms and 2 studios are more comfortable, with a modern look. Reception is only open 3–11pm. There is a rustic restaurant serving French gastronomic dishes.

🍴 EAT

☻ La Pen'Tière – *21 Route d'Etroeungt, exit S on N 2, Route de Lacapelle. ✆03 27 61 03 45. www.lapentiere.com. Closed last two weeks Jul and Sat lunch.* This restaurant opened in an old farmhouse is perfect for big appetites, with a starter buffet, grilled meats on the open fire, and local dishes. The atmosphere is festive, often with live singing.

Sains-du-Nord
The **Maison du Bocage** (*rue J.B. Lebas* ⊙*open Apr–Oct Mon–Fri 2–6pm, weekends and public holidays 2.30–6.30pm; ☺3.50€; ✆03 27 59 82 24, www.ecomusee-avesnois.fr*), a branch of the Eco-musée, has been established in a 19C farm. Exhibitions present life and work in the woodlands and pastures of the Avesnois (stock farming, cheese-making etc).

☻☻ Auberge de Châtelet – *Les Haies-à-Charmes, 59440 Dourlers. ✆03 27 61 06 70. www.aubergeduchatelet.com. Closed mid- to end-Aug, Sun and public holiday evenings.* Charmingly rustic interior with exposed beams, panelling and tiled floor is an ideal place to stop for lunch if you've been out walking. Try the *boulette d'Avesnes* a variety of the famed *maroilles* cheese .

☻☻ L'Estaminet – *83 Grand-Rue, 59550 Maroilles. ✆03 27 77 78 80. Closed Sun evening, Mon.* The unassuming facade gives no hint of this establishment's popularity, and yet it is always packed. Chalk its reputation up to the particularly warm decor and reception, and the plentiful, savoury cuisine centreing on maroilles, a flavourful local cheese.

🛍 SHOPPING

Le Verger Pilote – *1810 Route de Landrecies, 59550 Maroilles. ✆03 27 84 71 10. Open Mon–Fri 9am–6pm.* This boutique sells all of the local specialities from the region, including Maroilles beers, pear cider, andouillettes and home made flamiches.

EVENTS AND FESTIVALS

Carnaval Saint-Pansard – The people of the small town of Trélon come out in force on the first Sunday in March.

Bailleul

Situated in the hilly area known as Monts de Flandre, the town of Bailleul was damaged in 1918 during the last German onslaught in this region, then rebuilt in authentic Flemish style.

The Shrove Tuesday Carnival, headed by the giant Gargantua, offers Doctor Picolissimo the opportunity of throwing tripe to the crowd. The drive through the Monts de Flandre shows that Flanders is not as flat as some people say. In July, the Fête des Épouvantails is celebrated by burning scarecrows and a popular ball.

SIGHTS
Grand-Place

In spite of having been destroyed eight times, Bailleul and its Grand-Place have always regained their typically Flemish atmosphere. Before settling down in a local tavern with a glass of "3 Monts" beer, have a closer look at the town hall and its belfry in neo-Flemish style. The brick façade decorated with corner stones features a proclamation balcony.

Rue du Musée

The street is lined with fine houses, in particular no 3, the town's cultural centre with its Marguerite-Yourcenar hall.

Belfry

🔊 Guided tours Jul–Sept Tue & Thu 11am, Fri 8pm, weekends 4pm; Apr–Jun & Sept weekends 4pm; Oct–Mar 1st Sun of month 4pm. ⊚2.50€. ✆03 28 43 81 00. www.montsdeflandre.fr.

The belfry towering over the town hall housed the cloth market in medieval times. There is a 13C Gothic room at ground level and from the watch-path at the top, the vast **panorama★** includes the plain and Monts de Flandre to the north and the slag heaps of the mining area to the south. When the weather is clear, the city of Lille is visible. The peal of bells chimes well-known Flemish tunes.

- ▶ **Population:** 14 146
- 🖉 **Michelin Local Map:** 302: E-3
- 🖩 **Info:** 3 Grand'Place, 59270 Bailleul. ✆03 28 43 81 00.
- ◑ **Location:** Almost on the border with Belgium, and 150 miles north of Paris via the A 1.
- ⊛ **Don't Miss:** A tour of the belfry with its superb view.
- ◔ **Timing:** Spend half a day here, and then maybe stay over for a relaxing lunch.
- 🖉 **Also See:** Lille.

Belfry

S. Sauvignier/MICHELIN

Lace-making today

In the 17C, lace-making was already a local tradition, but it reached its height during the 19C, when there were as many as 800 lace-makers in the area. The first school was founded in 1664. Lace-making declined from 1900 onwards because of the introduction of machines. Today the tradition lives on. The International Lace-making Weekend takes place every third year (third weekend in July, scheduled for 2010) with the participation of lace-makers worldwide.

Musée Benoît-Depuydt

24 rue du musée. ⊙*Open Wed–Mon 2–5.30pm.* ⊛*3.60€, no charge 1st Sunday in the month.* ℘*03 28 49 12 70. www.montsdeflandre.fr.*
Founded in 1859, this elegant museum displays glazed earthenware from Delft and Northern France, porcelain from China and Japan, 16C to 18C furniture and carved wood as well as paintings from the Flemish, French and Dutch schools. Note in particular a breast-feeding Virgin Mary by Gérard David and an Adoration of the Magi by Pieter Brueghel. In addition, a large tapestry from Flanders (18C) and 19C portraits hang in the museum.

Maison de la Dentelle

6 Rue du Collège. ♿ ⊙*Open Mon–Sat 1.30–5pm.* ⊛*1.50€.* ℘*03 28 41 25 72.*
The school occupies a Flemish-style house; the pediment is decorated with a lace-maker and her spinning wheel. Every year some 100 students learn the technique of bobbin lace-making.

Conservatoire Botanique National de Bailleul

Hameau de Haendries. ⊙*Open Mon–Fri 8.30am-noon, 1.30–6pm. June–Sept.* ⊛*3€.* (*⚫guided tours, 5€*). ℘*03 28 49 93 07. www.cbnbl.org.*
Housed on the 30ha/74-acre estate of a restored Flemish farm, this national botanical conservatory specialises in vegetation from Northern France. The medicinal garden contains some 700 plants and the botanical gardens are dedicated to the preservation of more than 600 endangered species. The GR 128 footpath, which crosses the Monts de Flandre, goes through the estate. Picnic tables, a viewing table and nature trails are available for visitors.

🚗 DRIVING TOUR

Northern heights

Allow half a day.

This itinerary will take you through the Flemish countryside into Belgium. On the way, you will see hills, mills, typical local taverns and taste "special" beer and soft cheese.

▶ *Follow D 23 north, then turn left on D 223.*

On your right (on the Belgian side) is **Mont Kemmel** crowned by a hotel. On the same side but closer is **Mont Rouge** (Rodeberg).

▶ *Turn left again on D 318.*

Mont Noir

Straddling the border between France and Belgium, Mont Noir (Black Hill), so called owing to its dark wooded slopes, is part of the Monts de Flandres range (altitude 170m/558ft). A path leads to the artificial grotto (1875) dedicated to Notre-Dame de la Salette.

Saint-Jans-Cappel

This village lies at the foot of Mont Noir, immortalised in *Archives du Nord (How Many Years),* the autobiographical work of writer and French Academy member **Marguerite Yourcenar** (1903–87) who spent her childhood years here.
From the **Parc Marguerite-Yourcenar★**, the view extends towards Ypres, Mont Rouge and Mont des Cats, surmounted by its monastery. The sea and Artois hills are visible in clear weather.
Within the Parc, the **Villa Mont-Noir★**, dating from the 1920s, is a cultural and literary centre which welcomes resident European writers.
Le sentier des jacinthes, a marked trail (2hr 30min) running along the slopes of Mont Noir, is dotted with the writer's quotations.
The **Musée Marguerite-Yourcenar** displays documents, photographs, a video presentation of her life and works as well as works by local artists who illustrate the beauty of the region (*⚫Guided visits (45min)* ⊙*open Mon–Fri 10am–noon & 2–4.30pm, Sun 3.30–5.30pm;* ⊛*4.50€;* ℘*03 28 42 20 20; www.montsdeflandre.fr).*

▶ *Follow D 10 north to Berthen and turn left.*

Mont des Cats

Also known as Catsberg (altitude 158m/514ft), this hill is part of the Monts de Flandres range. It lies in pleasant undulating countryside where fields of hops, poplar trees, and red roofs form the "humanised landscape" defined by geographer Brunhes.

Gourmets know this area for its wonderful cheeses which are similar to Port-Salut. On top of the hill are the neo-Gothic buildings of a Trappist monastery – **Abbaye Notre-Dame-du-Mont** – founded in 1826 and restored since that time.

Centre Charles Grimminck

&. 🕐*Open Apr–Sept Mon 2–6.30pm, Wed–Sat 10am–noon & 2–6.30pm, Sun noon–1pm & 2–6.30pm; Oct–Mar Mon & Wed–Sat 2.30–5.30pm, Sun noon–1pm & 2.30–5.30pm.* ✆*No charge.* ℘*03 28 43 83 70. www.montsdeflandre.fr.*
The centre consists of an exhibition hall, a shop selling products from the monastery and a room where the monks' daily life is the subject of an audio-visual presentation.

▶ *Turn back and follow D 10 to Boeschepe.*

Boeschepe

The village of Boeschepe at the foot of Mont des Cats has a restored windmill, the **Ondankmeulen**, the mill of ungratefulness (🚶 *guided tours (30min) Apr–Oct Sun 3–6pm, rest of the year on request;* ✆*1.50€. ℘03 28 42 50 70),* next to a delightful bar *(estaminet)*, which sells some 50 different kinds of beer.

▶ *Follow D 139 past the Belgian border and continue to Poperingue.*

Poperinge

The inhabitants are known as **Kei-koppen**, "Tough Heads". On the Grand'Place, a stone weighing 1 650kg/3 638lb testifies to this reputation.

The Cathédrale St-Bertinus, a Flemish hall-church, is a fine example of the transition from the Romanesque style to the Gothic style.

▶ *Leave Poperinge via N 308 towards Dunkerque and turn left to Watou, also in Belgium.*

Watou

This village is ideal for anyone wishing to sample the authentic atmosphere of an *estaminet* (a bar), where the locals drink beer while playing various games.

▶ *Return to Bailleul along D 10.*

ADDRESSES

🛏 STAY

⊜⊜ **Auberge du Vert Mont** – *1318 Rue du Mont-Noir, 59299 Bœschepe.* ℘*03 28 49 41 26. Closed Mon lunch off-season. 7 rooms.* ⊑*6.50€. Restaurant* ⊜⊜.
This red brick inn perches upon the village heights. Smart bedrooms overlook the valley. Pleasant country-style dining room decorated with wooden clogs, barrels and wheels. Kids' games and a small animal park.

🍽 EAT

⊜ **Estaminet 'De Vierpot'**– *125 complexe Joseph-Decanter, 59299 Bœschepe, 12km/7.2mi N of Bailleul via D10.* ℘*03 28 49 46 37. Closed Mon, Apr–Jun & Sept; Jul–Aug; Mon–Tue, Oct–Mar.* This inviting tavern at the foot of a restored mill is a model of northern hospitality. Typical decor dating from the 1900s, with an old stove and wooden benches. The menus offer *planches flamande*s, quiches, crepes, and a choice of more than 50 beers.

A COLD BREW

Ferme-brasserie Beck – *Eckelstraete.* ℘*03 28 49 03 90. Sat from 7pm, Sun from 5pm. Closed Dec–Feb.* Guided tours of the farm-brewery and tasting sessions.

Bavay★

This small town with low houses is known for its natural mint-flavoured candies called "Chiques de Bavay". At the time of Caesar Augustus, Bagacum was an important town in Roman Belgium, situated at the junction of seven roads that led to Utrecht, Boulogne, Cambrai, Soissons, Reims, Trier and Cologne.

A BIT OF HISTORY
Grand' Place
The brickwork of the 17C belfry contrasts with the 18C town hall, built of granite, next to it. A fluted column in the square supports a statue of Brunhilda, Queen of Austrasia, who legend says built the seven routes of Bavay in just three days and three nights.

Remains of the Roman City
In 1942 Canon Biévelet began excavating a site cleared by bombing in 1940. The excavations revealed remains of a large group of monumental buildings: a civil basilica, a forum, a portico above a horseshoe-shaped underground gallery (*cryptoporticus*) and a room over a deep cellar stand along an east-west axis.

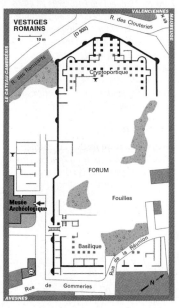

- ▶ **Population:** 3 581
- ⌖ **Michelin Local Map:** 302: K-6
- ℹ **Info:** Maison du Patrimoine, r. Saint-Maur, 59570 Bavay. ℘03 27 39 81 65. www.bavay.com.

A few houses have also been found south of the walls built after the invasions of the second half of the 3C.

VISIT
Musée Archéologique
2 rue de Gommeries. ⊙*Open Apr–Sept Wed–Mon 9am–6pm; Oct–Mar Mon–Fri 9am–noon & 2–5.30pm, weekends 10.30am–12.30pm & 2–6pm.* ⊛*4.50€. ℘03 27 63 13 95. http://museesavesnois. site.voila.fr.*
This museum has two large exposition rooms featuring everyday life of Bavay during the time of the Romans, when it was an important centre for pottery. One window houses a collection of fine **bronze figurines★**.

ADDRESSES

A SWEET SHOP
La Romaine – *30 pl. Charles-de-Gaulle. ℘03 27 63 10 06. Daily (except Mon) 7am–7pm. Closed 15 Jul–15 Aug.* This establishment guards the secret of the renowned 'Chiques de Bavay' – sweets flavoured with apple, cherry or coffee. They were purportedly in-vented by the wives of soldiers under Napoléon I who often chewed tobacco in order to spit out the lead they had ingested while ripping open gun-powder bags with their teeth. Their wives came up with these recipes to give them an alternative to the tobacco-chewing habit.

A BREWERY
Brasserie au Baron – *place des Rocs, Gussignies. ℘03 27 66 88 61.* Visits of the microbrewery.

Bergues★★

Bergues is a peaceful and prosperous Flemish town whose historic ramparts overlook scenic pastures famous for producing butter, cheese, and wool.
The yellow-ochre tones of the buildings are reflected in the waters of the moat and canals which partly surround the town. Despite wartime damage, Bergues has retained its old character with winding streets, large squares and the silent quays along the edge of the River Colme.

A BIT OF HISTORY

The Walled Town The walls, pierced by four gateways and surrounded by a deep moat, date partly from the Middle Ages (Bierne Gate, Beckerstor, curtain wall east of Cassel Gate) and partly from the 17C. These fortifications were used by the French troops during the defence of Dunkirk, forcing the Germans to use Stukas and flame-throwers to breach them.

🐾 WALKING TOUR

Allow approx 2hr 30mins.

Belfry

🕐*Open 10am–noon, 2–6pm; weekends & public holidays, 10am–1pm & 3–6pm.*
🕐*Closed Sun (Nov–Feb), 1 Jan, 1 May 1 and 11 Nov & 25 Dec.* ⊜*2.50€.*
☎*03 28 68 71 06.*
Erected during the 14C, remodelled in the 16C and dynamited by the Germans in 1944, the belfry (54m/ 177ft high) was rebuilt by Paul Gélis who sought to preserve the main structure of the former edifice while simplifying the exterior decoration. It is made of yellow bricks known as "sand bricks" and is surmounted by the lion of Flanders; the **carillon** comprises 50 bells (*contact tourist office for information on recitals*).

Porte de Cassel

This 17C gateway has a **drawbridge** and a triangular pediment featuring a carved sun, Louis XIV's emblem.

▶ **Population:** 4 209
🕭 **Michelin Local Map:**
302: C-2
🛈 **Info:** Pl. de la République, 59380 Bergues. ☎03 28 68 71 06. www.bergues.fr.

Belfry

Y. Tierny/ MICHELIN

Rempart Ouest

The western rampart was built in 1635. Beyond the **Poudrière du Moulin** stands the **Tour Nekestor** and the **Porte de Bierne** (16C) with its drawbridge, offering views of the **ruins of a medieval tower** and some **ancient locks**.

Rempart Nord

The northern rampart links the **Porte de Dunkerque**, which overlooks the beginning of the inner canal, the **Tour Guy-de-Dampierre** (1286) and the first **Porte d'Hondschoote**.

Couronne d'Hondschoote★

On the north side of the walls, Vauban used the branches of the River Colme to build an extensive system of bastions completely surrounded by large moats which serve as a bird sanctuary today.

Couronne and abbaye de St-Winoc

The Couronne de St-Winoc was designed to protect the abbey of the same name. It comprises three mighty **bastions**

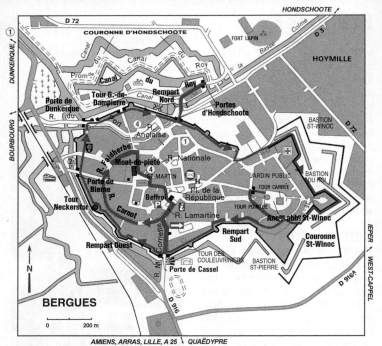

BERGUES

0   200 m

AMIENS, ARRAS, LILLE, A 25 ↘ QUAËDYPRE

WHERE TO STAY		WHERE TO EAT	
Camping Le Bois des Forts..............①		Le Cornet d'Or.................................①	
Hôtel Au Tonnelier...........................④		Taverne Le Bruegel..........................④	

(1672–92): the St-Winoc bastion, the King's bastion and the St-Pierre bastion. Most of the buildings of the Benedictine **abbey** were destroyed during the Revolution; all that survives is the 18C marble front door, the Tour Pointue (rebuilt in 1815) and the 12C–13C tower of the transept, supported by reinforced buttresses.

Rempart Sud

Follow the southern rampart past three small 13C round towers, the Faux-Monnayeurs and Couleuvriniers towers, to return to the Porte de Cassel.

Rues Carnot and Faidherbe

These streets are lined with lovely 18C buildings including the **Hôtel de Hau de Staplande**, 22 rue Carnot.

Mont-de-piété

This elegant building with a Baroque gable is constructed of brick and white stone. It was designed by **Wenceslas Coebergher** (1561–1634), a painter, architect, economist and engineer who introduced the first pawnshops (*monts-de-piété*). This pawnshop was inaugurated in 1633 and today houses the **Musée du Mont-de-piété** (◉open mid-Apr–Oct Wed–Mon 10am–noon, 2–5pm; ⊗3.60€; ☎03 28 68 13 30; www.bergues-tourisme.fr). An outstanding painting exhibited here is *Hurdy-Gurdy Player*, a vast canvas by **Georges de la Tour** (1593–1652) exhibited on the first floor. There are also works by several 16C–17C Flemish artists including a sketch by Rubens, and portraits by Van Dyck, Cossiers and Simon de Vox. The natural history section includes an extensive collection of birds and butterflies.

ADDRESSES

🛏 STAY

🛏 **Camping Le Bois des Forts** – *59380 Coudekerque, 700m/.5mi northwest of Coudekerque-Village, on D 72.* ✆*03 28 61 04 41.* 🏕 *130 pitches.* This discreet campsite has lovely spaces and well-maintained sanitary blocks. The spaces close to the main road can be noisy.

🛏 **Au Tonnelier** – *4 Rue du Mont de Piété.* ✆*03 28 68 70 05. www.au tonnelier.com. 25 rooms.* 🛏*10€. Restaurant* 🛏🛏. Located near the church, this village house is decorated by flower-filled window boxes in the summer. Come in through the old café and take a seat in the cheerful dining room. Newly renovated rooms.

🍴 EAT

🍴 **Taverne le Bruegel** – *1 Rue du Marché-aux-Fromages.* ✆*03 28 68 19 19. www.lebruegel.com. Closed first week of Jan.* A typical, congenial tavern in the oldest house in Bergues, dating back to 1597. Carbonnade and other Flemish specialities are served in an engaging decor featuring brick walls and wooden furniture.

🍴🍴 **Le Cornet d'Or** – *26 Rue de l'Espagnole.* ✆*03 28 68 66 27. Closed Sun evening and Mon.* Don't be put off by this restaurant's rather austere façade – the traditional cuisine with a nicely modern touch has a solid reputation in these parts. The dining room, sporting exposed beams and floral bouquets, is plush and cosy.

🎭 SHOWTIME

La Nuit du Miroir aux Alouettes, Anno 1585 – *Beffroi, Place de la Republique.* ✆*03 28 68 71 06. 12€ (children 6 €).* An interactive historical event in the walled town. Tickets and reservations at the Office du Tourisme.

Boulogne-sur-Mer★★

Boulogne, once a Roman city, has a rough but appealing look and busy streets. Today it is the largest European centre of the fish trade and home of an international fish-processing complex. Boulogne's illustrious citizens include the literary historian **St Beuve**, (1804–69), the engineer **Frédéric Sauvage** (1786–1857), the inventor of the propeller used in steam navigation, and the Egyptologist **Auguste Mariette**.

A BIT OF HISTORY

Boulogne is linked to Bonaparte, who from 1803 to 1805 kept his troops mustered at the **Boulogne Camp** in readiness to invade England.

On 26 August 1805, a year after being crowned emperor, Napoleon finally abandoned his project in order to set his Grande Armée against the Austrians. In August 1840 the future Napoleon III tried to raise the town against Louis-

- ▶ **Population:** 135 116
- ⌖ **Michelin Local Map:** 301: C-3
- **Info:** 24 quai Gambetta, 62203 Boulogne-Sur-Mer. ✆03 21 10 88 10. www.tourisme-boulognesurmer.com.
- ▶ **Location:** Accessible from the A 16. Amid the newer shopping streets of the ville basse are some of the best food shops in the whole region.
- **Don't Miss:** Nausicaä; the ville haute.
- **Timing:** Nausicaä will consume around two hours (best visited in the afternoon). Allow a half day to tour the town.
- **Kids:** Nausicaä and its aquariums; the beach at Portel.
- **Also See:** Hardelot; the coast, and Desvres.

Philippe, but the attempt floundered and he was imprisoned in Ham Fort.

The Father of Egyptology – The young man from Boulogne, who was working at the Louvre Museum in Paris, left for Cairo in 1850, entrusted with the task of finding Coptic manuscripts. Instead he discovered Memphis, the ancient capital of the Pharaohs. During the following 30 years, **Auguste Mariette** (1821–81) travelled throughout Egypt and was responsible for numerous excavation projects. He also founded the Boulaq Museum, which later became Cairo's Egyptian Museum, and set up the department of Egyptian Antiquities. In 1879 he was promoted to the rank of pasha by the Egyptian authorities.

NAUSICAÄ★★★

Centre National de la Mer. 👥👤 ♿
🕐 *Open Jul–Aug, 9.30am–7.30pm; Sept–Jun 9.30am–6.30pm.* 🕐*Closed 3 weeks in Jan, 25 Dec.* ✇17.40€ *(children 11.20€).* ✆*03 21 30 99 99.*
www.nausicaa.fr.

Designed by architect Jacques Rougerie, who specialises in buildings with a maritime theme, and Christian Le Conte, a specialist in museography, **Nausicaä** is the largest sea-life centre in Europe. It aims to provide information about fauna in warm and cold ocean environments and to man-

age marine resources and the trades linked to them.

The building is dappled with bluish light and filled with aquatic music. There are 36 aquariums with more than 10 000 marine animals from the world's seas.

Journey through the World's Seas – The circular aquarium contains jellyfish. Exhibits show the reproduction cycle of species from tropical seas and the Mediterranean.

Next comes the **Espace Diamant des Thons**, a strange aquarium shaped like a reverse pyramid and containing a shoal of *sérioles* (of the tuna family).

Man and the Sea – A long circular corridor illustrates the relationship between man and the sea going back thousands of years. A **celestial dome** forms the setting of the area devoted to resources from the sea and to the dangers which threaten the coastline.

Tropical Lagoon Village – You then arrive on the beach of 'Paradise' island surrounded by the greenish-blue waters of a **lagoon**. From the pontoon, you can observe the lagoon full of colourful fish on one side, and the open sea with characteristic shoals of fish on the other.

Underwater Observatory – The underwater observatory reveals Californian sea-lions diving and swimming through the waves. The **aerial observatory** shows the same sea-lions stretched out on the rocks in a typical Californian setting of cliffs and log cabins.

An escalator leads to the **hands-on basin**, full of cod, pollack and turbot, where children can stroke thorn-back rays.

The tour takes you to a reduced-scale fish farm where new fish-farming techniques are described. The adjacent area is devoted to various fishing techniques and a film shows night work aboard a trawler in the North Sea.

The visit ends with the spectacular **Anneau des sélaciens**, a panoramic circular tank filled with sharks.

Off the foyer are a cinema (130 seats), a multimedia library, souvenir shops, a restaurant, bar and cafeteria.

Penguins at Nausicaä

©Anne-Sophie Flament/Nausicaä

LA VILLE BASSE

The **outer harbour** is protected by two jetties, of which the Digue Carnot is 3 250m/over 2mi long.

The **inner harbour** consists of a tidal dock reserved for ferries, small trawlers and yachts and the Napoleon and Loubet docks for the big fishing boats.

Quai Gambetta, overlooked by tall buildings, is busiest when the trawlers unload their catch, some sold on the spot.

Beach – 👫 Already quite well known in the 18C, the fine, white-sand beach became very fashionable from the mid-19C onwards. Because of its facilities for children and summer leisure activities, the town has been awarded the "Station Kid" label. Sailing, landsailing and speedsail are also available.

Église St-Nicolas – The church, standing in place Dalton where the market is held (*Wednesdays and Saturdays*), is the oldest in Boulogne despite its Classical façade. It was built from 1220 to 1250, and underwent many alterations in the 16C (apse, transept, chancel vaults, chapels) and in the 18C when the nave was rebuilt. The 17C high altar features spiral columns and a fine painting of *The Flagellation* by Lehmann, a pupil of Ingres.

LA VILLE HAUTE★★

The upper town, enclosed by ramparts, stands on the site of the old Roman *castrum* or fortified town. It is overlooked by the enormous dome of Notre-Dame basilica and is popular with tourists in summer, offering pleasant strolls along the ramparts or through the streets and past the historic buildings of the walled town.

Ramparts – The fortifications were built in the early 13C on the foundations of the Gallo-Roman walls and were strengthened in the 16C to 17C.

The ramparts form a rectangle reinforced by the **castle** to the east, and accessed by four gates – Gayole, Dunes, Calais and **Degrés** which is pedestrian only – flanked by two towers. The parapet walkway is accessible from each gateway and offers lovely **views**★ of the town and the port.

At the western corner the **tour Gayette**, a former jail, was the site of the take-off for the balloon flight in 1785 by **Pilâtre de Rozier** and Romain who were attempting to cross the Channel; they crashed near Wimille, just north of Boulogne.

A pyramid-shaped monument surmounted by a statue stands in the garden between Boulevard Auguste-Mariette and the ramparts: it is dedicated to **Mariette** the Egyptologist, whom the statue shows in Egyptian costume.

▷ *Walk through the western Porte des Dunes to place de la Résistance and place Godefroy-de-Bouillon.*

Library – This is located in the old Annonciades Convent. The 17C buildings and the cloisters house study and exhibition rooms, while the main reading room occupies the 18C chapel with its superb coffered ceiling, visible through the windows from the square.

Belfry – 👣 *Tours Mon–Fri 8am –6pm, Sat 8am –noon.* ✆*No charge.* ✆*03 21 80 13 12.* The 13C Gothic belfry (*access through the Hôtel de Ville*), has a 12C base (the former keep from the castle of the counts of Boulogne) and an 18C octagonal section at the top. It houses Gallo-Roman statues and regional antique furniture as well as a beautiful stained-glass window portraying Godefroy de Bouillon.The top of the belfry (183 steps) offers an extensive **view**★ of Boulogne and its surroundings.

Port, Boulogne-sur-Mer

Y. Tierny/ MICHELIN

▶ *Place de la Résistance leads into place Godefroy-de-Bouillon located at the junction of the four main streets.*

Hôtel de Ville – The 18C façade of red brick with stone dressings, contrasts sharply with the primitive Gothic belfry.

Hôtel Desandrouin – To the right as you come out of the town hall stands this Louis XVI mansion where Napoleon stayed several times from 1803 to 1811.

▶ *Follow rue de Puits-d'Amour alongside Hôtel Desandrouin and turn right.*

Rue Guyale – The merchants' guildhall used to stand on this street, which has been restored and reveals the back of the Annonciades Convent and the rough-stone façades of the old houses.

▶ *From place Godefroy-de-Bouillon take rue de Lille.*

At no 58 is the oldest **house** in Boulogne (12C). The Basilique Notre-Dame stands on the left. Rue du Château on the right leads to the former residence of the counts of Boulogne.

Basilique Notre-Dame

Access via the south transept in rue de Lille. ◷*Open Apr–Aug 9am–noon, Sept–Mar 10am–noon & 2–5pm.*
The basilica was built from 1827 to 1866 on the site of the old cathedral (destroyed after the Revolution) and has preserved the Romanesque crypt.
The superb, soaring **dome**★ with its circle of large statues rises behind the chancel; in the central chapel, stands the wooden statuette of Our Lady of Boulogne (Notre-Dame de Boulogne), crowned with precious stones.
Crypt – ◷*Open Tue–Sun 2–5pm.* ✑*2€.* ℘*03 21 30 22 70.* Under the basilica, a labyrinth of underground passages links 14 chambers.
One of them houses the **Treasury**★ which contains religious statues and objects from churches in the region, and the relic of the Holy Blood offered

by Philip the Fair to Our Lady of Boulogne.
Continue through several rooms to the **crypt of the painted pillars** dating from the 11C, discovered during the construction of the new basilica.

▶ *Take rue du Château opposite.*

Château-musée★

Rue de Bernet. ◷*Open Wed–Sun 10am–12.30pm & 2–5.30pm, Sun and public holidays 10am–12.30pm, 2.30–6pm.* ✑*3€ (under 18, free). Free first Sun of month.* ℘*03 21 10 02 20.* www.ville-boulogne-sur-mer.fr.
Formerly the residence of the counts of Boulogne, this polygonal building was the first in western Europe to abandon the traditional keep. Flanked by round towers, it protected the most vulnerable part of the ramparts facing the plateau.
The archaeology of the Mediterranean is represented by an Egyptian section (sarcophagi and numerous funerary objects, the gift of Mariette the Egyptologist) and also by a beautiful group of **Greek vases**★★ dating from 5–6C BC, among them a black-figure jug portraying the suicide of Ajax.
Beyond this are rooms containing porcelain, ceramics and earthenware from French and foreign manufacturers.
Among the ethnographic collections, the **Eskimo and Aleutian masks**★★ brought back from a voyage to North America by the anthropologist Pinart, and the objects from the South Sea Islands including a Maori battle canoe from New Zealand, are particularly interesting.
The enormous guard-room displays collections from the Middle Ages and the Renaissance: copper and brassware, sculptures, Gothic furniture and woodwork, paintings, and coins.

ADDITIONAL SIGHTS
Maison de la Beurière★

◷*Open mid-Jun to mid-Sept Tue–Sun 10am–1pm, 3–6pm; mid-Sept–mid-Jun Wed & Sat 10am–noon, 2–5pm.* ✑*2€.* ℘*03 21 30 14 52.* www.ville-boulogne-sur-mer.fr.

Fish Trade Centre

Industrial trawlers unload their catch around midnight; coastal-fishing boats come back in the early hours of the morning. The catch is offered for sale and refrigerated during the fish auction (*la criée*) which starts between 6 and 7am. The batches are then sent round to factories for processing. This is completed by 11am and the parcels end up at the harbour station (112 unloading bays, 24 refrigerated-transport companies) to be dispatched to various destinations: Paris/Rungis, Strasbourg, Lyon, Marseille, Bordeaux… and abroad, where they arrive the same day or the next morning at the latest.

In the ancient seafaring quarter, at the time known as "la Beurière ", but today as St-Pierre, 4 000 people used to live, a third of the entire Boulonnais population. From this time there remains just one narrow, stepped street and five or six houses. The others were destroyed during the Second World War. Here, in one of the last dwellings, dated 1870, a small museum illustrates the life of a seafaring family around 1900.

EXCURSIONS
Colonne de la Grande Armée★★
3km/2mi north by N 1 and turn left on a small road. ⏱*Closed mid-Jun–Sept Wed–Sun, 10.30am–12.30pm & 2.30–6.30pm; rest of year, Fri–Sun 10am–noon & 2–4pm.* ⏱*Closed 1 Jan, 1 May, 1 and 11 Nov, 25 Dec.* ⊚3€. ℘03 21 80 43 69. http://wimille.monuments-nationaux.fr.

Designed by the architect **Eloi Labarre** (1764–1833) to commemorate the Boulogne Camp, the column was started in 1804 but only finished under Louis-Philippe. The column is of marble from nearby Marquise, rises 54m/177ft high and is 4m/13ft in diameter.

On its base, a bronze low-relief sculpture portrays Field Marshal Soult offering the plans of the column to the Emperor.

A staircase (*263 steps*) leads to the square platform (190m/623ft above sea level) from where the **panorama★★** extends over the lush countryside of the Boulogne region and, on a clear day, across the Channel as far as the white cliffs of Dover.

Monument de la légion d'honneur
2km/1.25mi north by D 940 and a path to the right.

This obelisk marks the site of the throne on which Napoleon I sat on 16 August 1804 for the second distribution of the Legion of Honour decorations (the first took place on 14 July 1804 at the Invalides in Paris).

Viewpoint of St-Étienne-au-Mont★
5km/3mi along D 52 then right up a steep hill (13% grade).

From the cemetery adjacent to the isolated hilltop church (altitude 124m/407ft), there is a fine **view★** of the Liane Valley; Boulogne, over which towers the dome of Notre-Dame basilica, can be seen downstream.

Le Portel
5km/3mi southwest.

👤👤 The town has been awarded the "Station Kid" label for the facilities its sandy **beach** dotted with rocks offers children. The resort faces a small isle on which stands **fort de l'Heurt**, built by Napoleon in 1804. A statue of Our Lady of Boulogne watches over the Epi jetty.

Hardelot-Plage⚐⚐
15km/9mi south by D 940 and D 113E.

This elegant seaside sporting resort and "Station Kid" features a magnificent, gently sloping beach of fine sand. Leisure facilities include paths for walking, riding and cycling; golf; sailing; kite-flying; and a country club with tennis courts and a swimming pool.

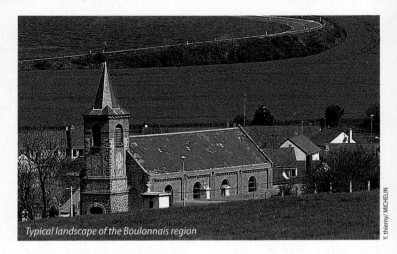

Typical landscape of the Boulonnais region

Y. thierry/ MICHELIN

The **château** north of the village, by the Lac des Miroirs, retains some of its 13C fortifications. In the 19C an Englishman had the château rebuilt in the style of Windsor Castle with crenellations and turrets. It now belongs to the city.

Forêt de Boulogne
10km/6mi east by D 341.

The road climbs the slopes of **Mont Lambert** (189m/620ft); a television aerial rises from the top. The forest covers 2 000ha/4 940 acres and contains forest roads, bridle paths, parking facilities and picnic areas. The lush Liane Valley borders the forest to the south and east.

🚗 DRIVING TOUR

Le Boulonnais★
75km/46mi round-trip– about 3hr.

The Boulonnais is a region of lush countryside. Its complex relief is due to differing geological formations: marble in Marquise, sandstone in Outreau and chalk in Desvres and Neufchâtel, where it lies under a layer of clay. In some places outcrops rise over 200m/656ft in altitude.

The plateau between Guînes and the River Aa is intermittently bare or dotted with copses; here and there great farms surrounded by thickets and pastures grow cereals and sugar beet.

The Wimereux, Liane, Hem and Slack valleys are deep and narrow, providing fertile ground for orchards (cider apples) and meadows. A local breed of cow is found here, in addition to the Northern Blue and the Flemish Red cows; sheep are put out to pasture with Boulonnais draughthorses.

The Boulonnais forms part of the nature park known as the **Parc Naturel Régional des Caps et Marais d'Opale** which includes the Boulonnais and Audomarois parks.

◯ *Leave Boulogne eastward along N 42; 3km/2mi on, beyond the roundabout, turn onto D 232.*

This picturesque road, edged with beeches and old elms, descends sharply into the freshness of the **Wimereux Valley** which is carpeted with meadows and scattered with copses.

Souverain-Moulin
The château and its outbuildings look very attractive in their leafy setting.

◯ *Take D 233 (east) to Belle, then turn left onto D 238 and right onto D 251. Turn right again onto D 127.*

The **Maison du Parc National Régional des Caps et Marais d'Opale** is situated in the **manoir du Huisbois** (◯open Mon–Fri 9am-noon & 2–6pm; 📞03 21

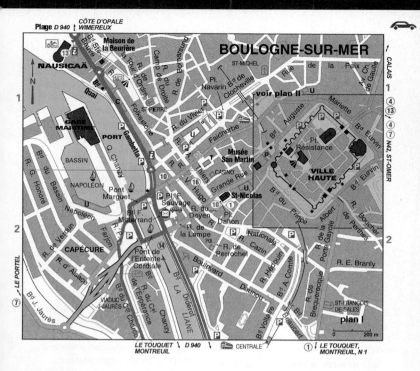

Plage *D 940* ▶ CÔTE D'OPALE
WIMEREUX

BOULOGNE-SUR-MER

WHERE TO STAY

Chambre d'hôte Le Clos d'Esch	①
Hôtel de la Ferme du Vert	④
Hôtel de la Plage	⑦
Hôtel Faidherbe	⑩
Hôtel Le Beaucamp	⑬
Hôtel Métropole	⑯

WHERE TO EAT

Chez Jules	①
Ferme-auberge de la Raterie	④
Ferme-auberge du Blaisel	⑦
Le Doyen	⑩
Restaurant de Nausicaà	⑬

87 90 90) a beautiful 17C house of local grey stone. The information centre provides documentation, a library, a video centre and exhibitions all relating to the Boulonnais.

◑ *From N 42 to Saint-Omer, turn left on D 224 to Licques.*

Licques

Licques is famous for its turkeys introduced in the area in the 17C by the monks of the local abbey.

ADDRESSES

🏠 STAY

Le Clos d'Esch (Bed and Breakfast) – *126 Rue de l'Église, 62360 Echinghen, 4km/2.4mi E of Boulogne. ✆03 21 91 14 34. www.leclosdesch.fr. Closed 23 Dec to end Jan. 🍴 4 rooms.* If you prefer the tranquillity of the country to the bustle of the city, this is definitely the place for you. At the centre of a small village, this renovated farm is a pleasing halt in a pastoral setting.

Hôtel de la Ferme du Vert – *62720 Wierre-Effroy,10km/6mi NE of Boulogne via N 42 and D 234. ✆03 21 87 67 00, www.fermeduvert.com. Closed 15 Dec to 20 Jan. 16 rooms. 🍴12€. Restaurant* 🍽️. Rest and relaxation are inevitable when you stay in this old farm built in the 19C. Each room is different, with simple, elegant interior design. The restaurant and cheese shop will delight connoisseurs.

Hôtel de la Plage – *168 bd Sainte-Beuve. ✆03 21 32 15 15. 42 rooms. 🍴7€.* Situated on the beachfront. Functional rooms facing the back are quiet, those facing the front have views of the sea from the 3rd floor.

Hôtel Faidherbe – *12 Rue Faidherbe. ✆03 21 31 60 93. www.hotel boulogne.com. Closed 25 Dec & 1 Jan. 30 rooms. 🍴8€.* This comfortable and cosy hotel is conveniently located halfway between the centre of town and the port. The themed rooms all have antique furnishings, colourful linens and well-equipped bathrooms.

Hôtel Métropole – *51 Rue Thiers. ✆03 21 31 54 30. www.hotel-metropole-boulogne.com. Closed 19 Dec to 5 Jan. 25 rooms. 🍴10€.* A practical hotel offering modern or rustic bedrooms, all air-conditioned, comfortable and well soundproofed. Dapper breakfast room opening onto a garden.

Hôtel Le Beaucamp – *62720 Wierre-Effroy,13km/8mi NE of Boulogne-sur-Mer by N 42. ✆03 21 30 56 13. www.le beaucamp.com. Closed 20 Dec to 20 Jan. 5 rooms.* Surrounded by 10ha/24ac of forest grounds this 19C manor is still in the same family. The rooms upstairs are most comfortable. Generous breakfast buffet.

🍴 EAT

Le Doyen – *11 Rue du Doyen. ✆03 21 30 13 08. Closed 15 days in Jan and Sun except holidays.* The small interior is nattily decorated in pastel hues, the welcome is warm indeed, and seafood is the mainstay of the delectable cuisine.

Ferme-auberge du Blaisel – *Chemin de la Lombarderie, 62240 Wirwignes, 12km/7.5mi SE of Boulogne-sur-Mer by D 341. ✆03 21 32 91 98. www.fermeaubergedublaisel.com. Closed 23 Dec to 5 Jan, Sun evening, & Wed.* A real working farm produces the freshest ingredients used at this restaurant. Rooms available if you need to sleep off your meal. Apple picking in the fall.

Restaurant de Nausicaä – *Blvd Ste-Bevue. ✆03 21 33 24 24. Closed Mon evenings.* This split-level seafood restaurant in the Centre National de la Mer commands panoramic views of the beach and harbour entrance.

Chez Jules – *8–10 Place Dalton. ✆03 21 31 54 12. www.chez-jules.fr. Closed two weeks end of Sep, 23 Dec–15 Jan, & Sun night off-season.* An unpretentious brasserie with a warm atmosphere and hearty dishes such as moules-frites, crêpes, fresh pasta, wood-fired pizzas and light dishes.

La Raterie – *1744 hameau de la Maloterie, 62720 Wierre-Effroy, 12km/7.2mi NE of Boulogne-sur-Mer via D 238. ✆03 21 92 80 90. www.ferm-auberge-laraterie.com. Closed Sun evening and Mon.* This pretty 18C farm inn, furnished with period pieces, a fireplace and a splendid enamelled stove, serves appetizing regional recipes. Vast bedrooms overlook the garden.

🛒 SHOPPING

Ferme du Puits du Sart – *62132 Hermelinghen. ✆03 21 85 00 79.* Producer of duck foie gras. Visits and sampling of different products.

Licques Volailles – *777, rue de l'Abbé Pruvost, 62850 Licques. ✆03 21 35 05 42.* Licques poultry, a breed that was created by local monks, is renowned throughout France. Worth tracking down.

Calais

Calais is the leading passenger port in France and the second in the world with a traffic totalling 20 million passengers a year. The town gave its name to the Pas-de-Calais, the strait known on the north side of the Channel as the Straits of Dover. The history of the town has been considerably influenced by its proximity to the English coast, only 38km/23.5mi away. The white cliffs of Dover are often clearly visible from the promenade and the vast sandy beach west of the entrance to Calais harbour. Calais is the ideal starting point for excursions along the Opal Coast to Le Touquet.

A BIT OF HISTORY
The Channel Tunnel

The "Chunnel" is the realisation of more than two centuries of dreams and unfinished projects.

From utopia to reality

Over the past 250 years there have been 27 proposals, the oldest of which was made in 1750 by M Desmarets, who wanted to rejoin Britain to the mainland by a bridge, a tunnel or a causeway. From 1834 onwards, Aimé Thomé de Gamond, who is known as the "Father of the Tunnel", put forward several different propositions, all of them technically viable.

First attempts

In 1880, 1 840m/over 1mi of galleries were dug out on the site called the "Puits des Anciens". 2 000m/ 1.25mi were tunnelled out on the English side before the work was stopped. A fresh approach was tried in 1922. The technical progress of the 1960s gave the project a boost but a 400m/433yd gallery was abandoned once again.

Birth of Eurotunnel

During a Franco-British summit conference in September 1981, the idea of building a fixed link was again mooted by British Prime Minister Margaret Thatcher and French President François

> **Population:** 104 852
> **Michelin Local Map:** 301: E-2
> **Info:** 12 bd Clemenceau, 62100 Calais, ☎03 21 96 62 40. www.ot-calais.fr.

Mitterrand. In October 1985, after an international competition, four projects were shortlisted and it was the Eurotunnel project which was finally selected, on 20 January 1986. A Franco-British treaty was signed on 12 February 1986 in Canterbury Cathedral with a view to the construction of the tunnel. The first link between France and England was established on 1 December 1990. The official opening of the tunnel and of the Shuttle service took place on 6 May 1994.

Facts and figures

Most of the tunnel lies at a depth of 40m/130ft below the seabed, in a layer of blue chalk. Enormous tunnel-digging machines bored their way through the rock at a rate of 800 to 1 000m/867 to 1 083yd a month.

The **trans-Channel link** consists, in fact, of two railway tunnels 7.60m/25ft in diameter connected every 375m/406yd to a central service gallery 4.80m/ 16ft in diameter built for the purposes of ventilation, security, and system maintenance. The tunnels contain a single track and the trains run in one direction only, taking passengers and freight. The tunnels have a total length of 50km/31mi of which 40km/24mi are beneath the Channel.

The Burghers of Calais

After his success at Crécy **Edward III** of England needed to create a powerbase in France. He began the siege of Calais on 3 September 1346, but eight months later had still not been able to breach the valiant defence led by the town governor, Jean de Vienne; in fact, it was famine that forced the inhabitants to capitulate in the end.

Six burghers, led by **Eustache de Saint-Pierre**, prepared to sacrifice themselves

The Burghers of Calais by Rodin

Y. Thierry/ MICHELIN

in order that the other citizens of Calais would be spared the sword. In thin robes, "barefoot, bareheaded, halters about their necks and the keys to the town in their hands," they presented themselves before the king to be delivered to the executioner. They were saved by the intercession of Edward's wife, Queen Philippa of Hainault.

Calais was in the hands of the English for over two centuries and was liberated only in 1558, by the Duke of Guise. This was a mortal blow to **Mary Tudor**, Queen of England, who said: "If my heart were laid open, the word "Calais" would be engraved on it."

Calais Lace

Together with Caudry-en-Cambrésis, Calais is the main centre of machine-made lace, employing about 2 000 workers using over 350 looms. Englishmen from Nottingham introduced the industry at the beginning of the 19C; quality was improved around 1830 when the first Jacquard looms were introduced. Three quarters of the lace made in Calais is exported. Traditional lace made with the Leavers machine is entitled to a quality label created in 1991, representing a peacock.

SIGHTS
Monument des Bourgeois de Calais★★

This famous work by **Rodin**, *The Burghers of Calais*, is located between the Hôtel de Ville and Parc St-Pierre. It dates from 1895 and exemplifies the sculptor's brilliance: the bronze group is simultaneously full of vitality and pathos. Each of the six life-size figures should be admired separately: their veins and muscles exaggerated, their forms tense and haughty. They express the heroic nobility of the men obliged to humiliate themselves before the king of England.

Hôtel de ville

The beautiful and graceful town hall is built of brick and stone in the 15C Flemish style yet dates only from the turn of the last century. The **belfry** (75m/246ft) can be seen for miles in all directions. Inside, a **stained-glass window** recalling the departure of the English diffuses the sunlight over the grand staircase.

Place d'Armes

Before the devastation of the war, this was the heart of medieval Calais. Only the 13C **watchtower** has survived. The belfry and the town hall beside it are popular subjects for artists.

To the left is the Bassin Ouest; to the right is the Bassin du Paradis and the rear harbour used as a marina.

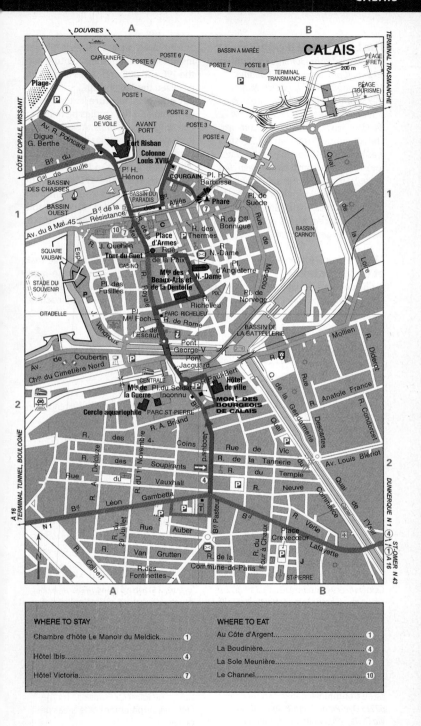

CALAIS

WHERE TO STAY	
Chambre d'hôte Le Manoir du Meldick	1
Hôtel Ibis	4
Hôtel Victoria	7

WHERE TO EAT	
Au Côte d'Argent	1
La Boudinière	4
La Sole Meunière	7
Le Channel	10

The Lighthouse (Le phare)

Guided visits (30min) Jun–Sep Mon–Fri 2–6.30pm, weekends & holidays 10am–noon, 2–6:30pm; Oct–May Wed 2–5.30pm, weekends 10am–noon & 2–5.30pm. 4.50€ *(children 2€).* 03 21 34 33 34. www.pharedecalais.com.
The lighthouse (53m/174ft tall; 271 steps) was built in 1848 to replace the watchtower beacon. From the top (*steep climb by stairs*) there is a surprisingly wide and splendid panoramic **view★★** over Calais, the harbour, the basins, the town's stadium, place d'Armes and the unexpectedly large Church of Our Lady.

Musée des Beaux-Arts et de la Dentelle★

Open Mon & Wed–Sat 10am–noon & 2–5.30pm (Sat 6.30pm), Sun 2–6.30pm. 4€ 03 21 46 48 40. www.calais.fr.

The fine arts and lace museum gives an insight into changes in sculpture over the 19C and 20C and styles of painting between the 17C and 20C.

19C and 20C sculpture features works by Rodin and the studies he made for *The Burghers of Calais*. Also works by Rodin's predecessors, including Carrière-Belleuse, Carpeaux, Barye, and his students, Bourdelle and Maillol.

Paintings from the 17C to the 20C by the Flemish and North-European schools. There are also works by modern and contemporary artists such as Jean Dubuffet, Félix Del Marle, Picasso, Fautrier, Lipchitz, Arp…

The **lace section**, in a former tulle-making factory, deals with machine-made and hand-made lace (the museum owns more than 400 000 samples of machine-made lace).

ADDRESSES

☜ STAY

Hôtel Victoria – *8 Rue du Cdt-Bonningue.* 03 21 34 38 32. www.hotel-victoria-calais.activehotels.com. *14 rooms.* 5.50€. Well situated opposite the lighthouse and a short walk from the Transmanche station, this small hotel is nothing fancy, but impeccably maintained.

Hôtel Ibis – *35 Blvd Jaquard.* 03 21 97 98 98. www.ibishotel.com. *66 rooms.* Comfortable, functional rooms in the centre of town with 24-hour front desk.

Le Manoir du Meldick (Bed and Breakfast) – *2528 Ave du Gén.-de-Gaulle, Le Fort Vert, 62730 Marck, 6km/3.6mi E of Calais via D 940 and D 119.* 03 21 85 74 34. www.manoir-du-meldick.com. *5 rooms.* Just a few minutes from the Calais port, yet far from its crowds, Meldick Manor is sure to please. Rooms are spacious and comfortable.

☝ EAT

La Boudinière – *2691 rte de Waldam, 62215 Oye-Plage,14km/8.5mi E of Calais via D 119.* 03 21 85 93 14. www.la boudiniere.com. *Closed Wed & evenings Mon–Fri off-season.*

Lost in the Calais countryside, this little restaurant serves traditional cuisine of excellent quality. The meat served here is top-rate – the owner-chef chooses and cuts the steaks himself. Friendly reception and quiet dining room.

La Sole Meunière – *1 Blvd de la Résistance.* 03 21 34 43 01. www.solemeuniere.com. *Closed Sun evening and Mon.* The house speciality is sole, cooked five different ways by the 'sole-ful' chef. Opt for a table by the bay windows for a view of the port. Also offered are other seafood dishes, local cheeses, desserts and fine wines.

Au Côte d'Argent – *1 digue G.-Berthe.* 03 21 34 68 07. *Closed mid-Feb, mid-Aug to early Sept, 24 Dec-early Jan, Wed eve Sept-Apr, Sun eve and Mon.* Dine in a setting that looks and feels like a boat, as you watch the ferries coming and going.

Le Channel – *3 Blvd de la Résistance.* 03 21 34 42 30. *Closed late-Jul–early Aug, 23 Dec to 18 Jan, Sun eve and Mon.* A last chance to sample French cuisine before heading for England ! Try the French interpretations of le 'steak pie' or 'jelly'.

Cambrai★

Cambrai stands in the centre of a rich cereal and sugar beet region, on the east bank of the River Escaut (or Scheldt). Traditionally, Cambric linen was made here, bleached in the sunny meadows then used to make handkerchiefs and fine lingerie. In gourmet terms, Cambrai is known for its small chitterling sausages *(andouillettes)*, its tripe and its mint-flavoured sweets *(bêtises de Cambrai)*. The town's heroes are the giants Martin and Martine who are said to have killed the local tyrant. The town is built of white limestone and is overlooked by the three towers of the belfry, the cathedral and St Gery's Church. Once a military stronghold, Cambrai today looks peaceful, a ring of boulevards having replaced the ramparts.

A BIT OF HISTORY

The "Swan of Cambrai"
In 1695 François de Salignac de La Mothe-Fénelon (1651–1715), a great lord and famous writer, was made archbishop of Cambrai. **Fénelon** was venerated for his gentleness and charity. " The charity of the "Swan of Cambrai" was often called upon during the War of the Spanish Succession; starving peasants from the surrounding Cambrai region poured into the archdiocese, where Fénelon welcomed them. On one occasion a cow was lost on the way. At once the archbishop set out on foot to find the animal, which he was able to return it to its poor owner.

🚶 WALKING TOUR
OLD TOWN *allow 2hr*

Porte de Paris
This town gate, a vestige of the medieval fortifications, is flanked by two round towers dating from 1390.

▶ *Follow avenue de la Victoire towards the town hall, visible at the end of the street. Place du St-Sépulcre appears shortly on the left.*

▶ **Population:** 33 738
🎣 **Michelin Local Map:** 302: H-6
ℹ **Info:** Office de tourisme, 48 r. de Noyon, 59400 Cambrai. ☎03 27 78 36 15. www.villedecambrai.com.

Cathédrale Notre-Dame
🕐*Open Mon–Thu & Sat, 8am–noon, 2–7pm; Fri, 2–7pm; Sun, 9am–12.30pm, 3–6pm.* 🕐*Closed Sun afternoons Oct–Easter.*
Originally dedicated to the Holy Sepulchre, the abbey church was elevated to the rank of cathedral after the Revolution. It was built in the 18C and has been altered several times since. The rounded chapels terminating the transept are decorated with *trompe-l'œil grisailles*, painted in 1760 by the Antwerp artist Martin Geeraerts. Fénelon's tomb was sculpted by David d'Angers in 1826.

Maison Espagnole
(Tourist office) This wooden house, its gables sheathed in slate, dates from the late 16C. You can see the medieval cellars and, on the first floor, the oak carvings which once adorned the façade. Note the 17C and 18C private mansions along rue du Grand-Séminaire, rue de

Companile of the Hôtel de Ville

S. Sauvignier/MICHELIN

Bêtises de Cambrai

These oblong mint-flavoured sweets with a yellow stripe on the side are, according to legend, the result of the fortunate mistake of a 19C confectioner's apprentice. His mother complained that he had once again blundered and made a mistake (*bêtise*), hence the name given to the mint humbugs which were nevertheless appreciated for their digestive and refreshing qualities. Another old legend tells how men who went to an important market held on the 24th day of every month would behave irresponsibly and waste their money on sweets made in front of them!

l'Epée and rue de Vaucelette. One of these, carefully restored, houses the fine arts museum.

As you walk across place Jean-Moulin, note the rounded east end of the chapel of the former St-Julien hospital.

Église St-Géry

🕐 *Open Mon–Sat, 10am–noon, 3–6pm; Sun, 8.15am–noon, 5.30–7.30pm.*
✆ *03 27 78 36 15.*

Overlooked by a tower (76m/249ft tall), the old church of St Aubert's Abbey replaced an older temple believed to have been dedicated to Jupiter Capitolinus. Construction of this austere Classical building lasted from 1698 to 1745. .

The beautiful **rood screen** (1632) is a good example of the Baroque style with its contrasting red and black marble and its carved decoration creating an impression of movement or even agitation. The monumental pulpit, installed in 1850, was the work of Cambrai crafts-

men. The north transept houses Rubens' enormous painting, **The Entombment★★**. The 14C bishop **statue** in the south transept was discovered in 1982 during excavations in the crypt.

▶ *Cross place du 9-Octobre to reach place Aristide-Briand.*

Place Aristide-Briand

The square was entirely rebuilt after the First World War and is dominated by the majestic lines of the **hôtel de ville**. Its reconstruction in the 1920s, together with that of the square itself, respected the 19C façade and its Louis XVI peristyle. The hall is surmounted by a columned bell-tower, flanked by the town's two jack-o'-the-clocks, Martin and Martine. According to legend these two individuals, who appear in parades as giants, were 14C blacksmiths who dealt with the lord ravaging the region by felling him with hammer blows. The bronze figures (2m/6.5ft tall), dressed as

Maison Espagnole with the chapel of the Grand-Séminaire in the background

©Nimbus/Fotolia.com

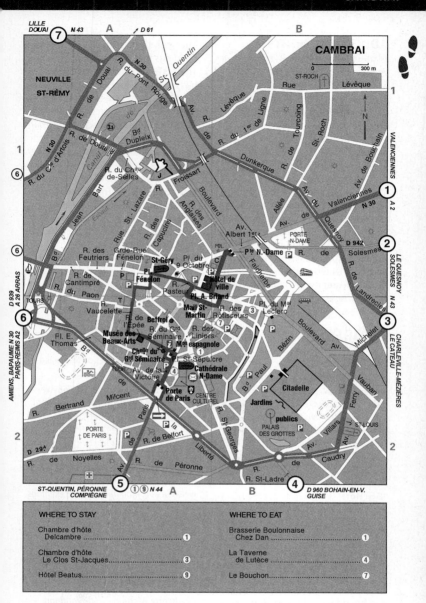

WHERE TO STAY		WHERE TO EAT	
Chambre d'hôte Delcambre	①	Brasserie Boulonnaise Chez Dan	①
Chambre d'hôte Le Clos St-Jacques	③	La Taverne de Lutèce	④
Hôtel Beatus	⑨	Le Bouchon	⑦

turbaned Moors, date from 1512; they strike the town bell with their hammers to sound the hour.

The southwest corner of the square marks the beginning of a long avenue, Mail St-Martin, offering a good view of the 15C–18C **belfry** (70m/230ft tall), all that remains of St Martin's Church.

Porte Notre-Dame

This part of the Baroque fortifications was built at the beginning of the 17C; it owes its name to the statue of the Virgin Mary that adorns the outer face. The gate is unusual for its diamond-shaped stones and its grooved columns. The sun representing Louis XIV was added to the pediment after the town was captured from the Spanish by the French.

ADDITIONAL SIGHTS
Musée des Beaux-Arts

&. ⊙Open Wed–Sun 10am–noon, 2–6pm. ∞3€. No charge 1st Sat–Sun in the month. ℘03 27 82 27 90. www.villedecambrai.com.

The town museum is housed in a mansion built for the Comte de Francqueville c. 1720. It has been restored and substantially extended, with the addition of two new buildings.

The **archaeology** department occupies the vaulted 18C cellars. Three themes recall the Gallo-Roman period: ceramics, housing and funerals. Exhibits from the Merovingian period include funerary artefacts from sites near Cambrai. The section devoted to osteo-archaeology gives a clearer insight into man during the Dark Ages.

The sculptures come from religious buildings that have been demolished. There is a fine 16C **rood screen★** originally in the chapel of St-Julien Hospital. **Alabaster statues** come from the former cathedral church. A painting by **Van der Meulen** illustrates the capture of Cambrai by Louis XIV in 1677.

The **Fine Arts** section features Dutch painting in the late 16C and 17C, including paintings by Van Veerendael and Rombouts. The 18C French School is represented by Berthelemy, de Lajoue, and Wille. From the 19C and 20C are works by Carolus Durand, Boudin, Utrillo, Marquet, Friesz etc.

The museum also has a sculpture collection, with works by Rodin, Camille Claudel, Bourdelle, Zadkine and the contemporary artist Georges Jeanclos.

ADDRESSES

⌂ STAY

⊖⊕ **Delcambre (Bed and Breakfast)** – Ferme de Bonavis, 59266 Banteux, 11km/ 6.6mi S of Cambrai via N 44. ℘03 27 78 55 08. www.bonavis.fr. ⊟. 3 rooms. This former coach inn with a pleasantly roomy interior was converted to a farm (still working) after WW II; guest rooms, with their high ceilings and parquet floors, are sober and quiet.

⊖⊕ **Hôtel Beatus** – 718 Ave de Paris. ℘03 27 81 45 70. www.hotelbeatus.fr. 32 rooms. ⊇9.50 €. Restaurant ⊖⊕. Shaded by large trees, this spacious hotel has contemporary rooms, some with Provencal decor. Some rooms open to the garden. Cosy lounge bar.

⊖⊕⊕ **Le Clos Saint-Jacques (Bed and Breakfast)** – 9 Rue St-Jacques. ℘03 27 74 37 61. www.leclosstjacques.com. ⊟. 5 rooms. ⊇9.50 €. Restaurant ⊖⊕. A beautiful residence in the centre of town, renovated while preserving the charming historic quality. Local terroir specialities served at meals.

⊈ EAT

⊖'Chez Dan' Brasserie Boulonnaise – 18 Rue des Liniers. Closed Tue. ℘03 27 81 39 77. Traditional northern hospitality

and the warm ambience keep customers coming back to this brasserie with a maritime décor.

⊖⊕ **La Taverne de Lutèce** – 68 Ave de la Victoire. ℘03 27 78 54 34. Closed at lunch. Come to this simple, rustic tavern and satisfy your appetite with a choice of traditional dishes and a few Picard and Flemish specialities.

⊖⊕ **Le Bouchon** – 31 Rue des Rôtisseurs. ℘03 27 78 44 55. Closed 3 weeks in Aug, Mon, Tue and Wed evenings and Sun. An affordable eatery serving ample portions. Eat elbow to elbow in this relaxed environment. Bistro-style cooking and a 'ch'ti' menu for sampling regional specialities.

⊞ SHOPPING

Confiserie Afchain – ZI de Cantinpré. ℘03 27 81 25 49. www.betises-de-cambrai.fr. Mon–Thu 8am–noon. Closed 3 wks in Aug, 2 wks in Dec. The self-proclaimed originator of the Bêtises de Cambrai bonbons. A small museum tells the story of this unusual invention.

Confiserie Despinoy – Rte Nationale. ℘03 27 83 57 57. Open Mon–Fri, 9am–3.30pm. Closed Aug. Another confectionary specialised in Bêtises de Cambrai.

Cassel★

Cassel is a small town that is Flemish both in its customs and appearance: an enormous cobbled main square (Grand' Place), narrow, winding streets and low whitewashed houses. The town stands at the top of Cassel Hill, the green slopes of which, formerly dotted with windmills, overlook the flat Flanders region. Local traditions are still celebrated: the religious fête with its mass, parades, traditional competitions; archery; the carnival; and the procession of the Reuze giants.

▶ **Population:** 2 290
◔ **Michelin Local Map:** 302: C-3

A tour of the terrace offers an excellent **panorama★★** (*viewing platforms*) over the picturesque jumble of Cassel's old rooftops, and beyond to the hills of Flanders and the plain, as far as the North Sea and the belfry of Bruges.
A local saying maintains that "from Cassel you can see five kingdoms: France, Belgium, Holland, England and, above the clouds, the Kingdom of Heaven".

A BIT OF HISTORY
"Cassel Hill"

The highest point of the region (176m/577ft high) and a link in the Flemish hill-range, the hill looks surprisingly large rising up in the middle of the Flemish plain; although about 30km/18mi from the coast, it is used as a landmark by sailors. Its peak is made up of a very hard ferruginous layer. To the east, **Mont des Récollets** (159m/ 521ft high) owes its name to a convent of Recollect nuns that stood here from 1615 to 1870.

Two World Wars

From October 1914 to April 1915 General **Marshall Foch** had his headquarters at Cassel. From here he followed the progress of the battle of Flanders, which was raging on the banks of the Yser. He stayed at the Hôtel de Schoebecque at no 32 in what is now rue du Maréchal-Foch.
In May 1940 members of the British expeditionary corps retreating towards Yser and Dunkirk fought a fierce rearguard action at Cassel, which enabled the allied forces to leave from Dunkirk.

SIGHTS
Public Gardens

The gardens at the top of the hill occupy the site of a medieval castle which once incorporated a collegiate church, the crypt of which remains. An equestrian statue of General Foch stands in the middle of the garden.

Casteel-Meulen (Moulin)

🕯 Guided visits (1hr) Apr–Sept Tue–Sun 10am–12.30pm, 2–6.30pm. Rest of year Sun, 10am–12.30pm, 2–6.30pm. ⏱Closed Dec. ⊚3€. Arrange visits through the Tourist Office on ✆03 28 40 52 55. www.ot-cassel.fr.
This 18C wooden **windmill** from Arneke was re-erected here to replace the castle's original windmill which burnt down in 1911. It produces flour (there is a bakery on the premises) and also linseed oil. Celebrations take place on 14 July.

Grand' Place

The main square, irregularly shaped and cobbled, extends along the hillside near the church. It has an attractive group of 16C–18C houses on its south side, among them the Hôtel de la Noble Cour.

Hôtel de la Noble Cour

A high roof dotted with blind dormer windows crowns the façade, which is entirely of stone – unusual in the North – pierced by large windows with alternately triangular and curvilinear pediments; the elegant Renaissance doorway, flanked by grey marble columns, is decorated with Fames in the spandrels and with Sirens and foliate scrolls on the frieze (⏱ temporarily closed for renovation until 2010). Pending its reopening, the museum stages temporary exhibitions.

Collégiale Notre-Dame

Foch often came here to pray and meditate in this Gothic Flemish church with three gables, three aisles, three apses and square tower over the transept.

EXCURSIONS
Steenvoorde

8km/5mi east by D 948.

This typical small Flemish town with painted houses under red-tiled roofs was once famous for its sheets; today it is known for its large dairy. The town celebrates the legend of its giant, Yan den Houtkapper, a woodcutter who made a pair of everlasting boots for Charlemagne; in return he was given a suit of armour, which he still wears for the town's processions.

Windmills – Three well-preserved windmills can be seen near the town. Two of them are wooden post mills: the **Drievemeulen** *(on D 948 west; Jul and Aug:* 90min guided tours through tourist office, *2€, 03 28 42 97 98)*, dating from 1776, is a typical oil mill; the **Noordmeulen** *(same hours as for Drievenmeulen)*, dating from 1576 with 18C working parts, is a wheat mill. The third, the **Steenmeulen** at Terdeghem *(on D 947 south)*, is a truncated brick mill, still in working order (1864). Apr-Sept, guided tours (90min), daily (except Fri and last Sun of month) 9am–noon, 2–6pm. 4€. 03 28 48 16 10. www.steenmeulen.com.

Wormhout

10km/6mi north via D 218 and D 916.

Moulin Deschodt – Guided visits (1h) 1st and 3rd Sun of Jun, 2nd Sun of Jul, 1st and 2nd Sun of Aug 3–6pm. 2€. 03 28 62 81 23. This wooden post mill is the last of 11 windmills which stood in the town in 1780.

Musée Jeanne-Devos – Open daily except Wed, 2–5pm, 1st two Sundays in the month 3–6pm. 2€. 03 28 62 81 23. This charming Flemish house, flanked by a dovecote and set within lovely gardens at the end of a cul-de-sac, is the old Wormhout presbytery (18C). It was inhabited by Jeanne Devos who collected, until her death in 1989, a multitude of objects from daily life. A photographer by profession, she left thousands of photographs portraying the ordinary and extraordinary lives of the villagers nearby.

ADDRESSES

♈/ EAT

La Taverne Flamande – *34 Grand'Place. 03 28 42 42 59. Closed Feb school holidays, end Aug, end Oct, Tue evening and Wed – reserv. recommended.* After paying your respects to giant hero Reuze Papa, come try the Flemish specialities served in this tavern with the summer terrace surveying the valley.

'T Kasteelhof – *8 Rue St-Nicolas. 03 28 40 59 29. Closed 3 wks in Jan, 1st wk Jul, 2 wks in Oct, Mon-Wed, 25 Dec. Reserv. recommended weekends.* Said to be the highest tavern in French Flanders! Come try the regional specialities and purchase local products in the adjoining shop. Saturday night and Sunday lunch Flemish tales are told to patrons as they dine.

Het Blauwershof – *9 Rue d'Eecke, 59270 Godewaersvelde, 12km/7.2mi E of Cassel via D 948 and D 18. 03 28 49 45 11. Closed Jan, 15 days in summer and Mon.* A genuine Flemish tavern whose name means 'Cheaters' Inn.' The decor is a typical hotchpotch, including an old stove, a mechanical piano, a crossbow and the effigy of Gambrinus, King of Beer.

Au Roi du Potje Vleesch – *31 Rue du Mont-des-Cats, 59270 Godewaersvelde; 12km/7.2mi E of Cassel via D 948 and D 18. 03 28 42 52 56. Closed Jan and Mon – reserv. weekends.* You must go through the delicatessen to find this tavern housed in a former slaughterhouse. The rustic Flemish decor sets the stage for a meal of regional cuisine, the famous potjevleesch (a meat stew) and Henri le Douanier beer, named after the village giant.

La Côte d'Opale★

The Opal Coast extends from Baie de Somme to the Belgian border, at the western end of the **Parc naturel régional des Caps et Marais d'Opale**. Its name derives from the opalescent colour of the breaking waves. A local painter, Édouard Lévêque, first used the name in 1911, but the landscapes had long been an inspiration for painters and writers such as Corot and Victor Hugo. The most spectacular part of the coastline lies between Boulogne and Calais, where the cliffs, worn away by the strong north-south current, skirt the Boulonnais hills.

🚗 DRIVING TOUR

9km/30mi – approx 2hr 30min

Boulogne-sur-Mer★
🕭 *See BOULOGNE-SUR-MER.*
Leave Boulogne by D 940.
D 940 is a winding coastal road that offers glimpses of the sea, the ports and the beaches, leading across hill crests which are intermittently bare or covered with closely cropped meadows.
To the north the road comes to the Escalles cran, resembling a mountain pass but at an altitude of less than 100m/328ft. Car parks flank the road, allowing access to the sea or to walks among the dunes.

Swimming Beaches
On a beach with lifeguards in attendance, pay attention to the colour of the flag flying near the lifeguard station:
● **Green** – *Lifeguards in attendance. Swimming authorised and not considered dangerous.*
● **Orange** – *Lifeguards in attendance. Swimming considered dangerous.*
● **Red** – *Swimming prohibited.*

🕭 **Michelin Local Map:** 301: C-2 to D-3
ℹ **Info:** Office du tourisme de la Terre des Deux Caps, pl. de la Mairie, 62179 Wissant ✆03 21 82 48 00.
▶ **Location:** The Opal coast borders the English Channel and the North Sea from Mers-les-Bains to Bray-Dune. Use the D 940 to explore.
☺ **Don't Miss:** Enjoy *moules et frites* and other seafood at Mers-les-Bains; they don't come any better than by the sea.
👪 **Kids:** Make the most of the beach as Wissant.
🕭 **Also See:** Marquenterre nature reserve. Cap Blanc Nez and Cap Gris Nez.

Wimereux ♨♨
The opening to the Wimereux Valley (🕭 *see Le BOULONNAIS*) is the site of a large and popular seaside resort for families, awarded the "Station Kid" label for the activities offered to children. A walk on the promenade built along the sand and pebble beach affords views of the Straits of Dover, the Grande Armée Column and Boulogne, where the promenade narrows to a path leading to **Pointe aux Oies**, site of the 6 August 1840 Napoleon III landing prior to his attempt to win over the garrison stationed there.

▶ *Between Wimereux and Ambleteuse, the road runs beside tall dunes.*

Ambleteuse
This picturesque village stands above the mouth of the River Slack, where boats can beach. Ambleteuse was formerly a naval base protected by **Fort d'Ambleteuse** (🕐 *open Jul–Aug weekends 3–7pm; Apr–Jun & Sept–Oct, Sun 3–7pm (last admission 1hr before closing); ≈3€. ✆03 20 54 61 54*), built by Vauban between 1685 and 1690. Napoleon based part of his flotilla here

Cap Gris-Nez

Y. Tierny / MICHELIN

"the Whales" (*Les Épaulards*) because from a distance it looks humpbacked and throws up spray.

Straight ahead, the **view**★ extends to the white English cliffs. On the French side you can see the folds of the coastline, Cap Blanc-Nez and Boulogne.

The **Musée du Mur de l'Atlantique** (⊙*open daily Jun–Sep 9am–7pm; Feb–May & Oct–Nov 9am–noon, 2–6pm; ⊛5.50€; ℘03 21 32 97 33; www.batterietodt.com)* is in the Todt battery, a World War II pillbox which served as a German launching base for 2m/6ft long missiles fired on England. There are collections of arms and uniforms, and a naval gun on rails (280 bore, made by Krupp in 1943), which is 35m/115ft long, could fire 15 times per hour and had a range of 62–86km/38.5–53.4mi.

at the time of the Boulogne Camp (⛐ *see BOULOGNE-SUR-MER*). Today it is a beach and Boulogne's harbour entrance.

The **Musée Historique de la Seconde Guerre Mondiale** (⛐ ⊙*open daily Apr–Oct, 10am–6pm (Jul–Aug 7pm); Nov & Mar weekends 10am–6pm); ⊛6.50€; ℘03 21 87 33 01; www.musee3945.com)* on the outskirts of Ambleteuse retraces the full story of World War II, from the conquest of Poland in 1939 to the Liberation. About 100 different uniforms are exhibited, with equipment worn or used by the armies involved in the war.

▶ *3km/2mi after Audresselles, turn left onto D 191.*

Cap Gris-Nez★★

This "grey-nose cape" looks out to the English coast less than 30km/19mi away. The gently sloping cliffs rise to 45m/148ft. The lighthouse (28m/92ft tall) with beams visible 45km/28mi away, was rebuilt after the war at the tip of a bare, windswept peninsula dotted with the remains of ruined German pillboxes. The Gris-Nez branch of CROSS, the organisation responsible for watching over waters where maritime traffic is the heaviest in the world, is underground. The crumbling debris from the cliffs mingles with the rocky reef known as

Wissant ⌂

👫 This splendid beach of fine, firm sand is well sheltered from the eastern winds and currents. It forms a vast curve between Cap Gris-Nez and Cap Blanc-Nez. Villas stand among the dunes overlooking the shore. The activities offered to children have earned the resort the "Station Kid" label.

The **Musée du Moulin** (⊙*open 2–6pm with prior reservation required; ⊛3€; ℘03 21 35 91 87, www.lemoulin-wissant. com)* is housed in a flour mill driven by hydraulic power. It is well preserved and features pinewood parts, cast-iron waterwheels and a conveyor belt.

Cap Blanc-Nez★★

The "white-nose cape" is a vertical mass of chalk cliffs rising 134m/440ft above the waves, offering extensive **views**★ of the English cliffs and the French coast from Calais to Cap Gris-Nez.

▶ *Retrace your steps to Mont d'Hubert.*

The **Musée National du Transmanche** (⊙*open mid-Apr–Oct Tue–Sun 2–6pm (last admission 45m before closing) ⊛3.80€; ℘03 21 85 57 42)* located on Mont d'Hubert, faces Cap Blanc-Nez; it retraces the turbulent history of the strait, which scientists and scholars have always used to promote their ideas. In 1751 Nicolas Desmarets was the first person to consider linking France to England. Later, Aimé Thomé de Gamond suggested a variety of options: a tunnel constructed of metal tubes, a concrete undersea vault, a pontoon, an artificial isthmus, a mobile bridge and a viaduct-bridge. Channel crossings were eventually achieved by balloon (Blanchard), plane (Blériot), steamboat (the first regular line was established in 1816), raft, on skis, etc.

Lower down the hill, near D 940, stands the monument to **Latham** (1883–1912), the pilot who attempted, unsuccessfully, to cross the Channel at the same time as Blériot.

ADDRESSES

🛏 STAY

😊 **La Grand' Maison Bed and Breakfast** – *Hameau de la Haute-Escalles, 62179 Escalles, 2km/1.2mi E of Cap-Blanc-Nez via D 243. ✆03 21 85 27 75.* 🛏 *6 rooms.* Here's an appealing 18C flower-filled farm facing the British Isles. Fans of hiking, horse riding or windsurfing will heartily appreciate this site between land and sea. The prestige guest rooms, equipped with TVs, are more comfortable. Three self-catering cottages.

😊😊😊 **La Goélette** – *13 digue de Mer, 62930 Wimereux. ✆03 21 32 62 44. www.lagoelette.com.* 🛏. *4 rooms.* Who could resist this charming villa from the early 1900s, ideally situated on the promenade? The rooms, all renovated, have recovered their original panache (mouldings, maritime pine furnishings). The blue and yellow rooms offer captivating views of the sea.

🍴 EAT

😊😊 **La Sirène** – *62179 Audinghen. ✆03 21 32 95 97. Closed 15 Dec–25 Jan, evenings except Sat Sept–Easter, Sun evening and Mon.* Situated on the Cap Gris-Nez beach, this restaurant commands a great view of the sea. Choose a table in one of the two large

Between **Sangatte** and Blériot-Plage, the chalets are built directly on the sea-washed dunes. It is here that the Channel Tunnel emerges.

Blériot-Plage

The beautiful beach extends along to Cap Blanc-Nez. At Baraques (*500m/550yd west of the resort*), near D 940, a monument commemorates the first aerial crossing of the Channel, by **Louis Blériot** (1872–1936). On 25 July 1909 he landed his aeroplane in a valley on the Dover cliffs, after a flight of approximately half an hour.

Calais
♿ *see CALAIS.*

dining rooms with large bay windows for a meal of grilled lobster (the house speciality) or other seafood dishes.

😊😊 **Liégeoise et Atlantic Hôtel** – *digue de Mer, 62930 Wimereux. ✆03 21 32 41 01. Closed Feb, Sun evening and Mon lunch.* For a satisfying seafood meal, choose between the roomy bar on the seafront promenade or the panoramic dining room upstairs. If you plan to stay over, be sure to obtain a room with a view of the ocean.

🏃 LEISURE ACTIVITIES

Eden 62 – *62930 Wimereux. ✆03 21 32 13 74. www.eden62.fr. Jul–Aug* 🌿 Guided tours of several natural areas along the Opal Coast: Platier d'Oye, Cap Gris-Nez, Cap Blanc-Nez, estuary and dunes of the Slack, Canche Bay and the Authie dunes.

Char à Voile Club – *Sea front, 62179 Wissant. ✆03 21 85 86 78, www.cvcco.com.* Sand yachting.

Station Kid – *62930 Wimereux.* Located on the Nord de Wimereux dike, the children's beach has a well-equipped play area. The Iodie Beach Club welcomes 3- to 12-year-olds. Dig'enfants offers other activities (workshops, shows): *✆03 21 33 90 41, www.wimereux-tourisme.fr.*

Douai★

Straddling the River Scarpe, Douai has preserved the 18C layout and buildings that gave it the aristocratic look Balzac evoked in his *Recherche de l'Absolu*. The town is proud of its belfry and the peripatetic peal of 50 bells which travels the length and breadth of France. A French bell-ringing school was founded in Douai by Jacques Lannoy, who still runs it today.

▶ **Population:** 518 727
🕐 **Michelin Local Map:** 302: G-5
🗐 **Info:** Office du tourisme de Douai, 70 pl. d'Armes 59500, Douai. ℘0327 88 26 79. www.ville-douai.fr.

A BIT OF HISTORY

Industrial, legal and intellectual centre – Light industry, a national printing works, and an important river freight trade all contribute to the town's economic prosperity. Douai is also a major legal centre, with a Court of Appeals, a relic of the Flanders Parliament from 1714 to the Revolution.

The town enjoys a distinguished reputation for intellectual activity, which began with the elegiac poetess **Marceline Desbordes-Valmore** (1786–1859) and continues through the many educational institutions which have taken the place of the 16C university, transferred to Lille in 1887.

Gayant's town – On 16 June 1479, Douai narrowly escaped falling into French hands. A procession was organised to thank the patron saint of the town and when peace with France was signed 60 years later, this annual event became more colourful with each corporation supplying a float decorated with symbolic characters. The wicker-workers' guild provided a *gayant* (giant in Picard dialect); a year later the fruit producers supplied him with a wife… the children soon followed.

Gayant's misfortunes – In 1770, the bishop of Arras forbade the procession, which celebrated a French defeat, and replaced it with another one on 6 July, intended to celebrate the arrival of French troops in Douai in 1667. The giants were given another lease of life in 1778, only to be wiped out again by the Revolution. They reappeared in 1801 and were given their present costumes 20 years later. Destroyed in 1918 and 1944, they were rebuilt each time with the same care.

🐾 WALKING TOUR

Start from **Porte de Valenciennes**, which is Gothic on one side (15C) and Classical on the other (18C) and walk to place d'Armes, a part-pedestrian zone with outdoor cafés and fountains. The

Jean Bellegambe (1470–1534)

This artist, who seems to have spent his entire life in Douai, was a likeable character with wide-ranging artistic talent.

He mastered the transition from the Gothic tradition (religious subjects treated with realistic detail and harmonious colours) to the Italian influence of the Renaissance (works decorated with columns, pilasters, shells and garlands) which he linked with the objective, intimate realism of the Flemish School and the intellectualism of the French School. The latter is marked by a choice of subjects which are sometimes difficult to understand.

Bellegambe worked a great deal for the abbeys of the Scarpe Valley, and Douai's landscape and buildings can often be recognised in his works: the belfry and town gates, the towers of the abbey church of Anchin, Flines woods and the watery landscapes of the River Scarpe and River Sensée.

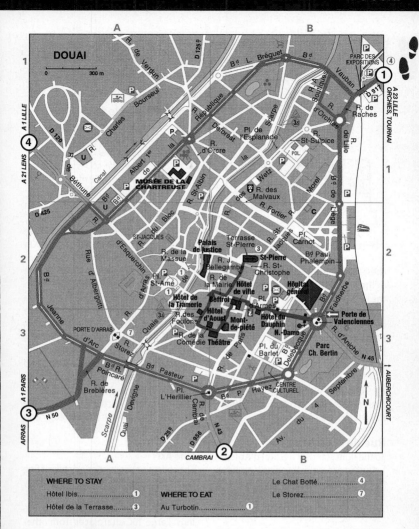

DOUAI

A 1 LILLE
A 21 LENS
A 1 PARIS
ARRAS
A 23 LILLE ORCHIES, TOURNAI
AUBERCHICOURT
CAMBRAI

MUSÉE DE LA CHARTREUSE
Palais de Justice
St-Pierre
Hôtel de ville
Hôpital général
Hôtel de la Tannerie
Beffroi
Hôtel d'Aoust
Mont-de-piété
Hôtel du Dauphin
N.-Dame
Théâtre
Porte de Valenciennes
Porte d'Arras
Parc Ch. Bertin

WHERE TO STAY		
Hôtel Ibis............①	WHERE TO EAT	Le Chat Botté.........④
Hôtel de la Terrasse.........③	Au Turbotin............①	Le Storez.........⑦

Hôtel du Dauphin is the only remaining 18C house here; its façade is adorned with trophies. It now houses the tourism office.

◯ *Walk along rue de la Mairie.*

Town Hall and Belfry★

◯*Open Jul and Aug ⚬⚬ guided tours (1hr), 10–11am, 2–6pm; rest of year, daily 11am (except Mon), 3–5pm. ⚬⚬3.50€. ℘03 27 88 26 79. www.ville-douai.fr.*
The construction of this Gothic ensemble, over which towers the austere belfry, began in 1380 and was resumed several times between 1471 and 1873.

Inside the **town hall** (*Hôtel de Ville*) the Gothic Council Chamber (15C), the old chapel (now the main hall), the White Salon with 18C wood panelling and the state room are open to visitors. The **belfry** is one of the best known in northern France and has been made famous not only by the description given by Victor Hugo who stopped briefly in the town in 1837, but also by Corot's fine painting, now in the Louvre. It is an imposing square Gothic tower, sombre and grim, completed in 1410; it stands 64m/210ft tall (40m/131ft from the ground to the platform).
The current **peal of 62 bells** on the fourth floor replaced those destroyed by

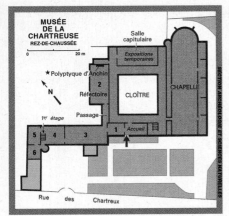

MUSÉE DE LA CHARTREUSE
REZ-DE-CHAUSSÉE

0   20 m

★ Polyptyque d'Anchin

N

Salle capitulaire

Expositions temporaires

2

Réfectoire

CLOÎTRE

CHAPELLE

1er étage   Passage

5   4   3   1   Accueil

6

Rue   des   Chartreux

SECTION ARCHÉOLOGIE ET SCIENCES NATURELLES

the Germans in 1917. They play the tune of the Scottish Puritans on the hour; on the half-hour, a boating song; at quarter past and quarter to the hour, a few notes of Gayant's tune.

From the top of the tower (192 steps), Douai and its industrial suburb may be seen through the louvre-boarding.

▶ *Follow the vaulted passageway and cross the courtyard of the town hall to rue de l'Université.*

Rue de la Comédie

To the right stands the **Hôtel d'Aoust**, a beautiful example of Louis XV architecturenwith a Rococo door and allegorical statues representing the four seasons on the façade overlooking the courtyard.

▶ *Continue along rue de la Comédie and turn right onto rue des Foulons.*

Rue des Foulons

Along the left-hand side of rue des Foulons, literally "Fullers' Street", a reminder of the linen-drapers of the Middle Ages, are 18C houses. At no 132, is the Louis XIII style **Hôtel de la Tramerie**.

▶ *Follow rue de la Mairie on the right then rue Gambetta to rue Bellegambe.*

Rue Bellegambe

The Modern Style boutique in rue Bellegambe (*opposite the church*) features a shop front decorated with sunflowers.

▶ *Walk back and turn left towards the town hall.*

SIGHTS
Musée de la Chartreuse★★

🕐 *Open Wed–Mon 10am–noon & 2–6pm.* 🚶 *Guided tours (1hr) possible.* 💶 *3€, no charge 1st Sunday in the month.* ☎ *03 27 71 38 80. www.ville-douai.fr.* The museum is installed in an interesting group of 16C, 17C and 18C buildings, which were once the old charter house. On the left is the Hôtel d'Abancourt; on the right, beneath a huge square tower, is the building in the Flemish Renaissance style constructed for the Montmorency family. This is where the first Carthusian monks settled in the 17C. They built the small cloisters, the refectory, the chapter-house and the chapel, which was completed in 1722. The great cloisters and the monks' cells were destroyed in the 19C. The museum is in two parts: the Fine Arts Section, and the Archaeology and Natural History Section.

Fine Arts

The collections consist principally of fine early paintings. **Rooms 1 to 3** – Early Flemish, Dutch (the Master of Manne, the Master of Flemalle) and Italian paintings. Large 16C altarpieces from other abbeys are on display here.

Especially noteworthy are **Anchin Polyptych**★ by Bellegambe (*room 2*) portraying the Adoration of the Cross or the Adoration of the Holy Trinity, and the Marchiennes Polyptych by Van Scorel (Utrecht School, 16C). Two masterpieces of the Italian Renaissance: Veronese's *Portrait of a Venetian Woman* and Carracci's *Scourging of Christ*, a work of rare intensity, are on display in room 3. The bronze *Venus of Castello* recalls the work of the famous sculptor and architect Giambologna.

Although he conducted most of his career in Italy, he was born in Douai in 1529 and trained in Flanders.

Rooms 4–6 – Relief map of Douai in 1709. 16C Flemish and Dutch Mannerism is exhibited: works by Roland Savery, the Antwerp artists Jean Matsys, son of Quentin, and Frans Floris, the Dutchmen Van Hemessen, Van Reymerswaele, Goltzius, Cornelis Van Haarlem etc.

Rooms 7–8 – Works by Rubens (*Céres and Pan*) and Jordaens (Study of a head); landscapes by Momper and Govaerts; a witchcraft scene by David Teniers.

Rooms 11–12 – The French School (17C–19C) is well represented here by portrait painters: Le Brun (*Louis XIV on Horseback*), Vivien, Largillière, Boilly, David (*Mme Tallien*) etc. Works by Impressionist painters are also on show: Renoir, Sisley and Pissaro and Post-Impressionists.

▶ *Return to the ground floor.*

Cloisters – The cloister vaults are pointed despite having been built in 1663, in the middle of the Classical period. The red brickwork contrasts pleasantly with the white stone of the ribs and the framing, carved with Baroque designs.

Chapter-house – The chapter-house was built in the same year as the cloisters (1663) and in the same style; it now holds temporary exhibitions.

Archaeology and Natural History
The evolution of man is traced from the Palaeolithic Age to AD 400 through the findings of excavations in the north of France (*first floor*). The collection includes a cast of Biache Man's skull, discovered at Biache-St-Vaast, about 13km/8mi from Douai; the man is thought to have lived about 250 000 years ago.

The Gallo-Roman period is illustrated through material found at Bavay (statuettes) and at Lewarde (busts). There are some interesting models of the Merovingian village of Brebières and the necropolis at Hordain.

Palais de Justice
💬 *Guided tour into the Parliament Chamber, Jul–Aug Sat 3.30pm.* 🎫*3.50€. www.ville-douai.fr.*
The law courts date from the early 16C but were almost entirely rebuilt in the 18C; they were once the refuge of Marchiennes Abbey and then became the seat of the Flanders Parliament. The old prison, from which a famous 18C French adventurer escaped, has been turned into an **exhibition centre** (*enter from the riverside*). The items on show illustrate the history of the town and the law courts.

The first-floor courtroom, called the **Grande Salle du Parlement** (1762), is furnished with a vast marble fireplace, carved Louis XV woodwork, a portrait of Louis XIV and allegorical paintings by Nicolas Brenet (1769). The brick façade overlooking the River Scarpe bears traces of the original Gothic arching.

EXCURSIONS
Flines-les-Raches
11km/7mi north-east by D 917 and D 938.
The village has a curious **church**, which is entered through a very old brick and sandstone belfry-porch (some say dating back to AD 800).

The narrow nave opens onto chapels from various periods. In the first two chapels on the right, the roof beams are decorated with historiated corbels; they bear the arms of Philippine Torck, Abbess of Flines from 1561 to 1571.

ADDRESSES

🏨 STAY

🛏️🍴 **Hôtel Ibis** – *Place St-Amé.* 📞*03 27 87 27 27. 42 rooms.* 🛏️*6.50€.*
The standards of Ibis hotels in a historic buildings dating back to the 16C and 18C. Rooms on 3rd floor have exposed ceiling beams.

🛏️🍴🍴🍴 **Hôtel de la Terrasse** – *36 terrasse St-Pierre.* 📞*03 27 88 70 04. 26 rooms.* 🛏️*8.50€. Restaurant* 🍴🍴.
The perfect starting place for a stroll along the nearby banks of the Scarpe. Functional, soundproofed rooms are housed in three separate buildings. The popular restaurant serves traditional cuisine in spacious dining rooms decorated with paintings and violins. Excellent wine list of over 800 bottles.

⍨/ EAT

🍴 **Le Storez** – *116 Rue Storez.* ☏*03 27 98 88 80. Closed Sun evening and Mon.* Opposite the Porte d'Arras, a remnant of the city's old ramparts, this brick house has been serving customers since 1896. Today's fare consists of dishes with a maritime accent, served in a retro-style decor.

🍴🍷 **Le Chat Botté** – *Château de Bernicourt, 59286 Roost-Warendin, 10km/ 6mi NE of Douai via D 917 and D 8.* ☏*03 27 80 24 44. Closed 1–15 Aug, Sun evening and Mon.* A moment of quietude in a shady park of the Château de Bernicourt. The restaurant, set up in the outbuildings, has a dining room decorated with coloured rattan chairs.

🍴🍷 **Au Turbotin** – *9 Rue de la Massue.* ☏*03 27 87 04 16. Closed 7–20 Feb; Aug, Sat lunch, Sun evening and Mon.* This former seed merchant's shop is brightly decorated and popular with people in the legal profession. Seafood menus.

🛒 SHOPPING

Aux Délices – *68 Rue de la Mairie, opposite the belfry.* ☏*03 27 88 69 19. Mon 2–7pm, Tue–Sat 9am–12.30pm, 2–7pm.* Caramel lovers come here to buy one of Douai's oldest specialities: Gayantines, milk caramel sweets with a butter caramel centre flavoured with vanilla or chicory.

🏃 SPORT AND RECREATION

Boating – *Jul–Aug Thu–Sun & public holidays 2pm–7pm; May–Jun & Sept weekends 3–7pm. (From the Palais de Justice landing stage). 4.50€.* This pleasant outing along the river Scarpe *(30min)*, takes you past banks lined with venerable old residences.

Rambling – There are many marked trails in the area. Ask for a map at the Office de Tourisme.

Dunkerque

Over 80 percent of the "heroic town" of Dunkirk was destroyed during World War II. Since its rebuilding, it has expanded rapidly, both commercially and industrially, owing to the enormous growth of its port. The town centre, renovated and extended, now offers visitors three fine museums, and the carnival brings in its fair share of popular rejoicing.

A BIT OF HISTORY
Jean Bart, the "king's official privateer"

During the wars fought by Louis XIV, the privateers of Dunkirk destroyed and captured 3 000 ships, took 30 000 prisoners and wiped out Dutch trade. The most intrepid of all the privateers was **Jean Bart** (1650–1702).

He was as famous as the privateers from St-Malo, Duguay-Trouin and Surcouf, and was a virtuoso of the North Sea trade routes. Unlike pirates, who were

> ▸ **Population:** 191 173
> ⚲ **Michelin Local Map:** 302: C-1
> ℹ **Info:** Beffroi, r. de l'Amiral-Ronarc'h, 59140 Dunkerque. ☏03 28 66 79 21. www.ot-dunkerque.fr.

outlaws attacking any and every passing ship and, in many cases, murdering the crews, privateers were granted "letters patent" from the sovereign entitling them to hound warships and merchant vessels. In 1694, Jean Bart saved the kingdom from famine by capturing 130 ships loaded with wheat. As a result, he was raised to the nobility and given the rank of Commodore.

It is said that Louis XIV announced the appointment personally. "Jean Bart, I have appointed you to the rank of Commodore." The brave seafarer is said to have replied, "Sire, you were right to do so."

Dunkirk Carnival

The carnival began at the end of the 19C. Before leaving town for several months to go fishing for cod in the frozen Icelandic waters, the *"visscherbende"* (groups of fishermen in Flemish) would organise a lively feast at the shipowners' expense. Afterwards they said goodbye and left. Today the Dunkirk Carnival is one of the most popular in the north of France. It means five weeks of mass hysteria: processions of over-excited people, accompanied by fifes and drums, winding through the streets, dancing side by side, and a long succession of popular balls (Bal des Corsaires, Nuit des Acharnés) with plenty to drink of course!

Church of the Dunes – Until the 7C the site on which Dunkirk stands was covered by sea. Its name, which means "church of the dunes," did not appear until 1067. Until the end of the 17C, possession of this poorly defended fishermen's town was fought over by Spanish, French, English and Dutch alike. In 1658 it was taken by Turenne after the Battle of the Dunes and fortified shortly after by Vauban.

Evacuation of Dunkirk (May-June 1940) – From 25 May to 4 June Dunkirk was the scene of a bloody battle at the time of the evacuation of Allied forces who were cut off from their bases after the German breakthrough at Sedan and the subsequent push toward the coast. The boats in Dunkirk's port and on the beaches from Malo to Bray-Dunes made the journey back and forth between the French coast and England. Despite the limpet mines, torpedoes, bombs and the pounding of heavy German shells, almost 350 000 men were rescued, about two-thirds of them British.

THE PORT★★

Dunkirk's harbour traffic is largely dependent on the importance of the town's industrial complex founded on steel, petroleum and petrochemical products. The shipyards closed down in 1987 after turning out more than 300 ships.

Since then, the eastern and western ports have been linked by a **deep-water canal** to the Nord-Pas-de-Calais region of France, Belgium and the Paris Basin. The port installations extend along 15km/9mi of coastline.

Port-Est

The eastern port is serviced by an outer harbour (80ha/198 acres) and three locks, with the largest, the Charles-de-Gaulle Lock (365×50m/400×55yd), able to accommodate ships up to 115 000 tonnes. The **harbour basin** (6km/4mi long) is divided into six open basins and specialised industrial basins, in addition to storage installations. Well equipped for ship repairs, the port has four dry docks and one floating dock.

WALKING TOUR
Approx 1hr.

Start from place du Minck (fish market) between the Bassin du Commerce and the Cale aux Pêcheurs and cross the old citadel district, where the customs forwarding agents are established today. The channel and the marina are on the right. Cross Trystam Lock and turn right toward the lighthouse.

Built between 1838 and 1843, the **lighthouse** (Closed for renovations through 2010, 03 28 63 33 39, www.museeportuaire.com) is 63m/207ft tall and its 6 000 watts produce beams which can be seen 48km/30mi away. From the top the **view** extends to the impressive harbour installations and the beach at Malo-les-Bains.

BOAT TRIPS
Guided boat tours Jul–Aug Tue–Fri 2:30pm & 4:30pm, weekends and public holidays, 3pm & 5pm; Mar–Jun & Sep–Oct hours vary, call 03 28 59 11 14 (landing stage) or 03 28 66 79 21

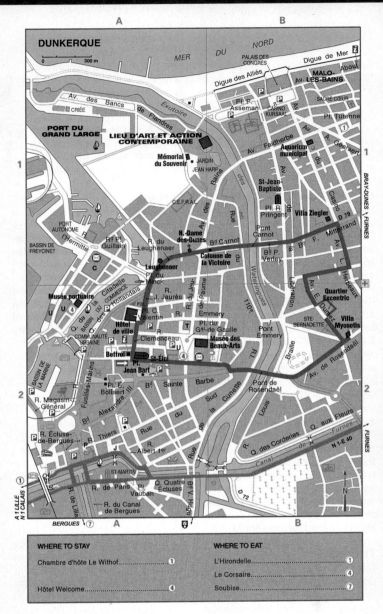

DUNKERQUE

MER DU NORD

PORT DU GRAND LARGE

LIEU D'ART ET ACTION CONTEMPORAINE

MALO-LES-BAINS

WHERE TO STAY		WHERE TO EAT	
Chambre d'hôte Le Withof............	①	L'Hirondelle....................	①
		Le Corsaire....................	④
Hôtel Welcome..................	④	Soubise......................	⑦

(tourist office). 8.50€ *(child 6.50€, family, 25€).*

Boats leave from the Place du Minck at the Bassin du Commerce, the largest of the three old basins, and cruise the entire length of the port.

The trip takes visitors past the tug basin, the workshops (dry docks), the various locks, the wet docks and storage areas, the sugar terminal (Transterminal Sucrier), the oil refinery and the petroleum wharves, etc.

THE TOWN
Belfry

🕐 *Guided panoramic visits (30mn) Mon–Sat 10am, 10.45am, 11.30am, 2pm, 2.45pm, 3.30pm, 4.15pm, 5pm & 5.45pm.* 2.90€ *(7–12 years, 2€).*
📞*03 28 66 79 21. www.ot-dunkerque.fr.*

Built in the 13C and heightened in 1440, this served as the bell-tower to **Église St-Éloi** which burnt down in 1558. This high tower (58m/190ft) contains a peal of 48 bells which play "Jean Bart's tune" on the hours and other popular tunes on the quarter hours. The tourist office is housed on the ground floor. A war memorial has been erected under the arch opposite Église St-Éloi.

SIGHTS
Musée Portuaire★

&. ♿️ ⏱️*Open Jul–Aug 10am–6pm. Rest of year Wed–Mon 10am–12.45pm, 1.30–6pm.* 🎟️*10€ (7–12 years, 8€).* ☎️*03 28 63 33 39. www.museeportuaire.fr.*

Laid out in a former tobacco warehouse dating from the 19C, this attractive museum gives an insight into the history and operating of the port of Dunkirk, Northern France's huge maritime gateway, through dioramas, model ships, maps, paintings, engravings and the tools once used by dockers.

In the 17C, Dunkirk became the main privateering harbour, with Jean Bart to defend it. *The Battle of Texel* (a copy of a painting by Isabey kept in the Musée de la Marine in Paris), engravings, and models of privateers' boats illustrate Bart's exploits.

Opposite the museum are several interesting ships including a three-master, the *Duchesse Anne*, once a sailing school ship (1901); a light vessel, the *Sandettie* (1949); and an old barge, the *Guilde* (1929), which houses an exhibition on inland navigation in its hold.

Musée des Beaux-Arts★ (Fine Arts Museum)

⏱️*Open Wed–Mon 10am–noon, 2–6pm.* 🎟️*4.50€, no charge 1st Sunday of the month.* ☎️*03 28 59 21 65.*

This museum (rebuilt in 1973) houses beautiful collections of 16C to 20C paintings and documents tracing Dunkirk's history. One room is dedicated to the privateer Jean Bart. Note the strange 17C money box in the shape of a chained captive from the Église St-Eloi. The money placed in it was used to buy back slaves.

Lieu d'Art et Action Contemporaine (LAAC) ★

⏱️*Open Tue–Sun 10am–midi & 2–5.30pm (Apr–Oct 6.30pm).* 🎟️*4.50€ (joint ticket with Beaux Arts Museum).* ☎️*03 28 29 56 00.*

Architect Jean Willerval bore in mind the existing garden when he built his modern concrete building sheathed in white ceramic. The museum is devoted to contemporary earthenware and glassware from 1950–1980, including CoBrA, César, Soulages, Warhol, and Télémaque. Working with the theme **"Dialogues in ceramics"**, the museum aims to increase public awareness of this art form.

The Museum of Contemporary Art stands in the middle of a **sculpture park**★ designed by landscape gardener Gilbert Samel. The paths climb outcrops and run down slopes, leading past great stone pieces by the sculptor Dodeigne, metal structures by Féraud and compositions by Viseux, Arman and Zvenijorovsky, all against the backdrop of the North Sea.

Duchesse Anne in front of Musée portuaire

S. Sauvignier/MICHELIN

ADDRESSES

☆ STAY

⊜☻ **Hôtel Welcome** – *37 r. Raymond-Poincaré.* ☏*03 28 59 20 70. 40 rooms.* ⌑*10.50€.* Functional rooms in bright cheerful colours and a modern bar with a billiard table. A modern, colourful setting in the dining room, serving traditional fare.

☝/ EAT

⊜☻ **Le Corsaire** – *6 quai Citadelle.* ☏*03 28 59 03 61. tetart.virginie@neuf.fr. Closed 24–31 Dec, Sun pm and Wed.* This restaurant near the harbour museum offers a view of the three-mast ship

"Duchesse Anne". Modern comfortable setting and seasonal cuisine.

⊜☻ **Soubise** – *49 rte de Bergues.* ☏*03 28 25 12 19. Closed 16–28 Apr, 23 Jul–18 Aug, 17 Dec–5 Jan, Sat–Sun.* This 18C posthouse bordering the canal now houses an extremely friendly restaurant. Traditional, well prepared and generously portioned dishes.

⊜☻☷ **L'Hirondelle** – *46 av. Faidherbe. Malo-les-Bains.* ☏*03 28 63 17 65. www. hotelhirondelle.com.* This friendly, family hotel is in the heart of a seaside resort; the rooms are gradually being made over in a pleasant, understated contemporary spirit. Seafood dishes complement a largely classic menu.

Guînes

Guînes, now a busy grain market town, was the seat of a powerful count, a vassal of the English crown for more than 200 years, from 1352 to 1558. Surrounded by forests and marshland, the town is the pleasant starting point for tours of the Trois Pays area. A *"son et lumière"* show takes place in June.

SIGHTS
Tour de l'Horloge★

▲☖⊙*Open Apr–Sept Mon–Sat 2–5pm.* ☎*6€ (children 3.50€).* ☏*03 28 59 21 65.* This clocktower built in 1763 offers panoramic views of Calais , the Opal Coast, and the Flanders plains.

At the foot of the tower is an interactive museum evoking the history of the town, from Viking invasions to the visit of Thomas Becket. Educational games for kids.

Écomusée Saint-Joseph-Village

▲☖⊙*Open Feb–Oct 10am–6pm (Jul & Aug 7pm).* ☎*10€(children 7–16 years 5€).* ☏*03 21 35 64 05. www.st-joseph-village.com.* This eco-museum reconstitutes the town the way it looked from 1900–1950, from the school and bakery to the mill.

▶ **Population:** 5 221
♨ **Michelin Local Map:** 301: E-2
❚ **Info:** Office du tourisme de Guînes, 14 r. Clemenceau, 62340. ☏03 21 35 73 73. www.calais-cotedopale.com.
◐ **Location:** 8km/5mi south of Calais.

Forêt de Guînes

✸The road from Guînes enters this hilly area which is densely covered with oak, beech, hornbeam and birch, and extends (785ha/1 940 acres) to the northern edge of the Boulonnais region.

The road ends at the **Clairière du Ballon**. To the left and slightly set back, the **Colonne Blanchard** in marble marks the landing spot of the balloon that on 7 January 1785 achieved the first aerial crossing of the Channel.

EXCURSIONS
Fortresse de Mimoyecques

○☛*Closed for renovations.* ☏*03 21 87 10 34, www.basev3-mimoyecques.com.* The launch site for the formidable V3 Howitzer in WW II was built here, but ended prematurely when Allied forces bombed Mimoyecques in July 1944.

Coupole d'**Helfaut-Wizernes**★★

This gigantic rocket-launching pad, built in 1943, is one of the most imposing relics of World War II. The site has now been turned into a *Centre d'Histoire de la Guerre et des Fusées* (centre devoted to the history of war and rockets), which serves both as a memorial and an instructive venue.

A BIT OF HISTORY

A project out of proportion – Following the destruction in 1943 of the Éperlecques Bunker, Hitler decided to build a new one. The Todt organisation built a protective dome 72m/236ft in diameter and 5m/16ft thick, railway tunnels to convey the rockets, and miles of underground galleries to stock them.

Tallboy versus V2 – In spite of the heavy bombing which lasted from March to September 1944 and involved 5t Tallboy bombs, the dome was hardly damaged but the advancing Allied forces in July 1944 forced the Germans to abandon the launching pad before it was completed.

First rockets to reach the stratosphere – Adjusted in a top secret centre headed by Wernher von Braun in Peenemünde, on an island in the Baltic Sea, V2 rockets were built by the prisoners of the DoraNordhausen concentration camp who were made to work day and night. These formidable 14m/46ft-high weapons comprised 22 000 pieces; they could achieve a speed of 5 800kph/3 604mph and reach a target 300km/186mi away. They marked the beginning of man's venture into space.

Race to conquer space – At the end of the war, Von Braun joined the Americans and became one of the initiators of the Apollo space programme. This signalled the start of a race to conquer space between America and the Soviet Union.

Michelin Local Map: 301: G-3
Location: Situated in the Pas-de-Calais, 5 km from the town of Saint-Omer.
Timing: Allow 2–3 hours for your visit.

VISIT

Open Jul–Aug 10am–7pm; Sept–Jun 9am–6pm. Closed 22 Dec–4 Jan. 9€ (children 6€). 03 21 93 27 27. www.lacoupole.com.

The tour starts in a tunnel through which travelled all trains arriving from Germany and continues along underground galleries intended for the storage of rockets. You then take a lift up a 40m/131ft shaft which brings you beneath the huge dome weighing 55 000t. Two exhibitions, relying heavily on audio-visual techniques (documentaries lasting 7 to 20min including rare archive pictures; laser show) present German secret weapons (V1 flying bombs and V2 rockets) and the life of the local population in northern France from 1940 to 1944.

One of the most moving sequences of the tour is focused on the last letter of a young member of the Resistance which shows up on a reconstruction of the Mur des Fusillés (execution wall) of the Lille citadel. An area is devoted to rockets and the conquest of space from 1945 to 1969 with models of Titan, Soyouz, Saturn, Ariane and a 20min film entitled *From the Earth to the Moon*.

A working model shows the firing site as it should have been; next to it, visitors can see a V1 flying bomb and an authentic V2 rocket, 14m/46ft high weighing 12t.

On the way back, the itinerary takes in the large octagonal hall, which remained unfinished, where rockets were prepared for launching (they were loaded with liquid oxygen and explosives) before being conveyed upright through two tunnels leading to two outside launching pads.

Lille★★

Lille, the lively capital of French Flanders, today enjoys a role as a regional and European metropolis thanks to its location at the major crossroads of Europe. This convivial city has acquired a new lease on life, successfully embracing its high-tech identity while maintaining its Baroque style and cultural treasures.

A BIT OF HISTORY
Life in Lille

The typical Lille citizen is reliable and hardworking, but also a *bon vivant* who likes his food and appreciates a beer. Place du Général-de-Gaulle, the pedestrianised place Rihour and nearby streets, particularly rue de Béthune with its cinemas, are always lively.

Cultural Activity

Lille is now a major cultural centre following the establishment of a philharmonic orchestra, the opening of Opéra du Nord in Lille, the lyric workshop in Tourcoing, the Northern France Ballet Company and the institution of several theatre companies such as the Théâtre du Nord. Several cultural festivals take place here every year; the autumn festival includes concerts, fine arts, and theatre and dance performances.

Folklore

Folklore still plays an active part in the city, as it does in much of northern France; every district of Lille has its own feast day (*ducasse*). Lille's **giants, Phinaert** and **Lydéric**, are paraded through the streets on holidays. According to legend, in about AD 600 a highwayman called Phinaert lived in a château where Lille stands today. One day the highwayman attacked the Prince of Dijon and his wife as they were on their way to England; the prince was killed, but his wife was able to escape and hide her baby before being caught herself. The baby was taken in by a hermit who baptised him Lydéric and had him suckled by a doe. Once grown to manhood, Lydéric vowed to avenge the death of his parents. He challenged

> **Population:** 226 800 – Metropolitan area 1 000 900
>
> **Michelin Local Map:** 302: G-4
>
> **Info:** Palais Rihour, pl. Rihour, 59000 Lille. ℘0 891 562 004. www.lilletourism.com.
>
> **Location:** 140 miles north of Paris, via the A 1, or 70 miles west via the A 27 from Brussels
>
> **Parking:** Plenty of car parks in the centre of the city, but these fill up early. Try the parking areas around the TGV station.
>
> **Don't Miss:** A walk in the Bois de Boulogne and around the Citadelle; take time out to explore the Old Town
>
> **Timing:** To get a feel for Lille you will need a few days here. If you have limited time, just explore the Old Town.
>
> **Kids:** The zoo in the Bois de Boulogne

Phinaert to a fight and slew the highwayman, then married the sister of King Dagobert and was entrusted with protecting the Flemish forests which had belonged to Phinaert.

The town's new look

Successful efforts over several years to preserve and restore the lovely 17C and 18C buildings and monuments of the old district have turned Lille into an attractive artistic city; at the same time, much modernisation has taken place: the rebuilding of the district known as St-Sauveur and of the Forum; the creation of Villeneuve-d'Ascq and Euralille.

The "Dallas" of northern France

Owing to its location at the centre of a network of major routes and waterways leading to Paris, Brussels, Dunkirk and

Grand'Place

B. Kaufmann/ MICHELIN

Antwerp, Lille has always been industrially and commercially important. The town is more than ever the economic centre of northern France. Business facilities (conference centre), traditional industries (textiles, mechanics), computer and technology giants, food production companies and research laboratories all co-exist here with the universities.

It has the third largest river port in France, an international airport at Lesquin, and the modernistic Lille-Europe station built for high-speed trains and Eurostar service to London and Brussels.

The city boasts the world's most modern metro, the **VAL**, an entirely automatic system. One line links Lille to Roubaix-Tourcoing.

A Turbulent History

Lille has had a turbulent history having been sometimes Flemish, sometimes French, sometimes under Austrian or Spanish control. The city has faced 11 sieges and destruction many times.

The Counts of Flanders

The name "l'Isle" (pronounced Lille) first appeared in 1066, in the charter of a donation to the collegiate church (*collégiale St-Pierre*) by Baudoin V, Count of Flanders, who owned a château on one of the islands in the River Deule. The town developed around this château. Although a French vassal, Flanders

was linked, at least economically, with England and the Holy Roman Empire. Faced with Philip Augustus' claims on the northern regions, a coalition was formed which included the counts of Boulogne, Hainaut and Flanders, King John of England and the Holy Roman Emperor Otto IV. The **Battle of Bouvines**, the first great French victory, concluded this war on 27 July 1214 with the defeat of King John and Otto IV.

The dukes of Burgundy and the Spanish

The marriage of Marguerite of Flanders to Philip the Bold in 1369 made Flanders part of the duchy of Burgundy. **Philip the Good** (1419–67) had Rihour Palace built, where he made the "Pheasant Vow" in 1454 promising to deliver Constantinople from the Turks.

The marriage of Marie of Burgundy, daughter of Charles the Bold, to Maximilian of Austria in 1477 brought the duchy of Burgundy, including Flanders, under Hapsburg control; the duchy later became Spanish when Charles V of Spain became emperor.

After the Wars of Religion, gangs of peasants in revolt devastated the countryside and sacked the churches. Lille escaped the assault of the "Howlers" (*Hurlus*) thanks only to the inhabitants' energetic defence, led by the innkeeper **Jeanne Maillotte**.

Lille becomes French

Following his marriage to Maria-Theresa of Spain in 1663, Louis XIV laid claim to the Low Countries, taking advantage of the rights of his wife to a part of Spain's heritage. In 1667 he personally directed the siege of Lille and triumphantly entered the city after only nine days of resistance, after which Lille became capital of the Northern Provinces. The Sun King hastened to have a citadel built by Vauban and enlarged the town.

Lille under Siege

In **September 1792**, 35 000 Austrians laid siege to Lille which was defended by only a small garrison. Cannonballs rained down on the town and many buildings were destroyed; nevertheless, the courageous inhabitants held on and the Austrians eventually raised the siege.

In early **October 1914**, when six Bavarian regiments tried to breach the fortifications, Lille was very poorly defended. The town was obliged to submit after three days of bloody resistance in which 900 buildings were destroyed. Prince Ruprecht of Bavaria, receiving the surrender, refused the sword of Captain de Pardieu "in recognition of the heroism of the French troops."

In **May 1940**, seven Nazi divisions and Rommel's armoured tanks attacked Lille. The 40 000 French soldiers held the city for three days before surrendering with military honours on June 1st.

Traditional economy

During the Middle Ages Lille became famous for its clothmaking; later the high-warp weavers who had been forced out of Arras by Louis XIV came to establish their tapestry workshops here.

Lille devoted itself to cotton and linen milling in the 18C, whereas nearby Roubaix and Tourcoing specialised in wool. Large-scale industry came to Lille at the end of the 18C, creating an urban proletariat with its accompanying miseries: by 1846 the rate of infant mortality in the slums in St-Sauveur reached 75% and the cellars where workers laboured

achieved a notoriety which Victor Hugo evoked in tragic verse.

Another of Lille's specialities was the milling of linseed, rapeseed and poppyseed to produce oil. Last but not least, the town was famous for the production of lace and ceramics.

SIGHTS
Palais des Beaux-Arts★★★

 ♿ 🕐*Open Mon 2–6pm & Wed–Sun 10am–7pm.* ❖*5.50€.* ℮*03 20 06 78 00, www.pba-lille.fr.*

The neo-Classic art museum, opened in 1892, was designed by architects Bérard and Delmas. A narrow building 70m/228ft long and 6.5m/19.5ft wide was added to the rear in 1997. It contains the café and restaurant on the ground floor.

Between the two buildings is the garden. The middle section has been given a glass surface that lets light into the temporary exhibition halls below.

The vast entrance hall extending the whole length of the façade is lit by two large coloured-glass chandeliers by Gaetano Pesce. There is free access to the atrium where the bookshop, tearoom and café-restaurant are situated (*garden entrance in rue de Valmy*).

Basement

Archaeology – Works from the Mediterranean basin: Egypt, Cyprus, Rome, Greece (three-legged toilet vase known as Exaleiptron, ceramics with black figures).

Middle Ages and Renaissance – The chased-bronze Lille incense-burner (12C Mosan art) is displayed in the centre of the first room. Next to it are a few ivory objets d'art from abbeys in northern France such as the *Old Man of the Apocalypse* (12C from St-Omer).

The vaulted galleries contain rare examples of Romanesque sculpture, including three fragments of a limestone high-relief carving representing the Deposition (c 1170). Note, in the last room, the famous *Wax head of a maiden* resting on a terracotta base (18C).

Relief maps★ – The large hall contains the plans of 15 towns situated on the northern borders of France at the time of Louis XIV.

Ground floor

Ceramics – A superb collection of 18C faience from Lille, Nevers, Strasbourg, Delft and Rouen, as well as German and Walloon sandstone exhibits and 18C porcelain from China and Japan.

Sculpture – The collection gives an overview of 19C French sculpture with Frémiet (*The Knight Errant*), Houdon (bust of *Le Fèvre de Caumartin*), David d'Angers (original terracotta low-relief sculptures from the Gutenberg memorial on place Kléber in Strasbourg), Camille Claudel (*Giganti, Mme de Massary*), and Bourdelle (*Penelope*, c. 1909).

First floor

The art collections are presented by schools around the atrium.

16C–17C Flemish School – Hermessan's *Vanity* (the museum's latest important acquisition) represents the 16C. Several characteristic canvases by Jordaens are displayed, ranging in theme from the religious (*The Temptation of Mary Magdalene*) to the mythological (*The Abduction of Europa*) or the rustic (*The Huntsman*); his study of cows was later taken up by Van Gogh.

17C Dutch School – Dutch masterpieces by De Witte (*Nieuwe Kerk in Delft*) and Ruysdael (*The Wheat Field*) hang with still-life paintings by Van der Ast and Van Beyeren, Van Goyen's *The Skaters* and Pieter Codde's *Melancholy*.

17C French School – Works by Charles de la Fosse (*The Keys to Paradise Are Given to St Peter*), Le Sueur, Chardin, Philippe de Champaigne (*Nativity*), La Hyre (*Pastoral Landscape*) and Largillière (*Jean-Baptiste Forest*).

18C and 19C French School – Remarkable works by Boilly (1761–1845), born at La Bassée near Lille, adorn the walls: *Le Jeu du Pied de Bœuf, Marat's Triumph* and numerous portraits. Note the charming paintings by Louis Watteau, who adopted Lille as his permanent home (*View of Lille*) and the work by his son François (*Alexander's Battle*). Other great painters represented include David

The Letter or The Young People by Francisco de Goya, Palais des Beaux-Arts

©Palais des Beaux-Arts de Lille

(*Belisarius Begging for Alms*), Delacroix, Géricault, Courbet and Puvis de Chavannes.

Italian and Spanish Schools – Italy is represented by Liss' *Moses Saved from the Waters*, Tintoretto's *Portrait of a Senator* and a sketch of *Heaven* by Veronese.

The few Spanish paintings are of a rare quality: *Time or The Old Women* and *The Letter or The Young People*, two **works**★ by **Goya**, kind and cruel satirist of his period; and El Greco's *St Francis Praying*.

Impressionists – The end of the 19C is represented by works from the **Masson Bequest**. The pre-Impressionist paintings include canvases by Boudin (*The Port of Camaret*), Jongkind (*The Skaters*) and Lépine. Impressionism itself is embraced in works by Sisley (*Port Marly, Winter: Snow Effects*), Renoir (*Young Woman in a Black Hat*) and Monet (*The Disaster, The Houses of Parliament*). Paintings by Vuillard, Carrière, Lebourg and several Rodin sculptures complete the collection.

Modern Artists – Figurative and abstract works on show are by Léger (*Women With a Blue Vase*), Gromaire (*Landscape of the Coalmining Region*), Poliakoff (*Composition no 2*), Sonia Delaunay (*Colour Rhythm 1076*) and Picasso (*Portrait of Olga, 1923*).

Drawings – This is one of the largest collections in France (about 4 000 works) especially Italian drawings, shown on a rotating basis as temporary expositions.

OLD LILLE★★

2hr 30min

The real renewal of Lille's old district began in 1965, when a few architecture enthusiasts decided to do something to recover the beauty of the 17C and 18C façades, hidden under unsightly rough-rendering. The restorations progressed well and whole blocks of buildings changed completely in appearance. Luxury shops, interior decorators and antique dealers settled in the area which is today an attractive place to explore.

Lille style

The distinctiveness of the Lille style is due to the particular mix of bricks and carved stone. Façades decorated with quarry stones shaped into lozenges (place Louise-de-Bettignies) first appeared in the early 17C; then came the period of the Flemish Renaissance (Vieille Bourse, the Maison de Gilles de la Boé) where the wealth of ornamentation reached its limit. By the end of the 17C the French influence began to be felt in the decoration of the houses and in their arrangement in aligned rows. Ground floors consist of arcades in close-grained sandstone that prevents humidity reaching the upper floors. The brick above alternates with limestone carved into cherubs, cupids, cornucopias, sheaves of wheat etc.

Place Rihour

The main building on this square is the **Palais Rihour** (🕓*open Mon–Sat 9.30am–6.30pm, Sun & holidays 10am–noon, 2–5pm; ⊜no charge; ℘0891 562 004; www.lilletourism.com)* which now houses the tourist office. This Gothic palace was built between 1454 and 1473 by Philip the Good, Duke of Burgundy. Outside are beautiful mullioned windows and the graceful octagonal brick turret. The groundfloor guard-room has tall, pointed arches. The chapel, or Conclave Room, is upstairs; the chapel for the Duke's private worship is reached by an elegant stone staircase.

Place du Général-de-Gaulle★

Reach the Place du Général-de-Gaulle via a busy pedestrian district lined with outdoor cafés. On the left, note the 17C houses built in a style that is a combination of Flemish and French. This form of architecture became commonplace in Lille after the town was taken over by Louis XIV. The Grand' Place or main square has always been the busy centre of Lille, and served as marketplace as early as the Middle Ages. The finest building in the square is the Vieille Bourse. *La Voix du Nord*, a daily newspaper, has its offices in the building (1936) with a stepped pediment beside the **Grand' Garde** (1717), which once housed the king's guard.

The **Colonne de la Déesse** (1845) rises in the middle of the square, a symbol of the city's heroic resistance during the siege of 1792.

Vieille Bourse★★

The exchange was built in 1653 by Julien Destrée, at the request of the tradesmen of Lille who wanted an exchange to rival those of the great cities in the Low Countries. It consists of 24 mansard-roofed houses around a courtyard that today houses used bookshops.

The profusion of decoration on the façade is due to the fact that Destrée was a wood sculptor. The caryatids and telamones, the garlands and masks above the outer windows, and the fruit and flowers carved on the inner court are all reminiscent of a Flemish chest. Bronze busts, and medallions and tablets honouring academics and sciences, can be seen under the arcades.

Place du Théâtre

The square is dominated by the imposing Nouvelle Bourse which houses the Chamber of Commerce and its neo-Flemish bell tower. Next to it stands the Louis XVI Opera.

Opposite the Nouvelle Bourse stands the "**Rang de Beauregard**," comprising houses adorned with pilasters sur-

Façade. Vieille Bourse

Y. Tierny / MICHELIN

mounted by elegant cartouches. The terrace, built in 1687, is the most characteristic and most interesting example of late-17C architecture in Lille.

Rue de la Bourse

The street is lined with 18C house-fronts decorated with cherubs and masks.

Rue de la Grande-Chaussée

The old arcaded sandstone houses have been renovated and now contain shops selling luxury goods. Some of the wrought-iron balconies and the upper part of the windows are very intricately worked. Note the first house on the right and nos 9, 23 (ship on the keystone of the window) and 29.

Rue des Chats-Bossus

The street acquired its curious name ("Street of the Humpback Cats") from an old tanner's sign. **L'Huîtrière**, a famous seafood restaurant, has a typical Art-Deco front dating from 1928.

Place Louise-de-Bettignies

The square bears the name of a First World War heroine. The **Demeure de Gilles de la Boé★**, at no 29 on a corner, was built in about 1636 and is a superb example of Flemish Baroque.

The abundant ornamentation includes cornices and prominent pediments. In the past this building stood on the edge of the Basse-Deûle port, in the days when there was a great deal of river traffic.

Rue de la Monnaie★

The Mint once stood in this street where the restored houses now attract antique dealers and interior decorators. On the left there is a row of 18C houses (note the apothecary's shop sign of a mortar and distilling equipment at no 3). The houses at nos 5 and 9 are decorated with dolphins, wheat-sheaves, palms etc.

At no 10 a statue of Notre-Dame-de-la-Treille adorns the front and at nos 12 and 14 the crow-stepped gable has been rebuilt. Neighbouring houses date from the first third of the 17C and flank the rusticated door (1649) of the Hospice Comtesse (**&** *see Additional Sights*).

◗ *Take the passageway opposite the Hospice Comtesse.*

AN OYSTER-LOVER'S PARADISE

◷◷ **À L'Huîtrière** – *3 rue des Chats-Bossus. ℘03 20 55 43 41. www.huitriere.fr. Closed 22 July–25 Aug, Sun evening and public holidays.* A first-rate establishment for fish and seafood lovers which has been duly acknowledged by the profession. The fish-monger's shop with its superb ceramic frescoes adjoins the dining room, decorated with light oak panelling, lamps and wall lights with pendants. The tables are ornamented with different varieties of fish and shellfish.

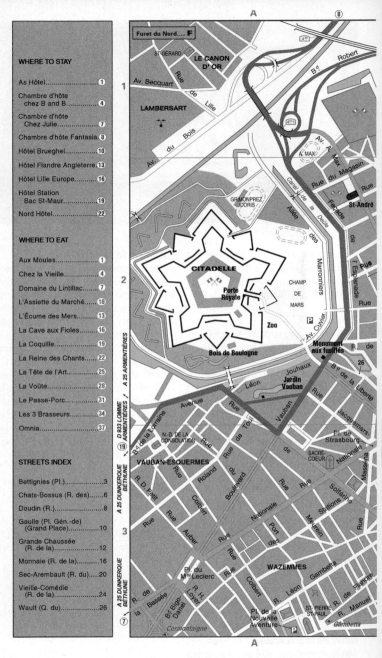

WHERE TO STAY

As Hôtel.......................... ①

Chambre d'hôte
chez B and B.............. ④

Chambre d'hôte
Chez Julie.................. ⑦

Chambre d'hôte Fantasia. ⑧

Hôtel Brueghel............... ⑩

Hôtel Flandre Angleterre. ⑬

Hôtel Lille Europe........... ⑯

Hôtel Station
Bac St-Maur............... ⑲

Nord Hôtel.................... ㉒

WHERE TO EAT

Aux Moules.................. ①

Chez la Vieille............... ④

Domaine du Lintillac....... ⑦

L'Assiette du Marché...... ⑩

L'Écume des Mers.......... ⑬

La Cave aux Fioles......... ⑯

La Coquille................. ⑲

La Reine des Chants...... ㉒

La Tête de l'Art............. ㉕

La Voûte..................... ㉘

Le Passe-Porc............... ㉛

Les 3 Brasseurs............. ㉞

Omnia........................ ㊲

STREETS INDEX

Bettignies (Pl.)................. 3

Chats-Bossus (R. des)....... 6

Doudin (R.)...................... 8

Gaulle (Pl. Gén.-de)
(Grand Place)............. 10

Grande Chaussée
(R. de la).................... 12

Monnaie (R. de la)........... 16

Sec-Arembault (R. du)..... 20

Vieille-Comédie
(R. de la).................... 24

Wault (Q. du)................. 26

On the left is the impressive **Cathédrale Notre-Dame-de-la-Treille**, a neo-Gothic construction that was never completed.

▶ *Return to rue de la Monnaie and walk straight ahead along rue de la Collégiale, then turn left onto rue Négrier and rue Royale.*

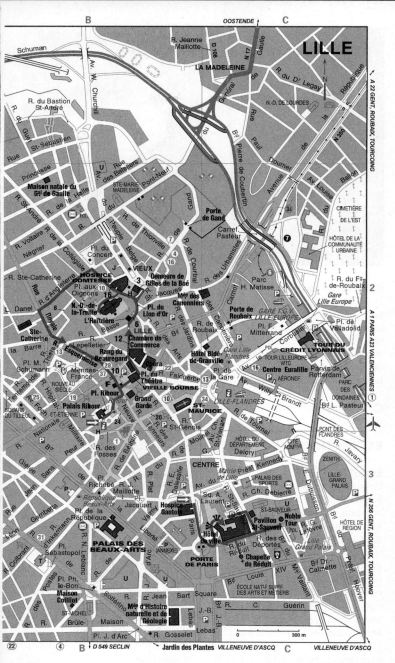

Rue Royale

This was the main route through the elegant district that was built during the 18C between the citadel and the old town. **Église Ste-Catherine**, with its austere 15C tower, stands on the left at the beginning of the street.

Fine French-style mansions line the street: note, at no 68, the former Hôtel de l'Intendance, built in 1787 by Lequeux, a local architect.

Houses on Place Louise-de-Bettignies

©Daniel Leppens/Bigstockphoto.com

Rue Esquermoise

The street is lined with 17C and 18C houses. At nos 6 and 4 cherubs are shown embracing or turning their backs on each other depending on whether or not they belong to the same house. Opposite is a superb restored house that belonged to a furrier (Gailliaerde).

▶ *Return to place Rihour via the Grand'Place.*

EAST OF THE TOWN CENTRE

Euralille

Covering an area of almost 70ha/173 acres beyond Lille city centre is a whole new urban district designed by Dutch town planner Rem Koolhaas. Since May 1993, Lille's railway station, which was renamed **Lille-Flandres**, has catered to most of the high-speed trains from Paris. Linked by a viaduct with four arches, the new station, **Lille-Europe**, easily recognisable by its huge glass frontage, was built as part of the Paris-London and London-Brussels routes using the Channel Tunnel and for the high-speed train services between Lille and Lyon, Bordeaux, Nice, Montpellier etc. Two towers span the new stations, the **Tour Lille-Europe WTC** designed by architect Claude Vasconi and the L-shaped **Tour du Crédit Lyonnais★** designed by Christian de Portzampac.

The **Centre Euralille** was designed by the acclaimed French architect Jean Nouvel. Its spacious walkways and two floors contain more than 130 shops, a hypermarket, restaurants and a cultural centre called the Espace Croisé. It also has a theatre, private apartments, and a business school.

Porte de Roubaix

This massive gate from the 1621 Spanish fortifications is composed of a sandstone base surmounted by a dripstone and a layer in brick. It was opened in 1875 to allow room for tramways and the moats have been turned into gardens. There is a similar gate 600m/656yd to the north, the **Porte de Gand**, reached via rue des Canonniers and rue de Courtrai.

QUARTIER ST-SAUVEUR
Allow 1hr30min

This former working-class district was known for the misery of its slums which inspired Emile Desrousseaux, author of the famous French lullaby *Le P'tit Quinquin (statue in rue Nationale on the corner of avenue Foch).*
The area has today been completely remodelled into a business centre around the town hall. Relics of the past remain dotted among the modern buildings.

Porte de Paris★

This gate, built from 1685 to 1692 by Simon Vollant in honour of Louis XIV, is the only example of a town gate which also served as a triumphal arch; it was formerly part of the ramparts. On the outward side, it appears as an arch decorated with the arms of Lille (a lily) and of France (three lilies). Victory stands at the top, honoured by Fames, about to crown Louis XIV represented in a medallion. From the inner side the gate has the appearance of a lodge.

Hôtel de Ville

The town hall was built from 1924 to 1927 and is overlooked by a tall belfry (104m/341ft). The two Lille giants, Lydéric and Phinaert are sculpted at its base.

Pavillon St-Sauveur

This is the wing of an 18C cloister, preserved when a hospice was demolished in 1959. The brick and stone arches are surmounted by clerestory windows decorated with flowered medallions.

Noble Tour

This keep with its truncated appearance is the only relic of the 15C fortifications; it has become a Resistance memorial. There is a beautiful work by the sculptor Bizette-Lindet.

ADDITIONAL SIGHTS
Hospice Comtesse★

🕐Open Mon 2–6pm, Wed – Sun 10am–12.30pm & 2–6pm. ⊕2.50€ (no charge first Sun in the month).
𝒫03 28 36 84 00.

The hospital was built in 1237 by Jeanne de Constantinople, Countess of Flanders, to ask for divine intervention on behalf of her husband Ferrand de Portugal, taken prisoner at Bouvines (see above). It was destroyed by fire in 1468 but was rebuilt and enlarged in the 17C and 18C. It became a hospice during the Revolution, then an orphanage. It changed again in 1939 and is today a museum of history and ethnography which also holds concerts and exhibitions.

The monumental 17C main entrance is built from rusticated sandstone.

Hospital ward – A long, sober building, rebuilt after 1470 on the old 13C foundations flanks the main courtyard. Inside, the immense proportions of the interior and its panelled timber **vault★★** in the shape of an upturned boat are striking. The ward contains two beautiful tapestries, woven in Lille in 1704. One represents Baudouin of Flanders with his wife and two daughters; the other portrays Jeanne, the hospital's founder, flanked by her first and second husbands. The **chapel**, which extends the length of the interior, was enlarged and isolated by a rood screen after the fire of 1649. The old 15C window and traces of mural paintings have been revealed on the right wall. The vault is decorated with the heraldic arms of the hospital's benefactors.

Museum – In the right wing. Furniture and artworks evoking the atmosphere of a 17C religious establishment; the kitchen features blue and white tiles from Holland and Lille; the Baroque overmantel in the dining room frames a 16C Nativity; the sombre Louis XIV panels of the parlour are decorated with a series of 17C votive offerings in the form of portraits of local children. The prayer room is lined with Louis XV wood panelling.

The former dormitory on the first floor has carved ceiling beams. It contains 17C Flemish and Dutch paintings and a superb 16C wooden Crucifixion from Picardy. The cross-bar and main section of the Cross are decorated with medallions depicting the Evangelists. Two rooms flanking the dormitory are filled with exhibits relating to regional history: architectural features, objets d'art, and paintings by Louis and François Watteau representing Lille in the 18C.

Maison Natale du Général de Gaulle

9 rue Princesse. ♿🕐Open Wed–Sat, 10am–1pm and 2–6pm & Sun 1.30–5.30pm (last admission 1hr before closing). ⊕6€. 𝒫03 28 38 12 05. www.maison-natale-degaulle.org.

Charles de Gaulle was born on 22 November 1890 in this whitewashed brick house in Lille, where his grandfather had a lace works. The old workshop and the house have been turned into a small museum exhibiting photographs and memorabilia. On display are De Gaulle's christening robe and a replica of the car in which the General and his wife were travelling on the day of the attempt on their lives in Le Petit-Clamart.

Citadelle★ (Citadel)

The Citadelle is permanently occupied by the military; ⬤ *guided visits possible by arrangement, call for information.* ℰ0 891 562 004.

This citadel is the largest and best preserved in France. It was Louis XIV's first project after the conquest of Lille and is a fine example of Vauban's genius; it is still occupied by the army today. It took three years to build (1667–70) using 2 000 men. The result was this stone-faced brick construction comprising five bastions and five demilune fortifications, which protect the moats formerly fed by the River Deûle. These defences used to enclose a real town.

The **porte Royale**, which bears a Latin inscription praising Louis XIV, gives onto a vast pentagonal parade ground surrounded by buildings by Simon Vollant: the Classical chapel, the officer's quarters and a superb restored arsenal. These stone and brick buildings are representative of the French-Lille style which developed during this period. The citadel could be completely self-sufficient as it had its own wells, bakery, brewery, tailors, cobblers etc.

In the **Bois de Boulogne** there is a small **zoo** (🕐*open daily Mar–Nov 9am–6pm (weekends 7pm),* ⬤*free entry* ℰ*03 28 52 07 00)* near the Champ de Mars, as well as a tropical house and a playground. The **jardin Vauban** on the Deûle Canal bank is typical of mid-19C country gardens, with its clumps of trees, winding paths, flower beds and ponds. A statue of the Lille poet Albert Samain (1859–1906) stands within it.

During the last two World Wars many French patriots were executed by firing squad in the outer moats. The **Monument aux Fusillés** by Félix Desruelle

stands in neighbouring square Daubenton; it dates from 1915 and commemorates the Lille citizens who were shot.

Musée des Canonniers

🕐*Open Mon–Sat 2–5pm.* 🕐*Closed public holidays, Jan to mid-Feb and the first two weeks in Aug.* ⬤6€. ℰ03 20 55 58 90. www.museedes canonniers.org.

Housed in the former Hôtel des Canonniers, once a convent. In 1804 the building was given by Napoleon to the Sainte-Barbe Brotherhood, a corporation of gunners founded in 1483. The military museum illustrates the history of the various sieges Lille had to withstand. Some 3 000 objects are on display: rifles from 1777 to 1945, swords, etc.

Musée d'Histoire Naturelle et de Géologie

🕐*Open Mon & Wed–Fri 9am–noon & 2–5pm, Sun and public holidays 10am–1pm & 2–6pm.* ⬤3€. *No charge 1st Sun of the month.* ℰ03 28 55 30 80.

The Natural History and Geology Museum was set up in 1822. Its collections were extended at the beginning of the 20C by two local geologists. Facing visitors as they enter the main hall are two impressive whale skeletons, the remains of creatures washed up on the coast.

The **zoology** collection on the left includes stuffed mammals and birds, reptiles, Batrachia, molluscs, fish, and insects. Dioramas are used to show French fauna in its natural habitat: huge boars, alert deer, beavers etc. The magnificent ornithological collection boasts more than 5 000 birds, including examples of species that are now extinct.

The section on the right deals with **geology**. Fossils and rocks illustrate the history of Northern Europe from 600 million years BC to the Gallo-Roman period. Numerous plant fossils found in old mine workings are the remains of the dense forest that covered the region 300 million years ago. The work of miners is illustrated by a reconstruction of a coal seam, with its narrow gallery and heavy cart..

ADDRESSES

🏨 STAY

B & B (Bed and Breakfast) –
78 Rue Caumartin. ℰ*03 20 13 76 57. Email: chezbandb@numericable.fr.* ⌑ *3 rooms.*
"B & B" as in Bed and Breakfast, as well as in Béatrice and Bernard, the current owners of this house built during the reign of Napoléon III. The comfortable rooms have been nicely refurbished; two of them have sloping ceilings. Cosy sitting room, breakfast room looking out onto the garden.

Station Bac St-Maur – *77 Rue de la Gare, Bac St-Maur, 62840 Sailly-sur-la-Lys, 7km/4.2mi SW of Armentières.* ℰ*03 21 02 68 20. www.stationbacsaintmaur. com. Closed Nov–Mar. 7 rooms.* ⌑*6.50€.*
Continue your travels while staying put by taking a room in this old train station converted into a hotel-restaurant. Fans of railway's golden years will enjoy lodging in one of the six compartments of this Orient-Express wagon dating from the 1930s.

Chez Julie – *8 Rue de Radinghem, 59134 Beaucamps-Ligny, 12km/7.2mi W of Lille. Take A 25, exit no 7, then D 62, Rte du Radinghem.* ℰ*03 20 50 33 82. www.chezjulie.fr.* ⌑ *3 rooms.* One quickly feels at home in this nice red-brick smallholding on the edge of a village near Lille. The pastel-toned bedrooms are well-maintained; a piano, a wood-burning stove and traditional Flemish games round out the breakfast room.

Hôtel Lille Europe – *Ave Le Corbusier, Euralille.* ℰ*03 28 36 76 76. www.hotel-lille-europe.com. 97 rooms.* ⌑ *8.50€.* This modern hotel between two stations in the centre of Euralille has soundproofed rooms and panoramic breakfast room.

Nord Hôtel – *48 Rue du Faubourg d'Arras.* ℰ*03 20 53 53 40. www.nord-hotel.com. 80 rooms.* ⌑*7.50€.*
Conveniently located near the Porte d'Arras metro station and easily accessible from the highway. Modern and spacious rooms.

Hôtel Flandre Angleterre – *13 Place de la Gare, 59000 Armentières.* ℰ*03 20 06 04 12. www.hotel-flandre angleterre-lille.com. 44 rooms.* ⌑ *8€.*

Situated opposite the train station and near the pedestrian streets, this family-run hotel presents modern rooms that are comfortable and cosy. Recommended for location and affordability.

As Hôtel – *98 Rue Louis-Braille, 59790 Ronchin, 3km/1.8mi SE of Lille.* ℰ*03 20 53 05 05. www.ashotel.com. 65 rooms.* ⌑ *8€ Restaurant* ⌑⌑*.*
This contemporary hotel offers functional and comfortable rooms, and a pleasant dining room in shades of yellow and black. A convenient stopover just off the A1 motorway.

Hôtel Brueghel – *5 Parvis St-Maurice, 59000 Armentières.* ℰ*03 20 06 06 69. www.hotel-brueghel.com. 60 rooms.* ⌑ *8.50€.* This Flemish-style house is conveniently located in the pedestrian part of town near the train station. The rooms have old-fashioned charm and modern bathrooms. The lift, the woodwork and the knick-knacks give the place a nostalgic appeal.

Fantasia (Bed and Breakfast) –
At the Port, 59118 Wambrechies. ℰ*06 16 44 09 82. www.peniche-fantasia.fr.* ⌑ *3 rooms.* Rooms on this charming old fashioned "peniche" boat moored at the port are wood pannelled and air conditioned.

🍴 EAT

Omnia – *9 Rue Esquermoise.* ℰ*03 20 57 55 66. http://omnia-restaurant.com.* Successively a cabaret, a brothel, a movie theatre, and a microbrewery, this Baroque-Roccoco bar ad restaurant is a popular establishment with bustling waiters and a festive atmosphere. Traditional fare plus a few regional specialities.

La Voûte – *4 Rue des Débris-Saint-Étienne.* ℰ*03 20 42 12 16. www.lapetite voute.com. Closed Sun, Mon evening.*
A friendly establishment specialising in homemade local dishes. A convivial atmosphere, checkered tablecloths on tables pushed closely together.

La Reine des Chants – *10 Rue Faidherbe.* ℰ*03 20 55 13 74.* A pretty yellow and blue restaurant in the centre of town specializing in dishes featuring the hearty potato in all its forms.

Chez la Vieille – *60 Rue de Gand.* *03 28 36 40 06. Closed 2 weeks in Aug Sun & Mon.* Go back in time in this traditional Flemish estimanet, favoured by locals for its authentic local cuisine and festive atmosphere.

Le Passe-Porc – *155 Rue de Solférino, 59000 Armentières. 03 20 42 83 93. Closed 15 Jul to 15 Aug and Sun. Reserv. required.* . A bistro after our own hearts. The tiled floor, wall seats and enamelled plaques on the walls act as the backdrop for a remarkable collection of pigs. The hearty ambience and plentiful fare are in perfect harmony with the amusing surroundings.

Aux Moules – *34 Rue de Béthune, 59000 Armentières 03 20 57 12 46.* A multitude of mussels (moules) and a few other Flemish specialities await customers in this 1930s style brasserie located in a lively pedestrian street. A must for bona fide shellfish fans and friends.

La Coquille – *60 Rue Saint-Étienne. 03 20 54 29 82. Closed Sun.* Exposed stone walls, beamed ceilings and tightly-packed wooden tables make for a country-style atmosphere in this low-key restaurant specialising in the fresh seasonal products.

Domaine de Lintillac – *43 Rue de Gand. 03 20 06 53 51. Closed 2 wks in Aug, Sun–Mon.* The red facade of the building will lead you directly to this rustic restaurant in Old Lille. Wicker baskets hang from the beams and the walls are lined with pots of preserves from southwest France. The plentiful cuisine of the Périgord region is dished up here.

La Tête de l'Art – *10 Rue de l'Arc, 59000 Armentières. 03 20 54 68 89. www.latetedelart-lille.com. Closed Mon evening, Tue evening, and last Sun of month. Reserv. essential.* A charming, lively restaurant is hidden behind the pink facade of this manor built in 1890. Follow the hallway to discover the inviting dining room where denizens of Lille gather for traditional meals. A good selection of wines at reasonable prices.

Restaurant La Cave aux Fioles – *39 Rue de Gand, 59000 Armentières. 03 20 55 18 43. www.lacaveauxfioles.com. Closed Sat lunch, Sun and public holidays. Reserv. required evenings.* Don't be put off by the gloomy passageway that leads to this restaurant housed in two 17C and 18C residences – the interior is unexpectedly warm and pleasant: brick, wood, beams and paintings by area artists. Convivial ambience; bistro cuisine.

L'Assiette du Marché – *61 Rue de la Monnaie. 03 20 06 83 61. www.assiette dumarche.com. Closed 3 weeks in Aug, & Sun.* Contemporary decor and a large skylight over the inner courtyard compliments the 18C architecture of this former treasury mint. Seasonal dishes.

L'Ecume des Mers – *10 Rue Pas. 03 20 54 95 40. www.ecume-des-mers.com. Closed Sun lunch.* Not far from the Grand' Place, this elegant restaurant specialises in seafood and seasonal game. Striking decor and a cosy mezzanine.

ON THE TOWN

L'Échiquier (*Bar of the Alliance Hotel*), *17 quai de Wault, 59000 Armentières. 03 20 30 62 62. www.alliance-lille. com. Mon–Sat 10am–1am, Sun and public holidays 10.30am–11pm. No musical events Jul–Aug.* This bar, installed in the majestic 17C setting of a former Minim convent, is attached to the Alliance Hotel. A harpist performs Mon–Thu 7.30pm–9.30pm, followed by a pianist Mon–Thu 10pm–11.30pm, Fri and Sat 7.30pm–11.30pm, Sun 4pm–7pm. Rich selection of champagne and cocktails.

Les 3 Brasseurs – *22 Place de la Gare (Opposite the Lille-Flandres train station), 59000 Armentières. 03 20 06 46 29. www.les3brasseurs.com. Daily 11am–12.30am. Closed Aug.* The pungent scent of hops greets visitors to this brasserie, a veritable Lille institution. Sample one or all of the four kinds on beer on draught drawn directly from the tuns behind the counter. Flammekueches, sauerkraut and regional fare are on hand for nibblers and the ravenous alike.

SHOWTIME

Useful tip: The Office de Tourisme publishes a weekly journal, *Sortir*, listing all of the city's current events, concerts and art exhibitions.

Théâtre Le Grand Bleu – *36 Ave Max-Dormoy. 03 20 09 88 44. www.legrandbleu.com. Ticket office*

9am–noon, 2pm–6pm. Closed Aug.
This performance hall caters to a young
audience. Some of its events appeal to
children as young as five years old, others
are designed for teens. Dance, circus,
theatre, storytelling, hip-hop, etc.

Orchestre National de Lille – *30 Place
Mendès-France, 59000 Armentières. ℰ03
20 12 82 40, www.onlille.com. Mon–Fri
9am–12.45pm, 2pm–6pm. Closed Aug.
Tickets from 10€.* Since 1976, The
Orchestre National de Lille gives an
average of 120 concerts per season.
Performances are held in the Lille area,
the Nord-Pas-de-Calais region and
abroad (30 countries altogether). The
varied repertoire features performances
for young audiences, original pieces,
established musicians and fresh talent

**Théâtre de Marionnettes du Jardin
Vauban** – *Rue Léon-Jouhaux, Chalet
des Chèvres in the Jardin Vauban, 59000
Armentières. ℰ03 20 42 09 95. Open
Easter–Oct. Tickets 4.50€.* An outdoors
puppet show of the Guignol tradition
starring characters of local repute, such
as Jacques de Lille and Jean-Jean La Plume.

Théâtre Mariska – *2 Place de la Gare,
59830 Cysoing, 15km/9mi SE of Lille via
D 955. ℰ03 20 79 47 03. www.mariska.fr.
8.30am–noon and 1.30–5.30pm. Closed
Aug. Tickets 5€.* Created in 1970, this
marionette puppet theatre is housed
in a typical Flemish residence. Impressive
collection of 120 puppets.

👫 SPORT AND LEISURE

Les Ballons Migrateurs – *3 Rue Boileux.
ℰ06 16 93 91 07. www.vol-en-ballon.com.*
Hot-air balloon flights at dawn or sunset
from Bondues or le Mont des Cats
(from €190).

Ch'ti vélo – *10 Ave Willy-Brandt. ℰ03
28 53 07 49. Daily 7.30am–7.30pm (Sat,
Sun and public holidays, 9am–7.30pm.
Reservations required.* Cycle hire.

🛍 SHOPPING

Le Furet du Nord – *15 Place du Gén.-
De-Gaulle. ℰ03 20 78 43 43. www.furet.
com. Mon–Sat 9.30am–7.30pm.* This
bookshop, founded in 1936, has over
7,000sq m and 9 different levels: a
bibliophile's paradise. Stairs, footbridges
and a number of passage-ways take you
to your chosen destination: books, games,
music, videos, comic books, stationery or
the ticket agency.

Leroux SAS – *86 Rue François-Herbo
(south-eastern suburb), 59310 Orchies.
ℰ03 20 64 48 00. www.leroux.fr. Write to
make a reservation.* A visit to this factory
teaches all about chicory – cultivated
locally – and demonstrates how it is
transformed into powder, liquid or
special, flavoured products.

Marché de Wazemmes – *59000
Armentières. ℰ08 90 39 20 04.* Tue,
Thu and especially Sun mornings, the
Wazemmes market takes over the Place
de la Nouvelle-Aventure. Food stands
alternate with second-hand bric-a-brac
in a merry market.

Rue Basse – *59000 Armentières.* This is
Lille's main street for antique dealers;
you will also find other unusual shops
here, selling furniture, decorative
objects, gifts and handcrafted jewellery.

Rue de Gand – Paved, animated and
highly colourful, La Rue de Gand is well
worth a visit. Butcher shops, taverns,
bars and especially restaurants line the
pavements.

♿ VISITS AND TOURS

Tourist packages – The Office de
Tourisme, *ℰ0 890 392 004*, offers a
variety of package deals (discovery,
Christmas market, culture, Lille flea
market, cabaret) that may include one
or several nights in a hotel, a City Tour,
museum admission or a show, etc.

Tour of Lille – A tour of Lille by mini-
bus (1hr) – *Dep. hourly from 10am to 5pm
(except 1pm); ♿ 10€ (children under
18 8€).* Rendez-vous at Palais Rihour.
Headset commentary in eight languages.
Schedule sometimes varies: enquire at
the Office de Tourisme, *ℰ03 20 21 94 21.*

♿ TRANSPORTATION

Lille Métropole City Pass –
This inclusive ticket gives you access
to Lille's public transport network
(Transpole) plus 25 interesting sites
and tourist attractions in Lille, Roubaix,
Tourcoing, Villeneuve-d'Ascq and
Wattrelos. The passes are valid 1 day
(18€), 2 days (30€) or 3 days (45€).
Information and sales in the Offices de
Tourisme of the cities cited, through
the Comité Départemental du Tourisme
du Nord and via *ℰ0 820 42 40 40,
www.lilletourism.com.*

Montreuil-sur-Mer★

Montreuil occupies a picturesque site★ on the edge of the plateau overlooking the Canche Valley. This peaceful town preserves a slightly nostalgic charm in its old streets lined with 17C and 18C houses, its citadel and shaded ramparts commanding vast horizons. Montreuil's proximity to the coast and particularly to Le Touquet attracts numerous tourists in summer.

A BIT OF HISTORY
Royal patronage

Montreuil developed around two buildings: the monastery founded in the 7C by the Bishop of Amiens, and the fortress built around 900 by the Count of Ponthieu.

In 1537 Emperor Charles V's troops forcibly seized the town, almost completely destroying it in the process. The ramparts were rebuilt by the engineers of François I, Henri IV and Louis XIII. In 1804, at the time of the Boulogne Camp, Napoleon stayed in Montreuil, and in 1916 British commander Douglas Haig made it his headquarters.

SIGHTS
Citadelle★

◷Open Mar–Oct Wed–Mon 10am–noon, 2–6pm. ◷Closed Dec–Feb. ◉3€. ℘03 21 06 10 83.

Montreuil citadel was built in the second half of the 16C, but contains elements of an 11C and 13C structure. It was completely remodelled in the 17C.

On the side facing the town, a demilunes protects the entrance.

Having crossed this, the tour encompasses the two 13C round towers which flank the royal château; Tour Berthe (14C), the tower that served as the entrance to the town until 1594 (it houses the emblems of the lords killed at Agincourt in 1415); the sentry walk, which offers attractive **views**★★ over the Canche Valley and Le Touquet marked

▶ **Population:** 2 428
♿ **Michelin Local Map:** 301: D-5
🛈 Info: 21 r. Carnot, 62170 Montreuil, ℘03 21 06 04 27. www.tourisme-montreuillois.com.
◑ **Location:** Just 11 miles inland from Le Touquet via the N 39, and 30 miles north of Abbeville along the N1.
🅿 **Parking:** Limited roadside parking.
🕭 **Don't Miss:** A tour of the ramparts, and the cobbled Rue Clape-en-Bas.
◷ **Timing:** You can easily spend a relaxed half day exploring the citadelle and the ramparts.
♿ **Also See:** The Gardens of Valloires, Le Touquet-Paris-Plage.

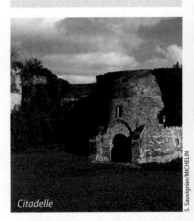

Citadelle

S. Sauvignier/MICHELIN

by its lighthouse; and the pillboxes built in 1840 and the 18C chapel.

Remparts★ (Ramparts)

♿The red-brick and white-stone walls with bastions date largely from the 16C-17C, though some elements of the 13C walls have remained on the west front.

◑ *Leave the citadel by the bridge and turn right onto the path that runs alongside the walls; continue for 300m/330yd towards the Porte de France gate.*

From the sentry walk there is a lovely perspective of the 16C curtain walls with their series of 13C towers.

🚶 It is possible to walk right round the ramparts (*1hr*) along a shaded path offering views over the countryside.

ADDRESSES

🛏 STAY

🛏 **L'Écu de France** – *5 porte de France. ℘03 21 06 01 89. Closed Wed–Thu in winter. 8 rooms. ⬦ 6€ Restaurant* 🍴🍴.
This inviting house with a spotless facade offers modern bedrooms in shades of red and yellow. At mealtime, generous portions of Flemish cooking are served in a medieval decor (swords hang on the walls!).

🍴🍴 **Manoir Francis** – *1 Rue de l'Église, 62170 Marles-sur-Canche, 5.5km/3.3mi SE of Montreuil via D 113. ℘03 21 81 38 80. www.manoirfrancis.com. 🛏 3 rooms.*
Guests must go through an enormous covered porch, then cross the yard abounding in poultry to reach this handsome 17C seigniorial farmhouse. Spacious bedrooms furnished with period pieces and a private sitting room. Magnificent breakfast room.

🍴🍴 **La Commanderie (Bed and Breakfast)** – *Allée des Templiers, 62990 Loison-sur-Créquoise. ℘03 21 86 49 87. www.lacommanderie.com. 🛏 Reserv. recommended in winter. 3 rooms. ⬦5€* A long alleyway leads to this splendid 12C residence, formerly belonging to knights of the Templar. The stylishly decorated rooms have been given girls' names. Beautiful antiques found throughout, and there is a pleasant park bordered by a river.

🍴🍴🍴 **Haute Chambre (Bed and Breakfast)** – *124 Route d'Hucqueliers, le Ménage hamlet, 62170 Beussent, 10km/6mi N of Montreuil via N 1 then D 127. ℘03 21 90 91 92. Closed 1–15 Sept and 15 Dec–15 Jan. 🛏 5 rooms.* If the Canche Valley is a tiara, the Haute Chambre is its brightest jewel. Rather difficult to find, this 1858 manor has been marvellously restored by the owners.

THE TOWN
Rue du Clape-en-Bas

This charming cobbled street is lined with low, whitewashed houses with mossy tiled roofs, typical of dwellings in the Canche Valley. Craftsmen work here during the season (weavers, potters).

Whether in the plush bedrooms or the idyllic park, you'll live the aristocratic life at your own rhythm here.

🍴 EAT

🍴 **L'Auberge d'Inxent** – *62170 Inxent, 9km/5.4mi N of Montreuil via D 127. ℘03 21 90 71 19. Closed mid-Jun–mid-Jul, mid-Dec–mid-Jan, Tue–Wed off-season & Mon Jul–Aug.* Located in the heart of the village, this pretty blue house dating from 1765 has always been an inn. Tasty cuisine of the Artois region. The garden is well worth a visit.

🍴🍴🍴 **Auberge La Grenouillère** – *62170 Madelaine-sous-Montreuil, 2.5km/ 1.5mi W of Montreuil via D 139 and secondary road. ℘03 21 06 07 22. Closed 20 Dec–3 Feb, 5–10 Sept, Wed except Jul– Aug & Tue.* In this charming country inn, the guest of honour is unquestionably the frog, whose presence can be seen on walls, on paintings, and, for enthusiasts, on the dinner plate. In summer the delectable fare is served outdoors. A few guest rooms.

🛒 SHOPPING

M. et Mme Leviel – *Fond des Communes, 62170 Montcravel. Closed Sun. ℘03 21 06 21 73.* Sales of dairy products, their speciality is *apérichèvres*, goat cheese hors-d'œuvres.

SHOWTIME

Son et lumière – 'Sound and Light' show – *'Les Misérables'*, a show based on Victor Hugo's *chef-d'œuvre*. Late July-early Aug, evenings. *Information at Tourism Office.*

TOURS

Visit of in the city – The Office de Tourisme offers guided tours. Jun–Sept, weekends. *7€. ℘03 21 06 04 27.*

Colline de
Notre Dame-De-Lorette★

In a dramatically bleak setting, under an often grey sky, the hill at Notre-Dame-de-Lorette (166m/544ft high) is the culminating point of the Artois hill range. It overlooks a battlefield and was the target of many attacks during the First World War. **General Pétain** had his command post at La Targette, 7km/4.3mi from Notre-Dame-de-Lorette hill, while the 33rd army corps pierced the German lines.

A BIT OF HISTORY

Notre-Dame-de-Lorette features in dispatches during the First World War, especially during the first battle of Artois from May to September 1915. Among the many other places mentioned are Carency, Ablain St-Nazaire, Souchez (monument to General Barbot and the 1 500 *"chasseurs alpins"* killed in May 1915), Neuville St-Vaast, Vimy and La Targette (German cemetery).

SIGHTS
Tour-lanterne

The main ossuary with its lantern tower (52m/170ft high) and the seven other ossuaries house the remains of 20 000 unknown soldiers. From the top floor, there is a vast **panorama**★ of the mining basin (*north*), the Vimy Memorial (*east*), the ruined church of Ablain St-Nazaire, the towers of Mont-St-Éloi and Arras (*south*).

- **Michelin Local Map:** 301: J-5 11km/7mi SW of Lens
- **Info:** 100 Rue Pasteur, 62153 Souchez ℘03 21 72 66 55.
- **Location:** The highest point of the Artois hills; 7 miles southwest of Lens by the D 58E, and from Béthune or Arras by the D 937 then D 58E.

Musée vivant 1914–1918

Open 9am–8pm. *Closed 1 Jan and 25 Dec.* ⊕4€. ℘03 21 45 15 80.
Located 100m/109yd from the basilica, the museum houses many objects (photographs, uniforms, shells, helmets, stereoscopic plates), and several reconstructions of underground shelters with laser effects, which recreate the environment of soldiers. Next to the museum, the Champ de bataille extends over an area of 3ha/7.4 acres with its maze of French and German trenches and its mementos of the First World War (guns, machineguns, turrets).

Musée de la Targette

48 Route Nationale to Neuville-Saint-Vaast, 7km southeast along D 937. & *Open 9am-8pm.* ⊕4€. ℘03 21 59 17 76.
The museum contains over 2 000 exhibits, including ancient weapons, but it is mainly devoted to the two World Wars and re-creates fighting in the Artois region with the help of reconstructed scenes.

Château d'Olhain★

Olhain Castle, set in a romantic lake at the bottom of a valley, is characteristic of fortified castles built in low-lying areas during the Middle Ages. It dates from the 13C–15C and is surrounded by agricultural lands.

- **Michelin Local Map:** 301: I-5
- **Info:** ℘03 21 27 94 76. www.chateau-olhain.com.
- **Location:** 5.6/3.5mi southeast of Bruay-la-Buissière.
- **Kids:** The nature park.
- **Also See:** Béthune, Lens.

VISIT
🕐 *Open Jul–Aug, weekends 3–6.30pm; Apr–Jun & Sept–Oct Sun and public holidays 3–6.30pm.* 👁4€.
The castle has retained its medieval structure. A drawbridge gives access to the courtyard and from there to a watchtower (*staircase with 100 steps*), a Gothic room known as the guard-room, cellars with 2–3m/6.5–10ft-thick walls, and a chapel. There is a pleasant stroll along the edge of the moat.

SURROUNDS
Dolmen de Fresnicourt
3km/2mi on D 57 and a little road to the right (signposted).

The "Fairies' Table" is situated on the edge of a small, once-sacred oakwood. It is an impressive sight, even though its capstone has slipped. The crest of the hill on which the megalith stands, separating Flanders from Artois, provides extensive views.

👥 Parc Départemental de Nature et de Loisirs
1km/0.5mi north on D 57E.
In this nest of greenery in the heart of the mining region, numerous facilities have been established: sports grounds, swimming pool, golf course, tennis courts, playgrounds, picnic areas, footpaths etc.

Le Quesnoy★

This quiet town of low, whitewashed houses lies in a lush setting of lakes close to Mormal Forest, and is a fine example of French military architecture.

FORTIFICATIONS★
The perfectly preserved fortifications still show clearly the unique qualities of the old stronghold. Built of coarse stone, flint and lime mortar covered with bricks, they form a polygon of defensive curtain walls with projecting bastions.
Despite apparently being in the style of Vauban these defences, particularly the bastions with projecting towers, in fact date in part from the time of Emperor Charles V (16C). Various all-season paths offer pleasant walks, enabling enthusiasts of military architecture to study the layout of the defences (information panels).

⊙ *Leave from place du Général-Leclerc and head for the postern gate by avenue d'Honneur des Néo-Zélandais.*

The gateway gives access to the moat, to the spot where the men of the New Zealand Rifle Brigade scaled the walls in November 1918. The Monument des Néo-Zélandais commemorates their exploits.

> ▶ **Population:** 4 917
> ♿ **Michelin Local Map:** 302: J-6
> 🅷 **Info:** 1 r. du Mar.-Joffre, 59530 Le Quesnoy. ☎03 27 20 54 70.
> ◐ **Location:** Between the Oise and the Cambrésis, via Valenciennes or Bavay by the N 49 and D 934, and from Cambrai by the D 942.
> 🅿 **Parking:** Limited parking within the fortifications (fee); park near the Étang du Pont Rouge.
> ◉ **Don't Miss:** A tour of the ramparts.
> 🕐 **Timing:** Tour the fortifications in the morning, then take a picnic in the forest.

⊙ *Follow the moat around the south front of the ramparts.*

From **Étang du Pont Rouge** continue to **Lac Vauban** which lies at the foot of the ramparts to each side of the Porte Fauroeulx.
The bridge provides a lovely view of the red-brick curtain walls and bastions and their reflection in the calm waters.

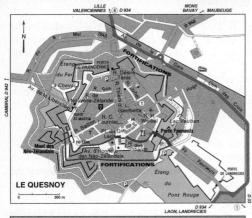

Hidden behind a large wooden doorway in the centre of town, this townhouse has a charming terrace garden and two simple yet comfortable rooms.

⊜⊜ **Le Château d'en Haut (Bed & Breakfast)** – *20 Route Nationale, 59144 Jenlain. ℰ03 27 49 71 80. http:// chateaudenhaut.free.fr. ⌂. 5 rooms.* An 18C castle with remarkable woodwork and paintings. Baldaquin beds and friendly welcome.

WHERE TO STAY	WHERE TO EAT
Chambre d'hôte la Petite Couronne..........① Château d'En Haut..........④	La Brumaudière..........①

ADDRESSES

⌂ STAY

⊜⊜ **La Petite Couronne (Bed & Breakfast)** – *3 Rue de la Couronne. ℰ03 27 36 37 87. mariannik. ledinwantellet@9online.fr. ⌂.*

⌾ EAT

⊜ **La Brumaudière** – *3 Route de Quesnoy, 59530 Locquignol. ℰ03 27 36 37 87. Closed 2 weeks in Mar, Sun–Thu evening.* Located in an old farmhouse, this bar-restaurant overlooks a small lake at the village entrance. Rustic decor with dantique farming tools on the walls, a fireplace, and traditional French cuisine.

St-Amand-les-Eaux

The town, set on the west bank of the River Scarpe, gets its name from St Amand, who founded an important Benedictine monastery in the 7C, and its hot springs, used for the treatment of rheumatism and respiratory disorders. The four mineral springs produce water bottled by the Société des Eaux Minérales de St-Amand, the fifth largest producer in France.

SIGHTS
Abbey

The last reconstruction of these monastic buildings was undertaken between 1625 and 1673. After the Revolution, only the impressive abbey tower and the magistrates' buildings remained.

▶ **Population:** 17 175
⟡ **Michelin Local Map:** 302: I-5
▤ **Info:** 89 Grand'Place, 59230 St-Amand-Les-Eaux. ℰ03 27 22 24 47. www.tourisme-porteduhainaut.fr.
◖ **Location:** Close to the border with Belgium, 30km/18mi from Lille via the D 955.
⟳ **Don't Miss:** Culinary specialities including acorn tarts, hazelnut-flavoured flat cake and the local "abbey beer".

Abbey Tower – Museum★

⟳*Open Wed–Mon 2–5pm & weekends 10am–12.30pm & 3–6pm (Oct–Mar 2–5pm). ⊛2€. ℰ03 27 22 24 55.*

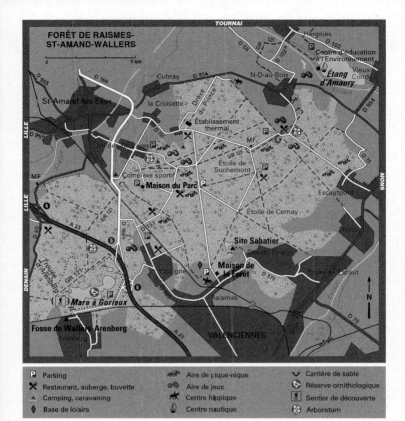

FORÊT DE RAISMES-ST-AMAND-WALLERS

Legend:
- **P** Parking
- ✖ Restaurant, auberge, buvette
- ▲ Camping, caravaning
- ◆ Base de loisirs
- 🐎 Aire de pique-nique
- ◎ Aire de jeux
- 🐎 Centre hippique
- ⚓ Centre nautique
- ↻ Carrière de sable
- 🦅 Réserve ornithologique
- 🧍 Sentier de découverte
- 🕸 Arboretum

This colossal 17C building (82m/269ft high) in a traditional Flemish Baroque style has a dramatic belltower and interior decorated with local faïence ceramics. The museum features well-preserved illuminated manuscripts.

Établissement thermal

4km/2.5mi east by D 954 and D 151.
Fontaine-Bouillon was known to the Romans for the curative powers of the spring water, the exploitation of which was renewed in the 17C under Vauban's direction. The waters and mud, bubbling up at a temperature of 26°C/82°F, are among the most radioactive in France; they are used for the treatment of rheumatism and for respiratory ailments.
The **Établissement thermal** *(1303 rte. de la Fontaine Bouillon, ⊙open Mar–Nov; ℘03 27 48 25 00; www.chainethermale. fr)*, which was rebuilt after WW II, also houses a hotel and a casino; its park (8ha/20 acres) extends into the forest along Drève du Prince, created for the visit of the future Napoléon III in 1805.

PARC NATUREL RÉGIONAL SCARPE-ESCAUT
Forêt de Raismes-St-Amand-Wallers★

This forest (4 600ha/11 370 acres) is an important section of the larger park. The flat sand and clay soil, with the quarries of former mining works, has resulted in marshes and small lakes throughout the forest of oak, beech and poplar groves. The **Maison de la Forêt** *(Étoile de la Princesse; ⅋⊙open Apr–Oct Wed 2–6pm, Sun and holidays, 3–6.30pm; ⊚2€ (children 1€); ℘03 27 36 72 72)* provides a wealth of information on the history of the forest, its fauna and flora and former mining activities. 🧍Amenities include a recreation area, picnic areas, trails, water sports and a bird sanctuary.

St-Omer★★

With its quiet streets lined with 17C and 18C pilastered mansions and houses with sculpted bays, and a cathedral with some of the finest furniture in France, St-Omer retains an aristocratic air. This refined atmosphere contrasts with the simpler nature of the northern suburbs, where low Flemish houses line the quays of the River Aa.

CATHEDRAL DISTRICT★★
Cathédrale Notre-Dame★★

The large and majestic cathedral is the most beautiful religious building in the region, standing in the heart of a peaceful area which was formerly the canons' "Notre-Dame cloister". The **chancel** dates from 1200, the transept from the 13C, and the nave from the 14C and 15C. The pier of the large south door is ornamented with a 14C Virgin Mary and the tympanum bears a Last Judgment in which the chosen are very few. In a corner of the chancel stands an octagonal Romanesque tower.

Works of Art★★

Among the numerous interesting pieces, note in particular:
◆ the 13C cenotaph (**1**) of St-Omer;
◆ the 16C mausoleum (**2**) of Eustache de Croy, Provost of the

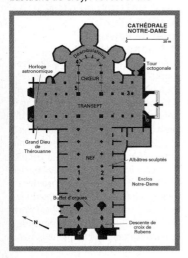

- ▶ **Population:** 15 747
- ⚲ **Michelin Local Map:** 301: G-3
- 🛈 **Info:** 4 r. du Lion d'Or, 62500 St-Omer. ✆03 21 98 08 51. www.tourisme-saint-omer.com.
- ◑ **Location:** Close to the channel port of Calais and 257km/160mi north of Paris.
- 🅿 **Parking:** Limited town centre parking; find a place (charged) near the cathedral, or the tourist information centre.
- ⊘ **Don't Miss:** A trip on the flat-bottomed boats.
- ◷ **Timing:** Leave at least 2 hours for the cathedral. With a wider viewpoint, you might spend 2 or 3 days discovering the region.
- 👥 **Kids:** The Fontinettes Barge Lift at Arques is fascinating.

St-Omer Chapter and Bishop of Arras. This striking work by the Mons artist Jacques Du Broeucq presents the deceased kneeling in his episcopal robes and also lying naked in the Antique manner;
◆ the 13C statue of Notre-Dame-des-Miracles (**3**), an object of pilgrimage;
◆ a 13C low-relief Nativity (**4**); the 8C tomb of St Erkembode (**5**), Abbot of St Bertin's;
◆ the Astronomical Clock with a mechanism dating from 1588 and the Flamboyant rose window above.

The **rue des Tribunaux** runs behind the east end of Notre-Dame and in front of the 17C **palais épiscopal**, which now houses the law courts, leading to place Victor-Hugo.

The square is the busy centre of St-Omer and features a fountain placed there to celebrate the birth of the Count of Artois, the future Charles X.

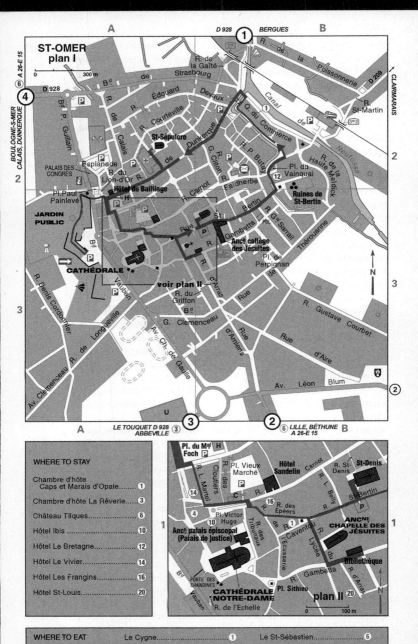

WHERE TO STAY

Chambre d'hôte Caps et Marais d'Opale	①
Chambre d'hôte La Rêverie	③
Château Tilques	⑥
Hôtel Ibis	⑩
Hôtel Le Bretagne	⑫
Hôtel Le Vivler	⑭
Hôtel Les Frangins	⑯
Hôtel St-Louis	⑳

WHERE TO EAT

Le Cygne	①	Le St-Sébastien	⑥
Le St-Charles	④		

Hôtel Sandelin and museum★

&. ⓈOpen Wed–Sun 10am–noon & 2–6pm. ⟨4.50€. ⌖03 21 38 00 94. www.musenor.com.
The house was built in 1777 for the Viscountess of Fruges. It is set between a courtyard and a garden, with a huge portal and an elegant Louis XV gate.

Ground Floor – The drawing rooms overlooking the gardens form a charming suite of rooms with finely carved wainscoting, 18C fireplaces, and Louis

XV furnishings. Among the paintings are Lépicié's *Rising of Fanchon*, the portrait of *Mme de Pompadour as Diana the Huntress* by Nattier and four works by Boilly. The woodcarving room (religious sculptures and medieval tapestries) and the Salle Henri Dupuis, containing ebony cabinets made in Antwerp, lead to the **Salle du Trésor** where exhibits include the famous gilt and enamelled **base of the St Bertin Cross★** (12C), a masterpiece of Mosan art. It is decorated with the Evangelists and enamelled scenes from the Old Testament and comes from the abbey of St Bertin, as does the beautiful ivory representing one of the old men of the Apocalypse. Note, too, the **cross reliquary** with its double crossbar (1210–20) from the abbey in Clairmarais.

First and Second Floors ★– Collection of local ceramics, and an outstanding series of **Delftware**.

WALKING TOUR
Jardin public★
A vast park (20ha/48 acres) is located on part of the old 17C ramparts, with formal French and English gardens, and views of the bastion, rooftops and the cathedral tower.

Place du Maréchal-Foch
The town hall was built between 1834 and 1841 using stone from the former abbey church dedicated to St Bertin. A theatre was set in the centre of the building. At 42 bis, the **Hôtel du Baillage** (now the Caisse d'Épargne savings bank) was originally the royal courthouse.

> Follow rue L.-Martel, place Victor-Hugo, rue des Epeers and rue St-Bertin.

Ruines de St-Bertin and Faubourg Nord
All that remains of the abbey are a few arches and the lower part of the tower (1460). Rue St Bertin provides a lovely view of the ruins surrounded by great trees. Via place du Vanquai, one can stroll through the Faubourg Nord (north suburb), along quai des Salines and quai du Commerce lined with low Flemish houses reflected in the River Aa.

> At the end of quai des Salines, turn left on rue de Dunkerque then right on rue St-Sépulcre.

Église St-Sépulchre
This hall-church (the three aisles are of the same width and height) was consecrated in 1387 and used to be the seat of the largest parish in the town. The name of the church, named after the Holy Sepulchre in France, comes from three local lords who went on the Crusades.

> Rue de Dunkerque leads back to place du Maréchal-Foch.

L'AUDOMAROIS
This region surrounding St-Omer, from the Latin word Audomarus meaning "Omer", forms part of the regional nature preserve. The area known as the Marais Audomarois, or Omer Marshes, is one of the most unusual parts of the park. *www.audomarois-online.com.*

Maison du Romelaëre
Open Apr–Jun & Sept Tue–Fri 2–6pm & Sun 3–6pm; Jul–Aug Sat 3–6pm. 03 21 38 52 95. www.parc-opale.fr.
This is the visitor centre for the Audomarois section of the **Parc Naturel Régional des Caps et Marais d'Opale**. The centre is also the starting point for footpaths, some within the Romelaëre Nature Reserve (observation and study trails).

Marais audomarois
The marshes stretch from Watten in the north to Arques just south of St-Omer, and from Clairmarais Forest to the Tilques watercress beds. Today the marshes encompass a series of small plots of land linked by **waterways**, which are used by large flat-bottomed boats known as *bacôves*. Join a **tour of the marshes** or hire your own boat.

Forêt de Rihoult-Clairmarais
4.5km/ 2.5mi east of St-Omer

🏃 Charlemagne hunted here in the oak groves; in the 12C the forest was the property of Cistercian monks.

The forest (1 167ha/2 884 acres) is now managed with tourists in mind (*picnic tables*), especially around **étang d'Harchelles**, the last of seven ponds dug by the Cistercians for peat and fish.

Arques

4km/2.5mi southeast on N 42.

Arques, which is an industrial town known chiefly for its crystal glassware, is also an important port at the junction of the canalised Aa and the Neuffossé Canal, linking the River Aa to the River Lys.

Arc International★

&. 🔍Guided tours (1hr30min) by request in advance, Mon–Sat 9am–12.30pm & 1.30–5.30pm. ⊚6.50€. Min. age 8 years. ℘03 21 12 74 74. www.arc-international.com.

Founded in 1825, the Verrerie-cristallerie d'Arques is now, under its new name, a world leader in fine tableware production. Every day, six million items are manufactured in glass, opal and crystal.

Maison du Parc Naturel Régional des Caps et Marais d'Opale

🕐Open Mon–Fri 8.30am–noon & 1.30–6pm. ℘03 21 87 90 90. www.parc-opale.fr.

Le Grand Vannage houses the Maison du Parc, a white-stone and pink-brick building spanning the Aa. The sluice gate room where the river level is regulated can be visited.

⏵ In Arques, take N 42 east toward Hazebrouck; about 1km/0.5mi beyond the bridge over the Aa, turn right onto a small road marked "Ascenseur des Fontinettes" which ends near a factory.

Ascenseur à Bateaux des Fontinettes★

🔼🔽 🕐Open daily mid-Jun–mid-Sept 3 –6.30pm; Apr–mid-Jun & mid-Sept–Oct weekends & holidays 3–6.30pm, 2–6pm, Sat, Sun 2–6pm (reserv. required). ⊚4€. ℘03 21 12 90 23. www.audomarois-online.com.

The barge lift, which was in use from 1888 to 1967 was built on the Neuffossé Canal to replace the five locks needed to negotiate the 13.13m/43ft drop in the canal. Displays in the engine room and a working model explain how it functioned.

Esquerdes

8km/5mi southwest along D 211.

This village lies in the Aa Valley and has been famous for papermaking since 1473. It still has several paper mills.

Maison du papier

🕐Open mid-Apr-Aug Tue-Sun 2-6pm. ⊚4€. ℘03 21 95 45 25.

Exhibitions explain papermaking techniques from early China to today.

ADDRESSES

🛏 STAY

🍴🛏 **Le Vivier** – 22 Rue Louis-Martel. ℘03 21 95 76 00. Closed early Jan and Sun evening, Mon lunch. 7 rooms. ⊇ 6.50€. Restaurant 🍴🛏. The perfect location for those who choose to stay in town. The rooms, with blonde wood furnishings, are quiet and well fitted out. The restaurant serves dishes with an accent on seafood.

🛏🛏 **La Rêverie (Bed & Breakfast)** – 19 Rue Jonnart, 62560 Fauquembergues, 17km/10.5mi SW of St-Omer by D 928, Rte de Berck-sur-Mer. ℘03 21 12 12 38. 🖨. 3 rooms. Meals 🍴🛏. A 19C house with well-preserved interior decor. A large garden and terrace.

🛏🛏 **Caps et Marais d'Opale (Bed & Breakfast)** – 11 quai du Commerce. ℘03 21 93 89 82. www.bb-opale.fr.🖨 3 rooms. ⊇ 6 €. An elegant manor house on the canal, with carved wood panelling and a pretty garden veranda.

🛏🛏 **Hôtel Le Bretagne** – 2 Pl. Vainquai. ℘03 21 38 25 78. www.hotellebretagne. com. 75 rooms. ⊇9€. Restaurant🍴🛏. An imposing modern building in the centre of town, with impeccable rooms and Parisian-style brasserie.

🛏🛏 **Ibis** – 2–4 Rue Henri-Dupuis. ℘03 21 93 11 11. www.ibishotel.com. 65 rooms. ⊇ 7 €. Located in a historic building in the centre of town. Contemporary, comfortable rooms on three levels.

Hôtel Saint-Louis – *25 Rue d'Arras. 03 21 38 35 21. www.hotel-saintlouis.com. 30 rooms. 9 €. Restaurant*. This hotel in the Cathedral district used to be a post office. Soundproofed rooms with light wood furnishings. Local specialties and seafood served in the restaurant.

Hôtel Les Frangins – *5 Rue Carnot. 03 21 38 12 47. www.frangins.fr. 26 rooms. 8 €. Restaurant*. Located in the historical centre of St-Omer, near shops and museums, 'Les frangins' – slang for 'the brothers' – offers renovated rooms that are practical and quiet.

Château Tilques – *62500 Tilques, 6km/3.7mi NW of St-Omer by N 43. 03 21 88 99 99. www.chateautilques.com. 53 rooms. 19€. Restaurant*. A 19C red brick castle surrounded by greenery. Rooms in the chateau have are classic in style, while the annex rooms are more contemporary. Restaurant in the former stables.

⑂ EAT

Le Cygne – *8 r. Caventou. 03 21 98 20 52. www.restaurantlecygne.fr. Closed 10–30 Aug, Sun evening and Mon except holidays.* Close to the cathedral, this restaurant has, rightly so, become the principal eatery in town serving traditional French cuisine, using the local produce.

Le Saint-Charles – *6 r. Minck. 03 21 88 57 38. Closed Thu evening & Sun.* Behind a retro facade is an intimate brasserie near the Cathedral, with a good value menu of grilled meats and fish dishes.

Le Saint-Sébastien – *2 Grand-Place, 62575 Blendecques. 03 21 38 13 05. Closed Sun evening & Mon.* A laidback restaurant in the centre of a tiny town just outside St-Omer. Family-friendly atmosphere, rustic décor and traditional French dishes.

Le Touquet-Paris-Plage ♨♨♨

Le Touquet lies between the sea and the forest, its parallel streets intersected by access roads to the beach. Villas and establishments with a certain old-world charm nestle among pine trees in a picturesque clash of architectural styles and a splash of bright colours: white walls with blue edging, red tiles, impeccable lawns and flower beds. At the end of the 19C, an English businessman capitalized on the tourism potential, building the first seaside residences.

The resort was almost immediately adopted by the English and took the name Le Touquet Paris-Plage in 1912. Since then it has developed into a year-round European resort with a sea-water therapy centre.

▶ **Population:** 5 299
✦ **Michelin Local Map:** 301: C-4
❚ **Info:** Palais de l'Europe, Pl. de l'Hermitage, 62520 Le Touquet-Paris-Plage. 03 21 06 72 00. www.letouquet.com.
◗ **Location:** On the coast, 68km/43mi south of Calais, and accessible by the A 16 (Junction 26 and then the N 39 to Étaples.
🅿 **Parking:** There is plenty of paid parking along the Digue-promenade, but in good weather you will need to be there early.
◐ **Don't Miss:** The maritime forest of the 'Jardins de la Manche'.
◕ **Timing:** The walk will occupy around half a day. Then hire a bike and spend time in the forest.
♣ **Kids:** The beach always has something going on for children to join in with.

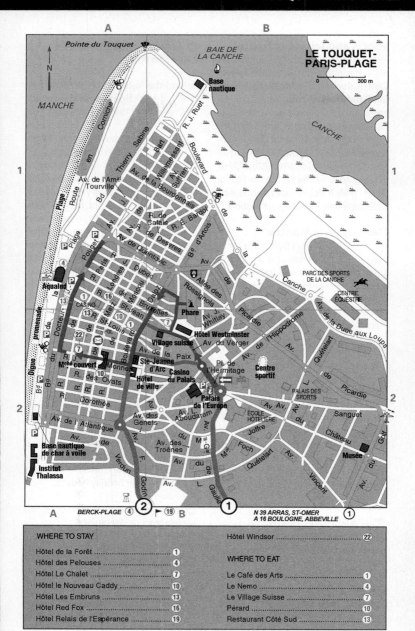

WHERE TO STAY

Hôtel de la Forêt	①
Hôtel des Pelouses	④
Hôtel Le Chalet	⑦
Hôtel le Nouveau Caddy	⑩
Hôtel Les Embruns	⑬
Hôtel Red Fox	⑯
Hôtel Relais de l'Espérance	⑲
Hôtel Windsor	㉒

WHERE TO EAT

Le Café des Arts	①
Le Nemo	④
Le Village Suisse	⑦
Pérard	⑩
Restaurant Côté Sud	⑬

VISIT
Digue-promenade

Along the seafront, the **promenade** is edged by numerous gardens and car parks. The south end leads to a sand-yachting club and the therapy centre.

The beach and port

The gently sloping beach is uncovered for 1km/0.5mi at low tide and stretches as far as the mouth of the River Authie. The **coast road** follows the line of the dunes and leads to the marina and the water sports club, sheltered by the Pointe du Touquet headland.

Sports and leisure activities

Near the attractive shopping galleries of the Hermitage district are the **Sports Centre**, the select **Casino du Palais** and the **Palais de l'Europe** where conferences and cultural exchanges take place. The **Museum** (🕐open Jun–Sept Wed –Mon 10am–1pm & 2–6pm (Sun 10am– 1pm & 3–6pm), Oct–May Wed–Mon 2– 6pm (Sun 3–6pm); ☞3.80€; ✆03 21 05 62 62) displays works by the Étaples School (1880–1914). It also includes paintings by Le Sidaner and a modern art section.

"Jardins de la Manche"

The forest (800ha/1900 acres) was planted in 1855; its maritime pine, birch, alder, poplar and acacia trees protect about 2000 luxury villas – either Anglo-Norman in style or resolutely modern – from the wind, with 45km/28mi of bridlepaths and 50km/31mi of forest tracks reserved for hikers.

🚶 **Four walks** start from place de l'Hermitage: **La Pomme de Pin** for "amateurs", **Le Daphné** for serious hikers, **La Feuille de chêne** for keen "explorers" and **L'Argousier** for really "experienced" hikers (*leaflets available from the tourist office*).

Three golf courses extend south of the forest. Along the River Canche are the **racecourse**, the **equestrian centre**, the **shooting range** (*archery*) and the **airport**.

🐾 WALKING TOUR

▷ *From place de l'Hermitage, take avenue du Verger.*

This is Le Touquet's most fashionable avenue, lined with flower beds and white-painted boutiques (1927) recalling the Art Deco style. Further on the **Hôtel Westminster** is one of the resort's most prestigious establishments with its red-brick façade and protruding windows.

▷ *Bear left and walk along rue St-Jean.*

The turreted **Village Suisse** (1905) is in mock medieval style. The shopping arcades have terraces upstairs.

▷ *Return to the hotel and follow avenue des Phares.*

Behind the hotel, the hexagonal column red-brick **lighthouse** was rebuilt by Quételart in 1949.

▷ *Cross avenue des Phares and follow rue J.-Duboc to boulevard Daloz.*

Villa Cendrillon (1923) on the corner of the boulevard has a pretty loggia and an unusual overlapping roof. At no 44 **Villa La Wallonne** stands at the beginning of the lively shopping centre. Note the façade of **Villa des Mutins** (1925) at no 78 with its two gables overlooking rue de Lens. **Villa Le Roy d'Ys** at no 45 looks like a traditional house from Normandy with its timber-framed stone walls. The **Hôtel de Ville** was built from local stone in 1931 in Anglo-Norman style with cemented timber-framing; it is flanked by a belfry (38m/125ft tall).

▷ *Take rue Jean-Monnet to the beach.*

Villa Le Castel (1904) at no 50 combines the neo-Gothic and Art Nouveau styles. Rue Jean-Monnet continues through the arch of the **covered market** (1927-32), a half-moon-shaped ensemble, and leads to boulevard Pouget on the seafront lined with other holiday houses.

▷ *Take avenue du Verger which leads back to place de l'Hermitage.*

EXCURSIONS
Stella-Plage

Leave Le Touquet along Ave F.-Godin for 5km/3mi, turn right onto D 144.
Behind the dunes that extend along the beach are villas dotted across the woods forming a continuation of the woods in Le Touquet.

St-Josse

10km/6mi southeast on N 39, D 143 and D 144 (views of Étaples).
St-Josse, which stands on a hill, was once the home of an abbey founded by Charlemagne in memory of St Josse,

a 7C pilgrim and hermit whose reliquary is venerated in the church's early-16C chancel. About 500m/550yd east, in the middle of a wooded close, stand St Josse's Chapel, which is a place of pilgrimage, and St Josse's fountain.

ADDRESSES

🛏 STAY

🍴 **Hôtel de la Forêt** – 73 Rue de Moscou. ✆03 21 05 09 88. Closed 15 Dec–15 Jan. 10 rooms. ⌑ 6.50€. This small family hotel in the centre of town is just 0.5km/0.3mi from the shore. Small, simple rooms, recently renovated and soundproofed.

🍴 **Le Chalet** – 15 Rue de la Paix. ✆03 21 05 87 65. www.lechalet.fr. 15 rooms. ⌑ 8.50€. Although only 50m/55yds from the beach, this hotel looks like it migrated here from the Alps. Spruce bedrooms decorated along a seaside or mountain theme.

🍴🍴 **Les Embruns** – 89 Rue de Paris. ✆03 21 05 87 61. www.letouquet-hotel-les-embruns.com. 22 rooms. ⌑ 9€. Located near the water, this attractive hotel has stylish rooms, some with balconies or overlooking the garden. Small sitting room and library.

🍴🍴 **Hôtel Le Nouveau Caddy** – 130 Rue de Metz, Place du Marché-Couvert. ✆03 21 05 83 95. www.le nouveaucaddy.com. Closed 4 –31 Jan. 20 rooms. ⌑ 8.50€. Overlooking the market square, close to the beach and shops, this welcoming hotel has simple rooms with a seasonal theme.

🍴🍴 **Hôtel Windsor** – 7 Rue Saint-Georges. ✆03 21 05 05 44. www.hotel-windsor.fr. 18 rooms. ⌑ 8€. Close to the beaches, with newly renovated rooms that range from singles to quads.

🍴🍴 **Hôtel Relais de l'Espérance** – 561 Ave d'Étaples, in Trépied, 62780 Cucq. ✆03 21 94 62 99. www.hotel-relais-de-l-esperance.com. 10 rooms. ⌑ 9€. On the Dieppe-Calais road at the edge of the Touquet forest, a short drive to the beaches. This hotel has modern rooms comfortably decorated and soundproofed.

🍴🍴 **Hôtel des Pelouses** – 465 Blvd Labrasse, 62780 Cucq. ✆03 21 94 60 86. www.lespelouses.com. Closed Dec–Feb. 26 rooms. ⌑8€. Restaurant 🍴🍴. Just 1.8km/1mi from the beaches, with modern and spacious rooms. Restaurant specialises in seafood. Children's menu.

🍴🍴 **Hôtel Red Fox** – 60 Rue de Metz. ✆03 21 05 27 58. www.hotelredfox.com. 53 rooms. ⌑13€. Comfortable, modern rooms in the centre of town, those on the top floor have a mansard roof.

🍴 EAT

🍴 **Restaurant Côté Sud** – 187 Blvd Jules-Pouget. ✆03 21 05 41 24. Closed Mon morning, Sun evening and Wed out of season . An attractive restaurant decorated in the colours of the south of France, with the sun-drenched food ito match: rabbit in rosemary sauce, and spicy red mullet, for example. Amazing sea views.

🍴🍴 **Pérard** – 67 Rue de Metz. ✆03 21 05 13 33. www.restaurantperard.com. Connoisseurs take note – fish soup is this restaurant's pride and joy! As with other seafood dishes, the ingredients come directly from their own fishmonger's shop next door.

🍴🍴 **Le Nemo** – Blvd de la Mer, Aqualud. ✆03 21 90 07 08. www.lenemo.com. Closed Dec–Jan. Enter this restaurant inspired by Jules Verne and dive 20 000 leagues under the sea. You'll find deep-sea diving suits, mariners' charts, woodwork, pewter pieces, marine curios. Pleasant terrace on the ocean side.

🍴🍴 **La Café des Arts** – 80 Rue de Paris. ✆03 21 05 21 55. A popular locals' establishment with a modern take on traditional French dishes and a good-value four course menu.

🍴🍴🍴 **Le Village Suisse** – 52 Ave St-Jean. ✆03 21 05 69 93. Closed 3 wks in Jan, Sun evening Oct–Easter, Tue lunch and Mon. Situated directly over the "village" shops, here's an elegant restaurant resembling a Swiss chalet. A comfortable, inviting dining room, courteous staff and delicious seasonal dishes.

🏃 SPORT AND LEISURE

Golf du Touquet – Ave du Golf, on A16, exit 26. ✆03 21 06 28 00. www.opengolf club.com. Open summer 7.30am–8pm, winter 8am–6pm. ⌘From 28€. Two 18-hole courses, one through the forest and the other along the sand dunes of the shore, and a 9-hole learning course.

Boobaloo – 38 Rue Saint-Louis. ✆03 21 05 66 47. Open weekends and school holidays 9am–7pm. Closed Jan. Cycle hire.

Valenciennes

This busy commercial town, located on the River Escaut (Scheldt), is surrounded by boulevards which replaced the former ramparts. Valenciennes was the northern capital of the steel industry and metallurgy. Today these industries have been replaced by car manufacturing, paints, pharmaceutical laboratories, mechanical engineering, and electronics. The presence of a science faculty has contributed to the development of the town, which is today an important cultural centre with fine arts collections. A culinary speciality of Valenciennes is *langue Lucullus*, smoked ox tongue covered in foie gras.

> ▶ **Population:** 357 395
> ⏱ **Michelin Local Map:** 302: J-5
> ℹ **Info:** Maison du tourisme de Valenciennes, 1 r. Askievre, 59300 Valenciennes ℘03 27 46 22 99. www.ville-valenciennes.fr.
> ◐ **Location:** Close to the Belgian border, southwest of Lille (56km/ 35 miles) and linked by the A 23.
> 🅿 **Parking:** Valenciennes is mostly one-way streets, but there are plenty of smal car parks.
> 🕐 **Timing:** A half day for the Musée des Beaux-Arts.
> 👥 **Kids:** The Parc d'attractions Le Fleury.

A BIT OF HISTORY
Athens of the North

Valenciennes earned this nickname because of the town's long-standing interest in the arts and the many artists who were born here: sculptors include André Beauneveu (14C) – the "image-maker" of Charles V , Antoine Pater (1670–1747); Saly (1717–76) who went to work for the court of Denmark, and **Carpeaux** (1827–75), who brought new life to French sculpture.

Famous local painters include the great **Antoine Watteau** (1684–1721) and Jean-Baptiste Pater (1695–1736) who both specialised in genre painting in the *fête galante* style; Louis and François Watteau, grand-nephew and great-nephew of Antoine; and in the 19C, the landscape painter Henri Harpignies (1819–1916).

SIGHTS
Maison espagnole

This 16C half-timbered, corbelled house built during the Spanish occupation now houses the tourist office.

Musée des Beaux-Arts★

&�🕐*Open Wed–Mon 10am–6pm (Thu 8pm).* ◉*4.90€.* ℘ *03 27 22 57 20.* This vast museum, which was built at the beginning of the last century, has a particularly large collection of works from the 15C–17C Flemish School (Rubens), 18C French works and 19C sculptures (Carpeaux). It has been renovated throughout with a bookshop and café.

EXCURSIONS
St-Saulve

2km/1.25mi northeast. Leave Valenciennes by avenue de Liège, N 30.
Chapelle du Carmel – *1 rue Barbusse.* 🕐*Open 9–11.30am & 1–5pm* ℘*03 27 46 24 98.* This Carmelite chapel, completed in 1966, was inspired by a model created by the sculptor Szekely and built to plans by the architect Guislain who favoured effects of mass and simple materials. The chapel is flanked by an asymmetrical bell tower. The interior is bathed in light from above the altar through stained-glass windows of geometric designs.

Sebourg

9km/5.5mi east. Leave town on the D 934, turn left on D 59 then right onto D 350.
This little market town attracts people from Valenciennes owing to its rural appearance and stretches over the verdant slopes of the Aunelle Valley.

The 12C–16C **church** (guided visits 9am–noon, 2–6.30pm 03 27 26 52 78) is for pilgrimages of St Druon; the 12C hermit who cures hernias; the 14C recumbent effigies of Henri of Hainault, Lord of Sebourg, and his wife.

Denain

10km/6mi southwest by N 30.

After the discovery of coal in 1828, this rural village became a major industrial centre. The town had up to 15 mine shafts at one time (the last one, the Puits du Renard, was closed in 1948 but its slag heap still dominates the town). It was in this town and in the countryside nearby that Zola came to seek inspiration for his work *Germinal*.

One large building (1852) remains of the mining community in avenue Villars; it is now the Academy of Music. It was here that the poet-miner Jules Mousseron (1868–1943) lived.

The **Cité Ernestine** (*park your car and take the alleyway between 138 and 140 rue Ludovic-Trarieux*) has retained its working-class atmosphere, with 20 or more semi-detached miners' houses. The **Cité Bellevue** to the north consists of a fine group of foremen's houses.

ADDRESSES

⁹⁄ EAT

Au Vieux St-Nicolas – *72 Rue de Paris* – 03 27 30 14 93. Closed 1 wk at Easter, 14 Jul –15 Aug. This restaurant in a house dating from 1735 is well-situated near the St-Géry church. The traditional cuisine is served under the kindly eye of a 16C statue in the back of the room.

✦ LEISURE

Parc d'attractions Le Fleury – 👪
5 Rue de Bouchain, 59111 Wavrechain-sous-Faulx. 03 27 35 71 16. www.lefleury. fr. Jul–Aug 9am–7pm; mid-Apr–Jun phone for open hours. Closed Oct-Apr. 9.50€. Water park and the petting zoo.

Villeneuve-d'Ascq★

In 1970 the *communes* of **Annappes, Flers and Ascq** were grouped together to form Villeneuve-d'Ascq, with the three old towns still hubs of activity. This town with its post-modern architecture, arts centre, and Val metro system linking it to Lille is also known for its parks and five lakes.

RURAL HERITAGE
Musée des Moulins

Guided tours (1–2hrs) Mon–Fri 10am–noon, 2–5pm. Closed Aug, mid-Dec–mid-Jan. 2.50€– 6€. 03 20 05 49 34. www.aram-nord.asso.fr.
In the 19C, the Lille region boasted some 200 mills. After 1976, three of them were reintroduced in Villeneuve-d'Ascq: the **Moulin des Olieux** (an oil mill dating from 1743), a traditional **flour mill** (1776)

▶ **Population:** 65 042

⚙ **Michelin Local Map:** 302: G-4

ℹ **Info:** Office du tourisme de Villebeuve-d'Ascq, Château de Flers, Chemin du Chat-Botté, 59652 03 20 43 55 75. www.villeneuvedascq-tourisme.eu.

▶ **Location:** The town lies 8km (5 miles) to the east of Lille, close to the border with Belgium.

🅿 **Parking:** See map for location of parking in the centre of the new town.

👁 **Don't Miss:** The windmill museum.

🕐 **Timing:** Visit in the morning, and stay for lunch.

👪 **Kids:** Forum des Sciences.

*Flour mill,
Musée des Moulins*

Y. Tierny/ MICHELIN

and a water mill. The museum exhibits the various mechanisms and tools used in the mills, by carpenters, millers, and woodcutters in the 18C and 19C.

Parc du Héron
The park is accessible from the castle by following the meander of the lake.
The Chemin du Grand Marais, a pleasant stroll beside the lake, leads to the sailing centre on the edge of Lac Héron. The path runs along the shore, past the bird sanctuary (73ha/180 acres) of herons, mallards, moorhens and partridges.

Musée du Terroir
12 carrière Delporte. Access via rue du 8-Mai. Open Mar–Nov Mon–Fri 2.30–6pm, 2nd and 4th Sun 3–6pm; rest of year Sun 9.30am–noon. 3€. 03 20 91 87 57. www.shvam.asso.fr.
Delporte Farm in the old centre of Annappes, built of Lezennes stone and brick, now houses the folk museum. A collection of agricultural tools is displayed, along with traditional workshops: foundry, locksmith's, joinery, saddler's, dairy etc.

Farms of Yesterday
There are more than 70 farms in Villeneuve-d'Ascq; the oldest date from the 17C and are built of brick, stone and flint. The **Ferme Lebrun** (1610) is now the home of race horses (*rue de la Liberté*). The **Ferme du Grand-Ruage** (19C) is still a working farm (*rue Colbert*). Others have been turned to other uses: a theatre (**Ferme Dupire**, *80 rue Yves-Decugis*), artists' studios (**Ferme d'En-Haut**, *rue Champollion*), nature centre (**Ferme du Héron**, 1816, *east of the lake*), the ideal starting point for guided nature walks.

SIGHTS
Musée d'Art Moderne★★
Closed for renovations. Call for information 03 20 19 68 68. http://mam.cudl-lille.fr.
Lying by a lawn above Lac du Héron, the huge building (1983) by architect Rolland Simounet suggests a set of brick and glass cubes. The sculpture park displays contemporary works by **Alexander Calder** and **Picasso**. The foyer leads to the permanent and temporary exhibitions, and to the reception and other services: library, cafeteria, classrooms used for courses in the plastic arts.

The collection – Roger Dutilleul's collection, which contains over 230 works mainly from the first half of the 20C, recognised the talent of artists who were not then understood: one of the first paintings he bought was Braque's *Houses and Tree* which had just been refused entry at the Salon d'Automne.

The collection contains many Fauvist, Cubist, primitive and abstract works. The Fauvists include Rouault, Derain and Van Dongen. Cubism is represented in paintings by **Braque** and **Picasso**. Several works by **Fernand Léger** follow his development from a 1914 landscape to his sketch for a mural (1938). One room is devoted to **Modigliani** paintings, drawings and the unique, white marble *Head of a Woman* (1913).

Works of abstract art featured are by Kandinsky, Klee and **De Staël**. De Staël knew Roger Dutilleul through the painter **Lanskoy**, who was the collector's protégé, and many examples of the latter's work are also on show. Other artists from the Paris School include **Charchoune**, **Buffet, Chapoval** and **Utrillo**.

Parc Archéologique Asnapio

Rue Carpeaux. ⊙*Open Jul–Aug Tue–Fri 2–5pm. Apr–Jun & Sept–Oct Wed 2–5pm, Sun 2–7pm.* ⊛*3€.* ℘*03 20 47 21 99.*

This 6ha/15 acre park contains reconstructions of regional dwellings from the Neolithic Era to the end of the Middle Ages: houses, barns, workshops.

Château de Flers

&⊙*Open Tue–Fri 9am–12.30pm & 2–6pm, Sat 9am–noon.* ⊛*No charge.* ℘*03 20 43 55 75.*

This Flemish castle built in 1661 is surrounded by a moat once spanned by a drawbridge. The brick buildings with stone clamping, surmounted by stepped gables, house the tourist office and an **archaeological museum**.

Mémorial Ascq 1944

77 rue Mangin in Ascq. &⊙*Open Jul–Aug Tue–Thu & Sun 2–5.30pm; Sept–Jun Wed & Sun 2–5.30pm.* ⊛*3€.* ℘*03 20 91 87 57.*

This museum is dedicated to the memory of 86 inhabitants of Ascq (the youngest was only 15) killed in 1944 and the trial of the Germans accused of their massacre. Eighty-six stones along the railway line to commemorate the tragedy.

Forum des Sciences-Centre F.-Mitterrand

1 Place de l'Hôtel-de-Ville. & ⊙*Open Tue–Fri 10am–5.30pm, weekends and public holidays 2.30–6.30pm.* ⊛*3€ to 5€ depending on the activities.* ℘*03 20 19 36 36. www.forum-des-sciences.tm.fr.*

👫 An introduction to new technologies, with a children's workshop and a planetarium.

ADDRESSES

🛏 STAY

⊝ **La Maison du Sart** – *64 av. de Flandre.* ℘*03 20 72 35 04. Closed 2 weeks in Aug. 2 rooms.* 🖵. Beautiful 1930s building with comfortable rooms and a rustic dining room. Bathroom not en-suite.

⊝⊜ **Ascotel** – *Ave Paul-Langevin, Cité Scientifique.* ℘*03 20 67 34 34. www.ascotel.fr. 83 rooms.* 🖵*12€. Restaurant*⊝⊜. In the heart of the city, Ascotel is a cubic establishment built of red brick. The pale yellow rooms are spacious and well fitted out. Modern restaurant.

🍴 EAT

⊝⊜ **L'Auberge de la Forge** – *160 r. de Lannoy.* ℘*03 20 19 19 69. www.auberge-de-la-forge.com. Closed evenings Fri–Sat.* Ample portions and a traditional menu with Flemish specialities await you at this address out of the city. Friendly service.

TOURS AND VISITS

Guided walking tours – *Rendez-vous at 2.45pm at the Château de Flers.* Walks are organized the 2nd Sunday of each month (no charge). Enquire at the Office de Tourisme.

INDEX

A

Abbaye de Jouarre 253
Abbaye de Port-Royal-des-Champs . 272
Abbaye de Prémontré 371
Abbaye de Royaumont 285
Abbaye des Vaux-de-Cernay 225
Abbaye et Jardins de Valloires...... 379
Abbaye St-Martin 349
Abbaye St-Nicolas-aux-Bois........ 371
Abbeville 296, 309
Accessibility.........................38
Acy.................................. 269
Acy-en-Multien 268
Age of Enlightenment 116
Ailly-sur-Somme 308
Airlines 39
Aisne 98
Albert 297
Ambleteuse.........................421
Amiens 299, 308
Ancienne Abbaye de St-Jean-
    des-Vignes, Soissons............. 366
André, Nélie.........................319
Arboretum de La Roche 284
Archon 377
Arc International 457
Arnauld, Angélique................. 272
Arques............................. 457
Arras 384
Art and Culture......................71
Artois 100
Atlantic Wall 91
ATMs 53
Aubigné, François d'............... 257
Audomarois........................ 456
Auguste, Phillippe...................115
Australian Memorial............... 342
Auvers, Château d' 209
Auvers-Sur-Oise.................... 208
Avesnes-sur-Helpe 392
Avesnois...........................101
Avesnois Region................... 392

B

Baie de Somme 368
Bailleul 397
Banks...............................53
Barbizon 210
Barbizon School, The 95, 210
Baroque architecture................85
Basic Information 52
Bavay............................. 400
Beaurain.......................... 378
Beauvais..........................313

Beaux Monts....................... 337
Bed & Breakfasts 46
Beer 63, 64
Bellegambe, Jean 424
Benedictine Order....................87
Bergues........................... 401
Bernay-en-Ponthieu............... 345
Bêtises de Cambrai 416
Bièvres 256
Billons.............................67
Blériot-Plage...................... 423
Blue-stone oratories............... 396
Blum, Léon........................ 256
Boeschepe 399
Books...............................29
Boudin..............................96
Bougival 154
Boulogne, Forêt de 408
Boulogne-sur-Mer.............403, 421
Boulonnais.........................101
Boulonnais, Le 408
Bourbons 69
Bourbons, The 115
La Bouteille 378
Bouvines, Battle of 435
Brasseries..........................48
Bray, Le Pays de 317
Bray-sur-Somme 308
Breteuil, Château de...............213
Brie................................63
Burelles........................... 377
Burghers of Calais, The 411
Business hours 52

C

Cabotans 303
Cakes..............................63
Calais..................... 411, 423
Calendar of Events 31
Calvin, Jean 355
Cambrai 415
Cambrésis 101
Camping............................46
Canoeing 22
Cap Blanc-Nez..................... 422
Capet, Hugh 361
Capetian Dynasty, The...............114
Cap Gris-Nez 422
Car 41
Car Insurance 42
Carnival, Dunkirk................. 429
Carnivals...........................64
Carolingians 68

Carrefour d'Eugénie 337
Car rental 43
Cartignies. 392
Cassel 419
Casteel-Meulen .419
Cathédrale, Chartres. 214
Cathedrale Notre-Dame, Amiens. . . . 300
Cathédrale St-Gervais-et-
    St-Protais, Soissons 366
Catsberg. 399
Cayeux-sur-Mer 369
Celts. 68
Centre d'accueil C. Grimminck 399
Cézanne, Paul 97
Chaalis, Abbaye de 318
Chaourse 377
Chapelle des Templiers 348
Chapelle Royale St-Frambourg. 364
Charles V. 115
Charles X. 118
Chartres 214
    Bell Tower. 217
    Église St-Pierre 222
    Grenier de Loëns 222
    Le COMPA. 222
    Maison Picassiette. 223
    Monument de Jean Moulin 222
    Musée de l'École 223
    Musée des Beaux-Arts 222
    Notre-Dame-de-la-Belle-Verrière 219
    Old Town 220
    Place du Cygne. 221
    Quartier St-André 220
    Virgin Mary's Veil 220
Château-Fort de Rambures 360
Château d'Auvers. 209
Château d'Écouen 148
Château d'If. 153
Château d'Olhain. 450
Château de Bagatelle 297
Château de Breteuil 213
Château de Chantilly 320
Château de Courances 262
Château de Dampierre. 224
Château de Ferrières. 233
Château de Flers 465
Château de Fontainebleau 235
Château de la Reine Blanche 327
Château de la Roche-Guyon 283
Château de Maintenon 258
Château de Montceaux 260
Château de Monte-Cristo 153
Château de Pierrefonds. 357
Château de Pont-Remy 309

Château de Rambouillet 278
Château de Raray. 364
Château de Thoiry. 289
Château de Vaux-le-Vicomte. . . . 291, 292
Château de Versailles 174
Château et Parc de Thoiry. 289
Cheese 62
Chemin des Dames 328
Children, Activities for 27
Chimes 66, 84
Cimetière National de Chambry 267
Cistercians 87
City Breaks. 14
Civil Architecture. 74
Clairière de l'Armistice 337
Classical architecture 85
Climate 14
Coach/Bus 40
Coach tours 23
Coal Mines 60
Coastal Flanders. 102
Coebergher 102
Colbert, Jean-Baptiste 171
Colline de Notre-Dame-de-Lorette. . 450
Colonne de la Grande Armée. 407
Compiègne 329
Confrérie du Puy Notre-Dame. 302
Conservation areas 26
Conservatoire Botanique
    National de Bailleul 398
Consulates 36
Corbie 308, 341
Corot, Camille. .94
Côte d'Opale, La. 421
Cottages. 46
Coucy-le-Château-Auffrique 342
Coupole d'Helfaut-Wizernes 433
Courances, Château de 262
Crécy-en-Ponthieu 344
Le Crotoy 368
Crouy-sur-Ourcq 269
Cruises. 25
Cultural Heritage Routes. 16
Currency. 52
Customs Regulations 37
Cycling 19
Le Cyclop 262

D

Dagny-Lambercy. 377
Dampierre, Château de 224
Daubigny, Charles-François 94
Debussy, Claude. 170
de Honnecourt, Villard 75

INDEX

Demeure de Gilles de la Boé 439
Denis, Maurice 97
Départements 59
Diagonal arches 80
Discounts 52
  Paris Museum Pass 141
Disney, Walt 226
Disneyland Resort Paris..........226
  Disneyland Park..................... 226
  Disney Studios 226
  Walt Disney Studios Park. 229
Dohis 377
Dolmen de Fresnicourt 451
Domaine de Villarceaux. 284
Domaine national de Saint-Cloud ... 160
Douai................................424
Doue 254
Drievemeulen........................ 420
Driving 41
Driving licence 42
Driving Tours.........................12
Ducasse 64
Dumas, Alexandre...................153
Dunkerque.......................... 428
Dunkirk............................. 428
Dupré, Jules.........................94
Duty-Free Allowances 38

E

Early Gothic..........................81
Écomusée Picarvie 375
Écouen, Château d' 148
Edward III.......................... 344
Église de Bouillancy 269
Electricity...........................52
Elevations...........................80
Embassies 36
Emergencies........................52
Empire, The........................118
Englancourt........................ 378
Eppe-Sauvage 395
Errard, Jean 90
Esquerdes 457
Étangs de Commelles. 327
Étrépilly............................ 268
Euralille............................ 442
Eurotunnel..........................39
Excursions to the UK................26

F

Faïence 91
Fairs 31
Farm Holidays.......................46
Fauna.............................. 106

Fauve................................97
Felleries 393
Fermes-auberges 48
Ferrières, Château de 233
Ferries...............................39
Festivals 31
First World War......................70
Fishing 22
Flamboyant Gothic...................81
Flanders 101
Flemish civil architecture 81
Flemish Cuisine 62
Flines-les-Raches.................... 427
Flora............................... 106
Flowers............................ 106
Flying buttresses.....................75
Fontainebleau, Fôret de 245
Fontainebleau 235
Fontainebleau, Château de 237
Food and Drink.................. 28, 62
Forestry 105
Forests 103
Forêt-Montiers 345
Forêt de Boulogne 408
Forêt de Chantilly 326
Forêt de Fontainebleau 245
Forêt de Marly 155
Forêt de Raismes-St-Amand-Wallers. 453
Forêt de Rambouillet 280
Forêt de St-Gobain 370
Formal Garden 106
Fortresse de Mimoyecques 432
Forum des Sciences-Centre
    F.-Mitterrand 465
Les Fontainettes 317
Fouquet, Nicolas 291
François I 71
French Brie......................... 103
French Revolution, The 70
French Vexin 103
Froissy............................. 308
Fruit 106

G

Gardens, Versailles 191
Gasoline 43
Gastronomy.........................48
Gâtinais............................ 103
Gayant.............................424
General Pétain 450
Getting Around 41
Getting There........................39
Giants 64
Gin 64

Go-Karting............................21
Gobelins.............................85
Golf 19
Gothic architecture..................75
Gourmet guide.......................48
Government 59
Grands Monts 339
Grisaille............................92
Gronard 377
Grottes-Refuges de Naours 353
Le Groupe des Trois.................96
Guînes............................. 432
Guinguettes 47

H

Hachette, Jeanne....................314
Hainaut.............................101
Handicrafts 28
Hangest-sur-Somme 309
Haras de Jardy 204
Hardelot-Plage...................... 407
Hardouin-Mansart, Jules.........85, 151,
                          159, 167, 172, 175
Hary............................... 377
Health..............................38
Henri IV........................ 74, 115
Henson horse breed, The 350
Hestrud............................ 394
High Gothic.........................81
Historial de la Grande Guerre 356
History.............................68
History Tours........................15
Horse farm..........................20
Horse Races........................161
Horse Riding 19
Hortillonnages 99, 303
Hostels.............................46
Hot-air Ballooning...................24
Hotels.............................45
Hôtel Sandelin and museum 454
Le Hourdel......................... 369
House of Valois, The 115
Hurepoix........................... 103

I

Île-de-France 8, 59, 206
L'Isle-Adam 252
Impressionism 95
Inland Flanders.....................102
Interior Decoration 72
Internet............................52

J

Jacquemart, Nélie 319
Jansenism 272
Jardin archéologique de St-Acheul .. 307
Jeantes 377
Joan of Arc........................115
Jouarre, Abbaye de................ 253
Jouy-en-Josas..................... 255

K

Kayaking............................22
Kermesse 64
Kite flying..........................20
Know Before You Go.................35

L

L'Audomarois 456
L'Isle-Adam 252
La Bouteille 378
Lachapelle-aux-Pots.................317
La Côte d'Opale 421
Laffitte, Jacques....................150
Landsailing 20
Landscape Garden 107
Landscape Painting 94
La Neuville......................... 308
Laon............................... 345
La Roche-Guyon 283
La Thiérache 376
La Tour, Quentin de................. 373
Lay brothers 88
Lebon, Joseph 384
Le Boulonnais...................... 408
Le Crotoy 368
Le Cyclop 262
Legislative Assembly 117
Le Groupe des Trois.................96
Le Hourdel 369
Le Nôtre 85
Le Portel.......................... 407
Le Quesnoy 451
Les Fontainettes 317
Le Shuttle-Eurotunnel...............39
Les Nieulles........................32
Le Tortoir 370
Le Touquet-Paris-Plage............. 458
le Vau, Louis 85
Lez-Fontaine...................... 394
Licques 409
Liercourt.......................... 309
Liessies 395
Lille............................... 434
Local crafts 17
Local Specialities....................28

INDEX

Long. 309
Longpré-les-Corps-Saints. 309
Longueil, René de 150
Mémorial de Longueval 298
Louis of Orléans 357
Louis XIII. 74
Louis XIV. 74, 177
Louis XV 74, 116
Louis XVI. 74
Louis XVIII 118
Louveciennes 153
Louvre, The 137
Luce, Maximilien .97

M
Mail 52
Maillotte, Jeanne. 435
Maintenon. 257
Maison de la baie de Somme et
    de l'Oiseau 368
Maison de la Dentelle. 398
Maison du Parc Naturel Régional
    des Caps et Marais d'Opale. 457
Maison littéraire de Victor Hugo 256
Maison Natale du Général de Gaulle. 443
Maisons-Laffitte. 150
Malmaison. 287
Manet, Édouard .96
Mansart. 85, 159, 167, 172, 175
Mansart, François 150
Mantois. 103
Mareuil-sur-Ourcq. 269
Marly, Forêt de .155
Marly, Machine of 154
Marly-Gomont 378
Marly-le-Roi 151
Marly Park 152
Maroilles. 392
Marquenterre 100, 350
May-en-Multien. 270
Meaux 259
Mémorial de Longueval 298
Mémorial de Pozières. 298
Mémorial de Thiepval 298
Mémorial de Villeroy 267
Mer de Sable 319
Merovingians 68
Metallurgy. 61
Metro, Paris 41
Meudon. 155
Mickey Mouse. 228
Military architecture. 90
Millet, Jean-François. 95, 210
Milly-La-Forêt. 261

Monasteries in Île-de-France. 86
Monastic buildings 88
Monastic Rules. .87
Monet, Claude 96
Money. 52
Monnet, Jean 263
Montceaux, Château de. 260
Montcornet. 377
Mont des Cats. 399
Montfort-l'Amaury 263
Mont Lambert 408
Montmorency. 157
Montmorency, Anne de. 320
Mont Noir. 398
Montreuil-sur-Mer. 448
Monts de Caubert 297
Mont St-Marc 338
Monument de la légion d'honneur . . 407
Monument des Bourgeois de Calais . .412
Monument Notre-Dame-de-
    la-Marne 268
Moret-Sur-Loing 265
Morgny-en-Thiérache 377
Morienval. 352
Motorhome Rental 43
Moulin, Jean 222
Moulin Edouard III. 344
Moustier-en-Fagne. 395
Multien 103
Musée Antoine-Lécuyer 373
Musée Antoine-Vivenel 336
Musée Benoît-Depuydt 398
Musée Boucher-de-Perthes. 296
Musée de l'Air et de l'Espace
    du Bourget 212
Musée de l'Île-de-France 172
Musée de la Chartreuse. 426
Musée de la Targette 450
Musée de la voiture et du tourisme. . 334
Musée Départemental de l'Oise 316
Musée de Picardie. 304
Musée des Antiquités nationales 169
Musée des Beaux-Arts, Amiens. 387
Musée des Canonniers. 444
Musée du Louvre. 136
Musée du Noyonnais 355
Musée du Second Empire. 333
Musée Français de la Photographie. . 256
Musée International d'Art Naïf 264
Musée National de la Céramique 173
Musée National de la Renaissance. . . 148
Musée National du Transmanche. . . . 422
Musée Rodin, Villa des Brillants 156
Musée Tourgueniev 154

Musée vivant 1914-1918 450
Musée Vivant du Cheval et du Poney 326
Mushrooms 106

N

Nabis 97
Naours 353
Napoleon 236, 237, 287
National Assembly 116
Nature 98
Nature Parks 25
Nausicaä 404
La Neuville 308
Les Nieulles 32
Nord-Pas-de-Calais 9, 58, 100, 382
Northern Folklore 64
Noyelles 369
Noyon 354

O

Oise 98
Opal Coast, The .421
Opening hours 52
Orangery, Versailles 196
Ourcq Valley 267

P

Palais des Beaux-Arts, Lille 436
Parc-mémorial de Beaumont-Hamel 298
Parc archéologique Asnapio 465
Parc Astérix 312
Parc de la Courneuve 166
Parc Départemental du Val-Joly 395
Parc du château de Versailles 191
Parc du Marquenterre 350
Parc Naturel Régional des Caps et
    Marais d'Opale 408
Parc naturel régional Scarpe-Escaut . 453
Parc Samara 309
Parc zoologique d'Amiens 307
Parfondeval 377
Paris
    Abbaye de St-Germain-des-Pré 131
    Arc de Triomphe 126
    Bercy 134
    Cathédrale Notre-Dame 129
    Centre George Pompidou 140
    Champs-Elysées 147
    Cité des Enfants 142
    Conservatoire des Arts et Métiers 144
    La Défense 133
    École Militaire 128
    Église Notre-Dame-du-Val-de-Grâce . 131
    Église St-Eustache 131

Église St-Séverin-St-Nicolas 131
Eiffel Tower 127
Faubourg-St-Honoré 147
La Géode 142
La Grande Arche 133
Hôtel de Cluny 141
Hôtel des Invalides 142
Hôtel de Ville 134
Institut de France 134
Invalides 125
L'Élysée 135
La Défense 133
La Géode 142
La Grande Arche 133
La Villette 134
Le Marais 132
Louvre 122
Louvre Museum 136, 138
Montmartre 134
Musée d'Orsay 140
Musée de l'Armée 142
Musée de l'Orangerie 141
Musée du Louvre 136
Musée du Moyen Âge 141
Musée National d'Art Moderne 140
Notre-Dame Cathedral 129
Opéra Garnier 128
Palais-Royal 127
Palais Bourbon 135
Palais de Chaillot 129
Palais de l'Élysée 135
Palais de la Découverte 143
Palais du Luxembourg 135
Palais L'Élysée 135
Panthéon 128
Place de la Concorde 126
Place Vendôme 147
Quartier Latin 136
Sainte-Chapelle 130
St-Germain-des-Prés 136
Tour Eiffel 127
Tuileries 133
La Villette 134
Paris and surrounds 8, 110
Parisis 102
Parking Regulations 43
Pays de Bray 98
Péguy, Charles 214
Péronne 307, 356
Pétain, General 450
Pétain, Marshal 328
Petrol 43
Philip the Good 435
Picardy 9, 58, 98

INDEX

Hotel De La Rapee Rest

Picardy Cuisine 62
Pierrefonds, Château de 339
Pissarro, Camille 95
Place du Général-de-Gaulle 438
Place Rihour 438
Plomion 376
Poissy 270
Pont-de-Sains 392
Pont-Ste-Maxence 364
Poperinge 399
Population 58
Porcelain 91
Porte d'Ardon 348
Porte de Bretagne 356
Porte de Paris 443
Porte de Roubaix 442
Porte de Soissons 349
Le Portel 407
Post 52
Post mills 89
Mémorial de Pozières 298
Pré carré 90
Prisces 377
Provins 274
Provins fairs 274
Public Holidays 53
Public Transport .41
Puppets 27, 303

Q

Quartier St-Leu, Amiens 302
Quartier St-Sauveur, Lille 442
Quesnoy, Le 451

R

Racine, Jean 273
Rail 39
Rail Europe 39
Raismes-St-Amand-Wallers, Forêt de 453
Rambouillet 278
Rambouillet, Château de 278
Rambures, Château-Fort de 360
Ramousies 393
Rancourt 298
Ravel, Maurice 263
Religious Architecture 74
Religious Orders .87
Renaissance architecture 84
Rental Cars 42
Restaurants 46
Restoration, The .118
Revolution 116
Rivers 99
Road Regulations 42

Robespierre, Maximilien de 384
La Roche-Guyon 283
Rock climbing 20
Rodin, Auguste 412
Romanesque architecture 75
Romans 68
Rousseau, Jean-Jacques 157, 319
Rousseau, Théodore 95, 210
Route des Crêtes 283
Rueil-Malmaison 287
Rural Housing in the North 88

S

Sailing 22
Sains-du-Nord 395
Saint-Jans-Cappel 398
Saint-Pierre, Eustache de 412
Sars-Poteries 393
Savignies 317
Sceaux 171
Sculpture 86
Sea-water Therapy 27
Seasons 14
Second Fontainebleau School 236
Second World War 71
Seine River 115
Senlis 361
Senlisis 102
Seurat, Georges .97
Sèvres 173
Ship 39
Shopping 28
Sightseeing 23
Skiing 21
Smoking 53
Soissons 366
Solre-le-Château 394
Somme 98
Souverain-Moulin 408
Spas 27
Speed Limits 43
Spires 75
St-Amand-les-Eaux 452
St-Cloud 159
St-Denis 162
St-Étienne-au-Mont 407
St-Germain-en-Laye 166
St-Germer-de-Fly 317
St-Gobain 370
St-Jean-aux-Bois 339
St-Josse 460
St-Leu-d'Esserent 371
St-Quentin 372
St-Riquier 374

St-Vaast, Ancienne Abbaye 387
St-Vaast-de-Longmont 365
St-Valery-sur-Somme 375
Stade de France 166
Stained Glass........................92
Ste-Périne 340
Steenvoorde 420
Stella-Plage........................ 460
Stock, Franz........................214
Suger, Abbot.......................162
Swimming 21

T

Telephones 53
Teschen table 213
TGV........................... 39, 41
Themed Tours.......................15
Mémorial de Thiepval 298
Thiérache...........................101
Thiérache, La.......................376
Time Line 68
Tipping 54
Todt Organisation 91
Tolls 43
Tortoir, Le......................... 370
Touquet-Paris-Plage, Le 458
Tourist Information Centres..........37
Tourist Offices......................35
Tourist Passes......................24
Tourist trains.......................23
Tower mills.........................89
Town halls 84
Traditional Games...................67
Traditions..................... 16, 64
Train...............................39
Transitional Gothic 80
Trees 104
Trélon 395

U

Useful Phrases 51
Useful Words........................49

V

Valenciennes....................... 462
Vallée de L'Ourcq.................. 267
Valleys.............................99
Valloires, Abbaye et Jardins de 379
Valois..............................102
Van Gogh 97, 208
VAT...............................28
Vauban 90
Vaulting 80
Vaux.............................. 308

Vaux-le-Vicomte, Château de 291
Vaux de Cernay..................... 225
Verne, Jules 307
Versailles, Château de 174
Versailles, Parc du château de 191
Versailles, Ville de 201
Versailles Classicism 85
Vervins 376
Vétheuil 284
Vieille Bourse 438
Villages of Paris 59
Ville de Versailles.................. 201
Villeneuve-d'Ascq.................. 463
Mémorial de Villeroy 267
Villers-Cotterêts................... 381
Vimeu 98
Vimeu Region...................... 297

W

Wagner, Richard.....................156
Walking.............................18
Wallers-Trélon...................... 395
Water mills.........................89
Water Sports 21
Watou 399
Weather 14
Websites...........................35
What to See and Do 18
When to Go 14
Where to Eat 46
Where to Stay 45
Wildlife Reserves....................27
Wimereux 421
Wimereux Valley 408
Wimy............................. 378
Windmills..................... 89, 420
Windsurfing 22
Wine 64
Wissant........................... 422
Wormhout........................ 420

INDEX

🏨 STAY

Abbaye de Jouarre 254
Abbaye et Jardins de Valloires 380
Amiens 310
Arras 390
Avesnes-sur-Helpe 396
Baie de Somme 369
Bailleul 399
Beauvais 317
Bergues 403
Boulogne-sur-Mer 410
Calais 414
Cambrai 418
Chartres 223
Château de Chantilly 327
Château de Ferrières 234
Château de Pierrefonds 359
Château de Vaux-le-Vicomte 293
Compiègne 340
Coucy-Le-Château-Aufrique 343
Douai 427

Dunkerque 432
La Côte d'Opale 423
Laon 349
La Roche-Guyon 285
Le Touquet-Paris-Plage 461
Lille 445
Maintenon 258
Milly-La-Forêt 262
Montreuil 449
Moret-sur-Loing 266
Noyon 355
Parc Astérix 313
Provins 277
Senlis 365
Soissons 367
St-Omer 457
St-Valery-sur-Somme 376
Valenciennes 463
Villeneuve-d'Ascq 465

🍷 EAT

Abbaye de Jouarre 254
Amiens 310
Arras 391
Avesnes-sur-Helpe 396
Baie de Somme 369
Bailleul 399
Beauvais 317
Bergues 403
Boulogne-sur-Mer 410
Calais 414
Cambrai 418
Cassel 420
Château de Chantilly 327
Château de Dampierre 225
Château de Pierrefonds 359
Château de Vaux-le-Vicomte 293
Compiègne 340
Corbie 342
Crécy-en-Ponthieu 345
Disneyland Resort Paris 232
Douai 428
Dunkerque 432
Grottes-Refuges de Naours 353
L'Isle-Adam 252
La Côte d'Opale 423

Laon 349
La Roche-Guyon 285
Le Touquet Paris-Plage 461
Lille 445
Maintenon 258
Marly-le-Roi 153
Milly-La-Forêt 262
Montfort-l'Amaury 264
Montmorency 158
Montreuil-sur-Mer 449
Moret-sur-Loing 266
Noyon 355
Paris 145
Poissy 272
Provins 277
Rueil-Malmaison 288
Senlis 365
Soissons 367
St-Amand-les-Eaux 452
St-Germain-en-Laye 171
St-Omer 458
St-Valery-sur-Somme 376
Vallée de l'Ourcq 270
Versailles 200, 205
Villeneuve d'Ascq 465

MAPS AND PLANS

THEMATIC MAPS

Principal Sights .... Inside front cover
Driving Tours. .... Inside back cover
Places to Stay 44
Geography of the region..............99
The Battle of the Marne............ 268

REGION MAPS

Paris and surrounds 111
Île-de-France 206-207
Picardy 294-295
Nord-Pas-de-Calais............ 382-383

MONUMENTS, MUSEUMS AND PARKS

Cathédrale d'Amiens 300
Ancienne abbaye St-Vaast d'Arras ... 387
Bavay: Roman remains.............. 400
Cathédrale St-Pierre de Beauvais.....315
Musée du château de Chantilly...... 322
Chantilly: Château and park..... 324-325
Chartres: Cathedral and crypt........219
Palais de Compiègne: 1st floor 331
Disneyland Resort Paris............. 227
Musée de la Chartreuse de Douai ... 426
Fontainebleau Palace.......... 237, 238
Grands appartements
    de Fontainebleau................ 240
Fontainebleau Gardens............. 244
Abbaye de Jouarre 254
Château de Pierrefonds............. 358
Rambouillet Park................... 278
Abbaye de Royaumont 286
Basilique de St-Denis 164
Cathédrale Notre-Dame de St-Omer . 454
Thoiry 290
Abbaye de Valloires 380
Vaux-le-Vicomte:
    Château and Gardens 292,293
Versailles:
    Construction 176
    Château.................... 180-181
    Park......................... 194-195

LOCAL MAPS FOR TOURING

L'Avesnois.......................... 393
Le Chemin des Dames 328
Forêt de Compiègne........336-337, 339
Forêt de Fontainebleau.....248-249, 250
Ourcq Valley 269
Forêt de Rambouillet 282
Forêt de Raismes-St-Amand-Wallers. 363
Forêt de St-Gobain 370
La Thiérache 378

TOWN PLANS

Amiens 304-305
Arras 388-389
Bergues........................... 402
Boulogne-sur-Mer................. 409
Calais.............................413
Cambrai 417
Chartres: Old town 215, 221
Coucy-le-Château.................. 343
Douai............................. 425
Dunkerque........................ 430
Laon...........................346-347
Lille...........................440-441
Paris...........................112-113
Provins 276
Le Quesnoy 452
St-Germain-en-Laye............... 168
St-Omer 455
Senlis 363
Le Touquet-Paris-Plage 459
Villeneuve-d'Ascq.................. 464

MAP LEGEND

	Sight	Seaside resort	Winter sports resort	Spa
Highly recommended	★★★	≜≜≜	✳✳✳	‡‡‡
Recommended	★★	≜≜	✳✳	‡‡
Interesting	★	≜	✳	‡

Selected monuments and sights

◉ ⇨	Tour - Departure point
🏠 ⸸	Catholic church
🏠 ⸸	Protestant church, other temple
▣ ▤ ⛩	Synagogue - Mosque
▬	Building
■	Statue, small building
⸸	Calvary, wayside cross
◎	Fountain
⟼	Rampart - Tower - Gate
⤬	Château, castle, historic house
∴	Ruins
∪	Dam
☼	Factory, power plant
☆	Fort
∩	Cave
▣	Troglodyte dwelling
⋔	Prehistoric site
▼	Viewing table
Ψ	Viewpoint
▲	Other place of interest

Abbreviations

A	Agricultural office (Chambre d'agriculture)	**P**	Local authority offices (Préfecture, sous-préfecture)
C	Chamber of Commerce (Chambre de commerce)	**POL.**	Police station (Police)
H	Town hall (Hôtel de ville)	▣	Police station (Gendarmerie)
J	Law courts (Palais de justice)	**T**	Theatre (Théâtre)
M	Museum (Musée)	**U**	University (Université)

Sports and recreation

🏇	Racecourse
⛸	Skating rink
≋ ▨	Outdoor, indoor swimming pool
🎥	Multiplex Cinema
⟁	Marina, sailing centre
⌂	Trail refuge hut
⊡━━━⊡	Cable cars, gondolas
⊡++++⊡	Funicular, rack railway
🚂	Tourist train
◆	Recreation area, park
🐗	Theme, amusement park
Ψ	Wildlife park, zoo
❋	Gardens, park, arboretum
◐	Bird sanctuary, aviary
🚶	Walking tour, footpath
😊	Of special interest to children

Special symbol

🏖	Beach

Additional symbols

ⓘ ▬ ═	Tourist information / Motorway or other primary route	✉	Post office
❶ ➊	Junction: complete, limited	☎	Telephone
⊨ ═	Pedestrian street	▭	Covered market
⋮====⋮	Unsuitable for traffic, street subject to restrictions	⋅✕⋅	Barracks
⸽⸽⸽ ----	Steps – Footpath	△	Drawbridge
🚆 🚉	Train station – Auto-train station	∪	Quarry
🚌 SNCF	Coach (bus) station	✕	Mine
━━━━	Tram	ⓑ Ⓕ	Car ferry (river or lake)
Ⓜ	Metro, underground	⛴	Ferry service: cars and passengers
℗	Park-and-Ride	⛵	Foot passengers only
♿	Access for the disabled	③	Access route number common to Michelin maps and town plans
		Bert (R.)...	Main shopping street
		AZ B	Map co-ordinates

REGIONAL AND LOCAL MAPS

To make the most of your journey, travel with Michelin maps at a scale of 1:200 000: **Regional maps nos 511, 513 and 514** and the new Local maps, which are illustrated on the map of France below.

And remember to travel with the latest edition of the **map of France no 721 (1:1 000 000)**, also available in atlas format: spiral bound, hard back, and the new mini-atlas – perfect for your glove compartment.

Michelin is pleased to offer a route-planning service on the Internet: **www.ViaMichelin.com.** Choose the shortest route, a route without tolls, or the Michelin recommended route to your destination; you can also access information about hotels and restaurants from *The Red Guide*, and tourist sites from *The Green Guide*.

Bon voyage!

Michelin Apa Publications Ltd

A joint venture between Michelin and Langenscheidt

58 Borough High Street, London SE1 1XF, United Kingdom

No part of this publication may be reproduced in any form
without the prior permission of the publisher.

© 2010 Michelin Apa Publications Ltd
ISBN 978-1-906261-88-7
Printed: November 2009
Printed and bound in Germany

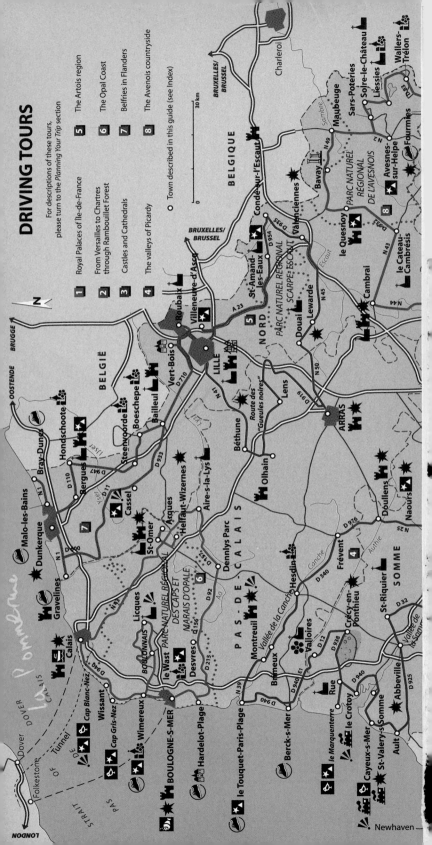

DRIVING TOURS

For descriptions of these tours,
please turn to the *Planning Your Trip* section

1 Royal Palaces of Île-de-France
2 From Versailles to Chartres through Rambouillet Forest
3 Castles and Cathedrals
4 The valleys of Picardy
5 The Artois region
6 The Opal Coast
7 Belfries in Flanders
8 The Avenois countryside

○ Town described in this guide (see Index)

0   30 km